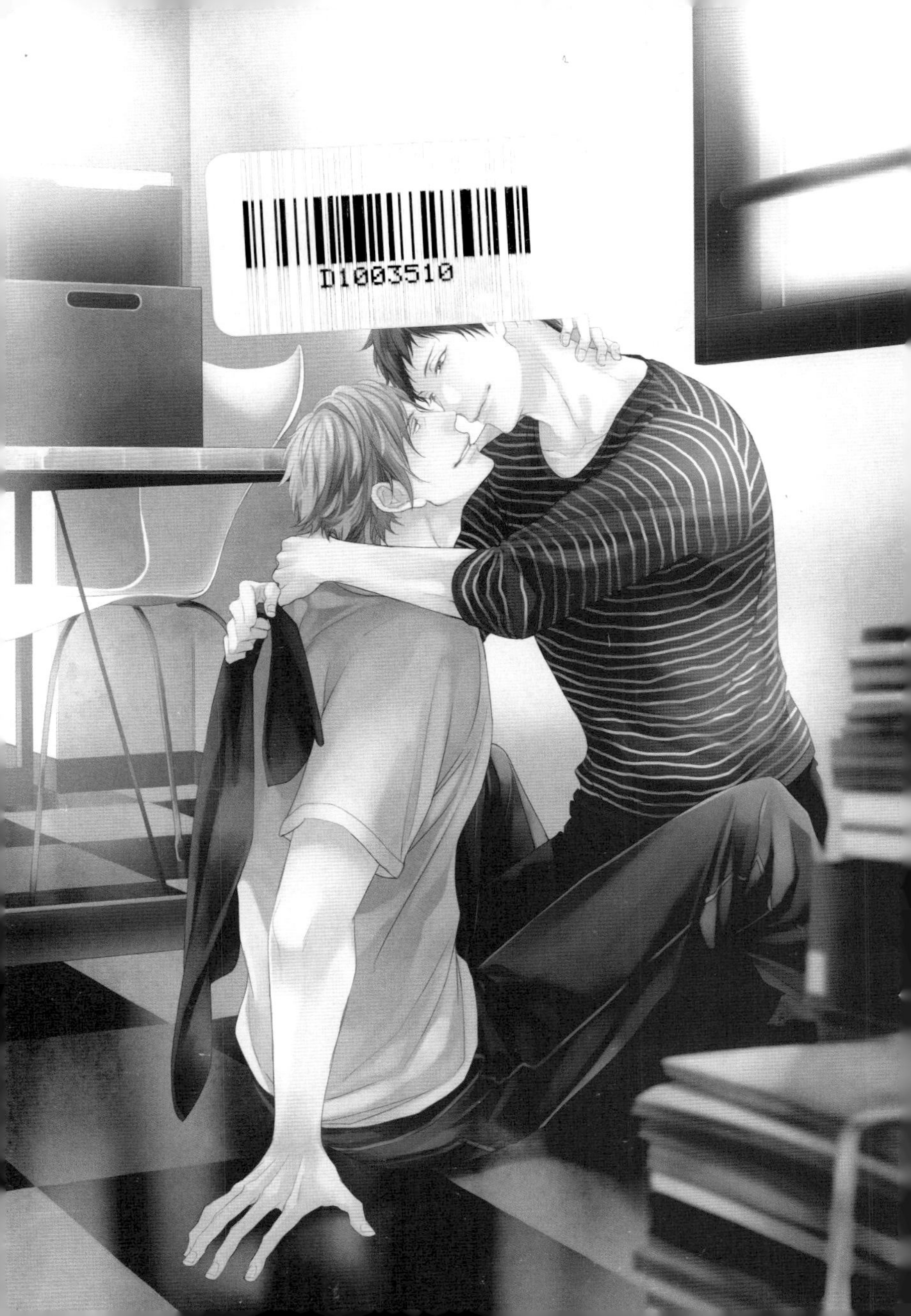

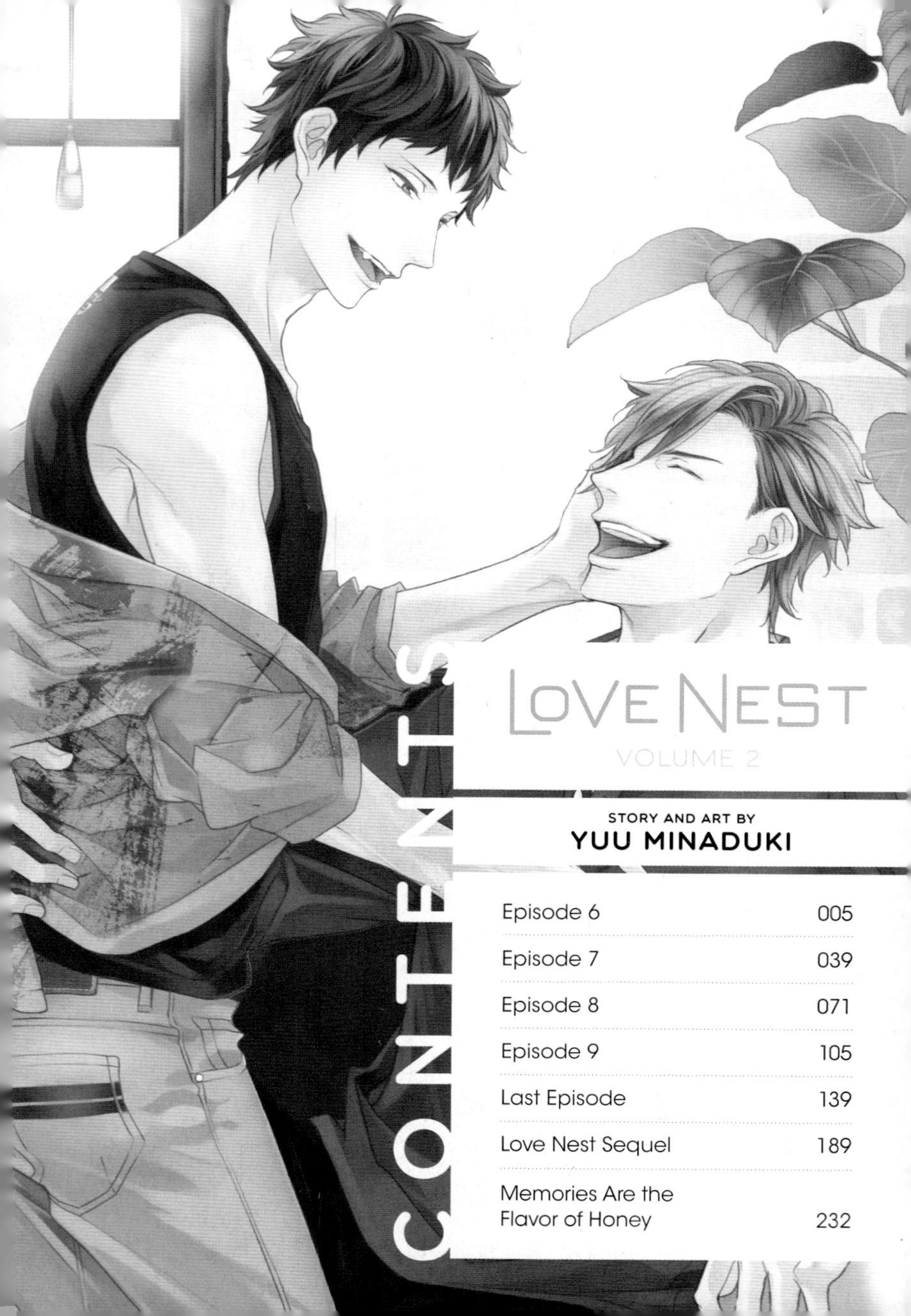

CONTENTS

LOVE NEST

VOLUME 2

STORY AND ART BY
YUU MINADUKI

LOVE NEST

STORY AND ART BY
YUU MINADUKI

2

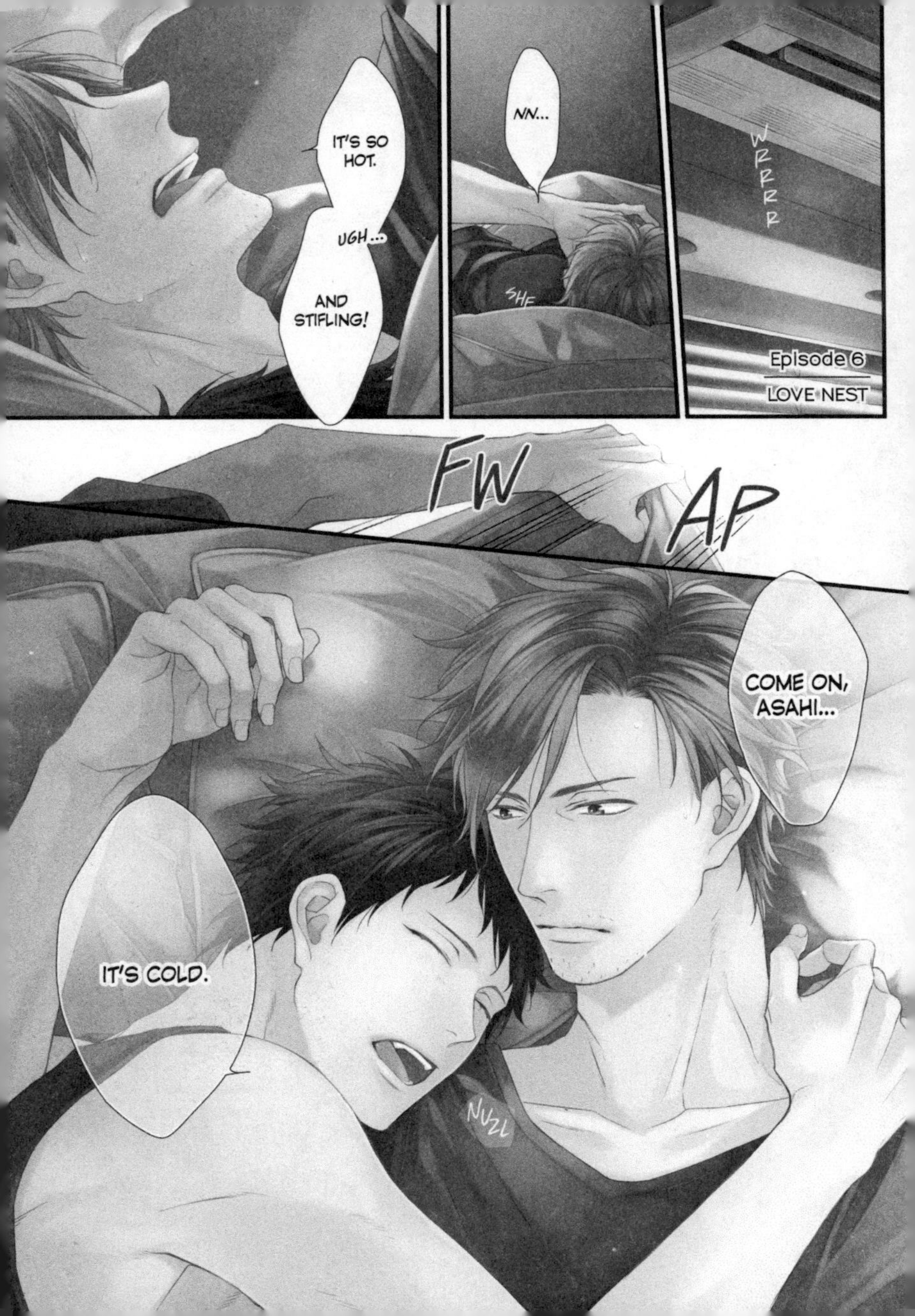
WRRRR
Episode 6
LOVE NEST
NN...
SHF
IT'S SO HOT.
UGH...
AND STIFLING!
FW AP
COME ON, ASAHI...
IT'S COLD.
NUZL

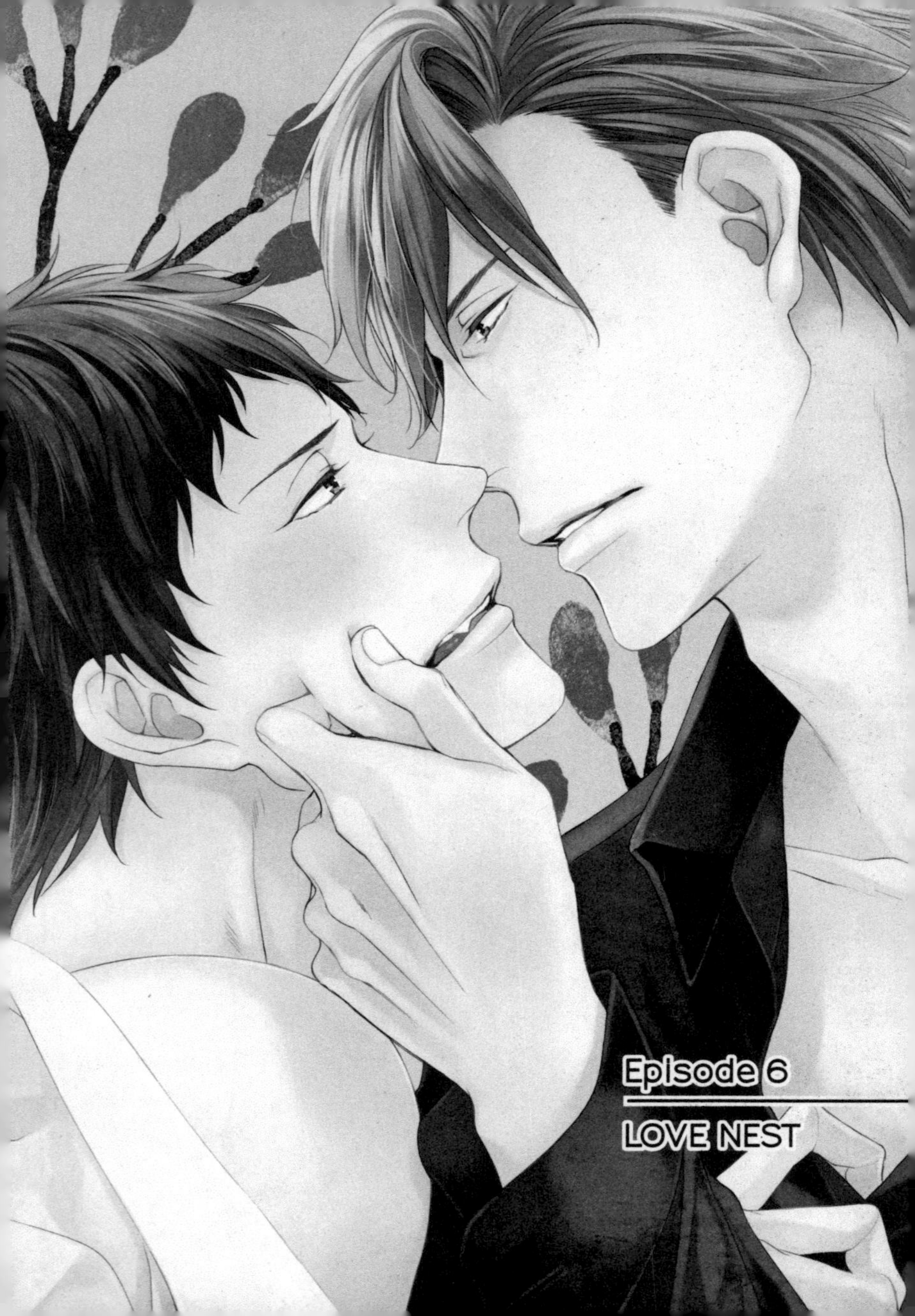
Episode 6
LOVE NEST

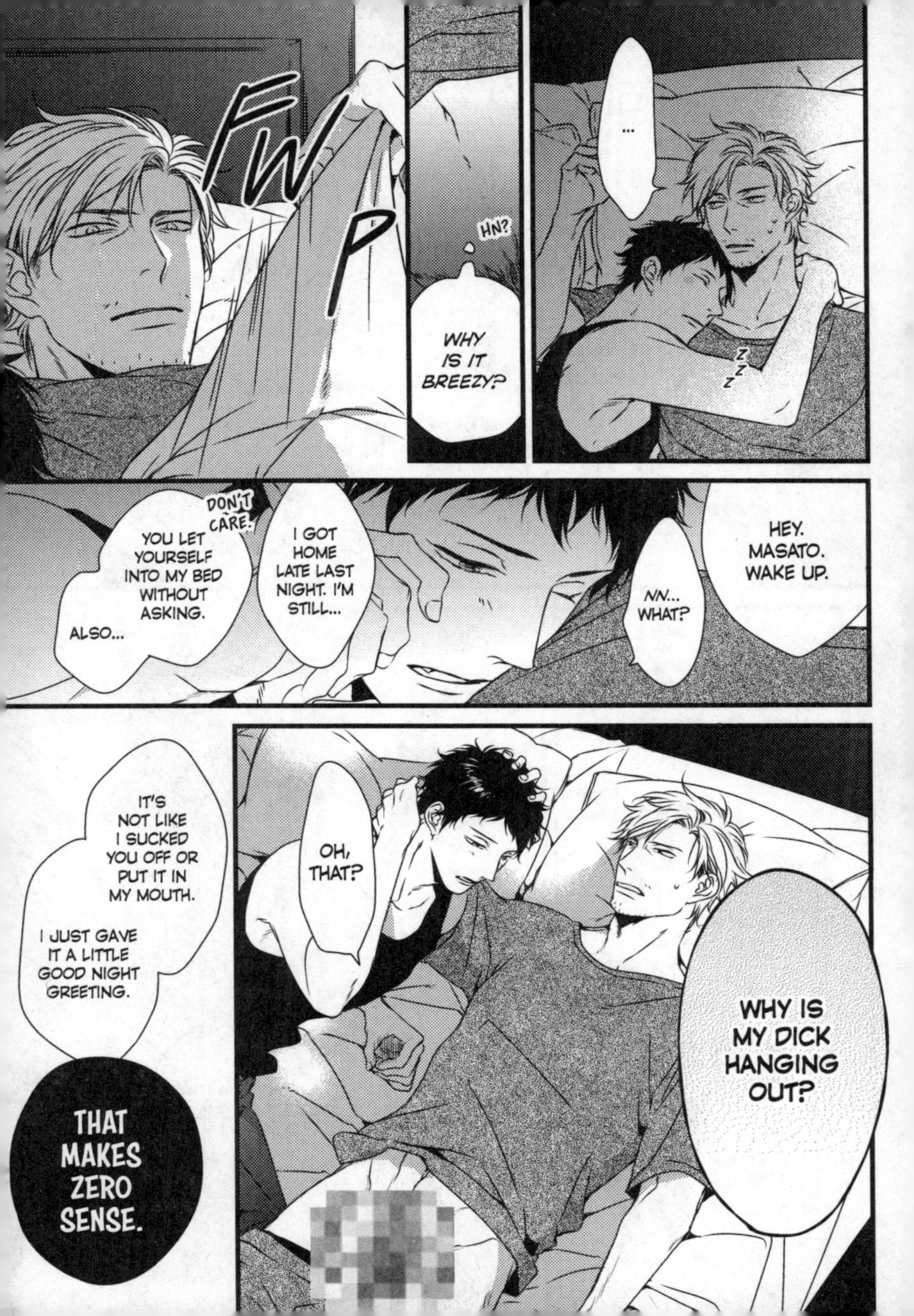
...
Z Z Z
HN?
WHY IS IT BREEZY?
FWP
HEY. MASATO. WAKE UP.
NN... WHAT?
I GOT HOME LATE LAST NIGHT. I'M STILL...
DON'T CARE.
YOU LET YOURSELF INTO MY BED WITHOUT ASKING.
ALSO...
WHY IS MY DICK HANGING OUT?
OH, THAT?
IT'S NOT LIKE I SUCKED YOU OFF OR PUT IT IN MY MOUTH.
I JUST GAVE IT A LITTLE GOOD NIGHT GREETING.
THAT MAKES ZERO SENSE.

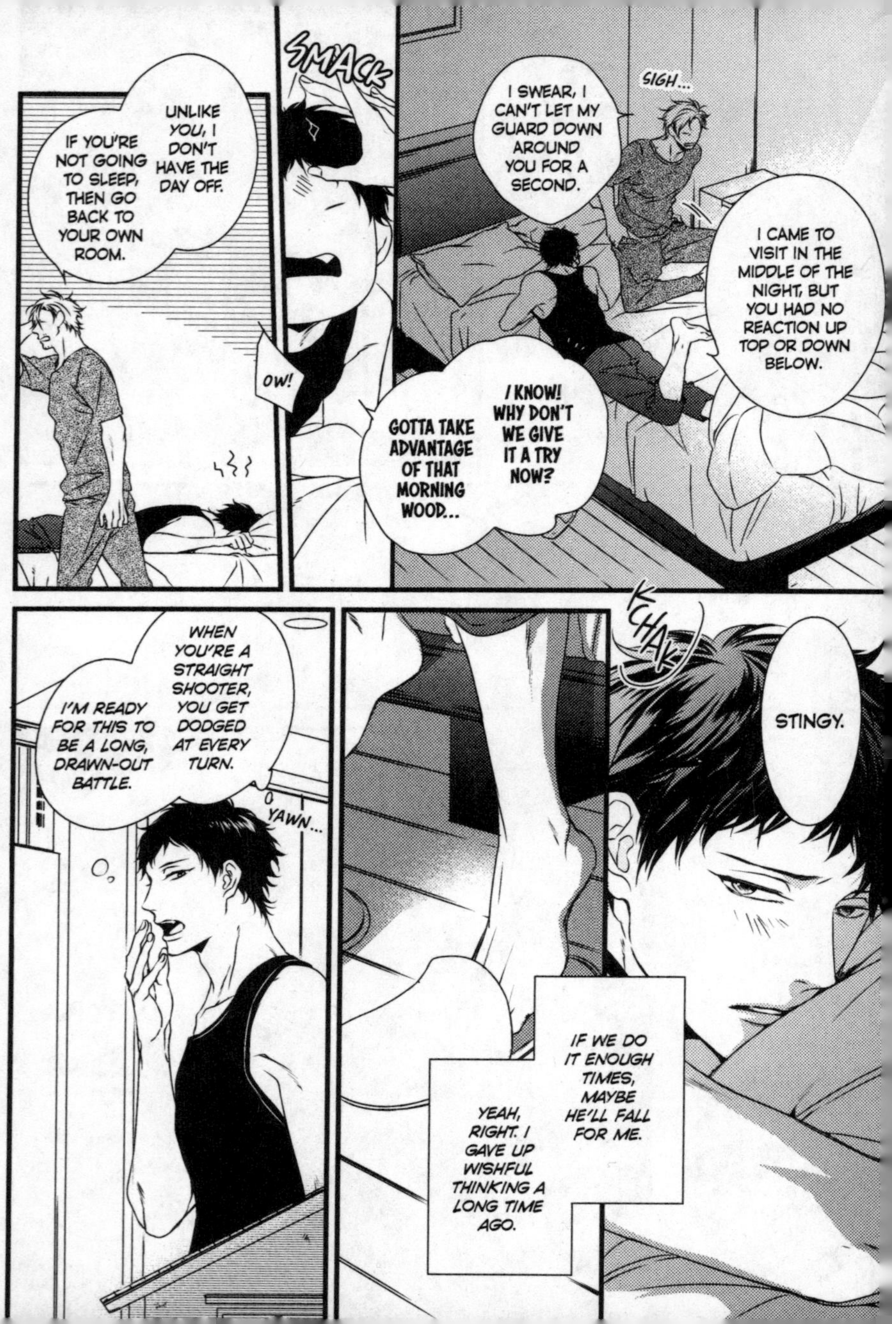
I CAME TO VISIT IN THE MIDDLE OF THE NIGHT, BUT YOU HAD NO REACTION UP TOP OR DOWN BELOW.
I KNOW! WHY DON'T WE GIVE IT A TRY NOW?
GOTTA TAKE ADVANTAGE OF THAT MORNING WOOD...
SMACK
OW!
SIGH...
I SWEAR, I CAN'T LET MY GUARD DOWN AROUND YOU FOR A SECOND.
UNLIKE YOU, I DON'T HAVE THE DAY OFF.
IF YOU'RE NOT GOING TO SLEEP, THEN GO BACK TO YOUR OWN ROOM.
KCHAK
STINGY.
IF WE DO IT ENOUGH TIMES, MAYBE HE'LL FALL FOR ME.
YEAH, RIGHT. I GAVE UP WISHFUL THINKING A LONG TIME AGO.
WHEN YOU'RE A STRAIGHT SHOOTER, YOU GET DODGED AT EVERY TURN.
I'M READY FOR THIS TO BE A LONG, DRAWN-OUT BATTLE.
YAWN...

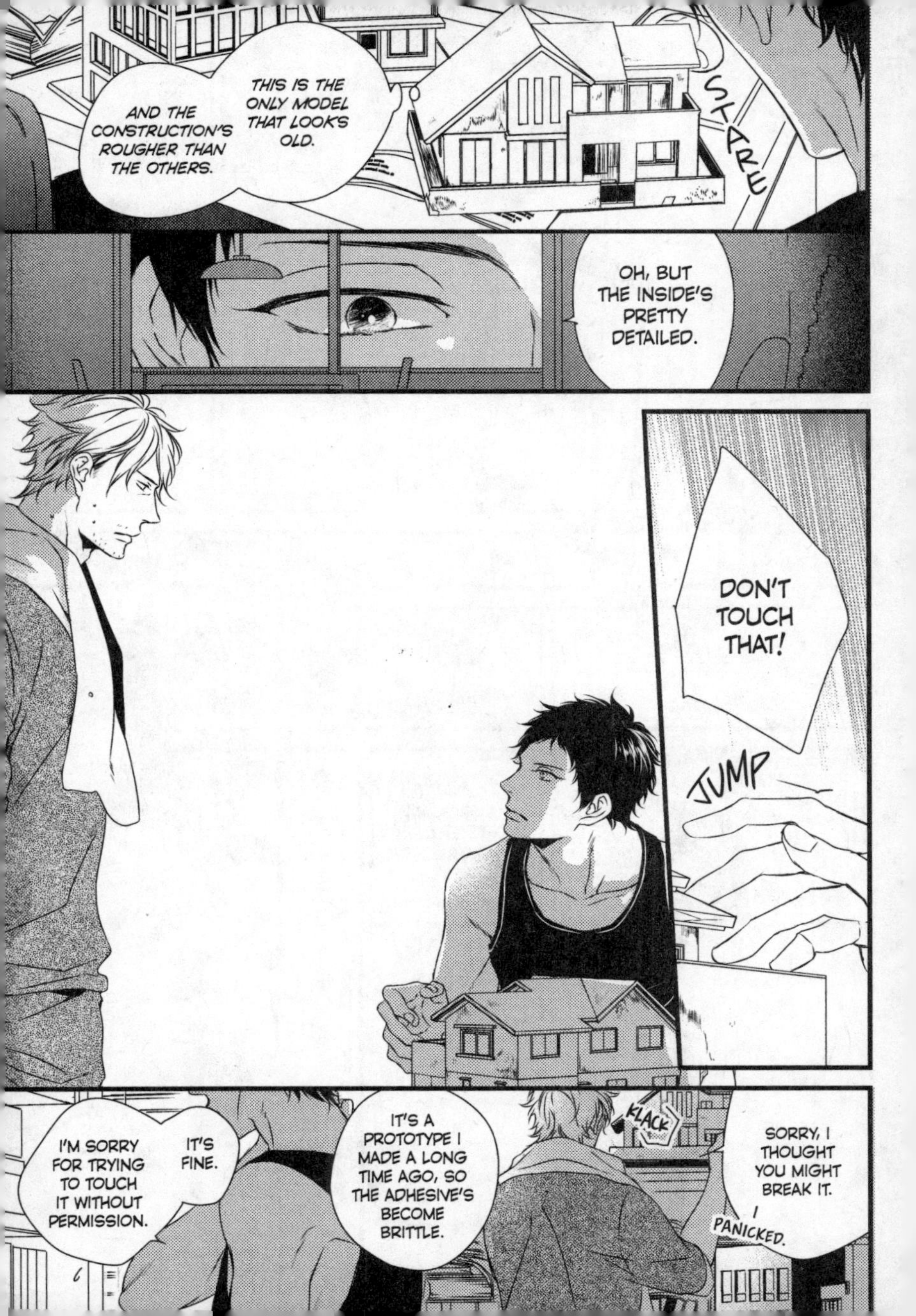
STARE
THIS IS THE ONLY MODEL THAT LOOKS OLD.
AND THE CONSTRUCTION'S ROUGHER THAN THE OTHERS.
OH, BUT THE INSIDE'S PRETTY DETAILED.
DON'T TOUCH THAT!
JUMP
SORRY, I THOUGHT YOU MIGHT BREAK IT.
I PANICKED.
KLACK
IT'S A PROTOTYPE I MADE A LONG TIME AGO, SO THE ADHESIVE'S BECOME BRITTLE.
IT'S FINE.
I'M SORRY FOR TRYING TO TOUCH IT WITHOUT PERMISSION.

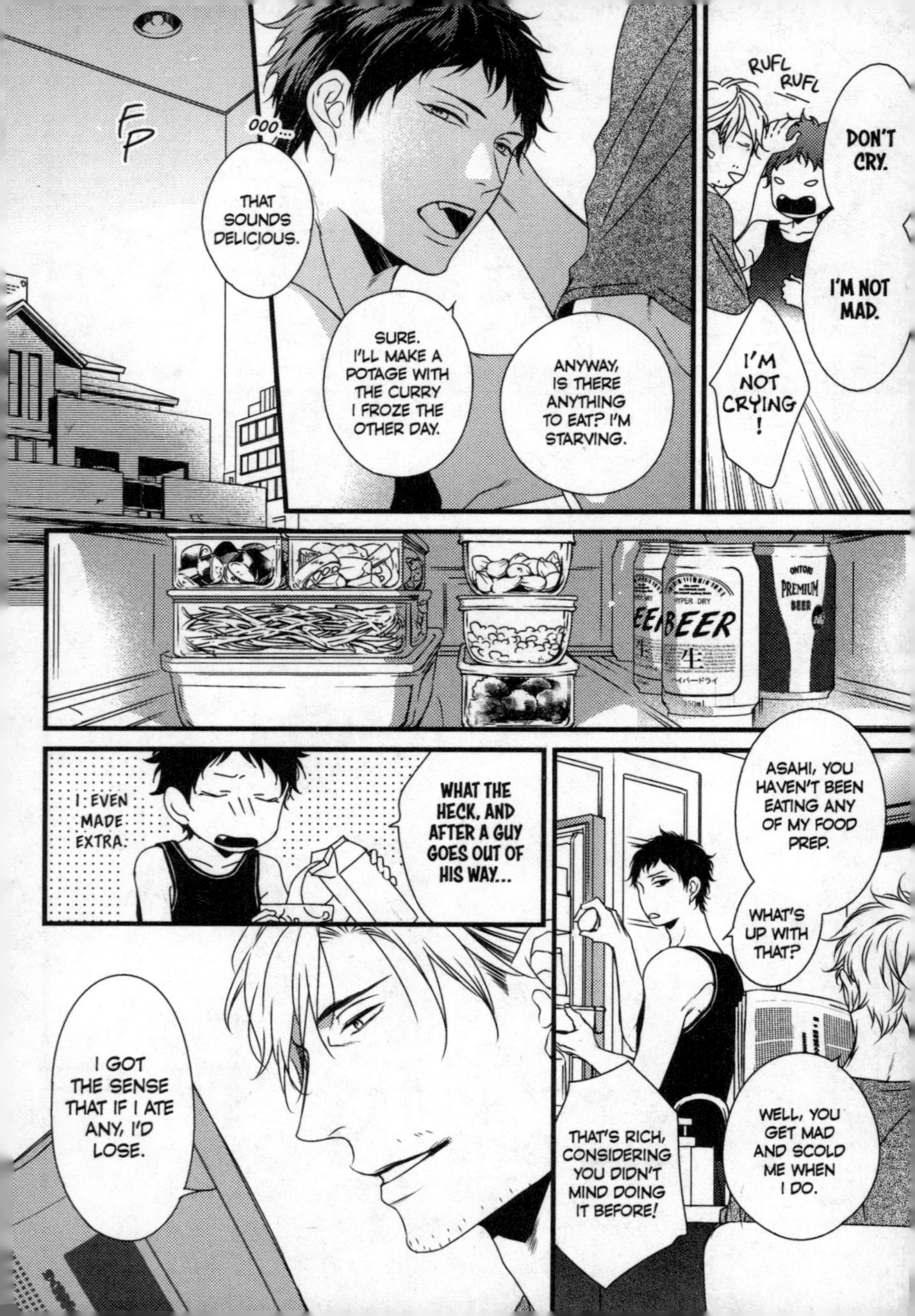

RUFL RUFL
DON'T CRY.
I'M NOT MAD.
I'M NOT CRYING!
FP
OOO...
ANYWAY, IS THERE ANYTHING TO EAT? I'M STARVING.
SURE. I'LL MAKE A POTAGE WITH THE CURRY I FROZE THE OTHER DAY.
THAT SOUNDS DELICIOUS.
ONTORI PREMIUM BEER
HYPER DRY BEER
ASAHI, YOU HAVEN'T BEEN EATING ANY OF MY FOOD PREP.
WHAT'S UP WITH THAT?
WELL, YOU GET MAD AND SCOLD ME WHEN I DO.
THAT'S RICH, CONSIDERING YOU DIDN'T MIND DOING IT BEFORE!
WHAT THE HECK, AND AFTER A GUY GOES OUT OF HIS WAY...
I EVEN MADE EXTRA.
I GOT THE SENSE THAT IF I ATE ANY, I'D LOSE.

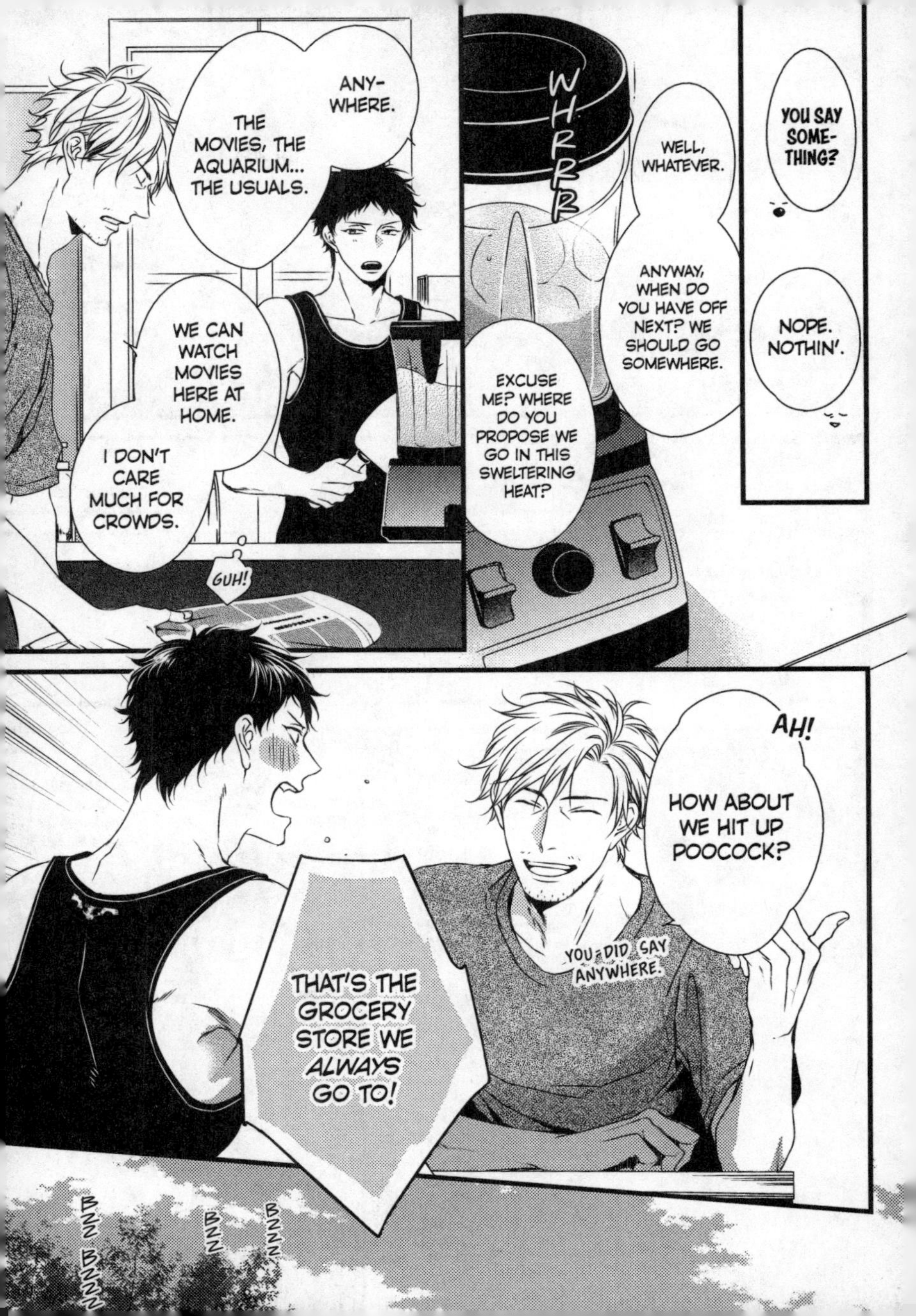
YOU SAY SOME-THING?
NOPE. NOTHIN'.
WHRRRR
WELL, WHATEVER.
ANYWAY, WHEN DO YOU HAVE OFF NEXT? WE SHOULD GO SOMEWHERE.
EXCUSE ME? WHERE DO YOU PROPOSE WE GO IN THIS SWELTERING HEAT?
ANY-WHERE.
THE MOVIES, THE AQUARIUM... THE USUALS.
WE CAN WATCH MOVIES HERE AT HOME.
I DON'T CARE MUCH FOR CROWDS.
GUH!
AH!
HOW ABOUT WE HIT UP POOCOCK?
YOU DID SAY ANYWHERE.
THAT'S THE GROCERY STORE WE *ALWAYS* GO TO!
BZZZ
BZZ
BZZZ

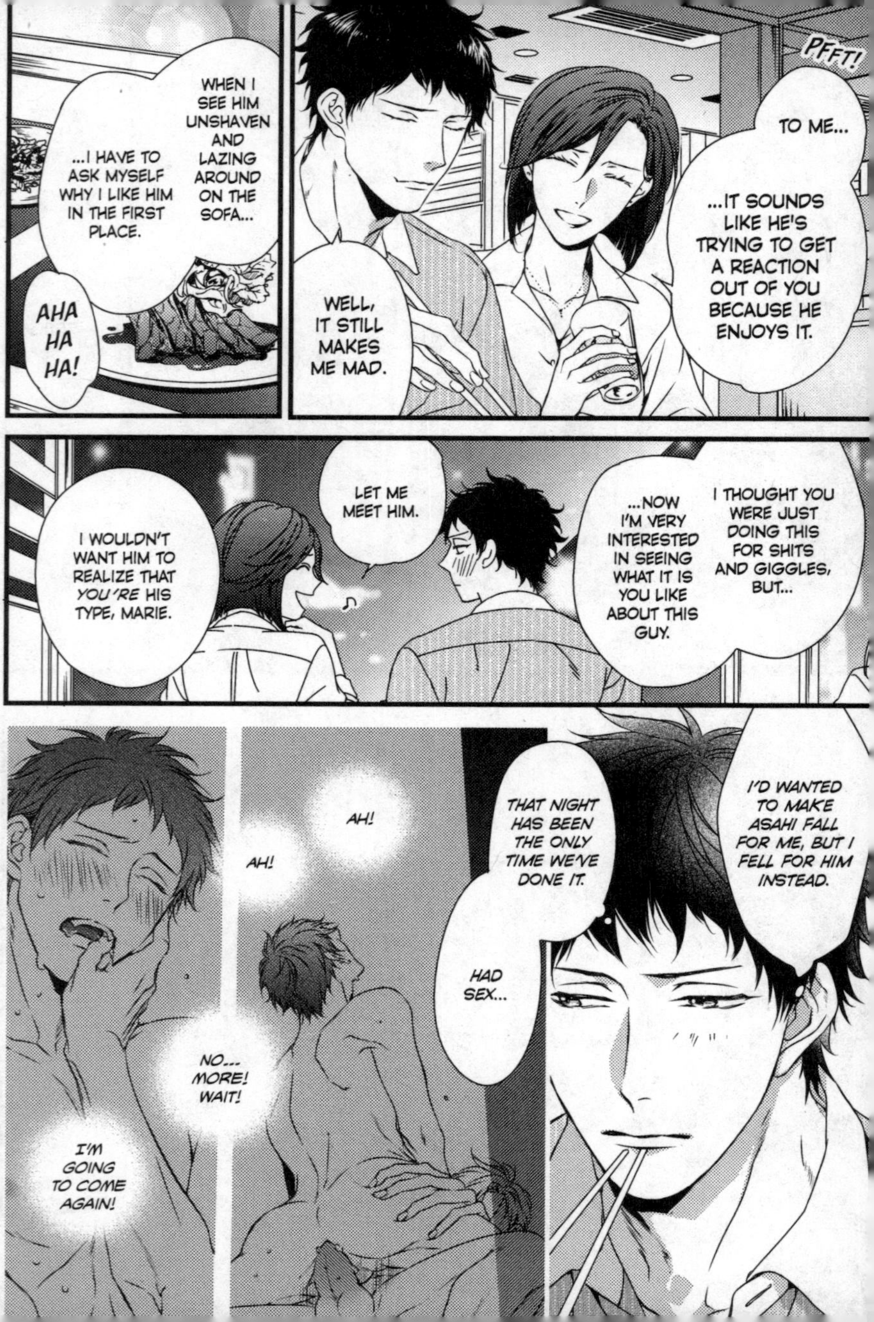
PFFT!
TO ME...
...IT SOUNDS LIKE HE'S TRYING TO GET A REACTION OUT OF YOU BECAUSE HE ENJOYS IT.
WELL, IT STILL MAKES ME MAD.
WHEN I SEE HIM UNSHAVEN AND LAZING AROUND ON THE SOFA...
...I HAVE TO ASK MYSELF WHY I LIKE HIM IN THE FIRST PLACE.
AHA HA HA!
I THOUGHT YOU WERE JUST DOING THIS FOR SHITS AND GIGGLES, BUT...
...NOW I'M VERY INTERESTED IN SEEING WHAT IT IS YOU LIKE ABOUT THIS GUY.
LET ME MEET HIM.
I WOULDN'T WANT HIM TO REALIZE THAT *YOU'RE* HIS TYPE, MARIE.
I'D WANTED TO MAKE ASAHI FALL FOR ME, BUT I FELL FOR HIM INSTEAD.
THAT NIGHT HAS BEEN THE ONLY TIME WE'VE DONE IT.
HAD SEX...
AH!
AH!
NO... MORE! WAIT!
I'M GOING TO COME AGAIN!

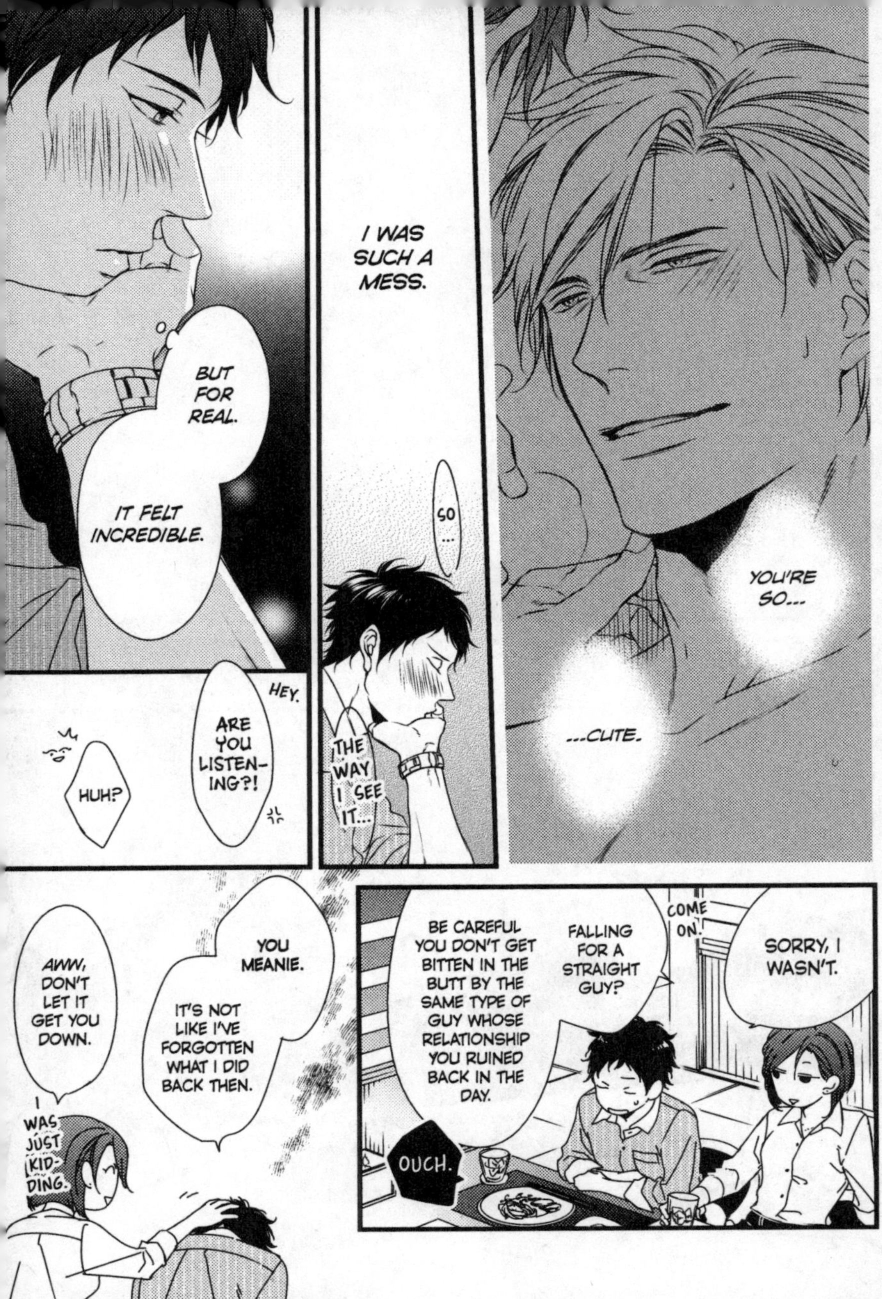
YOU'RE SO...
...CUTE.
I WAS SUCH A MESS.
SO...
THE WAY I SEE IT...
BUT FOR REAL.
IT FELT INCREDIBLE.
HEY.
ARE YOU LISTENING?!
HUH?
SORRY, I WASN'T.
COME ON.
FALLING FOR A STRAIGHT GUY?
BE CAREFUL YOU DON'T GET BITTEN IN THE BUTT BY THE SAME TYPE OF GUY WHOSE RELATIONSHIP YOU RUINED BACK IN THE DAY.
OUCH.
YOU MEANIE.
IT'S NOT LIKE I'VE FORGOTTEN WHAT I DID BACK THEN.
AWW, DON'T LET IT GET YOU DOWN.
I WAS JUST KIDDING.

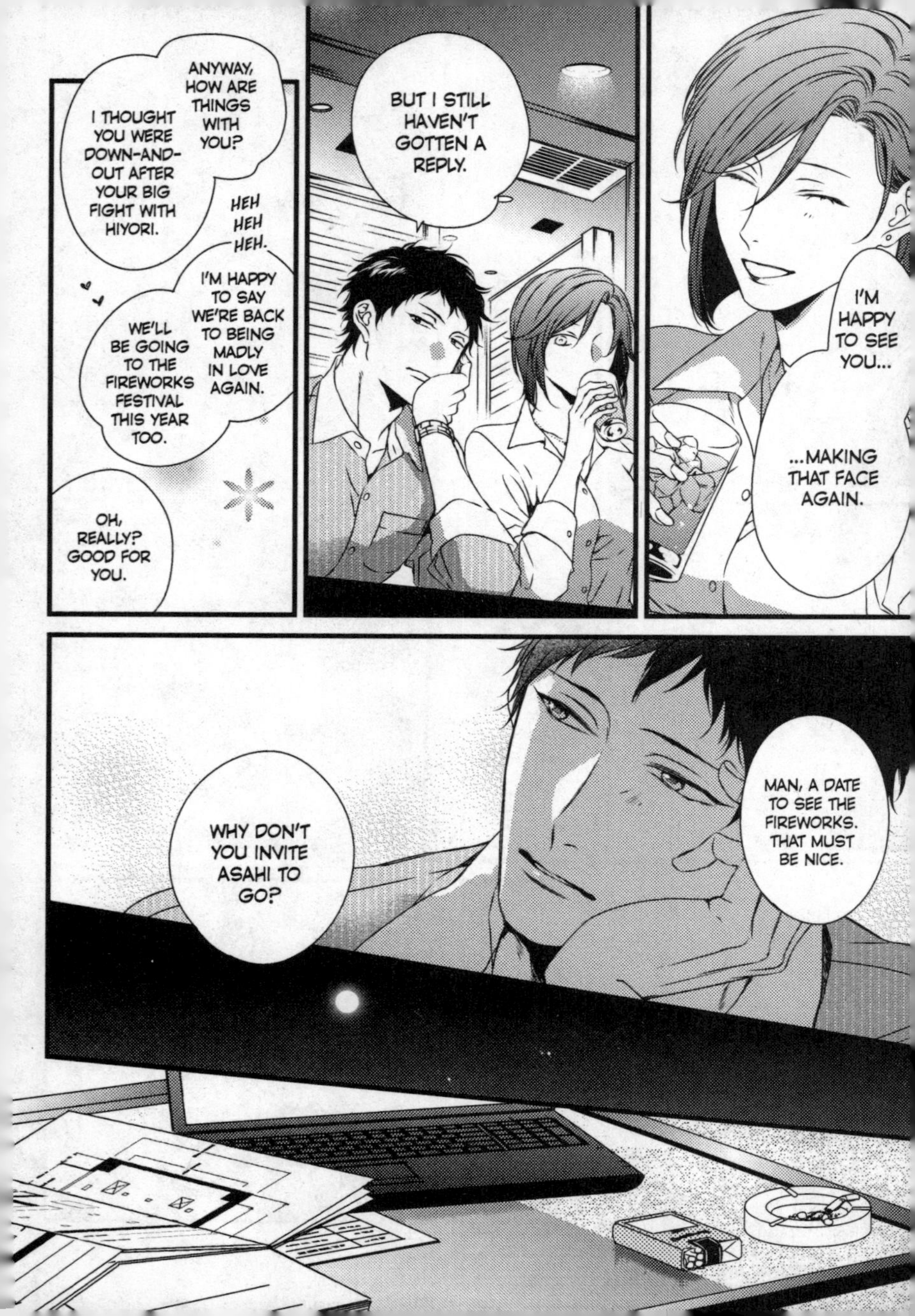
I'M HAPPY TO SEE YOU...
...MAKING THAT FACE AGAIN.
BUT I STILL HAVEN'T GOTTEN A REPLY.
ANYWAY, HOW ARE THINGS WITH YOU?
I THOUGHT YOU WERE DOWN-AND-OUT AFTER YOUR BIG FIGHT WITH HIYORI.
HEH HEH HEH.
I'M HAPPY TO SAY WE'RE BACK TO BEING MADLY IN LOVE AGAIN.
WE'LL BE GOING TO THE FIREWORKS FESTIVAL THIS YEAR TOO.
OH, REALLY? GOOD FOR YOU.
MAN, A DATE TO SEE THE FIREWORKS. THAT MUST BE NICE.
WHY DON'T YOU INVITE ASAHI TO GO?

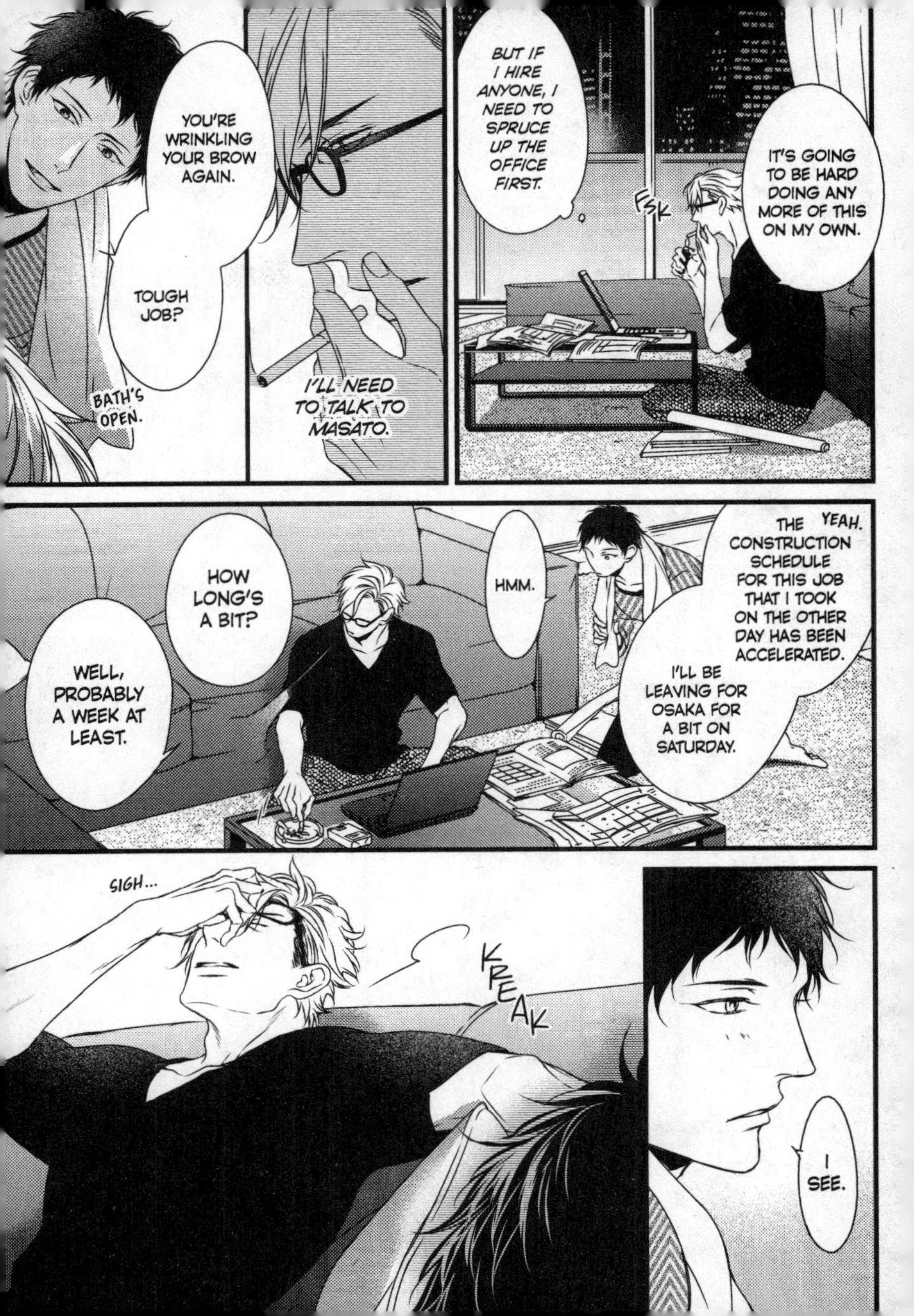
IT'S GOING TO BE HARD DOING ANY MORE OF THIS ON MY OWN.
FSK
BUT IF I HIRE ANYONE, I NEED TO SPRUCE UP THE OFFICE FIRST.
I'LL NEED TO TALK TO MASATO.
YOU'RE WRINKLING YOUR BROW AGAIN.
TOUGH JOB?
BATH'S OPEN.
YEAH.
THE CONSTRUCTION SCHEDULE FOR THIS JOB THAT I TOOK ON THE OTHER DAY HAS BEEN ACCELERATED.
I'LL BE LEAVING FOR OSAKA FOR A BIT ON SATURDAY.
HMM.
HOW LONG'S A BIT?
WELL, PROBABLY A WEEK AT LEAST.
I SEE.
SIGH...
KREAK

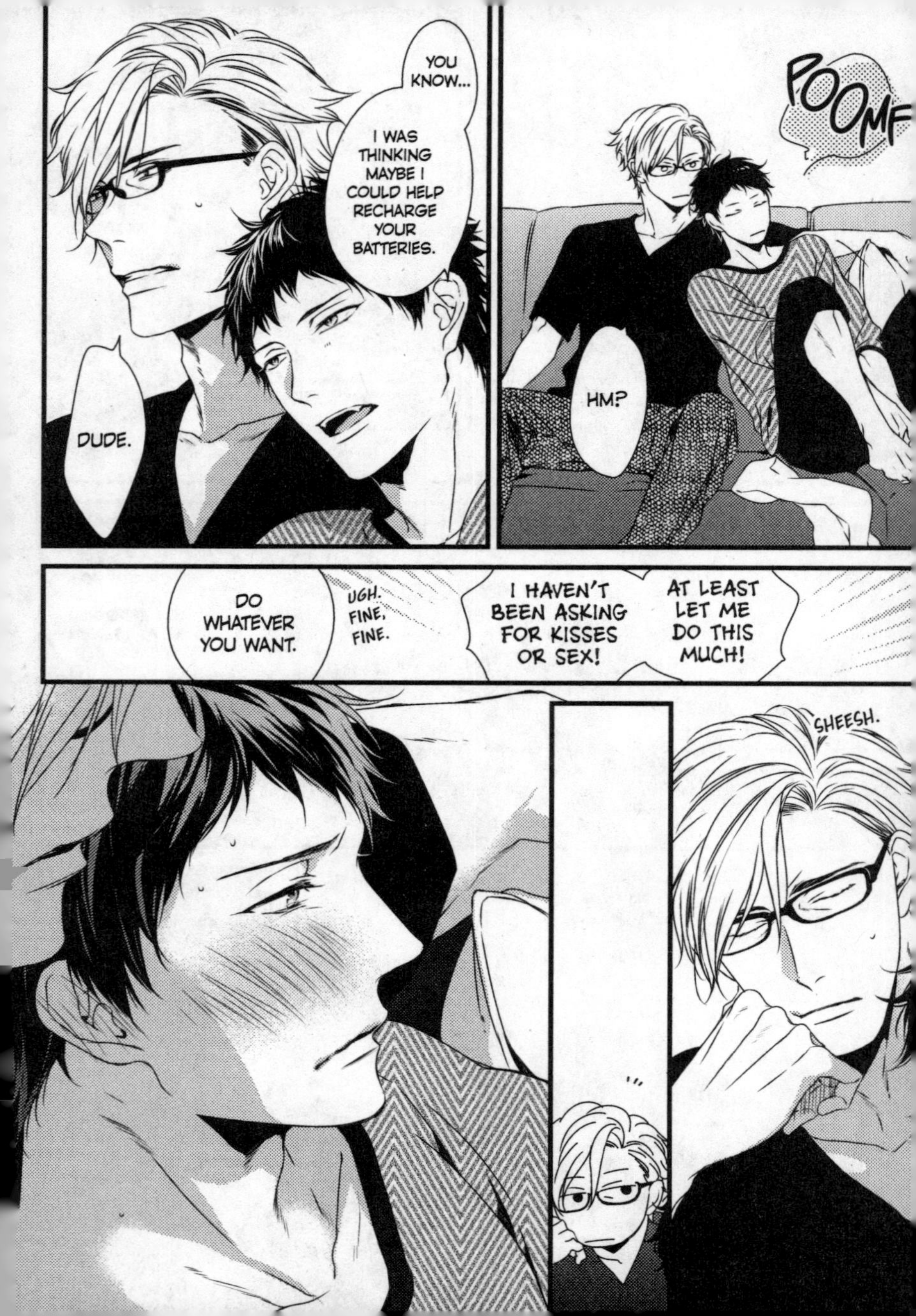
POOMF
HM?
YOU KNOW...
I WAS THINKING MAYBE I COULD HELP RECHARGE YOUR BATTERIES.
DUDE.
AT LEAST LET ME DO THIS MUCH!
I HAVEN'T BEEN ASKING FOR KISSES OR SEX!
UGH. FINE, FINE.
DO WHATEVER YOU WANT.
SHEESH.
...

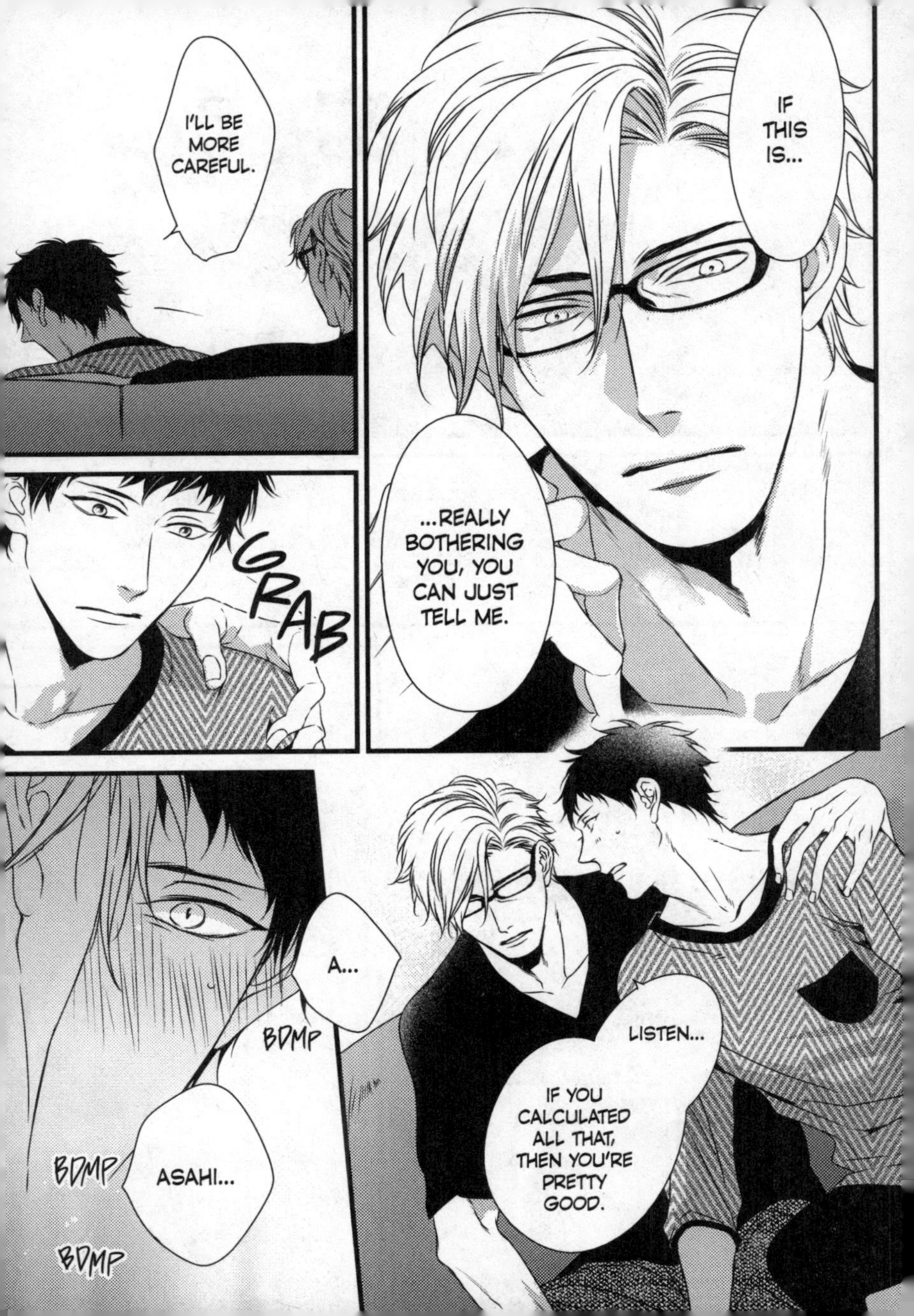
IF THIS IS...
...REALLY BOTHERING YOU, YOU CAN JUST TELL ME.
I'LL BE MORE CAREFUL.
GRAB
LISTEN...
IF YOU CALCULATED ALL THAT, THEN YOU'RE PRETTY GOOD.
A...
BDMP
ASAHI...
BDMP
BDMP

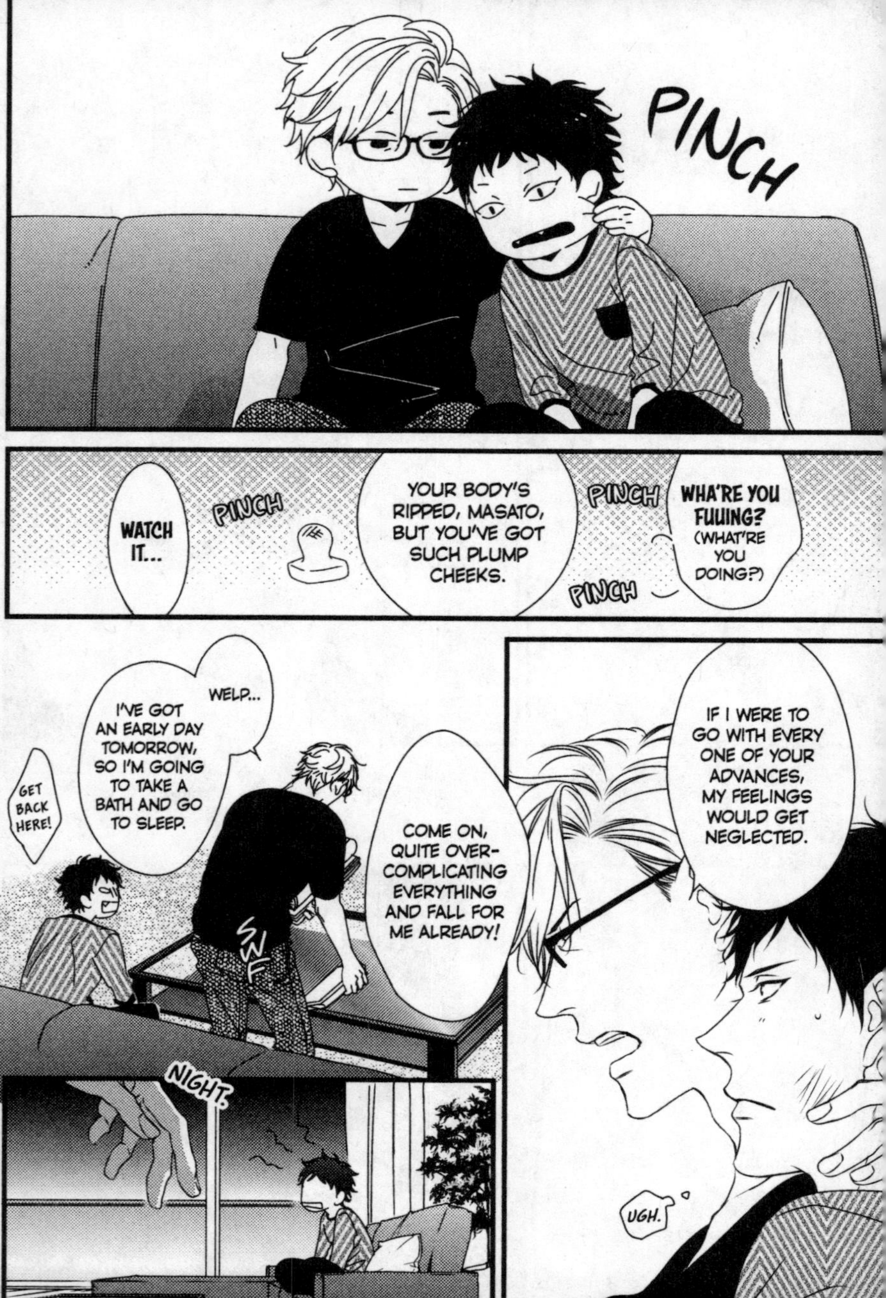
PINCH
WHA'RE YOU FUUING? (WHAT'RE YOU DOING?)
PINCH
PINCH
YOUR BODY'S RIPPED, MASATO, BUT YOU'VE GOT SUCH PLUMP CHEEKS.
PINCH
WATCH IT...
IF I WERE TO GO WITH EVERY ONE OF YOUR ADVANCES, MY FEELINGS WOULD GET NEGLECTED.
UGH.
COME ON, QUITE OVER-COMPLICATING EVERYTHING AND FALL FOR ME ALREADY!
WELP...
I'VE GOT AN EARLY DAY TOMORROW, SO I'M GOING TO TAKE A BATH AND GO TO SLEEP.
GET BACK HERE!
SWF
NIGHT.

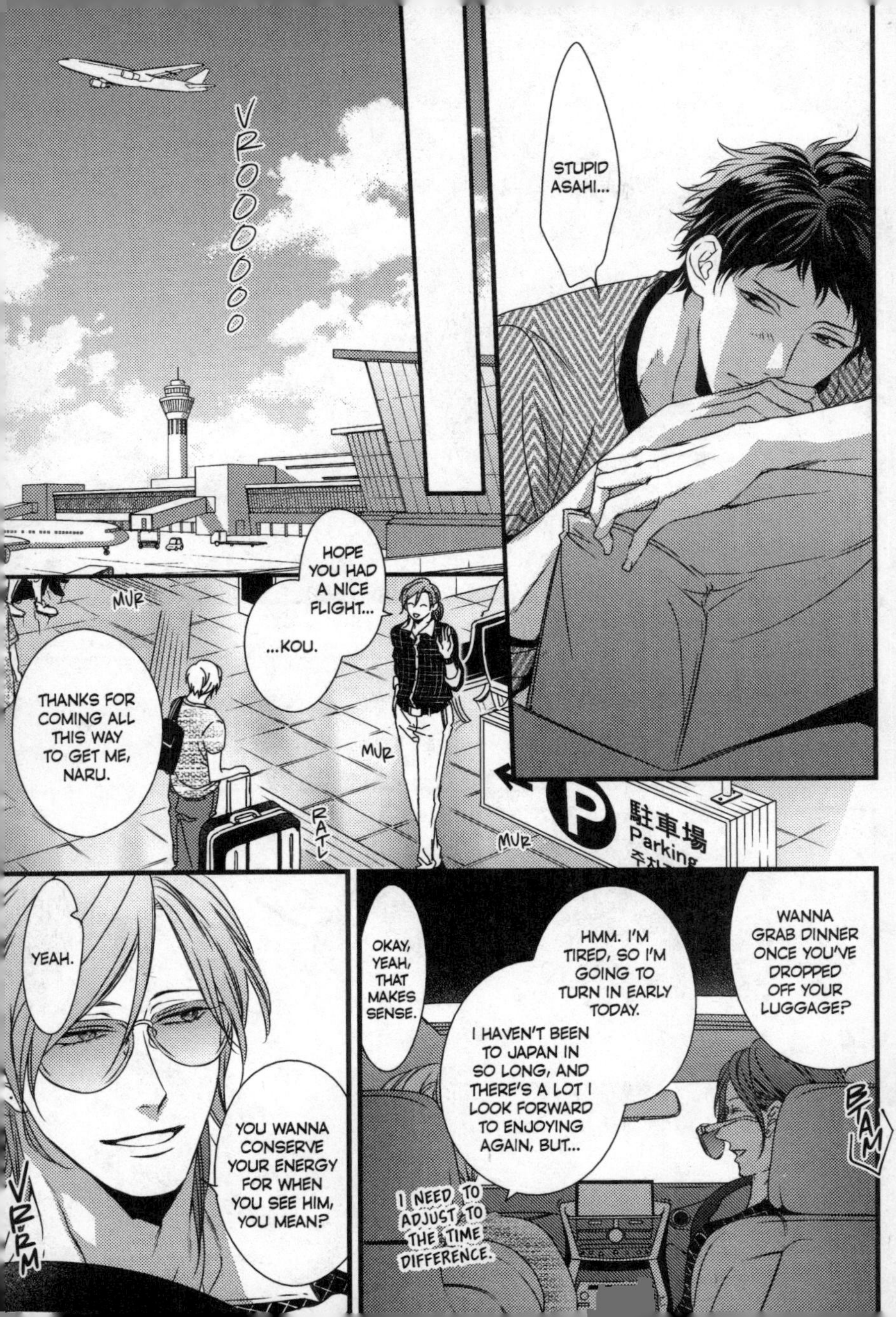
STUPID ASAHI...
VROOOOOOOOO
HOPE YOU HAD A NICE FLIGHT...
...KOU.
MUR
THANKS FOR COMING ALL THIS WAY TO GET ME, NARU.
MUR
RATL
MUR
P
駐車場
Parking
BTAM
WANNA GRAB DINNER ONCE YOU'VE DROPPED OFF YOUR LUGGAGE?
HMM. I'M TIRED, SO I'M GOING TO TURN IN EARLY TODAY.
I HAVEN'T BEEN TO JAPAN IN SO LONG, AND THERE'S A LOT I LOOK FORWARD TO ENJOYING AGAIN, BUT...
I NEED TO ADJUST TO THE TIME DIFFERENCE.
OKAY, YEAH, THAT MAKES SENSE.
YEAH.
YOU WANNA CONSERVE YOUR ENERGY FOR WHEN YOU SEE HIM, YOU MEAN?
VRRM

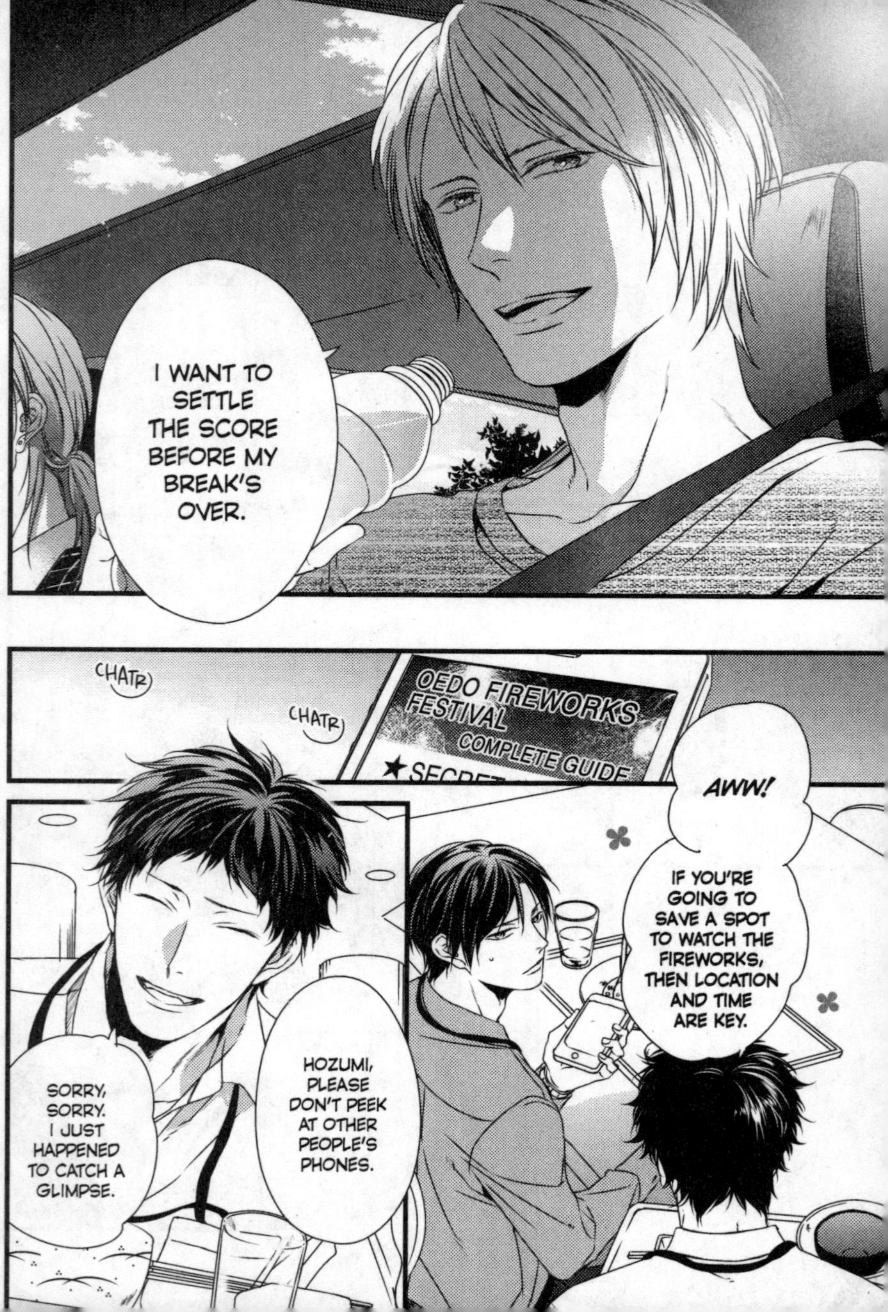
I WANT TO SETTLE THE SCORE BEFORE MY BREAK'S OVER.
CHATR
CHATR
OEDO FIREWORKS FESTIVAL COMPLETE GUIDE
★SECRET
AWW!
IF YOU'RE GOING TO SAVE A SPOT TO WATCH THE FIREWORKS, THEN LOCATION AND TIME ARE KEY.
HOZUMI, PLEASE DON'T PEEK AT OTHER PEOPLE'S PHONES.
SORRY, SORRY. I JUST HAPPENED TO CATCH A GLIMPSE.

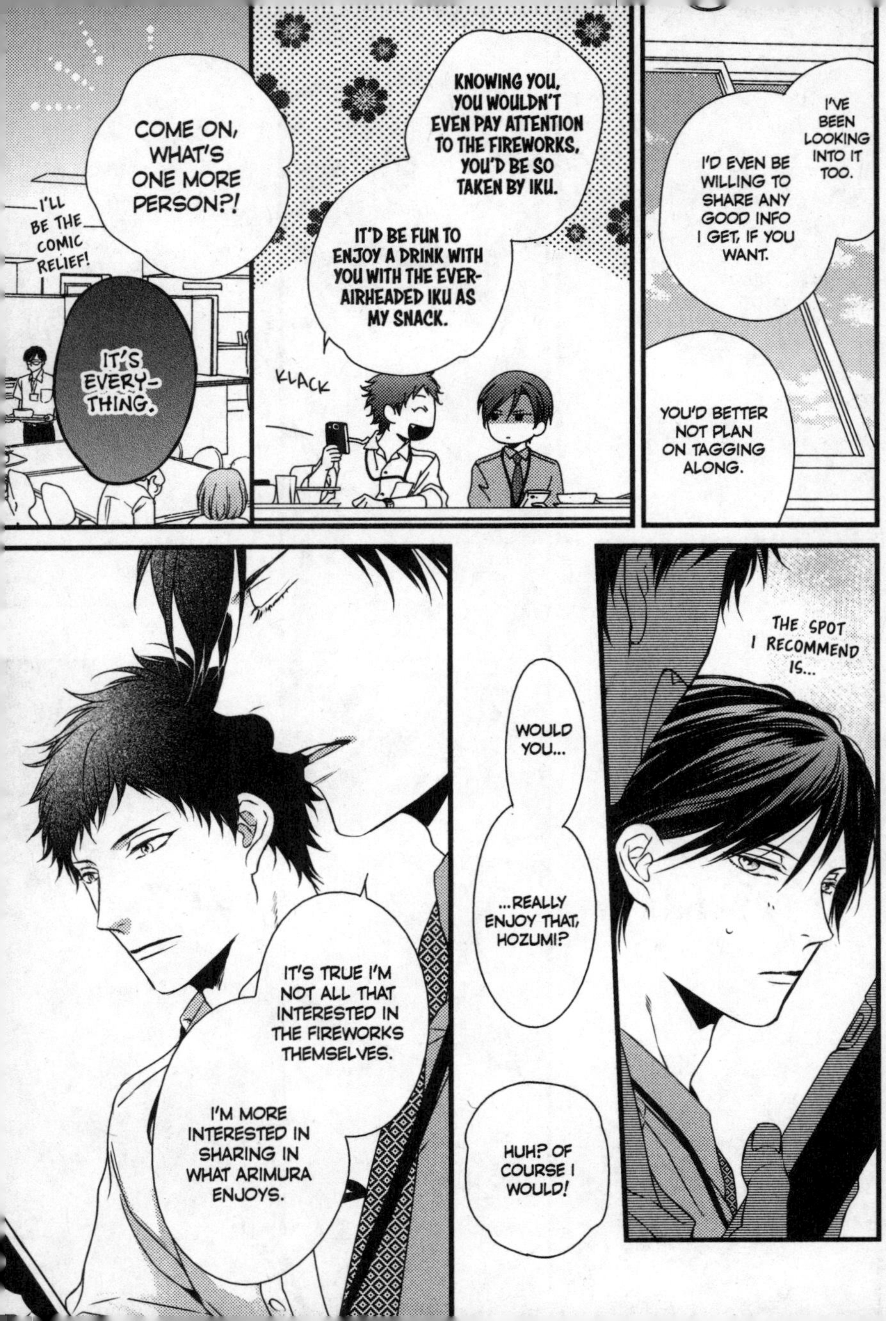
I'VE BEEN LOOKING INTO IT TOO.
I'D EVEN BE WILLING TO SHARE ANY GOOD INFO I GET, IF YOU WANT.
YOU'D BETTER NOT PLAN ON TAGGING ALONG.
KNOWING YOU, YOU WOULDN'T EVEN PAY ATTENTION TO THE FIREWORKS, YOU'D BE SO TAKEN BY IKU.
IT'D BE FUN TO ENJOY A DRINK WITH YOU WITH THE EVER-AIRHEADED IKU AS MY SNACK.
KLACK
COME ON, WHAT'S ONE MORE PERSON?!
I'LL BE THE COMIC RELIEF!
IT'S EVERY-THING.
THE SPOT I RECOMMEND IS...
WOULD YOU...
...REALLY ENJOY THAT, HOZUMI?
HUH? OF COURSE I WOULD!
IT'S TRUE I'M NOT ALL THAT INTERESTED IN THE FIREWORKS THEMSELVES.
I'M MORE INTERESTED IN SHARING IN WHAT ARIMURA ENJOYS.

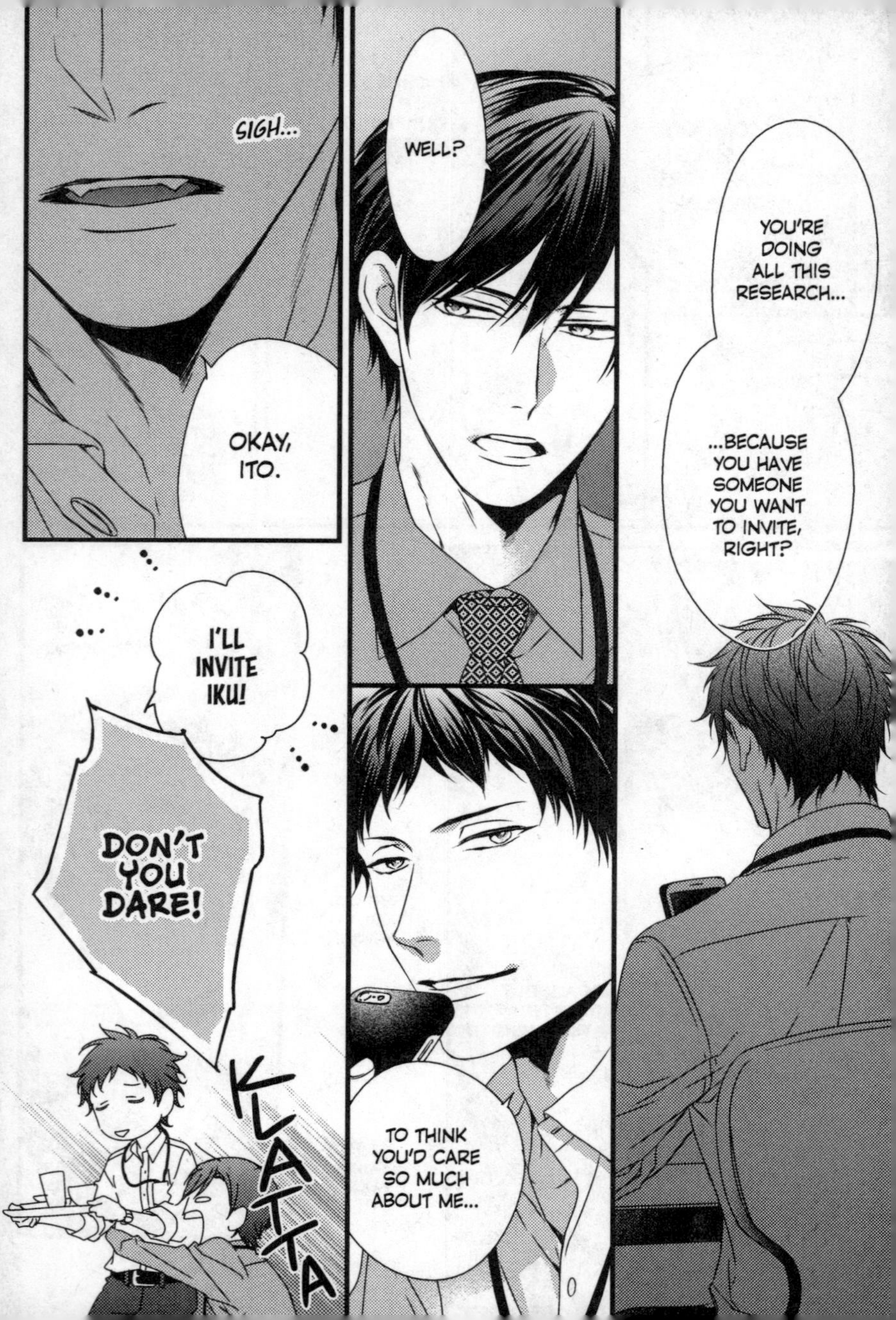
YOU'RE DOING ALL THIS RESEARCH...
...BECAUSE YOU HAVE SOMEONE YOU WANT TO INVITE, RIGHT?
WELL?
SIGH...
OKAY, ITO.
TO THINK YOU'D CARE SO MUCH ABOUT ME...
...
...
...
I'LL INVITE IKU!
...
...
DON'T YOU DARE!
KLATTA

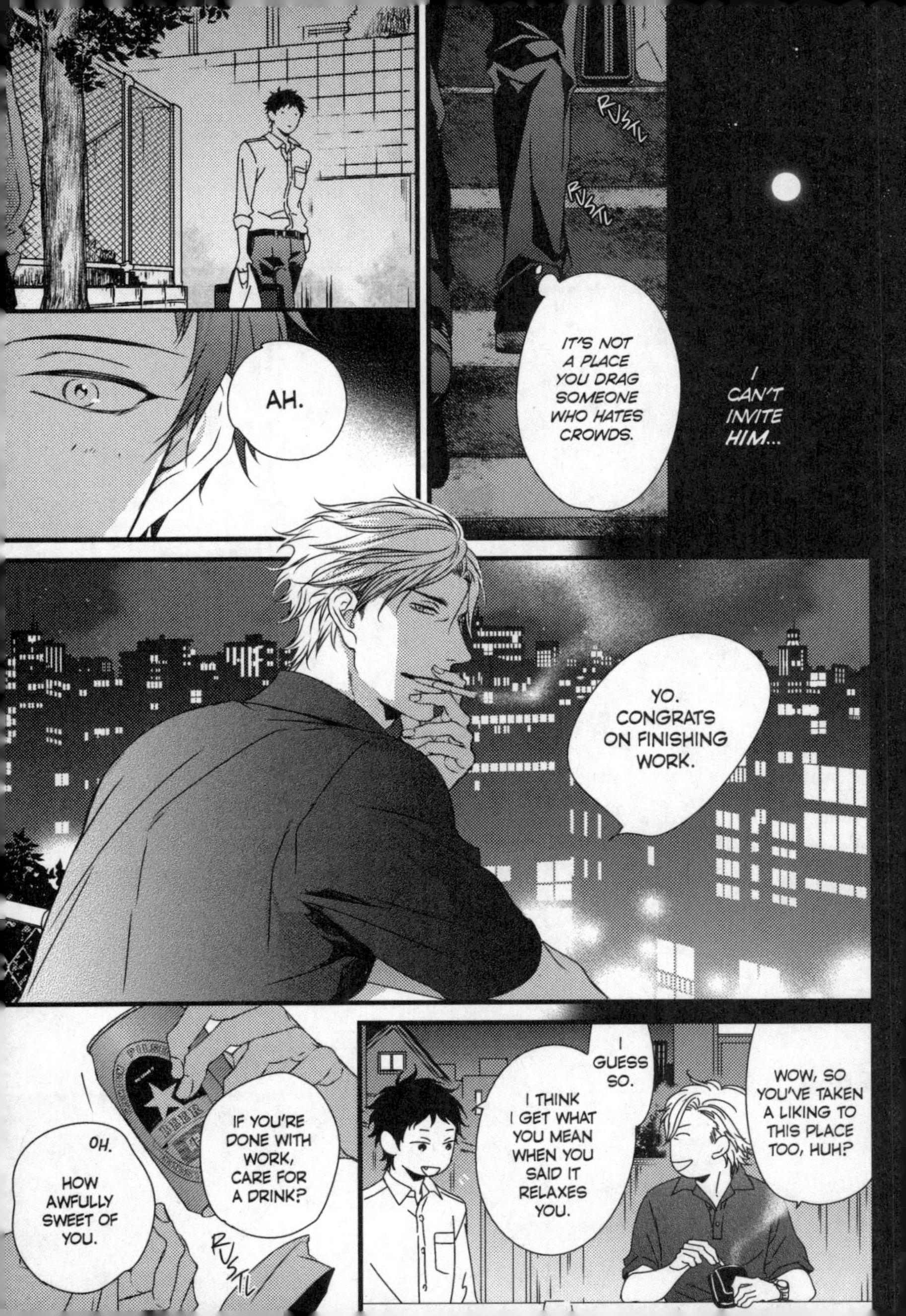
I CAN'T INVITE HIM...
RUSTLE
RUSTLE
IT'S NOT A PLACE YOU DRAG SOMEONE WHO HATES CROWDS.
AH.
YO. CONGRATS ON FINISHING WORK.
WOW, SO YOU'VE TAKEN A LIKING TO THIS PLACE TOO, HUH?
I GUESS SO.
I THINK I GET WHAT YOU MEAN WHEN YOU SAID IT RELAXES YOU.
IF YOU'RE DONE WITH WORK, CARE FOR A DRINK?
OH.
HOW AWFULLY SWEET OF YOU.
RUSTLE

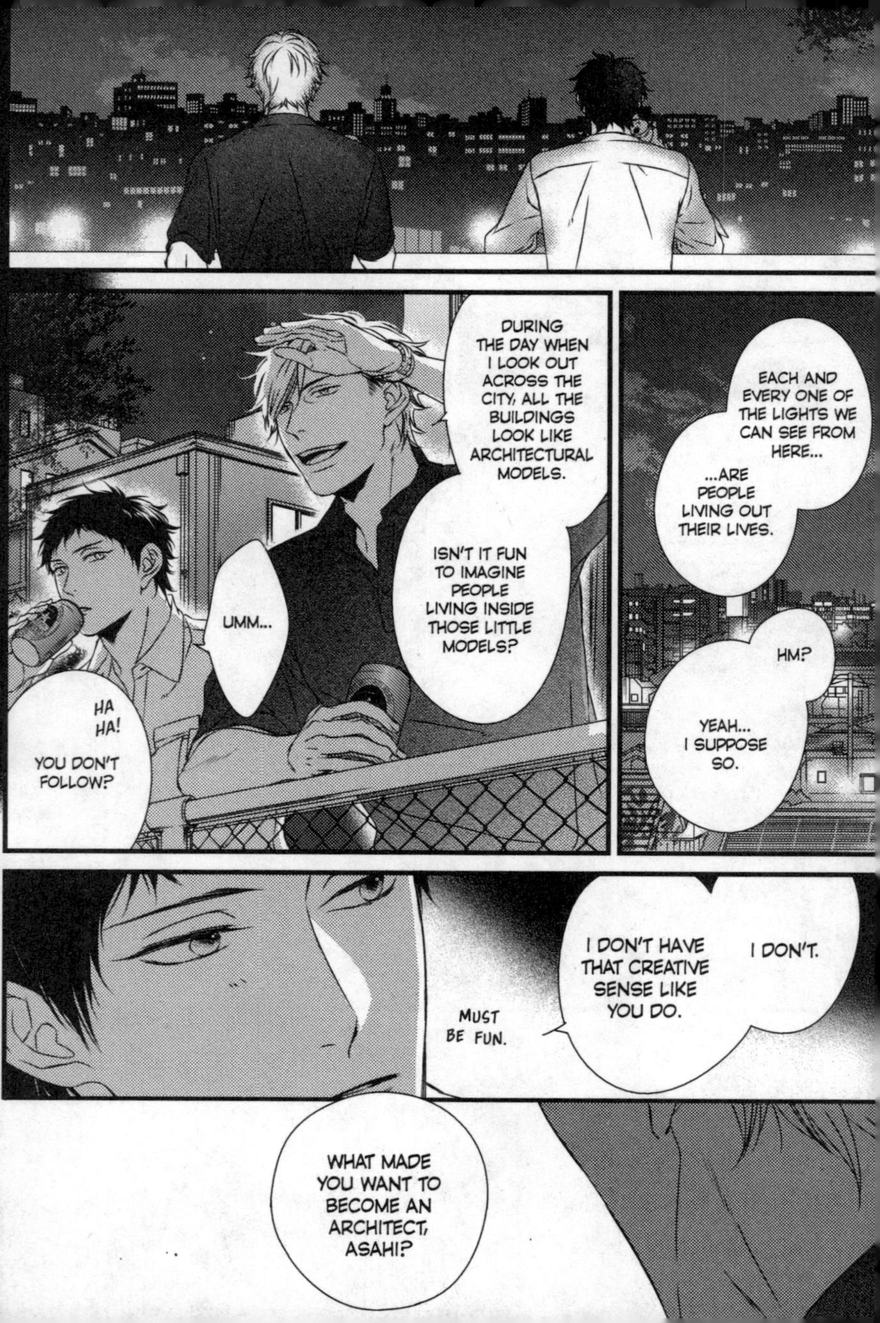
EACH AND EVERY ONE OF THE LIGHTS WE CAN SEE FROM HERE...
...ARE PEOPLE LIVING OUT THEIR LIVES.
HM?
YEAH... I SUPPOSE SO.
DURING THE DAY WHEN I LOOK OUT ACROSS THE CITY, ALL THE BUILDINGS LOOK LIKE ARCHITECTURAL MODELS.
ISN'T IT FUN TO IMAGINE PEOPLE LIVING INSIDE THOSE LITTLE MODELS?
UMM...
HA HA!
YOU DON'T FOLLOW?
I DON'T.
I DON'T HAVE THAT CREATIVE SENSE LIKE YOU DO.
MUST BE FUN.
WHAT MADE YOU WANT TO BECOME AN ARCHITECT, ASAHI?

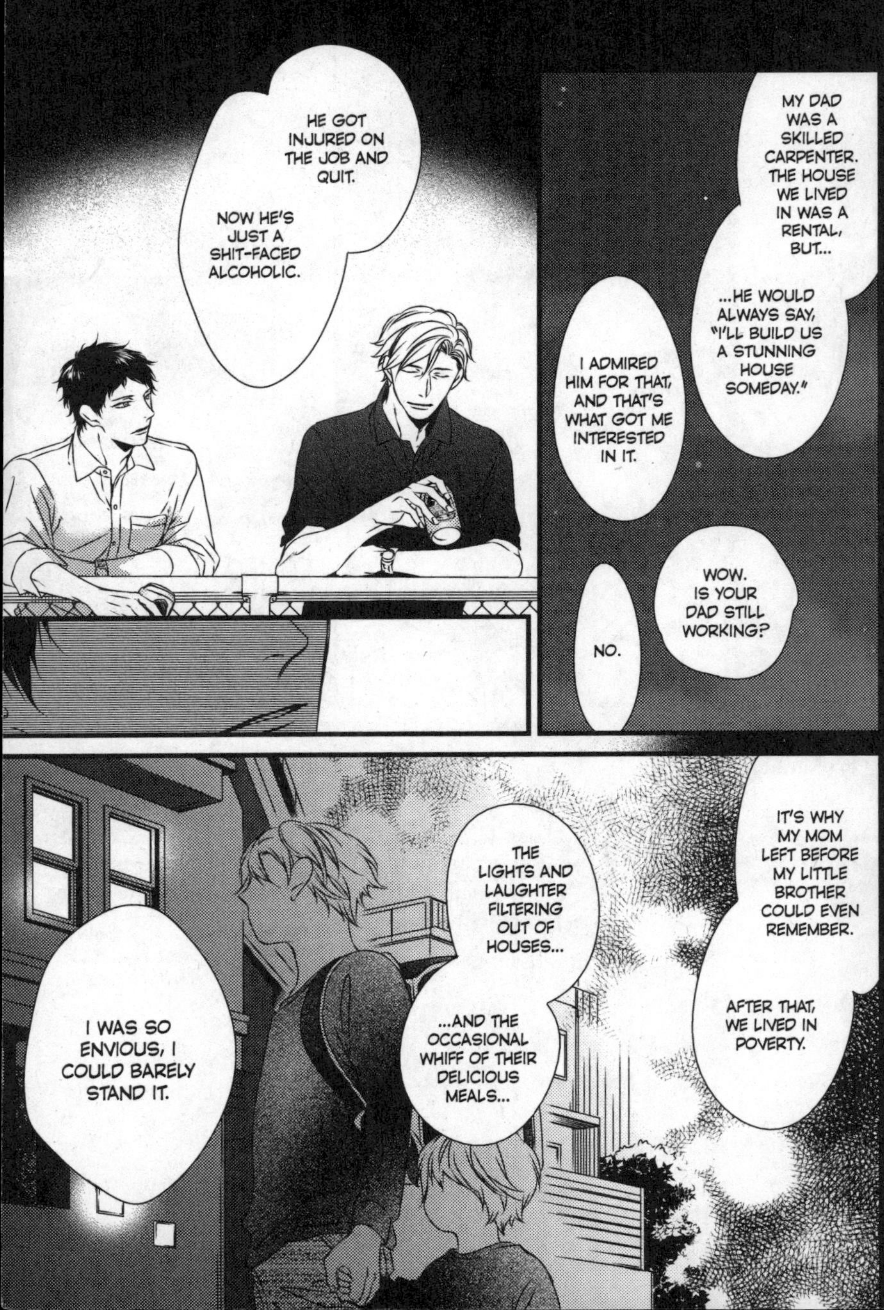
MY DAD WAS A SKILLED CARPENTER. THE HOUSE WE LIVED IN WAS A RENTAL, BUT...
...HE WOULD ALWAYS SAY, "I'LL BUILD US A STUNNING HOUSE SOMEDAY."
I ADMIRED HIM FOR THAT, AND THAT'S WHAT GOT ME INTERESTED IN IT.
WOW. IS YOUR DAD STILL WORKING?
NO.
HE GOT INJURED ON THE JOB AND QUIT.
NOW HE'S JUST A SHIT-FACED ALCOHOLIC.
IT'S WHY MY MOM LEFT BEFORE MY LITTLE BROTHER COULD EVEN REMEMBER.
AFTER THAT, WE LIVED IN POVERTY.
THE LIGHTS AND LAUGHTER FILTERING OUT OF HOUSES...
...AND THE OCCASIONAL WHIFF OF THEIR DELICIOUS MEALS...
I WAS SO ENVIOUS, I COULD BARELY STAND IT.

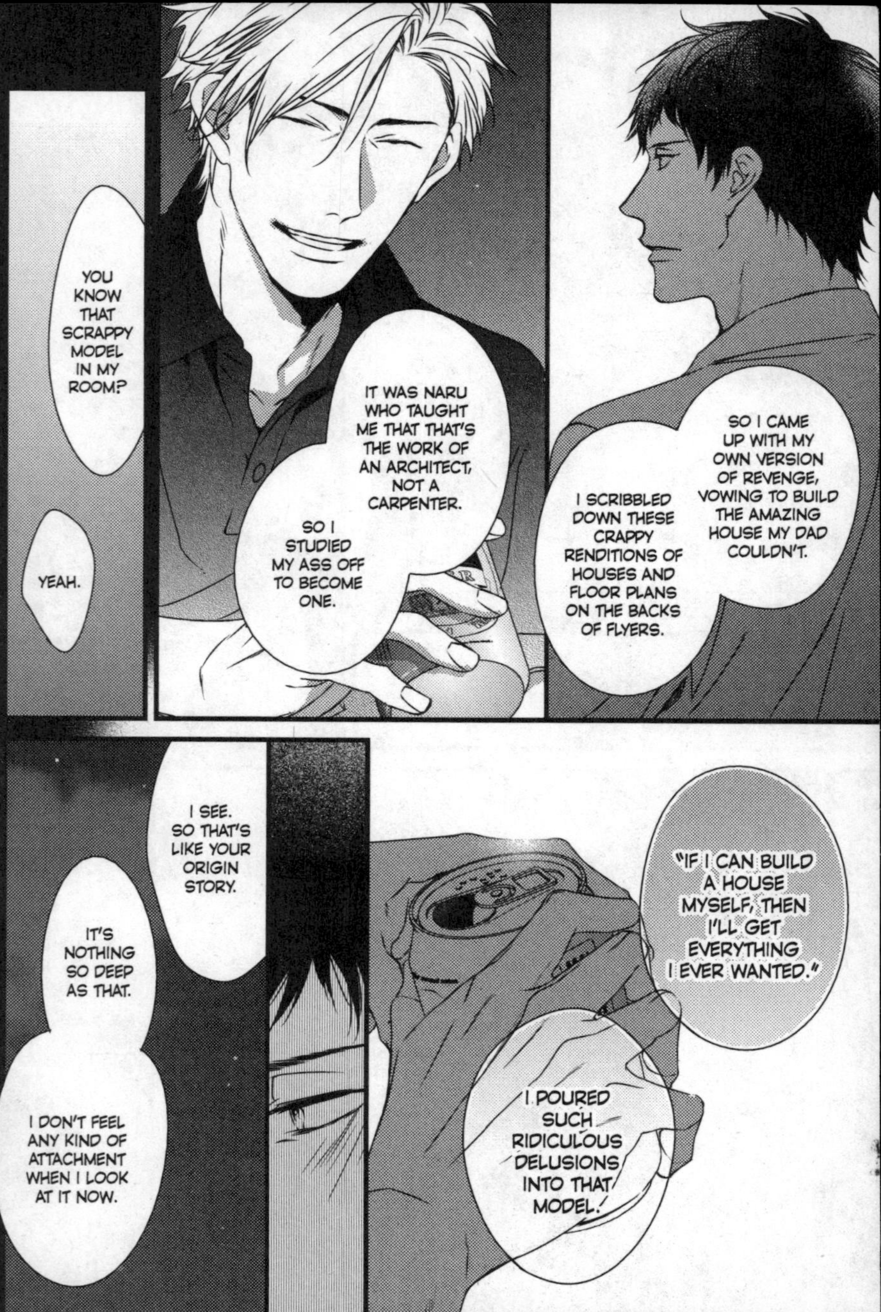
SO I CAME UP WITH MY OWN VERSION OF REVENGE, VOWING TO BUILD THE AMAZING HOUSE MY DAD COULDN'T.
I SCRIBBLED DOWN THESE CRAPPY RENDITIONS OF HOUSES AND FLOOR PLANS ON THE BACKS OF FLYERS.
IT WAS NARU WHO TAUGHT ME THAT THAT'S THE WORK OF AN ARCHITECT, NOT A CARPENTER.
SO I STUDIED MY ASS OFF TO BECOME ONE.
YOU KNOW THAT SCRAPPY MODEL IN MY ROOM?
YEAH.
"IF I CAN BUILD A HOUSE MYSELF, THEN I'LL GET EVERYTHING I EVER WANTED."
I POURED SUCH RIDICULOUS DELUSIONS INTO THAT MODEL.
I SEE. SO THAT'S LIKE YOUR ORIGIN STORY.
IT'S NOTHING SO DEEP AS THAT.
I DON'T FEEL ANY KIND OF ATTACHMENT WHEN I LOOK AT IT NOW.

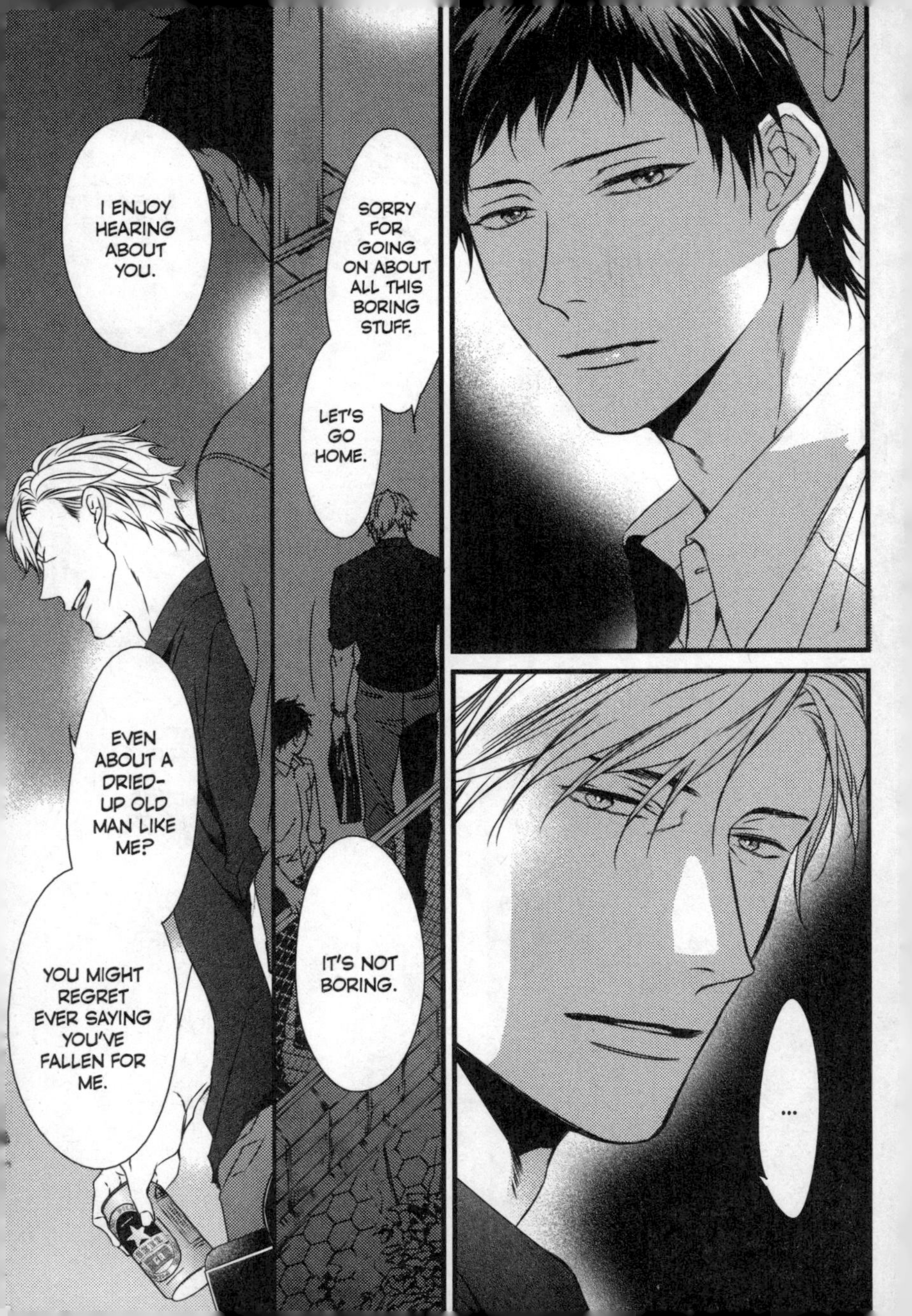
...
SORRY FOR GOING ON ABOUT ALL THIS BORING STUFF.
LET'S GO HOME.
IT'S NOT BORING.
I ENJOY HEARING ABOUT YOU.
EVEN ABOUT A DRIED-UP OLD MAN LIKE ME?
YOU MIGHT REGRET EVER SAYING YOU'VE FALLEN FOR ME.

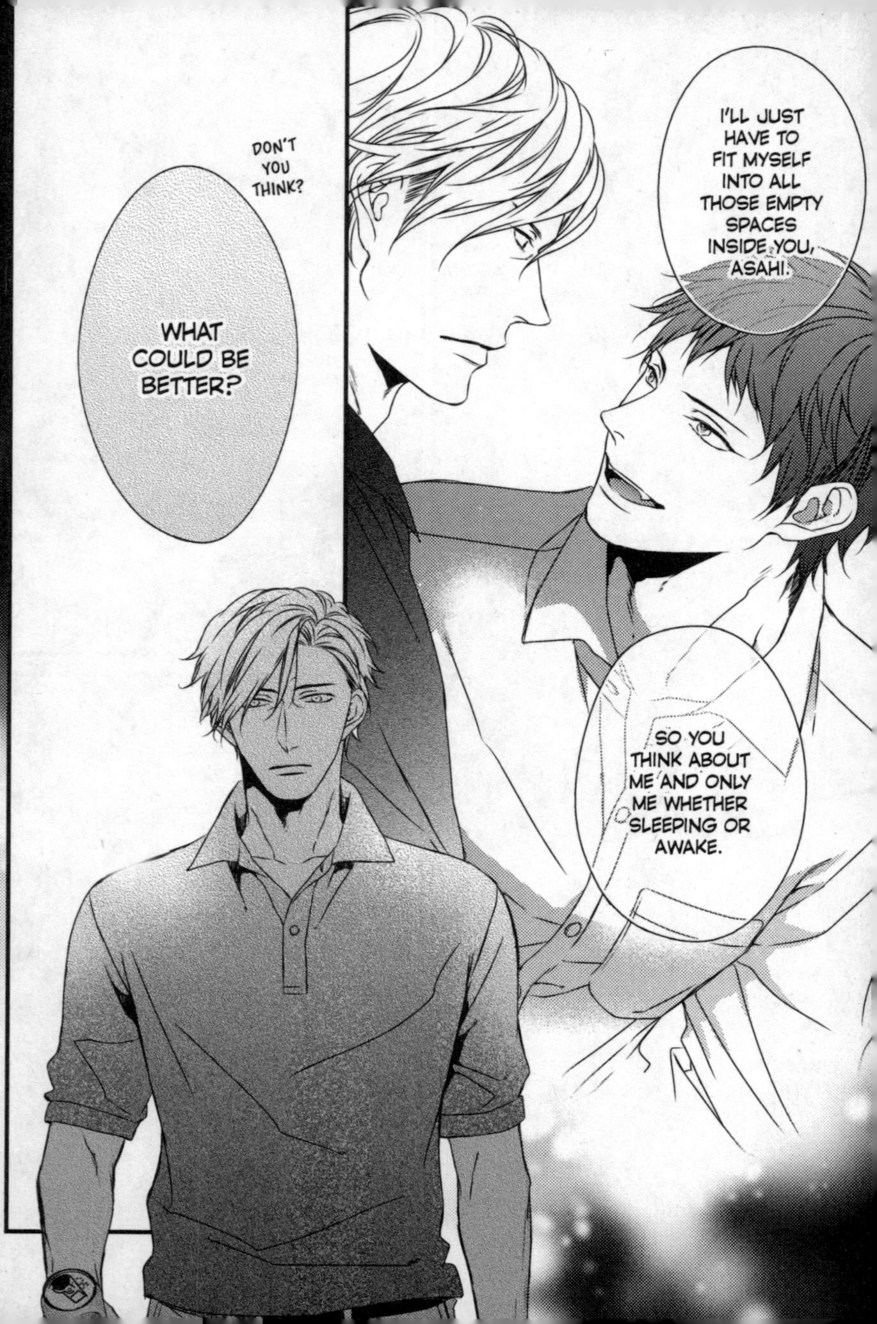
I'LL JUST HAVE TO FIT MYSELF INTO ALL THOSE EMPTY SPACES INSIDE YOU, ASAHI.
SO YOU THINK ABOUT ME AND ONLY ME WHETHER SLEEPING OR AWAKE.
DON'T YOU THINK?
WHAT COULD BE BETTER?

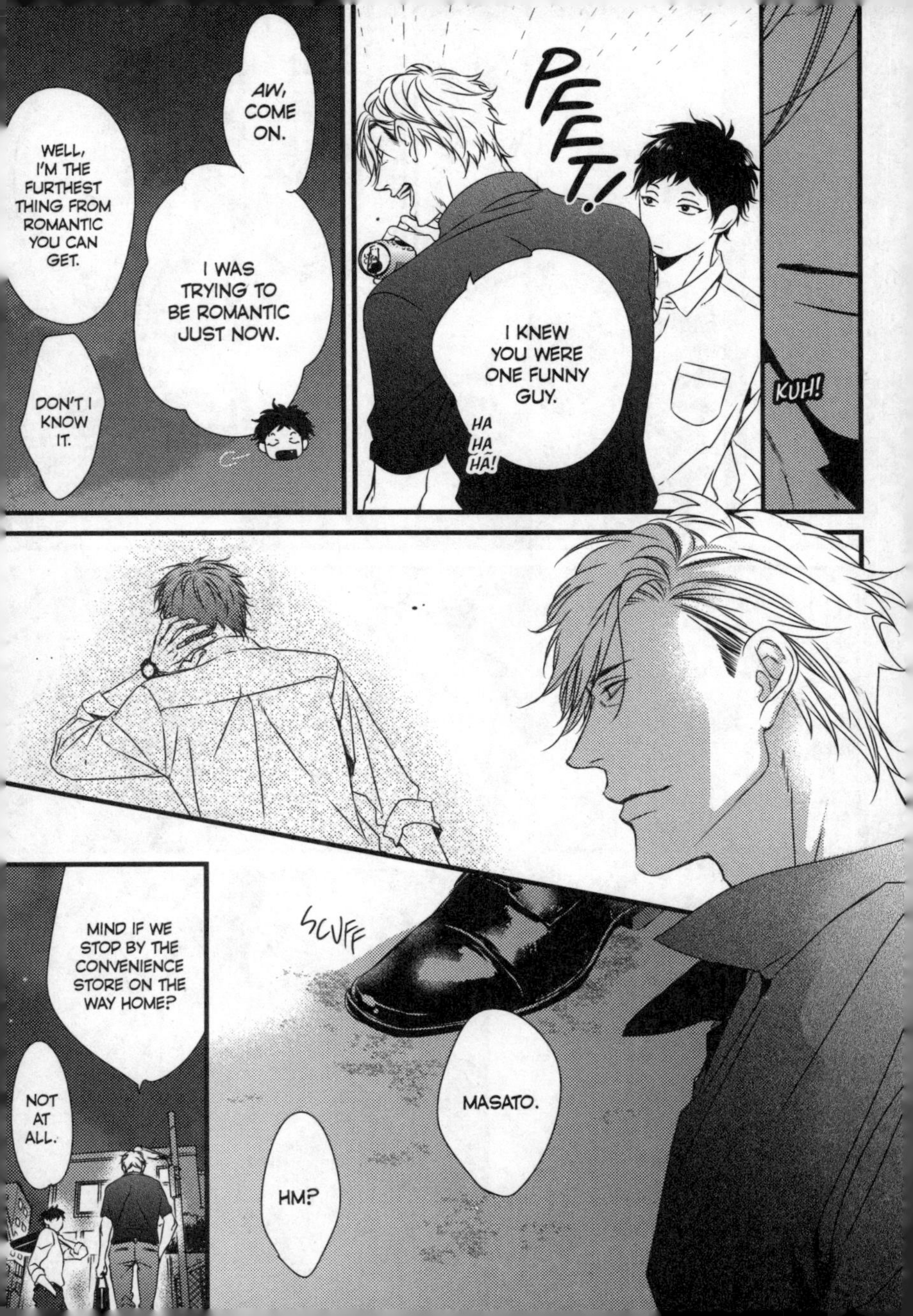
PFFT!
KUH!
I KNEW YOU WERE ONE FUNNY GUY.
HA HA HÃ!
WELL, I'M THE FURTHEST THING FROM ROMANTIC YOU CAN GET.
AW, COME ON.
I WAS TRYING TO BE ROMANTIC JUST NOW.
DON'T I KNOW IT.
SCUFF
MASATO.
HM?
MIND IF WE STOP BY THE CONVENIENCE STORE ON THE WAY HOME?
NOT AT ALL.

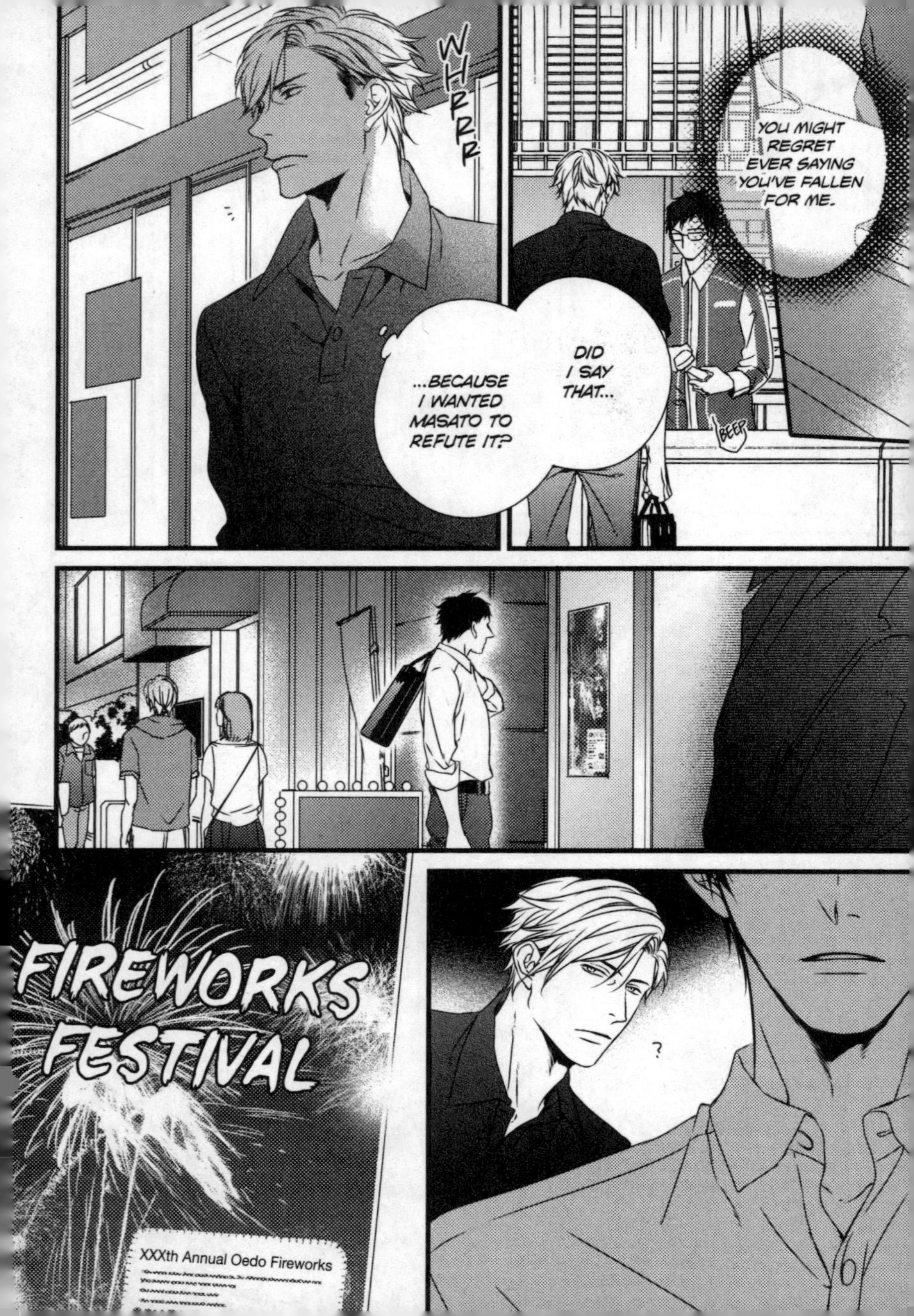
YOU MIGHT REGRET EVER SAYING YOU'VE FALLEN FOR ME.
BEEP
DID I SAY THAT...
...BECAUSE I WANTED MASATO TO REFUTE IT?
WHRRR
?
FIREWORKS FESTIVAL
XXXth Annual Oedo Fireworks

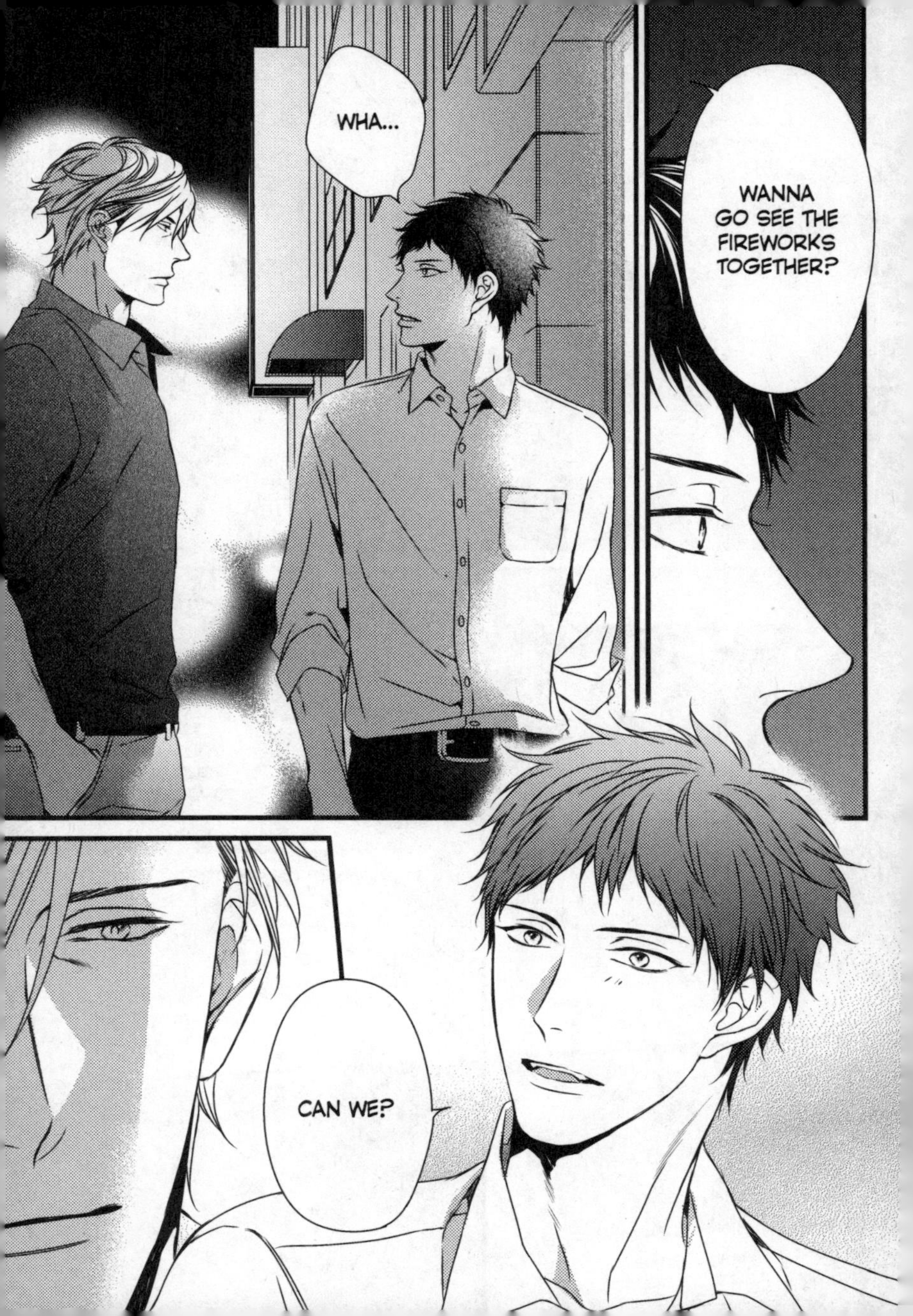
WANNA GO SEE THE FIREWORKS TOGETHER?
WHA...
CAN WE?

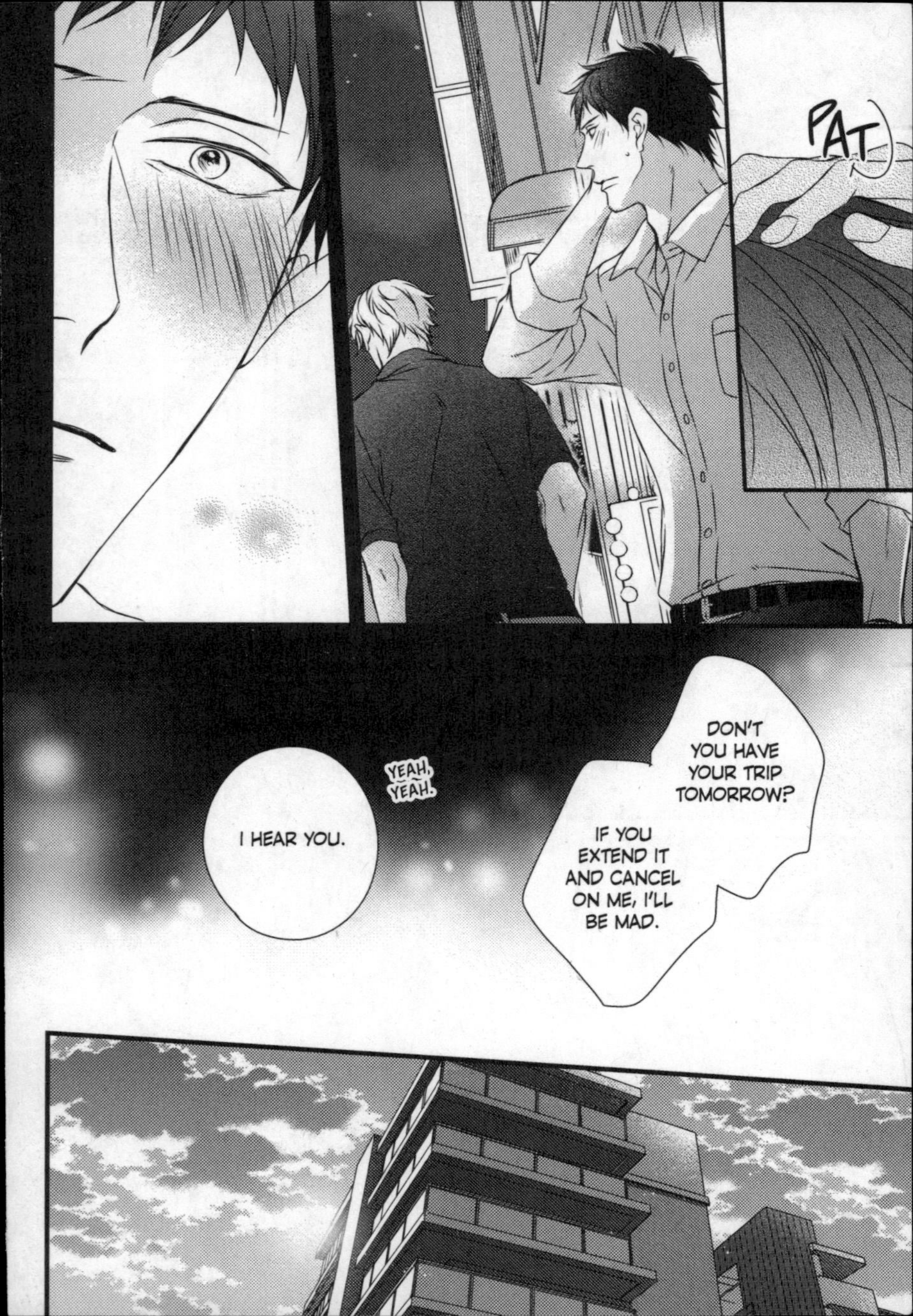
PAT
DON'T YOU HAVE YOUR TRIP TOMORROW?
IF YOU EXTEND IT AND CANCEL ON ME, I'LL BE MAD.
YEAH, YEAH.
I HEAR YOU.

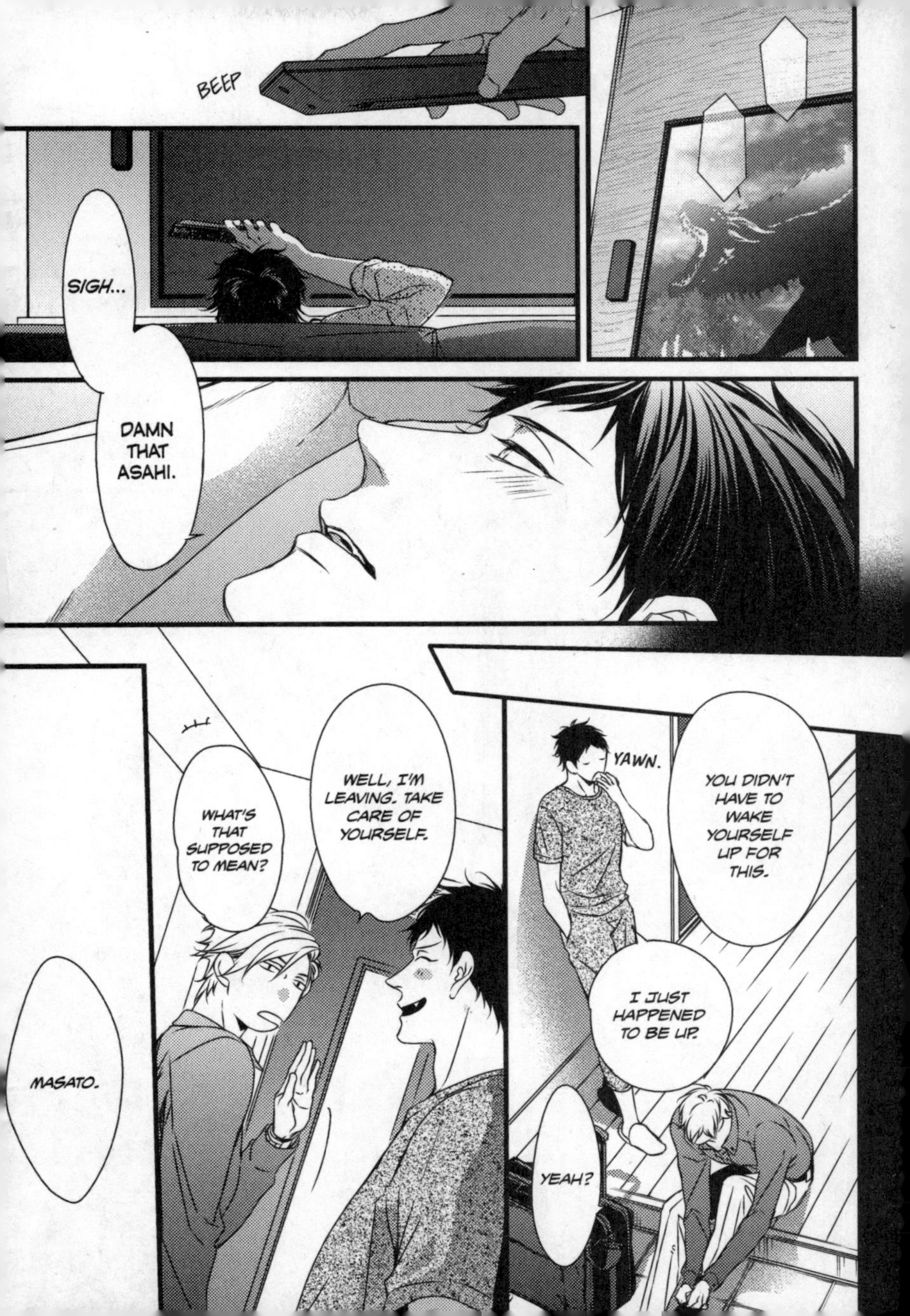
BEEP
SIGH...
DAMN THAT ASAHI.
YAWN.
YOU DIDN'T HAVE TO WAKE YOURSELF UP FOR THIS.
I JUST HAPPENED TO BE UP.
YEAH?
WELL, I'M LEAVING. TAKE CARE OF YOURSELF.
WHAT'S THAT SUPPOSED TO MEAN?
MASATO.

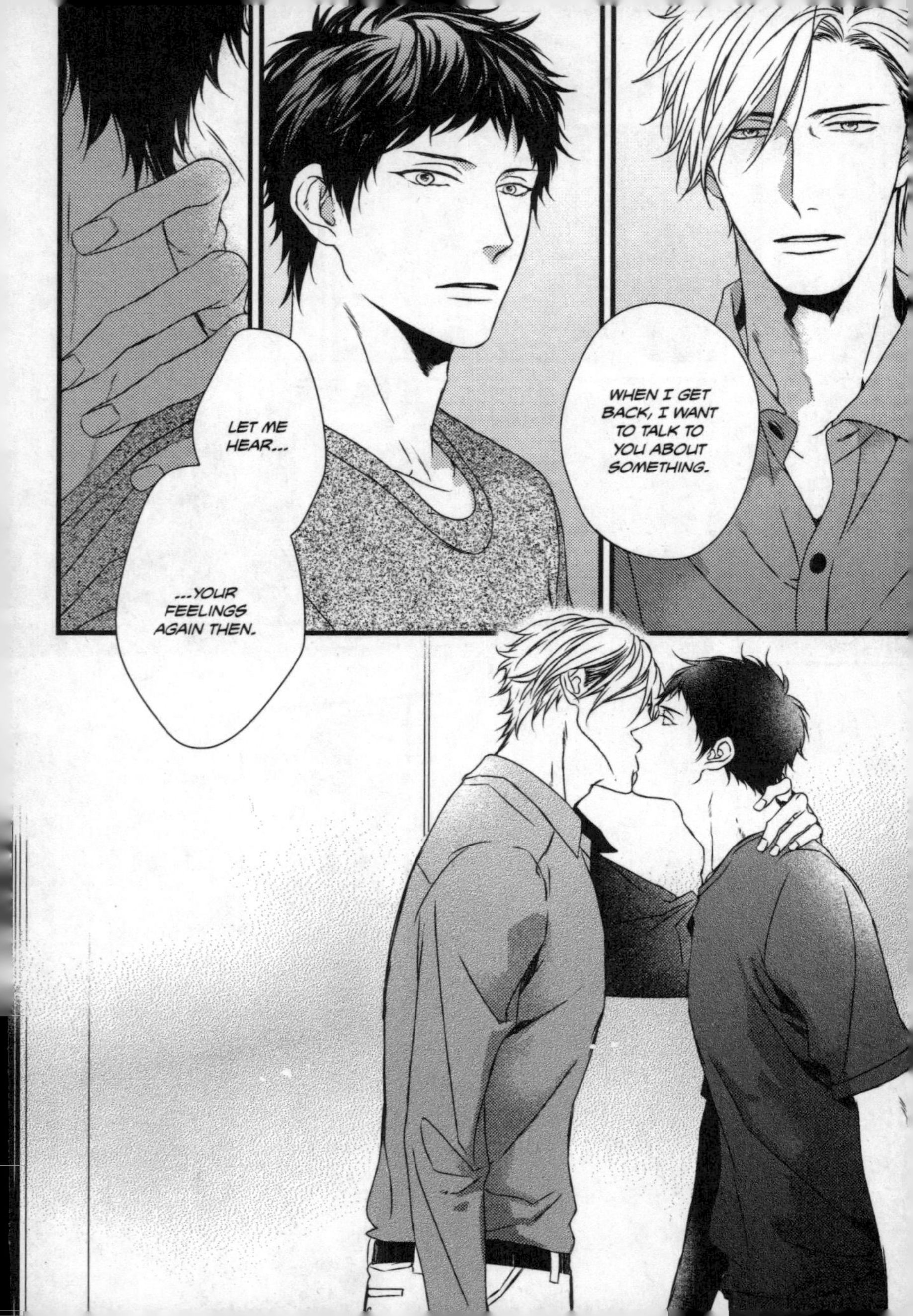
WHEN I GET BACK, I WANT TO TALK TO YOU ABOUT SOMETHING.
LET ME HEAR...
...YOUR FEELINGS AGAIN THEN.

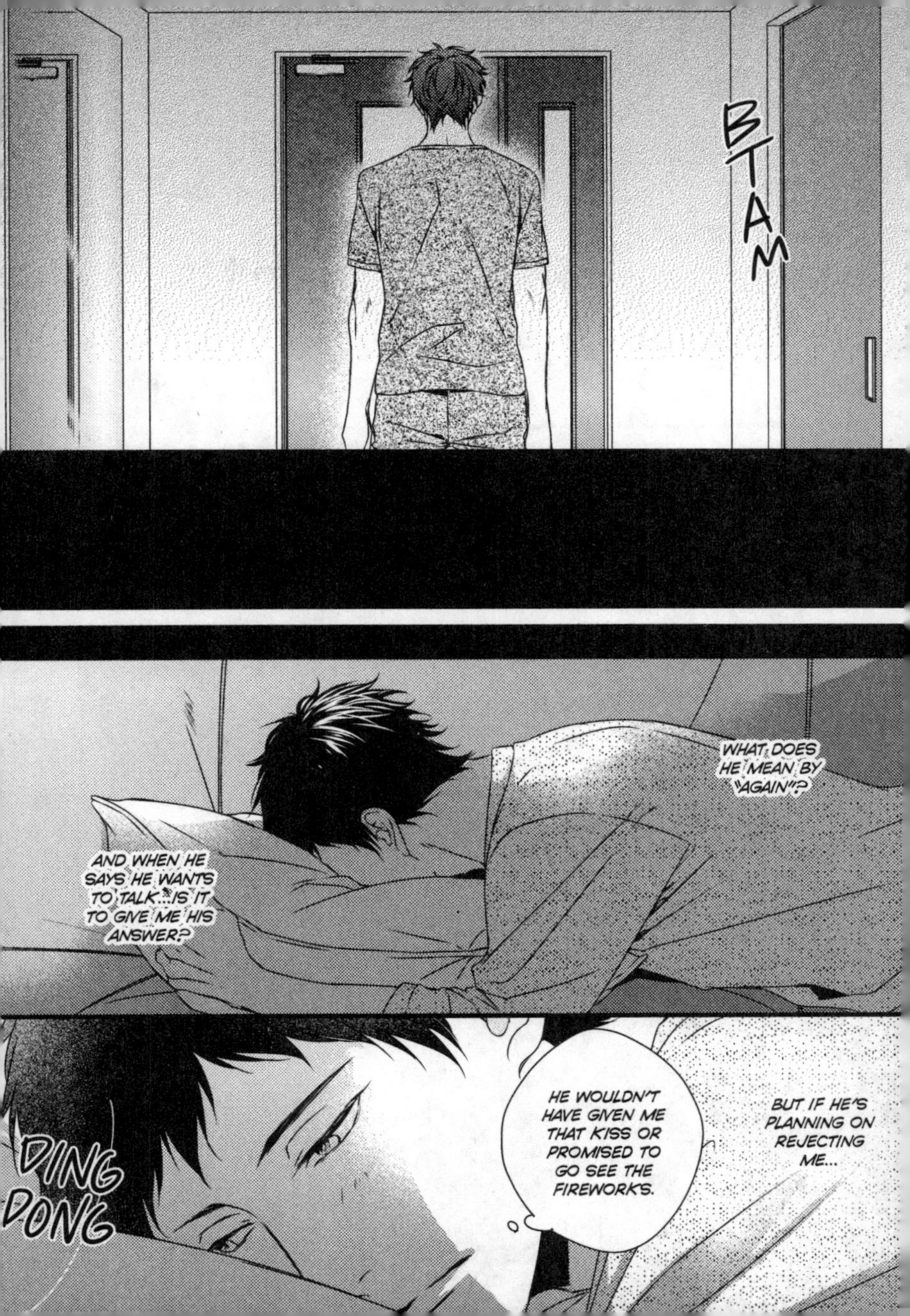
BTAM
WHAT DOES HE MEAN BY "AGAIN"?
AND WHEN HE SAYS HE WANTS TO TALK...IS IT TO GIVE ME HIS ANSWER?
BUT IF HE'S PLANNING ON REJECTING ME...
HE WOULDN'T HAVE GIVEN ME THAT KISS OR PROMISED TO GO SEE THE FIREWORKS.
DING DONG

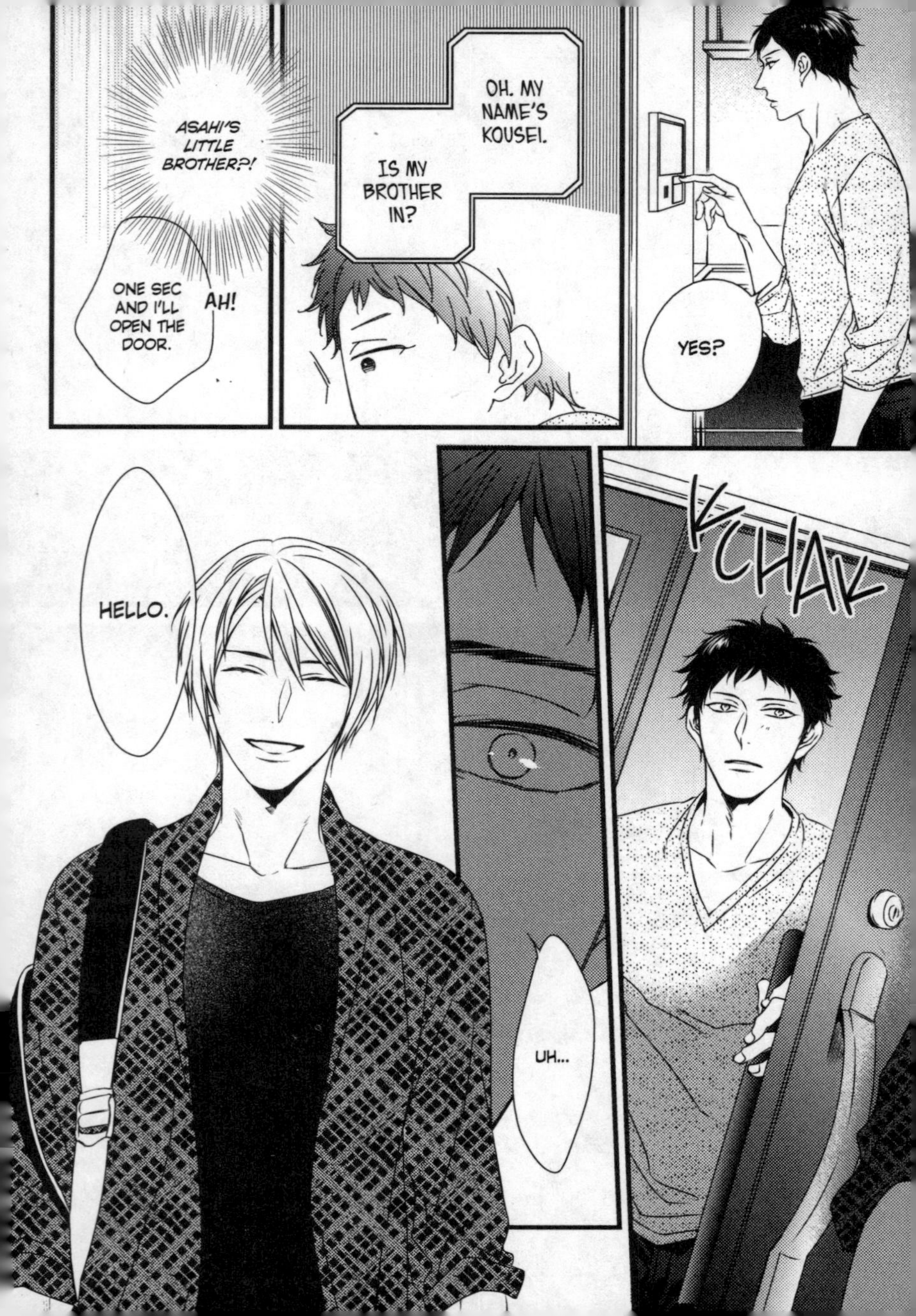
YES?
OH. MY NAME'S KOUSEI.
IS MY BROTHER IN?
ASAHI'S LITTLE BROTHER?!
AH!
ONE SEC AND I'LL OPEN THE DOOR.
K'CHAK
UH...
HELLO.

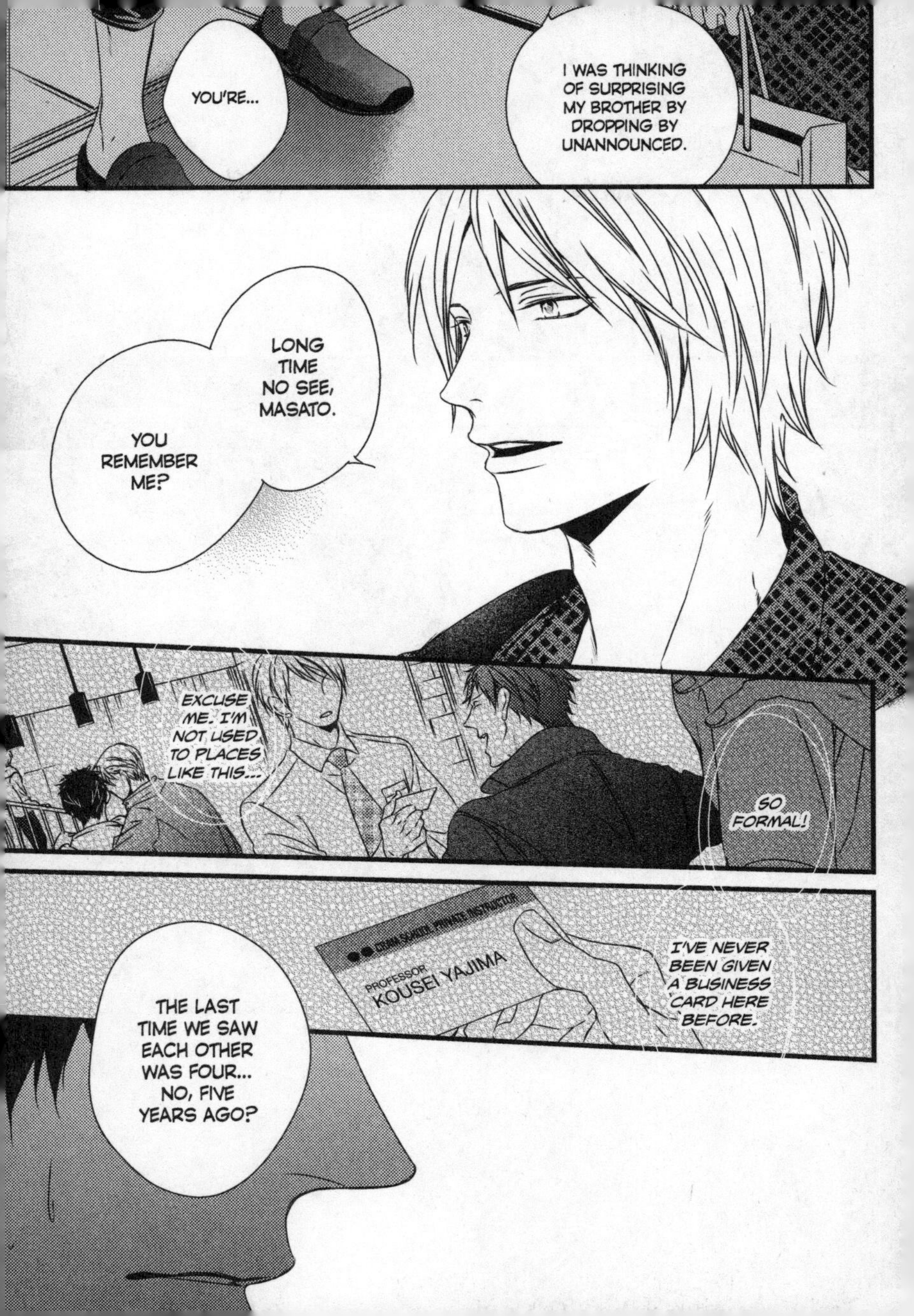
I WAS THINKING OF SURPRISING MY BROTHER BY DROPPING BY UNANNOUNCED.
YOU'RE...
LONG TIME NO SEE, MASATO.
YOU REMEMBER ME?
SO FORMAL!
EXCUSE ME. I'M NOT USED TO PLACES LIKE THIS...
I'VE NEVER BEEN GIVEN A BUSINESS CARD HERE BEFORE.
CRAM SCHOOL PRIVATE INSTRUCTOR
PROFESSOR
KOUSEI YAJIMA
THE LAST TIME WE SAW EACH OTHER WAS FOUR... NO, FIVE YEARS AGO?

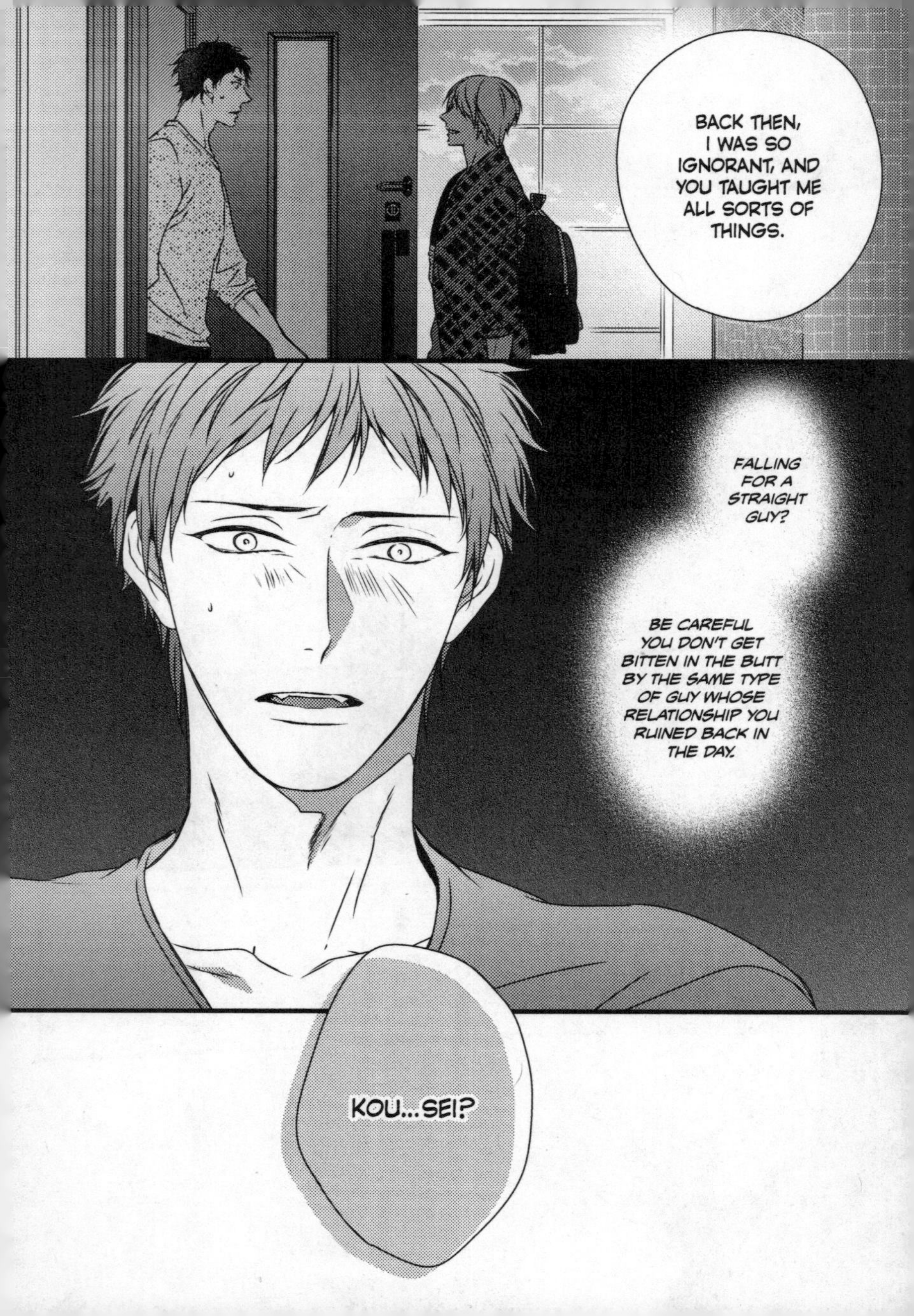
BACK THEN, I WAS SO IGNORANT, AND YOU TAUGHT ME ALL SORTS OF THINGS.
FALLING FOR A STRAIGHT GUY?
BE CAREFUL YOU DON'T GET BITTEN IN THE BUTT BY THE SAME TYPE OF GUY WHOSE RELATIONSHIP YOU RUINED BACK IN THE DAY.
KOU...SEI?

Episode 7

LOVE NEST

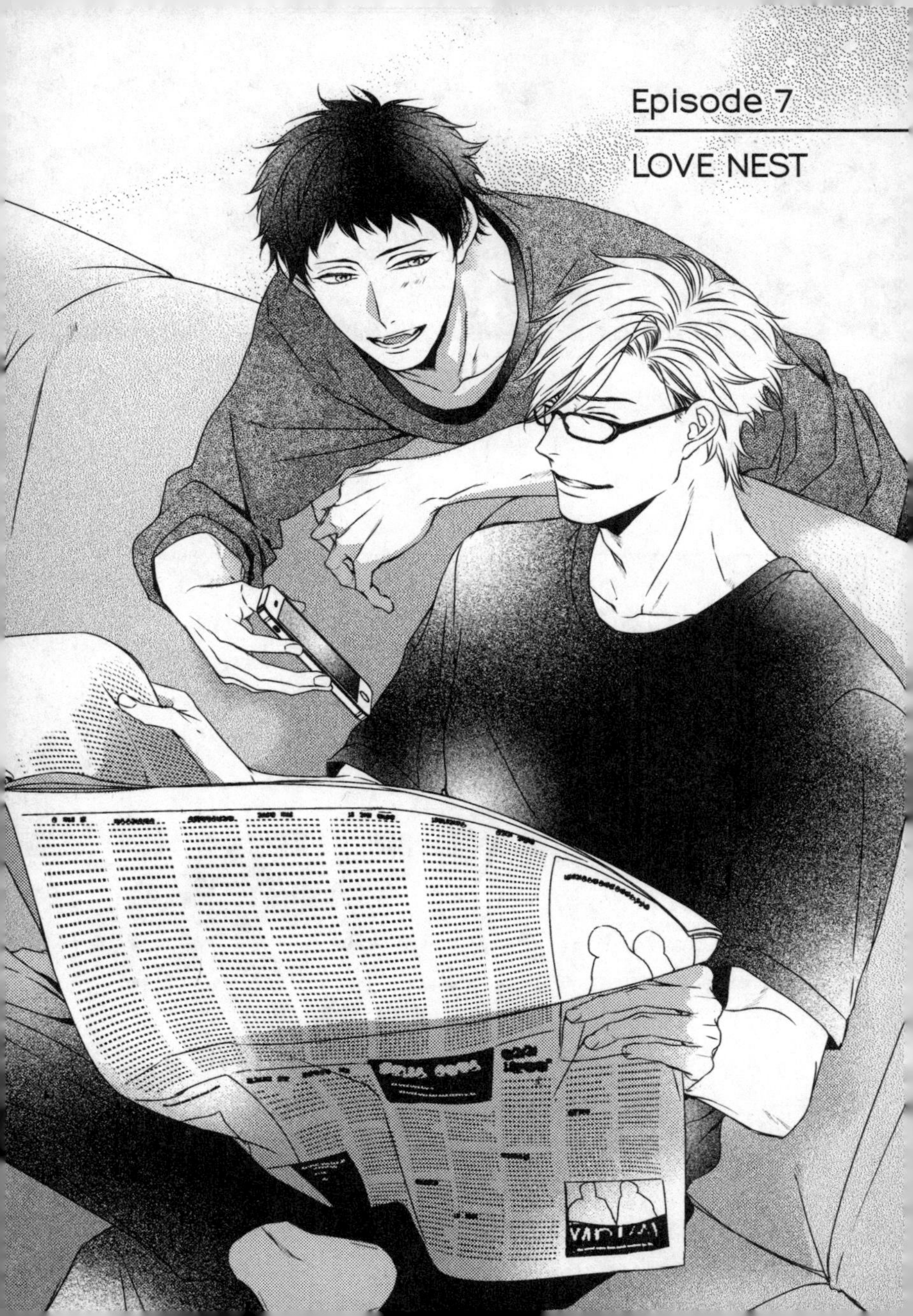

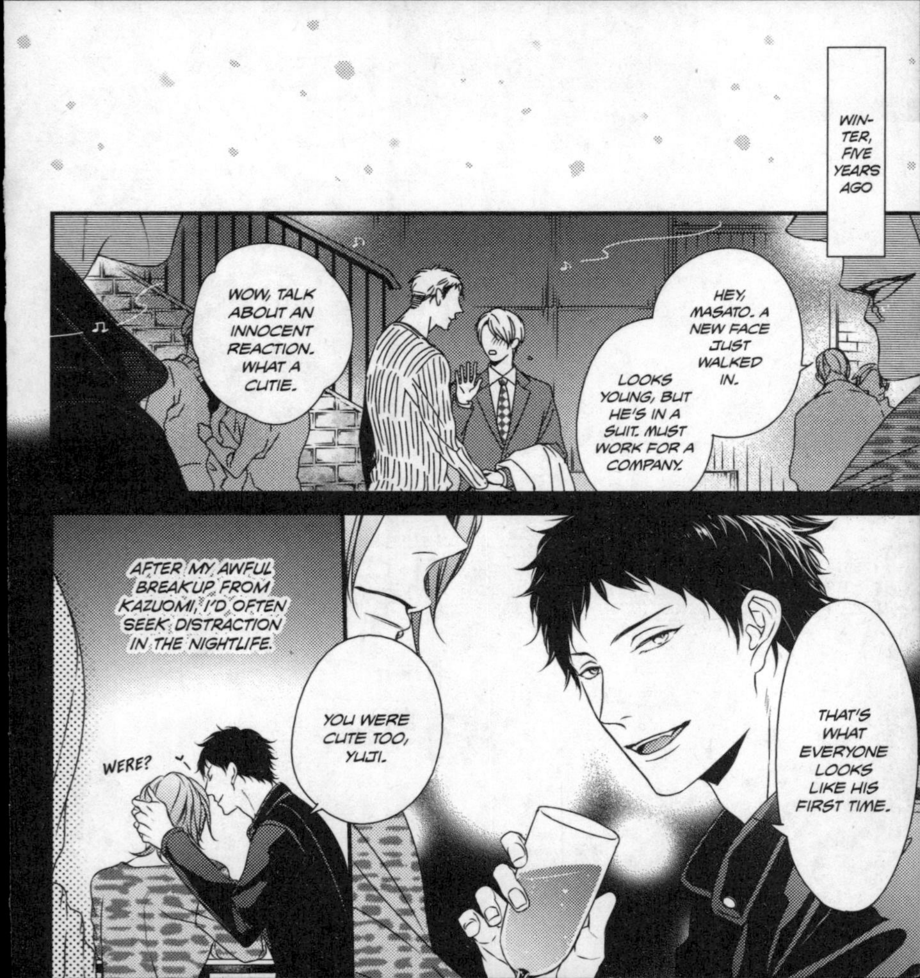
WIN-TER, FIVE YEARS AGO
HEY, MASATO. A NEW FACE JUST WALKED IN.
LOOKS YOUNG, BUT HE'S IN A SUIT. MUST WORK FOR A COMPANY.
WOW, TALK ABOUT AN INNOCENT REACTION. WHAT A CUTIE.
THAT'S WHAT EVERYONE LOOKS LIKE HIS FIRST TIME.
YOU WERE CUTE TOO, YUJI.
AFTER MY AWFUL BREAKUP FROM KAZUOMI, I'D OFTEN SEEK DISTRACTION IN THE NIGHTLIFE.
WERE?

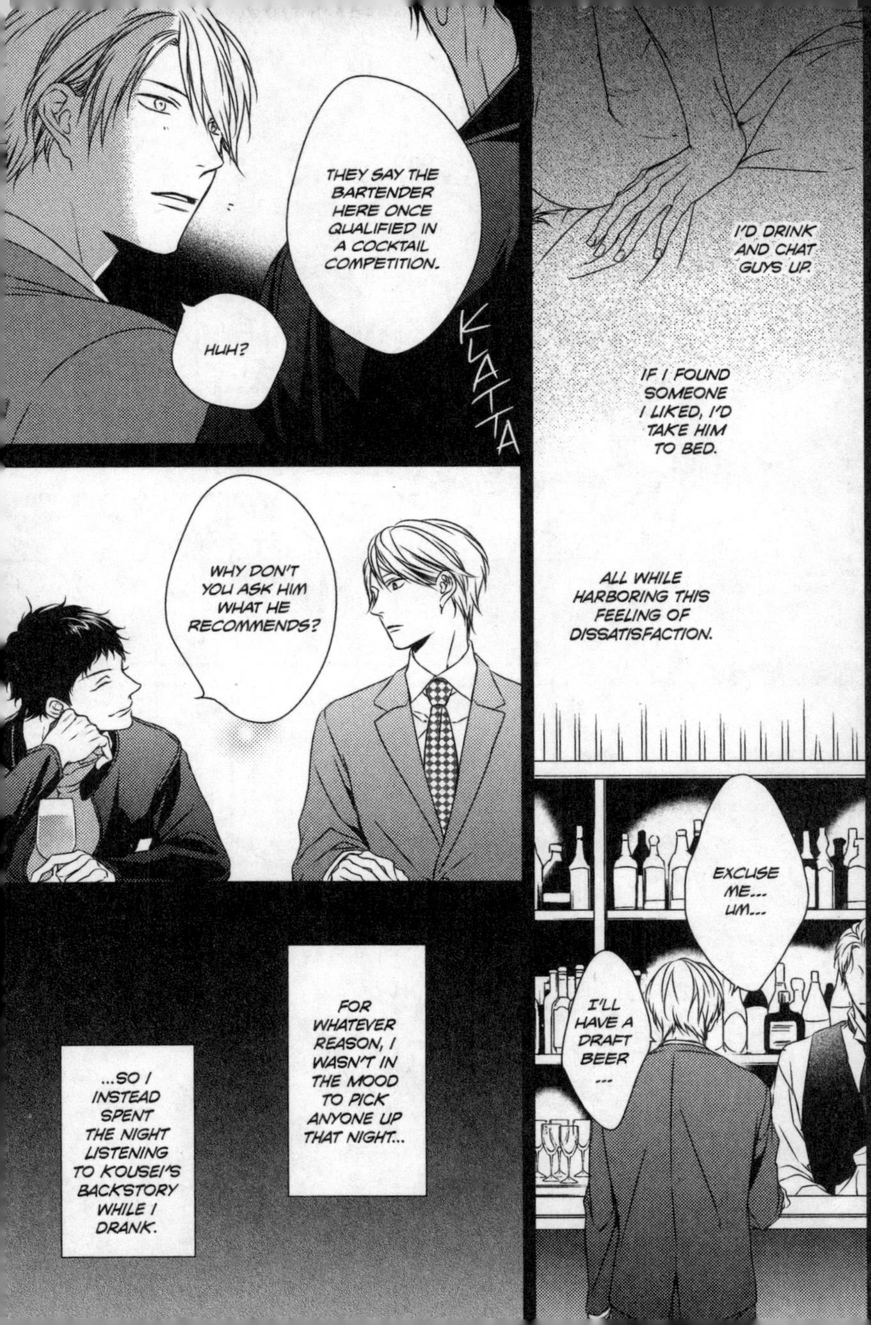
I'D DRINK AND CHAT GUYS UP.
IF I FOUND SOMEONE I LIKED, I'D TAKE HIM TO BED.
ALL WHILE HARBORING THIS FEELING OF DISSATISFACTION.
EXCUSE ME... UM...
I'LL HAVE A DRAFT BEER...
THEY SAY THE BARTENDER HERE ONCE QUALIFIED IN A COCKTAIL COMPETITION.
KLATTA
HUH?
WHY DON'T YOU ASK HIM WHAT HE RECOMMENDS?
FOR WHATEVER REASON, I WASN'T IN THE MOOD TO PICK ANYONE UP THAT NIGHT...
...SO I INSTEAD SPENT THE NIGHT LISTENING TO KOUSEI'S BACKSTORY WHILE I DRANK.

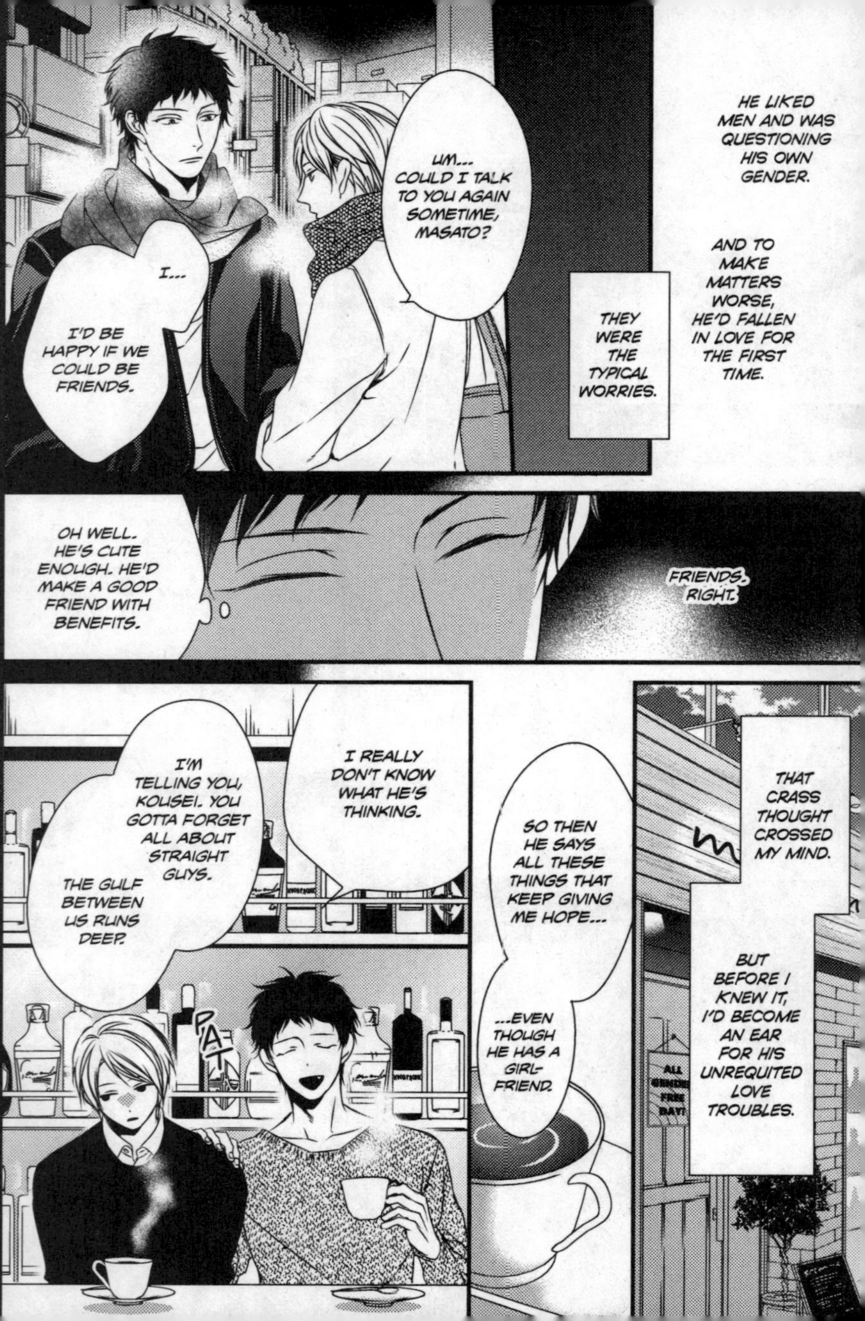
HE LIKED MEN AND WAS QUESTIONING HIS OWN GENDER.
AND TO MAKE MATTERS WORSE, HE'D FALLEN IN LOVE FOR THE FIRST TIME.
THEY WERE THE TYPICAL WORRIES.
UM... COULD I TALK TO YOU AGAIN SOMETIME, MASATO?
I...
I'D BE HAPPY IF WE COULD BE FRIENDS.
FRIENDS. RIGHT.
OH WELL. HE'S CUTE ENOUGH. HE'D MAKE A GOOD FRIEND WITH BENEFITS.
THAT CRASS THOUGHT CROSSED MY MIND.
BUT BEFORE I KNEW IT, I'D BECOME AN EAR FOR HIS UNREQUITED LOVE TROUBLES.
SO THEN HE SAYS ALL THESE THINGS THAT KEEP GIVING ME HOPE...
...EVEN THOUGH HE HAS A GIRL-FRIEND.
I REALLY DON'T KNOW WHAT HE'S THINKING.
I'M TELLING YOU, KOUSEI. YOU GOTTA FORGET ALL ABOUT STRAIGHT GUYS.
THE GULF BETWEEN US RUNS DEEP.
PAT

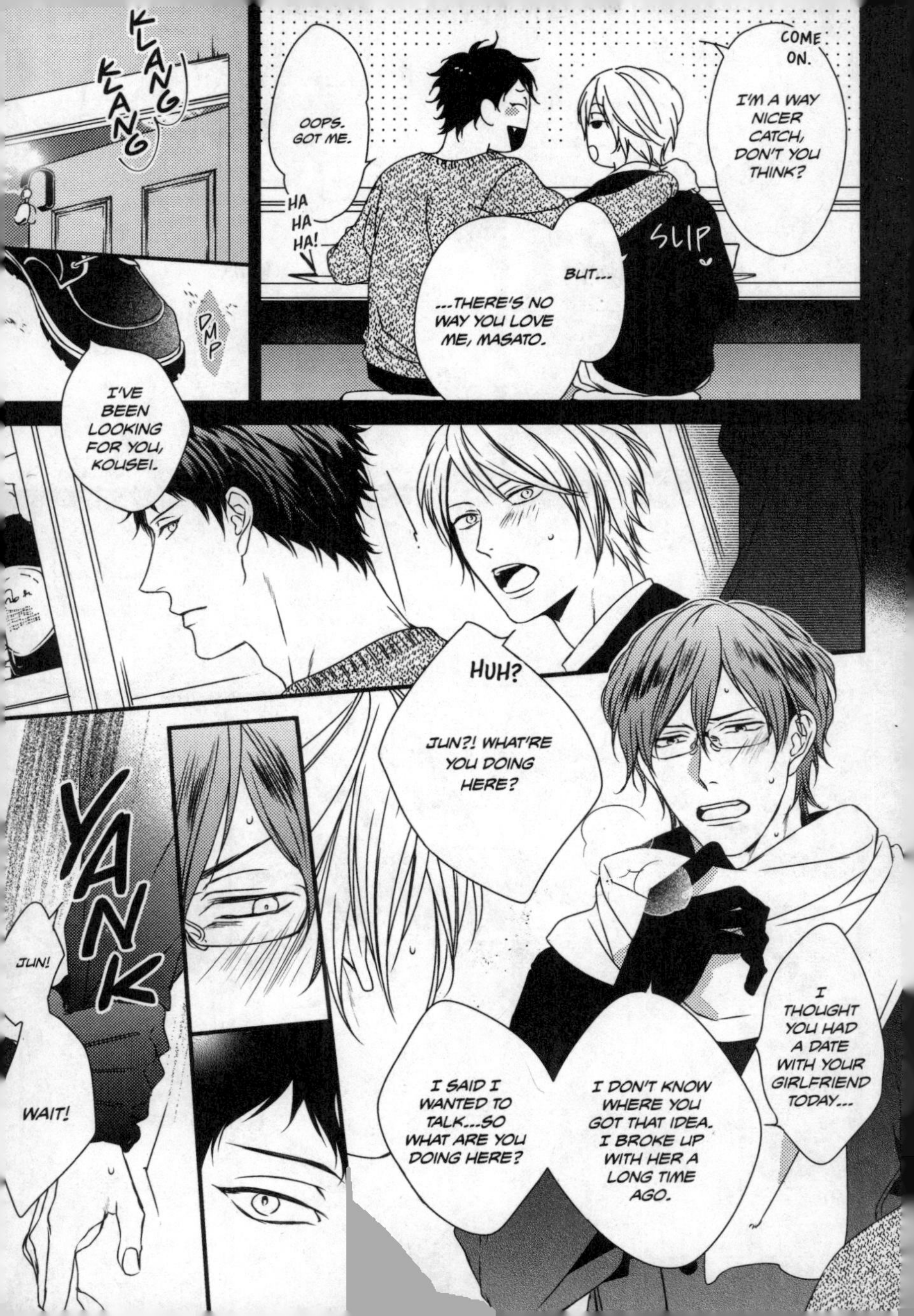
COME ON.
I'M A WAY NICER CATCH, DON'T YOU THINK?
OOPS. GOT ME.
HA HA HA!
SLIP
BUT...
...THERE'S NO WAY YOU LOVE ME, MASATO.
KLANG
KLANG
DMP
I'VE BEEN LOOKING FOR YOU, KOUSEI.
HUH?
JUN?! WHAT'RE YOU DOING HERE?
I THOUGHT YOU HAD A DATE WITH YOUR GIRLFRIEND TODAY...
I DON'T KNOW WHERE YOU GOT THAT IDEA. I BROKE UP WITH HER A LONG TIME AGO.
I SAID I WANTED TO TALK...SO WHAT ARE YOU DOING HERE?
YANK
JUN!
WAIT!

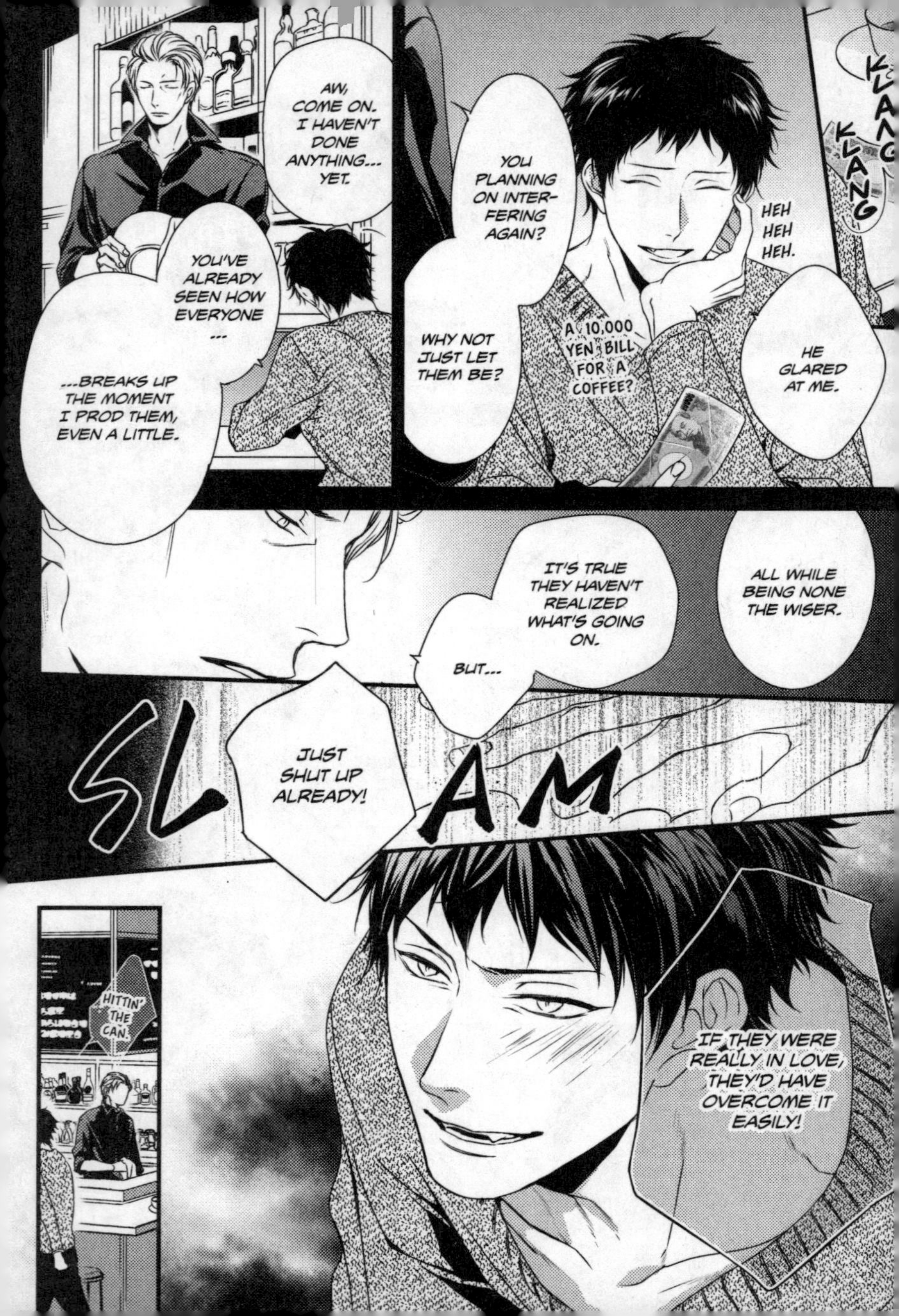
KLANG KLANG KLANG
HE GLARED AT ME.
A 10,000 YEN BILL FOR A COFFEE?
HEH HEH HEH.
YOU PLANNING ON INTER-FERING AGAIN?
WHY NOT JUST LET THEM BE?
AW, COME ON. I HAVEN'T DONE ANYTHING... YET.
YOU'VE ALREADY SEEN HOW EVERYONE ...
...BREAKS UP THE MOMENT I PROD THEM, EVEN A LITTLE.
ALL WHILE BEING NONE THE WISER.
IT'S TRUE THEY HAVEN'T REALIZED WHAT'S GOING ON.
BUT...
SLAM
JUST SHUT UP ALREADY!
IF THEY WERE REALLY IN LOVE, THEY'D HAVE OVERCOME IT EASILY!
HITTIN' THE CAN.

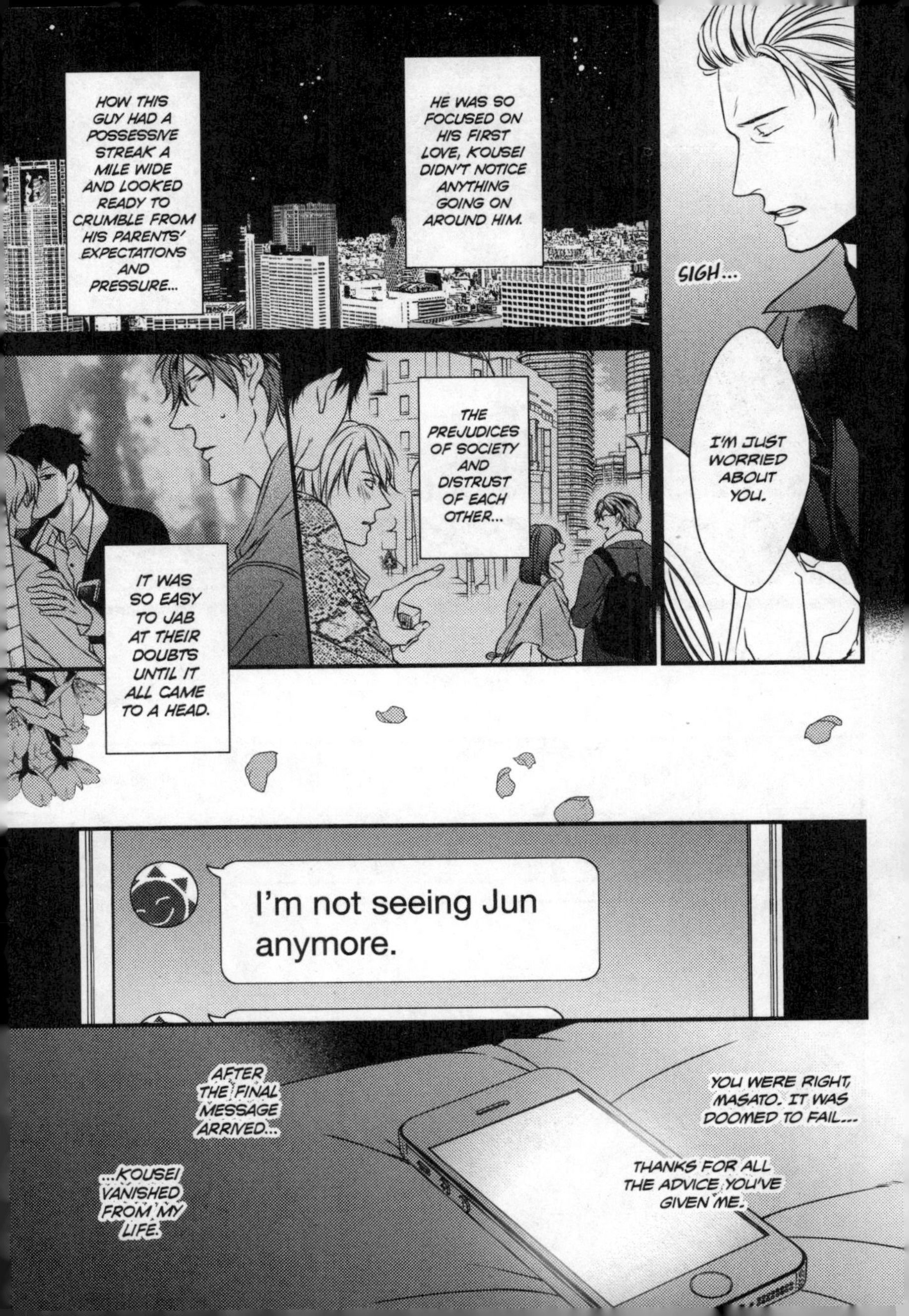
SIGH...
I'M JUST WORRIED ABOUT YOU.
HE WAS SO FOCUSED ON HIS FIRST LOVE, KOUSEI DIDN'T NOTICE ANYTHING GOING ON AROUND HIM.
HOW THIS GUY HAD A POSSESSIVE STREAK A MILE WIDE AND LOOKED READY TO CRUMBLE FROM HIS PARENTS' EXPECTATIONS AND PRESSURE...
THE PREJUDICES OF SOCIETY AND DISTRUST OF EACH OTHER...
IT WAS SO EASY TO JAB AT THEIR DOUBTS UNTIL IT ALL CAME TO A HEAD.
I'm not seeing Jun anymore.
YOU WERE RIGHT, MASATO. IT WAS DOOMED TO FAIL...
THANKS FOR ALL THE ADVICE YOU'VE GIVEN ME.
AFTER THE FINAL MESSAGE ARRIVED...
...KOUSEI VANISHED FROM MY LIFE.

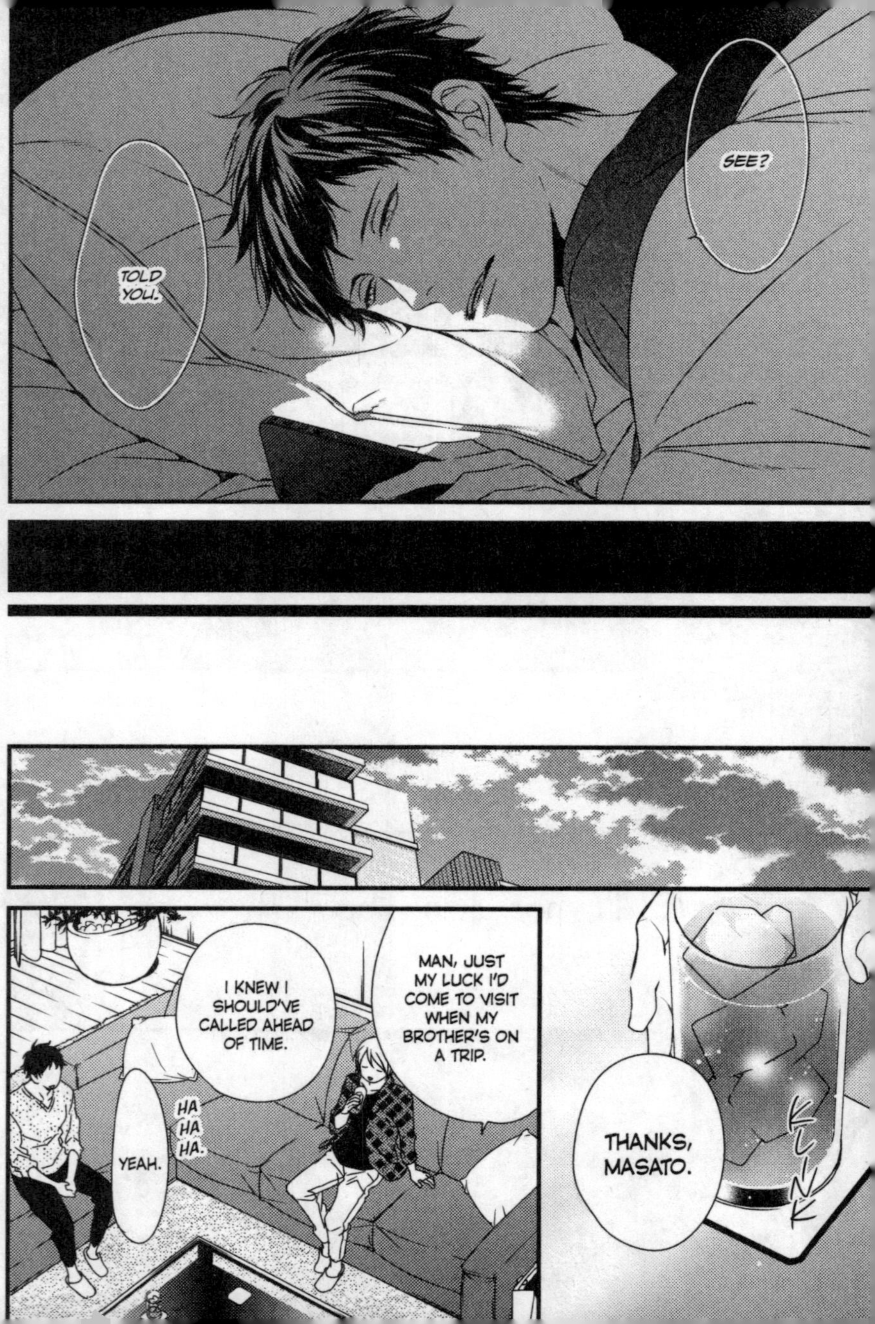
SEE?
TOLD YOU.
THANKS, MASATO.
KL-I-N-K
MAN, JUST MY LUCK I'D COME TO VISIT WHEN MY BROTHER'S ON A TRIP.
I KNEW I SHOULD'VE CALLED AHEAD OF TIME.
HA HA HA.
YEAH.

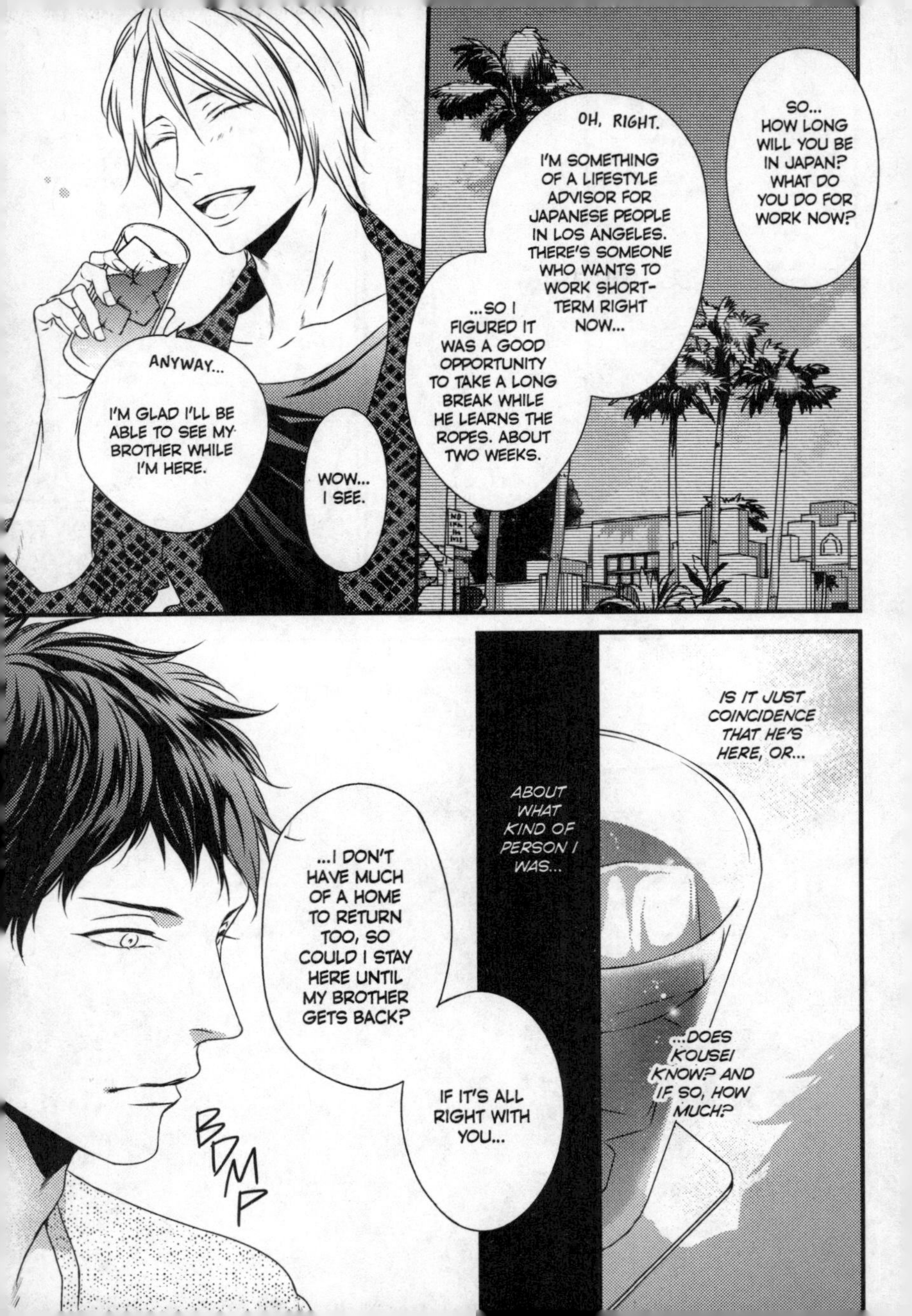
SO... HOW LONG WILL YOU BE IN JAPAN? WHAT DO YOU DO FOR WORK NOW?
OH, RIGHT.
I'M SOMETHING OF A LIFESTYLE ADVISOR FOR JAPANESE PEOPLE IN LOS ANGELES. THERE'S SOMEONE WHO WANTS TO WORK SHORT-TERM RIGHT NOW...
...SO I FIGURED IT WAS A GOOD OPPORTUNITY TO TAKE A LONG BREAK WHILE HE LEARNS THE ROPES. ABOUT TWO WEEKS.
WOW... I SEE.
ANYWAY...
I'M GLAD I'LL BE ABLE TO SEE MY BROTHER WHILE I'M HERE.
IS IT JUST COINCIDENCE THAT HE'S HERE, OR...
ABOUT WHAT KIND OF PERSON I WAS...
...DOES KOUSEI KNOW? AND IF SO, HOW MUCH?
...I DON'T HAVE MUCH OF A HOME TO RETURN TOO, SO COULD I STAY HERE UNTIL MY BROTHER GETS BACK?
IF IT'S ALL RIGHT WITH YOU...
BDMP

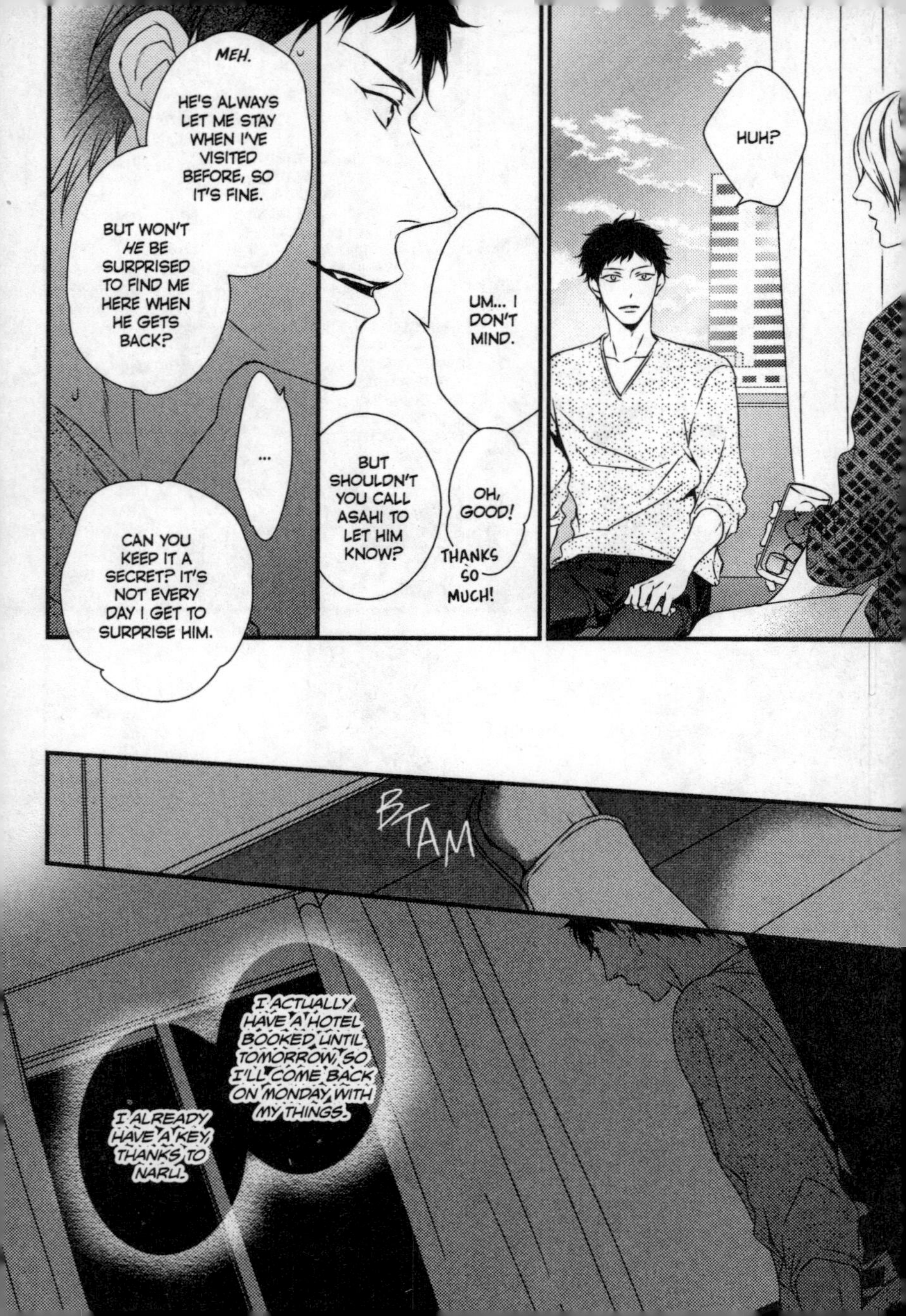
HUH?
UM... I DON'T MIND.
OH, GOOD!
THANKS SO MUCH!
BUT SHOULDN'T YOU CALL ASAHI TO LET HIM KNOW?
MEH.
HE'S ALWAYS LET ME STAY WHEN I'VE VISITED BEFORE, SO IT'S FINE.
BUT WON'T HE BE SURPRISED TO FIND ME HERE WHEN HE GETS BACK?
...
CAN YOU KEEP IT A SECRET? IT'S NOT EVERY DAY I GET TO SURPRISE HIM.
BTAM
I ACTUALLY HAVE A HOTEL BOOKED UNTIL TOMORROW, SO I'LL COME BACK ON MONDAY WITH MY THINGS.
I ALREADY HAVE A KEY, THANKS TO NARU.

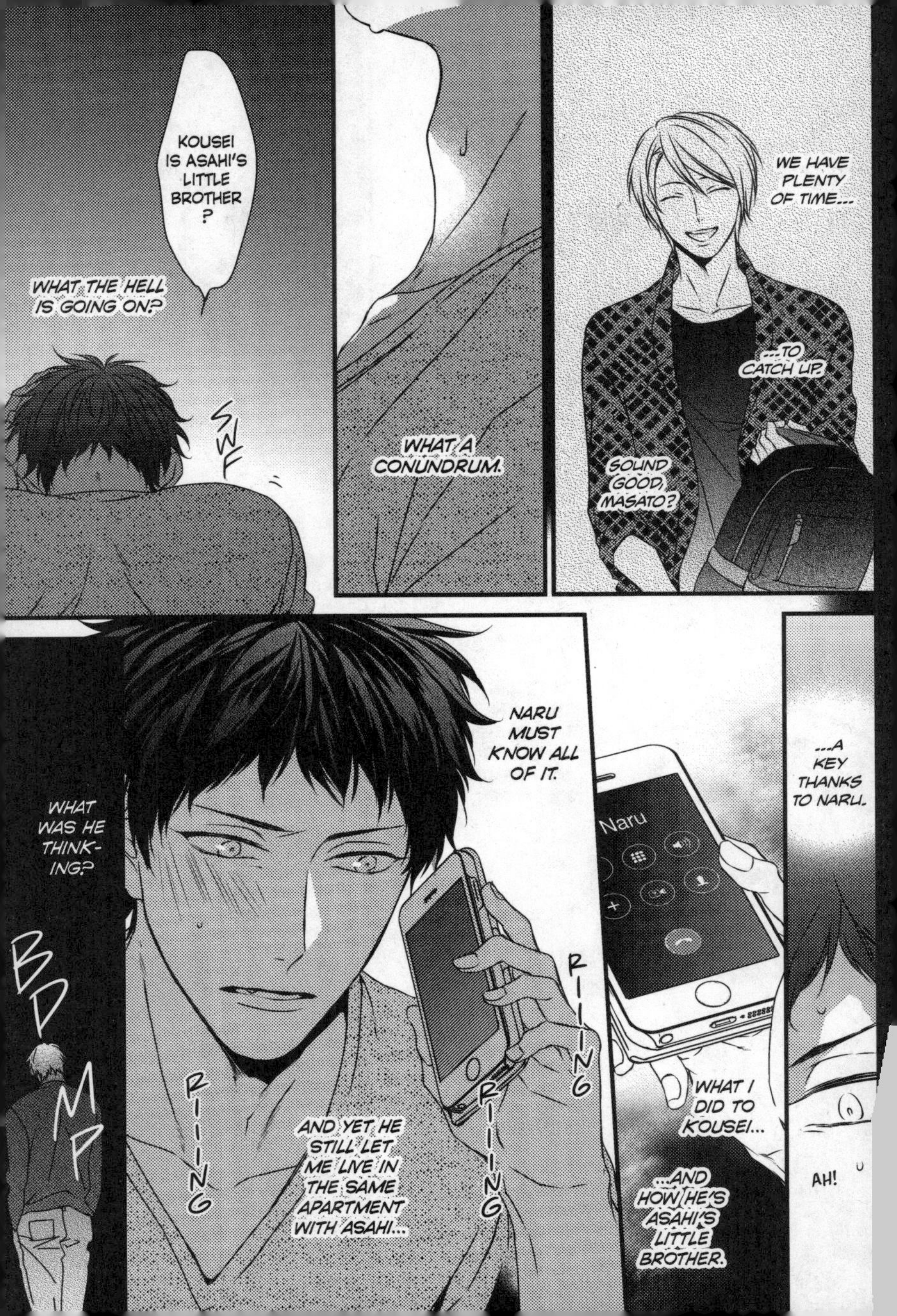
WE HAVE PLENTY OF TIME...
...TO CATCH UP.
SOUND GOOD, MASATO?
WHAT A CONUNDRUM.
KOUSEI IS ASAHI'S LITTLE BROTHER?
WHAT THE HELL IS GOING ON?
SWF
...A KEY THANKS TO NARU.
AH!
Naru
NARU MUST KNOW ALL OF IT.
WHAT I DID TO KOUSEI...
...AND HOW HE'S ASAHI'S LITTLE BROTHER.
RIIING
RIIIING
AND YET HE STILL LET ME LIVE IN THE SAME APARTMENT WITH ASAHI...
RIIING
WHAT WAS HE THINKING?
BDMP

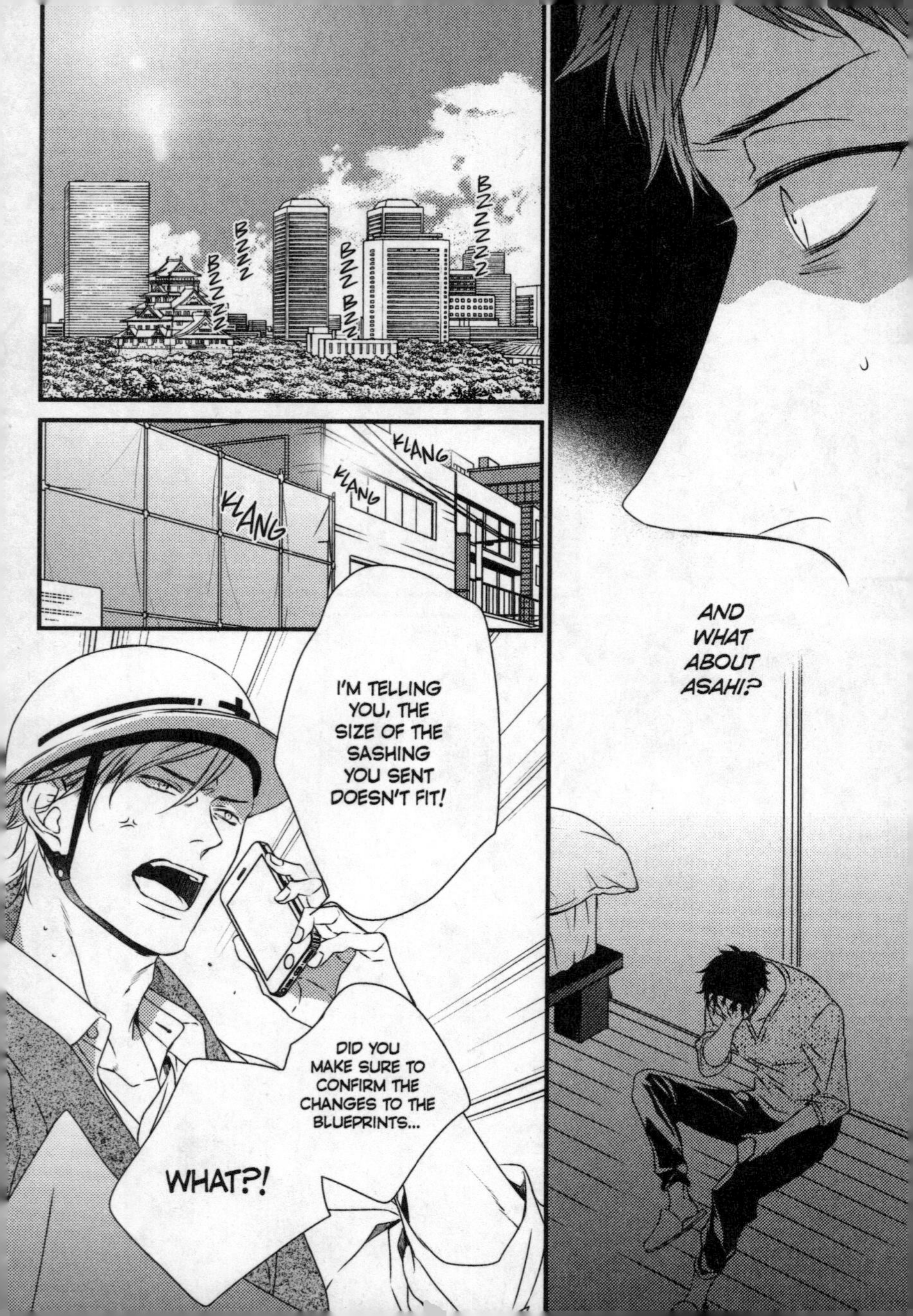
AND WHAT ABOUT ASAHI?
BZZZZZZ
BZZ
BZZ
BZZZ
BZZZZZ
KLANG
KLANG
KLANG
I'M TELLING YOU, THE SIZE OF THE SASHING YOU SENT DOESN'T FIT!
DID YOU MAKE SURE TO CONFIRM THE CHANGES TO THE BLUEPRINTS...
WHAT?!

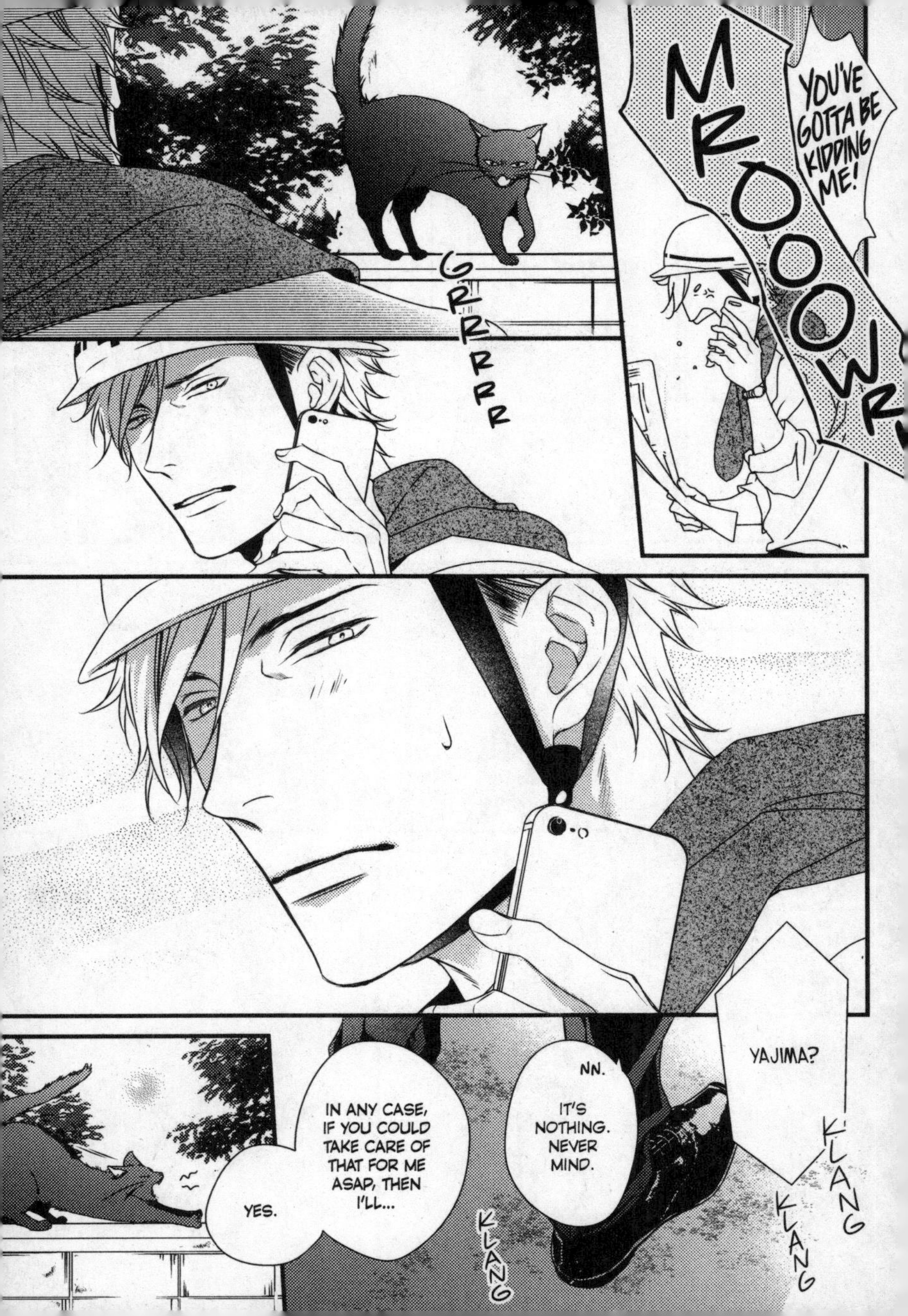
MROOOOWR!
YOU'VE GOTTA BE KIDDING ME!
GRRRRRR
YAJIMA?
KLANG
KLANG
NN.
IT'S NOTHING. NEVER MIND.
IN ANY CASE, IF YOU COULD TAKE CARE OF THAT FOR ME ASAP, THEN I'LL...
YES.
KLANG

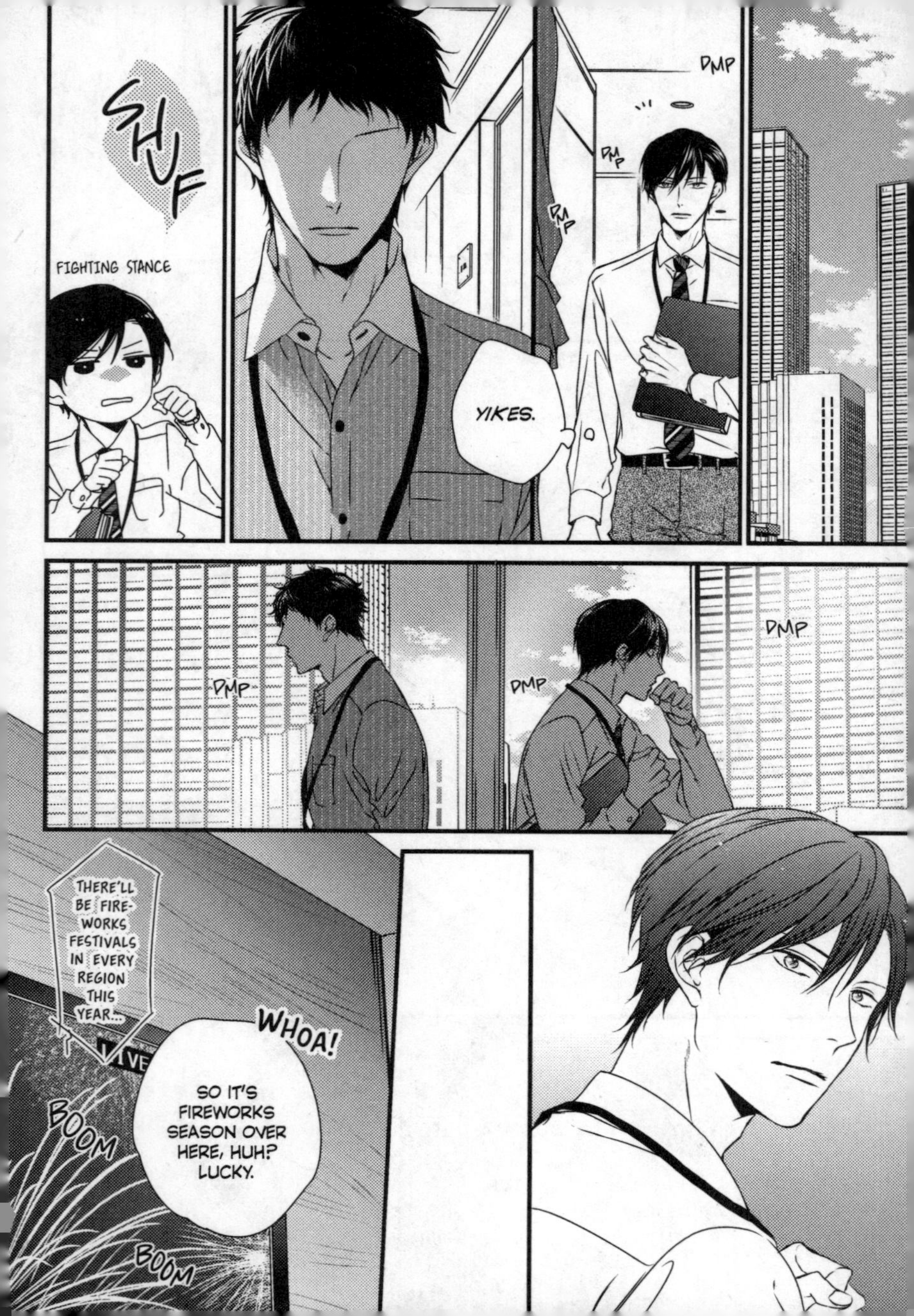
DMP
DMP
DMP
YIKES.
SHUF
FIGHTING STANCE
DMP
DMP
DMP
THERE'LL BE FIRE-WORKS FESTIVALS IN EVERY REGION THIS YEAR...
WHOA!
SO IT'S FIREWORKS SEASON OVER HERE, HUH? LUCKY.
BOOM
BOOM

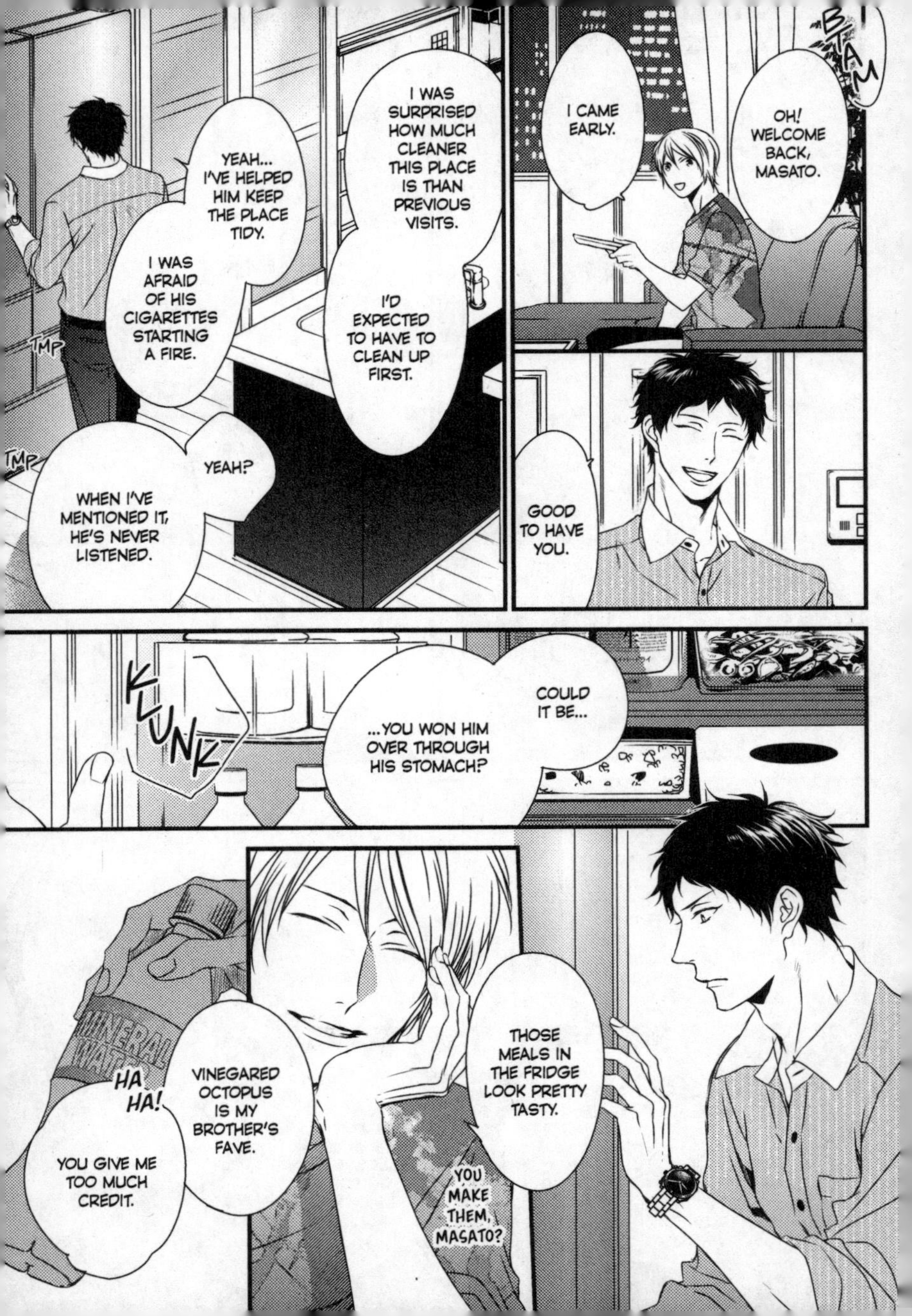
BTAM
OH! WELCOME BACK, MASATO.
I CAME EARLY.
GOOD TO HAVE YOU.
I WAS SURPRISED HOW MUCH CLEANER THIS PLACE IS THAN PREVIOUS VISITS.
I'D EXPECTED TO HAVE TO CLEAN UP FIRST.
YEAH... I'VE HELPED HIM KEEP THE PLACE TIDY.
I WAS AFRAID OF HIS CIGARETTES STARTING A FIRE.
TMP
YEAH?
WHEN I'VE MENTIONED IT, HE'S NEVER LISTENED.
TMP
COULD IT BE...
...YOU WON HIM OVER THROUGH HIS STOMACH?
KLUNK
THOSE MEALS IN THE FRIDGE LOOK PRETTY TASTY.
YOU MAKE THEM, MASATO?
VINEGARED OCTOPUS IS MY BROTHER'S FAVE.
HA HA!
YOU GIVE ME TOO MUCH CREDIT.

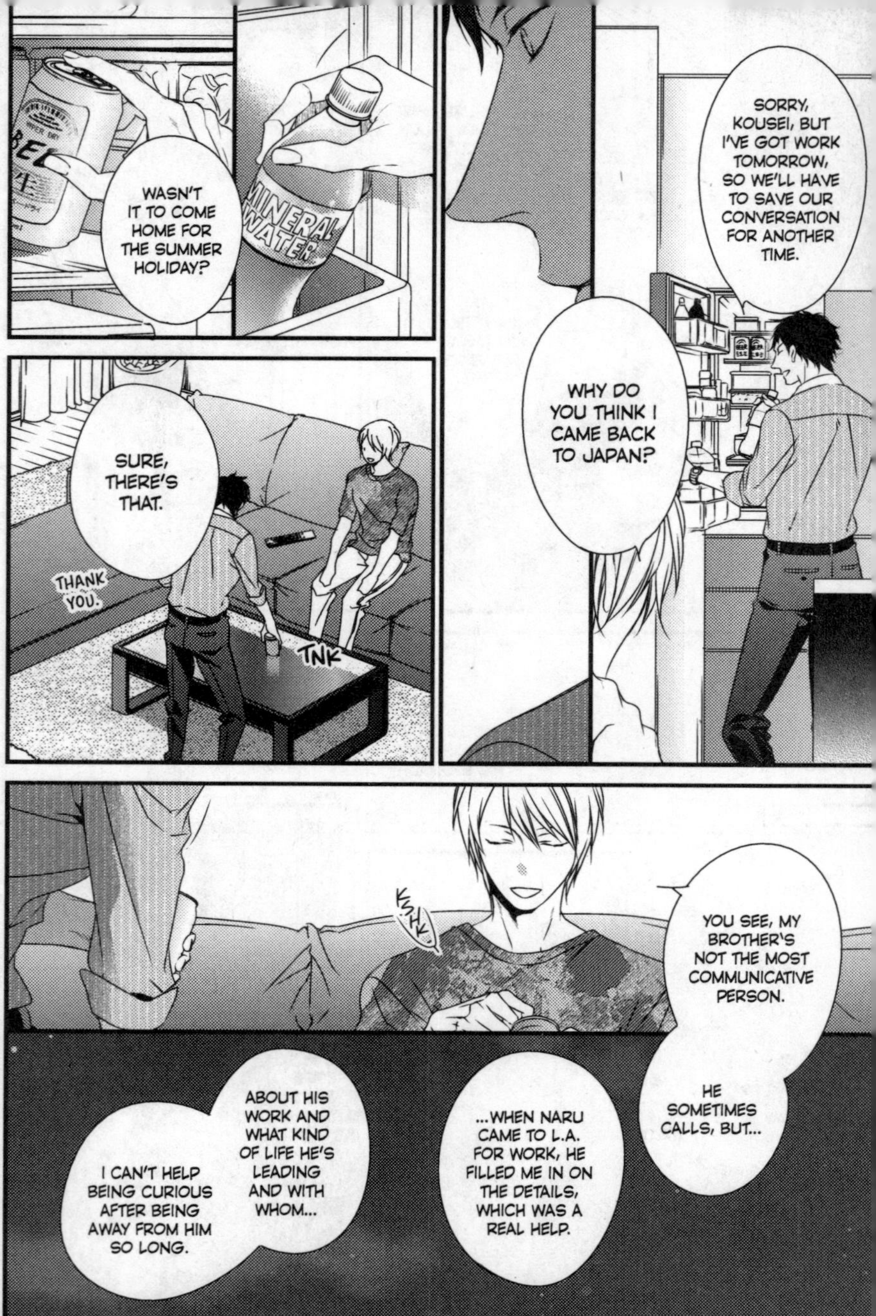
SORRY, KOUSEI, BUT I'VE GOT WORK TOMORROW, SO WE'LL HAVE TO SAVE OUR CONVERSATION FOR ANOTHER TIME.
WHY DO YOU THINK I CAME BACK TO JAPAN?
MINERAL WATER
WASN'T IT TO COME HOME FOR THE SUMMER HOLIDAY?
SURE, THERE'S THAT.
TNK
THANK YOU.
KSHK
YOU SEE, MY BROTHER'S NOT THE MOST COMMUNICATIVE PERSON.
HE SOMETIMES CALLS, BUT...
...WHEN NARU CAME TO L.A. FOR WORK, HE FILLED ME IN ON THE DETAILS, WHICH WAS A REAL HELP.
ABOUT HIS WORK AND WHAT KIND OF LIFE HE'S LEADING AND WITH WHOM...
I CAN'T HELP BEING CURIOUS AFTER BEING AWAY FROM HIM SO LONG.

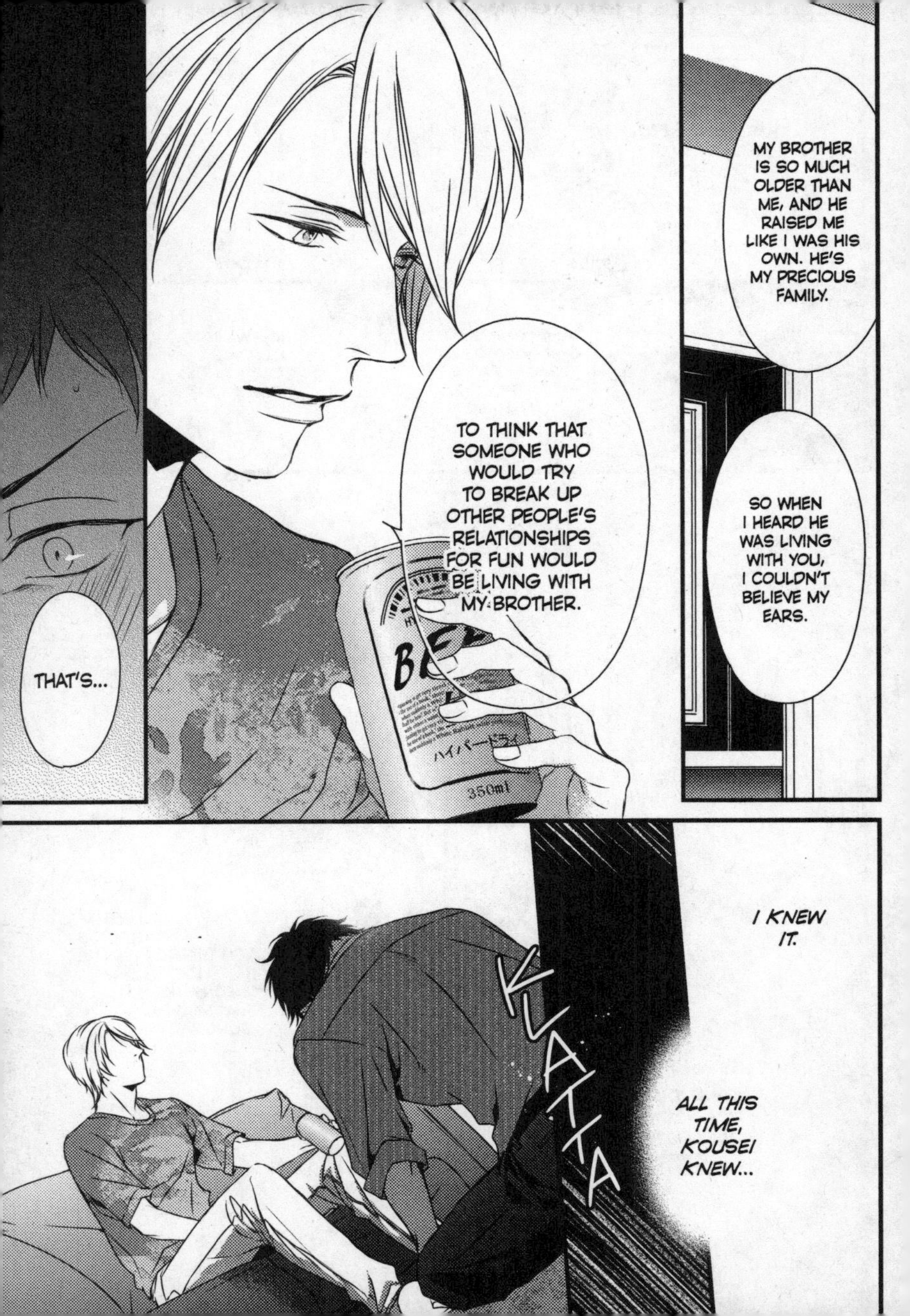
MY BROTHER IS SO MUCH OLDER THAN ME, AND HE RAISED ME LIKE I WAS HIS OWN. HE'S MY PRECIOUS FAMILY.
SO WHEN I HEARD HE WAS LIVING WITH YOU, I COULDN'T BELIEVE MY EARS.
TO THINK THAT SOMEONE WHO WOULD TRY TO BREAK UP OTHER PEOPLE'S RELATIONSHIPS FOR FUN WOULD BE LIVING WITH MY BROTHER.
THAT'S...
I KNEW IT.
KLATTA
ALL THIS TIME, KOUSEI KNEW...

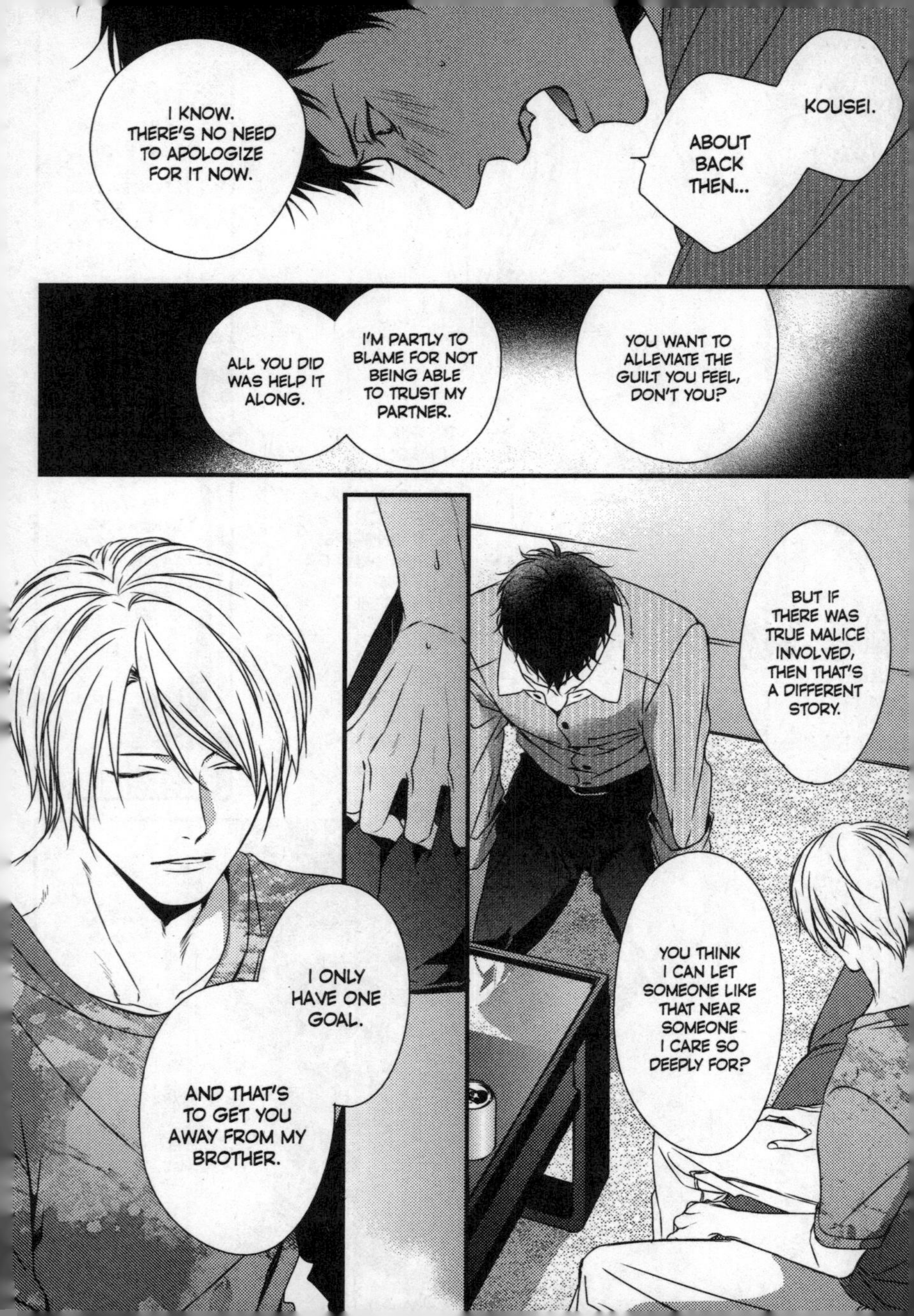
KOUSEI.
ABOUT BACK THEN...
I KNOW. THERE'S NO NEED TO APOLOGIZE FOR IT NOW.
YOU WANT TO ALLEVIATE THE GUILT YOU FEEL, DON'T YOU?
I'M PARTLY TO BLAME FOR NOT BEING ABLE TO TRUST MY PARTNER.
ALL YOU DID WAS HELP IT ALONG.
BUT IF THERE WAS TRUE MALICE INVOLVED, THEN THAT'S A DIFFERENT STORY.
YOU THINK I CAN LET SOMEONE LIKE THAT NEAR SOMEONE I CARE SO DEEPLY FOR?
I ONLY HAVE ONE GOAL.
AND THAT'S TO GET YOU AWAY FROM MY BROTHER.

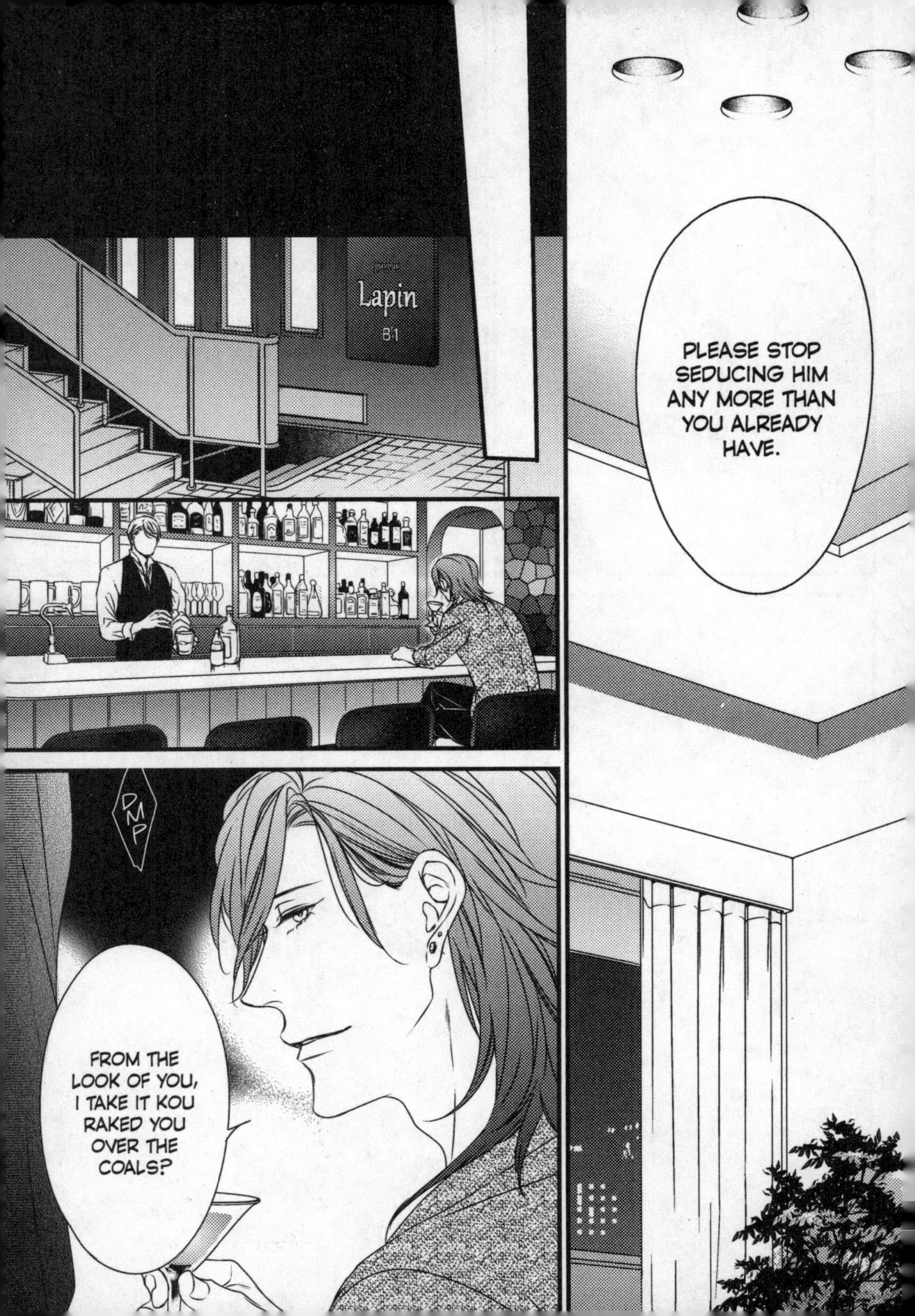
PLEASE STOP SEDUCING HIM ANY MORE THAN YOU ALREADY HAVE.
Lapin
B1
DMP
FROM THE LOOK OF YOU, I TAKE IT KOU RAKED YOU OVER THE COALS?

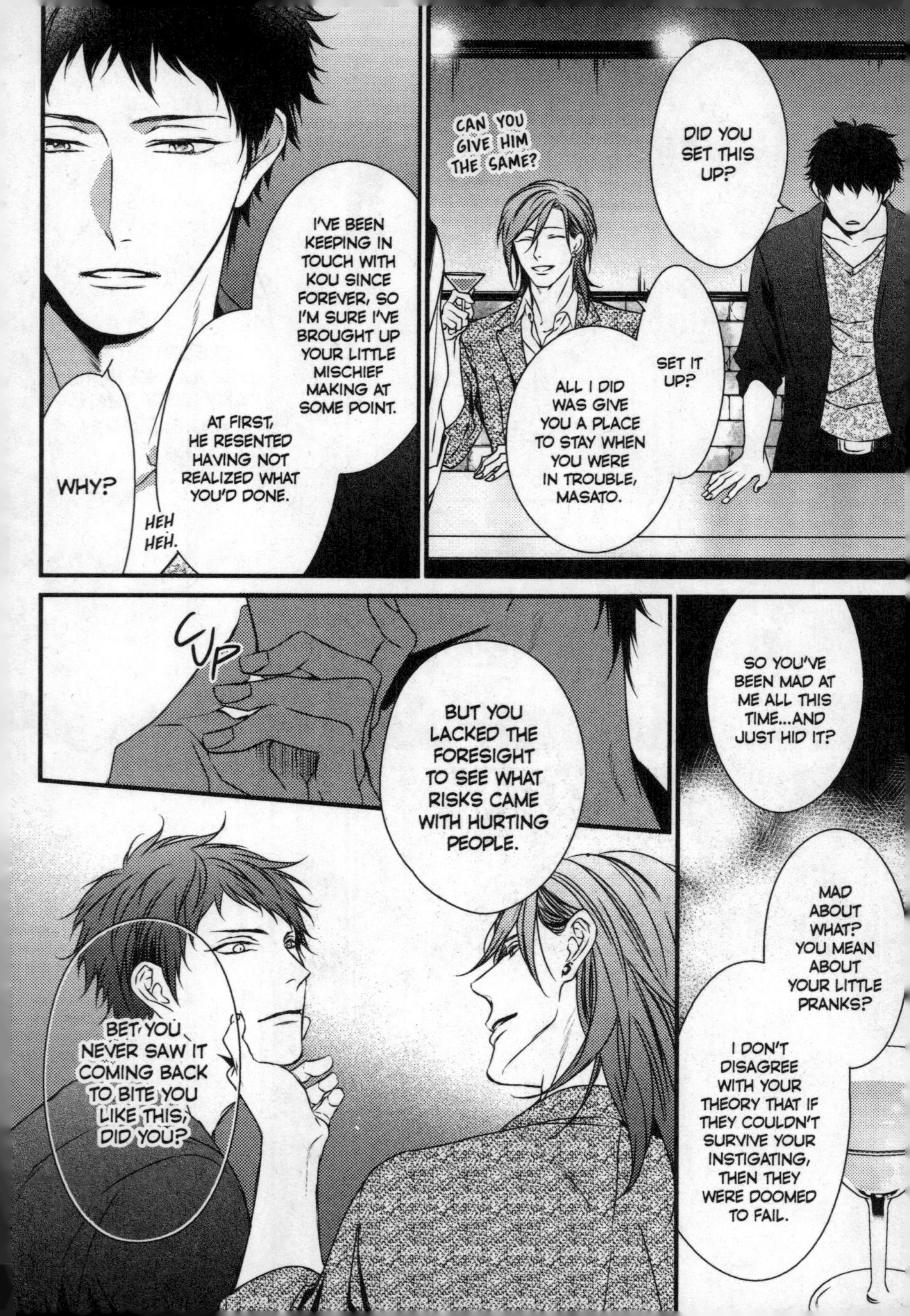
DID YOU SET THIS UP?
CAN YOU GIVE HIM THE SAME?
SET IT UP?
ALL I DID WAS GIVE YOU A PLACE TO STAY WHEN YOU WERE IN TROUBLE, MASATO.
I'VE BEEN KEEPING IN TOUCH WITH KOU SINCE FOREVER, SO I'M SURE I'VE BROUGHT UP YOUR LITTLE MISCHIEF MAKING AT SOME POINT.
AT FIRST, HE RESENTED HAVING NOT REALIZED WHAT YOU'D DONE.
WHY?
HEH HEH.
SO YOU'VE BEEN MAD AT ME ALL THIS TIME...AND JUST HID IT?
MAD ABOUT WHAT? YOU MEAN ABOUT YOUR LITTLE PRANKS?
I DON'T DISAGREE WITH YOUR THEORY THAT IF THEY COULDN'T SURVIVE YOUR INSTIGATING, THEN THEY WERE DOOMED TO FAIL.
CUP
BUT YOU LACKED THE FORESIGHT TO SEE WHAT RISKS CAME WITH HURTING PEOPLE.
BET YOU NEVER SAW IT COMING BACK TO BITE YOU LIKE THIS, DID YOU?

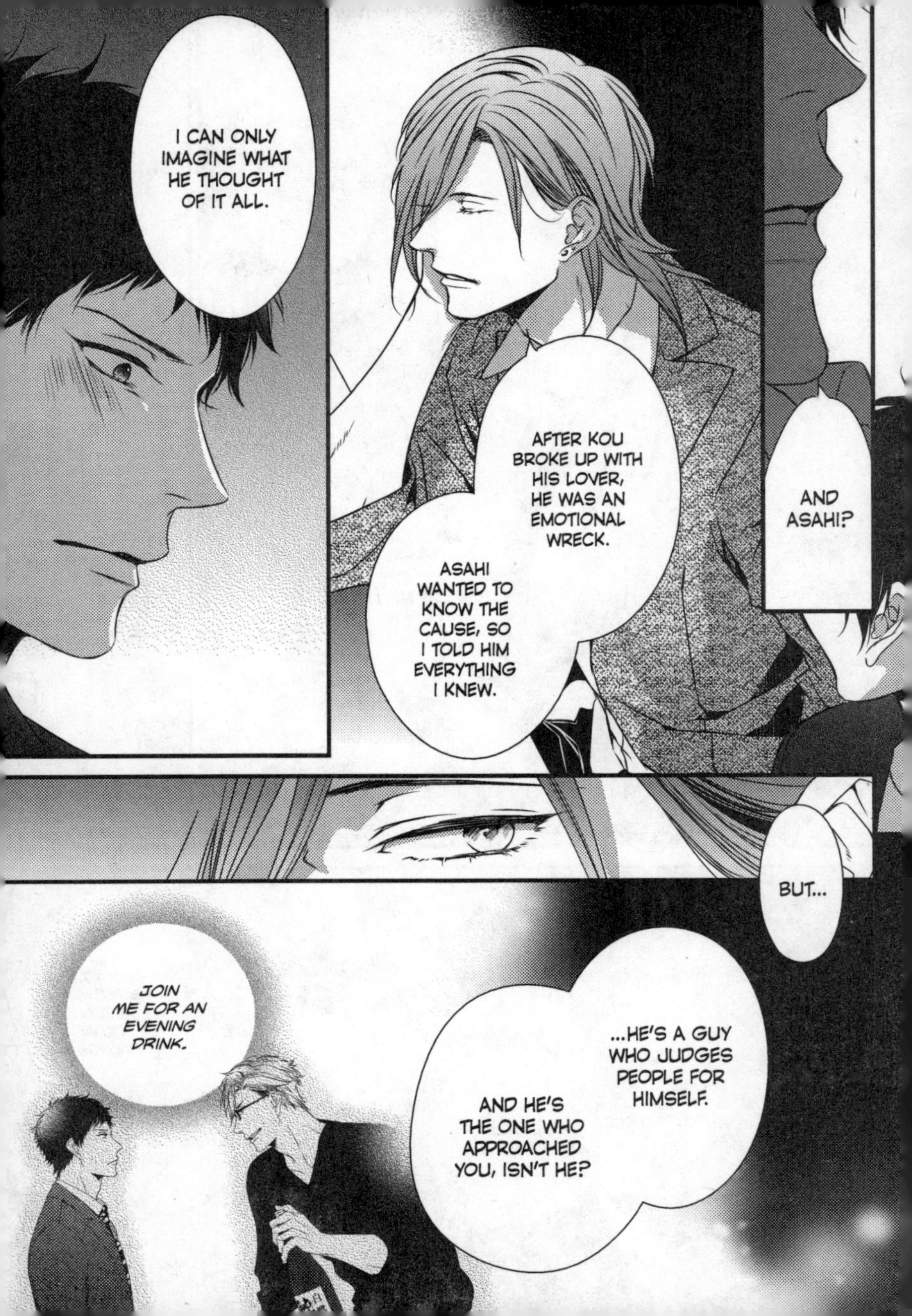
AND ASAHI?
AFTER KOU BROKE UP WITH HIS LOVER, HE WAS AN EMOTIONAL WRECK.
ASAHI WANTED TO KNOW THE CAUSE, SO I TOLD HIM EVERYTHING I KNEW.
I CAN ONLY IMAGINE WHAT HE THOUGHT OF IT ALL.
BUT...
...HE'S A GUY WHO JUDGES PEOPLE FOR HIMSELF.
AND HE'S THE ONE WHO APPROACHED YOU, ISN'T HE?
JOIN ME FOR AN EVENING DRINK.

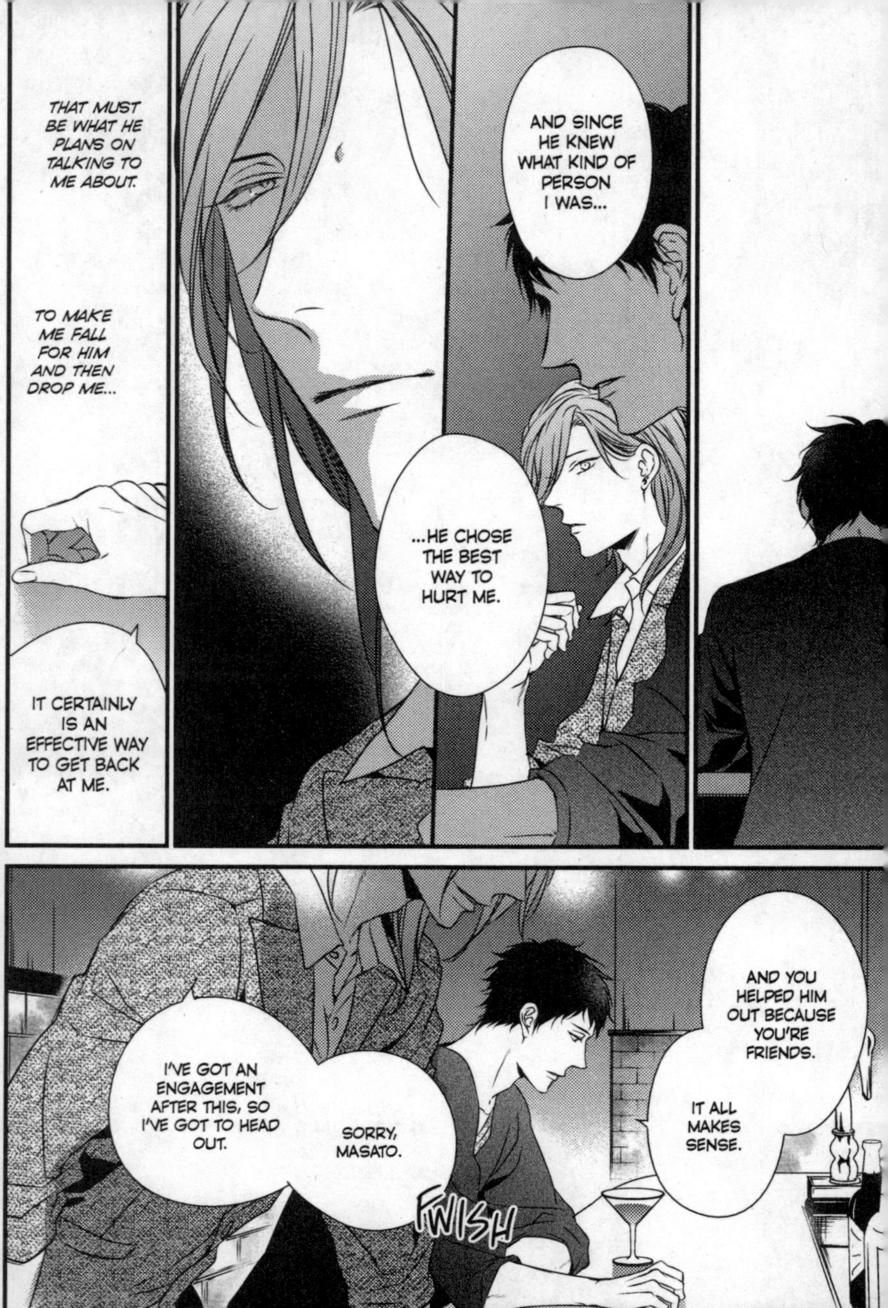
AND SINCE HE KNEW WHAT KIND OF PERSON I WAS...
...HE CHOSE THE BEST WAY TO HURT ME.
THAT MUST BE WHAT HE PLANS ON TALKING TO ME ABOUT.
TO MAKE ME FALL FOR HIM AND THEN DROP ME...
IT CERTAINLY IS AN EFFECTIVE WAY TO GET BACK AT ME.
AND YOU HELPED HIM OUT BECAUSE YOU'RE FRIENDS.
IT ALL MAKES SENSE.
FWISH
SORRY, MASATO.
I'VE GOT AN ENGAGEMENT AFTER THIS, SO I'VE GOT TO HEAD OUT.

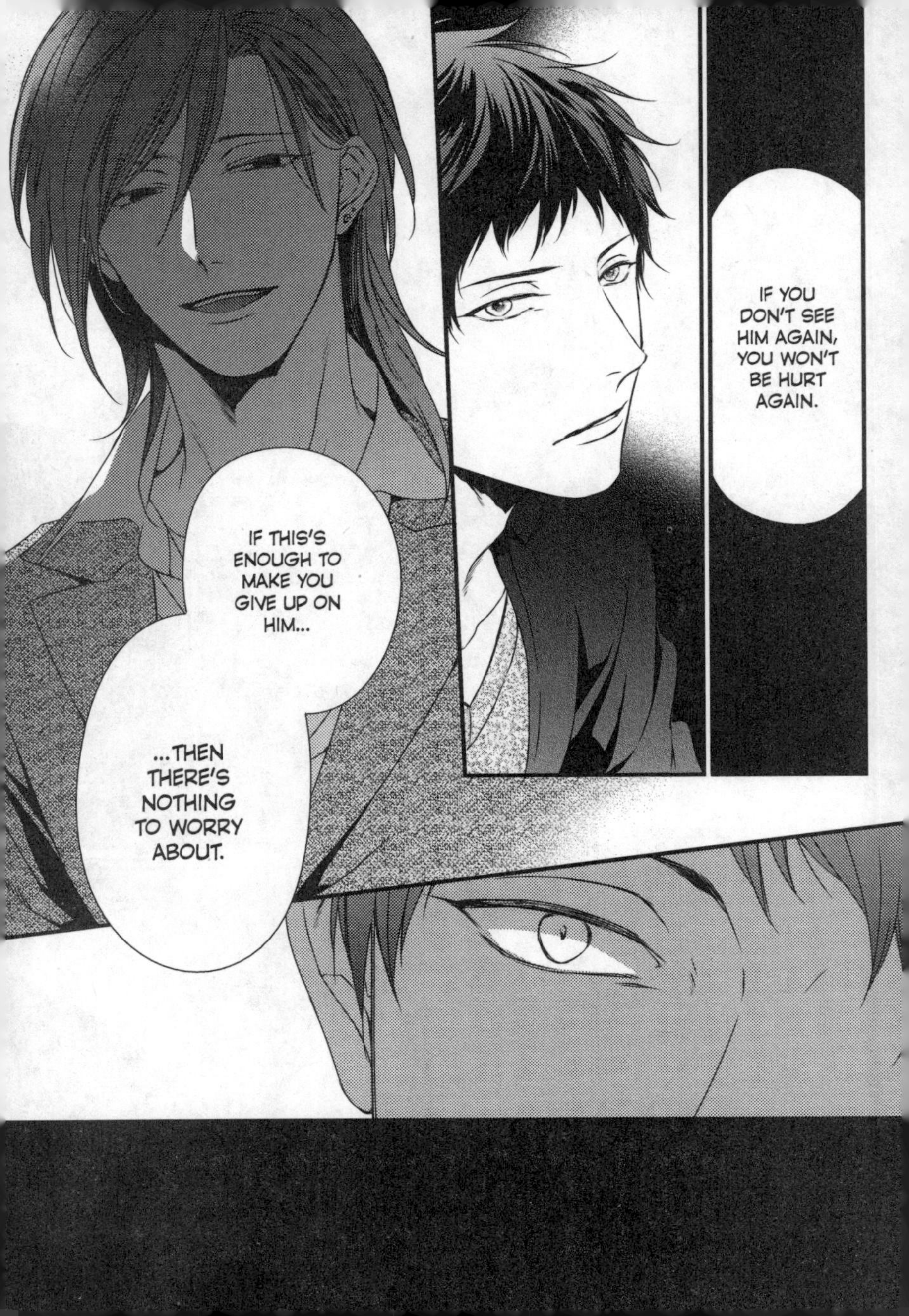
IF YOU DON'T SEE HIM AGAIN, YOU WON'T BE HURT AGAIN.
IF THIS'S ENOUGH TO MAKE YOU GIVE UP ON HIM...
...THEN THERE'S NOTHING TO WORRY ABOUT.

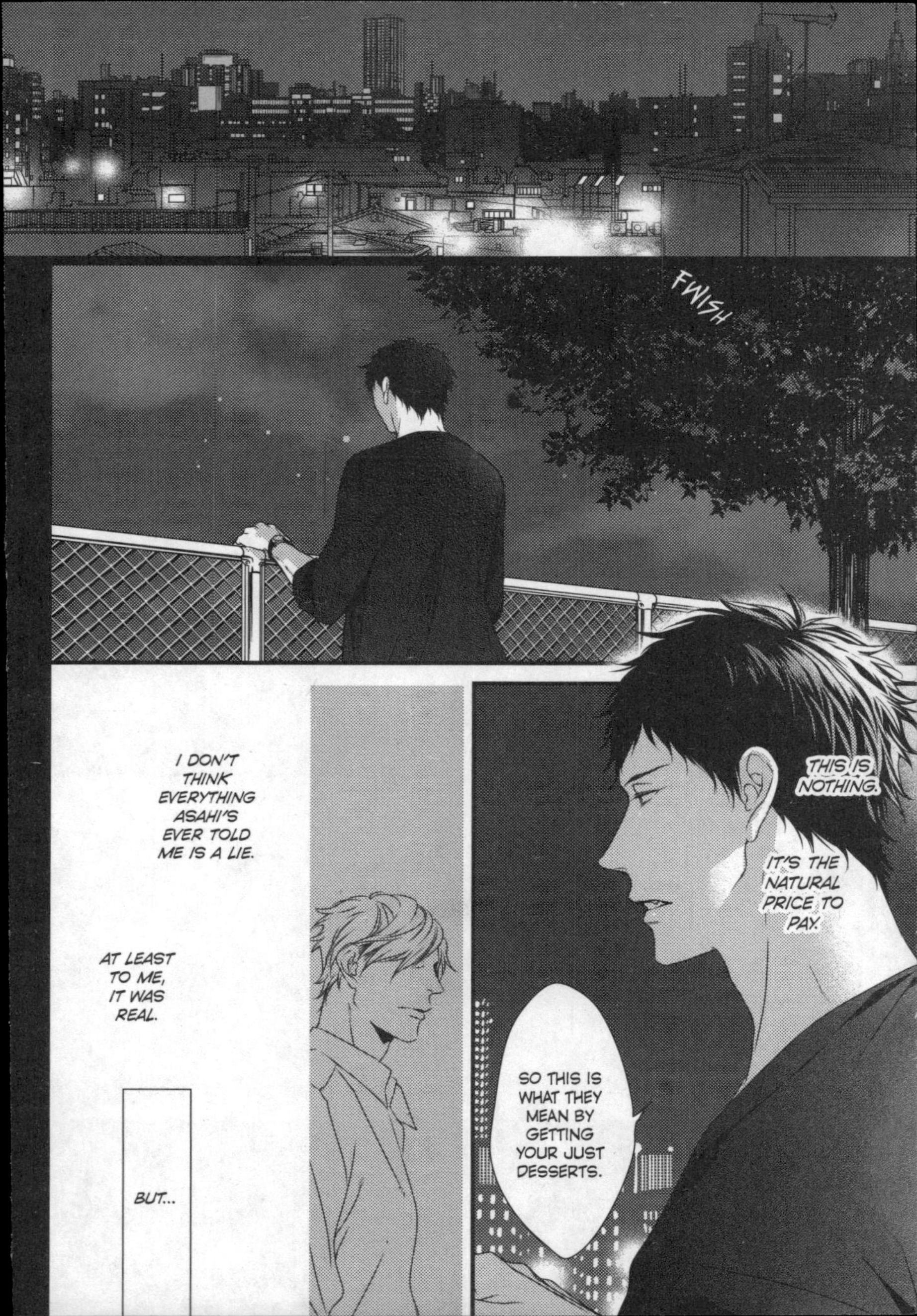
FWISH
THIS IS NOTHING.
IT'S THE NATURAL PRICE TO PAY.
SO THIS IS WHAT THEY MEAN BY GETTING YOUR JUST DESSERTS.
I DON'T THINK EVERYTHING ASAHI'S EVER TOLD ME IS A LIE.
AT LEAST TO ME, IT WAS REAL.
BUT...

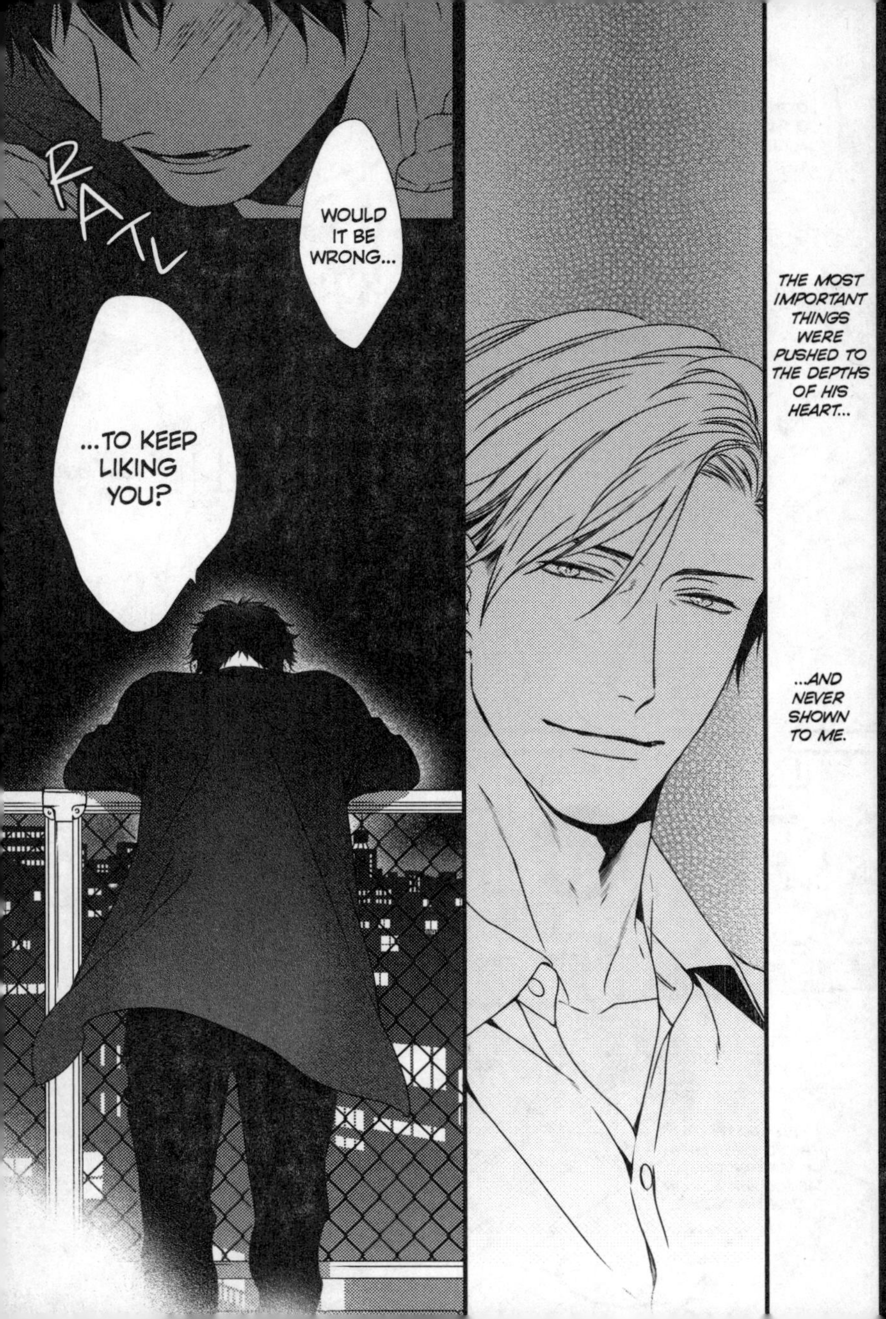
THE MOST IMPORTANT THINGS WERE PUSHED TO THE DEPTHS OF HIS HEART...
...AND NEVER SHOWN TO ME.
RATV
WOULD IT BE WRONG...
...TO KEEP LIKING YOU?

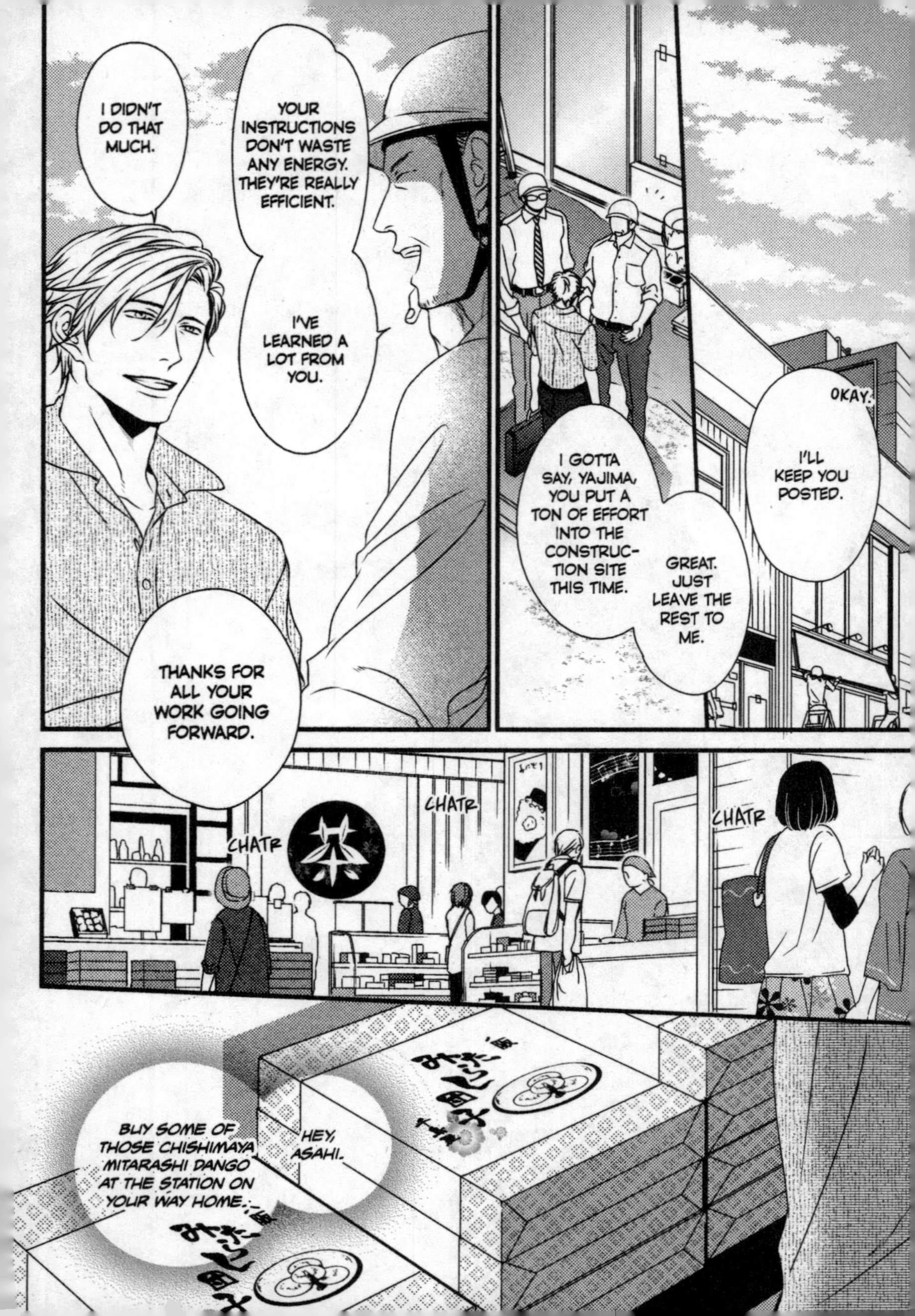
OKAY. I'LL KEEP YOU POSTED.
I GOTTA SAY, YAJIMA, YOU PUT A TON OF EFFORT INTO THE CONSTRUCTION SITE THIS TIME.
GREAT. JUST LEAVE THE REST TO ME.
YOUR INSTRUCTIONS DON'T WASTE ANY ENERGY. THEY'RE REALLY EFFICIENT.
I'VE LEARNED A LOT FROM YOU.
I DIDN'T DO THAT MUCH.
THANKS FOR ALL YOUR WORK GOING FORWARD.
CHATR
CHATR
CHATR
HEY, ASAHI.
BUY SOME OF THOSE CHISHIMAYA MITARASHI DANGO AT THE STATION ON YOUR WAY HOME.

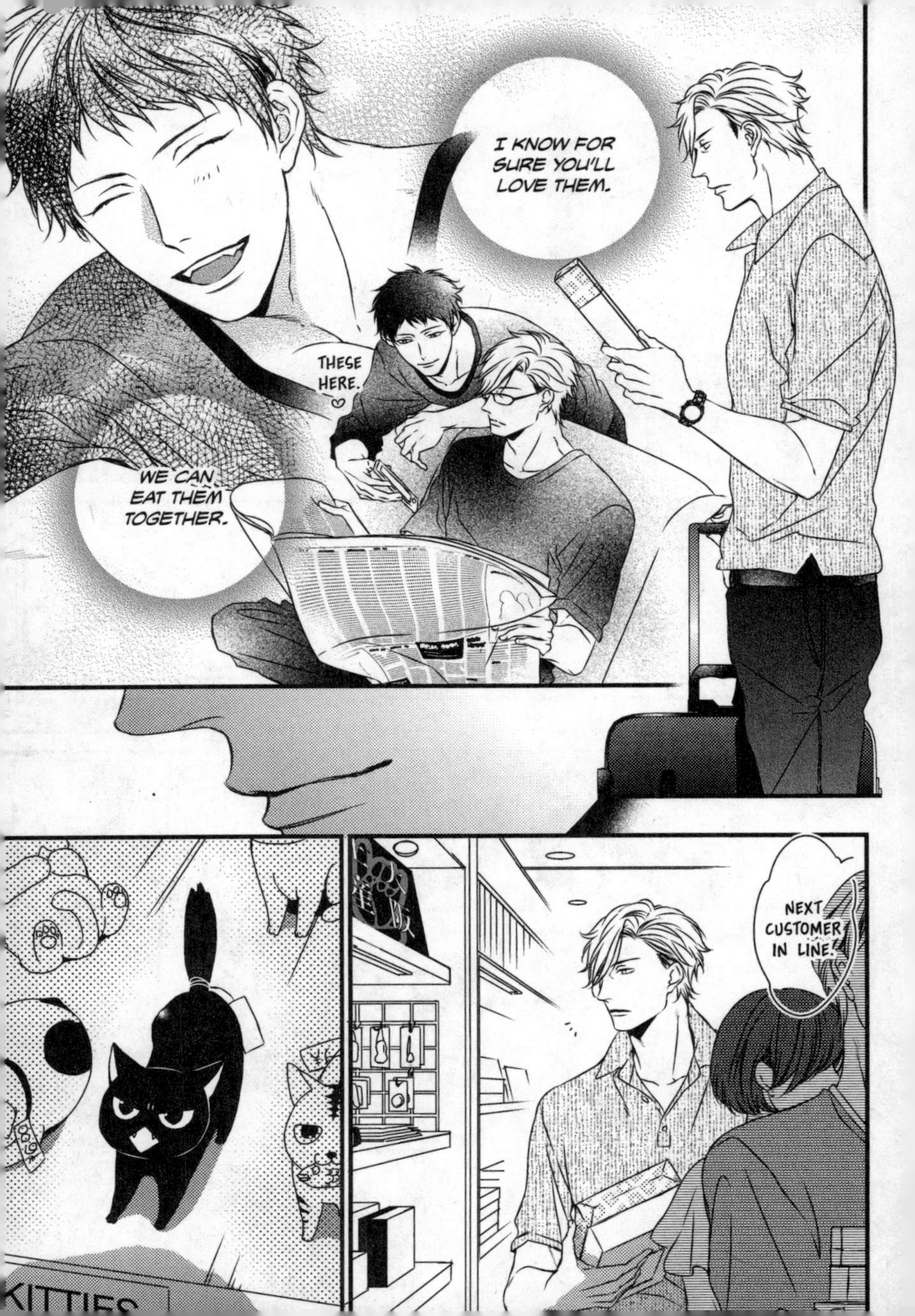
I KNOW FOR SURE YOU'LL LOVE THEM.
THESE HERE.
WE CAN EAT THEM TOGETHER.
NEXT CUSTOMER IN LINE.
KITTIES

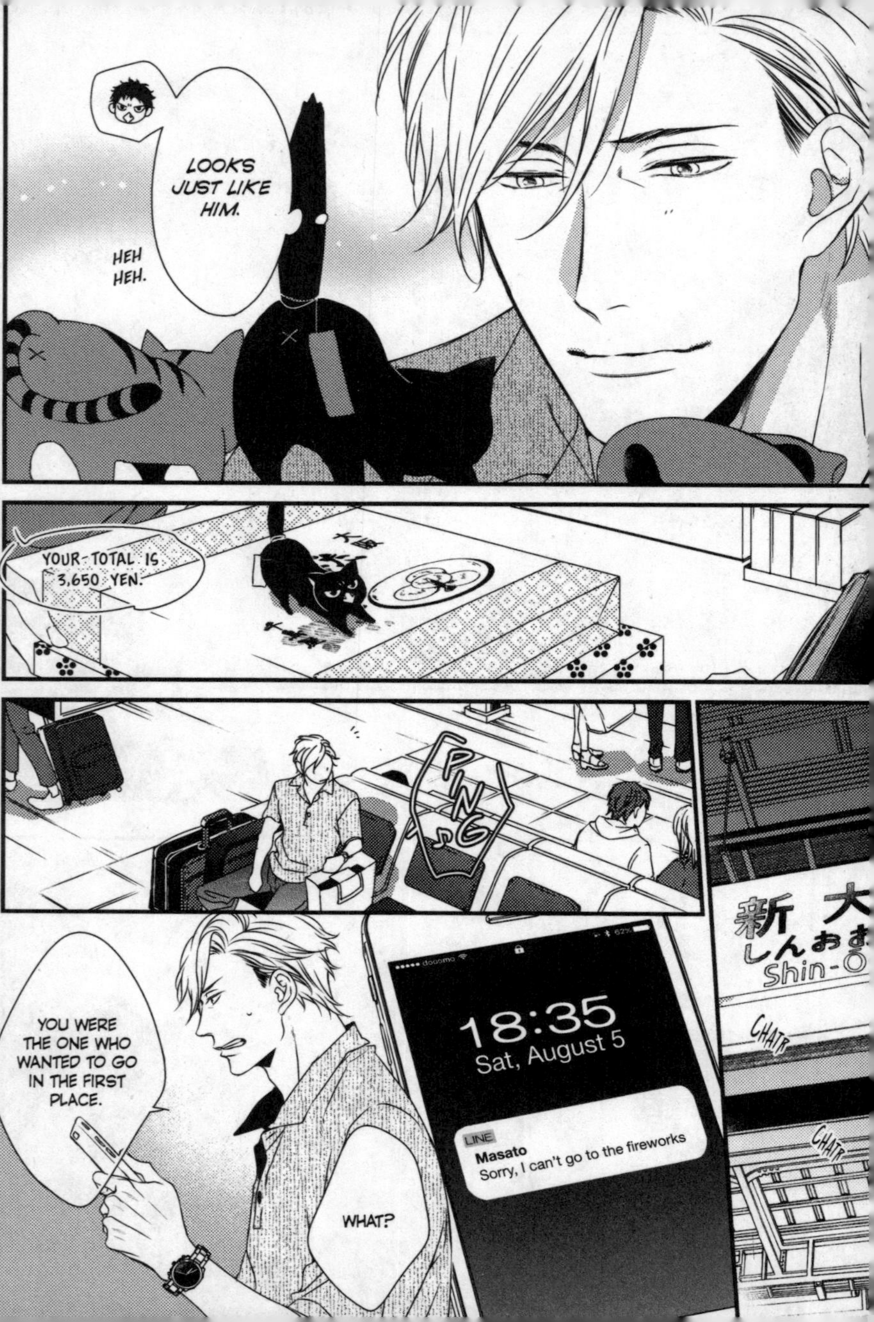

LOOKS JUST LIKE HIM.
HEH HEH.
YOUR TOTAL IS 3,650 YEN.
新大
Shin-O
CHATR
CHATR
PING
18:35
Sat, August 5
LINE
Masato
Sorry, I can't go to the fireworks
WHAT?
YOU WERE THE ONE WHO WANTED TO GO IN THE FIRST PLACE.

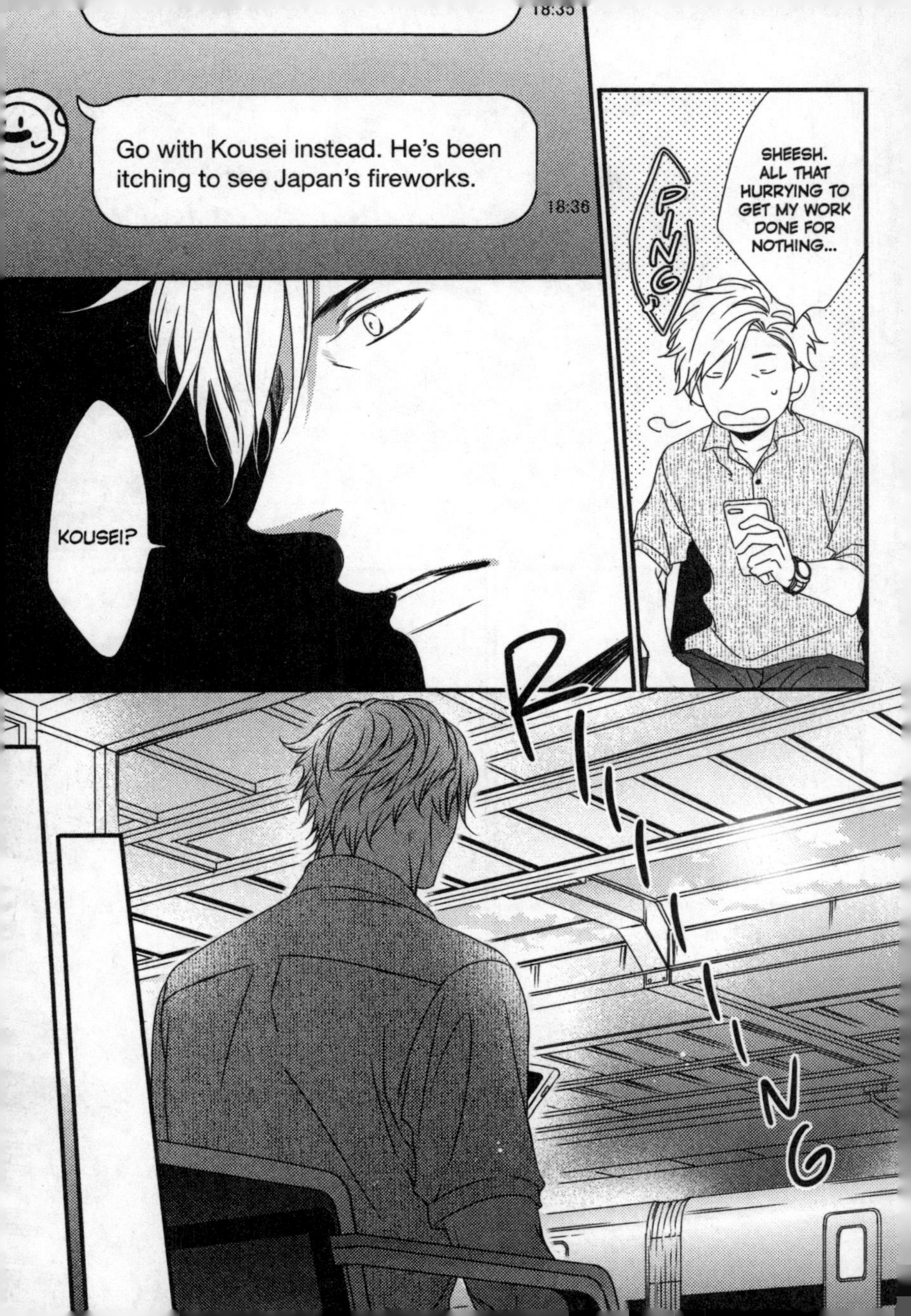
PING
SHEESH. ALL THAT HURRYING TO GET MY WORK DONE FOR NOTHING...
18:35
Go with Kousei instead. He's been itching to see Japan's fireworks.
18:36
KOUSEI?
RIIIIIIING

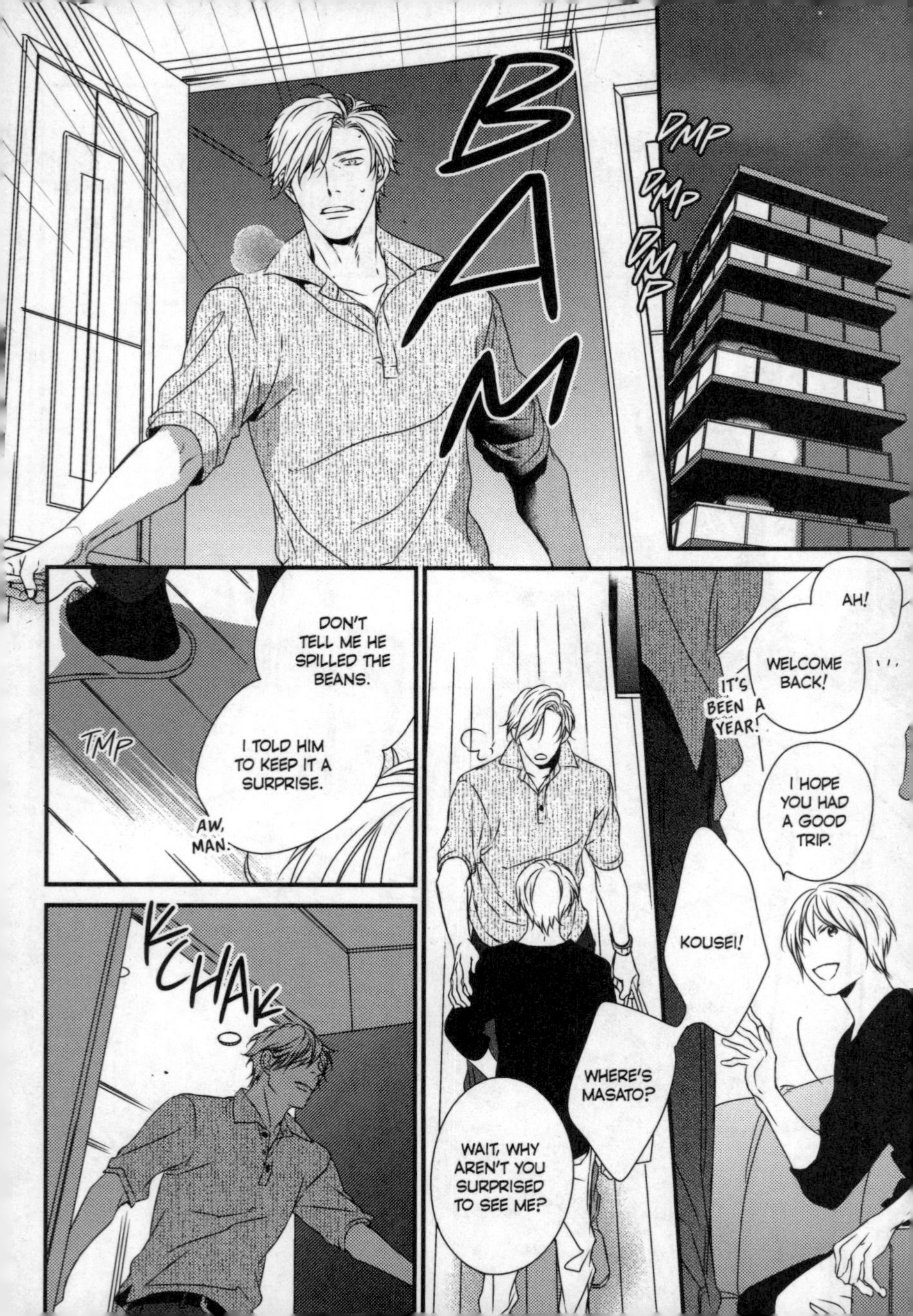
DMP
DMP
DMP
BAM
AH!
WELCOME BACK!
IT'S BEEN A YEAR!
I HOPE YOU HAD A GOOD TRIP.
KOUSEI!
WHERE'S MASATO?
WAIT, WHY AREN'T YOU SURPRISED TO SEE ME?
DON'T TELL ME HE SPILLED THE BEANS.
I TOLD HIM TO KEEP IT A SURPRISE.
AW, MAN.
TMP
KCHAK

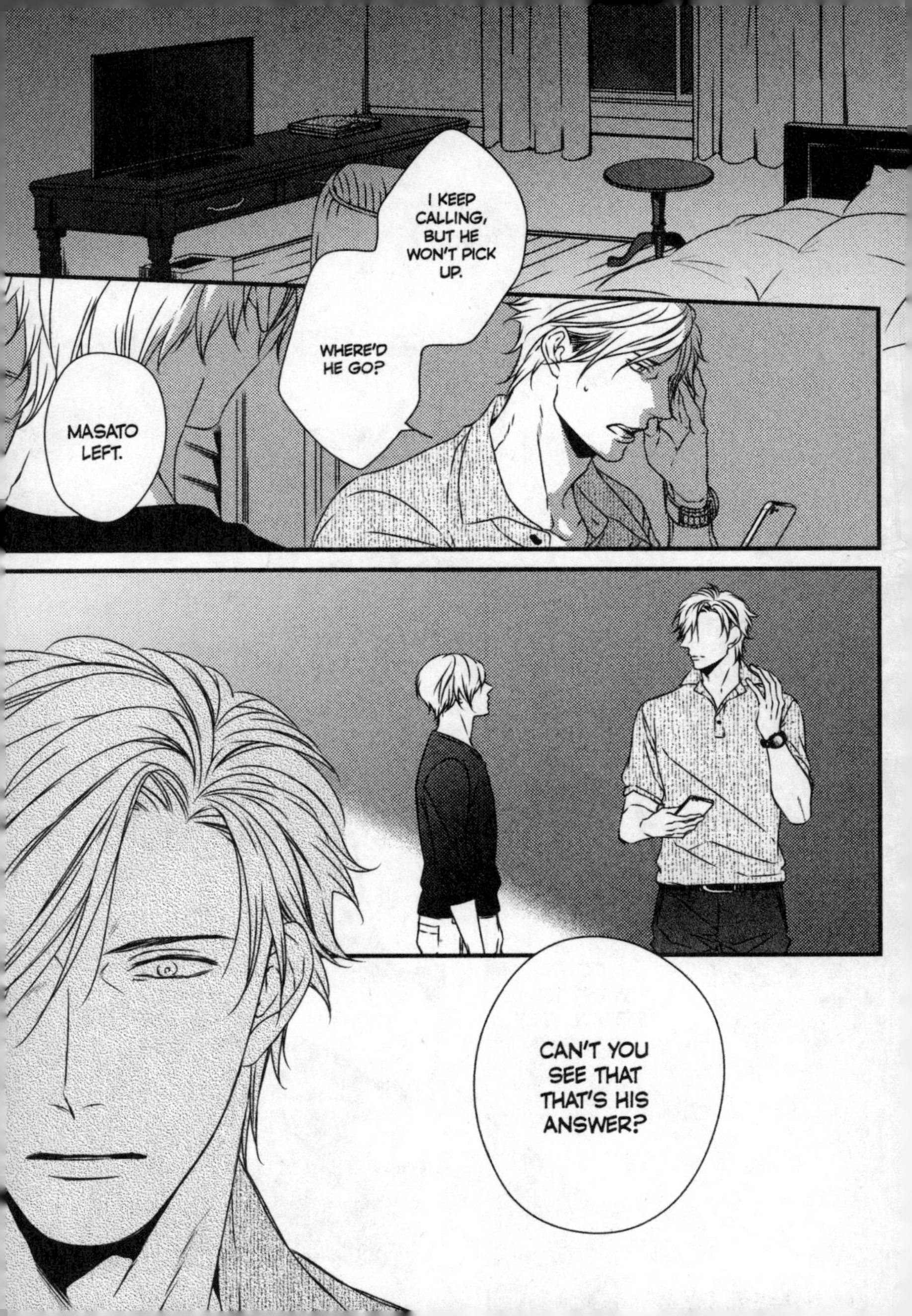
I KEEP CALLING, BUT HE WON'T PICK UP.
WHERE'D HE GO?
MASATO LEFT.
CAN'T YOU SEE THAT THAT'S HIS ANSWER?

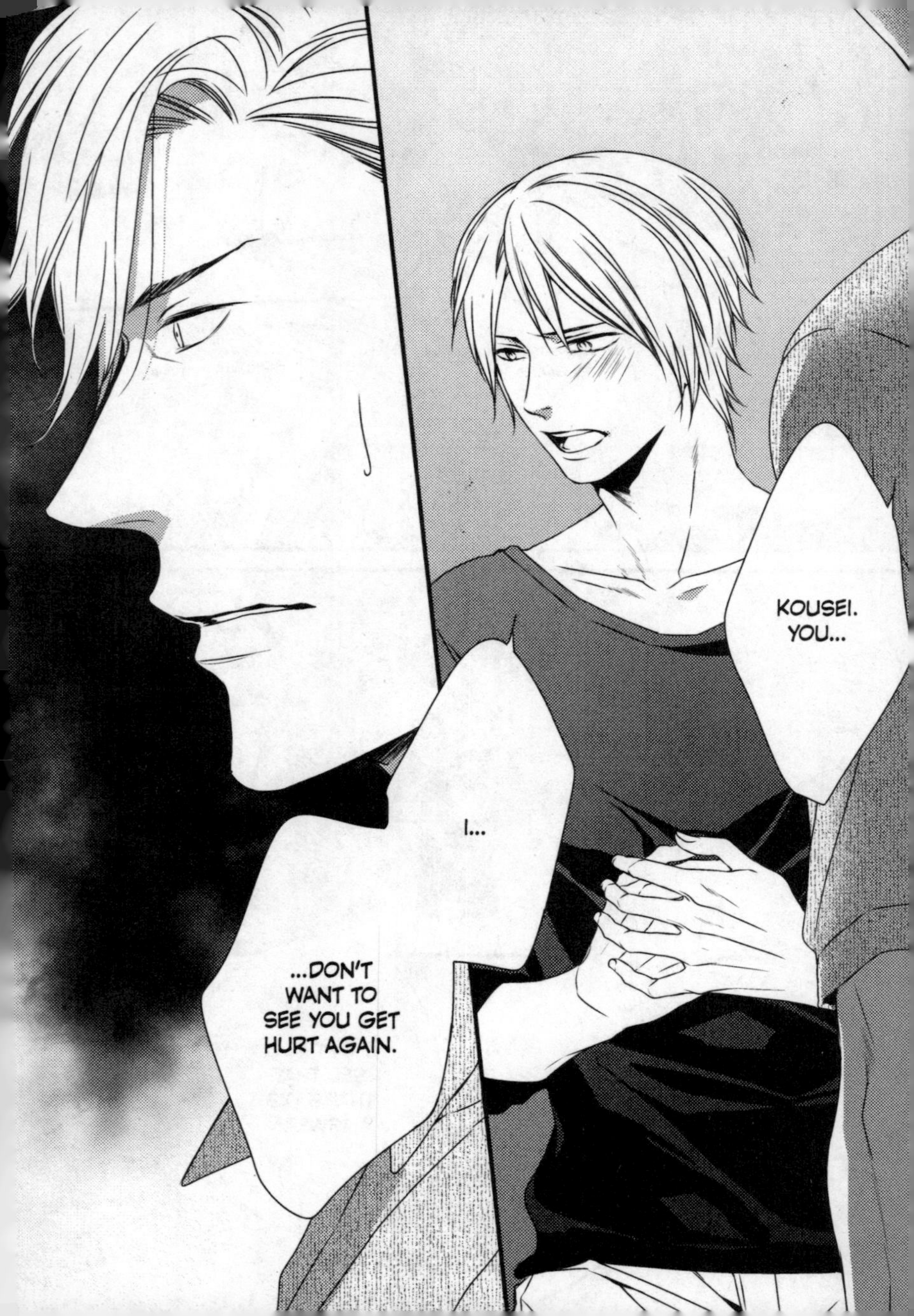
KOUSEI. YOU...
I...
...DON'T WANT TO SEE YOU GET HURT AGAIN.

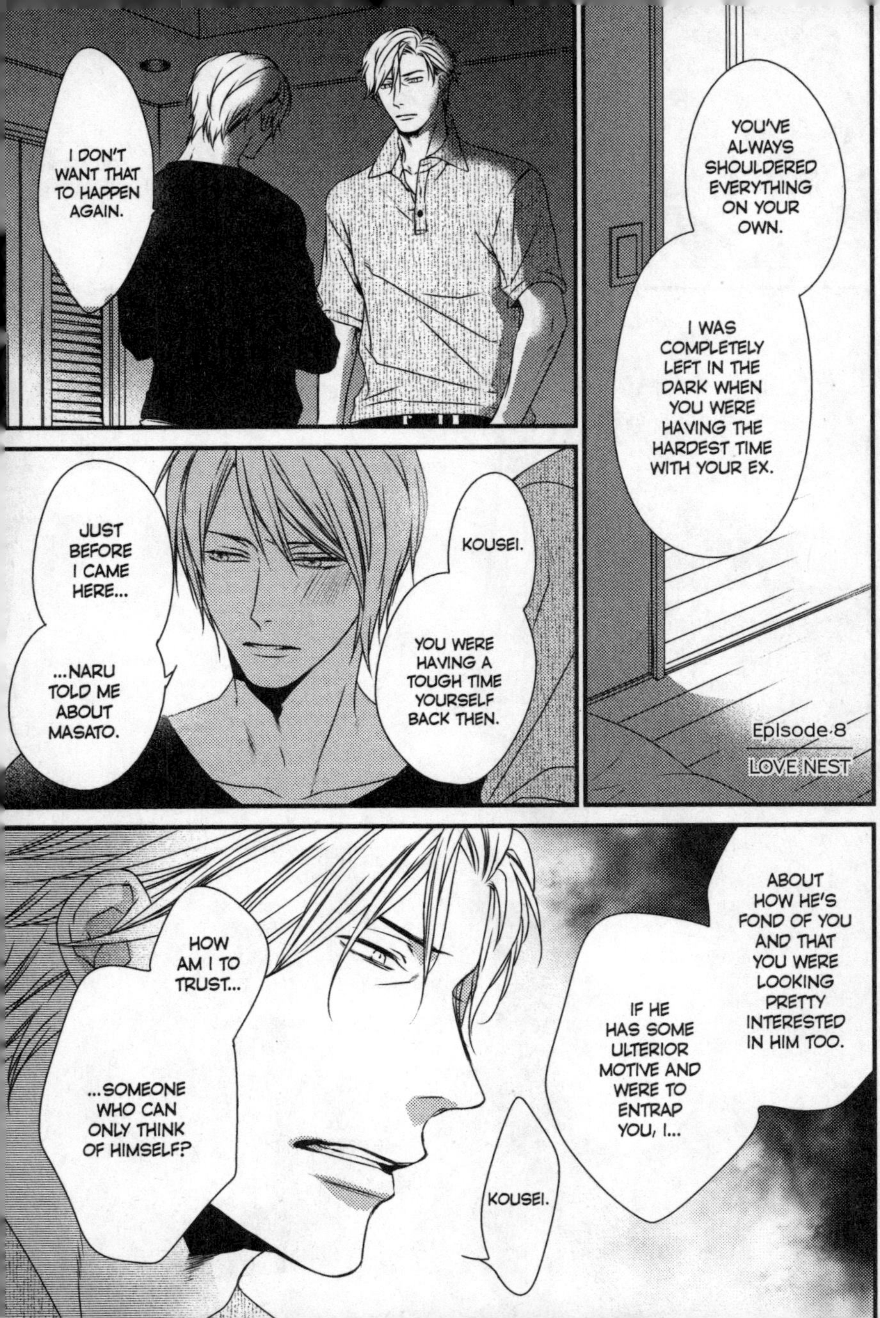
YOU'VE ALWAYS SHOULDERED EVERYTHING ON YOUR OWN.
I WAS COMPLETELY LEFT IN THE DARK WHEN YOU WERE HAVING THE HARDEST TIME WITH YOUR EX.
Episode 8
LOVE NEST
I DON'T WANT THAT TO HAPPEN AGAIN.
KOUSEI.
YOU WERE HAVING A TOUGH TIME YOURSELF BACK THEN.
JUST BEFORE I CAME HERE...
...NARU TOLD ME ABOUT MASATO.
ABOUT HOW HE'S FOND OF YOU AND THAT YOU WERE LOOKING PRETTY INTERESTED IN HIM TOO.
IF HE HAS SOME ULTERIOR MOTIVE AND WERE TO ENTRAP YOU, I...
KOUSEI.
HOW AM I TO TRUST...
...SOMEONE WHO CAN ONLY THINK OF HIMSELF?

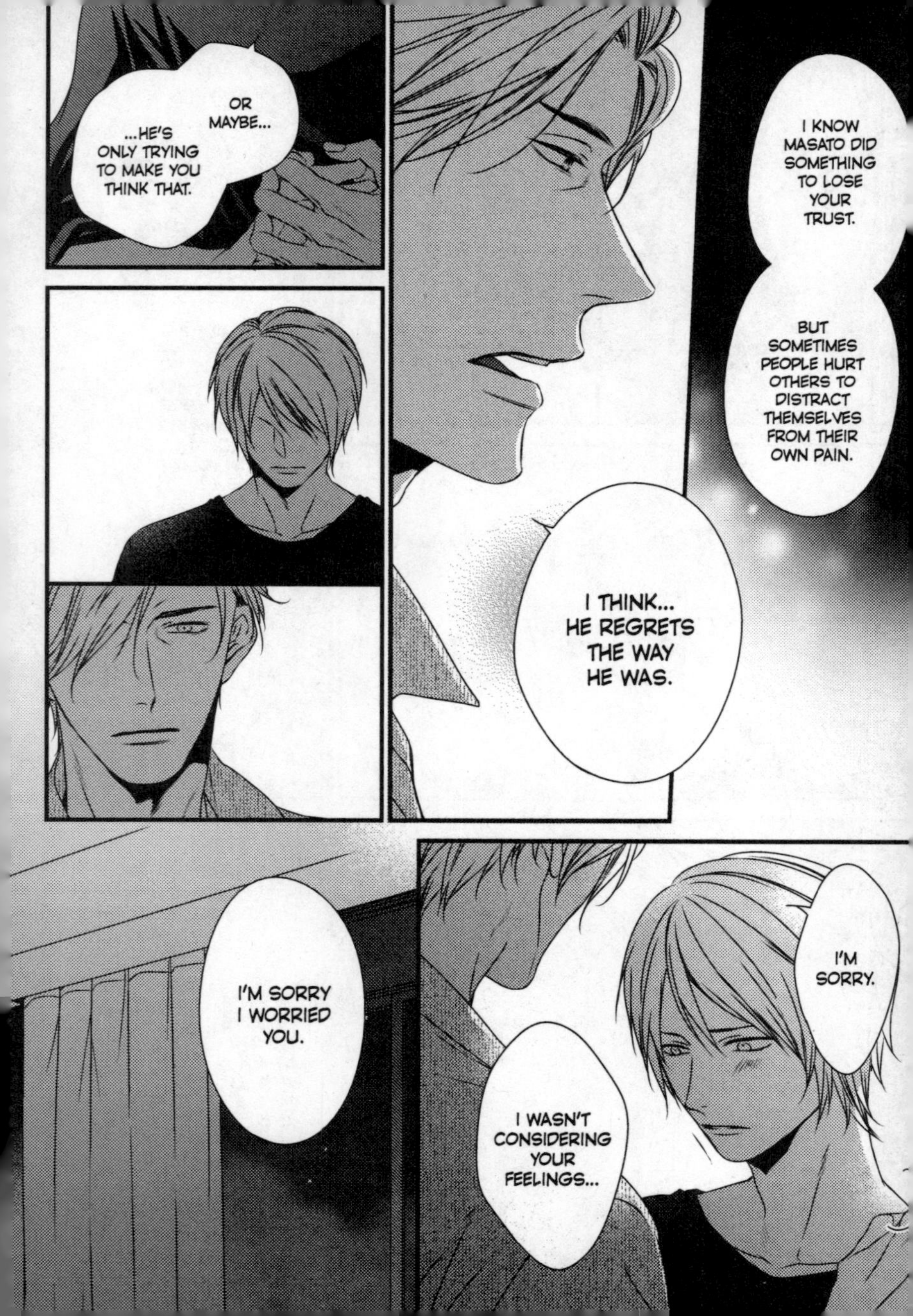
I KNOW MASATO DID SOMETHING TO LOSE YOUR TRUST.
BUT SOMETIMES PEOPLE HURT OTHERS TO DISTRACT THEMSELVES FROM THEIR OWN PAIN.
I THINK... HE REGRETS THE WAY HE WAS.
OR MAYBE...
...HE'S ONLY TRYING TO MAKE YOU THINK THAT.
I'M SORRY.
I WASN'T CONSIDERING YOUR FEELINGS...
I'M SORRY I WORRIED YOU.

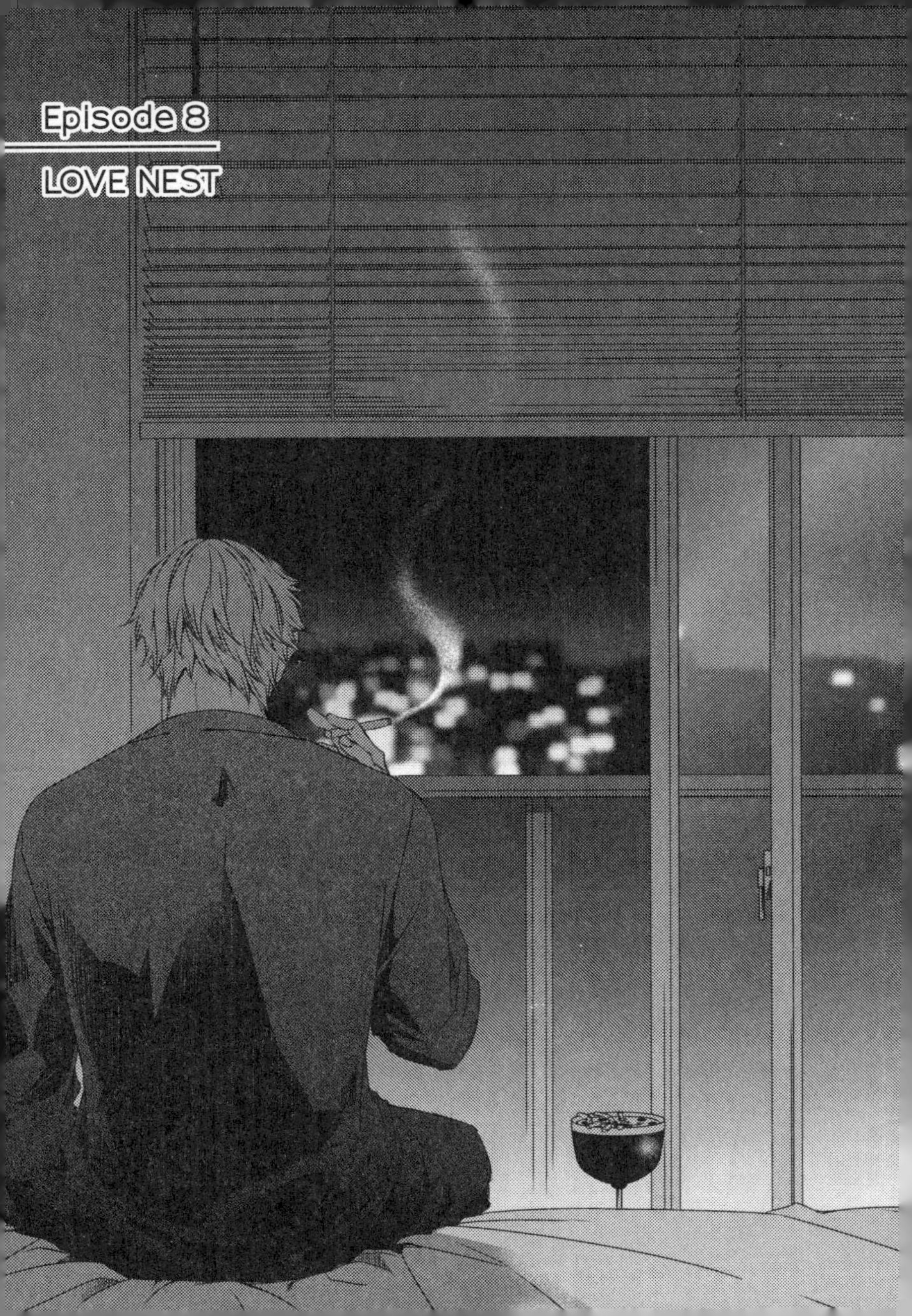
Episode 8
LOVE NEST

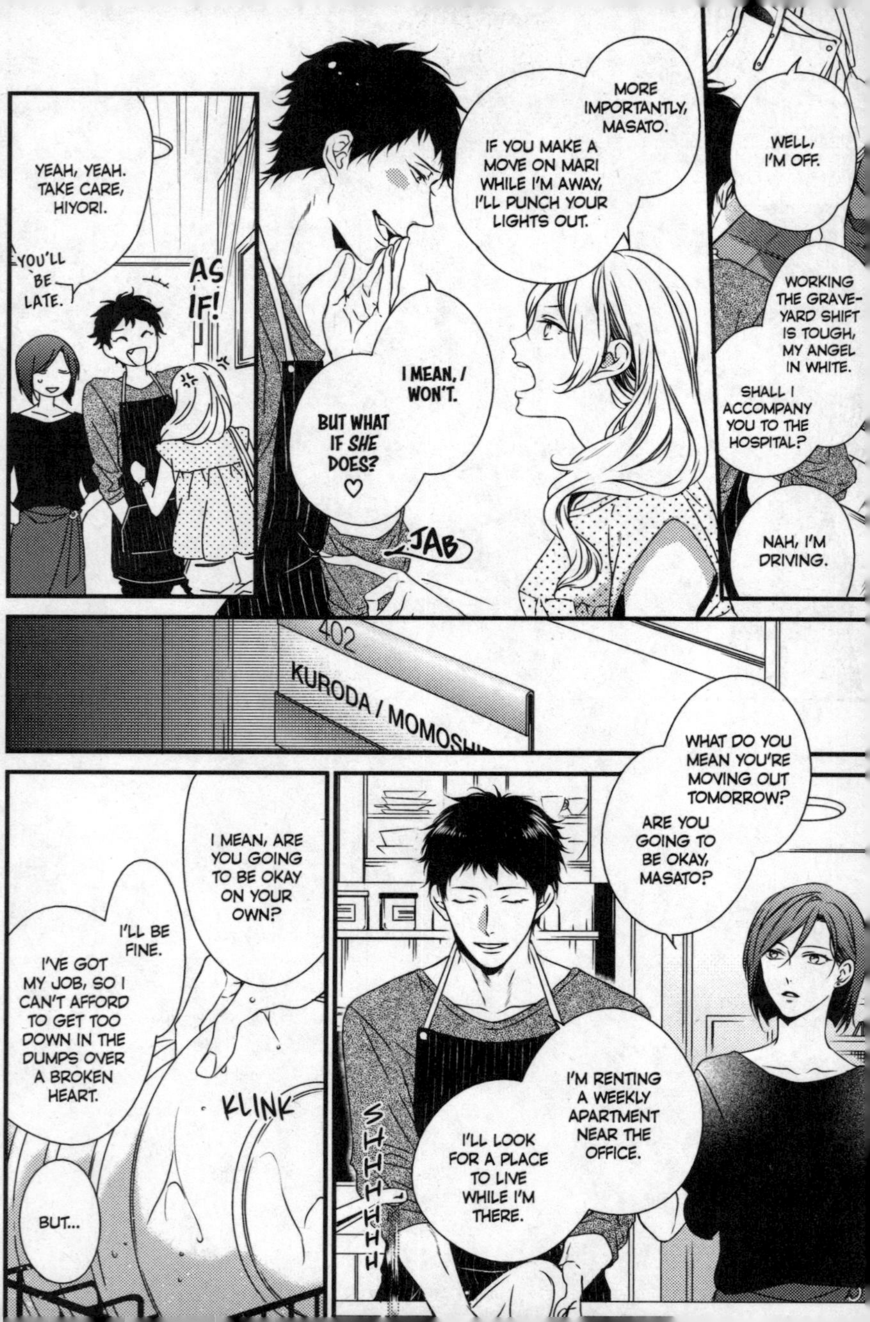
WELL, I'M OFF.
WORKING THE GRAVEYARD SHIFT IS TOUGH, MY ANGEL IN WHITE.
SHALL I ACCOMPANY YOU TO THE HOSPITAL?
NAH, I'M DRIVING.
MORE IMPORTANTLY, MASATO.
IF YOU MAKE A MOVE ON MARI WHILE I'M AWAY, I'LL PUNCH YOUR LIGHTS OUT.
I MEAN, I WON'T.
BUT WHAT IF SHE DOES? ♡
JAB
YEAH, YEAH. TAKE CARE, HIYORI.
YOU'LL BE LATE.
AS IF!
402
KURODA / MOMOSHI
WHAT DO YOU MEAN YOU'RE MOVING OUT TOMORROW?
ARE YOU GOING TO BE OKAY, MASATO?
I'M RENTING A WEEKLY APARTMENT NEAR THE OFFICE.
I'LL LOOK FOR A PLACE TO LIVE WHILE I'M THERE.
SHHHHHHHHH
I MEAN, ARE YOU GOING TO BE OKAY ON YOUR OWN?
I'LL BE FINE.
I'VE GOT MY JOB, SO I CAN'T AFFORD TO GET TOO DOWN IN THE DUMPS OVER A BROKEN HEART.
KLINK
BUT...

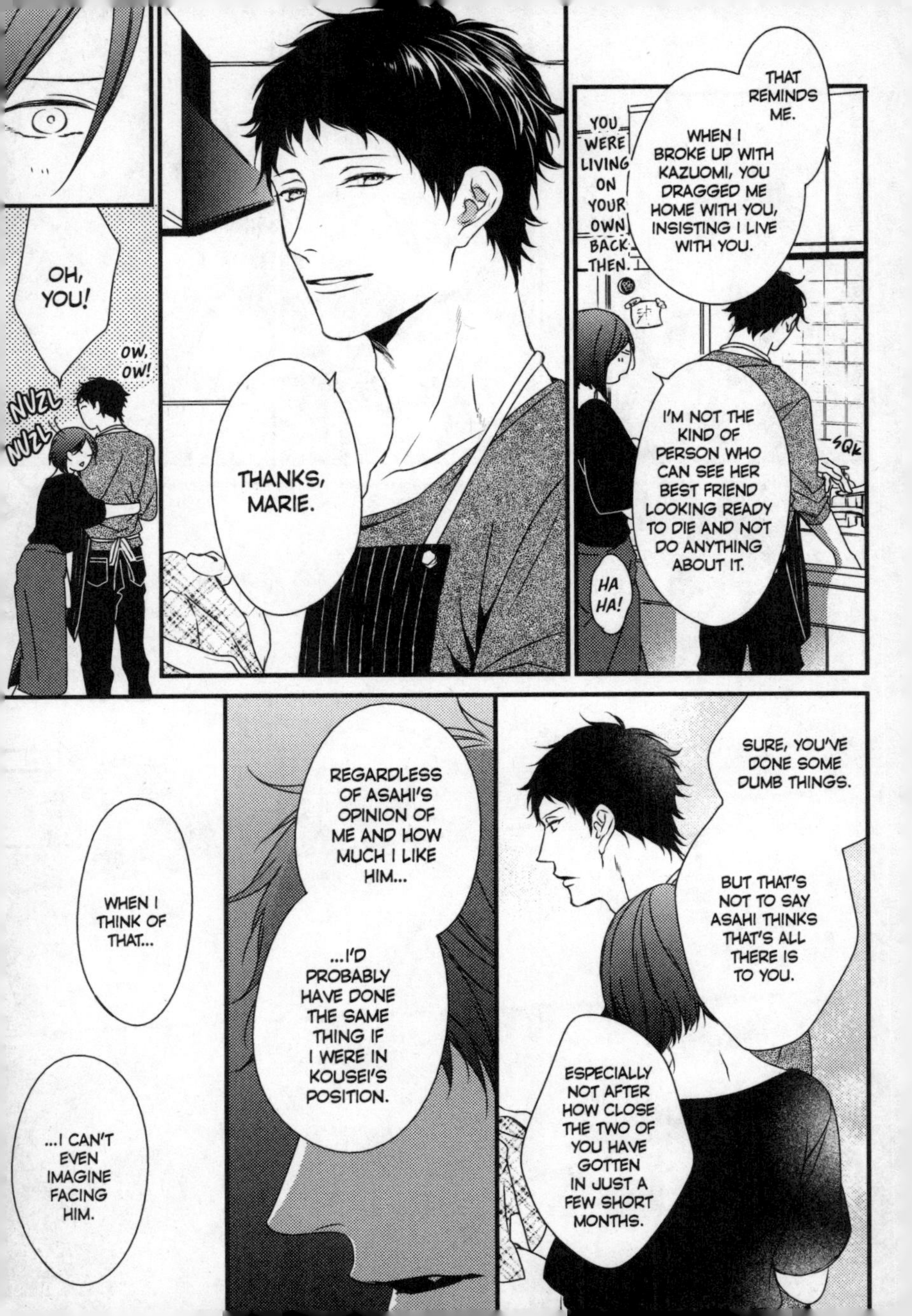
THAT REMINDS ME.
WHEN I BROKE UP WITH KAZUOMI, YOU DRAGGED ME HOME WITH YOU, INSISTING I LIVE WITH YOU.
YOU WERE LIVING ON YOUR OWN BACK THEN.
SQK
I'M NOT THE KIND OF PERSON WHO CAN SEE HER BEST FRIEND LOOKING READY TO DIE AND NOT DO ANYTHING ABOUT IT.
HA HA!
THANKS, MARIE.
OH, YOU!
OW, OW!
NUZL NUZL
SURE, YOU'VE DONE SOME DUMB THINGS.
BUT THAT'S NOT TO SAY ASAHI THINKS THAT'S ALL THERE IS TO YOU.
ESPECIALLY NOT AFTER HOW CLOSE THE TWO OF YOU HAVE GOTTEN IN JUST A FEW SHORT MONTHS.
REGARDLESS OF ASAHI'S OPINION OF ME AND HOW MUCH I LIKE HIM...
...I'D PROBABLY HAVE DONE THE SAME THING IF I WERE IN KOUSEI'S POSITION.
WHEN I THINK OF THAT...
...I CAN'T EVEN IMAGINE FACING HIM.

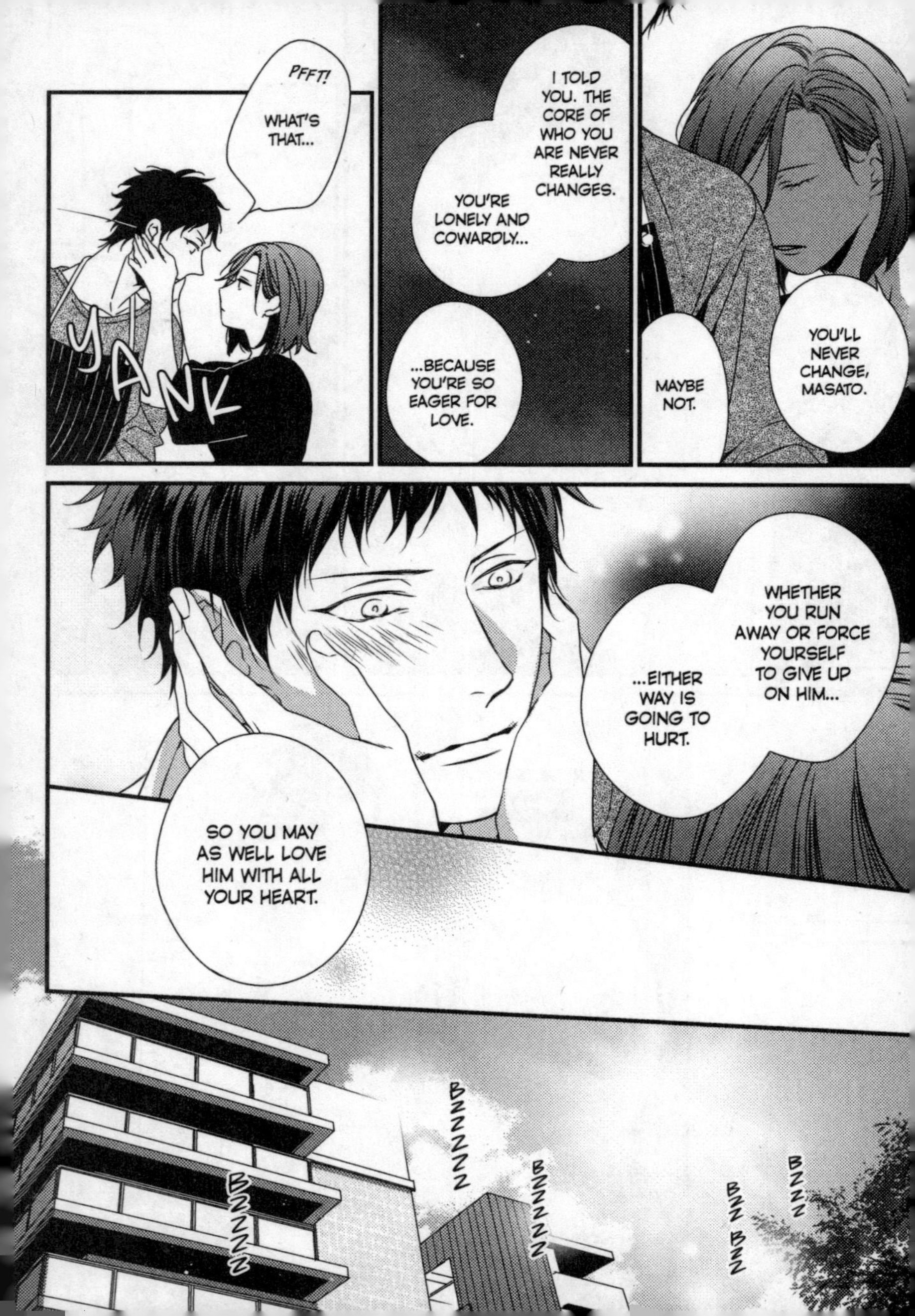
YOU'LL NEVER CHANGE, MASATO.
MAYBE NOT.
I TOLD YOU. THE CORE OF WHO YOU ARE NEVER REALLY CHANGES.
YOU'RE LONELY AND COWARDLY...
...BECAUSE YOU'RE SO EAGER FOR LOVE.
PFFT!
WHAT'S THAT...
YANK
WHETHER YOU RUN AWAY OR FORCE YOURSELF TO GIVE UP ON HIM...
...EITHER WAY IS GOING TO HURT.
SO YOU MAY AS WELL LOVE HIM WITH ALL YOUR HEART.
BZZZ
BZZ BZZ
BZZZZZ
BZZZZZZ
BZZZZ

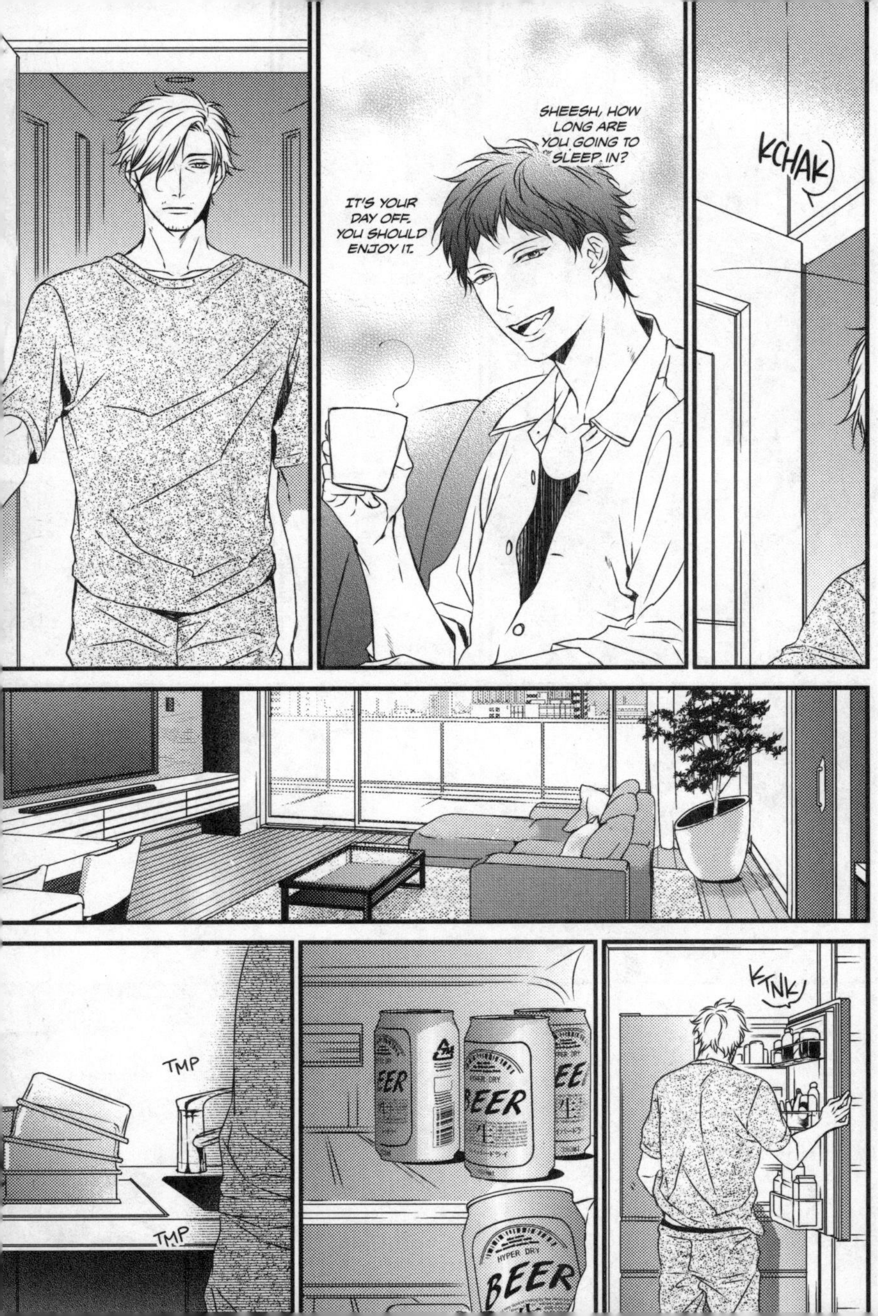
KCHAK
SHEESH, HOW LONG ARE YOU GOING TO SLEEP IN?
IT'S YOUR DAY OFF. YOU SHOULD ENJOY IT.
KTNK
HYPER DRY
BEER
TMP
TMP

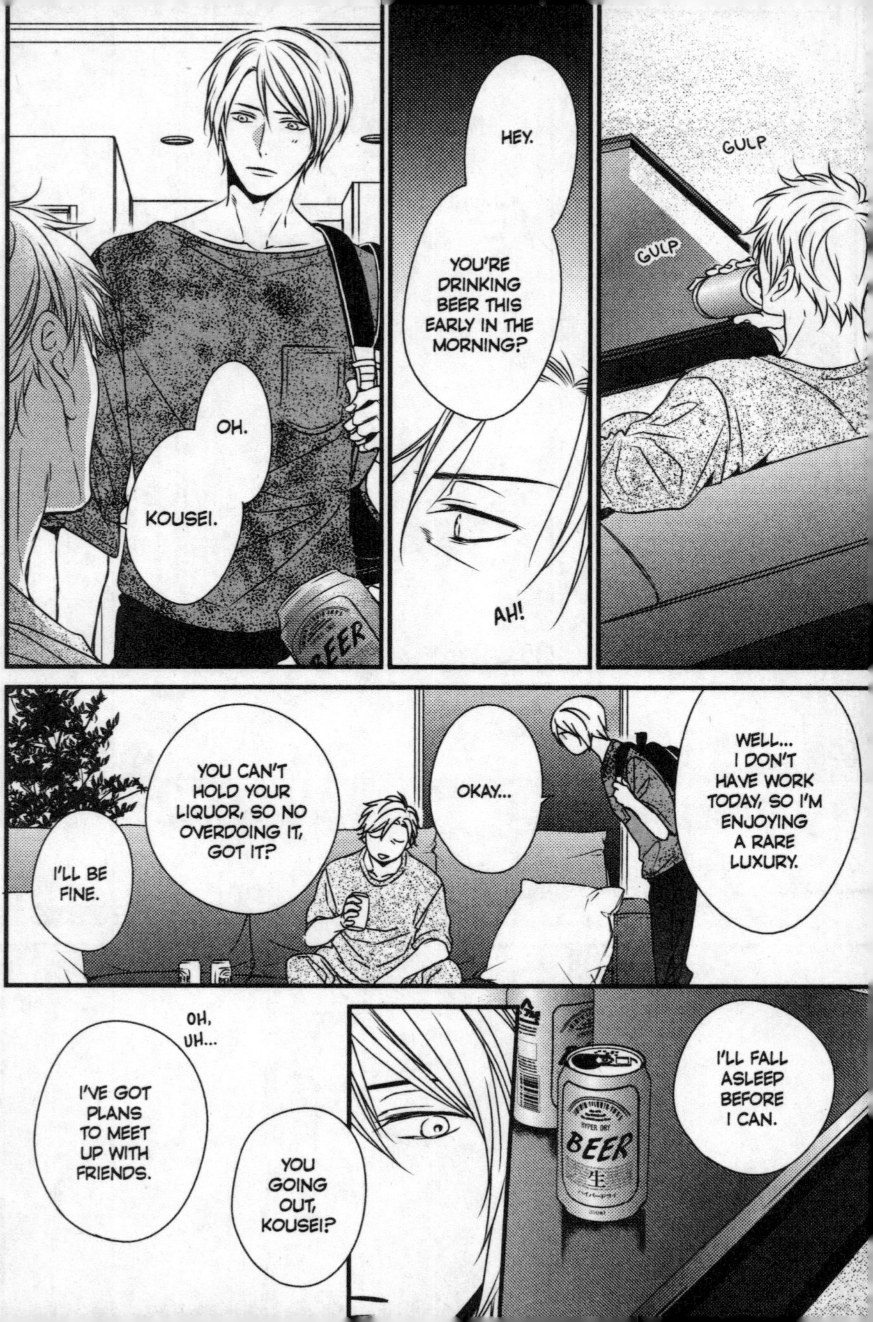
GULP
GULP
HEY.
YOU'RE DRINKING BEER THIS EARLY IN THE MORNING?
AH!
OH.
KOUSEI.
WELL... I DON'T HAVE WORK TODAY, SO I'M ENJOYING A RARE LUXURY.
OKAY...
YOU CAN'T HOLD YOUR LIQUOR, SO NO OVERDOING IT, GOT IT?
I'LL BE FINE.
I'LL FALL ASLEEP BEFORE I CAN.
BEER
YOU GOING OUT, KOUSEI?
OH, UH...
I'VE GOT PLANS TO MEET UP WITH FRIENDS.

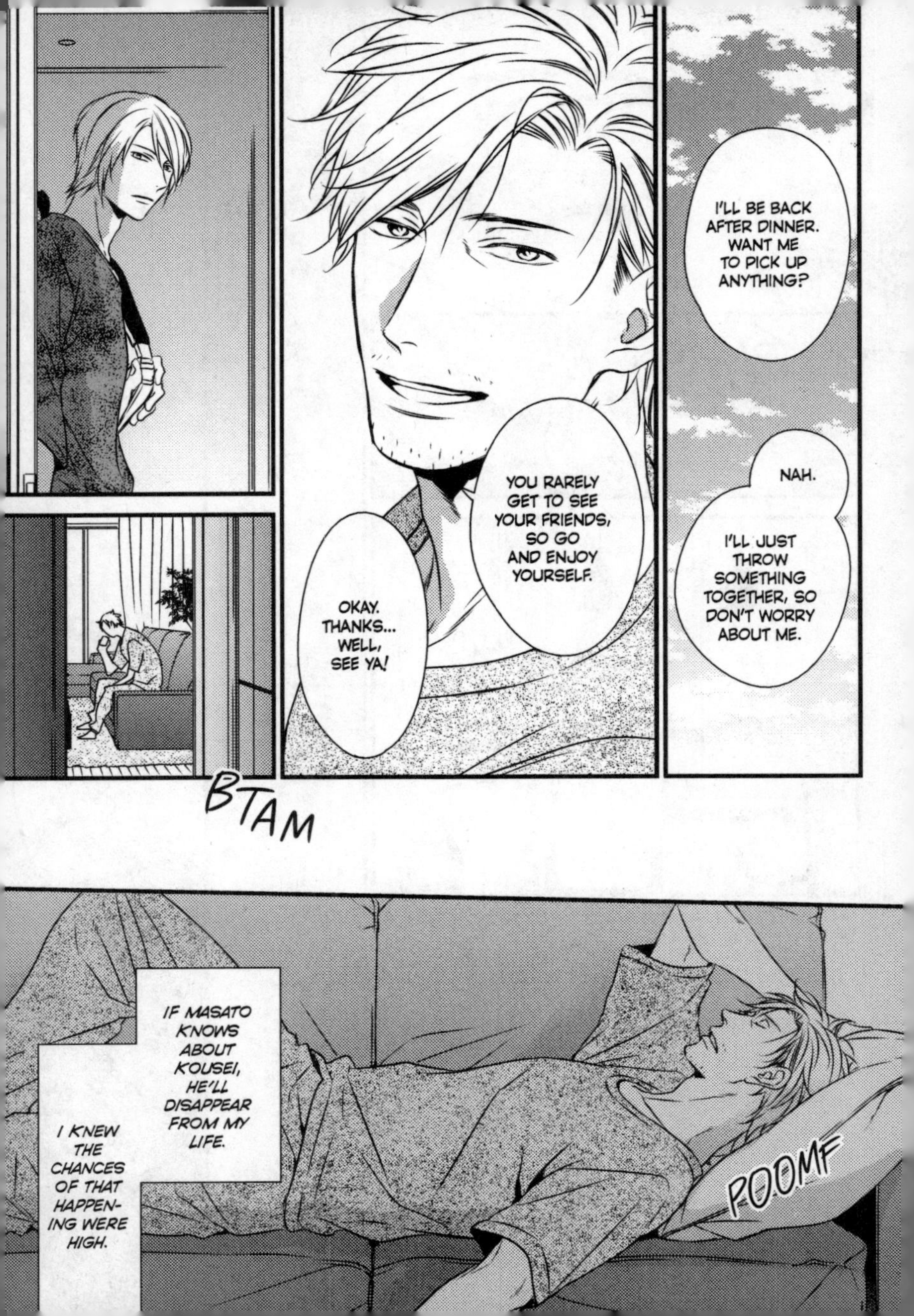
I'LL BE BACK AFTER DINNER. WANT ME TO PICK UP ANYTHING?
NAH.
I'LL JUST THROW SOMETHING TOGETHER, SO DON'T WORRY ABOUT ME.
YOU RARELY GET TO SEE YOUR FRIENDS, SO GO AND ENJOY YOURSELF.
OKAY. THANKS... WELL, SEE YA!
BTAM
IF MASATO KNOWS ABOUT KOUSEI, HE'LL DISAPPEAR FROM MY LIFE.
I KNEW THE CHANCES OF THAT HAPPEN-ING WERE HIGH.
POOMF

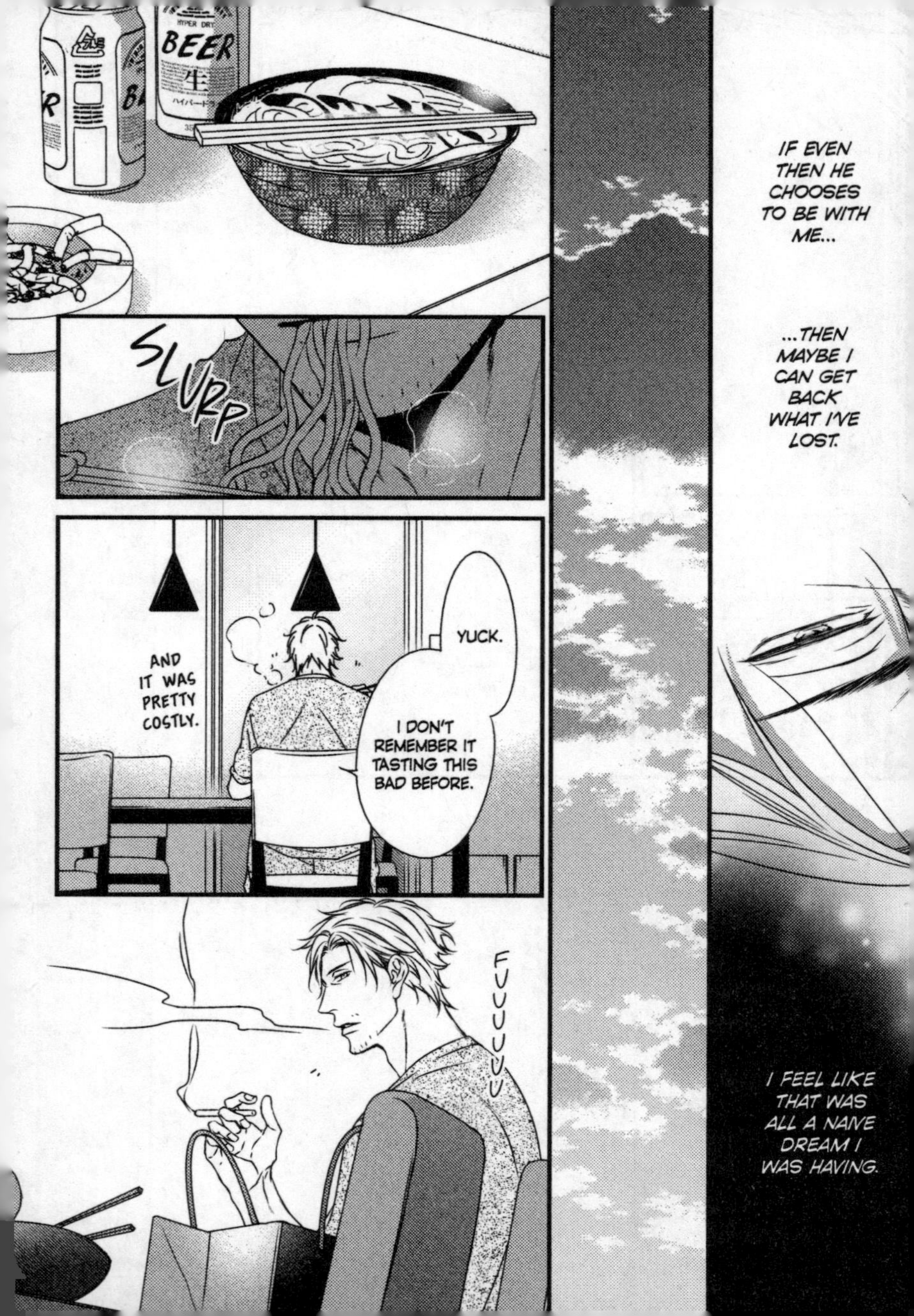
IF EVEN THEN HE CHOOSES TO BE WITH ME...
...THEN MAYBE I CAN GET BACK WHAT I'VE LOST.
I FEEL LIKE THAT WAS ALL A NAIVE DREAM I WAS HAVING.
HYPER DRY
BEER
生
SLURP
YUCK.
I DON'T REMEMBER IT TASTING THIS BAD BEFORE.
AND IT WAS PRETTY COSTLY.
FUUUUUU

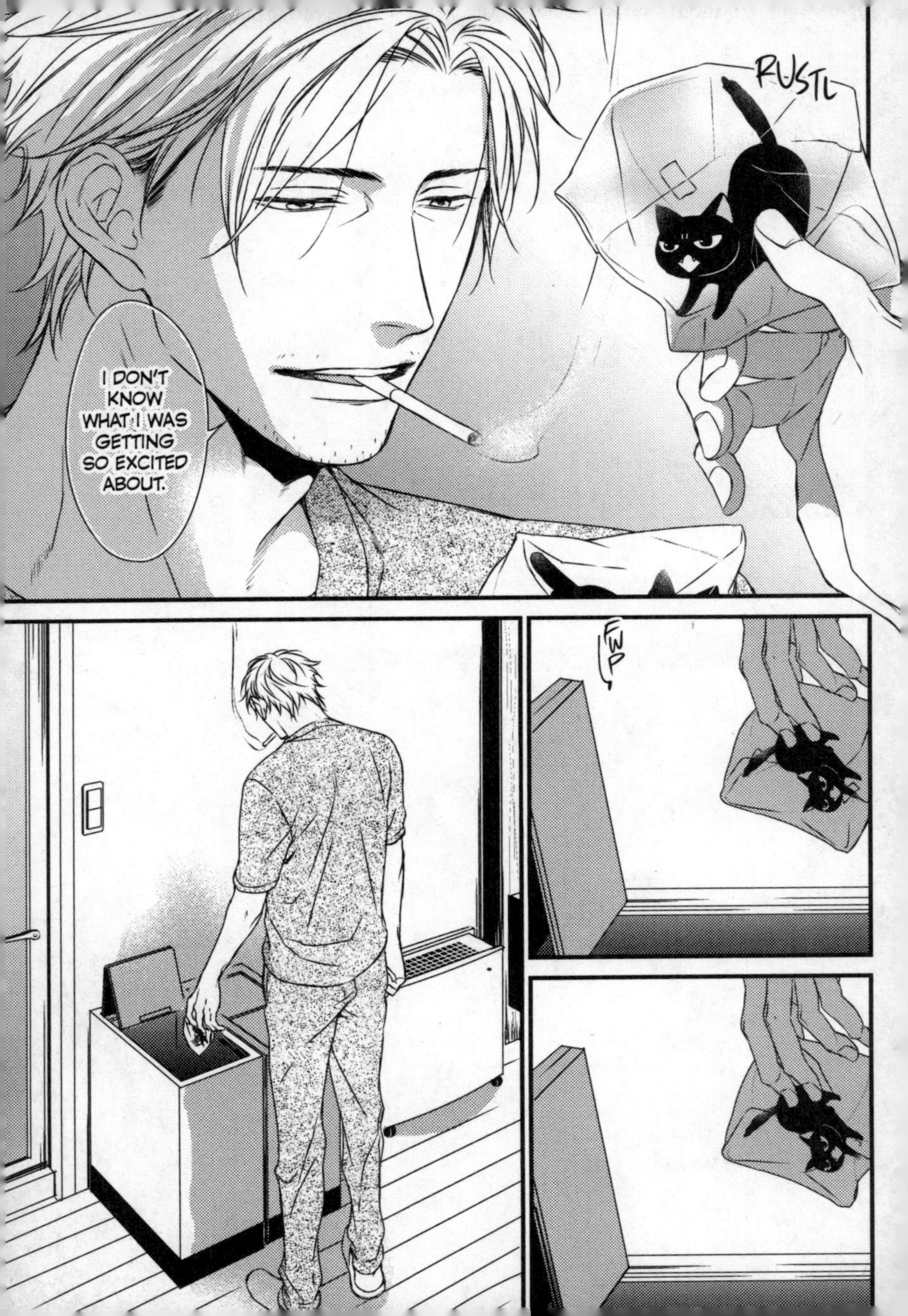
RUSTL
I DON'T KNOW WHAT I WAS GETTING SO EXCITED ABOUT.
FWP

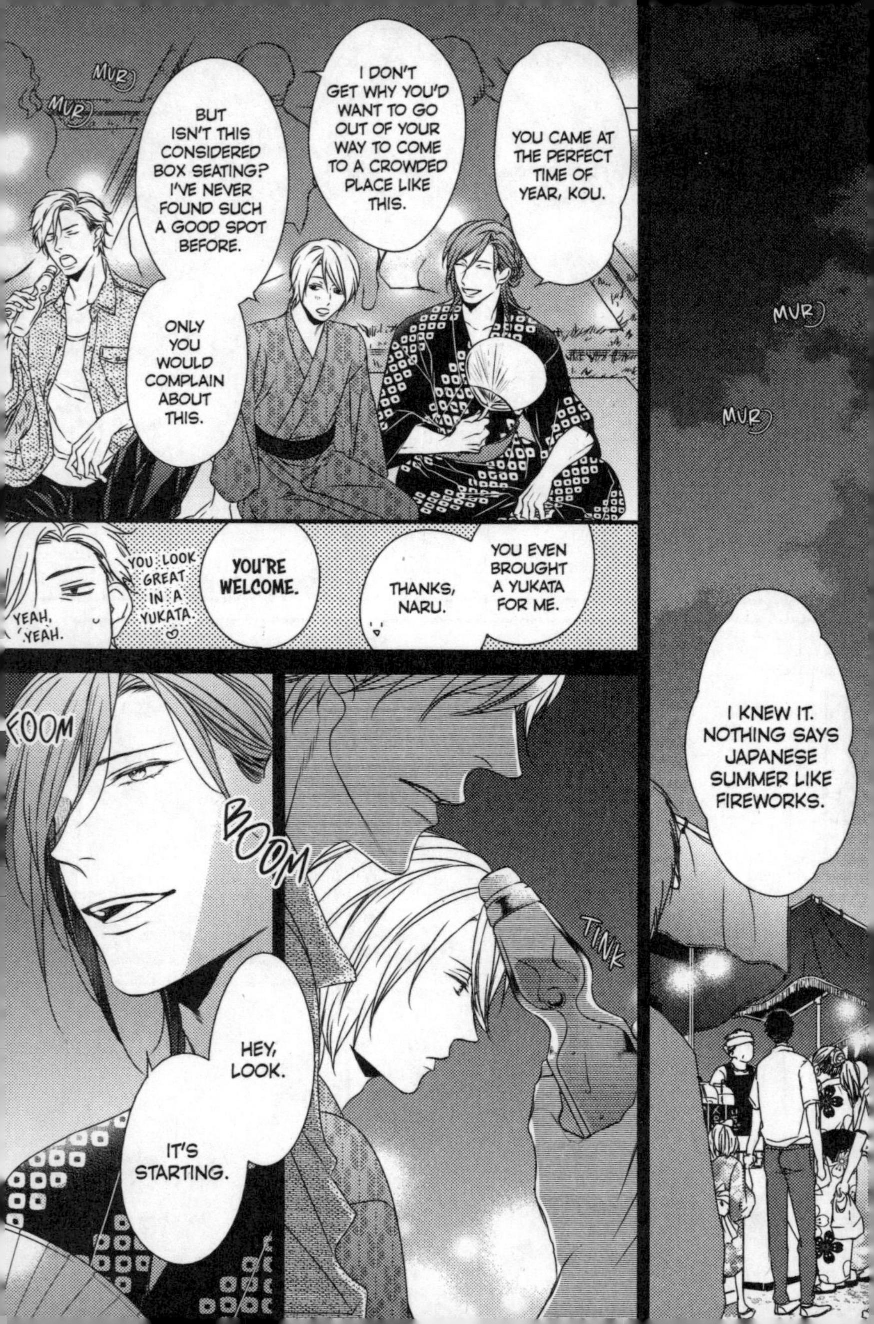
MUR
MUR
I KNEW IT. NOTHING SAYS JAPANESE SUMMER LIKE FIREWORKS.
YOU CAME AT THE PERFECT TIME OF YEAR, KOU.
I DON'T GET WHY YOU'D WANT TO GO OUT OF YOUR WAY TO COME TO A CROWDED PLACE LIKE THIS.
BUT ISN'T THIS CONSIDERED BOX SEATING? I'VE NEVER FOUND SUCH A GOOD SPOT BEFORE.
MUR
MUR
ONLY YOU WOULD COMPLAIN ABOUT THIS.
YOU EVEN BROUGHT A YUKATA FOR ME.
THANKS, NARU.
YOU'RE WELCOME.
YOU LOOK GREAT IN A YUKATA.
YEAH, YEAH.
TINK
FOOM
BOOM
HEY, LOOK.
IT'S STARTING.

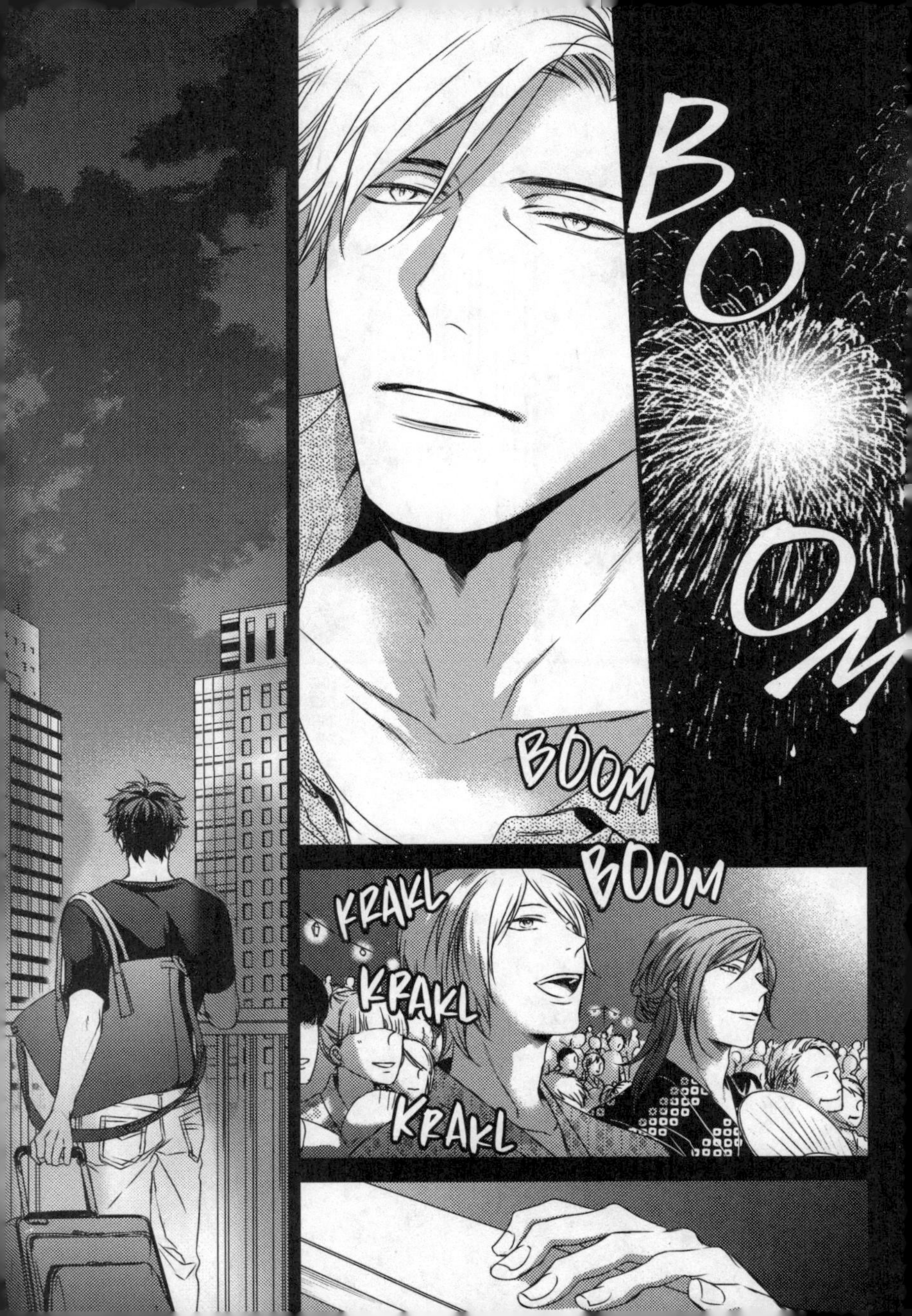
BOOM
BOOM
BOOM
KRAKL
KRAKL
KRAKL

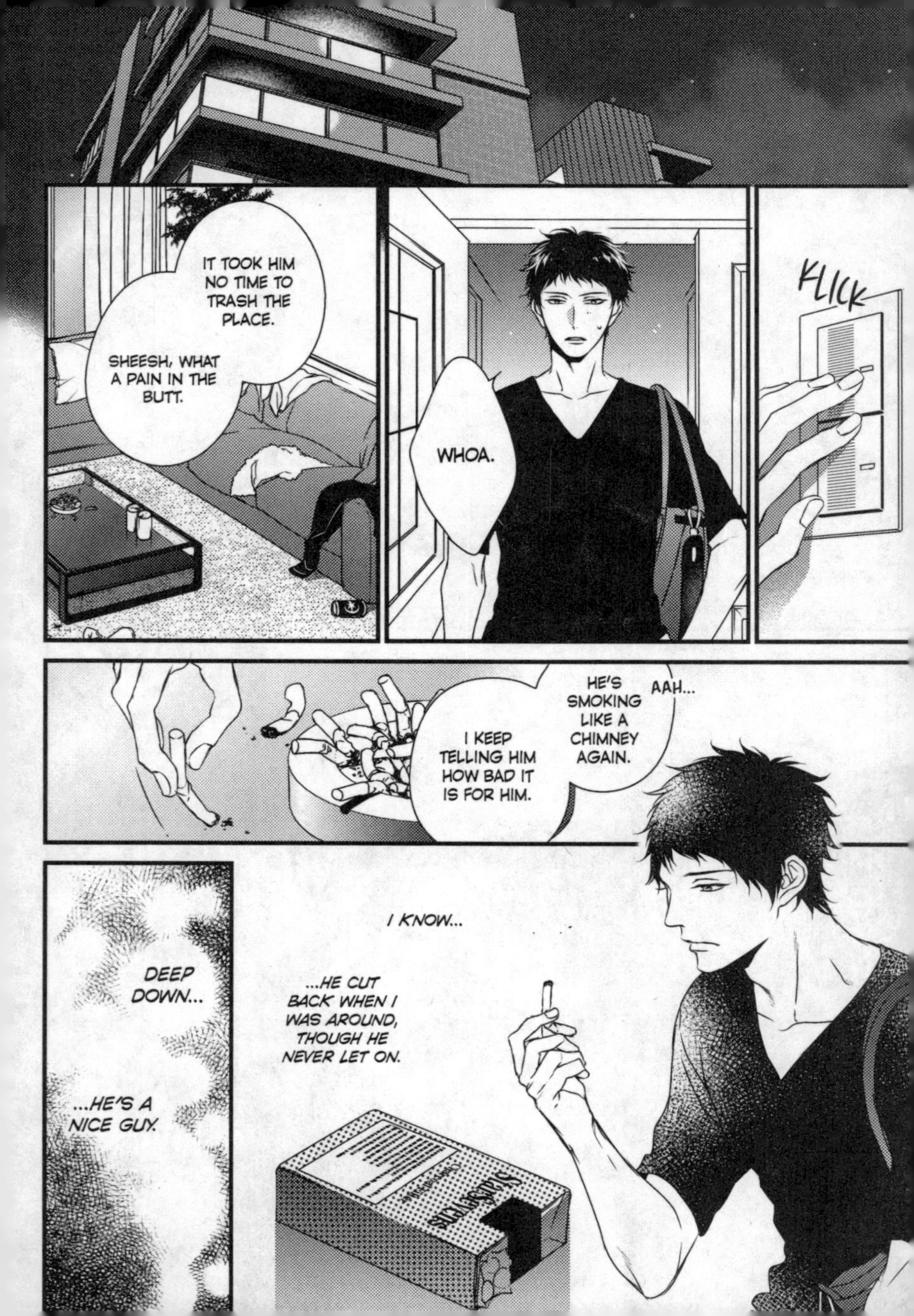
KLICK
WHOA.
IT TOOK HIM NO TIME TO TRASH THE PLACE.
SHEESH, WHAT A PAIN IN THE BUTT.
AAH...
HE'S SMOKING LIKE A CHIMNEY AGAIN.
I KEEP TELLING HIM HOW BAD IT IS FOR HIM.
I KNOW...
...HE CUT BACK WHEN I WAS AROUND, THOUGH HE NEVER LET ON.
DEEP DOWN...
...HE'S A NICE GUY.

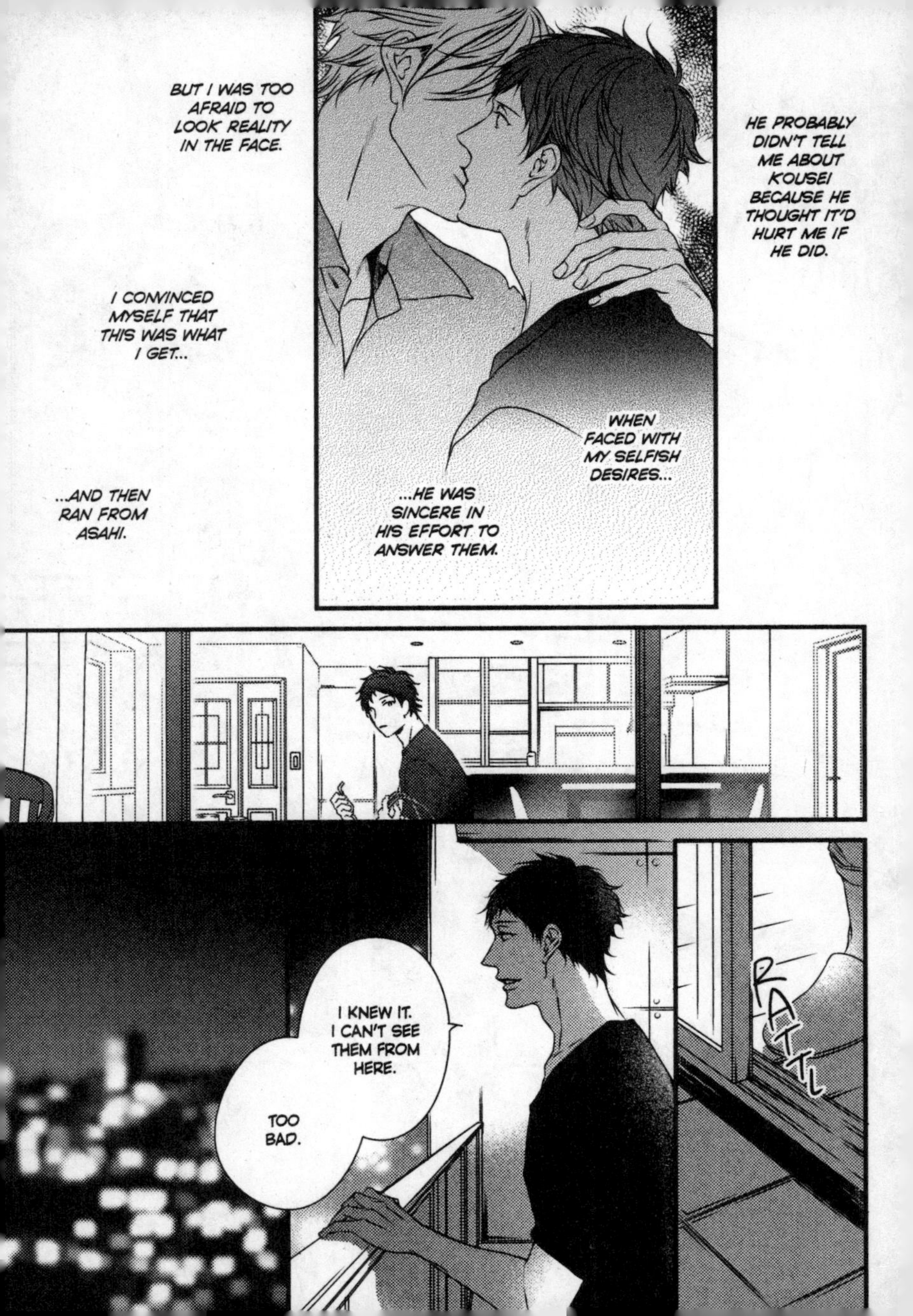
HE PROBABLY DIDN'T TELL ME ABOUT KOUSEI BECAUSE HE THOUGHT IT'D HURT ME IF HE DID.
WHEN FACED WITH MY SELFISH DESIRES...
...HE WAS SINCERE IN HIS EFFORT TO ANSWER THEM.
BUT I WAS TOO AFRAID TO LOOK REALITY IN THE FACE.
I CONVINCED MYSELF THAT THIS WAS WHAT I GET...
...AND THEN RAN FROM ASAHI.
RATTL
I KNEW IT. I CAN'T SEE THEM FROM HERE.
TOO BAD.

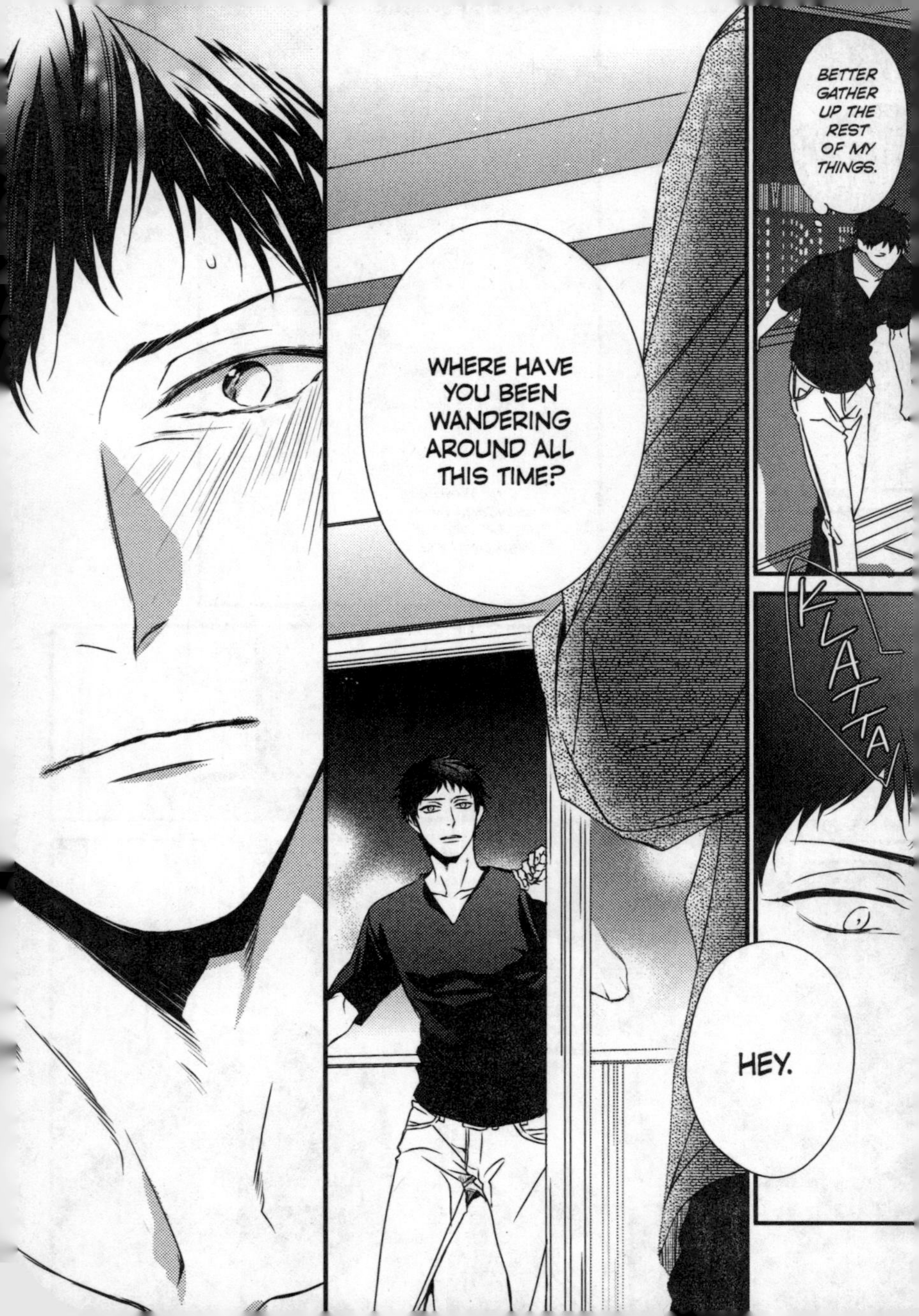
BETTER GATHER UP THE REST OF MY THINGS.
KLATTA
HEY.
WHERE HAVE YOU BEEN WANDERING AROUND ALL THIS TIME?

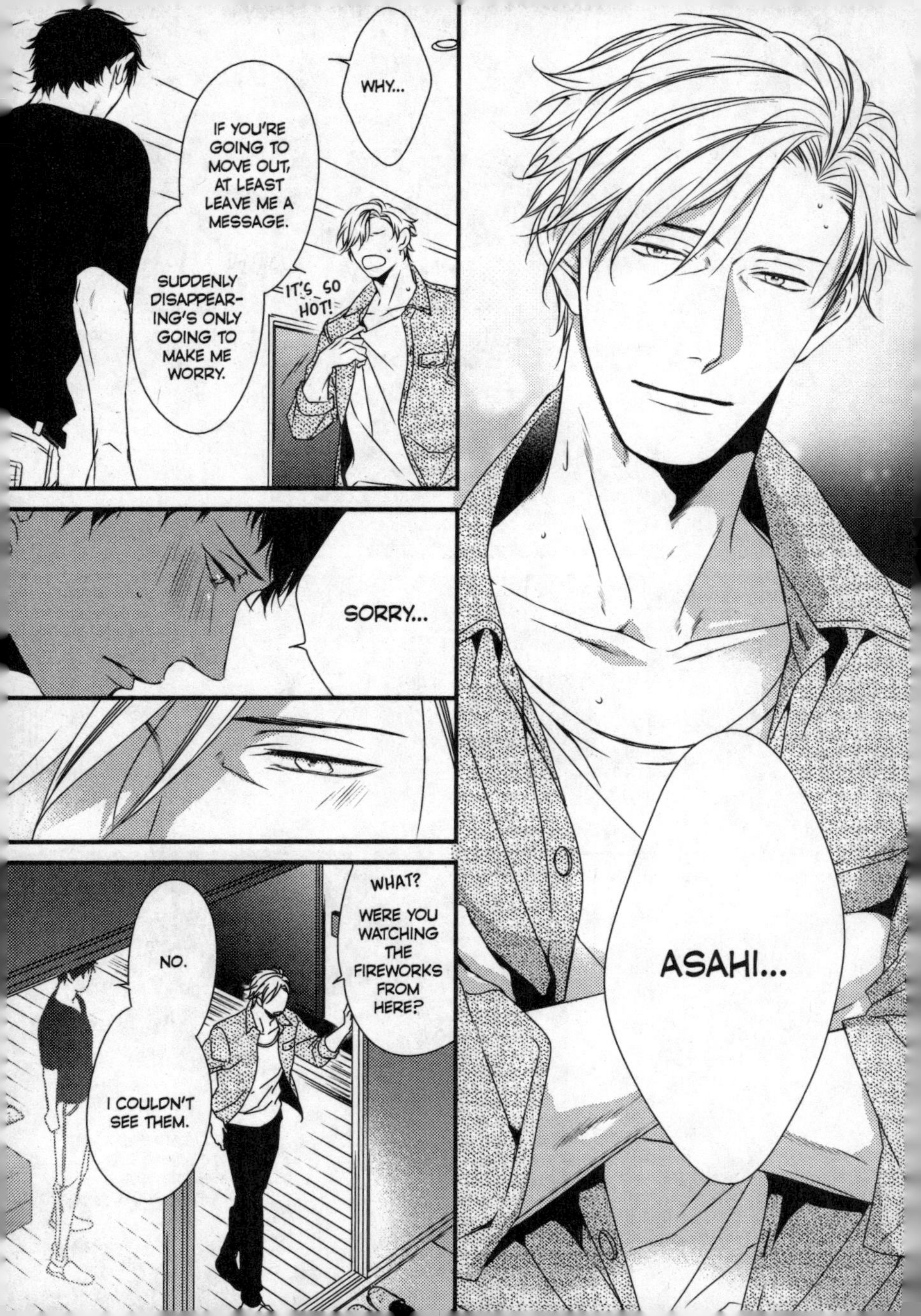
ASAHI...
WHY...
IF YOU'RE GOING TO MOVE OUT, AT LEAST LEAVE ME A MESSAGE.
IT'S SO HOT!
SUDDENLY DISAPPEAR-ING'S ONLY GOING TO MAKE ME WORRY.
SORRY...
WHAT?
WERE YOU WATCHING THE FIREWORKS FROM HERE?
NO.
I COULDN'T SEE THEM.

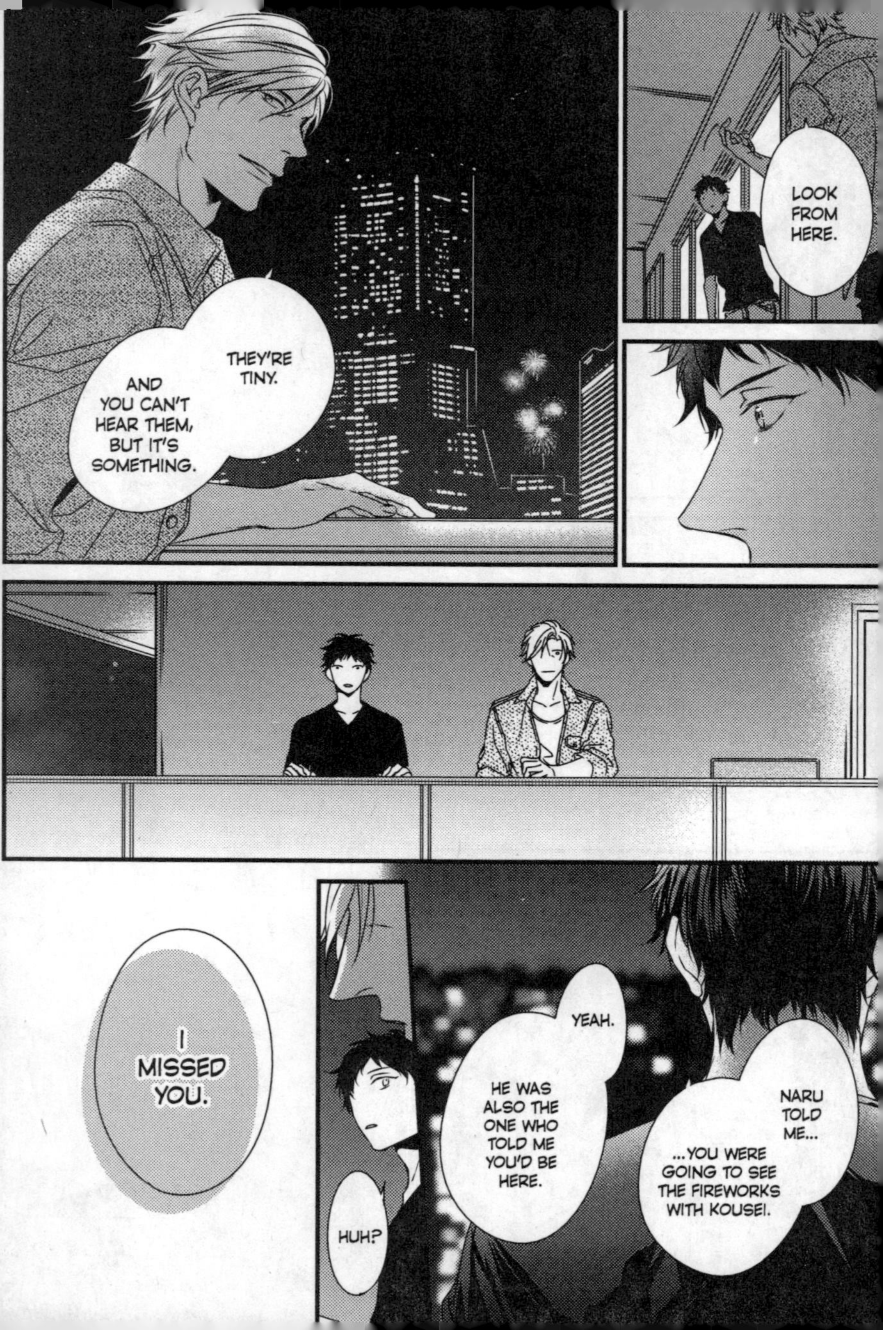
LOOK FROM HERE.
THEY'RE TINY.
AND YOU CAN'T HEAR THEM, BUT IT'S SOMETHING.
NARU TOLD ME...
...YOU WERE GOING TO SEE THE FIREWORKS WITH KOUSEI.
YEAH.
HE WAS ALSO THE ONE WHO TOLD ME YOU'D BE HERE.
HUH?
I MISSED YOU.

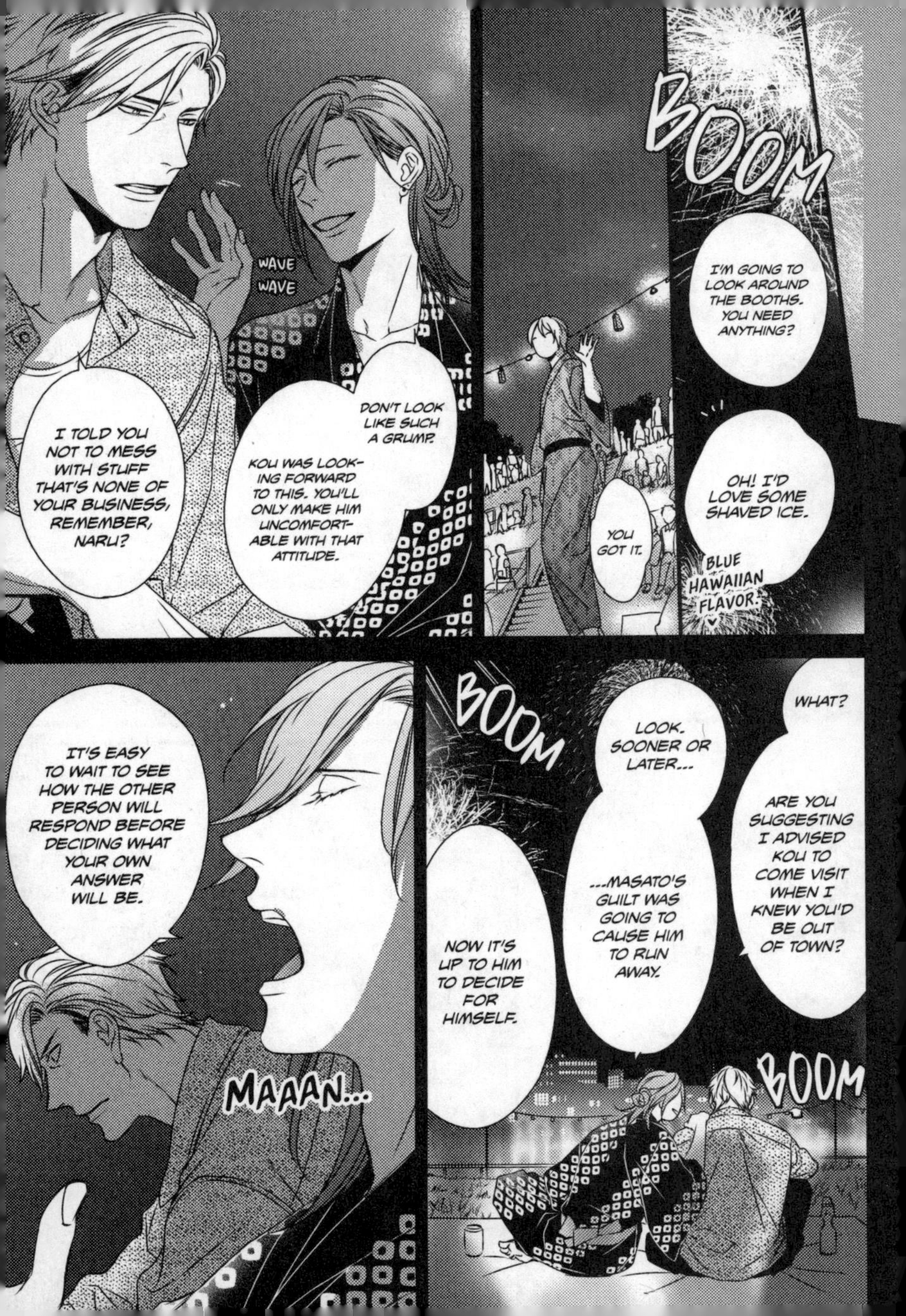
BOOM
I'M GOING TO LOOK AROUND THE BOOTHS. YOU NEED ANYTHING?
OH! I'D LOVE SOME SHAVED ICE.
BLUE HAWAIIAN FLAVOR.
YOU GOT IT.
WAVE WAVE
DON'T LOOK LIKE SUCH A GRUMP.
KOU WAS LOOKING FORWARD TO THIS. YOU'LL ONLY MAKE HIM UNCOMFORTABLE WITH THAT ATTITUDE.
I TOLD YOU NOT TO MESS WITH STUFF THAT'S NONE OF YOUR BUSINESS, REMEMBER, NARU?
WHAT?
ARE YOU SUGGESTING I ADVISED KOU TO COME VISIT WHEN I KNEW YOU'D BE OUT OF TOWN?
LOOK. SOONER OR LATER...
...MASATO'S GUILT WAS GOING TO CAUSE HIM TO RUN AWAY.
BOOM
NOW IT'S UP TO HIM TO DECIDE FOR HIMSELF.
BOOM
IT'S EASY TO WAIT TO SEE HOW THE OTHER PERSON WILL RESPOND BEFORE DECIDING WHAT YOUR OWN ANSWER WILL BE.
MAAAN...

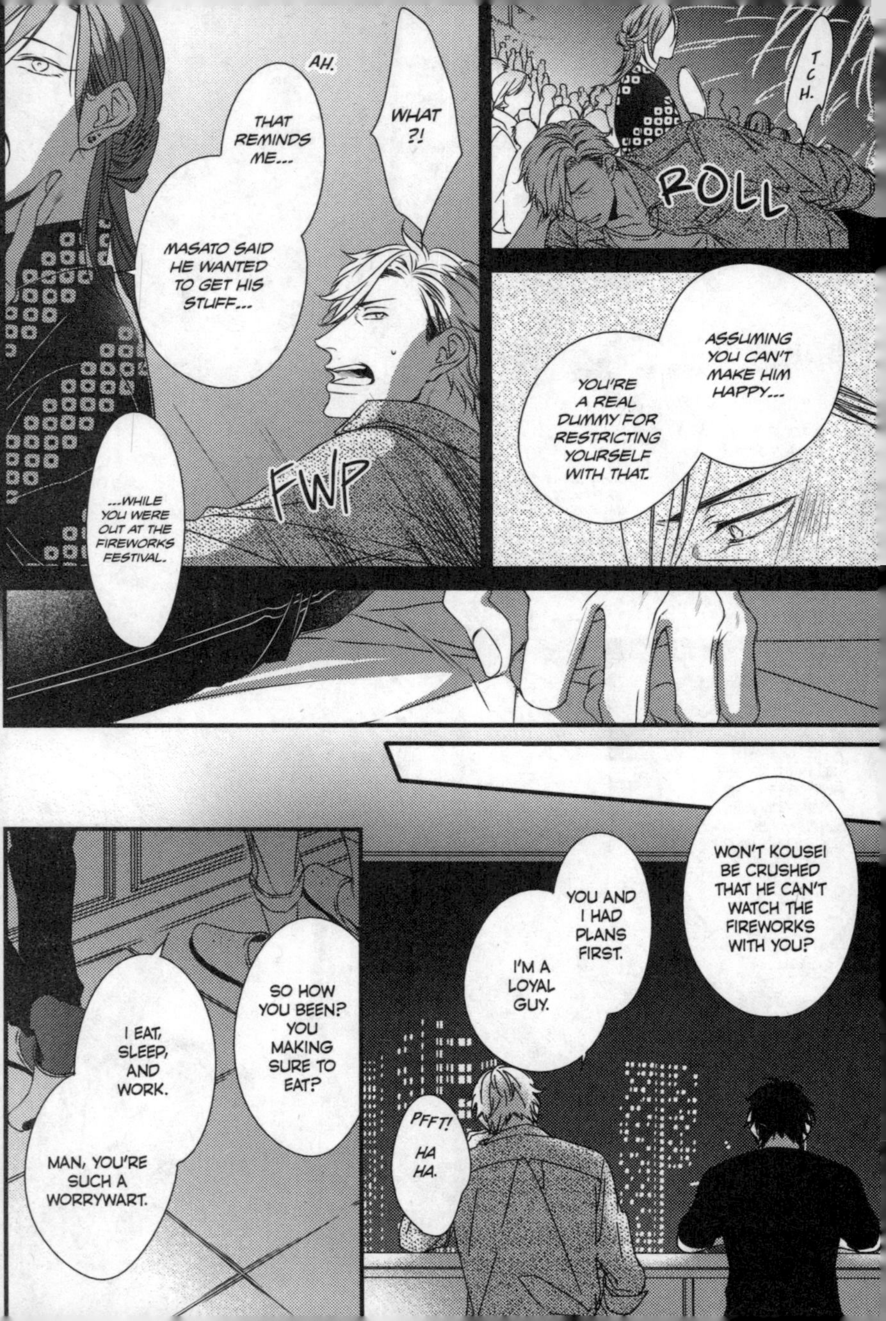

TCH.
ROLL
ASSUMING YOU CAN'T MAKE HIM HAPPY...
YOU'RE A REAL DUMMY FOR RESTRICTING YOURSELF WITH THAT.
AH.
THAT REMINDS ME...
MASATO SAID HE WANTED TO GET HIS STUFF...
WHAT ?!
FWP
...WHILE YOU WERE OUT AT THE FIREWORKS FESTIVAL.
WON'T KOUSEI BE CRUSHED THAT HE CAN'T WATCH THE FIREWORKS WITH YOU?
YOU AND I HAD PLANS FIRST.
I'M A LOYAL GUY.
PFFT!
HA HA.
SO HOW YOU BEEN? YOU MAKING SURE TO EAT?
I EAT, SLEEP, AND WORK.
MAN, YOU'RE SUCH A WORRYWART.

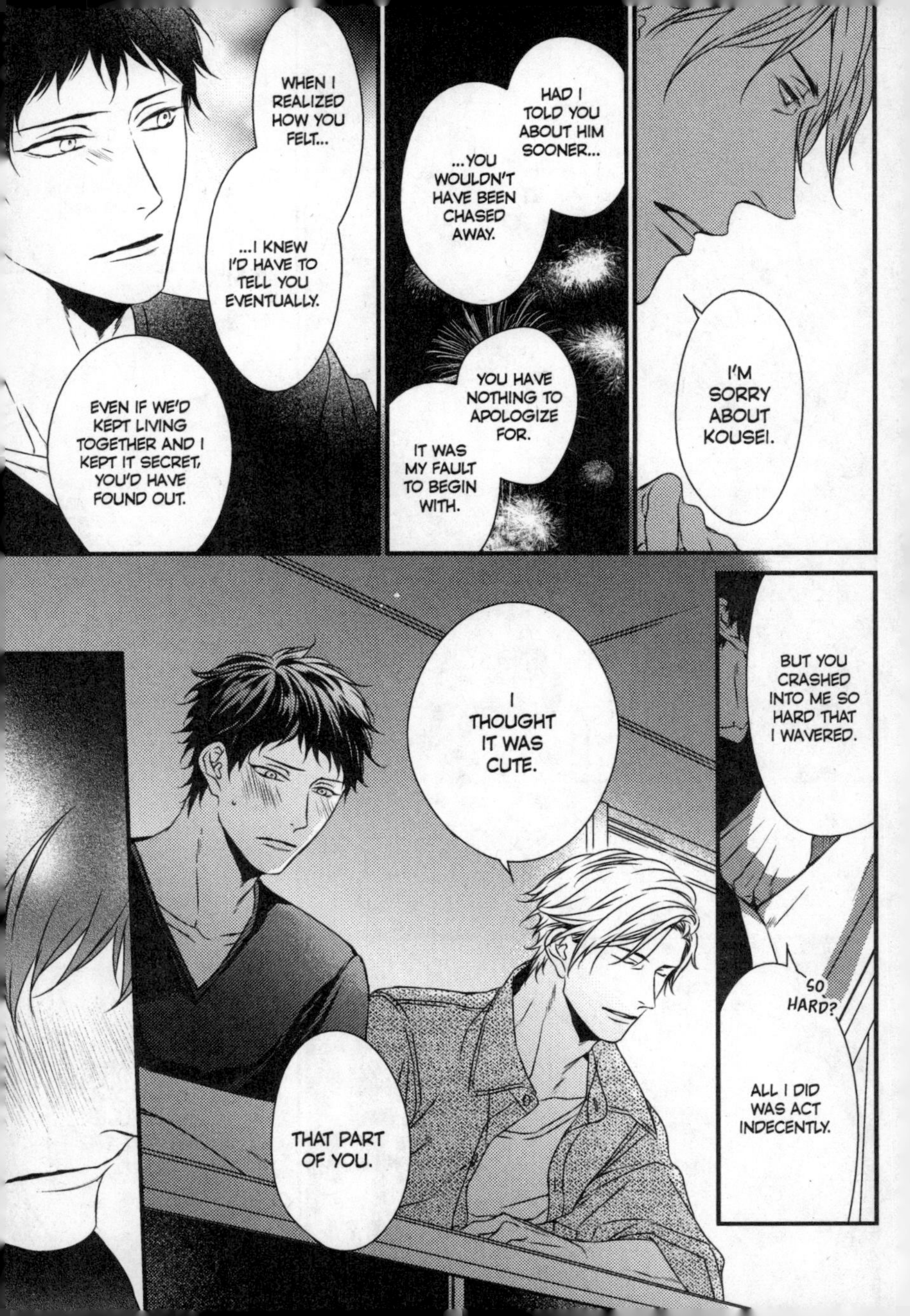
I'M SORRY ABOUT KOUSEI.
HAD I TOLD YOU ABOUT HIM SOONER...
...YOU WOULDN'T HAVE BEEN CHASED AWAY.
YOU HAVE NOTHING TO APOLOGIZE FOR.
IT WAS MY FAULT TO BEGIN WITH.
WHEN I REALIZED HOW YOU FELT...
...I KNEW I'D HAVE TO TELL YOU EVENTUALLY.
EVEN IF WE'D KEPT LIVING TOGETHER AND I KEPT IT SECRET, YOU'D HAVE FOUND OUT.
BUT YOU CRASHED INTO ME SO HARD THAT I WAVERED.
SO HARD?
ALL I DID WAS ACT INDECENTLY.
I THOUGHT IT WAS CUTE.
THAT PART OF YOU.

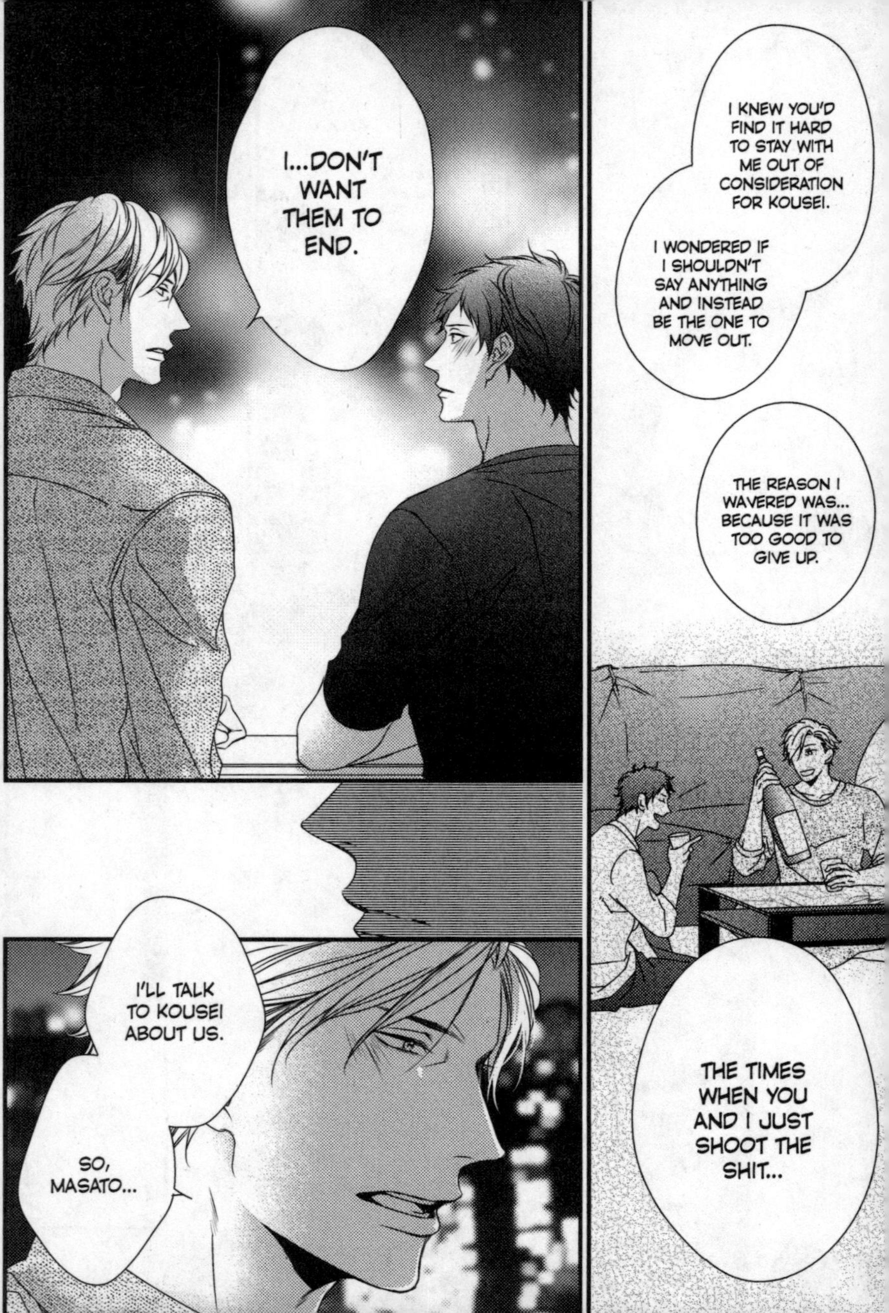
I KNEW YOU'D FIND IT HARD TO STAY WITH ME OUT OF CONSIDERATION FOR KOUSEI.
I WONDERED IF I SHOULDN'T SAY ANYTHING AND INSTEAD BE THE ONE TO MOVE OUT.
THE REASON I WAVERED WAS... BECAUSE IT WAS TOO GOOD TO GIVE UP.
THE TIMES WHEN YOU AND I JUST SHOOT THE SHIT...
I...DON'T WANT THEM TO END.
I'LL TALK TO KOUSEI ABOUT US.
SO, MASATO...

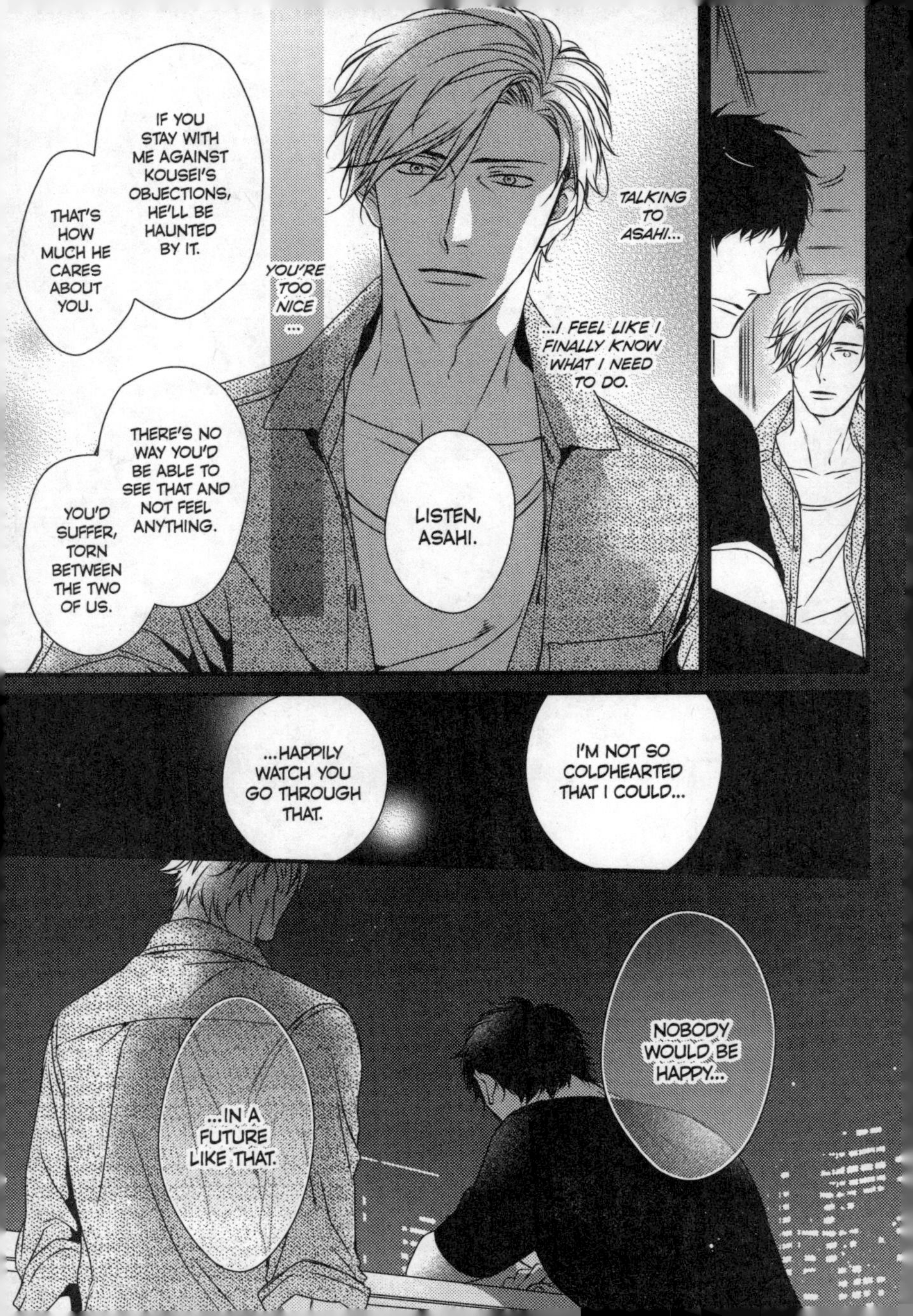
TALKING TO ASAHI...
...I FEEL LIKE I FINALLY KNOW WHAT I NEED TO DO.
YOU'RE TOO NICE ...
IF YOU STAY WITH ME AGAINST KOUSEI'S OBJECTIONS, HE'LL BE HAUNTED BY IT.
THAT'S HOW MUCH HE CARES ABOUT YOU.
LISTEN, ASAHI.
THERE'S NO WAY YOU'D BE ABLE TO SEE THAT AND NOT FEEL ANYTHING.
YOU'D SUFFER, TORN BETWEEN THE TWO OF US.
I'M NOT SO COLDHEARTED THAT I COULD...
...HAPPILY WATCH YOU GO THROUGH THAT.
NOBODY WOULD BE HAPPY...
...IN A FUTURE LIKE THAT.

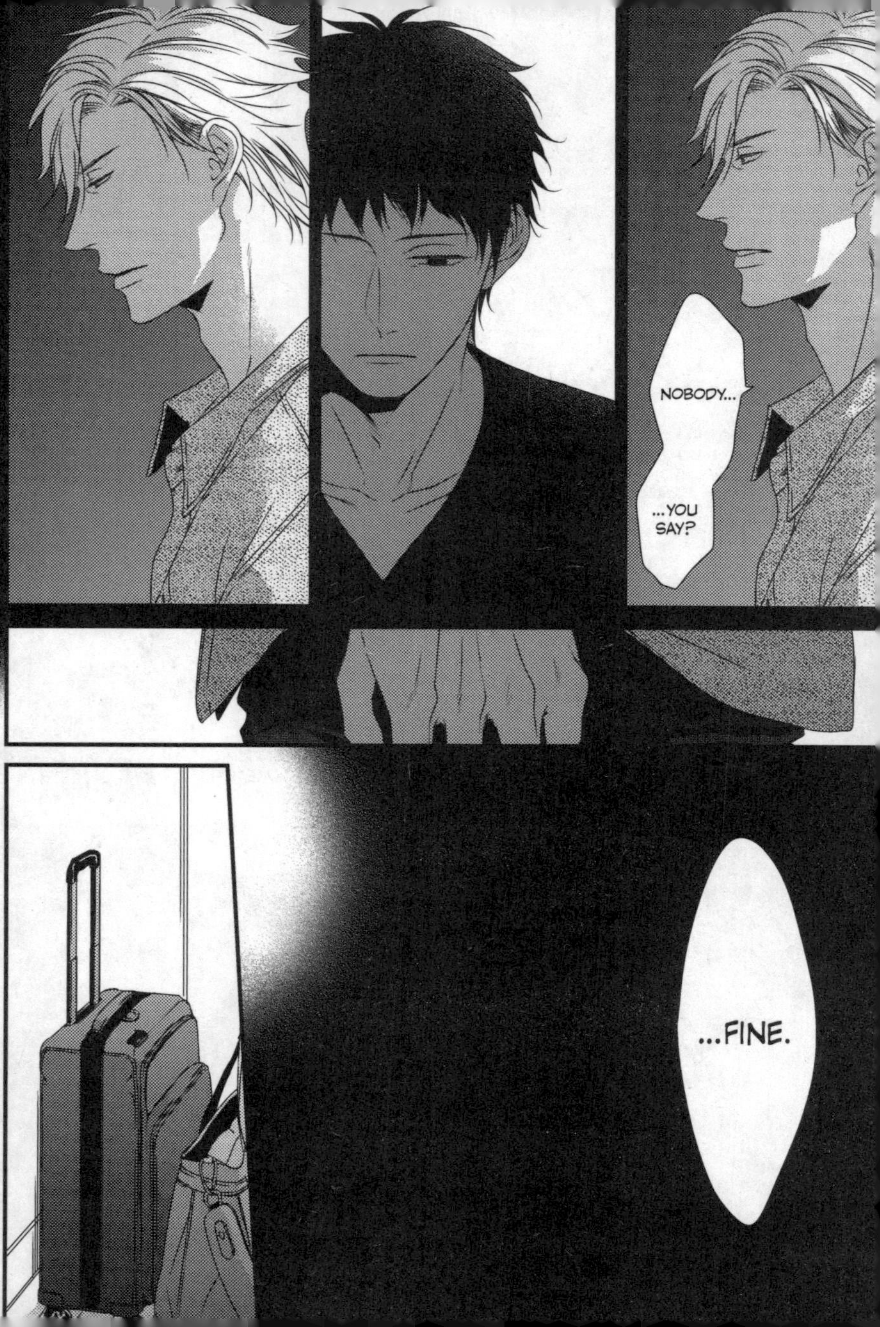
NOBODY...
...YOU SAY?
...FINE.

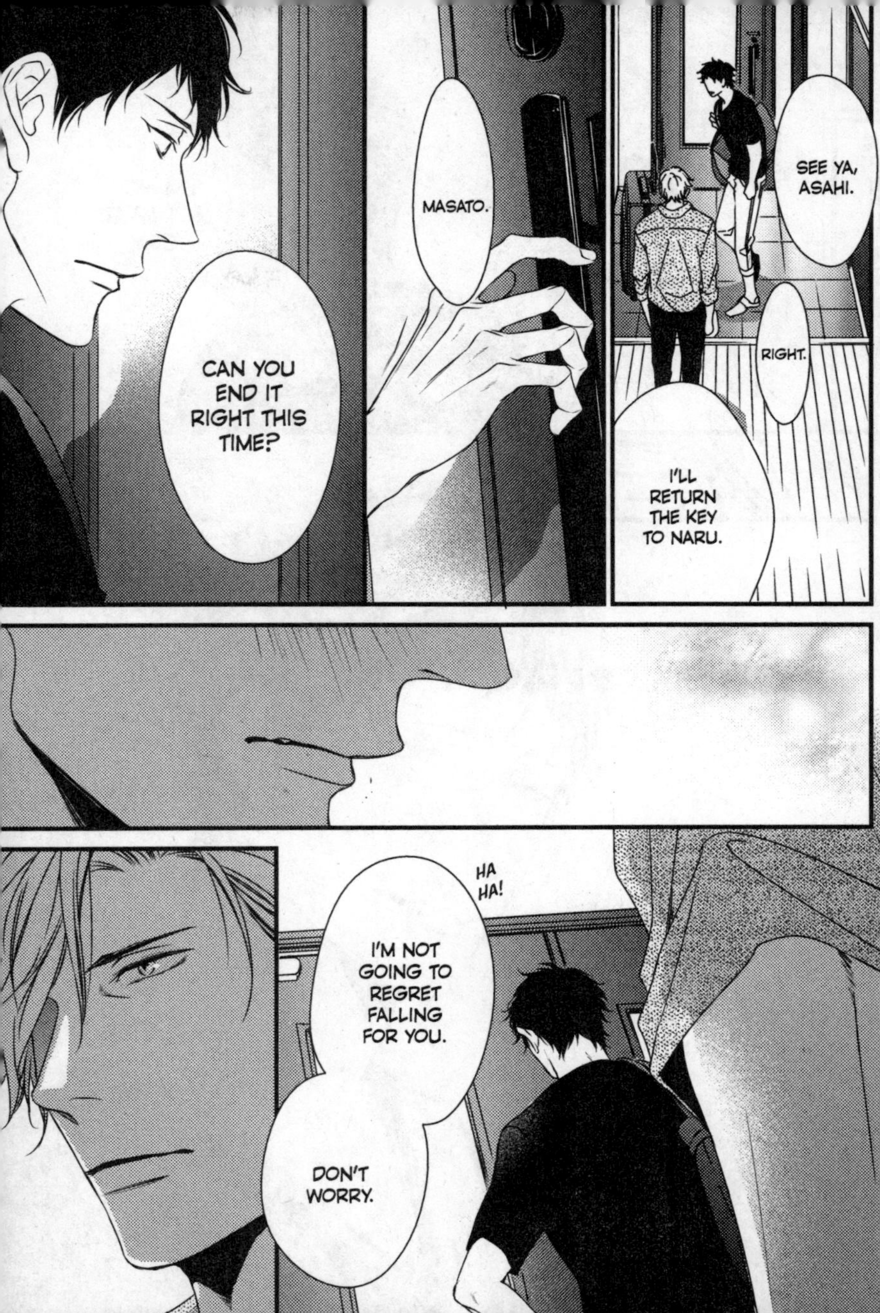
SEE YA, ASAHI.
RIGHT.
I'LL RETURN THE KEY TO NARU.
MASATO.
CAN YOU END IT RIGHT THIS TIME?
HA HA!
I'M NOT GOING TO REGRET FALLING FOR YOU.
DON'T WORRY.

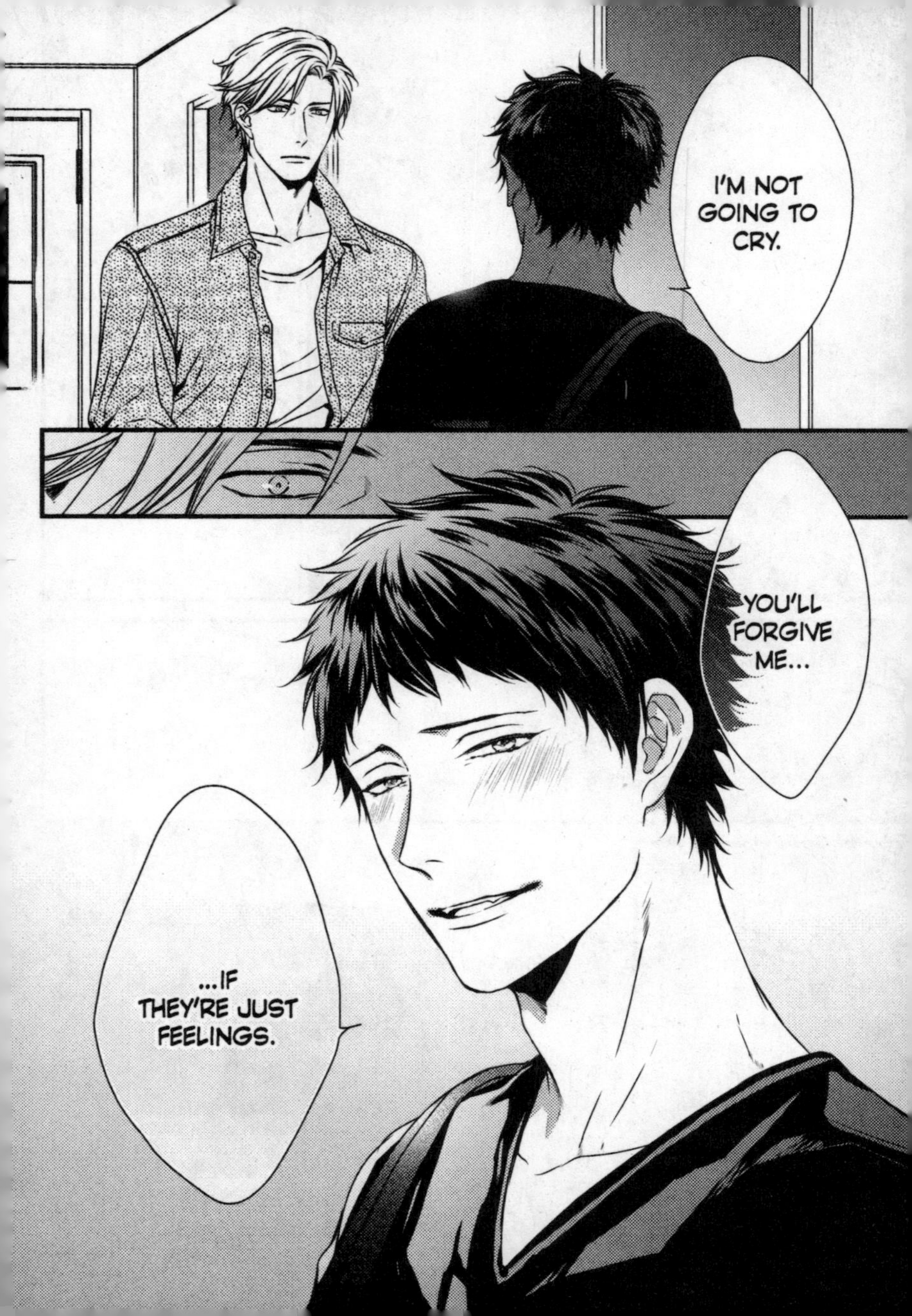
I'M NOT GOING TO CRY.
YOU'LL FORGIVE ME...
...IF THEY'RE JUST FEELINGS.

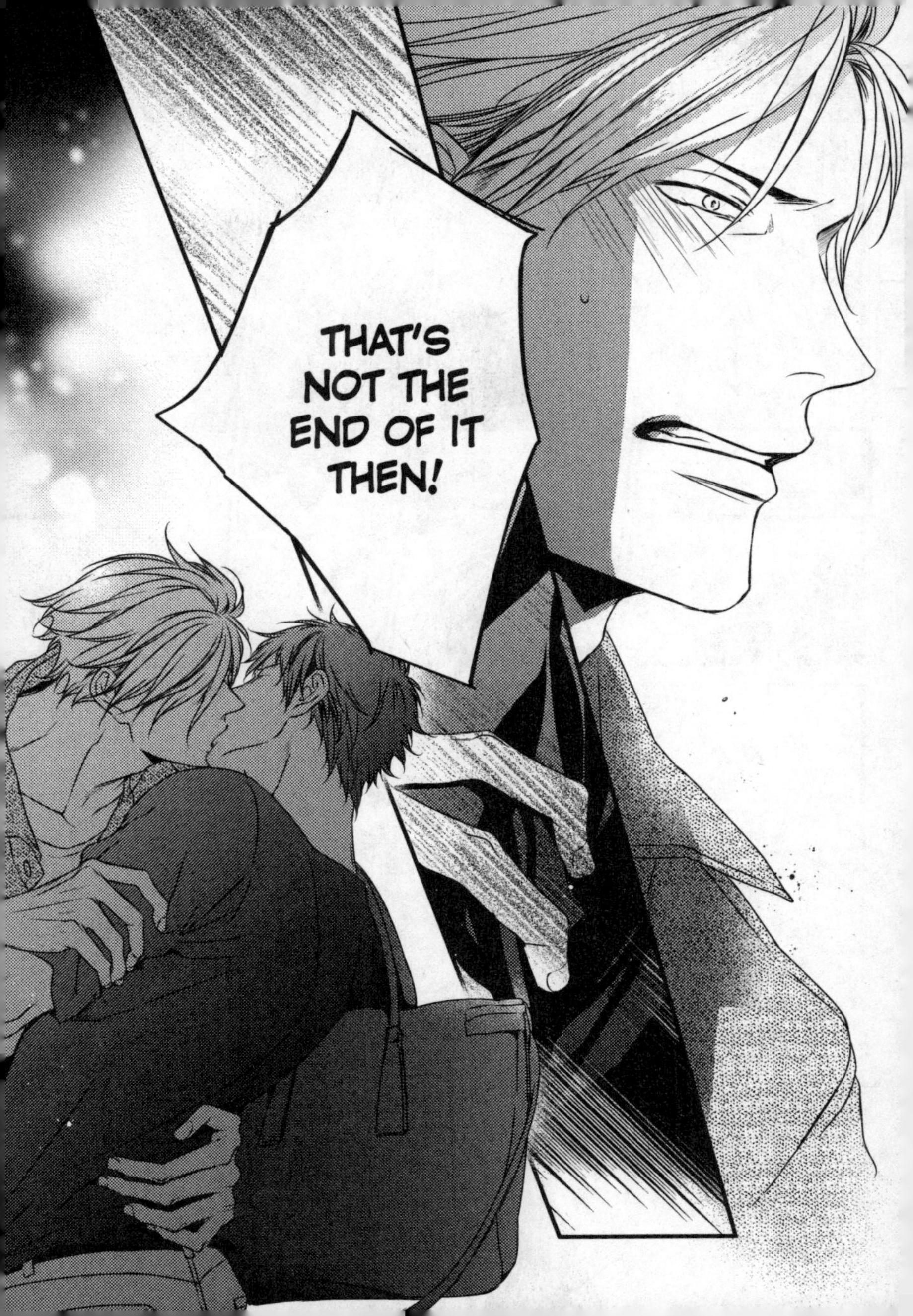
THAT'S NOT THE END OF IT THEN!

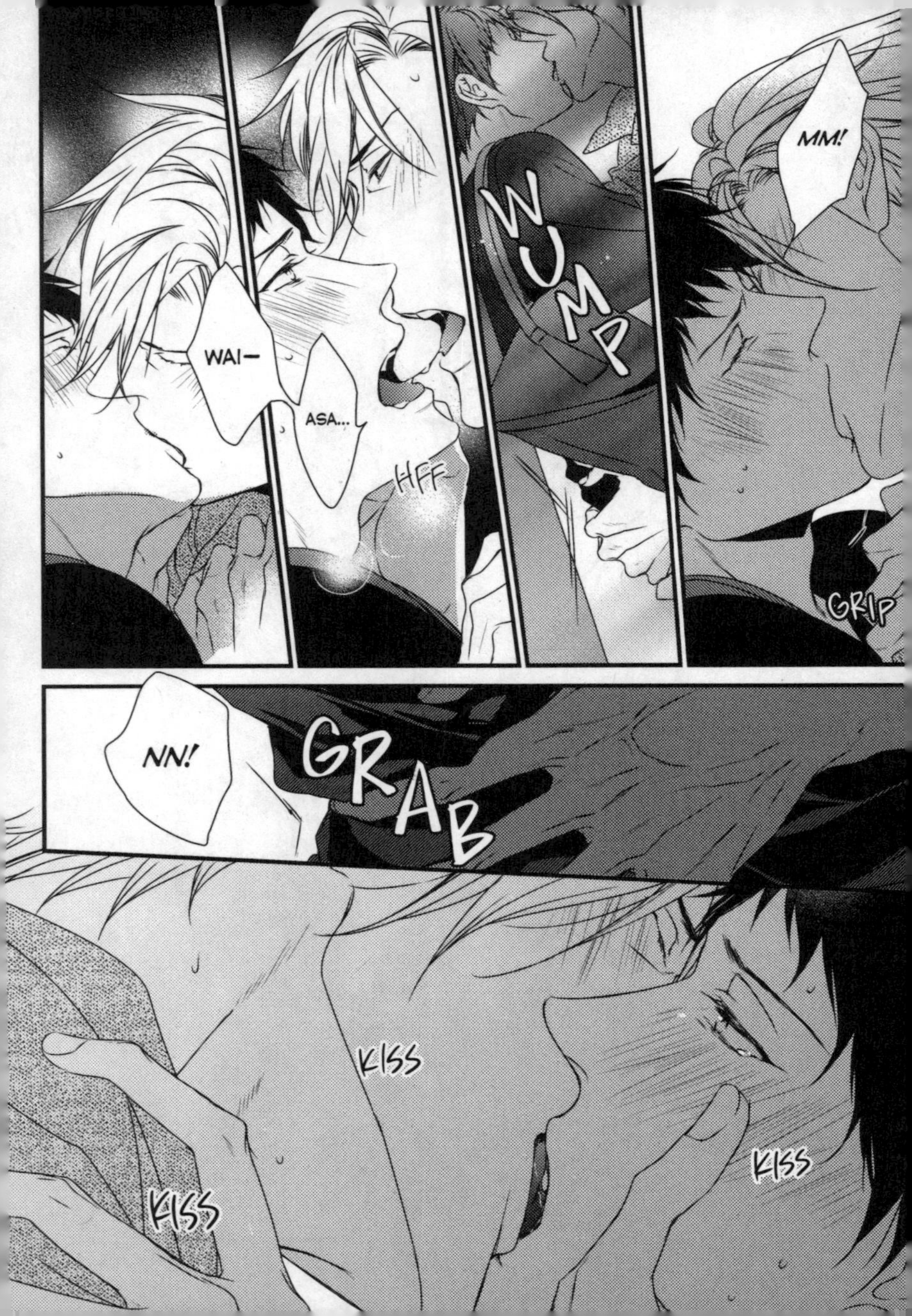
MM!
GRIP
WUMP
ASA...
HFF
WAI—
NN!
GRAB
KISS
KISS
KISS

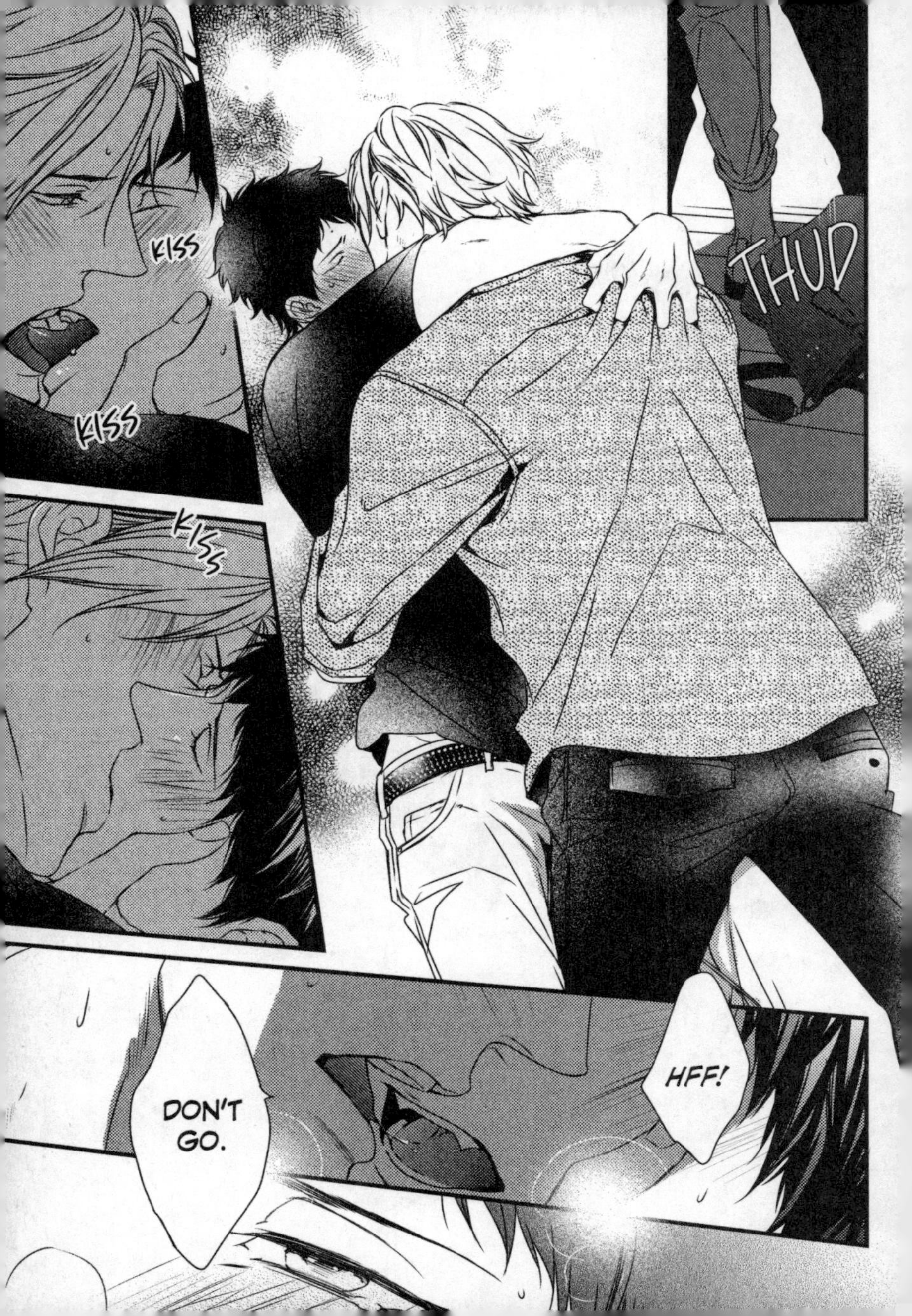
THUD
KISS
KISS
KISS
HFF!
DON'T GO.

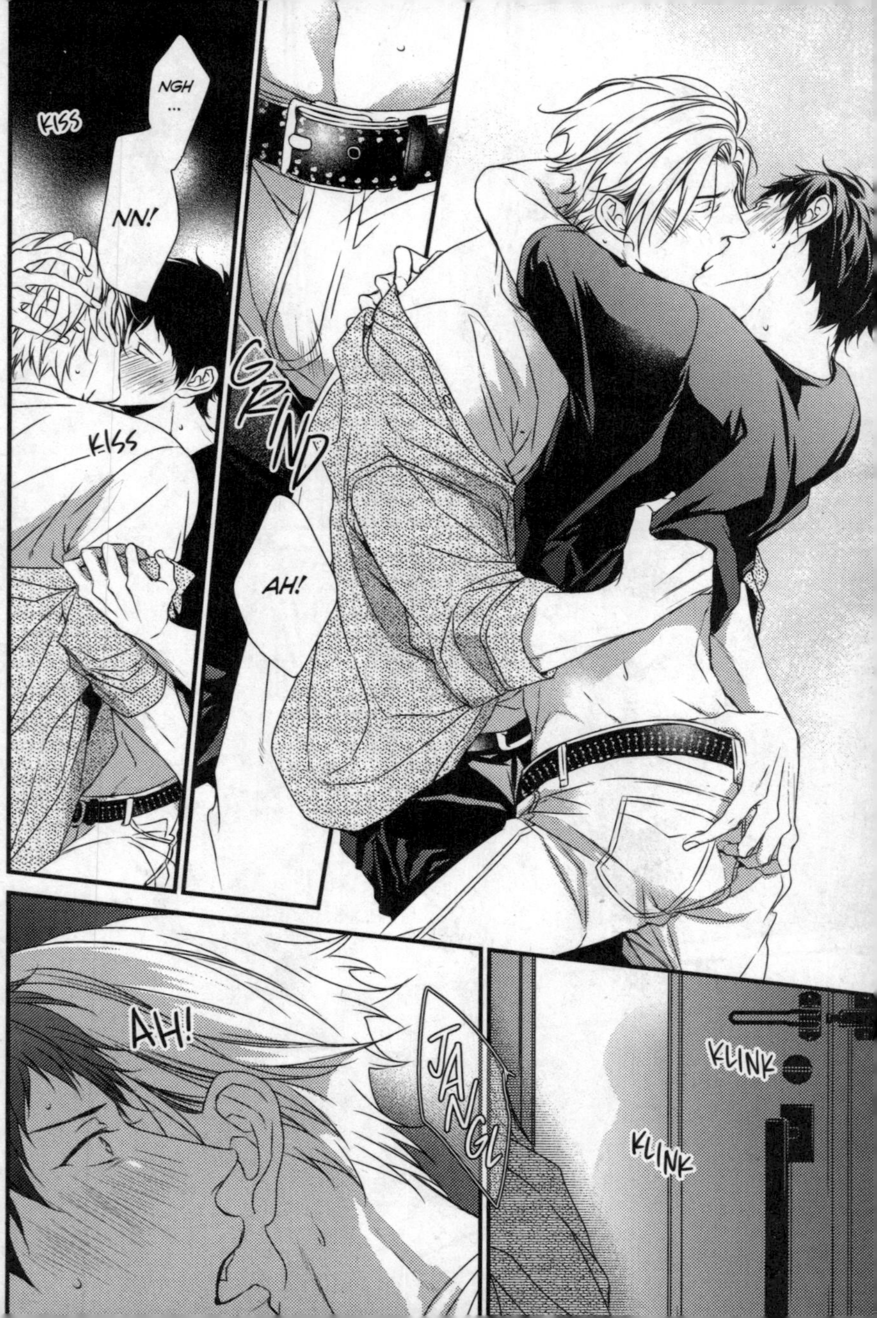
GRIND
AH!
NGH ...
KISS
NN!
KISS
KLINK
KLINK
JANGL
AH!

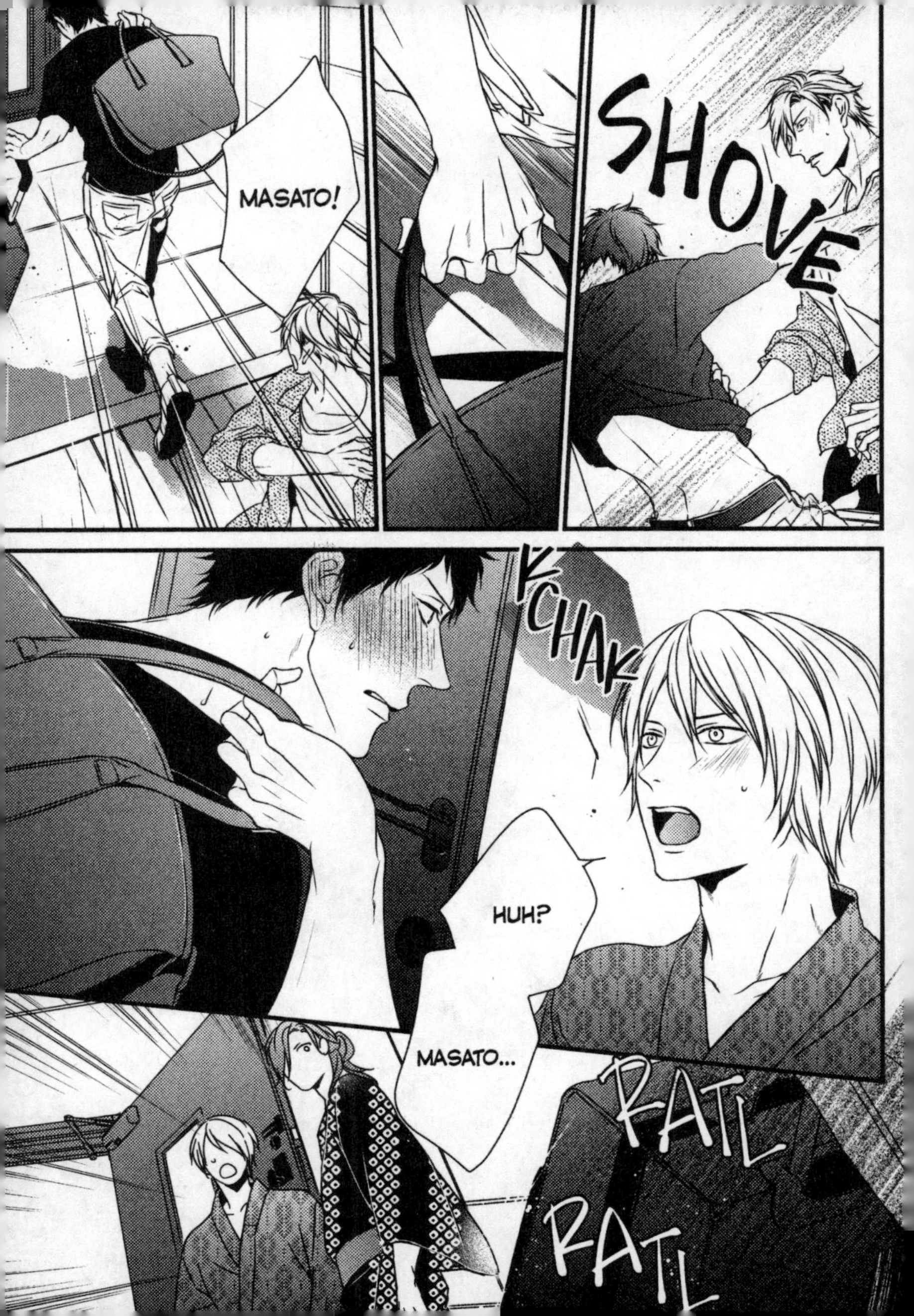
SHOVE
MASATO!
KCHAK
HUH?
RATL RATL
MASATO...

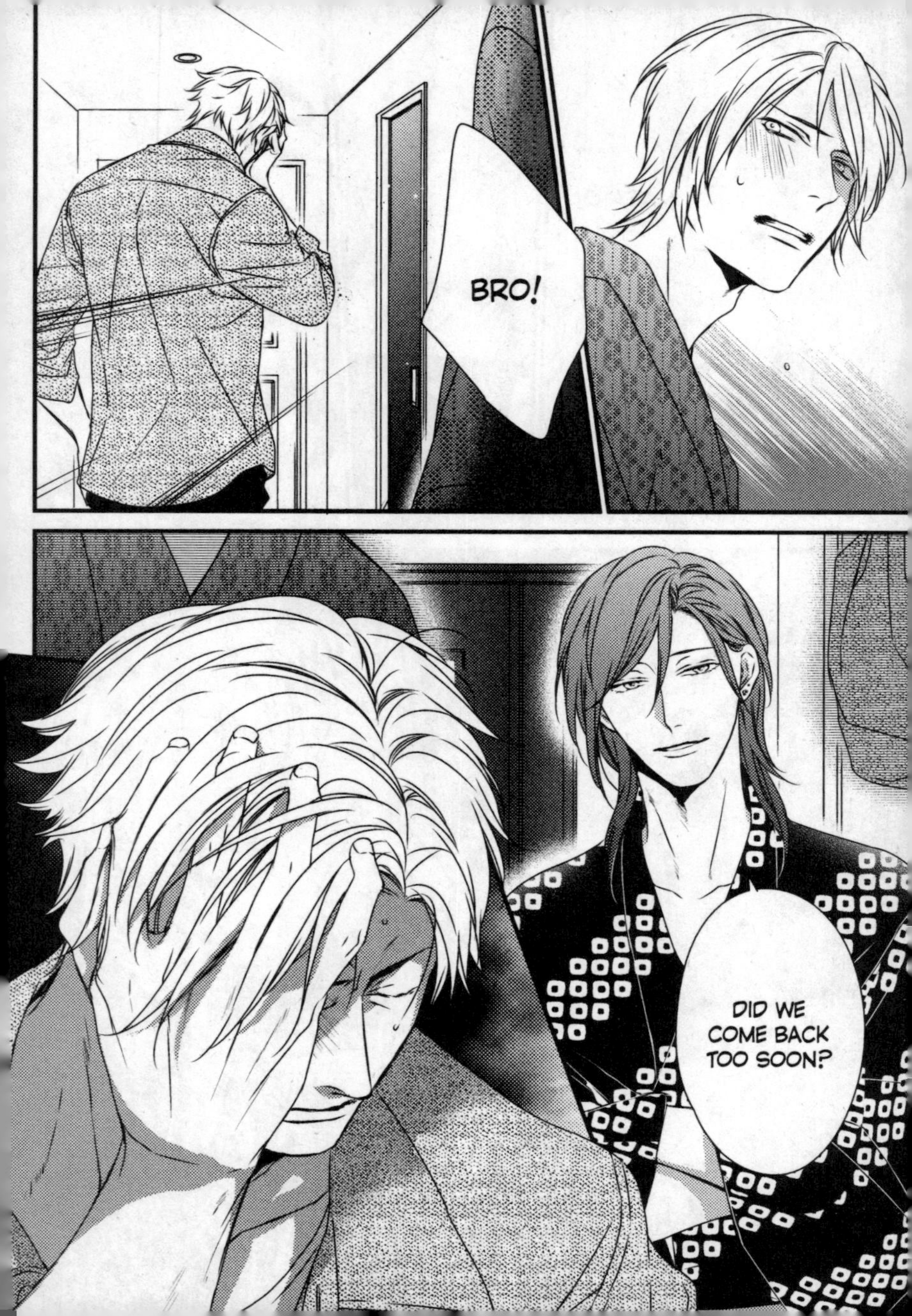
BRO!
DID WE COME BACK TOO SOON?

LOVE NEST

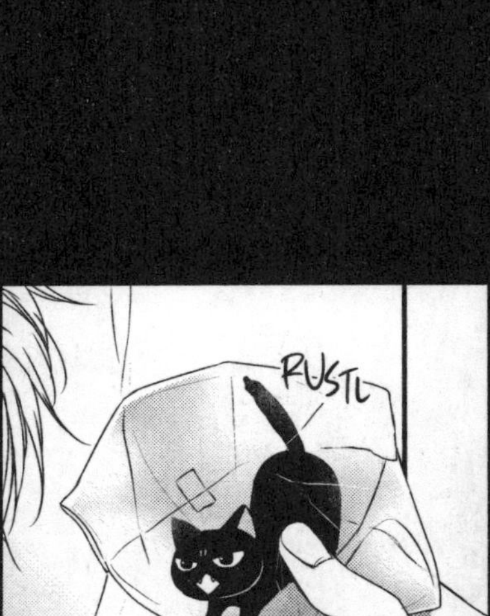
RUSTL

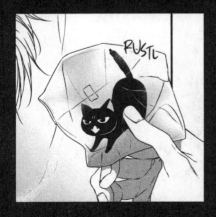

WHAT STAMINA.

I'D HAVE LOVED TWO MORE HOURS...

BRO...

TAKE 1

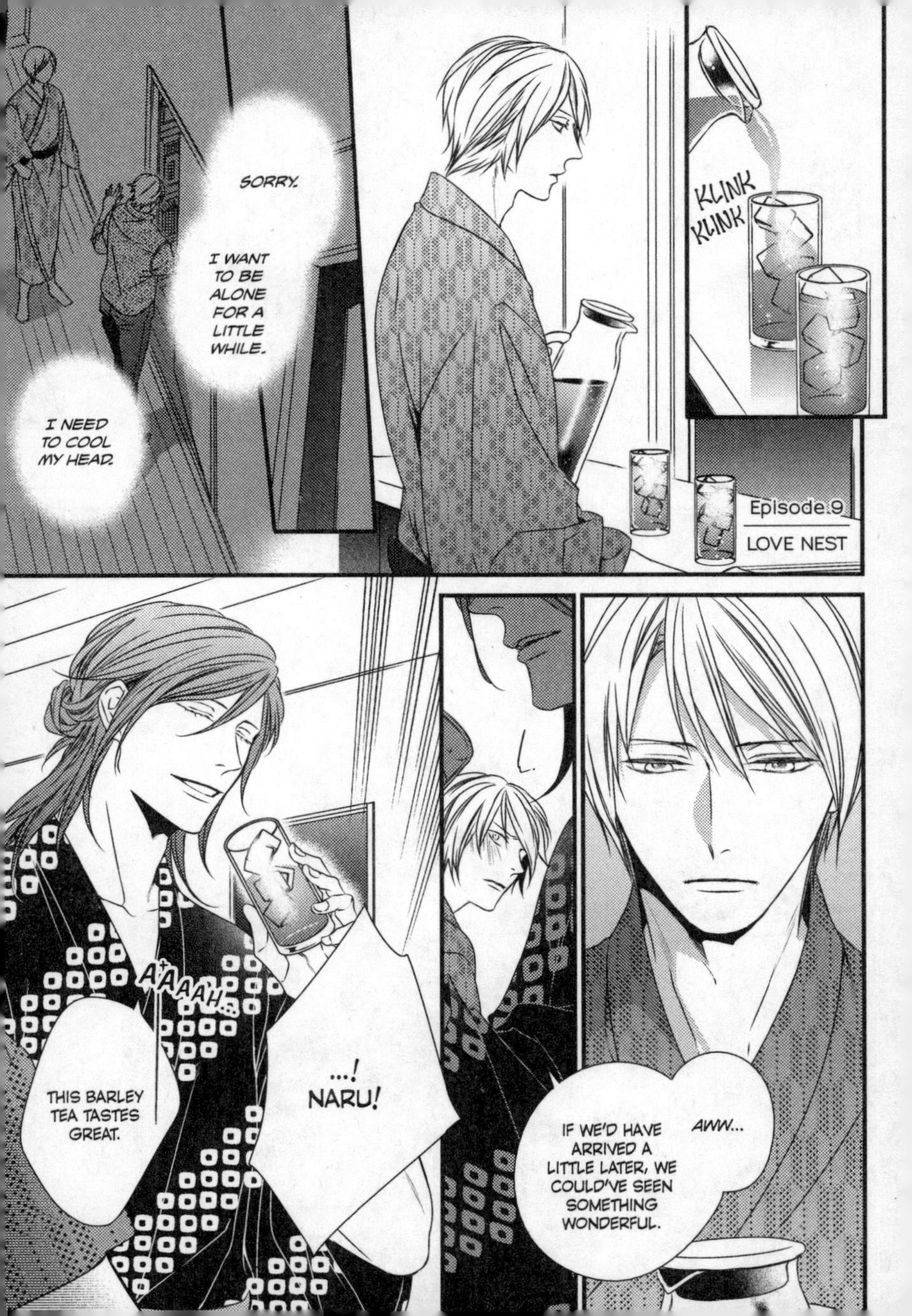
KLINK
KLINK
SORRY.
I WANT TO BE ALONE FOR A LITTLE WHILE.
I NEED TO COOL MY HEAD.
Episode.9
LOVE NEST
AWW...
IF WE'D HAVE ARRIVED A LITTLE LATER, WE COULD'VE SEEN SOMETHING WONDERFUL.
...! NARU!
A-AAAAH...
THIS BARLEY TEA TASTES GREAT.

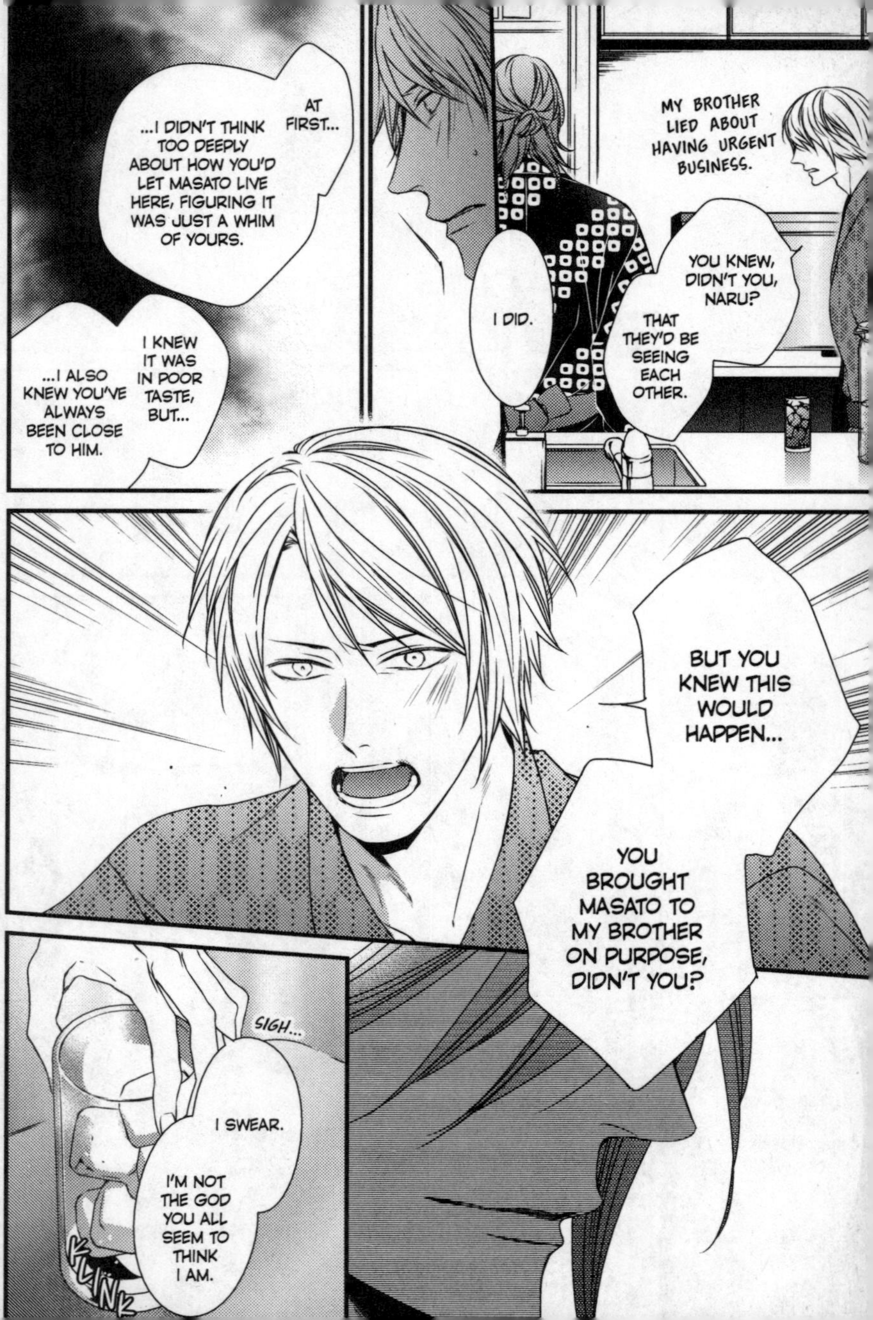
MY BROTHER LIED ABOUT HAVING URGENT BUSINESS.
YOU KNEW, DIDN'T YOU, NARU?
THAT THEY'D BE SEEING EACH OTHER.
I DID.
AT FIRST...
...I DIDN'T THINK TOO DEEPLY ABOUT HOW YOU'D LET MASATO LIVE HERE, FIGURING IT WAS JUST A WHIM OF YOURS.
I KNEW IT WAS IN POOR TASTE, BUT...
...I ALSO KNEW YOU'VE ALWAYS BEEN CLOSE TO HIM.
BUT YOU KNEW THIS WOULD HAPPEN...
YOU BROUGHT MASATO TO MY BROTHER ON PURPOSE, DIDN'T YOU?
SIGH...
I SWEAR.
I'M NOT THE GOD YOU ALL SEEM TO THINK I AM.
KLINK

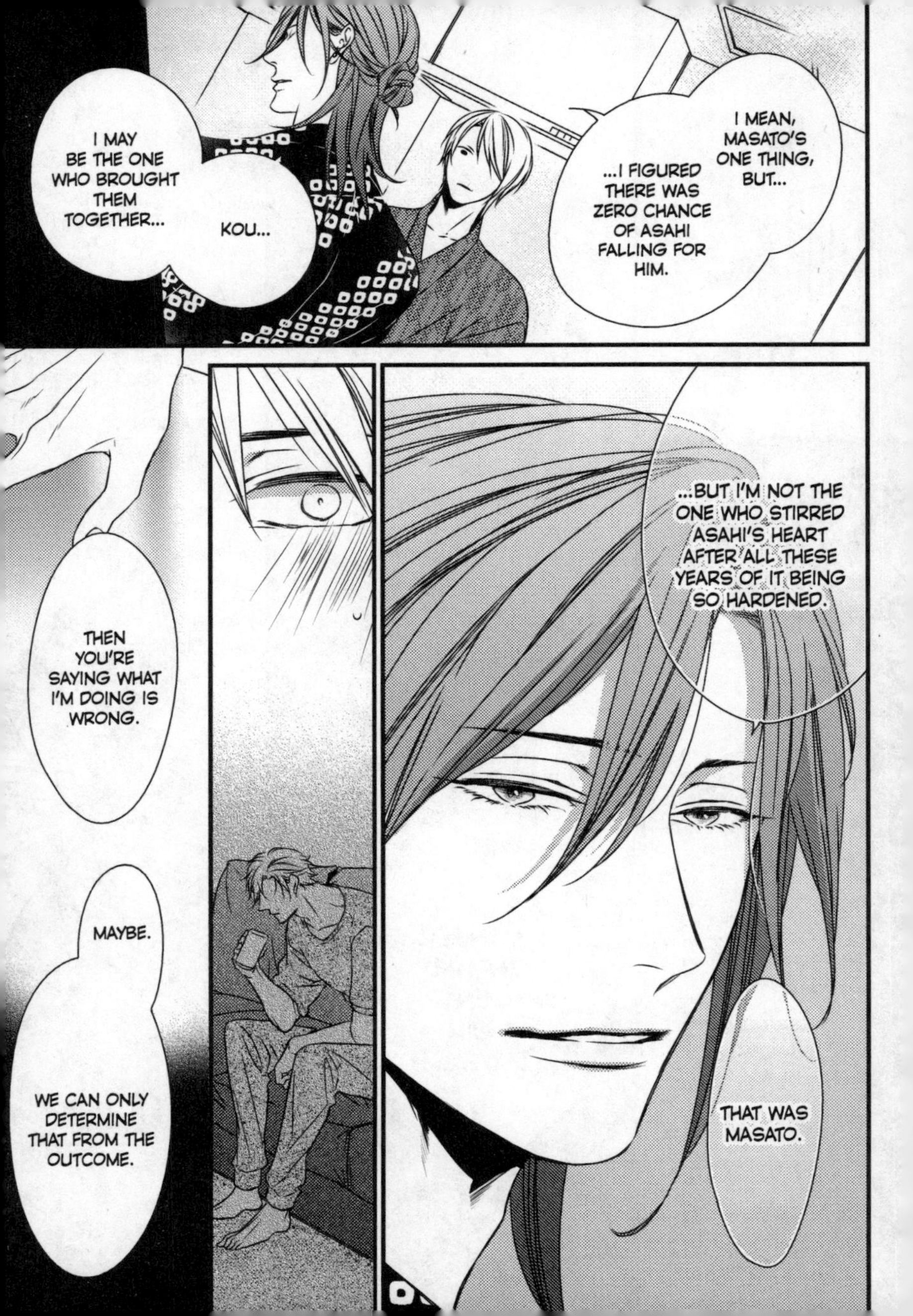
I MEAN, MASATO'S ONE THING, BUT...
...I FIGURED THERE WAS ZERO CHANCE OF ASAHI FALLING FOR HIM.
I MAY BE THE ONE WHO BROUGHT THEM TOGETHER...
KOU...
...BUT I'M NOT THE ONE WHO STIRRED ASAHI'S HEART AFTER ALL THESE YEARS OF IT BEING SO HARDENED.
THAT WAS MASATO.
THEN YOU'RE SAYING WHAT I'M DOING IS WRONG.
MAYBE.
WE CAN ONLY DETERMINE THAT FROM THE OUTCOME.

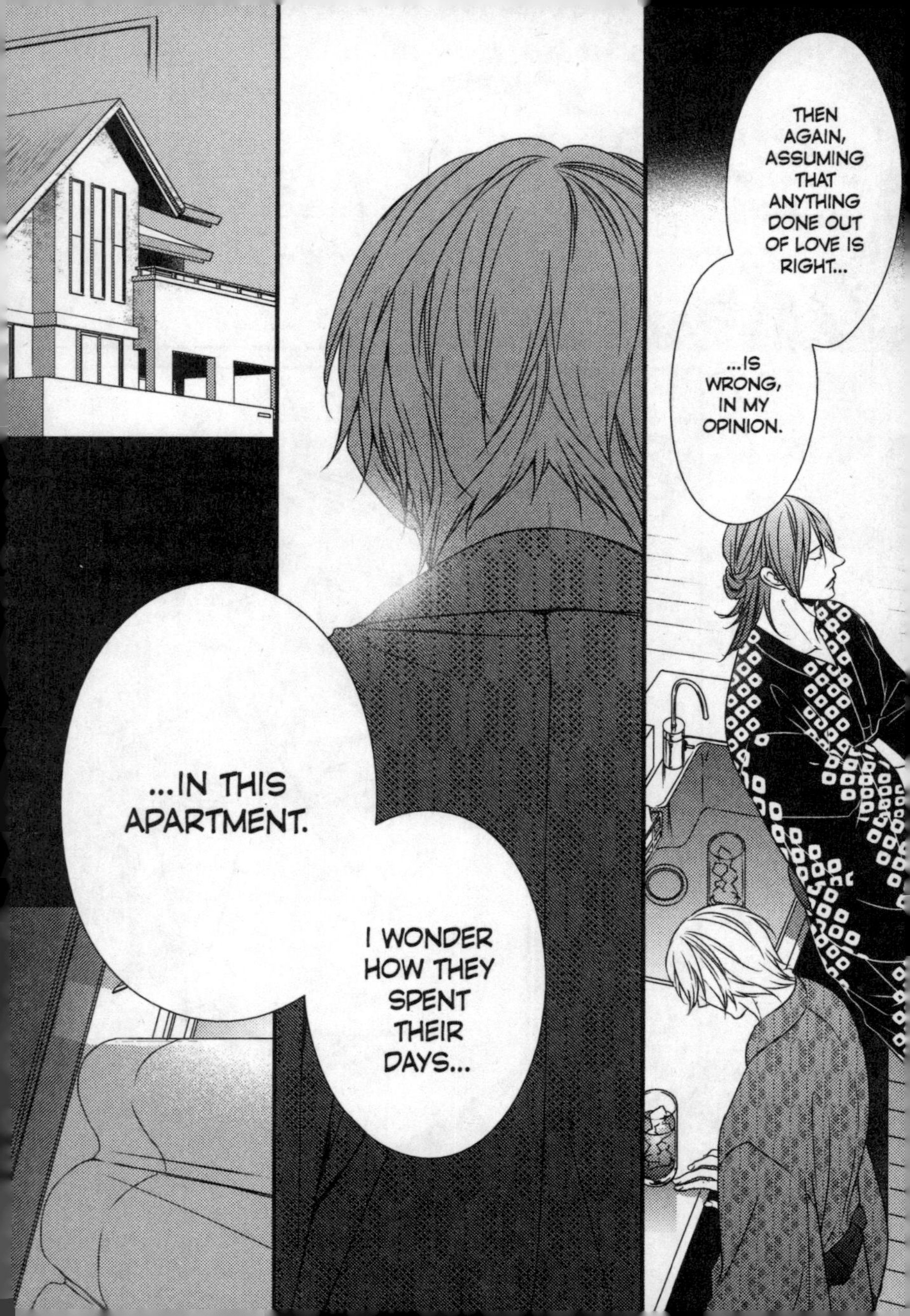
THEN AGAIN, ASSUMING THAT ANYTHING DONE OUT OF LOVE IS RIGHT...
...IS WRONG, IN MY OPINION.
I WONDER HOW THEY SPENT THEIR DAYS...
...IN THIS APARTMENT.

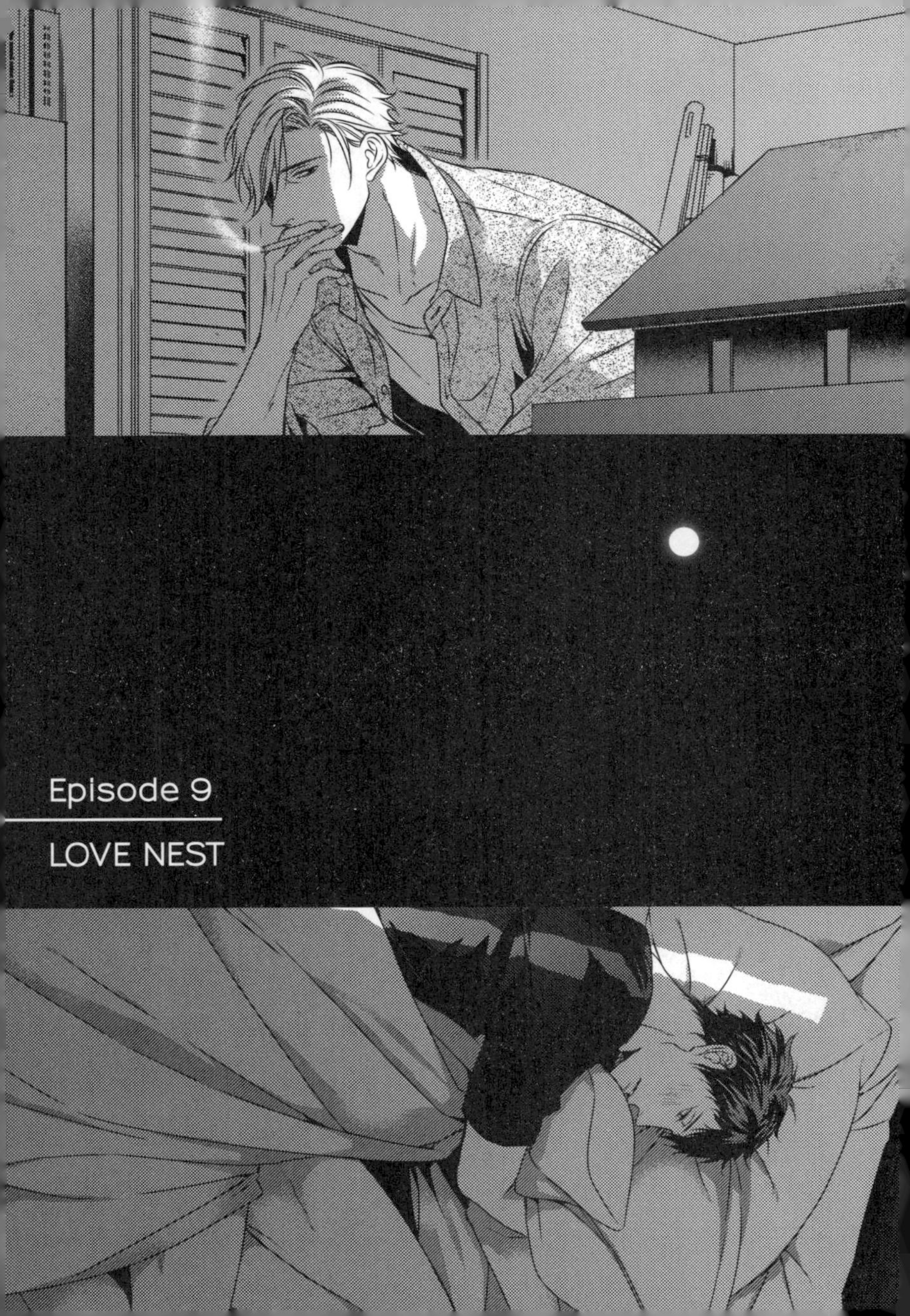
Episode 9
LOVE NEST

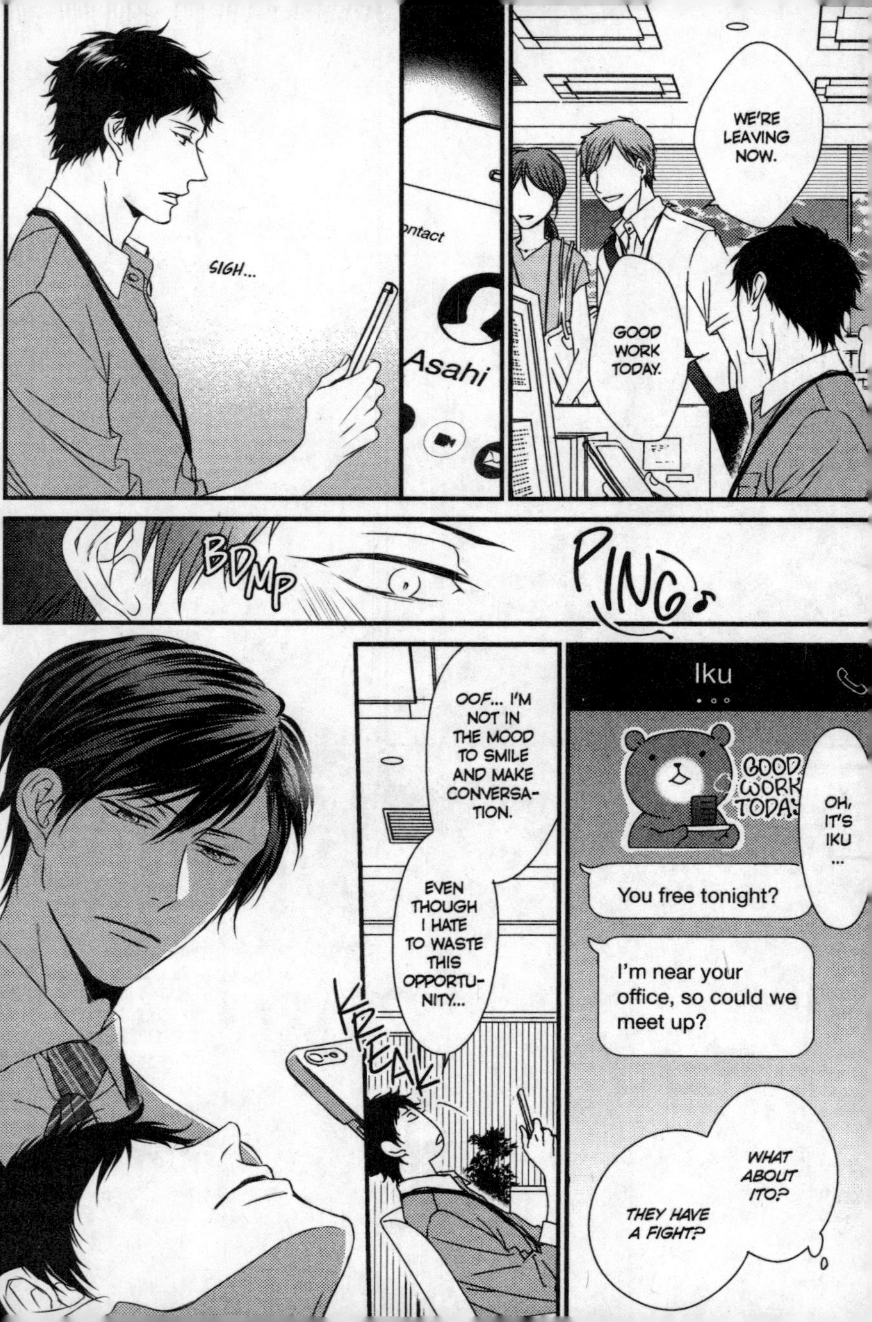
WE'RE LEAVING NOW.
GOOD WORK TODAY.
ontact
Asahi
SIGH...
PING♪
BDMP
Iku
GOOD WORK TODAY
OH, IT'S IKU ...
You free tonight?
I'm near your office, so could we meet up?
WHAT ABOUT ITO?
THEY HAVE A FIGHT?
OOF... I'M NOT IN THE MOOD TO SMILE AND MAKE CONVERSATION.
EVEN THOUGH I HATE TO WASTE THIS OPPORTUNITY...
KREEAK

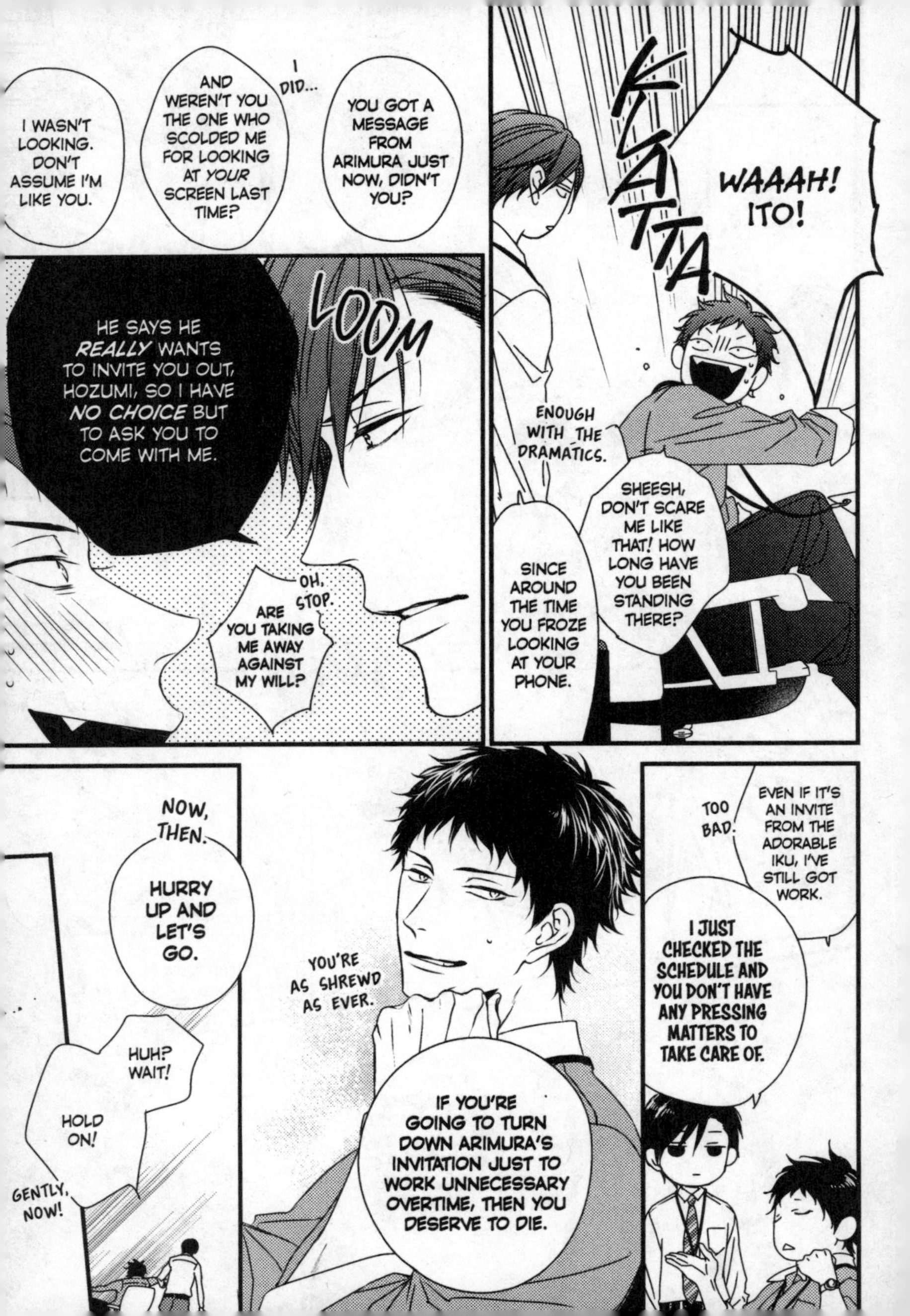

KLATTA
WAAAH! ITO!
ENOUGH WITH THE DRAMATICS.
SHEESH, DON'T SCARE ME LIKE THAT! HOW LONG HAVE YOU BEEN STANDING THERE?
SINCE AROUND THE TIME YOU FROZE LOOKING AT YOUR PHONE.
YOU GOT A MESSAGE FROM ARIMURA JUST NOW, DIDN'T YOU?
I DID...
AND WEREN'T YOU THE ONE WHO SCOLDED ME FOR LOOKING AT *YOUR* SCREEN LAST TIME?
I WASN'T LOOKING. DON'T ASSUME I'M LIKE YOU.
LOOM
HE SAYS HE *REALLY* WANTS TO INVITE YOU OUT, HOZUMI, SO I HAVE *NO CHOICE* BUT TO ASK YOU TO COME WITH ME.
OH, STOP.
ARE YOU TAKING ME AWAY AGAINST MY WILL?
EVEN IF IT'S AN INVITE FROM THE ADORABLE IKU, I'VE STILL GOT WORK.
TOO BAD.
I JUST CHECKED THE SCHEDULE AND YOU DON'T HAVE ANY PRESSING MATTERS TO TAKE CARE OF.
IF YOU'RE GOING TO TURN DOWN ARIMURA'S INVITATION JUST TO WORK UNNECESSARY OVERTIME, THEN YOU DESERVE TO DIE.
YOU'RE AS SHREWD AS EVER.
NOW, THEN.
HURRY UP AND LET'S GO.
HUH? WAIT!
HOLD ON!
GENTLY, NOW!

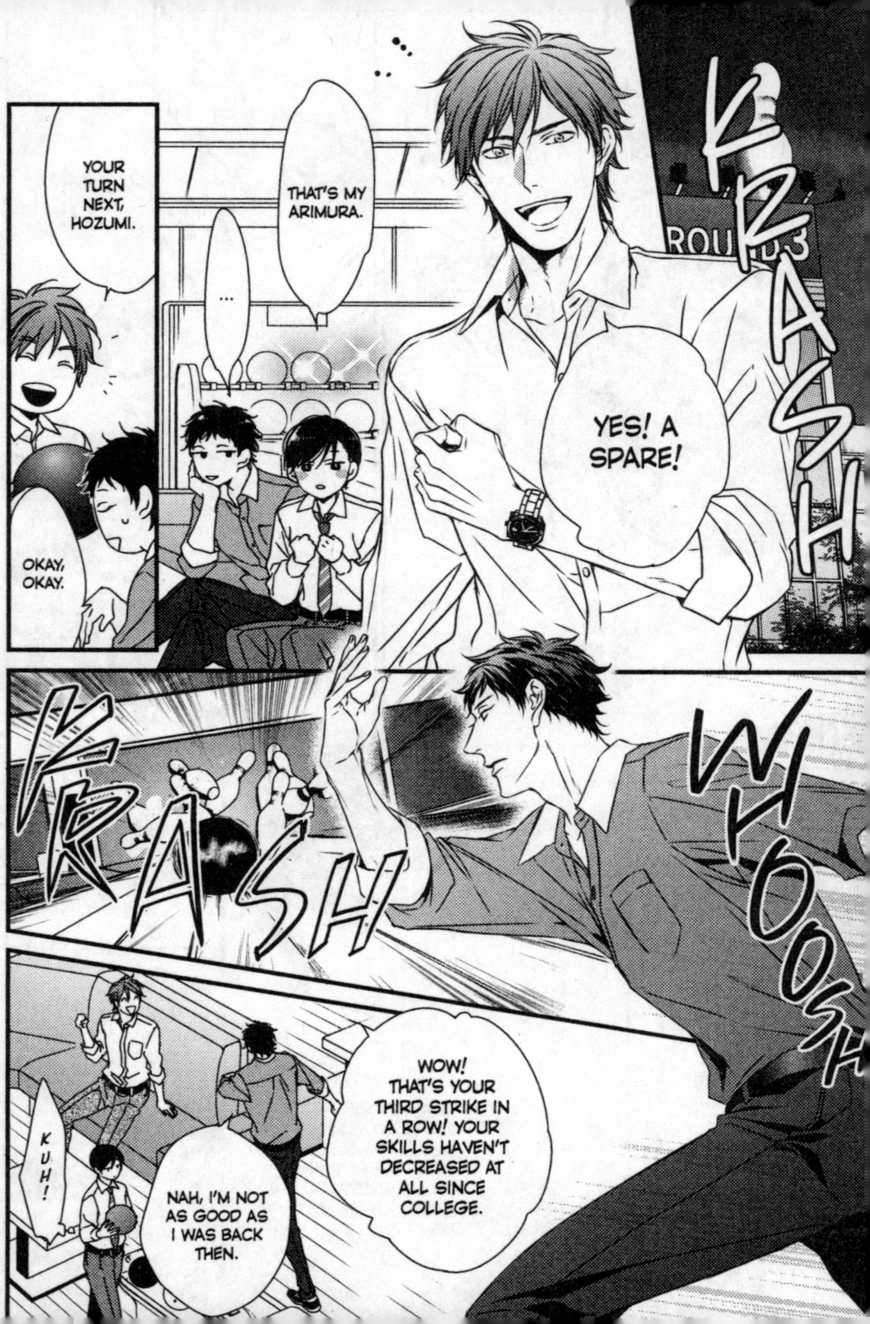
KRASH
YES! A SPARE!
...
THAT'S MY ARIMURA.
...
YOUR TURN NEXT, HOZUMI.
OKAY, OKAY.
WHOOSH
KRASH
WOW! THAT'S YOUR THIRD STRIKE IN A ROW! YOUR SKILLS HAVEN'T DECREASED AT ALL SINCE COLLEGE.
NAH, I'M NOT AS GOOD AS I WAS BACK THEN.
KUH!

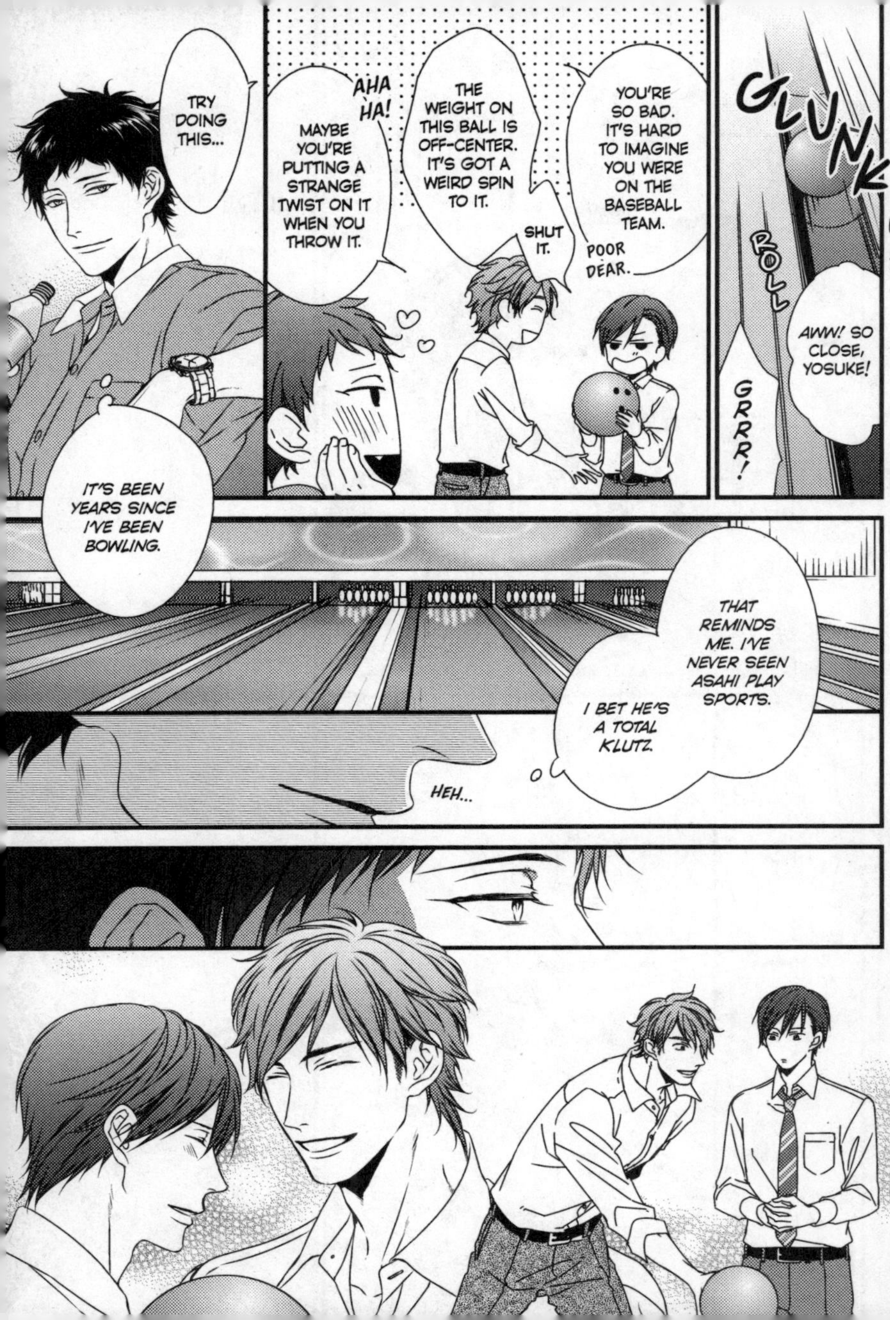
GLUNK
ROLL
KLATTA
AWW! SO CLOSE, YOSUKE!
GRRR!
YOU'RE SO BAD. IT'S HARD TO IMAGINE YOU WERE ON THE BASEBALL TEAM.
POOR DEAR.
THE WEIGHT ON THIS BALL IS OFF-CENTER. IT'S GOT A WEIRD SPIN TO IT.
SHUT IT.
AHA HA!
MAYBE YOU'RE PUTTING A STRANGE TWIST ON IT WHEN YOU THROW IT.
TRY DOING THIS...
IT'S BEEN YEARS SINCE I'VE BEEN BOWLING.
THAT REMINDS ME. I'VE NEVER SEEN ASAHI PLAY SPORTS.
I BET HE'S A TOTAL KLUTZ.
HEH...

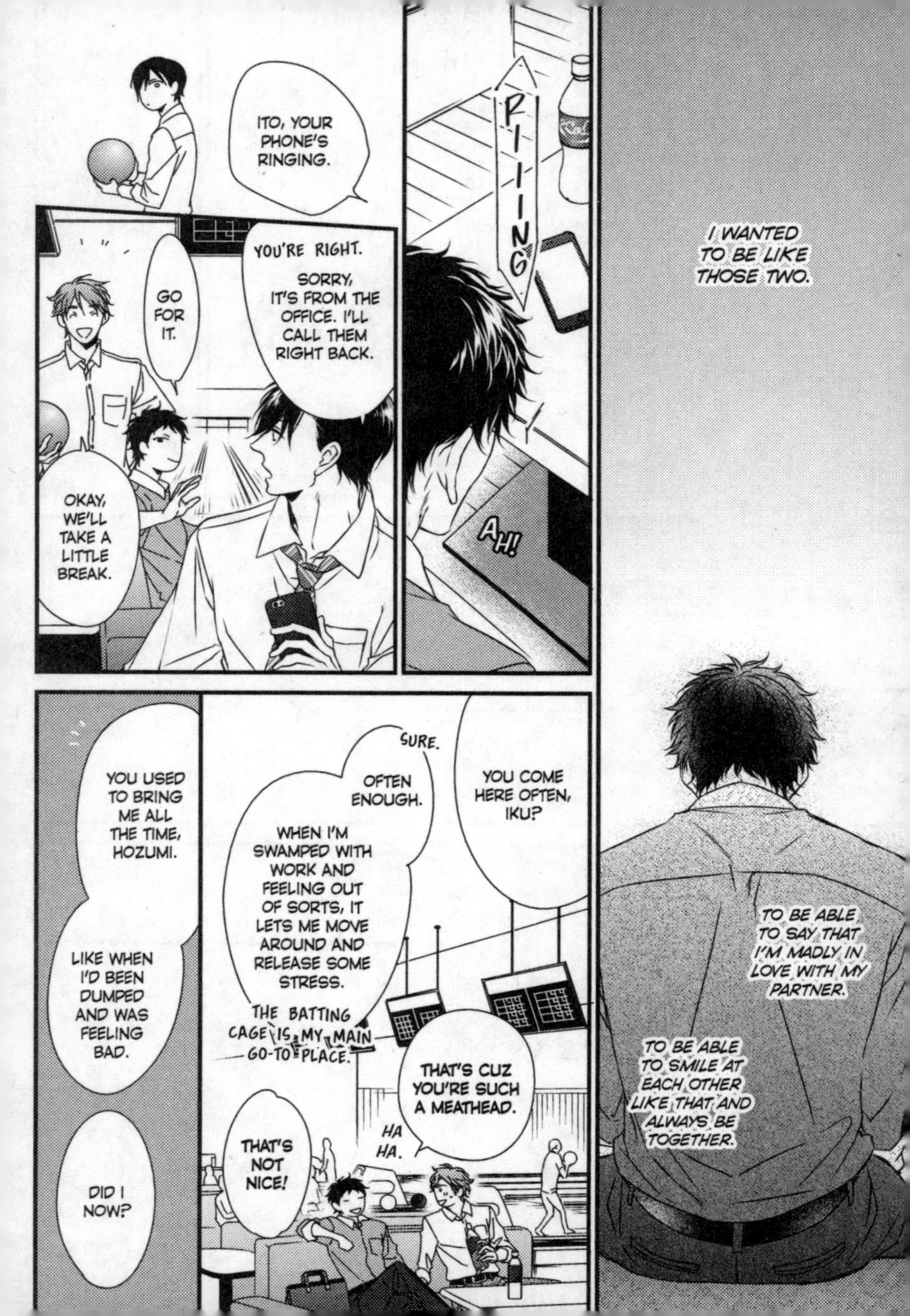
I WANTED TO BE LIKE THOSE TWO.
TO BE ABLE TO SAY THAT I'M MADLY IN LOVE WITH MY PARTNER.
TO BE ABLE TO SMILE AT EACH OTHER LIKE THAT AND ALWAYS BE TOGETHER.
RIIIING
AH!
ITO, YOUR PHONE'S RINGING.
YOU'RE RIGHT.
SORRY, IT'S FROM THE OFFICE. I'LL CALL THEM RIGHT BACK.
GO FOR IT.
OKAY, WE'LL TAKE A LITTLE BREAK.
YOU COME HERE OFTEN, IKU?
SURE.
OFTEN ENOUGH.
WHEN I'M SWAMPED WITH WORK AND FEELING OUT OF SORTS, IT LETS ME MOVE AROUND AND RELEASE SOME STRESS.
THE BATTING CAGE IS MY MAIN GO-TO PLACE.
THAT'S CUZ YOU'RE SUCH A MEATHEAD.
HA HA.
THAT'S NOT NICE!
YOU USED TO BRING ME ALL THE TIME, HOZUMI.
LIKE WHEN I'D BEEN DUMPED AND WAS FEELING BAD.
DID I NOW?

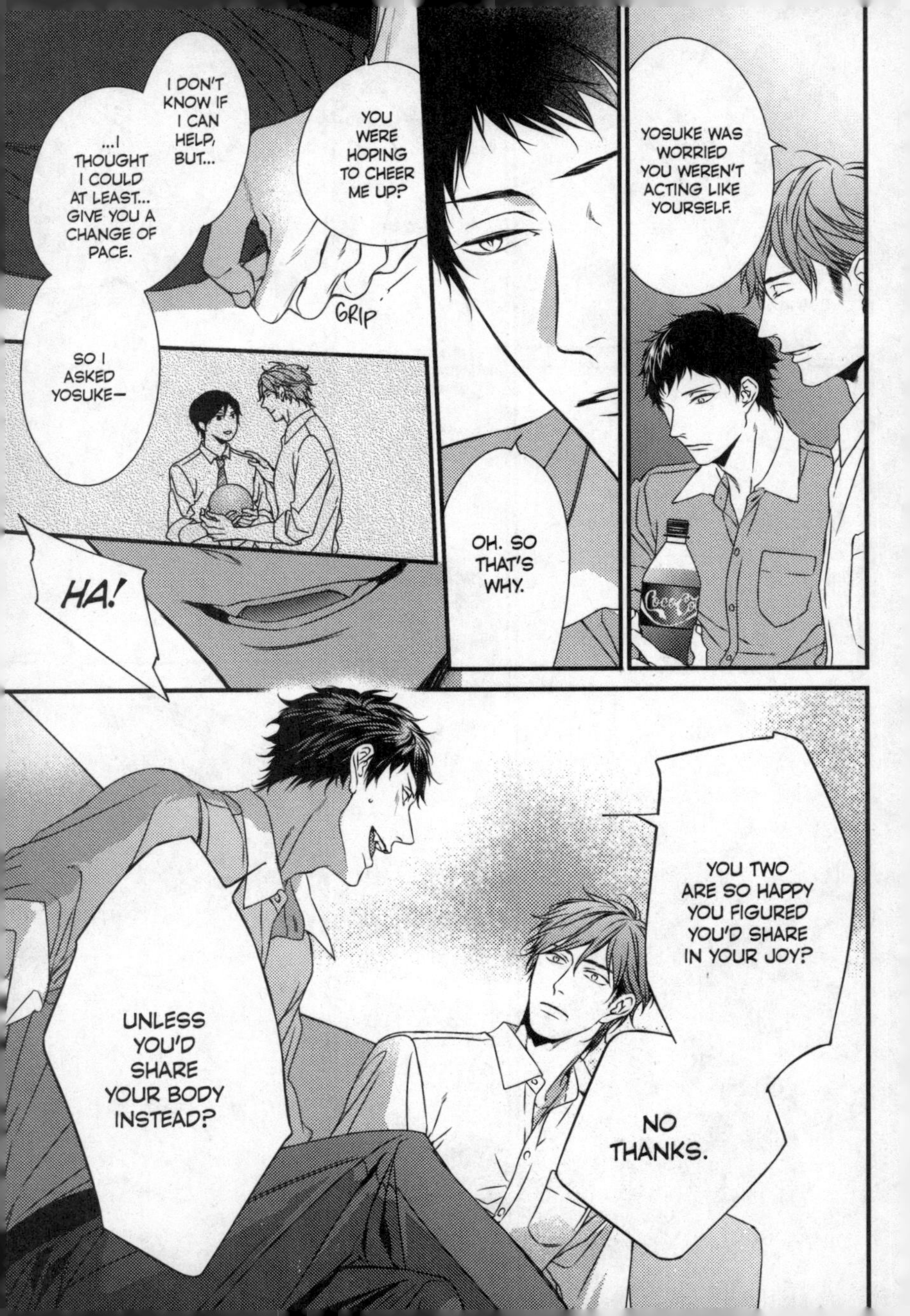
YOSUKE WAS WORRIED YOU WEREN'T ACTING LIKE YOURSELF.
OH. SO THAT'S WHY.
YOU WERE HOPING TO CHEER ME UP?
I DON'T KNOW IF I CAN HELP, BUT...
...I THOUGHT I COULD AT LEAST... GIVE YOU A CHANGE OF PACE.
GRIP
SO I ASKED YOSUKE—
HA!
YOU TWO ARE SO HAPPY YOU FIGURED YOU'D SHARE IN YOUR JOY?
UNLESS YOU'D SHARE YOUR BODY INSTEAD?
NO THANKS.

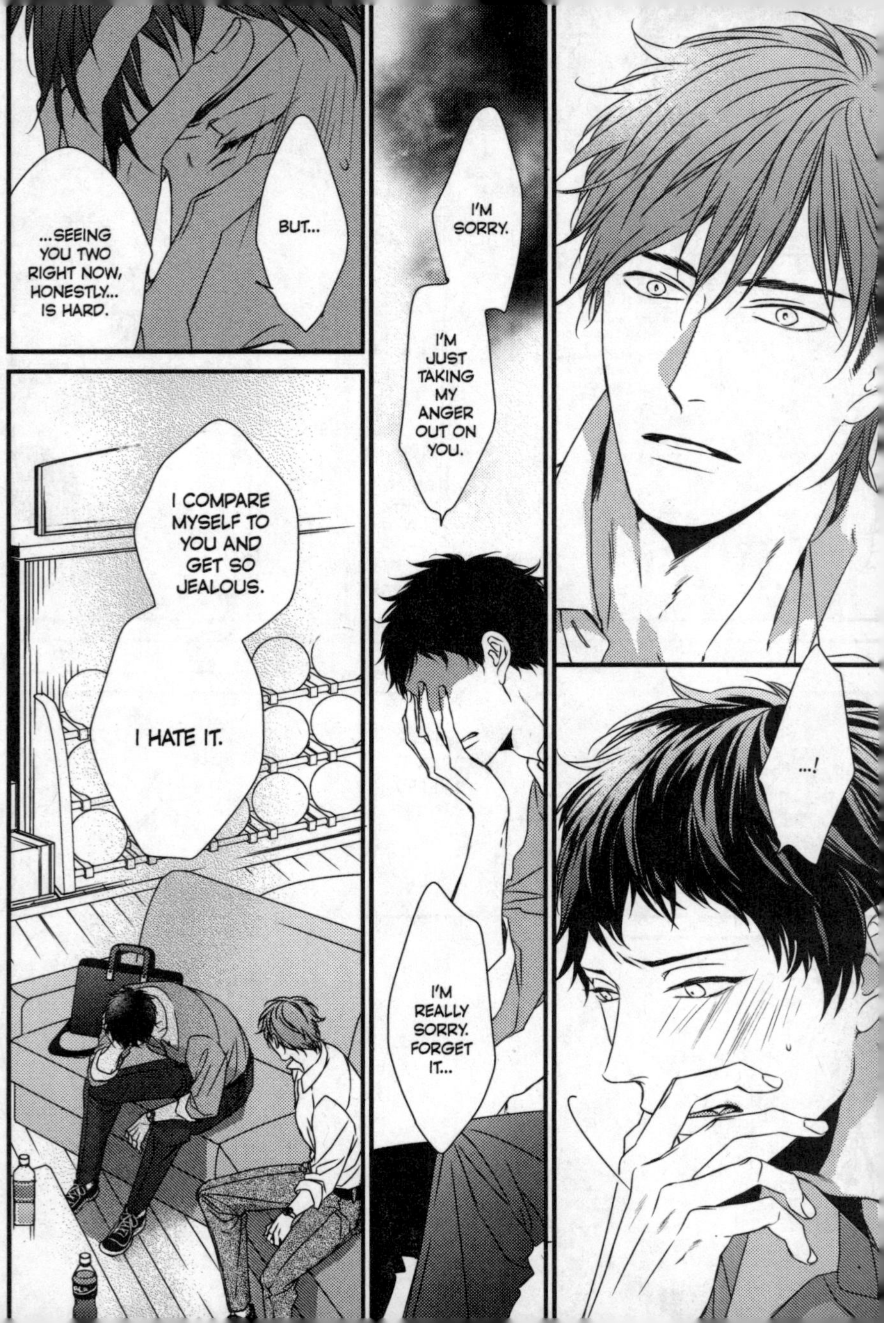
...SEEING YOU TWO RIGHT NOW, HONESTLY... IS HARD.
BUT...
I COMPARE MYSELF TO YOU AND GET SO JEALOUS.
I HATE IT.
I'M SORRY.
I'M JUST TAKING MY ANGER OUT ON YOU.
I'M REALLY SORRY. FORGET IT...
...!

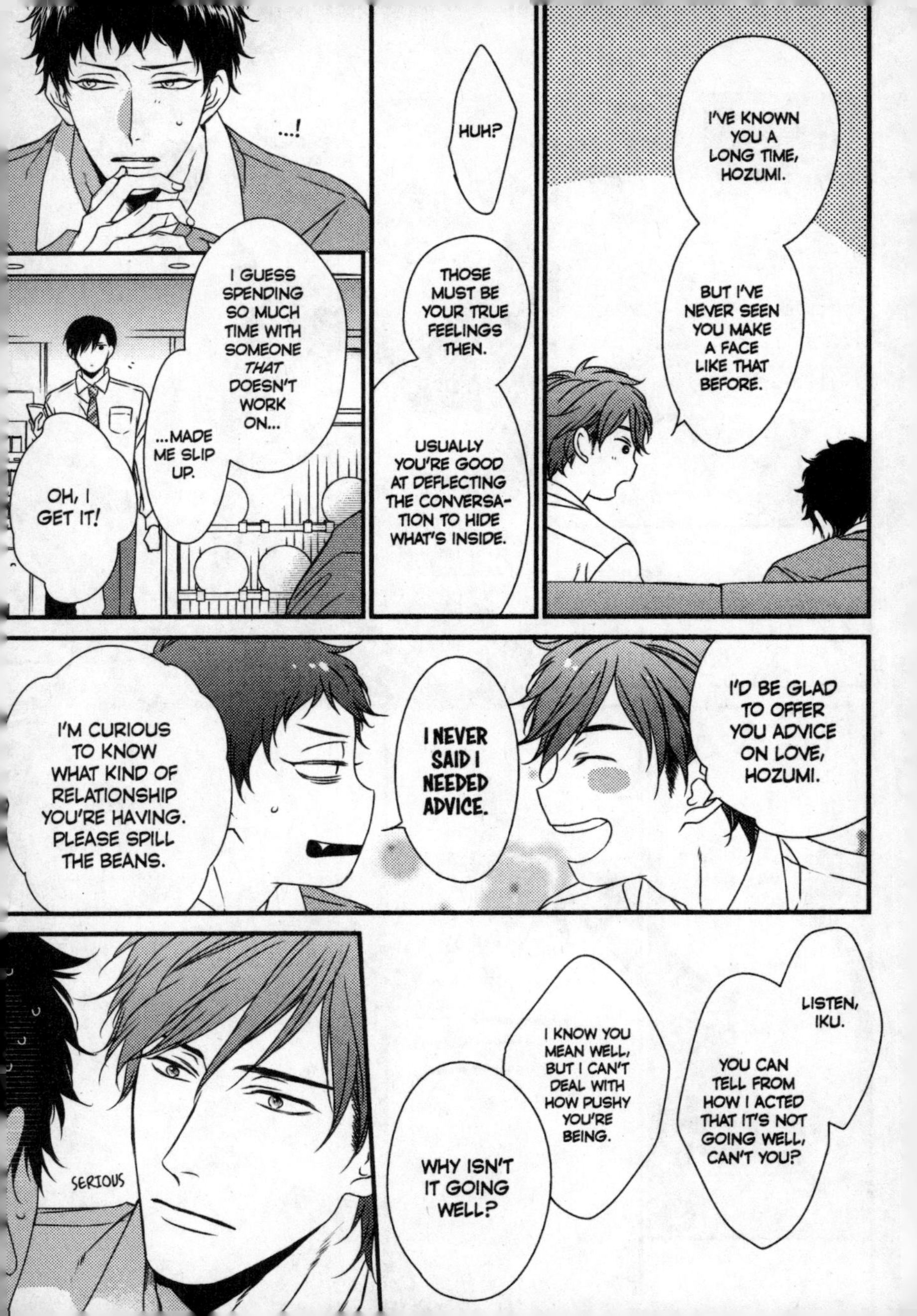
I'VE KNOWN YOU A LONG TIME, HOZUMI.
BUT I'VE NEVER SEEN YOU MAKE A FACE LIKE THAT BEFORE.
HUH?
THOSE MUST BE YOUR TRUE FEELINGS THEN.
USUALLY YOU'RE GOOD AT DEFLECTING THE CONVERSA-TION TO HIDE WHAT'S INSIDE.
...!
I GUESS SPENDING SO MUCH TIME WITH SOMEONE *THAT* DOESN'T WORK ON...
...MADE ME SLIP UP.
OH, I GET IT!
I'D BE GLAD TO OFFER YOU ADVICE ON LOVE, HOZUMI.
I NEVER SAID I NEEDED ADVICE.
I'M CURIOUS TO KNOW WHAT KIND OF RELATIONSHIP YOU'RE HAVING. PLEASE SPILL THE BEANS.
LISTEN, IKU.
YOU CAN TELL FROM HOW I ACTED THAT IT'S NOT GOING WELL, CAN'T YOU?
I KNOW YOU MEAN WELL, BUT I CAN'T DEAL WITH HOW PUSHY YOU'RE BEING.
WHY ISN'T IT GOING WELL?
SERIOUS

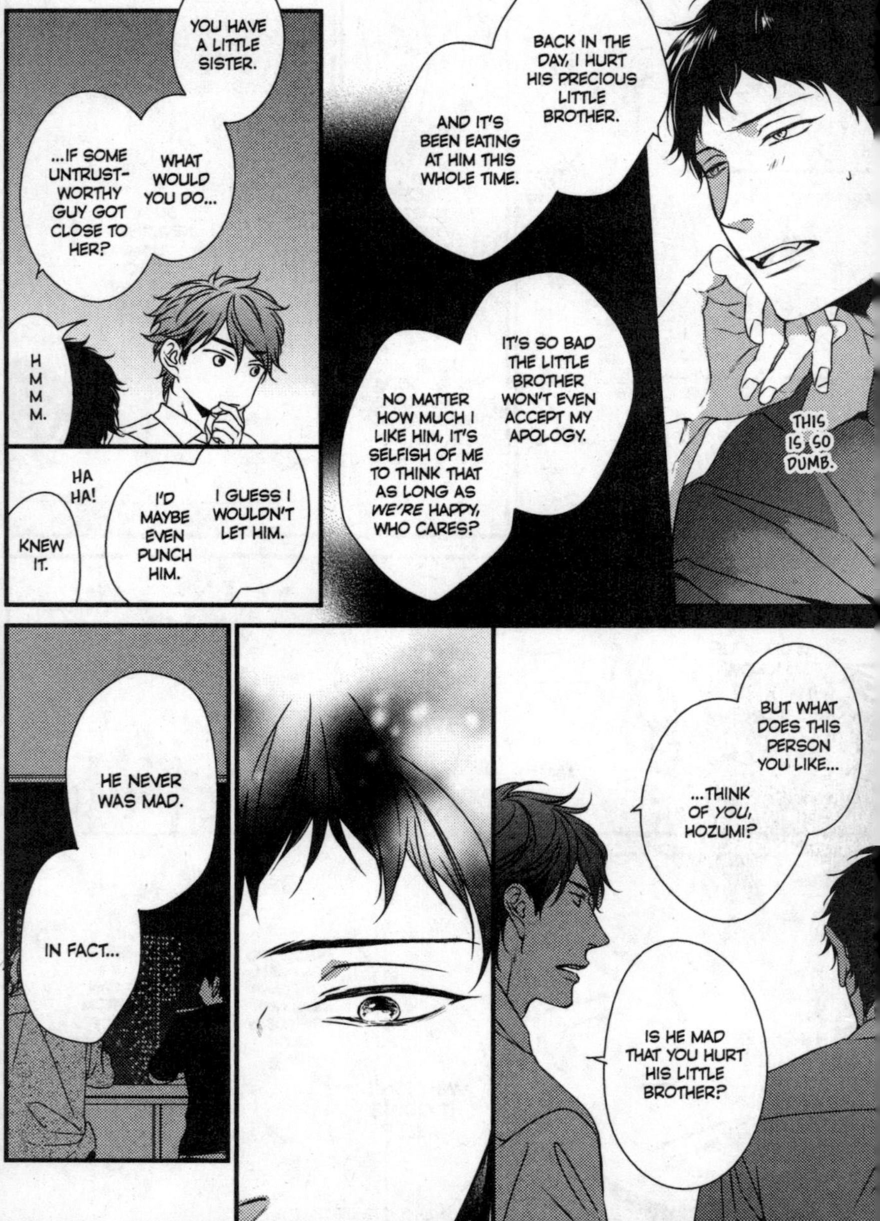
BACK IN THE DAY, I HURT HIS PRECIOUS LITTLE BROTHER.
AND IT'S BEEN EATING AT HIM THIS WHOLE TIME.
IT'S SO BAD THE LITTLE BROTHER WON'T EVEN ACCEPT MY APOLOGY.
NO MATTER HOW MUCH I LIKE HIM, IT'S SELFISH OF ME TO THINK THAT AS LONG AS *WE'RE* HAPPY, WHO CARES?
THIS IS SO DUMB.
YOU HAVE A LITTLE SISTER.
WHAT WOULD YOU DO...
...IF SOME UNTRUST-WORTHY GUY GOT CLOSE TO HER?
HMMM.
I GUESS I WOULDN'T LET HIM.
I'D MAYBE EVEN PUNCH HIM.
HA HA!
KNEW IT.
BUT WHAT DOES THIS PERSON YOU LIKE...
...THINK OF *YOU*, HOZUMI?
IS HE MAD THAT YOU HURT HIS LITTLE BROTHER?
HE NEVER WAS MAD.
IN FACT...

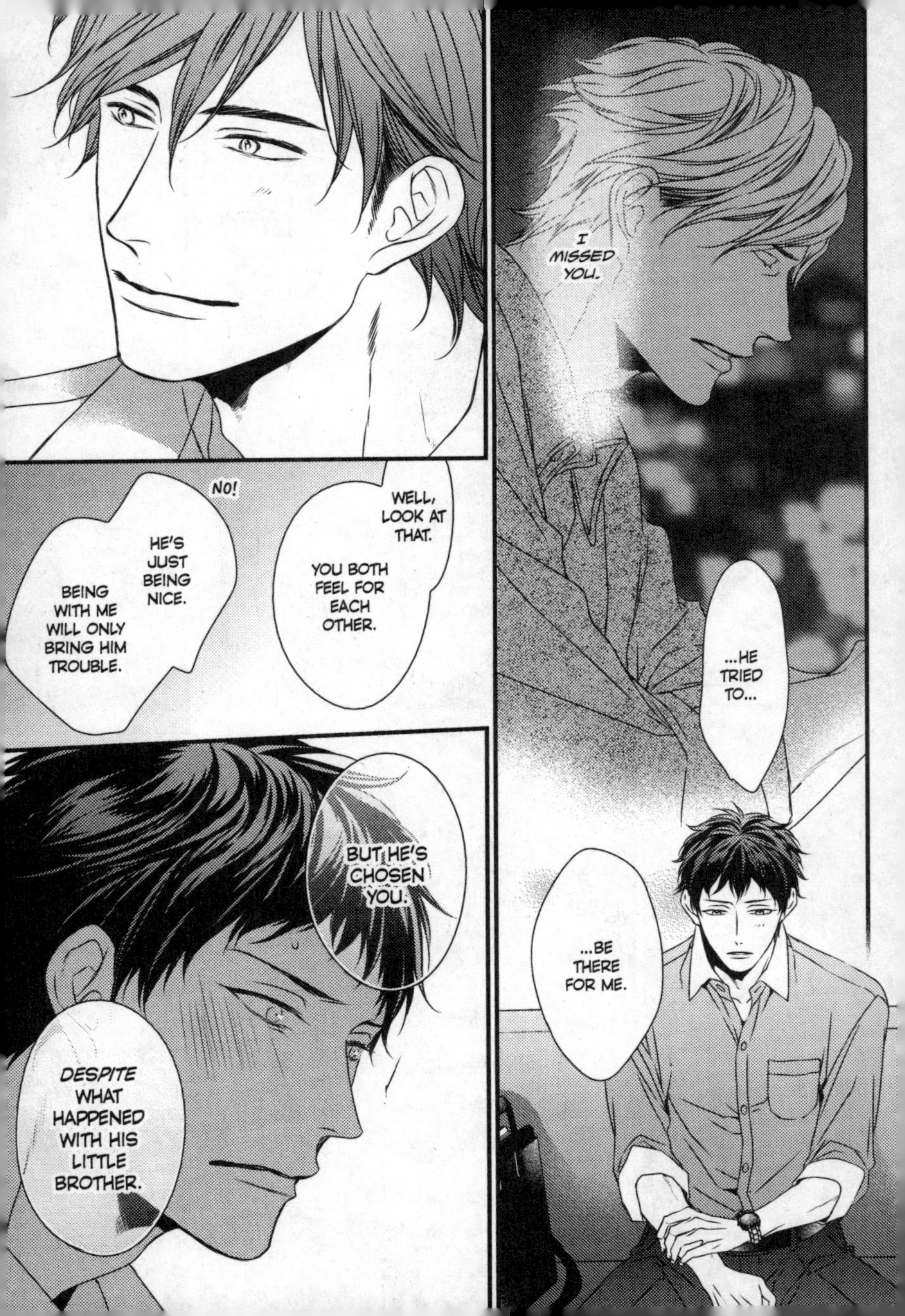
I MISSED YOU.
...HE TRIED TO...
...BE THERE FOR ME.
WELL, LOOK AT THAT.
YOU BOTH FEEL FOR EACH OTHER.
NO!
HE'S JUST BEING NICE.
BEING WITH ME WILL ONLY BRING HIM TROUBLE.
BUT HE'S CHOSEN YOU.
DESPITE WHAT HAPPENED WITH HIS LITTLE BROTHER.

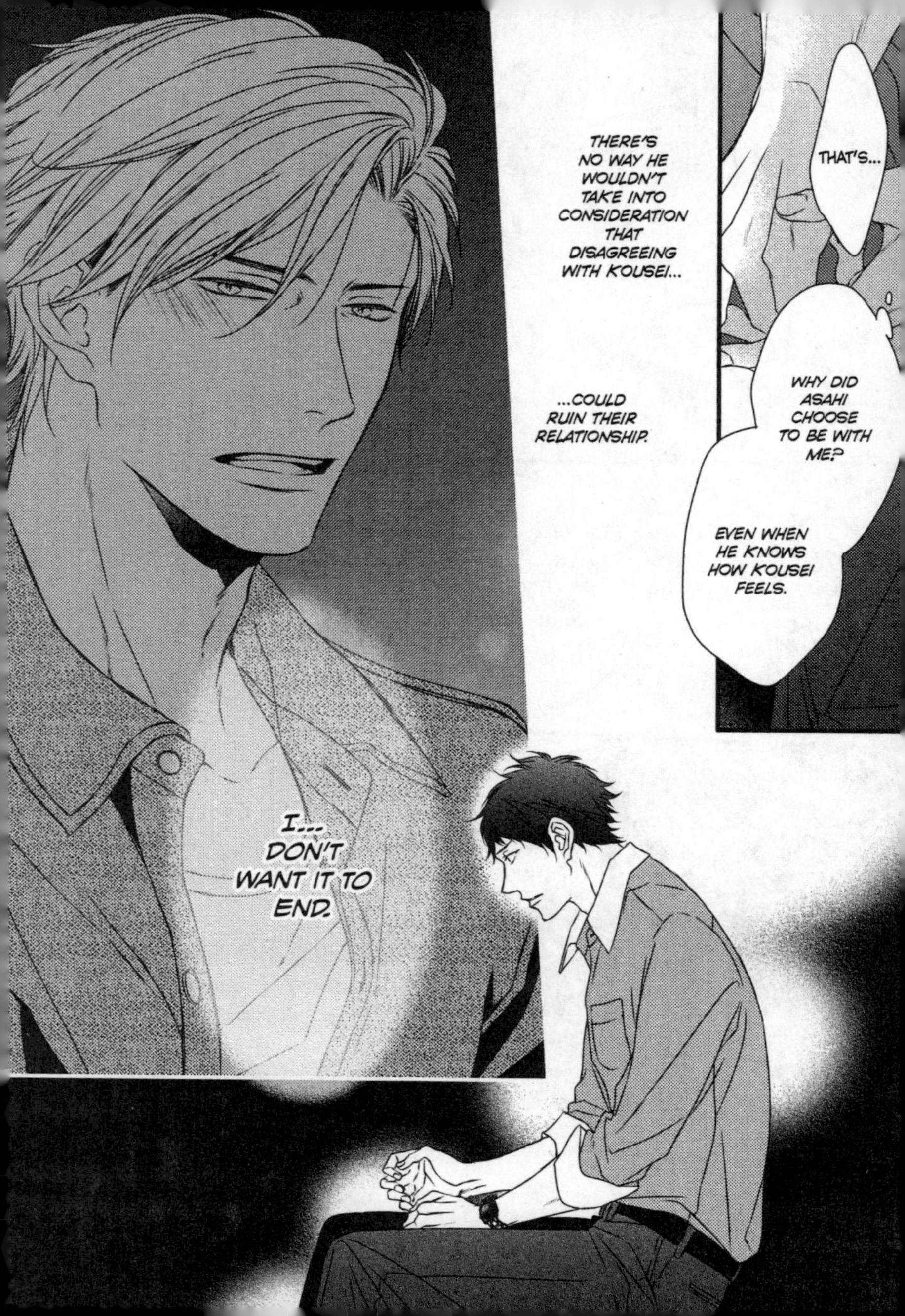
THAT'S...
WHY DID ASAHI CHOOSE TO BE WITH ME?
EVEN WHEN HE KNOWS HOW KOUSEI FEELS.
THERE'S NO WAY HE WOULDN'T TAKE INTO CONSIDERATION THAT DISAGREEING WITH KOUSEI...
...COULD RUIN THEIR RELATIONSHIP.
I... DON'T WANT IT TO END.

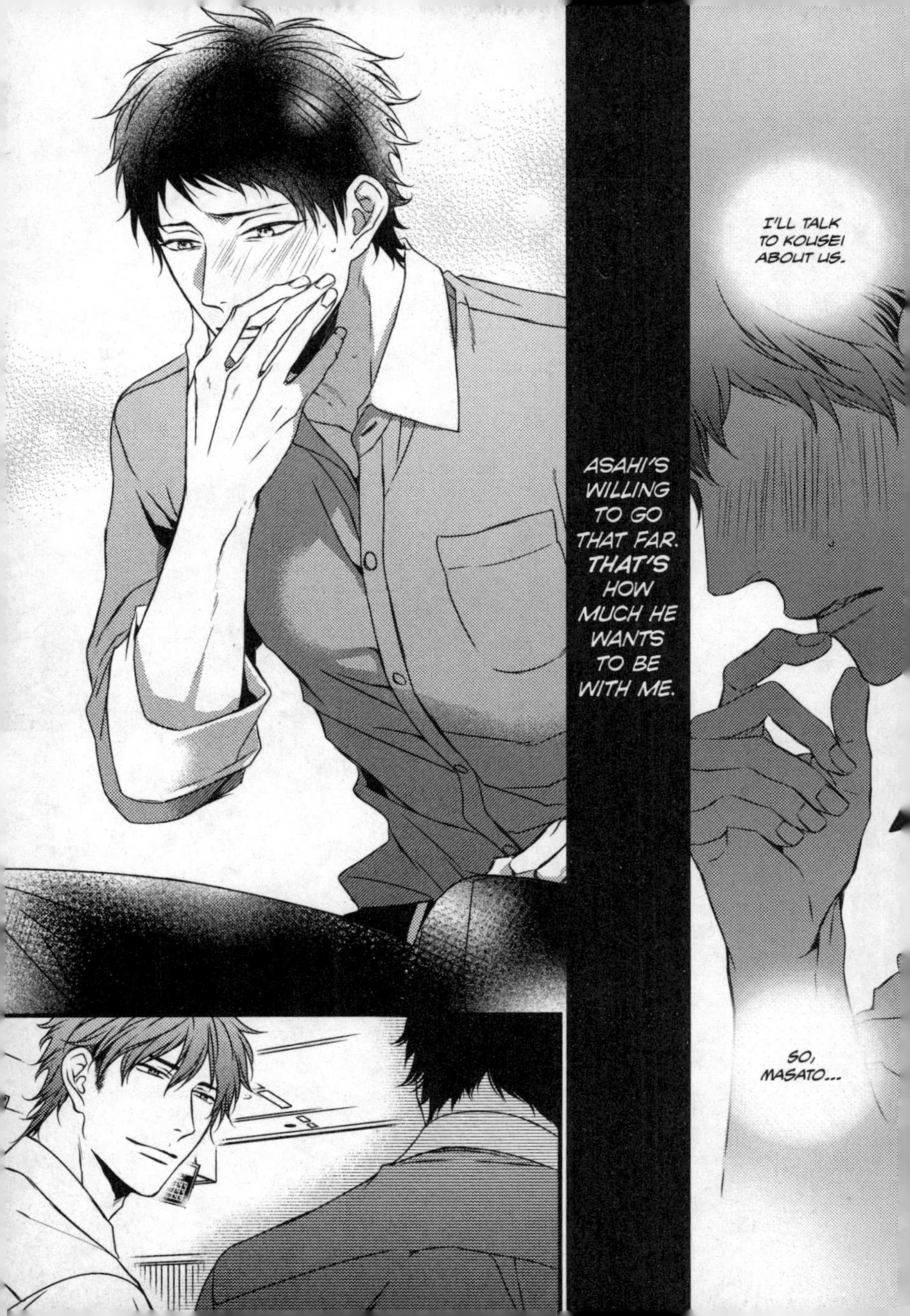
I'LL TALK TO KOUSEI ABOUT US.
SO, MASATO...
ASAHI'S WILLING TO GO THAT FAR. THAT'S HOW MUCH HE WANTS TO BE WITH ME.

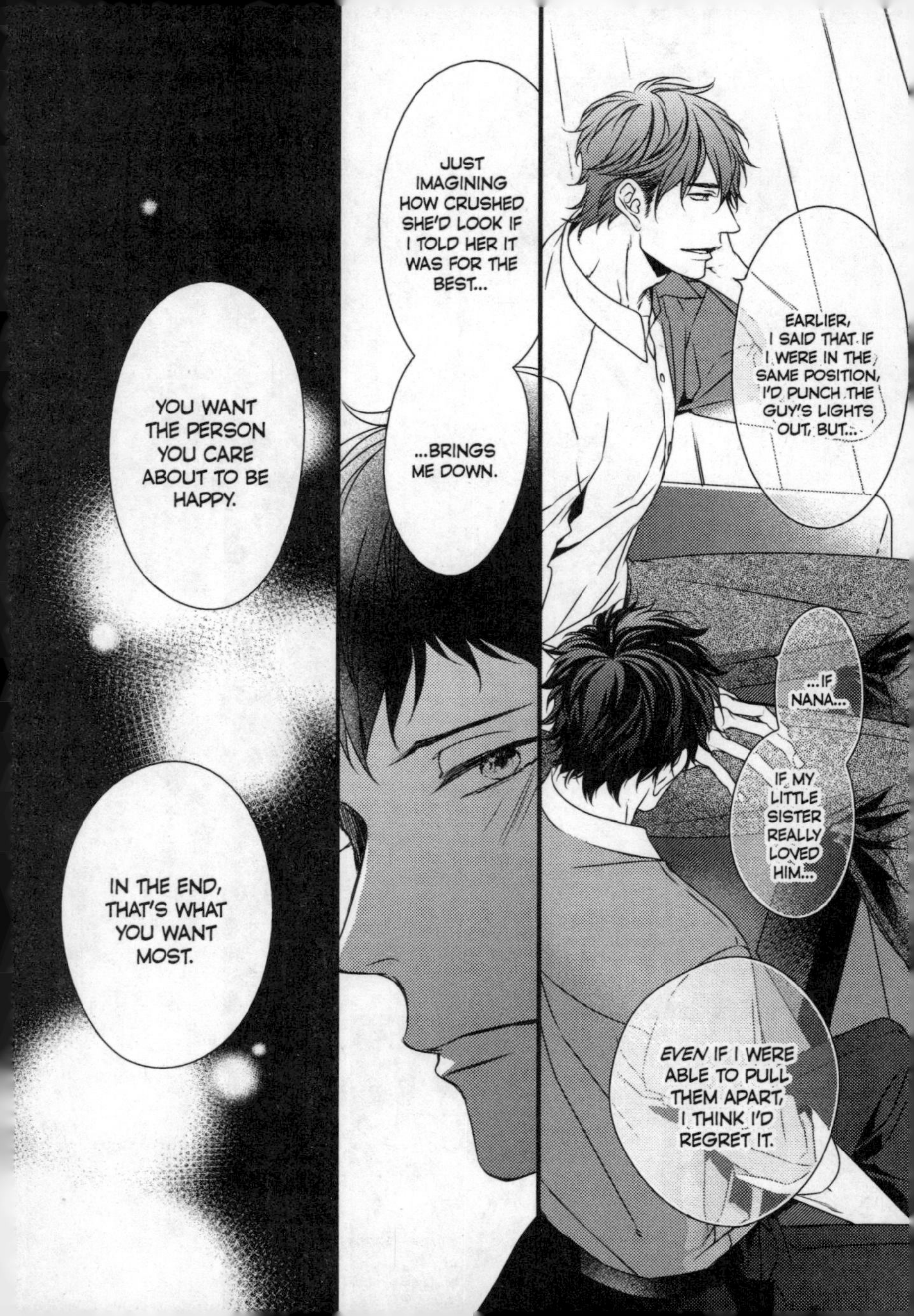
EARLIER, I SAID THAT IF I WERE IN THE SAME POSITION, I'D PUNCH THE GUY'S LIGHTS OUT, BUT...
...IF NANA...
IF MY LITTLE SISTER REALLY LOVED HIM...
EVEN IF I WERE ABLE TO PULL THEM APART, I THINK I'D REGRET IT.
JUST IMAGINING HOW CRUSHED SHE'D LOOK IF I TOLD HER IT WAS FOR THE BEST...
...BRINGS ME DOWN.
YOU WANT THE PERSON YOU CARE ABOUT TO BE HAPPY.
IN THE END, THAT'S WHAT YOU WANT MOST.

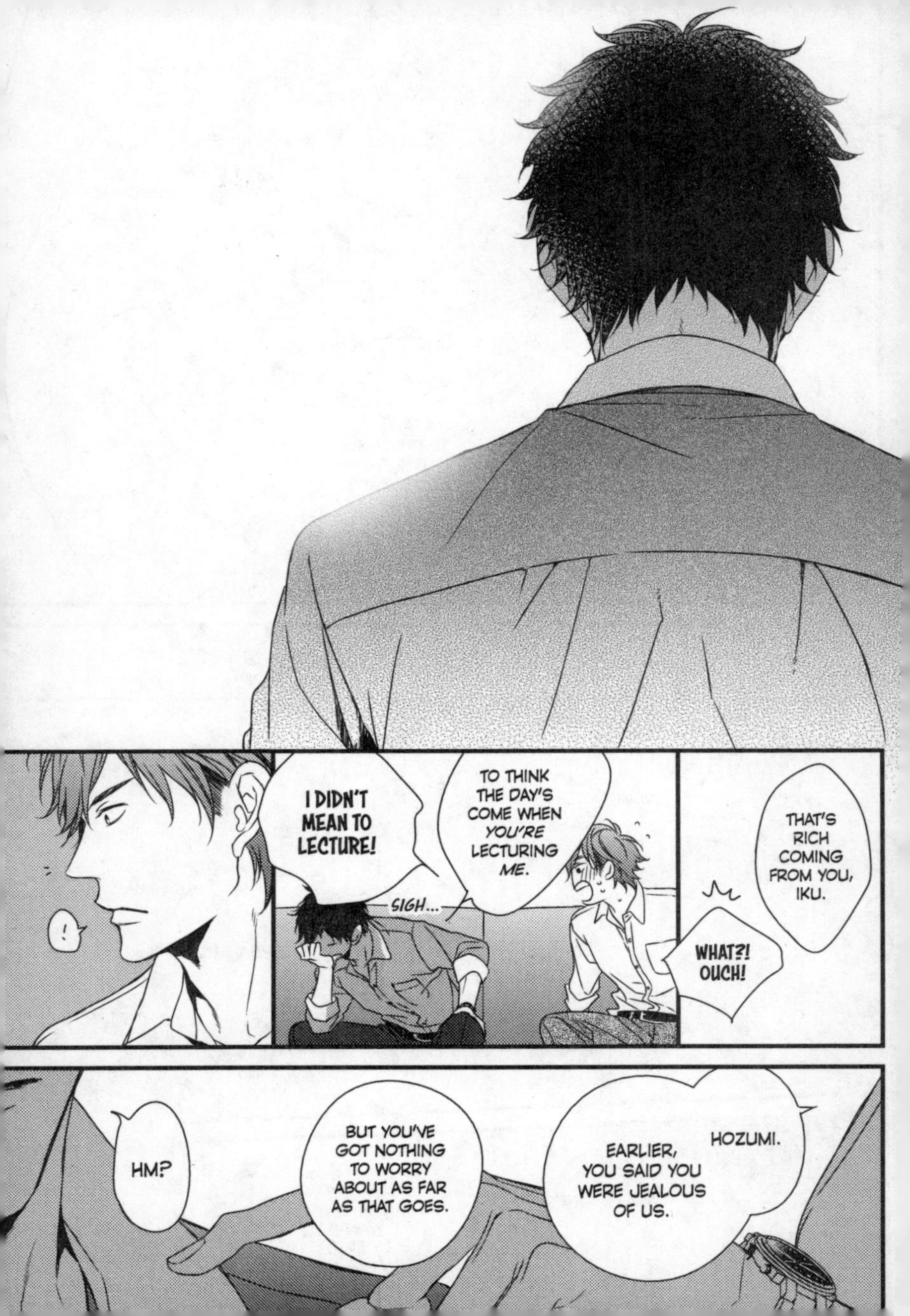
THAT'S RICH COMING FROM YOU, IKU.
WHAT?! OUCH!
TO THINK THE DAY'S COME WHEN *YOU'RE* LECTURING *ME*.
I DIDN'T MEAN TO LECTURE!
SIGH...
!
HOZUMI.
EARLIER, YOU SAID YOU WERE JEALOUS OF US.
BUT YOU'VE GOT NOTHING TO WORRY ABOUT AS FAR AS THAT GOES.
HM?

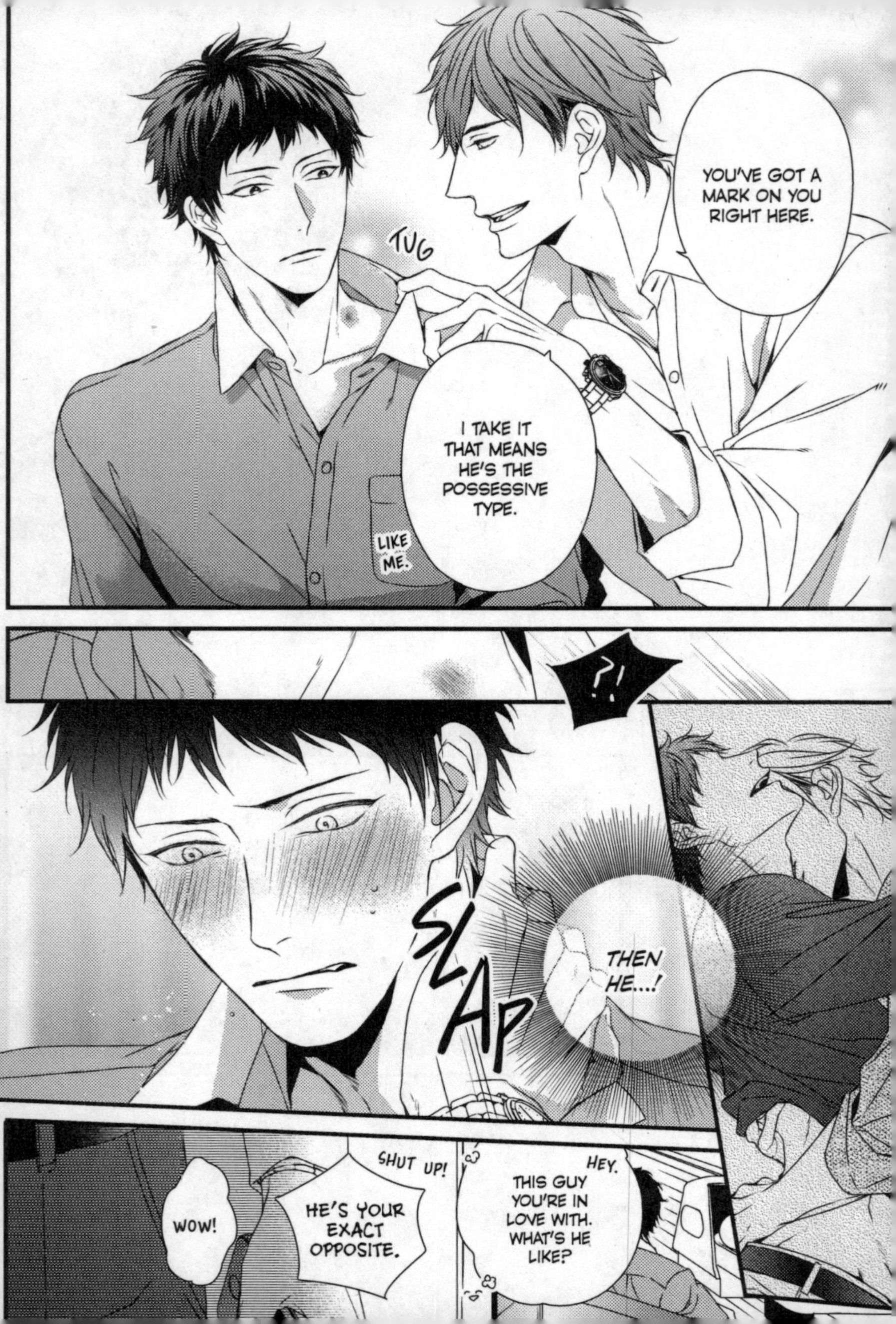
YOU'VE GOT A MARK ON YOU RIGHT HERE.
TUG
I TAKE IT THAT MEANS HE'S THE POSSESSIVE TYPE.
LIKE ME.
?!
THEN HE...!
SLAP
HEY.
THIS GUY YOU'RE IN LOVE WITH. WHAT'S HE LIKE?
SHUT UP!
HE'S YOUR EXACT OPPOSITE.
WOW!

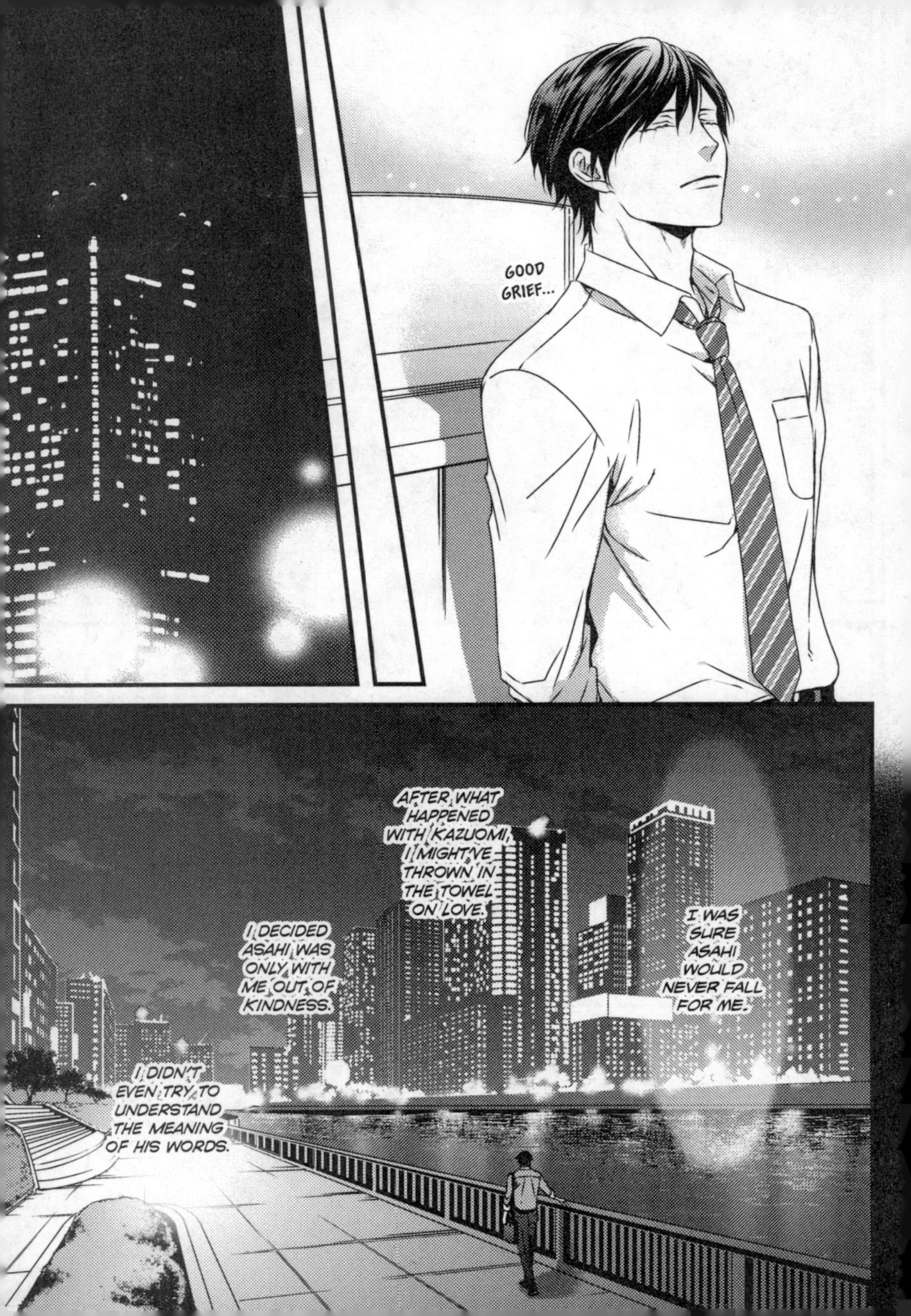
GOOD GRIEF...
AFTER WHAT HAPPENED WITH KAZUOMI, I MIGHT'VE THROWN IN THE TOWEL ON LOVE.
I WAS SURE ASAHI WOULD NEVER FALL FOR ME.
I DECIDED ASAHI WAS ONLY WITH ME OUT OF KINDNESS.
I DIDN'T EVEN TRY TO UNDERSTAND THE MEANING OF HIS WORDS.

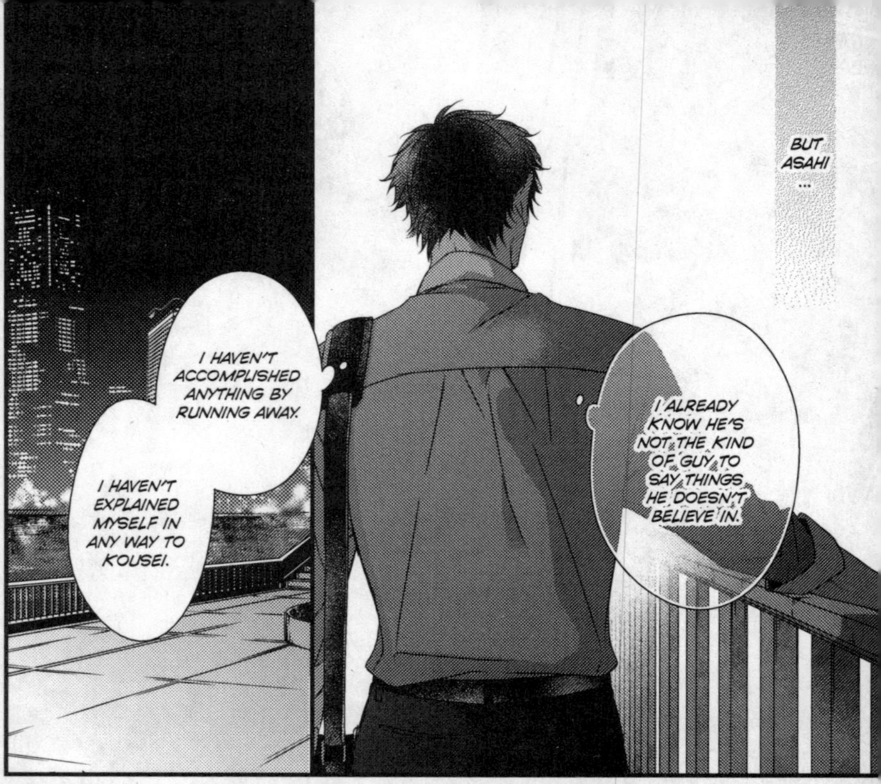
BUT ASAHI...
I ALREADY KNOW HE'S NOT THE KIND OF GUY TO SAY THINGS HE DOESN'T BELIEVE IN.
I HAVEN'T ACCOMPLISHED ANYTHING BY RUNNING AWAY.
I HAVEN'T EXPLAINED MYSELF IN ANY WAY TO KOUSEI.

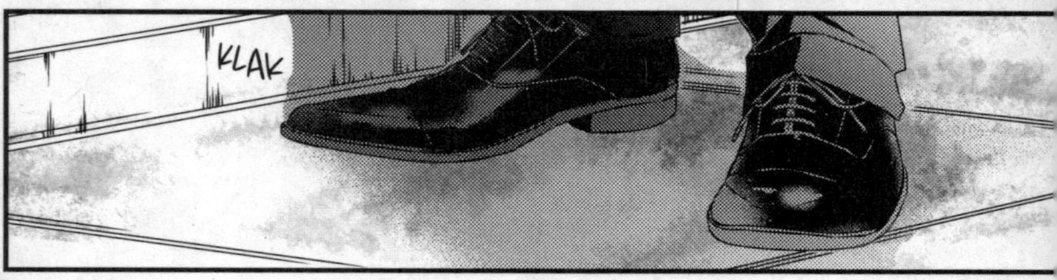
KLAK

NO MATTER WHAT I SAY, IT'S UNLIKELY HE'LL BELIEVE ME.

I DON'T KNOW HOW TO GET IT ACROSS TO HIM.

AND YET...

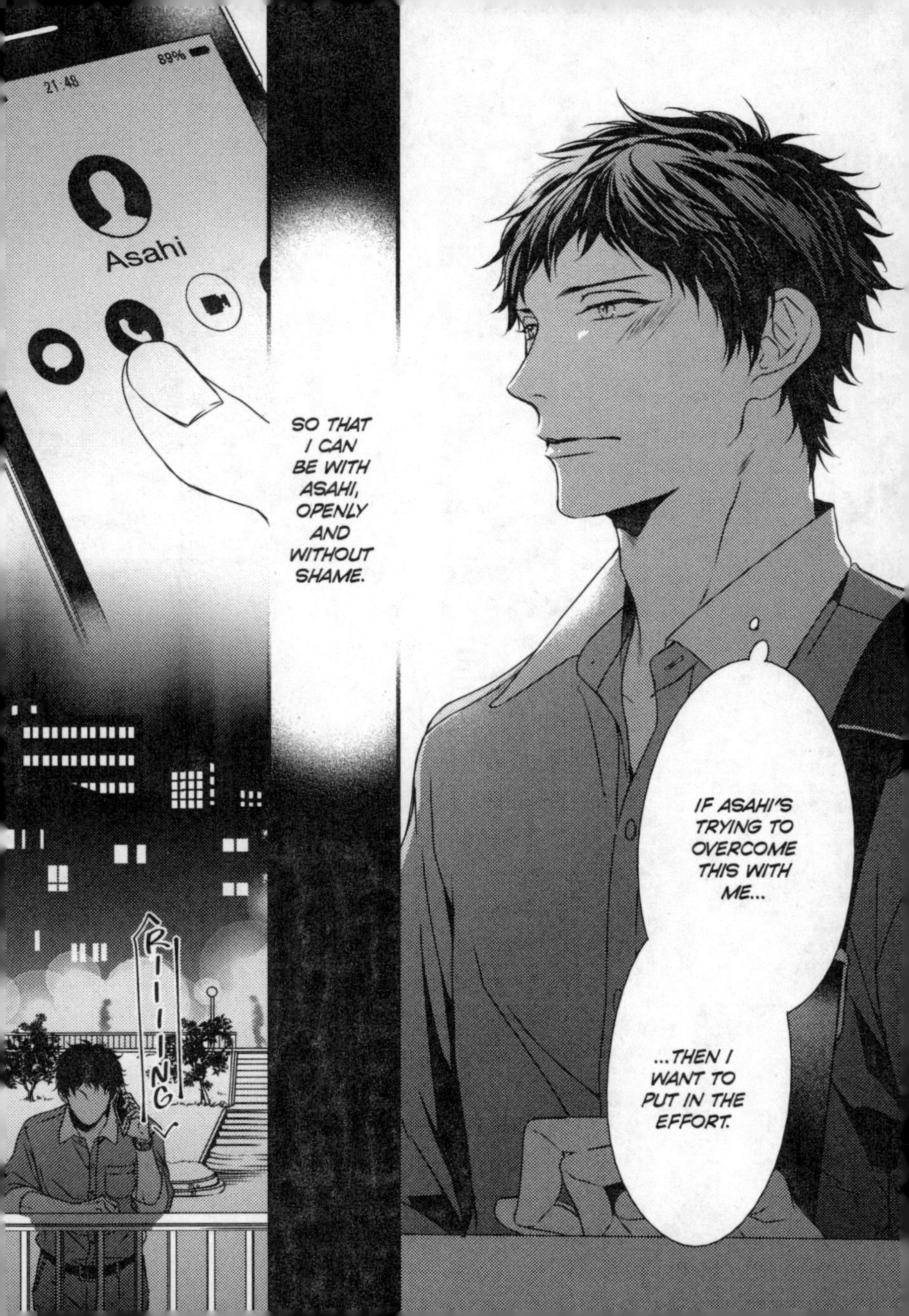
IF ASAHI'S TRYING TO OVERCOME THIS WITH ME...
...THEN I WANT TO PUT IN THE EFFORT.
SO THAT I CAN BE WITH ASAHI, OPENLY AND WITHOUT SHAME.
21:48
89%
Asahi
RIIIING

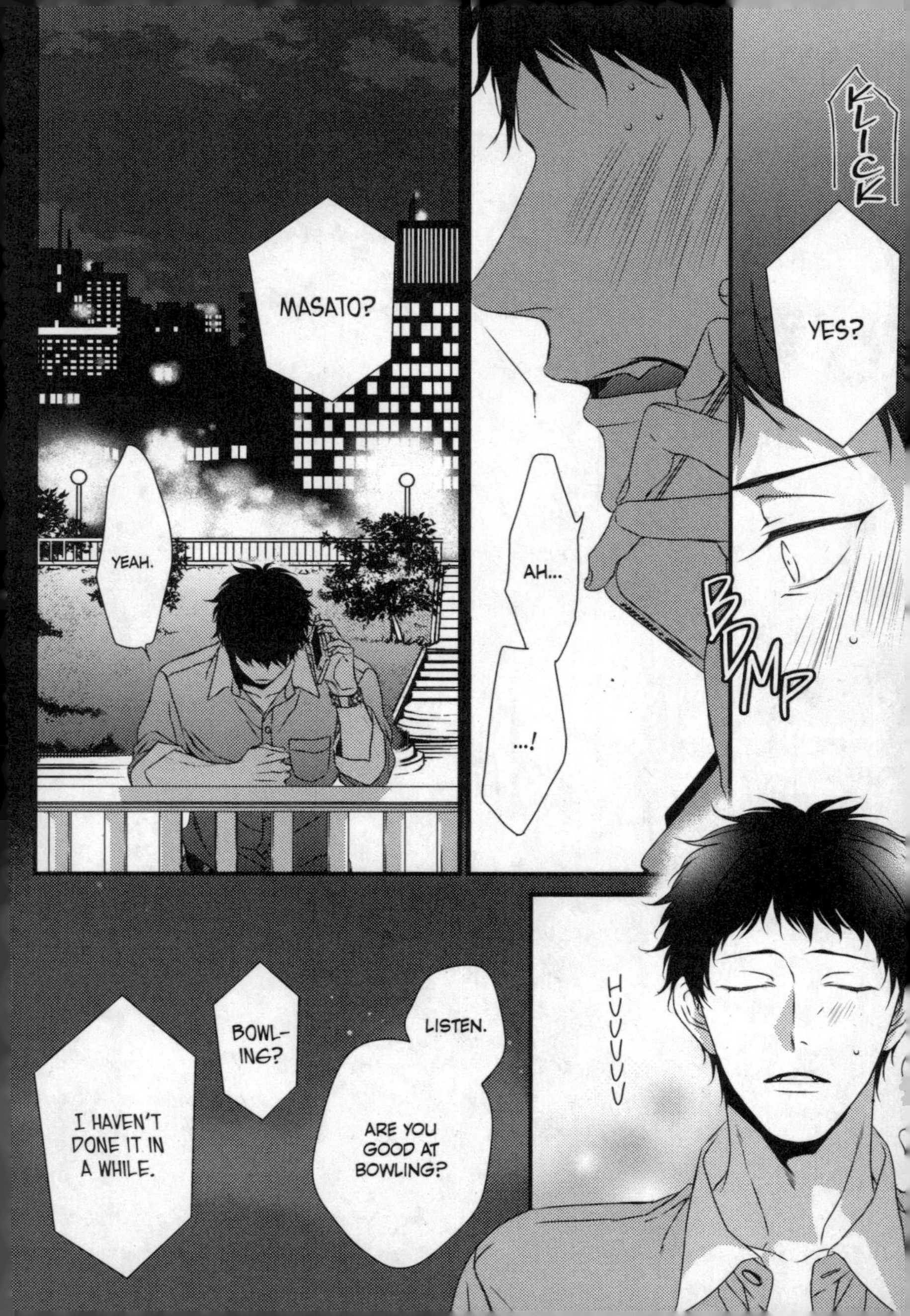
KLICK
YES?
BDMP
AH...
...!
MASATO?
YEAH.
HUUUUUU
LISTEN.
ARE YOU GOOD AT BOWLING?
BOWLING?
I HAVEN'T DONE IT IN A WHILE.

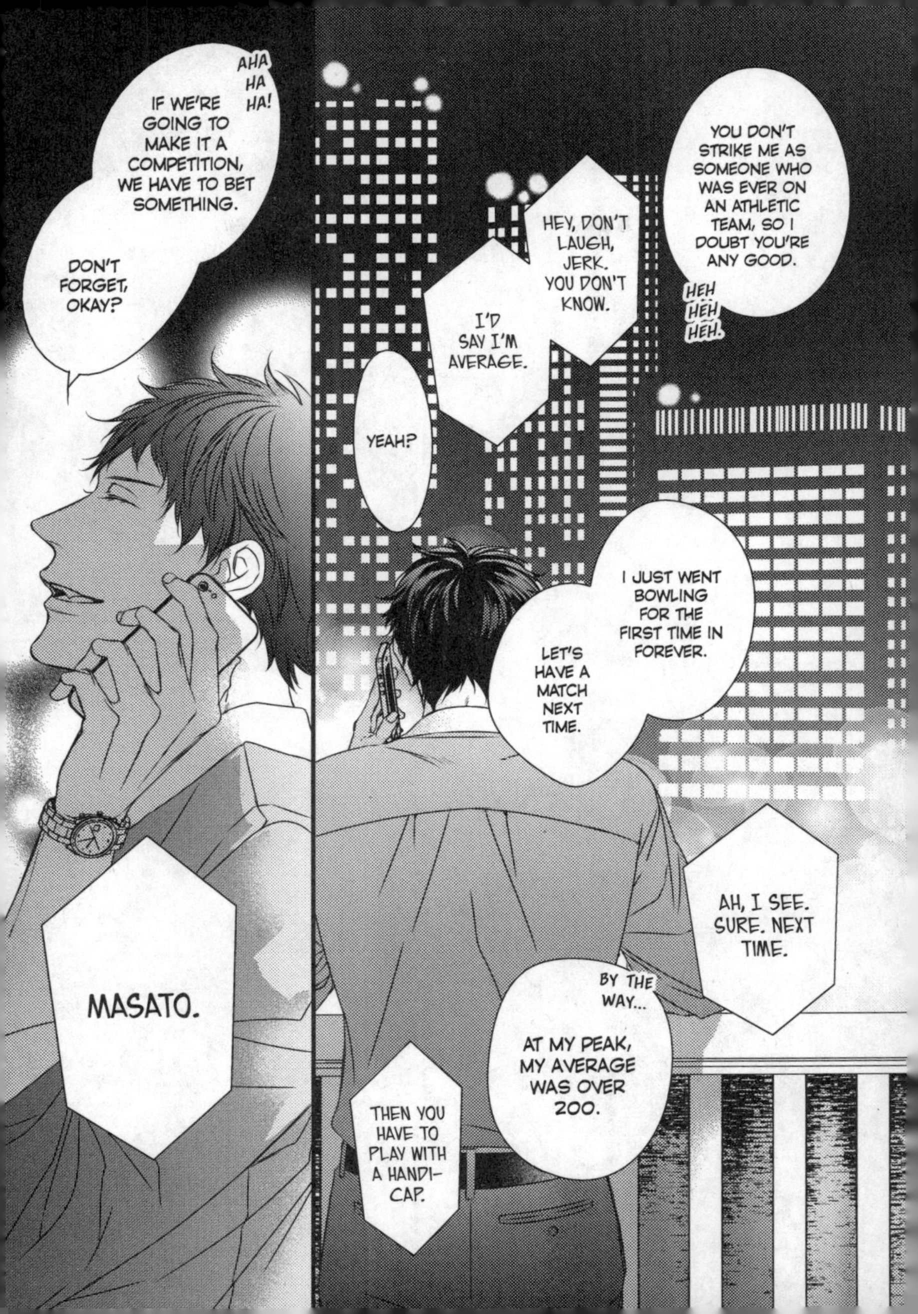
YOU DON'T STRIKE ME AS SOMEONE WHO WAS EVER ON AN ATHLETIC TEAM, SO I DOUBT YOU'RE ANY GOOD.
HEH HEH HEH.
HEY, DON'T LAUGH, JERK. YOU DON'T KNOW.
I'D SAY I'M AVERAGE.
YEAH?
I JUST WENT BOWLING FOR THE FIRST TIME IN FOREVER.
LET'S HAVE A MATCH NEXT TIME.
AH, I SEE. SURE. NEXT TIME.
BY THE WAY...
AT MY PEAK, MY AVERAGE WAS OVER 200.
THEN YOU HAVE TO PLAY WITH A HANDI-CAP.
AHA HA HA!
IF WE'RE GOING TO MAKE IT A COMPETITION, WE HAVE TO BET SOMETHING.
DON'T FORGET, OKAY?
MASATO.

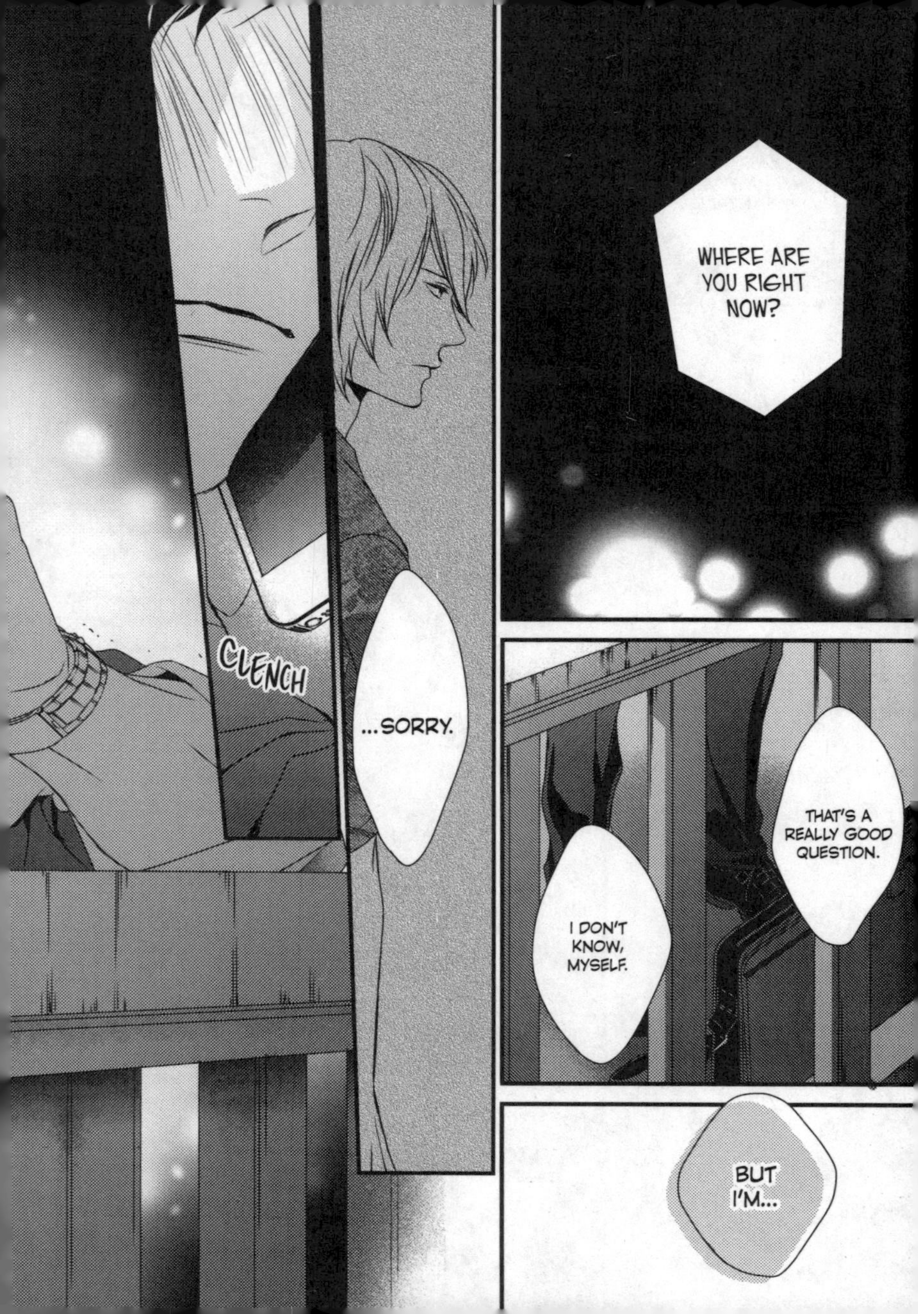
WHERE ARE YOU RIGHT NOW?
THAT'S A REALLY GOOD QUESTION.
I DON'T KNOW, MYSELF.
BUT I'M...
...SORRY.
CLENCH

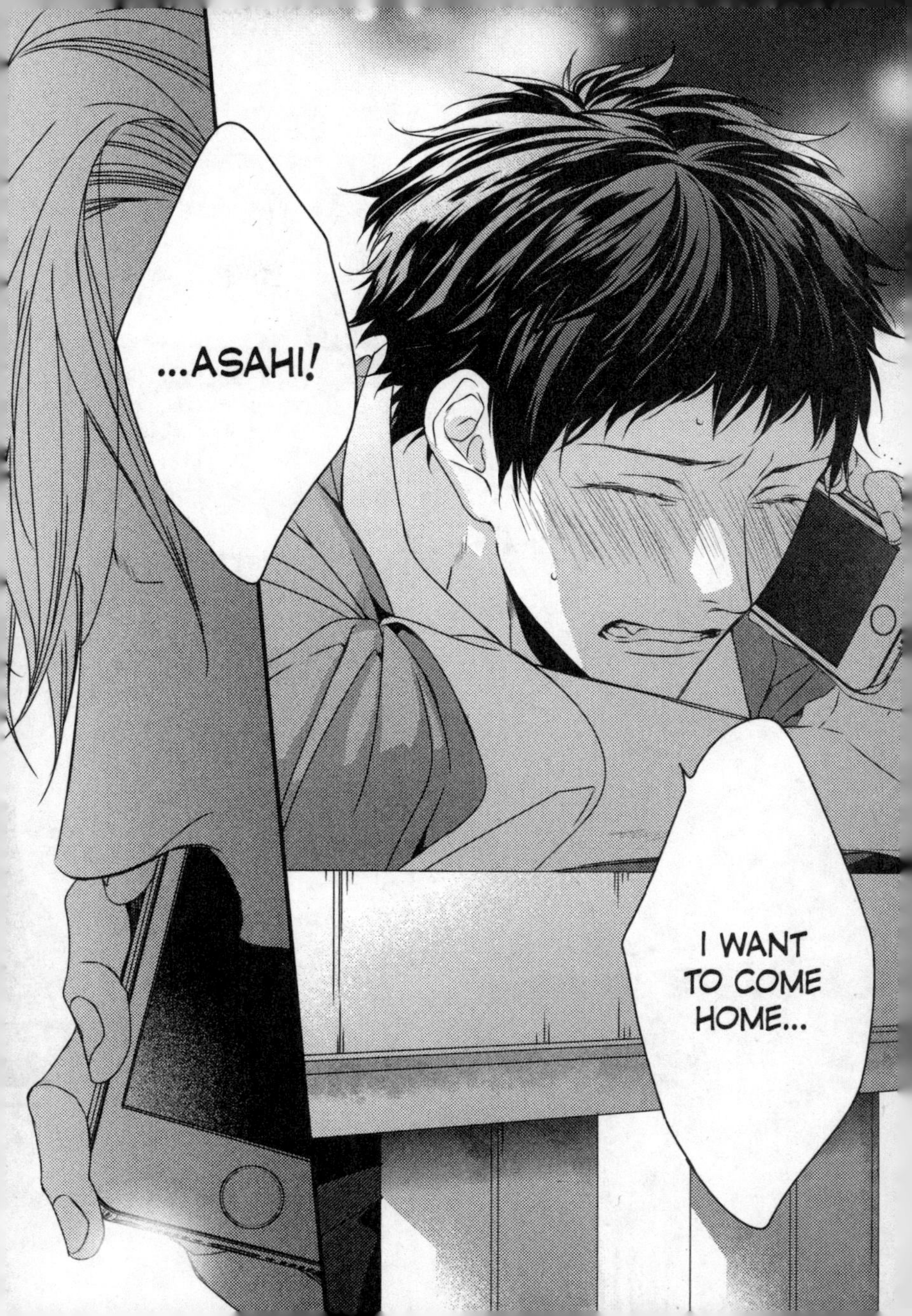
...ASAHI!
I WANT TO COME HOME...

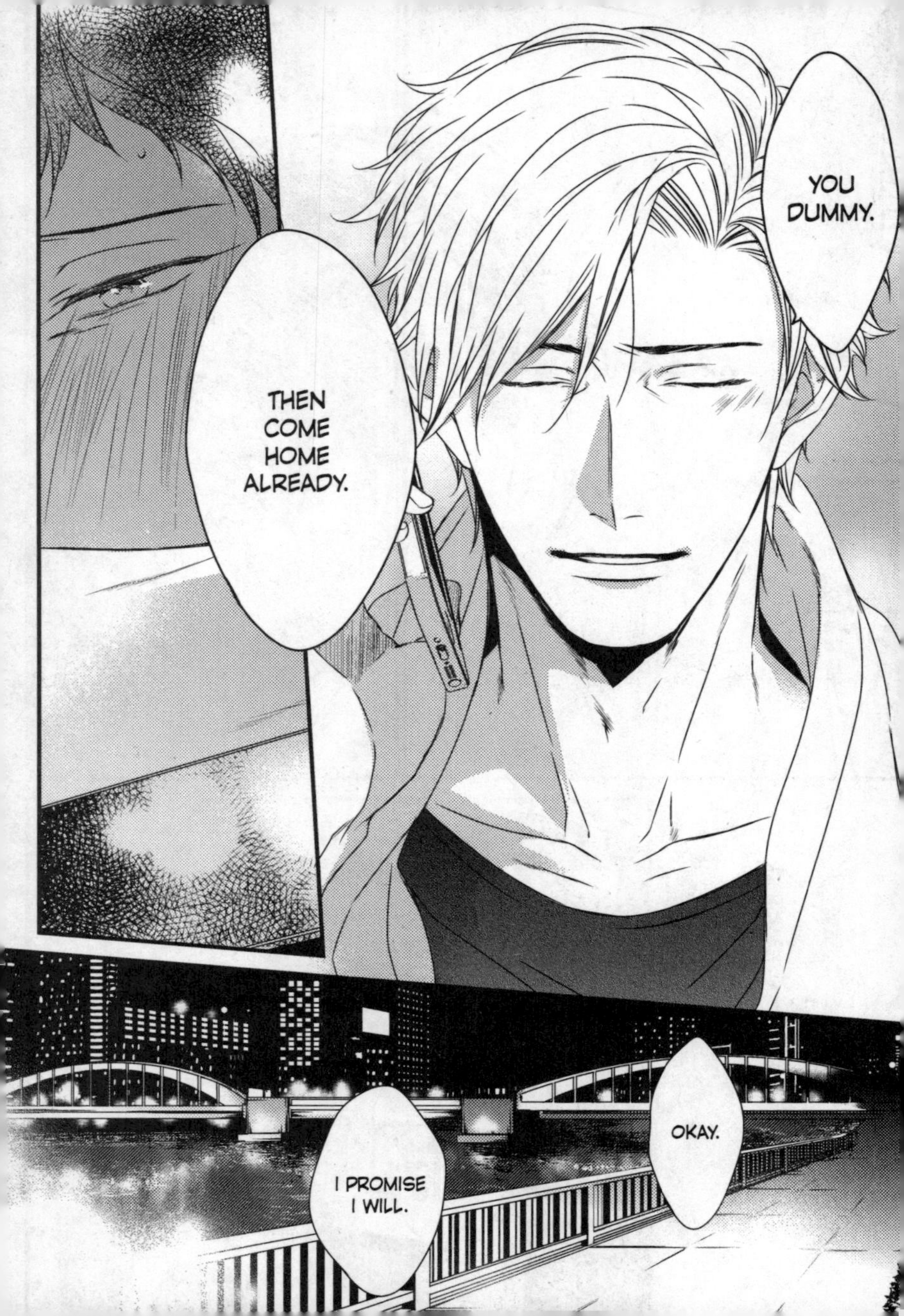
YOU DUMMY.
THEN COME HOME ALREADY.
OKAY.
I PROMISE I WILL.

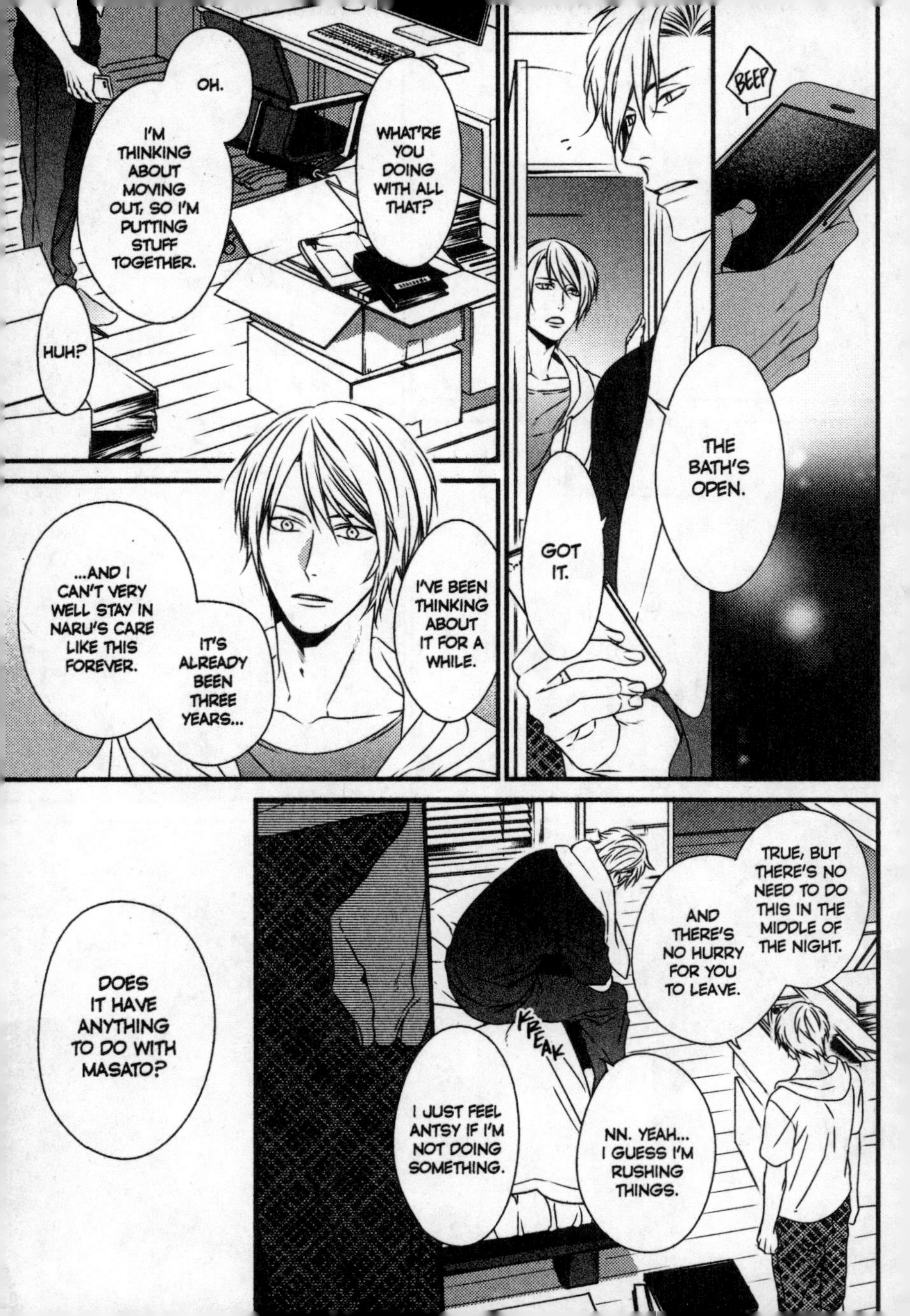
BEEP
THE BATH'S OPEN.
GOT IT.
WHAT'RE YOU DOING WITH ALL THAT?
OH.
I'M THINKING ABOUT MOVING OUT, SO I'M PUTTING STUFF TOGETHER.
HUH?
I'VE BEEN THINKING ABOUT IT FOR A WHILE.
IT'S ALREADY BEEN THREE YEARS...
...AND I CAN'T VERY WELL STAY IN NARU'S CARE LIKE THIS FOREVER.
TRUE, BUT THERE'S NO NEED TO DO THIS IN THE MIDDLE OF THE NIGHT.
AND THERE'S NO HURRY FOR YOU TO LEAVE.
KREAK
NN. YEAH... I GUESS I'M RUSHING THINGS.
I JUST FEEL ANTSY IF I'M NOT DOING SOMETHING.
DOES IT HAVE ANYTHING TO DO WITH MASATO?

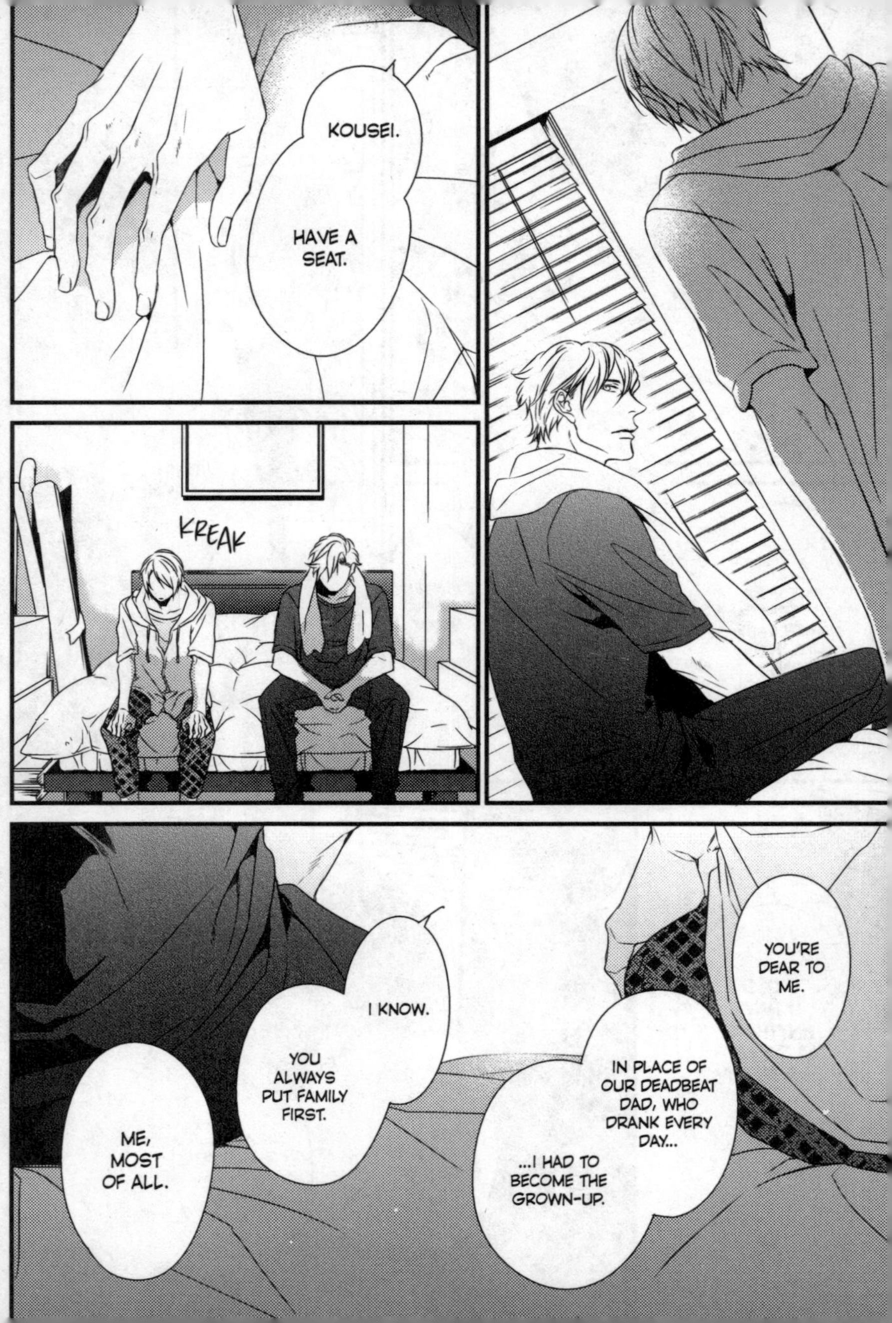
KOUSEI.
HAVE A SEAT.
KREAK
YOU'RE DEAR TO ME.
IN PLACE OF OUR DEADBEAT DAD, WHO DRANK EVERY DAY...
...I HAD TO BECOME THE GROWN-UP.
I KNOW.
YOU ALWAYS PUT FAMILY FIRST.
ME, MOST OF ALL.

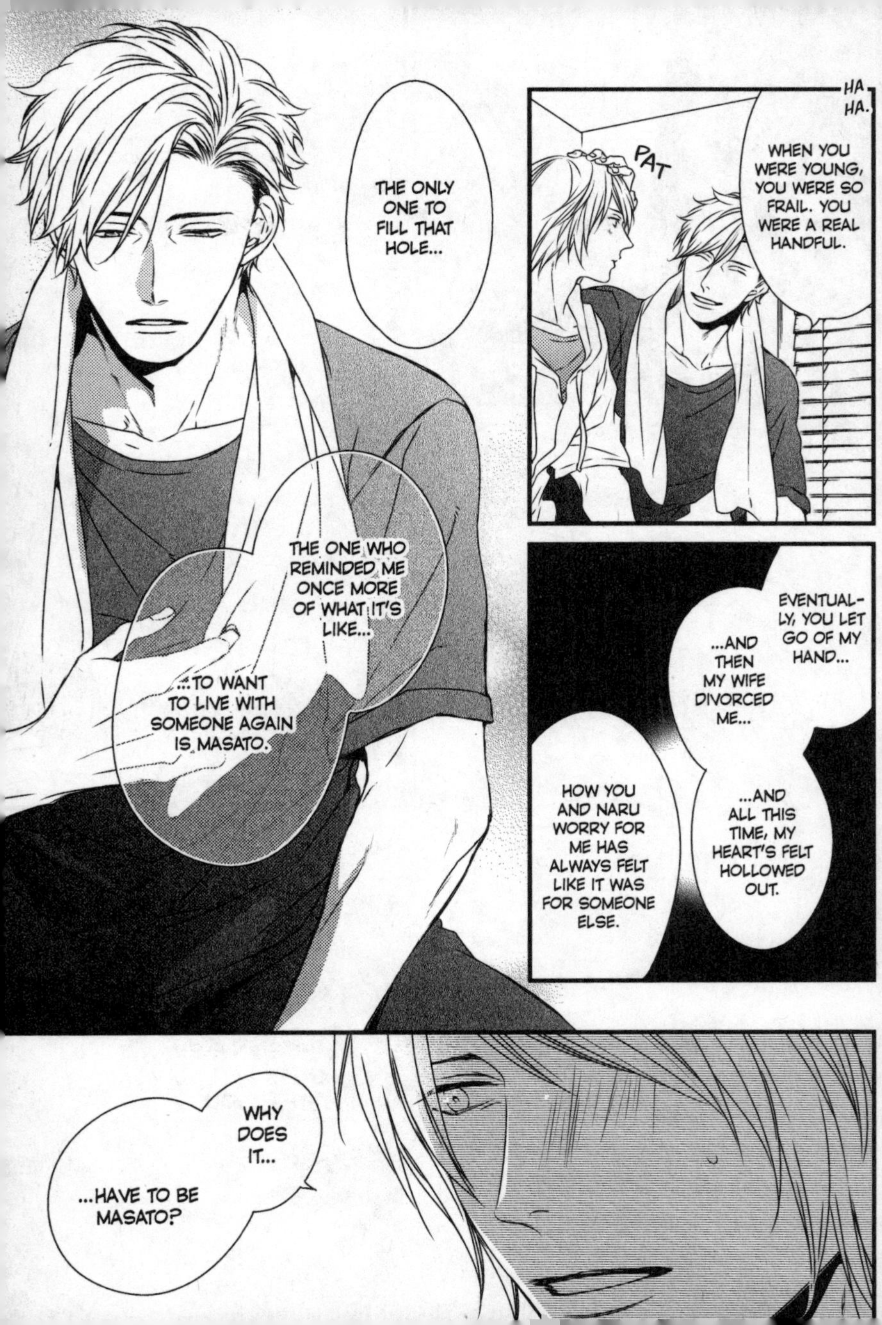
HA HA.
PAT
WHEN YOU WERE YOUNG, YOU WERE SO FRAIL. YOU WERE A REAL HANDFUL.
EVENTUAL-LY, YOU LET GO OF MY HAND...
...AND THEN MY WIFE DIVORCED ME...
...AND ALL THIS TIME, MY HEART'S FELT HOLLOWED OUT.
HOW YOU AND NARU WORRY FOR ME HAS ALWAYS FELT LIKE IT WAS FOR SOMEONE ELSE.
THE ONLY ONE TO FILL THAT HOLE...
THE ONE WHO REMINDED ME ONCE MORE OF WHAT IT'S LIKE...
...TO WANT TO LIVE WITH SOMEONE AGAIN IS MASATO.
WHY DOES IT...
...HAVE TO BE MASATO?

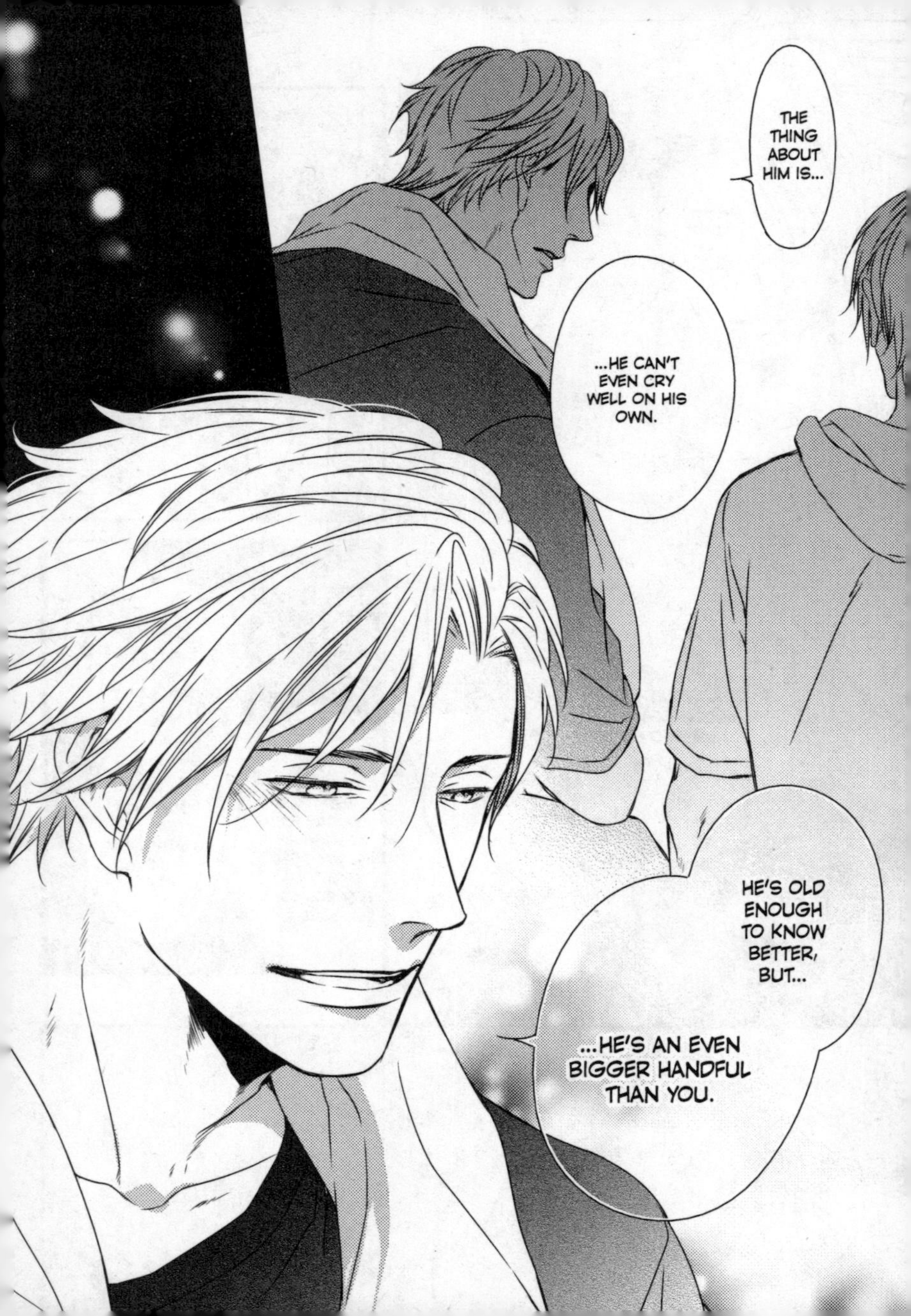
THE THING ABOUT HIM IS...
...HE CAN'T EVEN CRY WELL ON HIS OWN.
HE'S OLD ENOUGH TO KNOW BETTER, BUT...
...HE'S AN EVEN BIGGER HANDFUL THAN YOU.

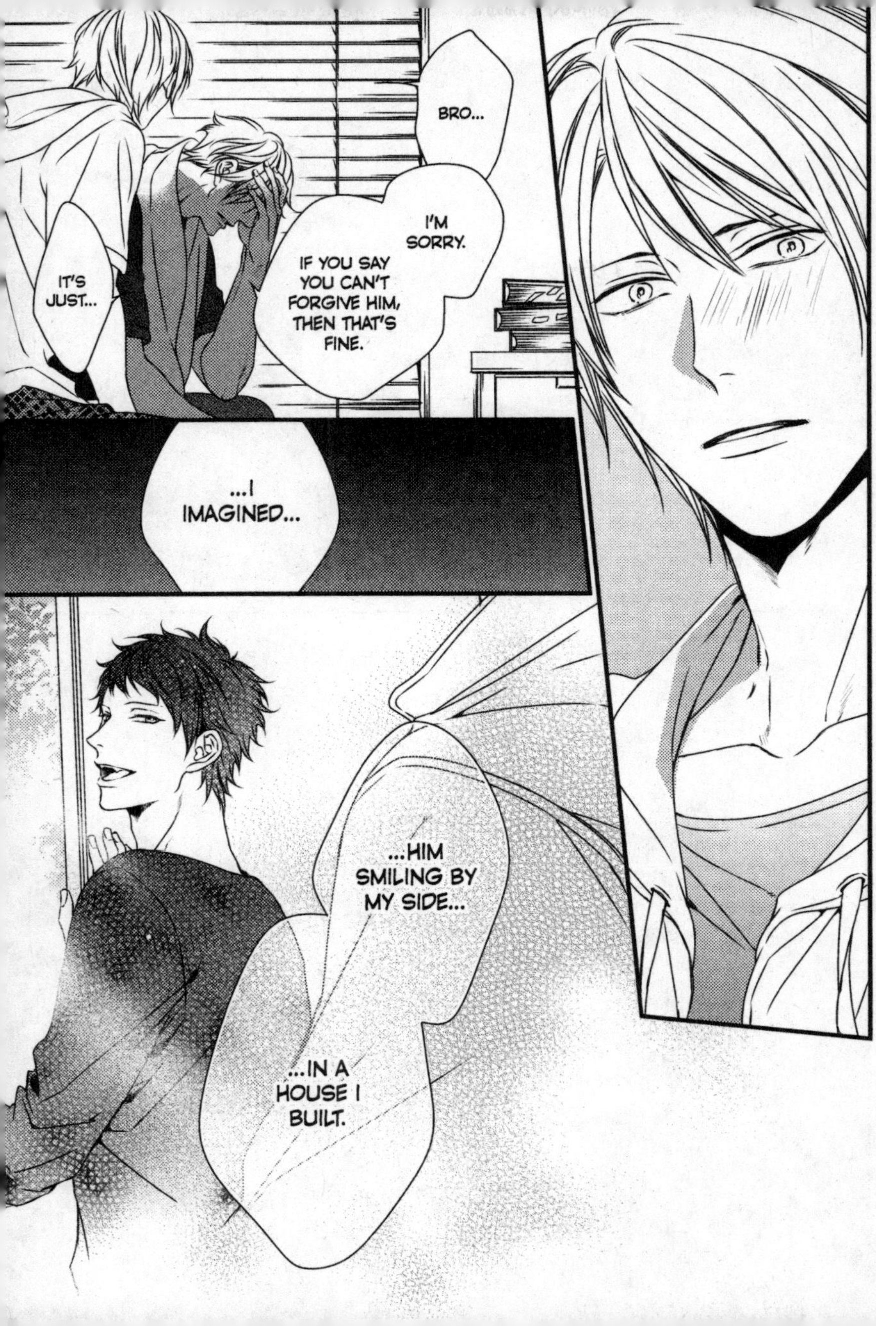
BRO...
I'M SORRY. IF YOU SAY YOU CAN'T FORGIVE HIM, THEN THAT'S FINE.
IT'S JUST...
...I IMAGINED...
...HIM SMILING BY MY SIDE...
...IN A HOUSE I BUILT.

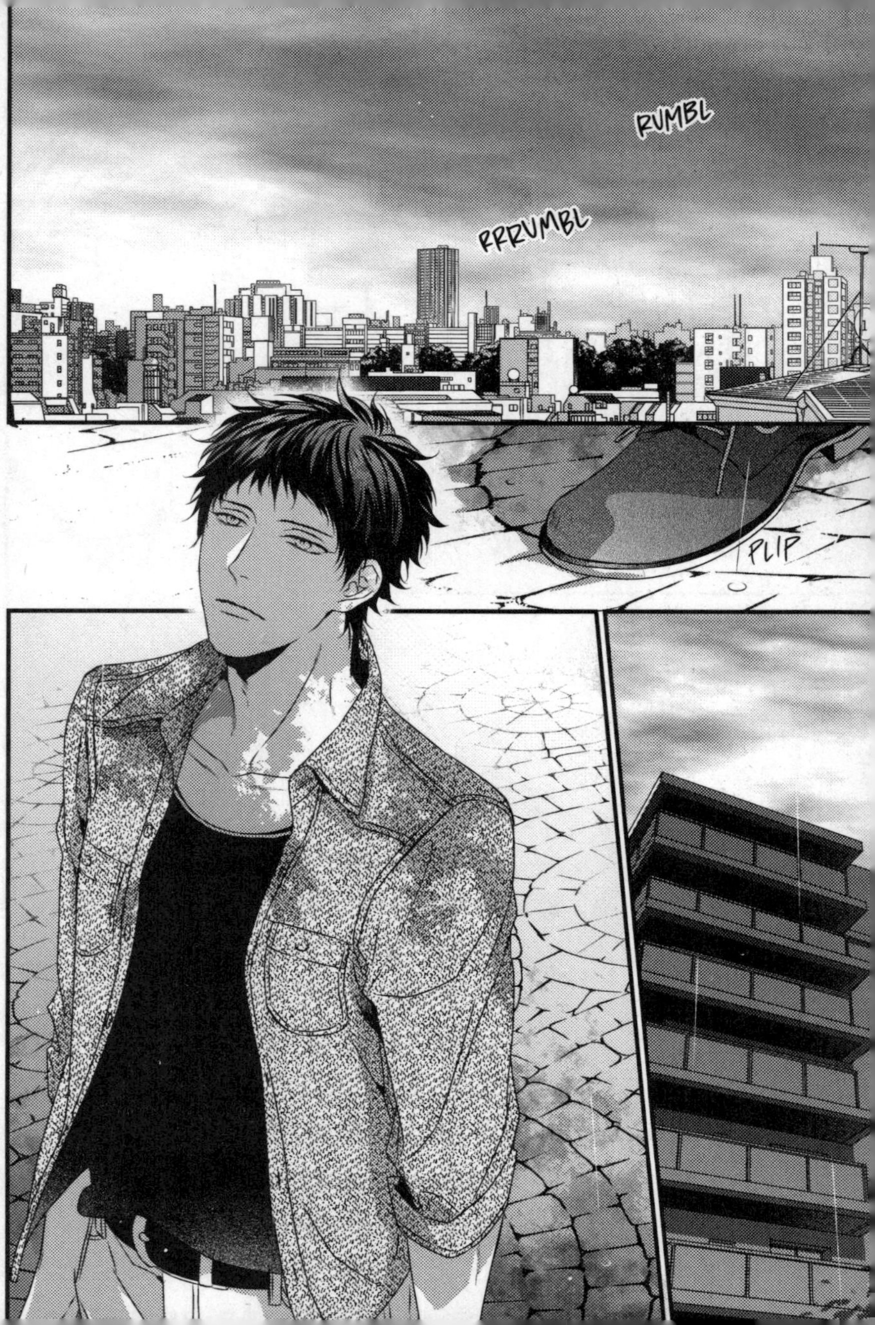
RUMBL
RRRUMBL
PLIP

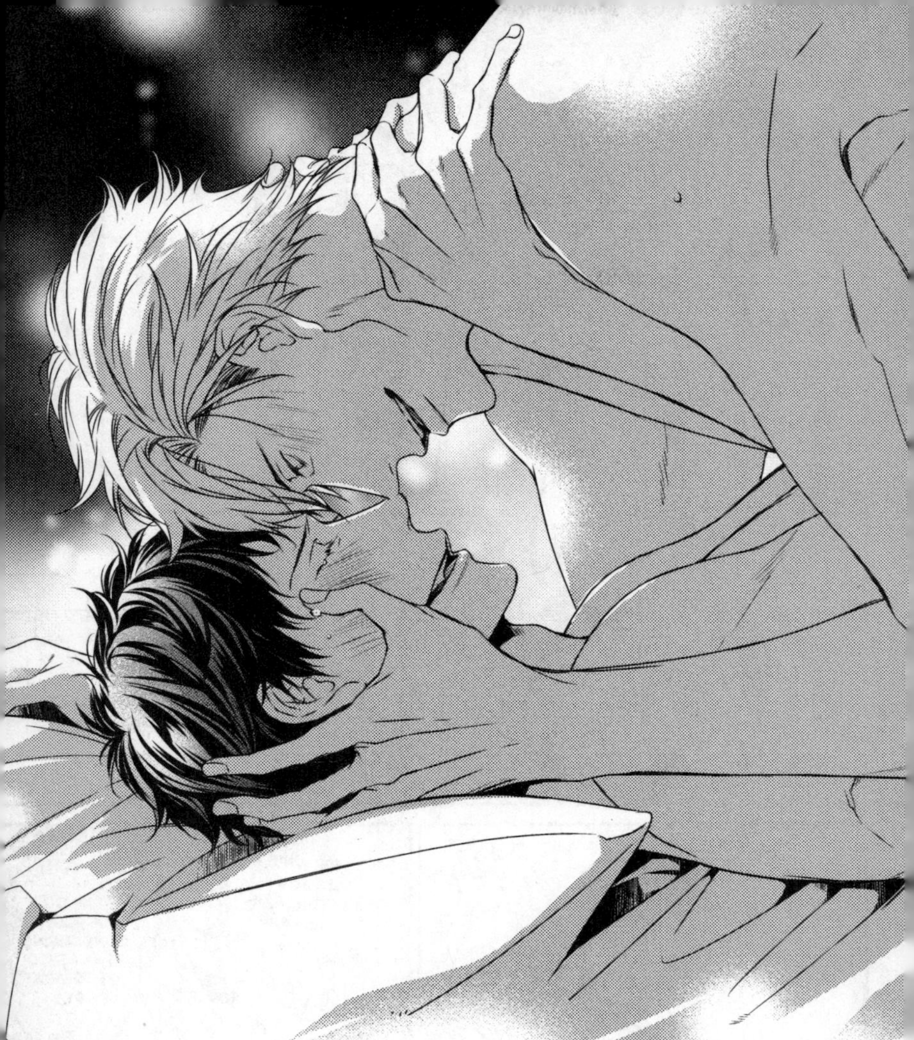

Last Episode

LOVE NEST

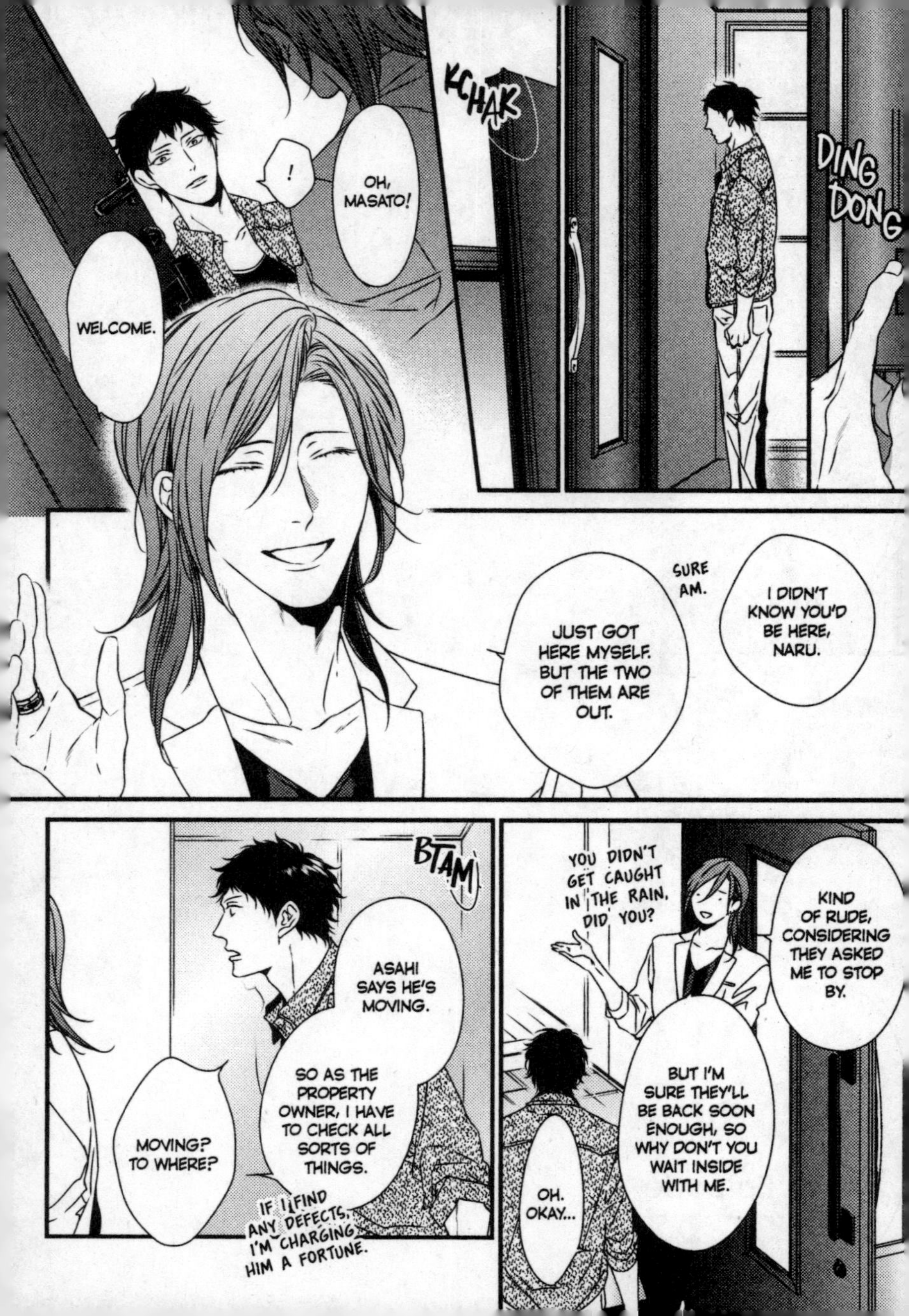
DING DONG
KCHAK
OH, MASATO!
!
WELCOME.
I DIDN'T KNOW YOU'D BE HERE, NARU.
SURE AM.
JUST GOT HERE MYSELF. BUT THE TWO OF THEM ARE OUT.
KIND OF RUDE, CONSIDERING THEY ASKED ME TO STOP BY.
YOU DIDN'T GET CAUGHT IN THE RAIN, DID YOU?
BUT I'M SURE THEY'LL BE BACK SOON ENOUGH, SO WHY DON'T YOU WAIT INSIDE WITH ME.
OH. OKAY...
BTAM
ASAHI SAYS HE'S MOVING.
SO AS THE PROPERTY OWNER, I HAVE TO CHECK ALL SORTS OF THINGS.
IF I FIND ANY DEFECTS, I'M CHARGING HIM A FORTUNE.
MOVING? TO WHERE?

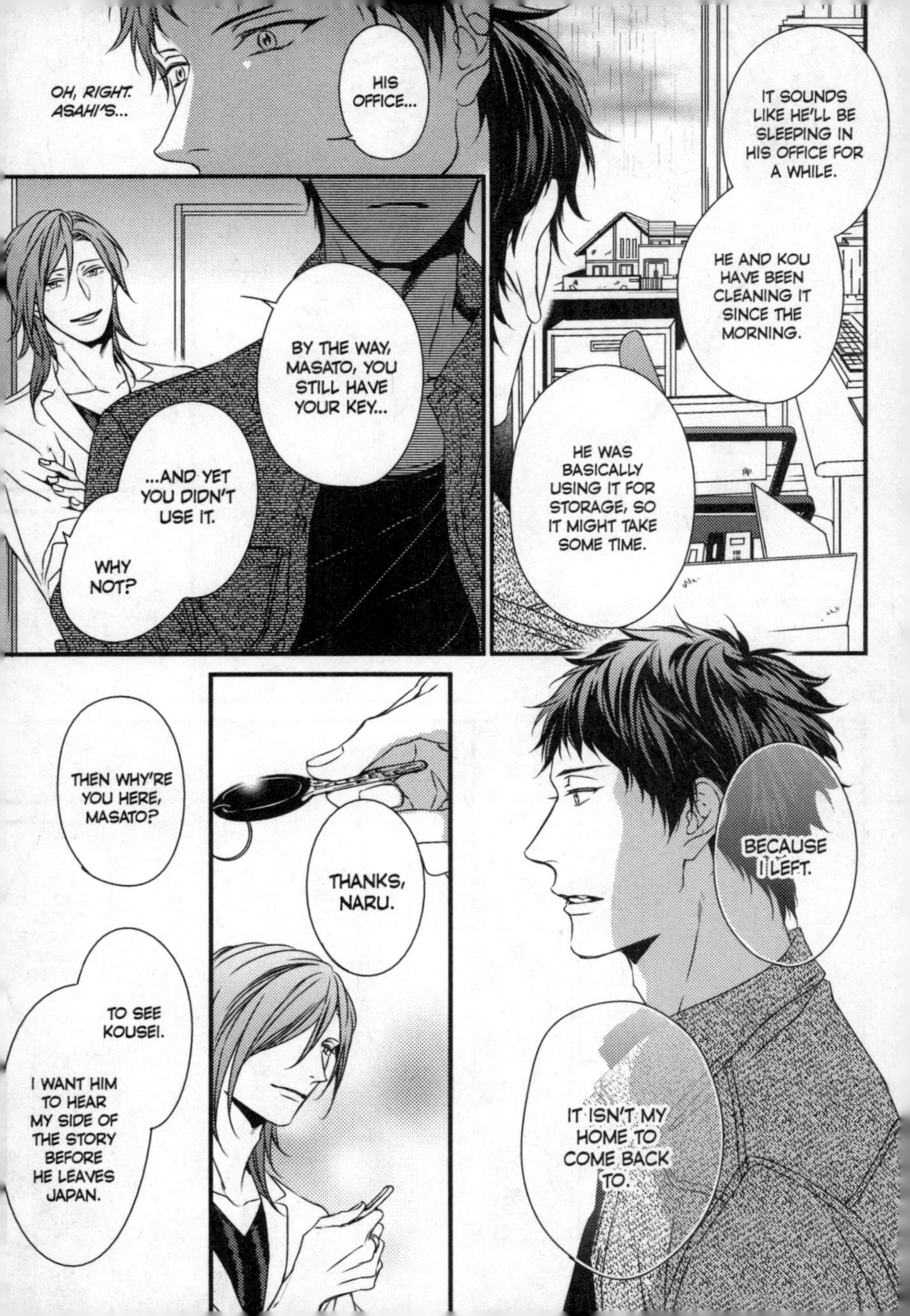
IT SOUNDS LIKE HE'LL BE SLEEPING IN HIS OFFICE FOR A WHILE.
HE AND KOU HAVE BEEN CLEANING IT SINCE THE MORNING.
HE WAS BASICALLY USING IT FOR STORAGE, SO IT MIGHT TAKE SOME TIME.
HIS OFFICE...
OH, RIGHT. ASAHI'S...
BY THE WAY, MASATO, YOU STILL HAVE YOUR KEY...
...AND YET YOU DIDN'T USE IT.
WHY NOT?
BECAUSE I LEFT.
IT ISN'T MY HOME TO COME BACK TO.
THANKS, NARU.
THEN WHY'RE YOU HERE, MASATO?
TO SEE KOUSEI.
I WANT HIM TO HEAR MY SIDE OF THE STORY BEFORE HE LEAVES JAPAN.

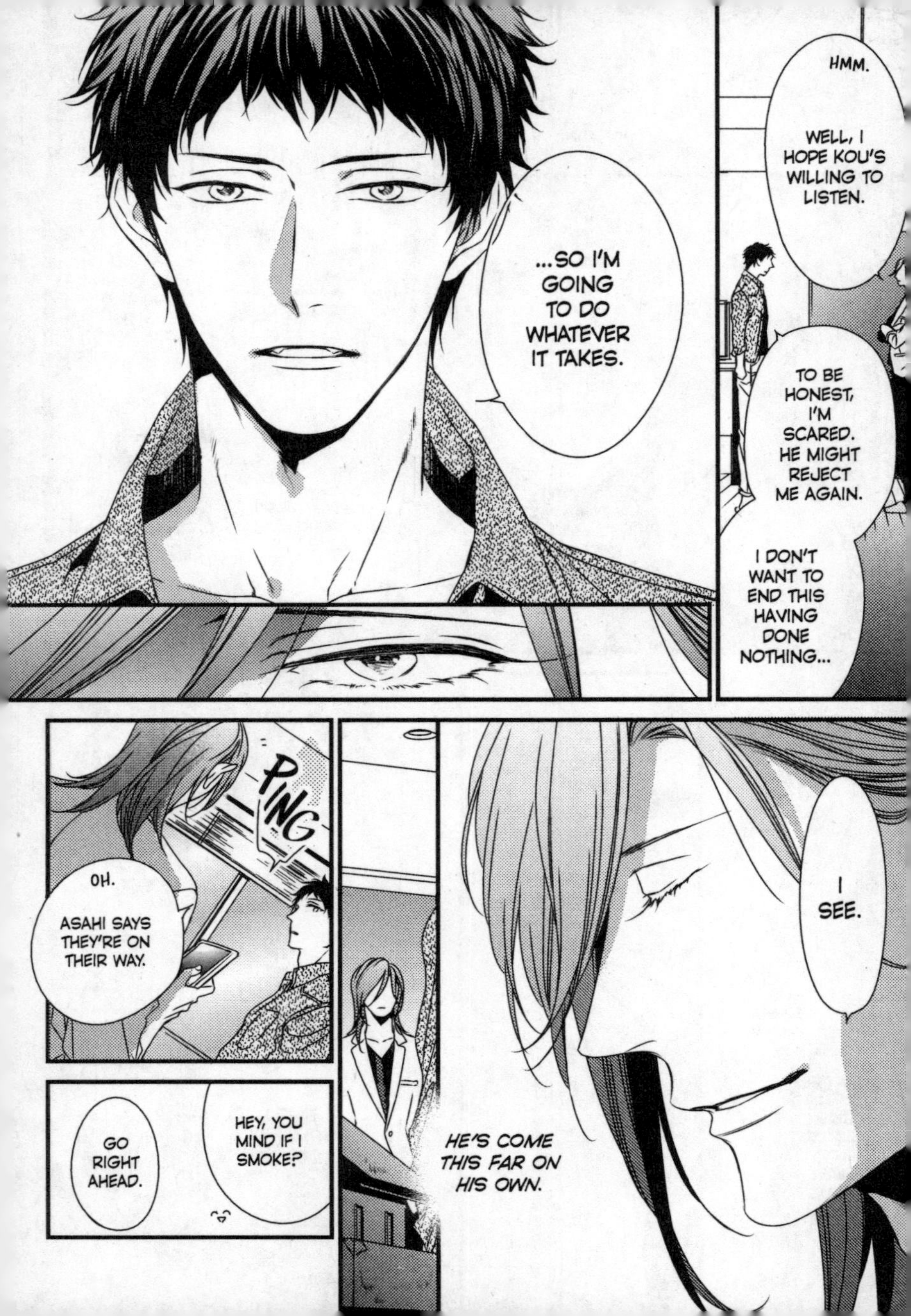
HMM.
WELL, I HOPE KOU'S WILLING TO LISTEN.
TO BE HONEST, I'M SCARED. HE MIGHT REJECT ME AGAIN.
I DON'T WANT TO END THIS HAVING DONE NOTHING...
...SO I'M GOING TO DO WHATEVER IT TAKES.
I SEE.
HE'S COME THIS FAR ON HIS OWN.
PING
OH.
ASAHI SAYS THEY'RE ON THEIR WAY.
HEY, YOU MIND IF I SMOKE?
GO RIGHT AHEAD.

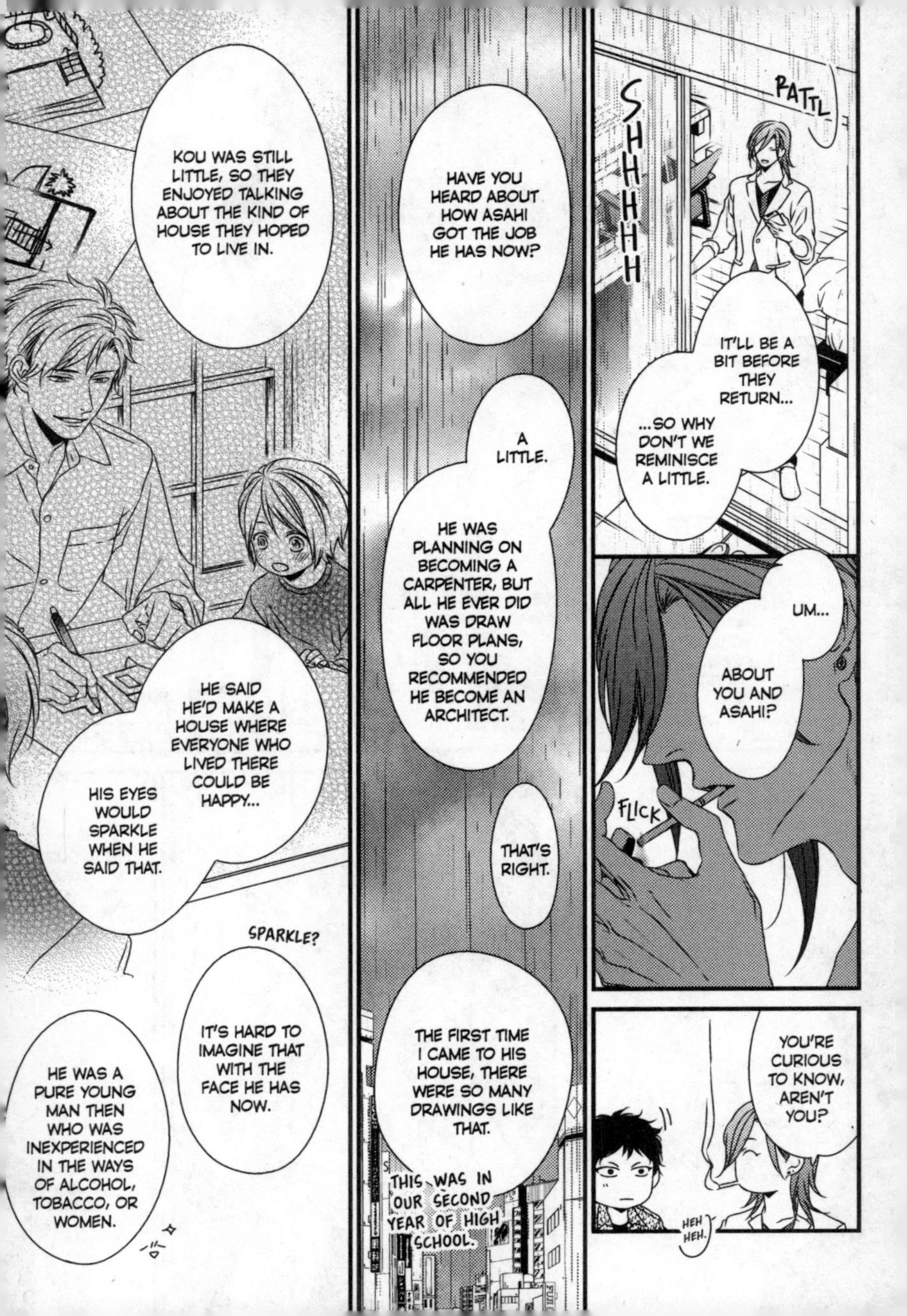
RATTL
SHHHHH
IT'LL BE A BIT BEFORE THEY RETURN...
...SO WHY DON'T WE REMINISCE A LITTLE.
UM...
ABOUT YOU AND ASAHI?
FLICK
YOU'RE CURIOUS TO KNOW, AREN'T YOU?
HEH HEH.
HAVE YOU HEARD ABOUT HOW ASAHI GOT THE JOB HE HAS NOW?
A LITTLE.
HE WAS PLANNING ON BECOMING A CARPENTER, BUT ALL HE EVER DID WAS DRAW FLOOR PLANS, SO YOU RECOMMENDED HE BECOME AN ARCHITECT.
THAT'S RIGHT.
THE FIRST TIME I CAME TO HIS HOUSE, THERE WERE SO MANY DRAWINGS LIKE THAT.
THIS WAS IN OUR SECOND YEAR OF HIGH SCHOOL.
KOU WAS STILL LITTLE, SO THEY ENJOYED TALKING ABOUT THE KIND OF HOUSE THEY HOPED TO LIVE IN.
HE SAID HE'D MAKE A HOUSE WHERE EVERYONE WHO LIVED THERE COULD BE HAPPY...
HIS EYES WOULD SPARKLE WHEN HE SAID THAT.
SPARKLE?
IT'S HARD TO IMAGINE THAT WITH THE FACE HE HAS NOW.
HE WAS A PURE YOUNG MAN THEN WHO WAS INEXPERIENCED IN THE WAYS OF ALCOHOL, TOBACCO, OR WOMEN.

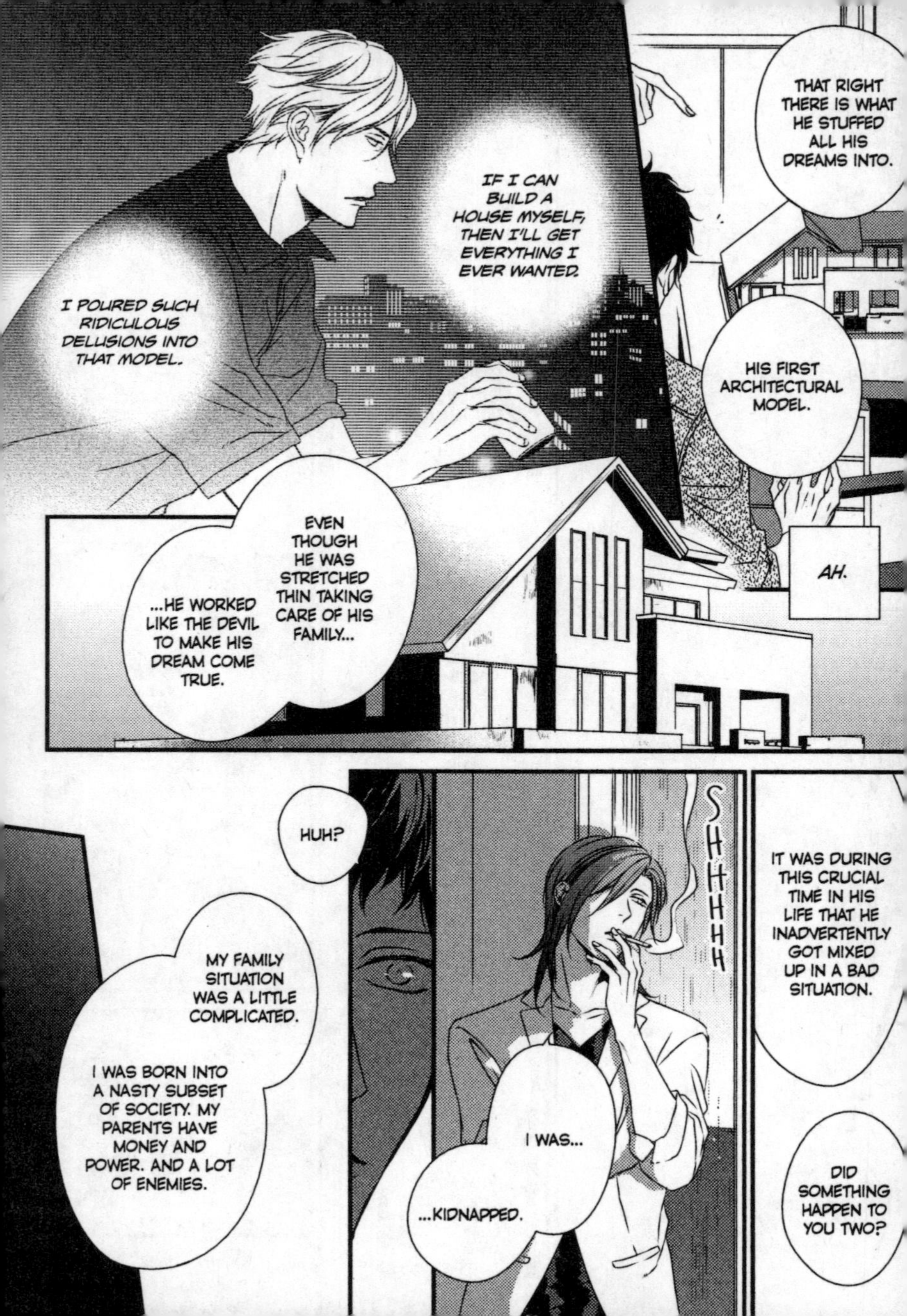
THAT RIGHT THERE IS WHAT HE STUFFED ALL HIS DREAMS INTO.
HIS FIRST ARCHITECTURAL MODEL.
AH.
IF I CAN BUILD A HOUSE MYSELF, THEN I'LL GET EVERYTHING I EVER WANTED.
I POURED SUCH RIDICULOUS DELUSIONS INTO THAT MODEL.
EVEN THOUGH HE WAS STRETCHED THIN TAKING CARE OF HIS FAMILY...
...HE WORKED LIKE THE DEVIL TO MAKE HIS DREAM COME TRUE.
IT WAS DURING THIS CRUCIAL TIME IN HIS LIFE THAT HE INADVERTENTLY GOT MIXED UP IN A BAD SITUATION.
DID SOMETHING HAPPEN TO YOU TWO?
SHHHHH
I WAS...
...KIDNAPPED.
HUH?
MY FAMILY SITUATION WAS A LITTLE COMPLICATED.
I WAS BORN INTO A NASTY SUBSET OF SOCIETY. MY PARENTS HAVE MONEY AND POWER. AND A LOT OF ENEMIES.

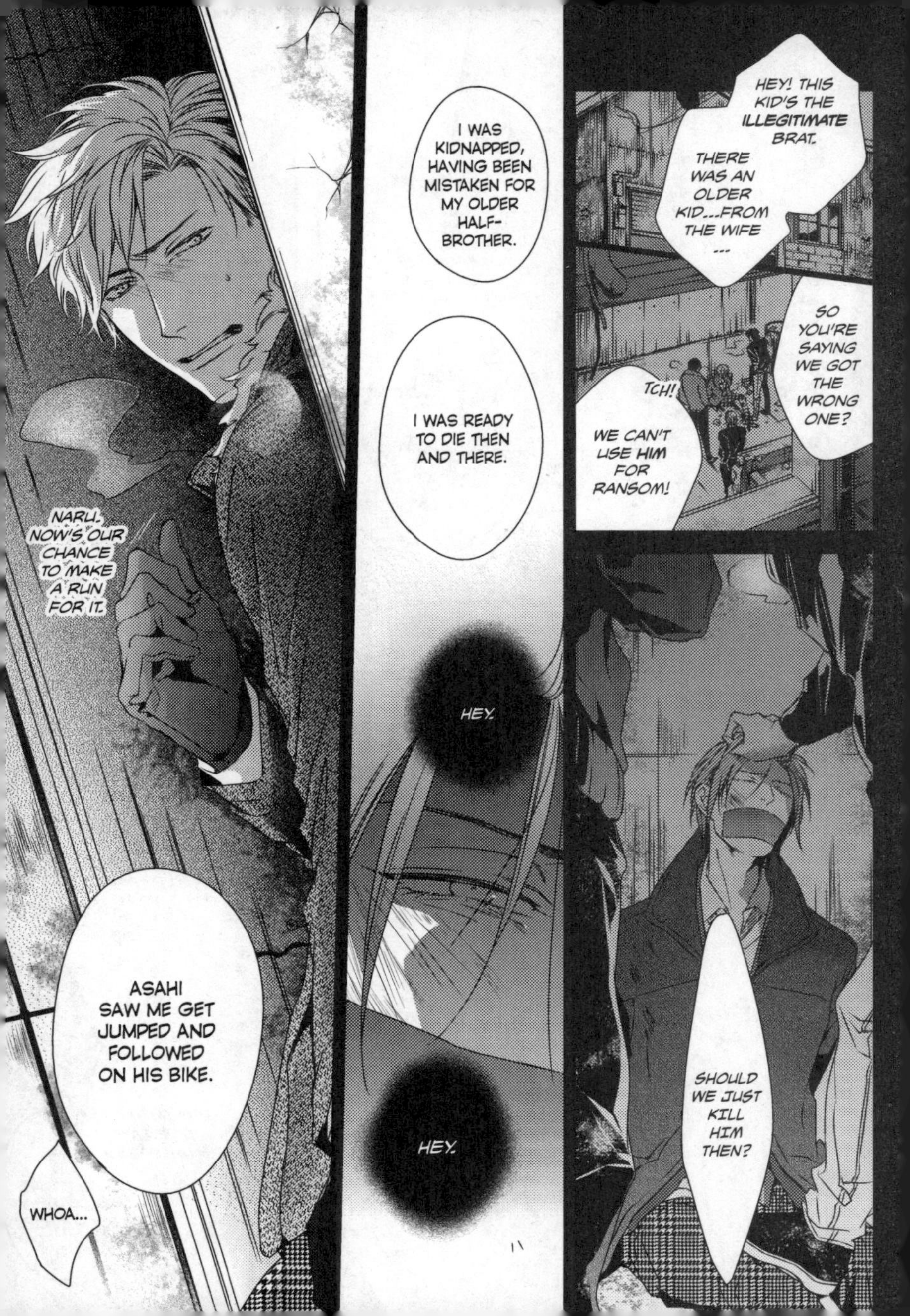
HEY! THIS KID'S THE ILLEGITIMATE BRAT.
THERE WAS AN OLDER KID...FROM THE WIFE...
SO YOU'RE SAYING WE GOT THE WRONG ONE?
TCH!
WE CAN'T USE HIM FOR RANSOM!
SHOULD WE JUST KILL HIM THEN?
I WAS KIDNAPPED, HAVING BEEN MISTAKEN FOR MY OLDER HALF-BROTHER.
I WAS READY TO DIE THEN AND THERE.
HEY.
HEY.
NARU. NOW'S OUR CHANCE TO MAKE A RUN FOR IT.
ASAHI SAW ME GET JUMPED AND FOLLOWED ON HIS BIKE.
WHOA...

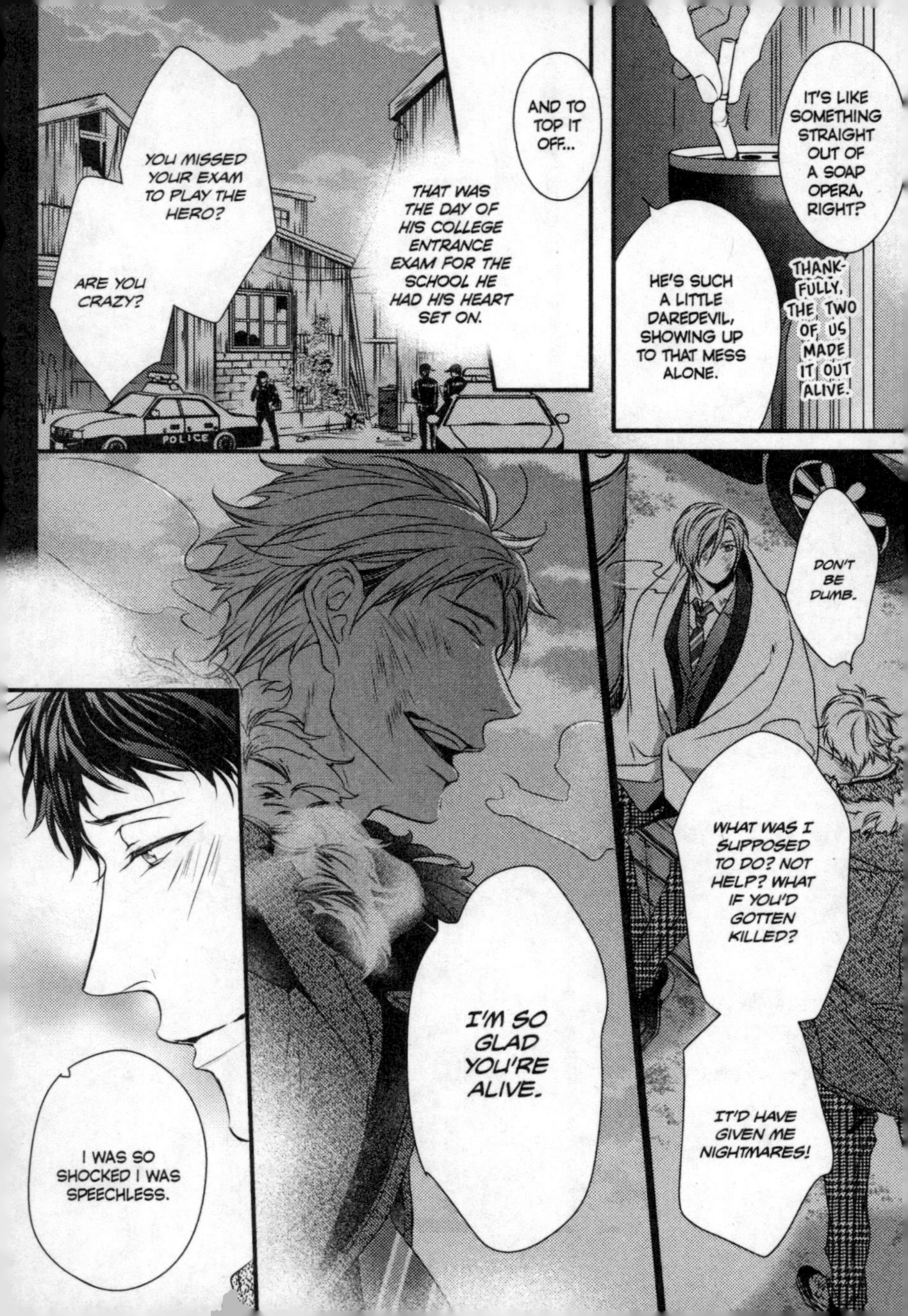
IT'S LIKE SOMETHING STRAIGHT OUT OF A SOAP OPERA, RIGHT?
HE'S SUCH A LITTLE DAREDEVIL, SHOWING UP TO THAT MESS ALONE.
THANK-FULLY, THE TWO OF US MADE IT OUT ALIVE.
AND TO TOP IT OFF...
THAT WAS THE DAY OF HIS COLLEGE ENTRANCE EXAM FOR THE SCHOOL HE HAD HIS HEART SET ON.
YOU MISSED YOUR EXAM TO PLAY THE HERO?
ARE YOU CRAZY?
POLICE
DON'T BE DUMB.
WHAT WAS I SUPPOSED TO DO? NOT HELP? WHAT IF YOU'D GOTTEN KILLED?
IT'D HAVE GIVEN ME NIGHTMARES!
I'M SO GLAD YOU'RE ALIVE.
I WAS SO SHOCKED I WAS SPEECHLESS.

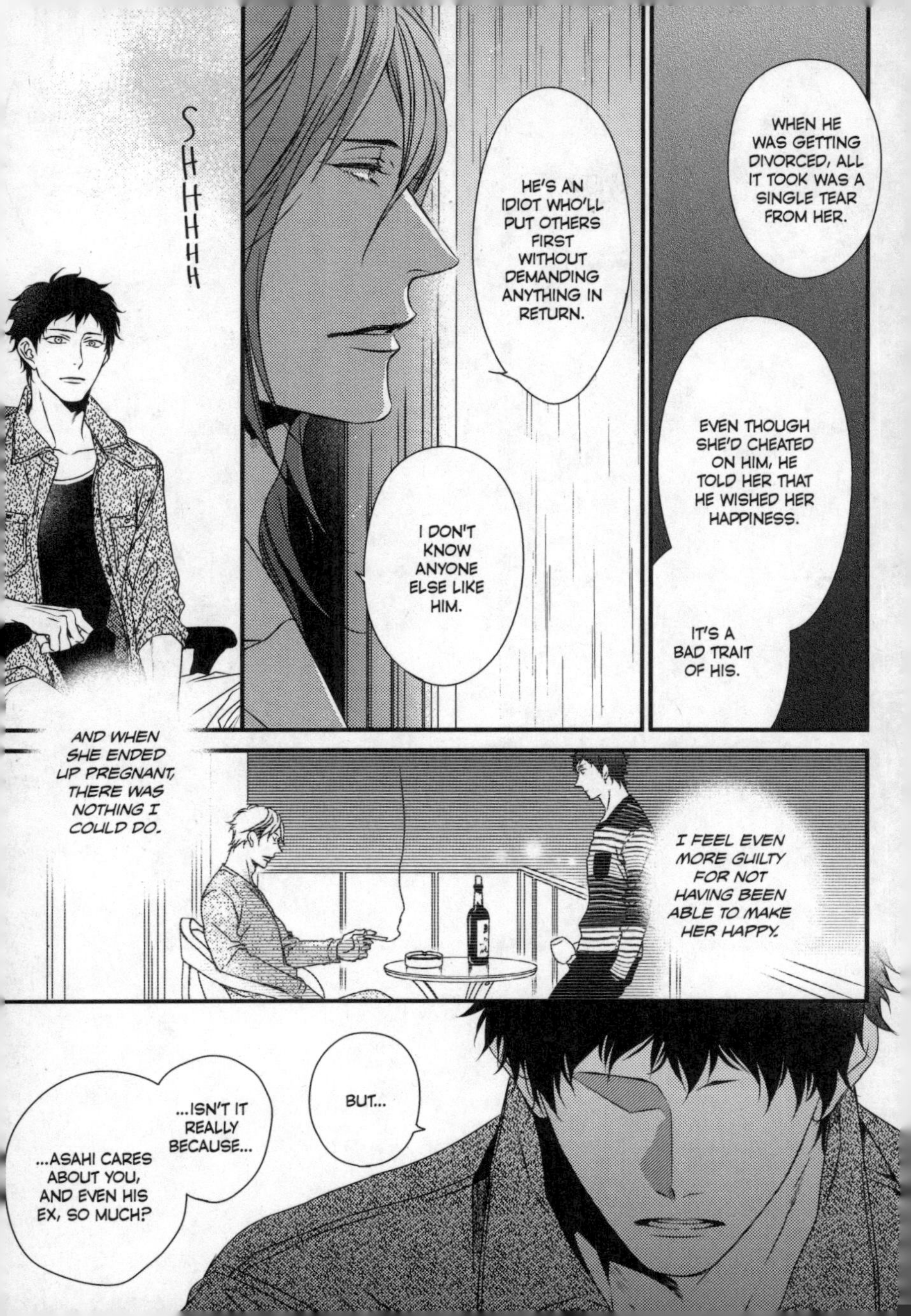
WHEN HE WAS GETTING DIVORCED, ALL IT TOOK WAS A SINGLE TEAR FROM HER.
EVEN THOUGH SHE'D CHEATED ON HIM, HE TOLD HER THAT HE WISHED HER HAPPINESS.
IT'S A BAD TRAIT OF HIS.
HE'S AN IDIOT WHO'LL PUT OTHERS FIRST WITHOUT DEMANDING ANYTHING IN RETURN.
I DON'T KNOW ANYONE ELSE LIKE HIM.
SHHHHH
I FEEL EVEN MORE GUILTY FOR NOT HAVING BEEN ABLE TO MAKE HER HAPPY.
AND WHEN SHE ENDED UP PREGNANT, THERE WAS NOTHING I COULD DO.
BUT...
...ISN'T IT REALLY BECAUSE...
...ASAHI CARES ABOUT YOU, AND EVEN HIS EX, SO MUCH?

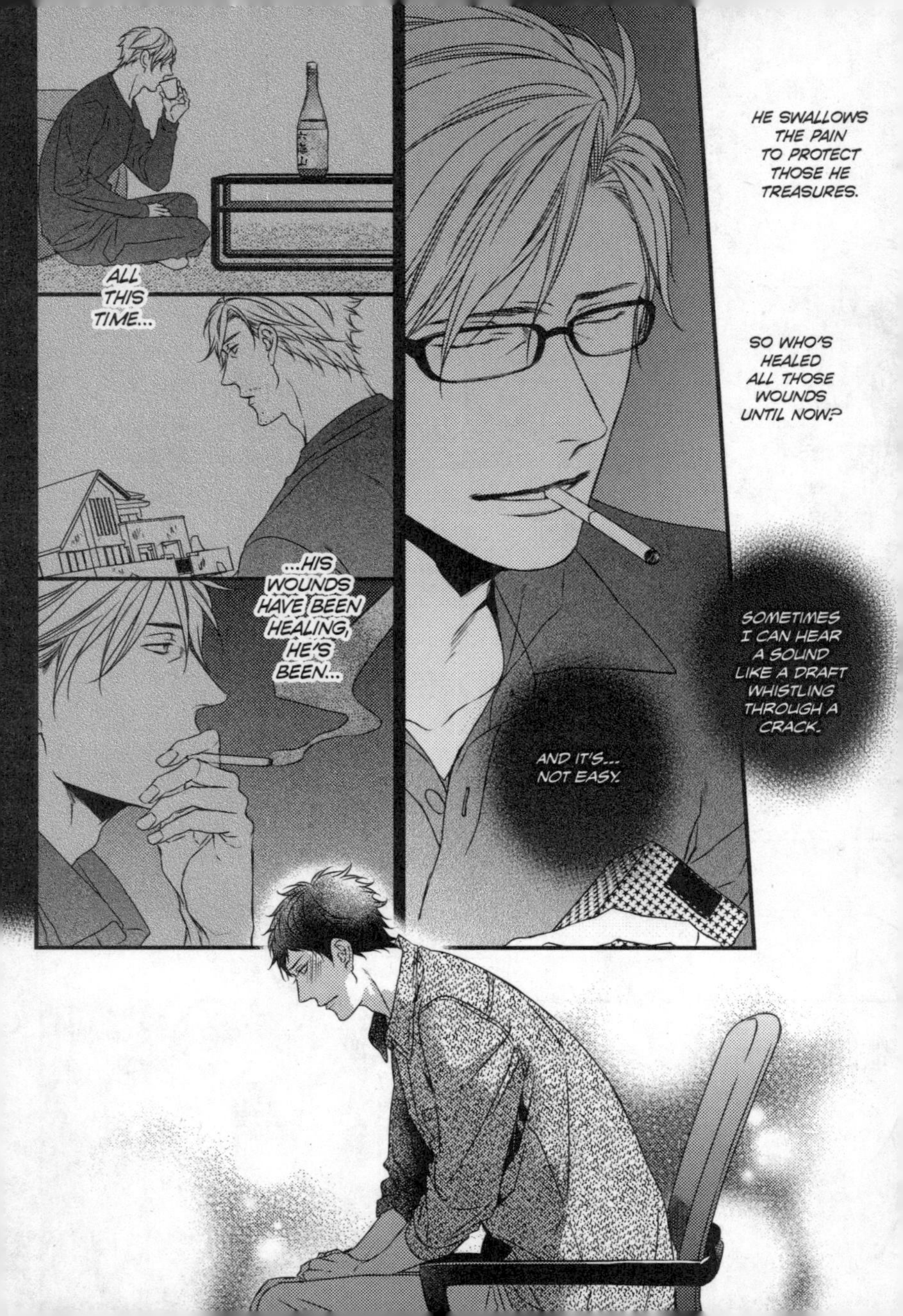
HE SWALLOWS THE PAIN TO PROTECT THOSE HE TREASURES.
SO WHO'S HEALED ALL THOSE WOUNDS UNTIL NOW?
SOMETIMES I CAN HEAR A SOUND LIKE A DRAFT WHISTLING THROUGH A CRACK.
AND IT'S... NOT EASY.
ALL THIS TIME...
...HIS WOUNDS HAVE BEEN HEALING, HE'S BEEN...

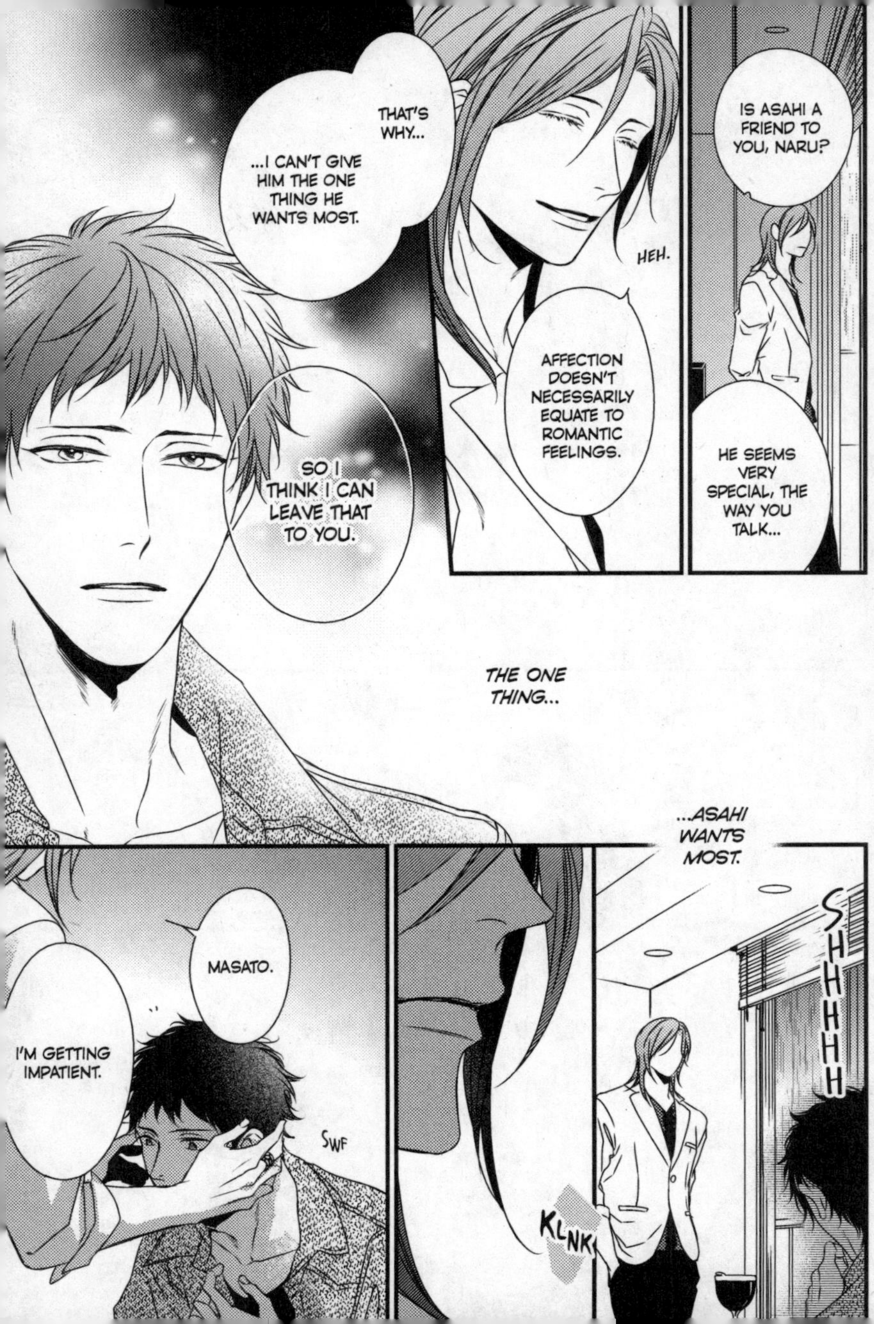
IS ASAHI A FRIEND TO YOU, NARU?
HE SEEMS VERY SPECIAL, THE WAY YOU TALK...
HEH.
AFFECTION DOESN'T NECESSARILY EQUATE TO ROMANTIC FEELINGS.
THAT'S WHY...
...I CAN'T GIVE HIM THE ONE THING HE WANTS MOST.
SO I THINK I CAN LEAVE THAT TO YOU.
THE ONE THING...
...ASAHI WANTS MOST.
SHHHHH
KLNK
MASATO.
I'M GETTING IMPATIENT.
SWF

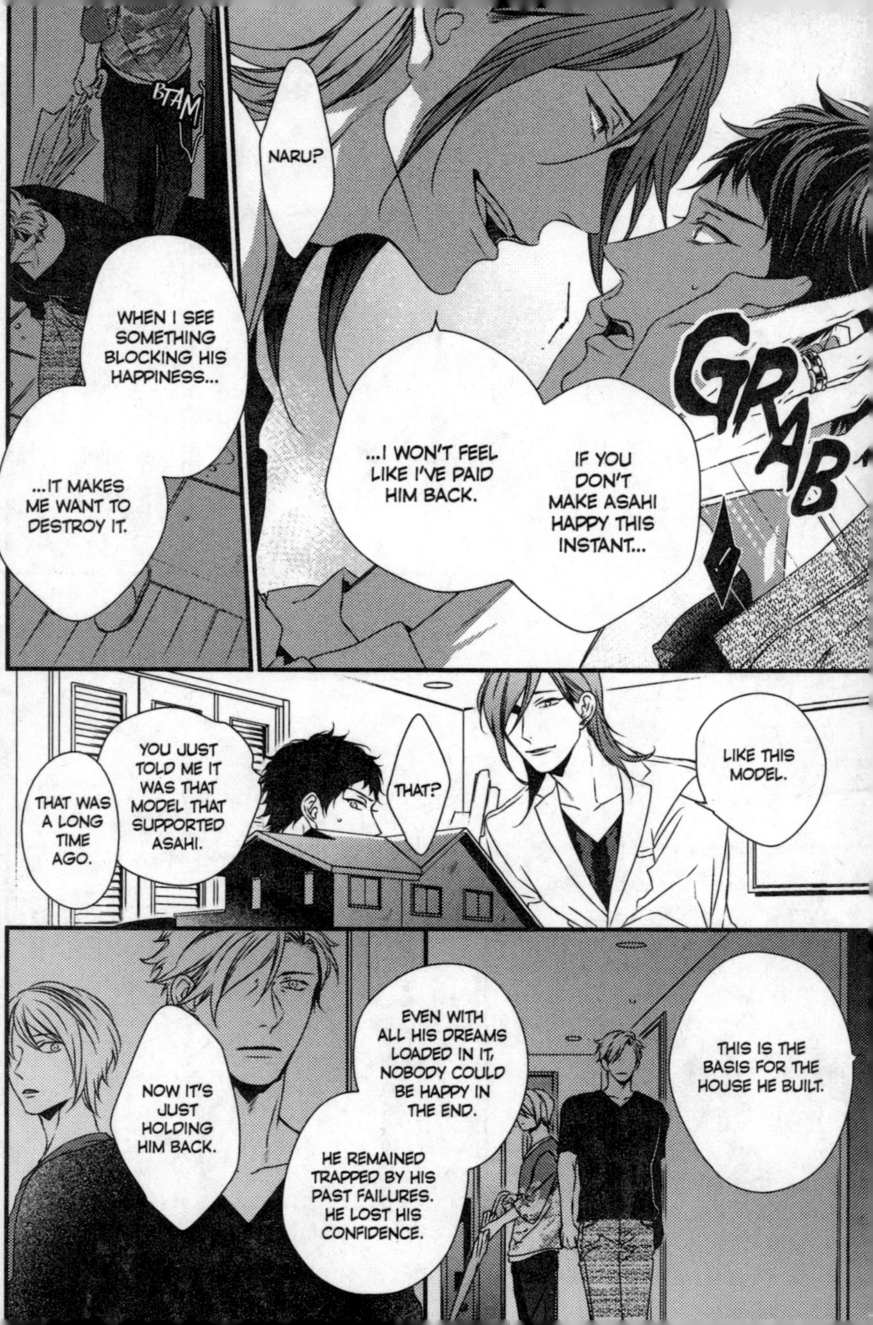
GRAB
NARU?
IF YOU DON'T MAKE ASAHI HAPPY THIS INSTANT...
...I WON'T FEEL LIKE I'VE PAID HIM BACK.
BTAM
WHEN I SEE SOMETHING BLOCKING HIS HAPPINESS...
...IT MAKES ME WANT TO DESTROY IT.
LIKE THIS MODEL.
THAT?
YOU JUST TOLD ME IT WAS THAT MODEL THAT SUPPORTED ASAHI.
THAT WAS A LONG TIME AGO.
THIS IS THE BASIS FOR THE HOUSE HE BUILT.
EVEN WITH ALL HIS DREAMS LOADED IN IT, NOBODY COULD BE HAPPY IN THE END.
HE REMAINED TRAPPED BY HIS PAST FAILURES. HE LOST HIS CONFIDENCE.
NOW IT'S JUST HOLDING HIM BACK.

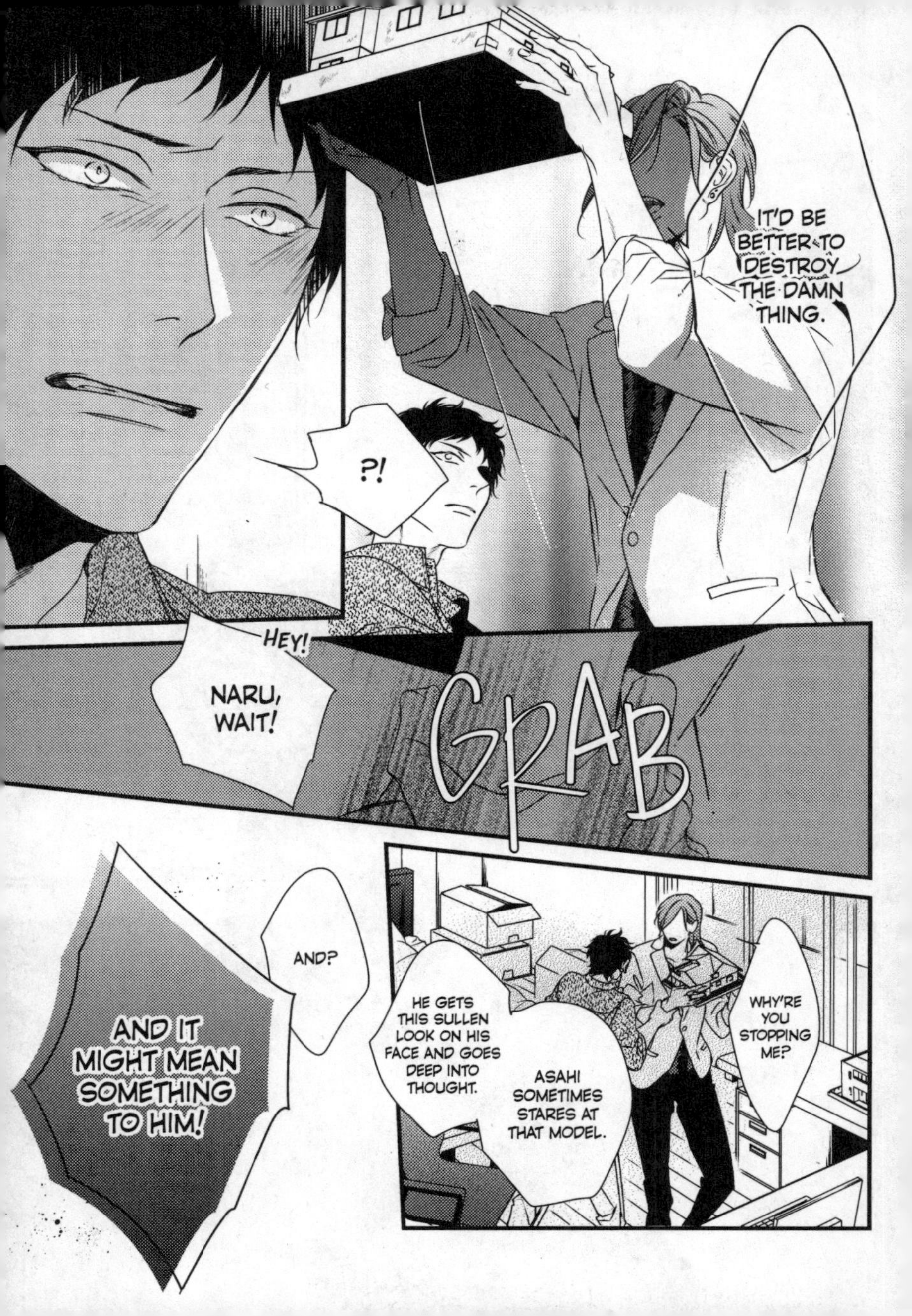
IT'D BE BETTER TO DESTROY THE DAMN THING.
?!
HEY!
NARU, WAIT!
GRAB
WHY'RE YOU STOPPING ME?
ASAHI SOMETIMES STARES AT THAT MODEL.
HE GETS THIS SULLEN LOOK ON HIS FACE AND GOES DEEP INTO THOUGHT.
AND?
AND IT MIGHT MEAN SOMETHING TO HIM!

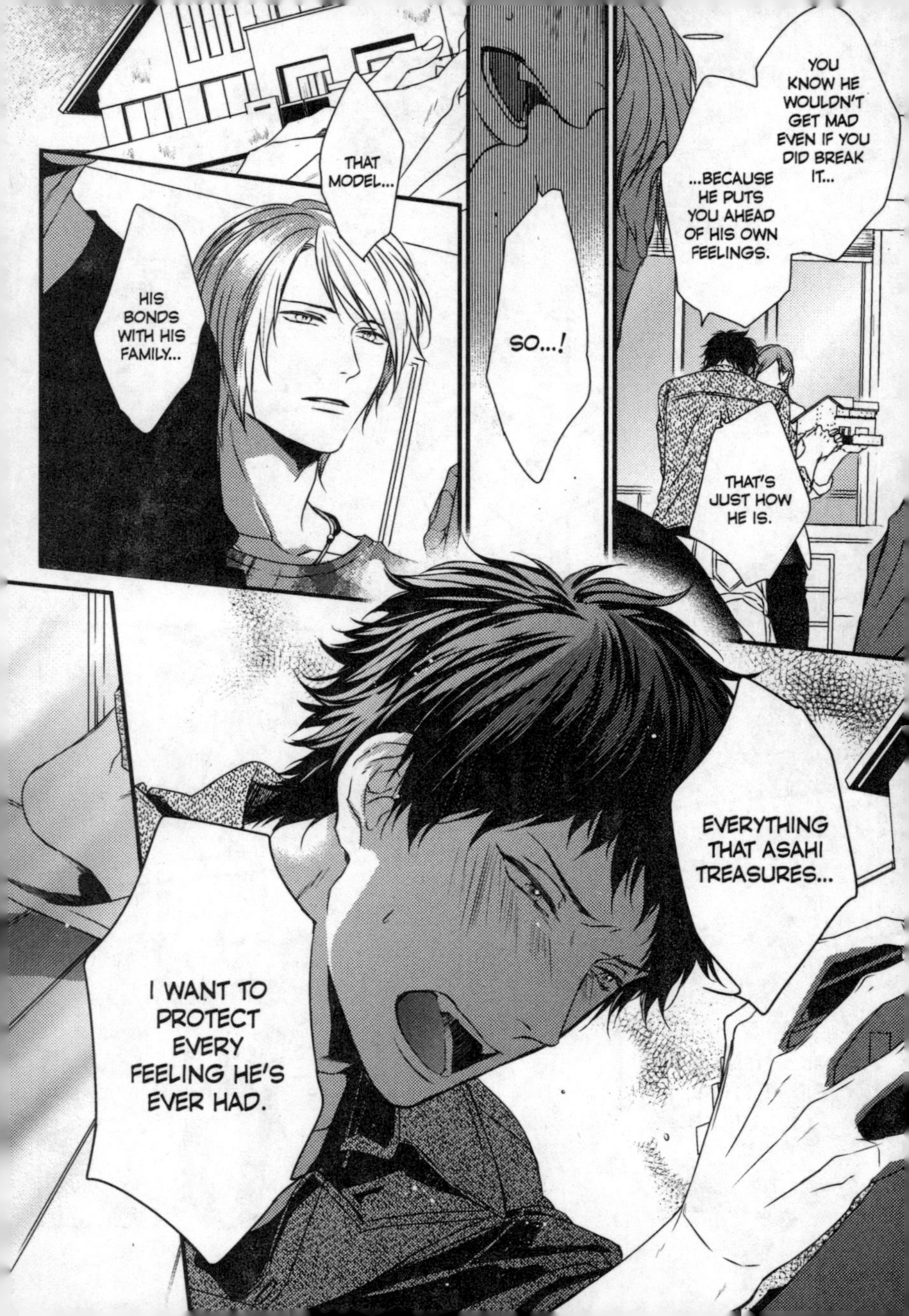
YOU KNOW HE WOULDN'T GET MAD EVEN IF YOU DID BREAK IT...
...BECAUSE HE PUTS YOU AHEAD OF HIS OWN FEELINGS.
THAT'S JUST HOW HE IS.
SO...!
THAT MODEL...
HIS BONDS WITH HIS FAMILY...
EVERYTHING THAT ASAHI TREASURES...
I WANT TO PROTECT EVERY FEELING HE'S EVER HAD.

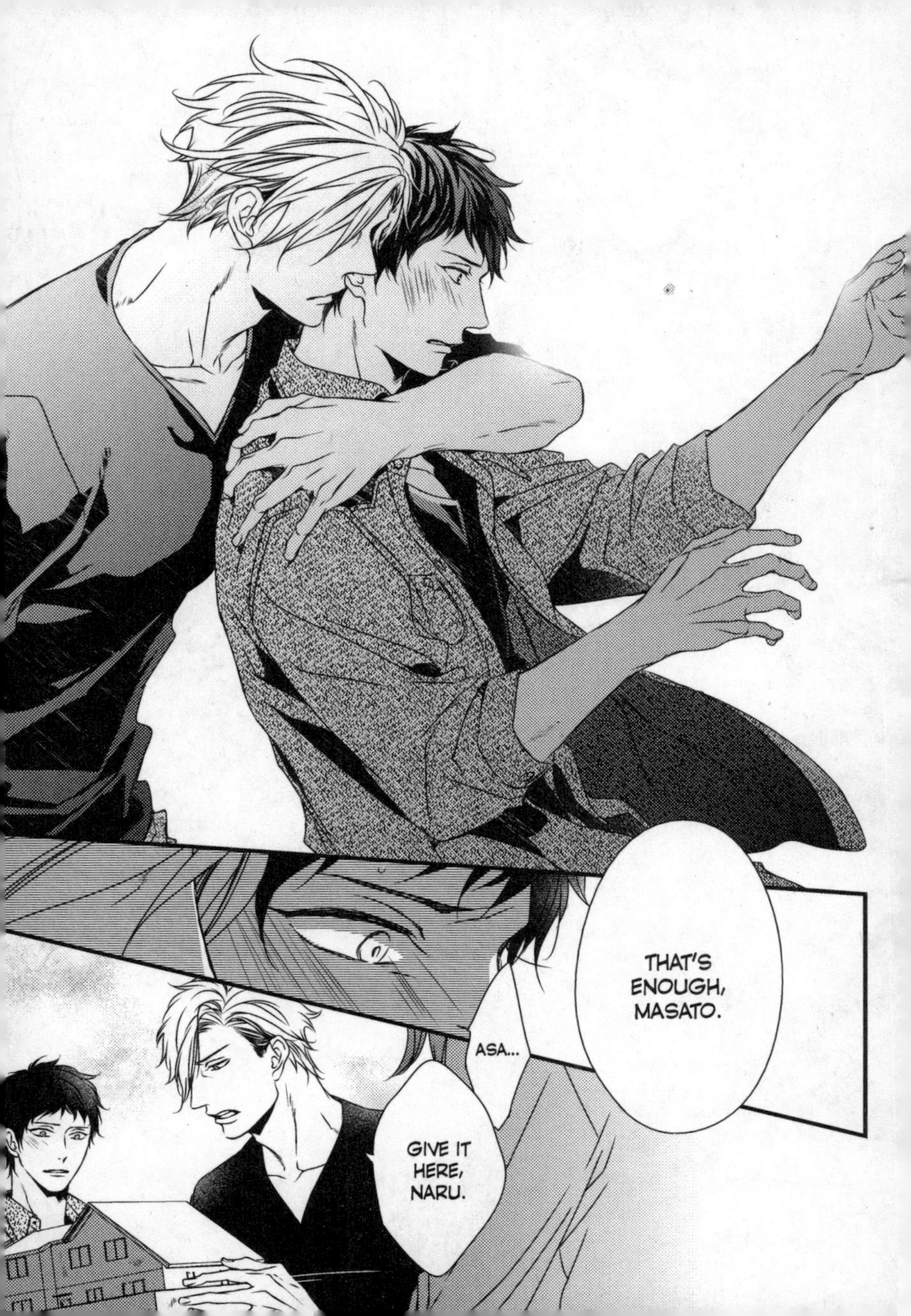
THAT'S ENOUGH, MASATO.
ASA...
GIVE IT HERE, NARU.

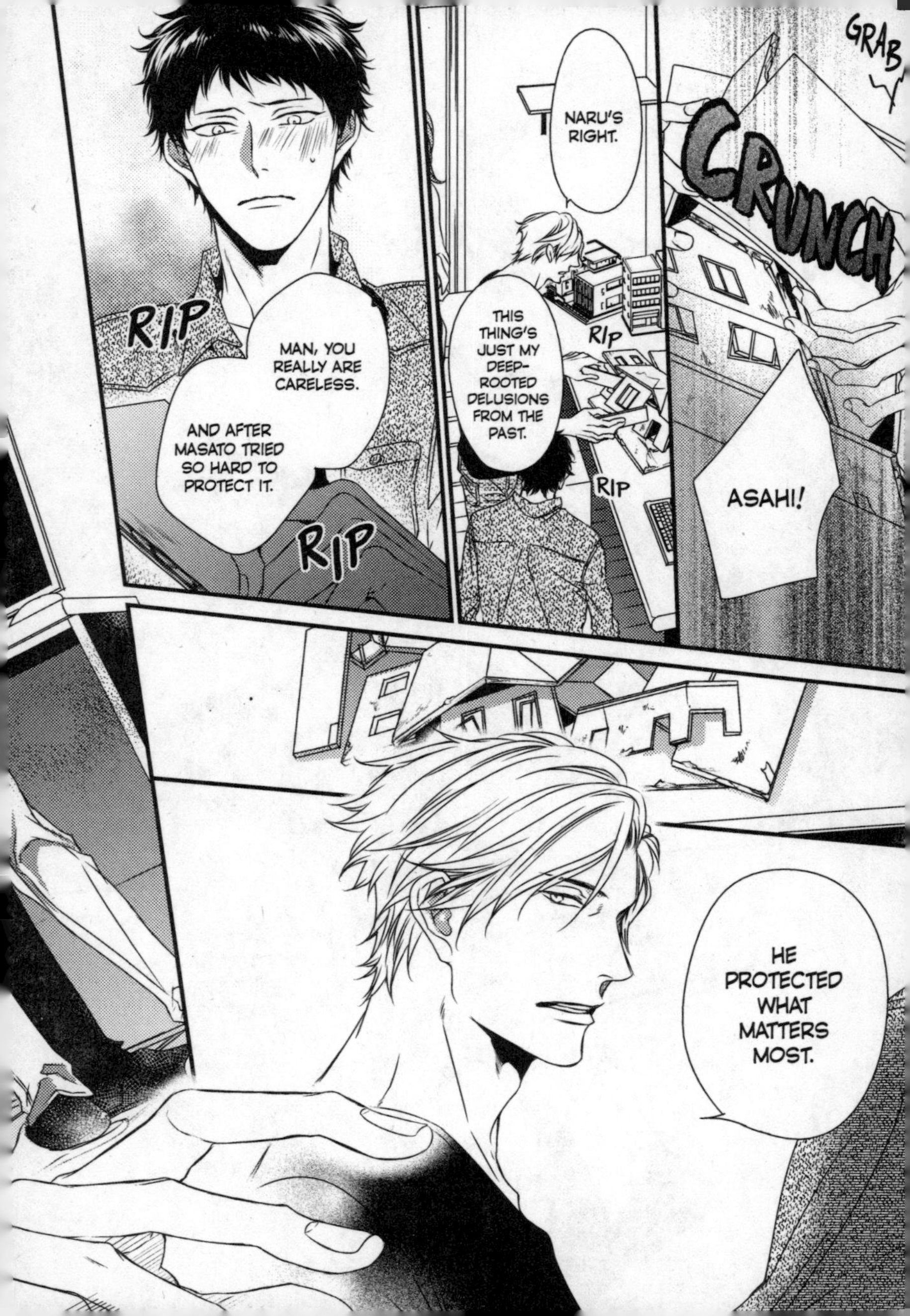
GRAB
CRUNCH
ASAHI!
NARU'S RIGHT.
THIS THING'S JUST MY DEEP-ROOTED DELUSIONS FROM THE PAST.
RIP
RIP
MAN, YOU REALLY ARE CARELESS.
AND AFTER MASATO TRIED SO HARD TO PROTECT IT.
RIP
RIP
HE PROTECTED WHAT MATTERS MOST.

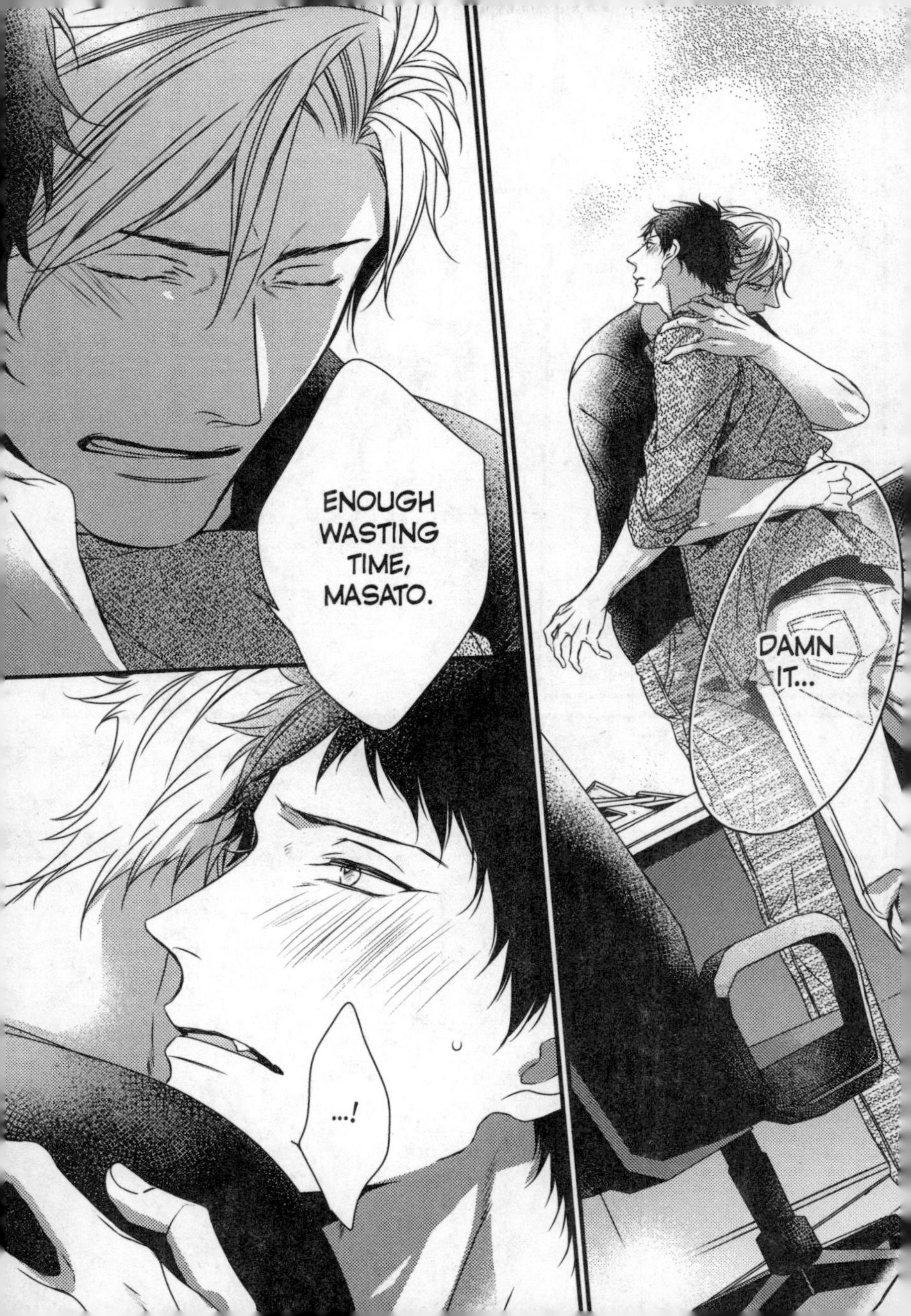
DAMN IT...
ENOUGH WASTING TIME, MASATO.
...!

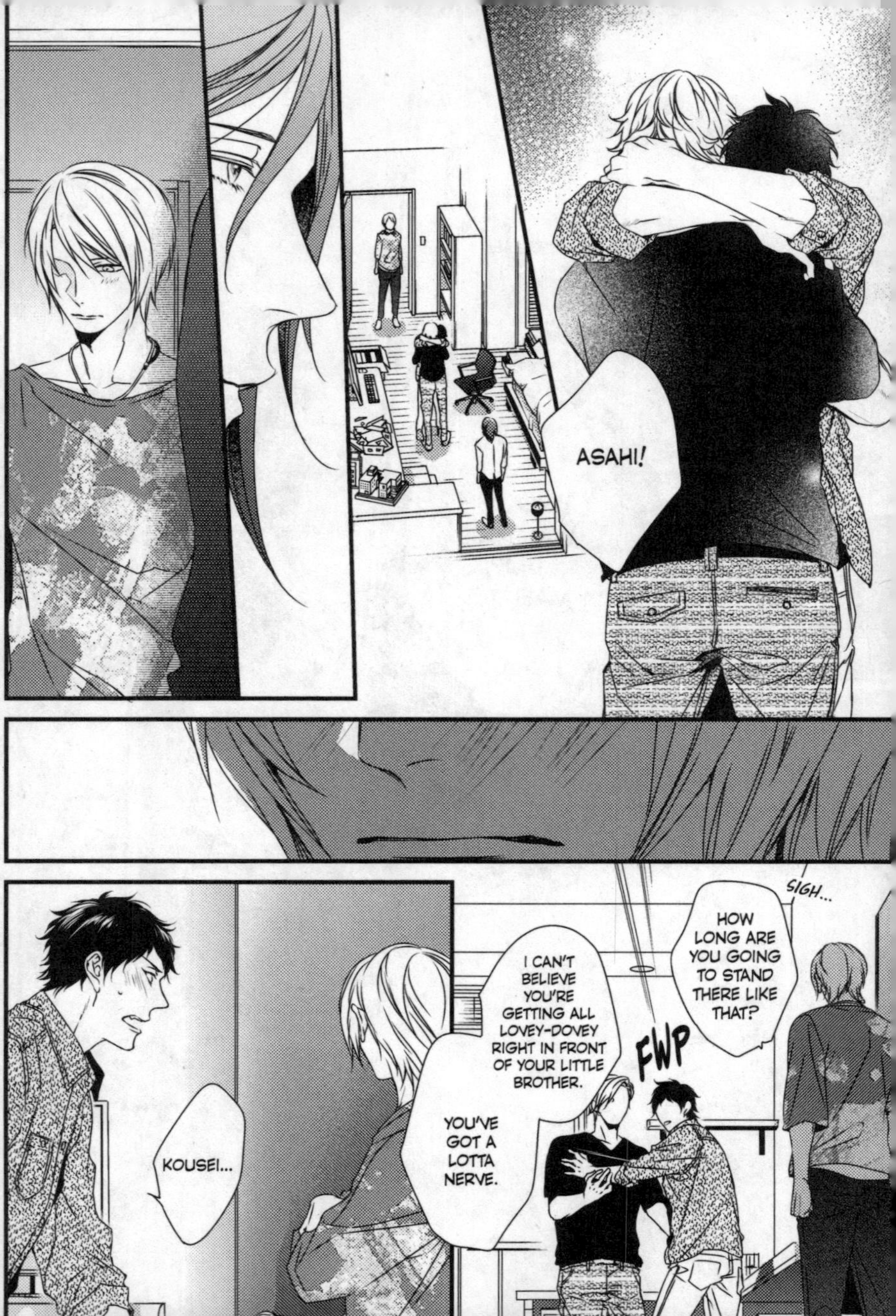
ASAHI!
SIGH...
HOW LONG ARE YOU GOING TO STAND THERE LIKE THAT?
FWP
I CAN'T BELIEVE YOU'RE GETTING ALL LOVEY-DOVEY RIGHT IN FRONT OF YOUR LITTLE BROTHER.
YOU'VE GOT A LOTTA NERVE.
KOUSEI...

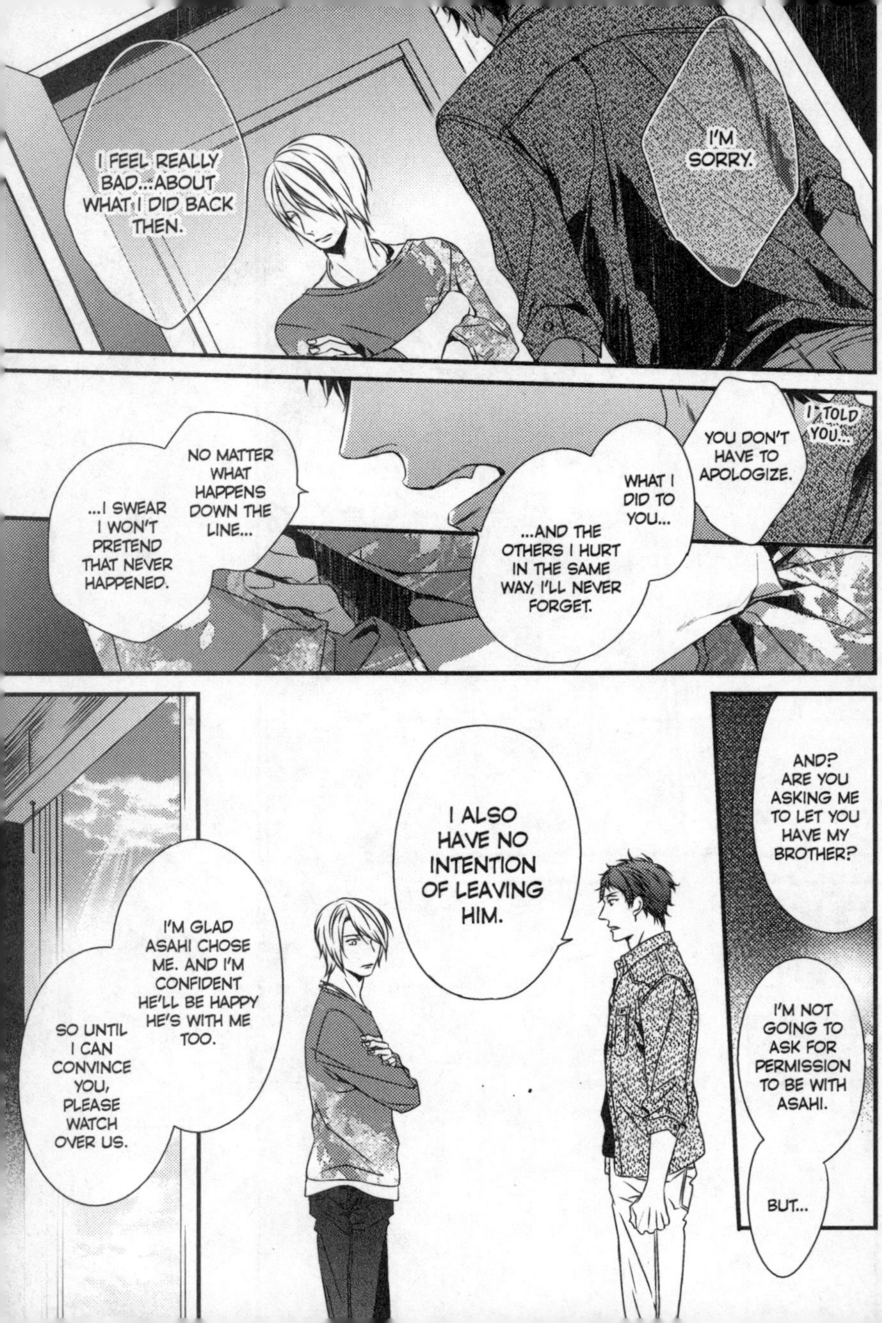
I'M SORRY.
I FEEL REALLY BAD...ABOUT WHAT I DID BACK THEN.
I TOLD YOU...
YOU DON'T HAVE TO APOLOGIZE.
WHAT I DID TO YOU...
...AND THE OTHERS I HURT IN THE SAME WAY, I'LL NEVER FORGET.
NO MATTER WHAT HAPPENS DOWN THE LINE...
...I SWEAR I WON'T PRETEND THAT NEVER HAPPENED.
AND? ARE YOU ASKING ME TO LET YOU HAVE MY BROTHER?
I'M NOT GOING TO ASK FOR PERMISSION TO BE WITH ASAHI.
BUT...
I ALSO HAVE NO INTENTION OF LEAVING HIM.
I'M GLAD ASAHI CHOSE ME. AND I'M CONFIDENT HE'LL BE HAPPY HE'S WITH ME TOO.
SO UNTIL I CAN CONVINCE YOU, PLEASE WATCH OVER US.

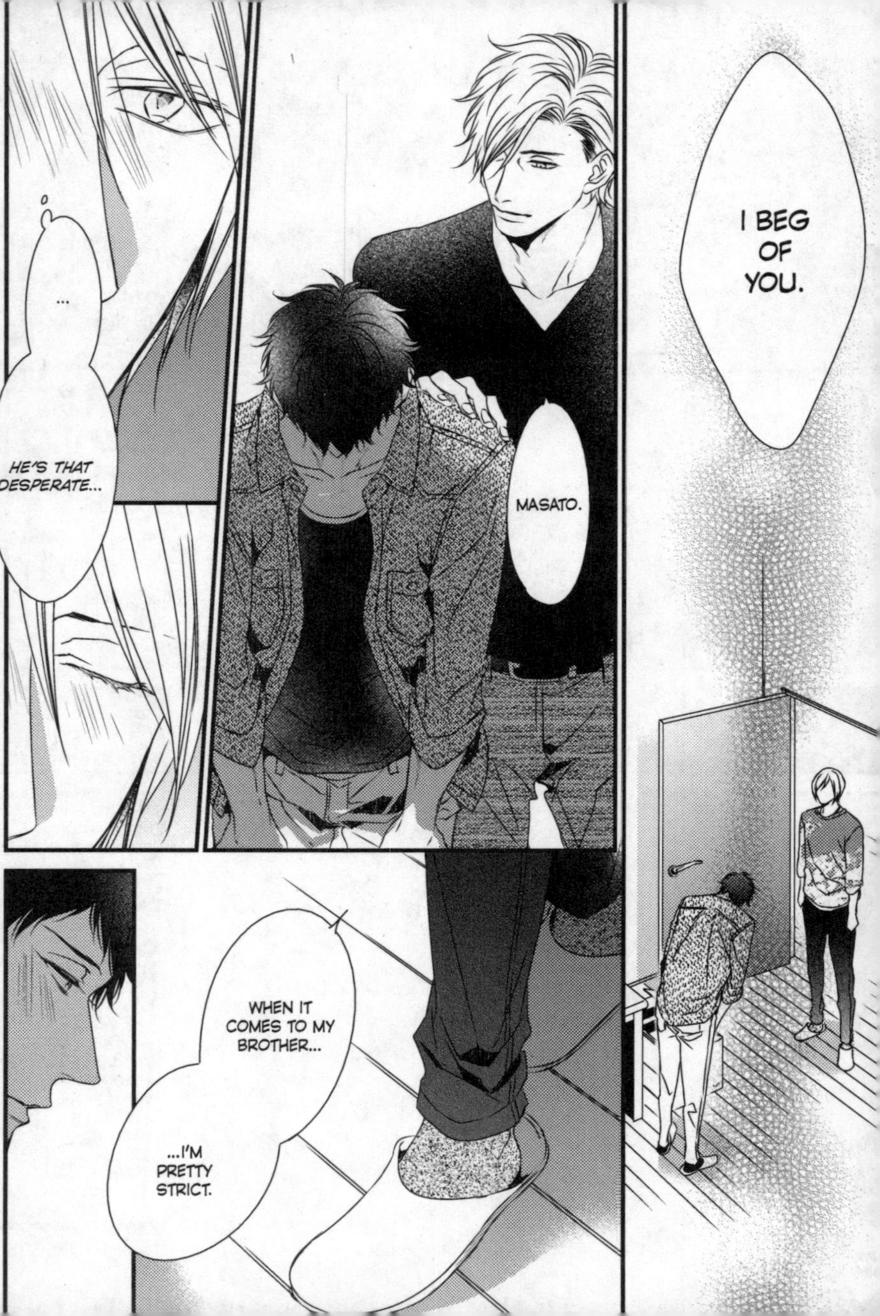
I BEG OF YOU.
MASATO.
...
HE'S THAT DESPERATE...
WHEN IT COMES TO MY BROTHER...
...I'M PRETTY STRICT.

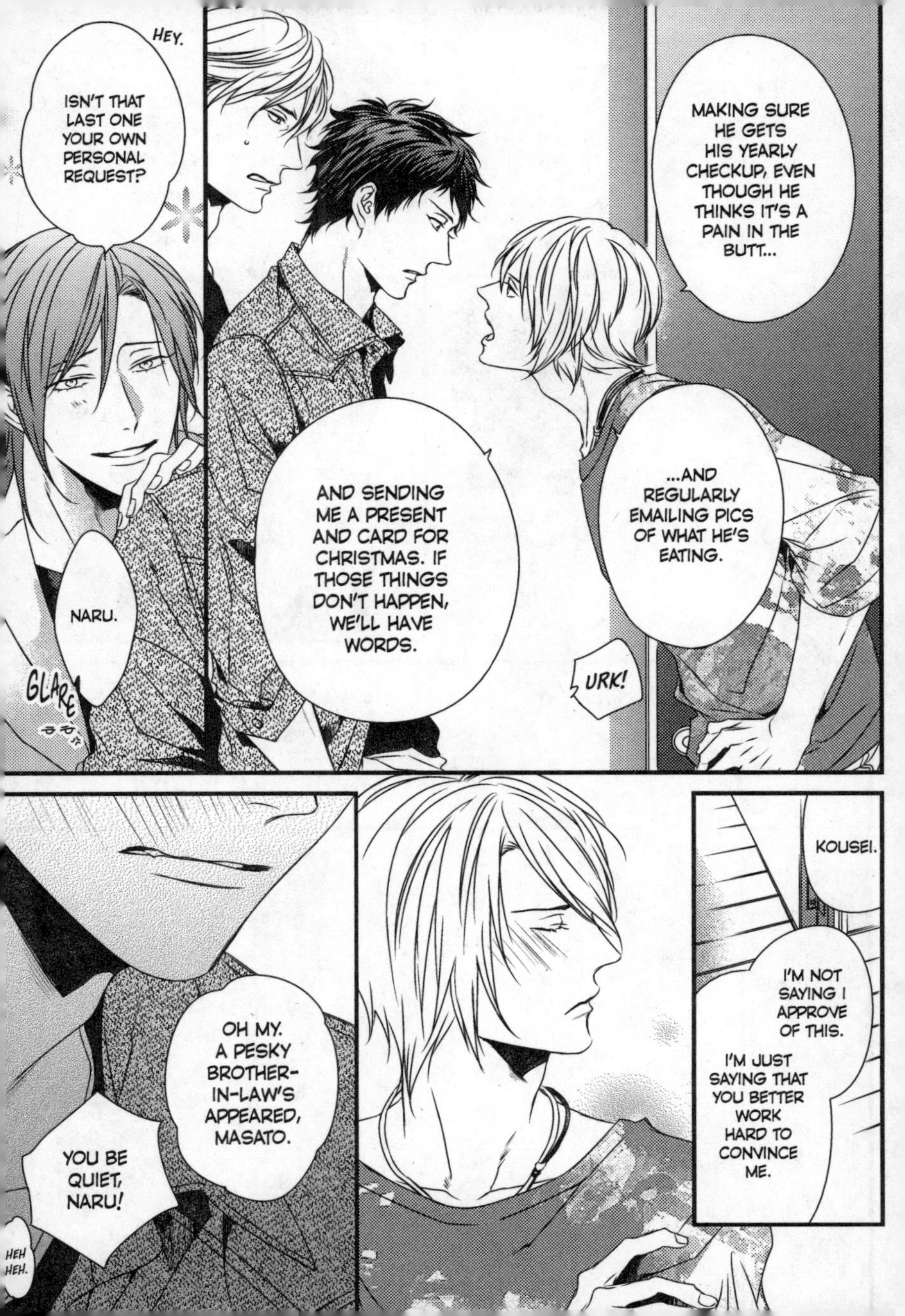
MAKING SURE HE GETS HIS YEARLY CHECKUP, EVEN THOUGH HE THINKS IT'S A PAIN IN THE BUTT...
...AND REGULARLY EMAILING PICS OF WHAT HE'S EATING.
AND SENDING ME A PRESENT AND CARD FOR CHRISTMAS. IF THOSE THINGS DON'T HAPPEN, WE'LL HAVE WORDS.
URK!
HEY.
ISN'T THAT LAST ONE YOUR OWN PERSONAL REQUEST?
NARU.
GLARE
KOUSEI.
I'M NOT SAYING I APPROVE OF THIS.
I'M JUST SAYING THAT YOU BETTER WORK HARD TO CONVINCE ME.
OH MY. A PESKY BROTHER-IN-LAW'S APPEARED, MASATO.
YOU BE QUIET, NARU!
HEH HEH.

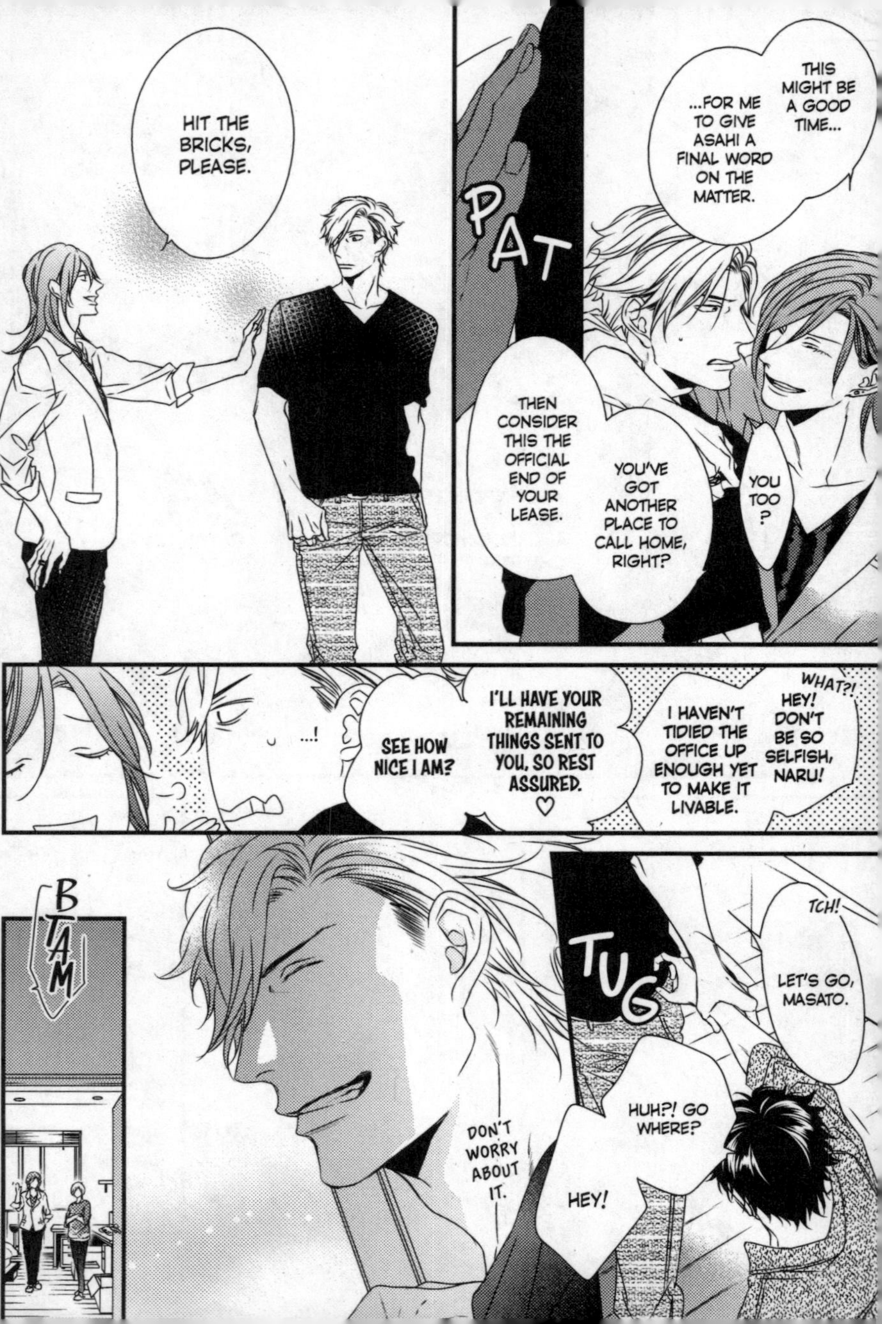
THIS MIGHT BE A GOOD TIME...
...FOR ME TO GIVE ASAHI A FINAL WORD ON THE MATTER.
PAT
YOU TOO?
YOU'VE GOT ANOTHER PLACE TO CALL HOME, RIGHT?
THEN CONSIDER THIS THE OFFICIAL END OF YOUR LEASE.
HIT THE BRICKS, PLEASE.
WHAT?!
HEY! DON'T BE SO SELFISH, NARU!
I HAVEN'T TIDIED THE OFFICE UP ENOUGH YET TO MAKE IT LIVABLE.
I'LL HAVE YOUR REMAINING THINGS SENT TO YOU, SO REST ASSURED. ♡
SEE HOW NICE I AM?
...!
TCH!
LET'S GO, MASATO.
TUG
HUH?! GO WHERE?
HEY!
DON'T WORRY ABOUT IT.
BTAM

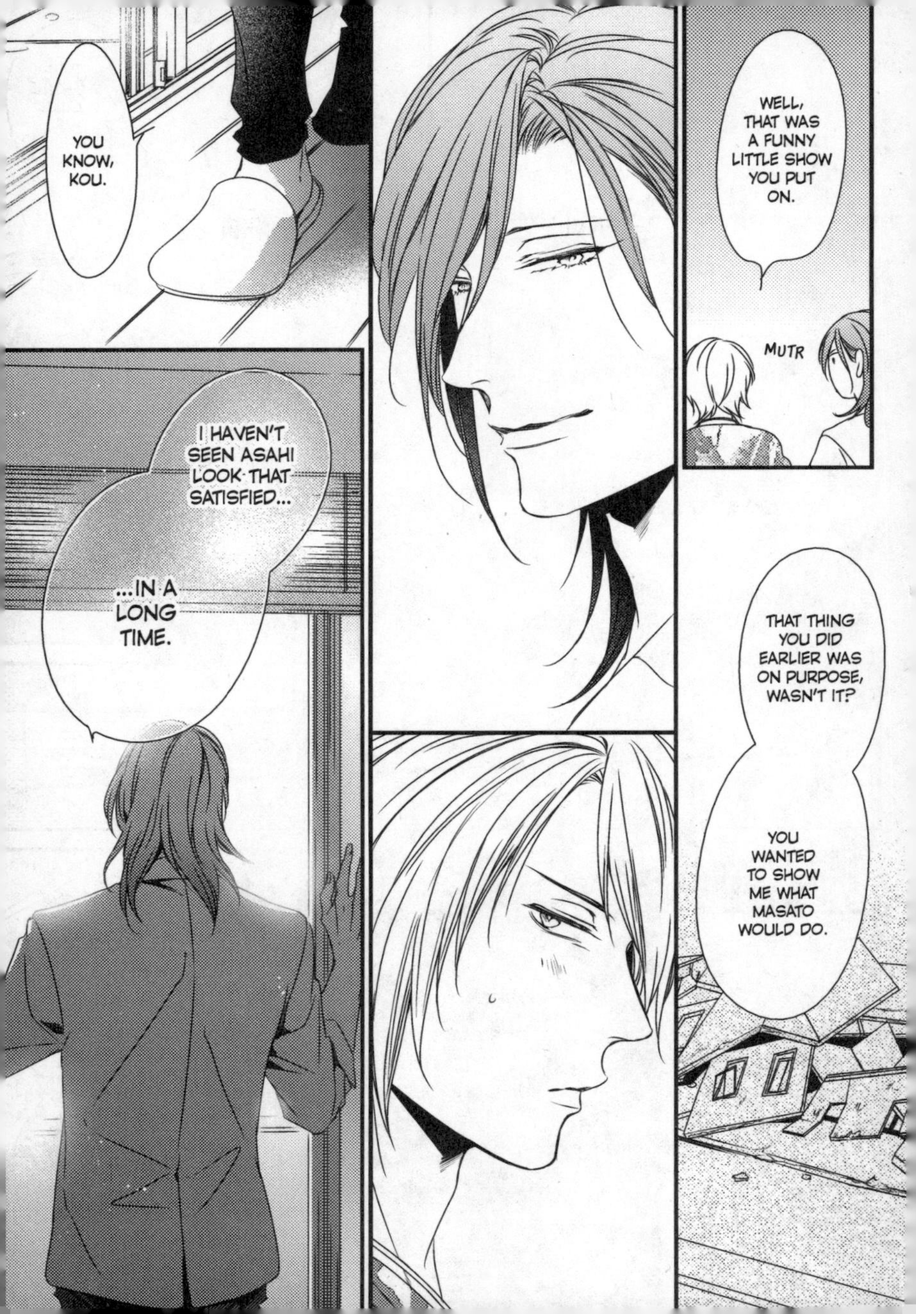
WELL, THAT WAS A FUNNY LITTLE SHOW YOU PUT ON.
MUTR
THAT THING YOU DID EARLIER WAS ON PURPOSE, WASN'T IT?
YOU WANTED TO SHOW ME WHAT MASATO WOULD DO.
YOU KNOW, KOU.
I HAVEN'T SEEN ASAHI LOOK THAT SATISFIED...
...IN A LONG TIME.

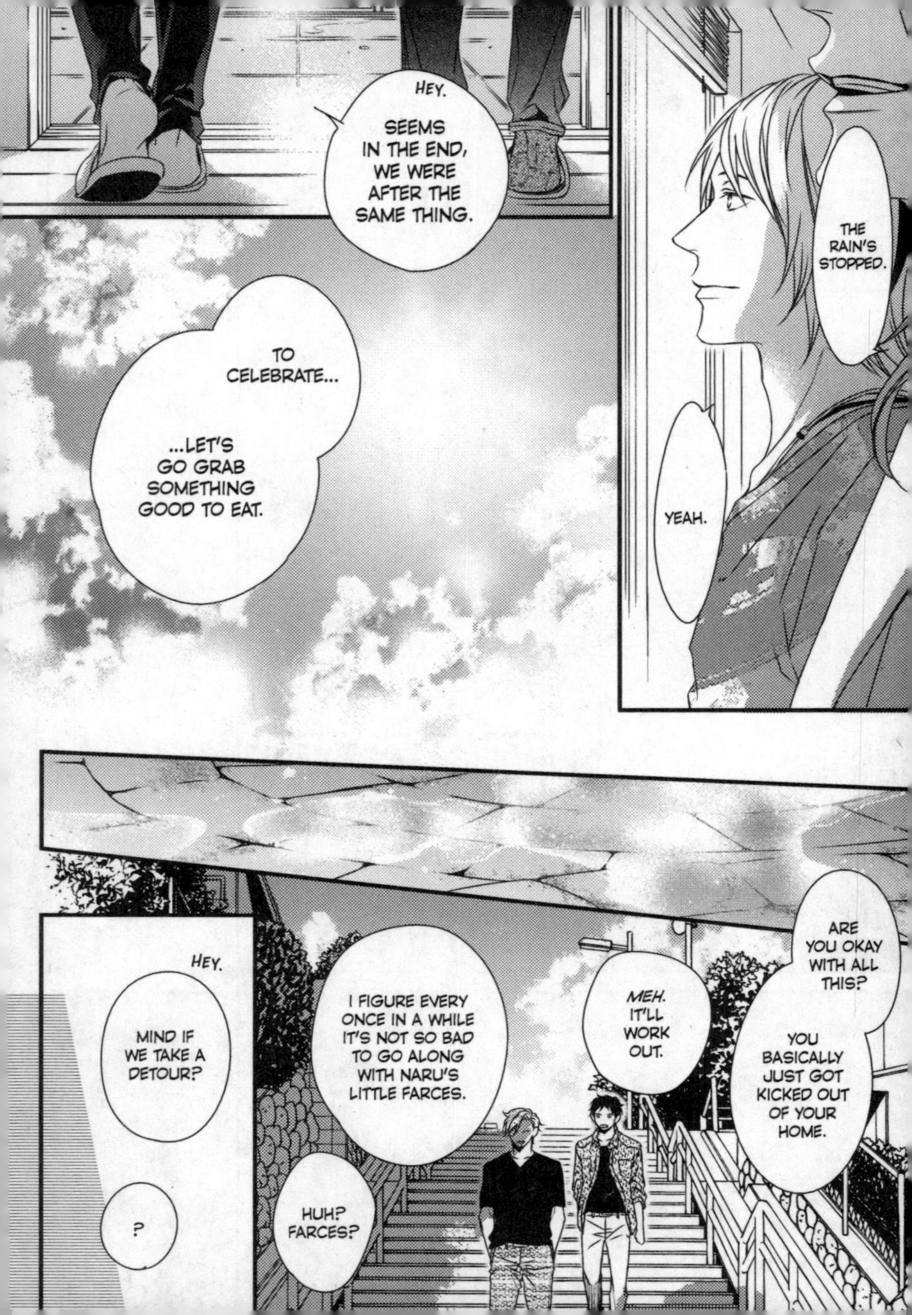
THE RAIN'S STOPPED.
YEAH.
HEY.
SEEMS IN THE END, WE WERE AFTER THE SAME THING.
TO CELEBRATE...
...LET'S GO GRAB SOMETHING GOOD TO EAT.
ARE YOU OKAY WITH ALL THIS?
YOU BASICALLY JUST GOT KICKED OUT OF YOUR HOME.
MEH. IT'LL WORK OUT.
I FIGURE EVERY ONCE IN A WHILE IT'S NOT SO BAD TO GO ALONG WITH NARU'S LITTLE FARCES.
HUH? FARCES?
HEY.
MIND IF WE TAKE A DETOUR?
?

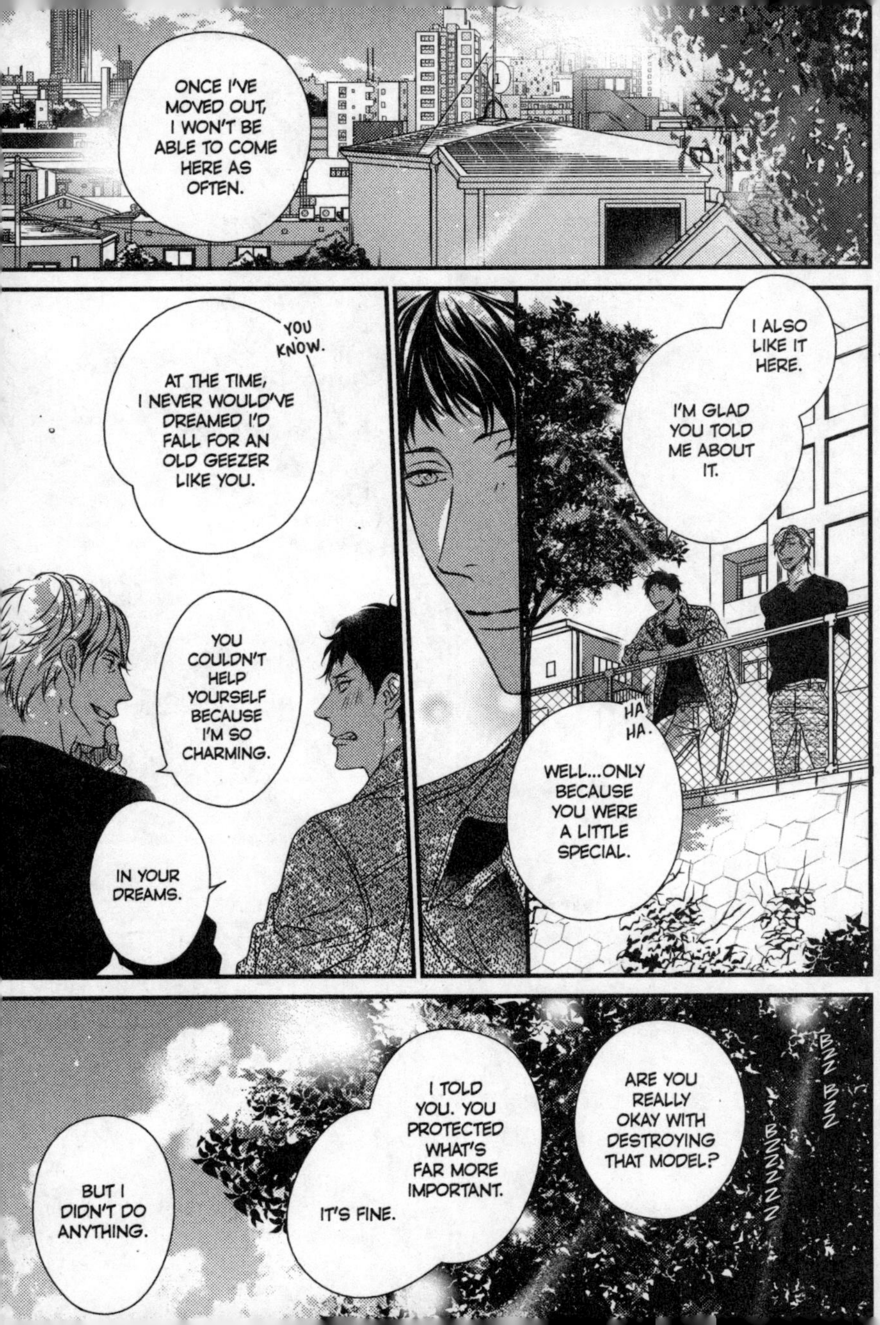
ONCE I'VE MOVED OUT, I WON'T BE ABLE TO COME HERE AS OFTEN.
I ALSO LIKE IT HERE.
I'M GLAD YOU TOLD ME ABOUT IT.
HA HA.
WELL...ONLY BECAUSE YOU WERE A LITTLE SPECIAL.
YOU KNOW.
AT THE TIME, I NEVER WOULD'VE DREAMED I'D FALL FOR AN OLD GEEZER LIKE YOU.
YOU COULDN'T HELP YOURSELF BECAUSE I'M SO CHARMING.
IN YOUR DREAMS.
BZZ BZZ BZZZZZ
ARE YOU REALLY OKAY WITH DESTROYING THAT MODEL?
I TOLD YOU. YOU PROTECTED WHAT'S FAR MORE IMPORTANT.
IT'S FINE.
BUT I DIDN'T DO ANYTHING.

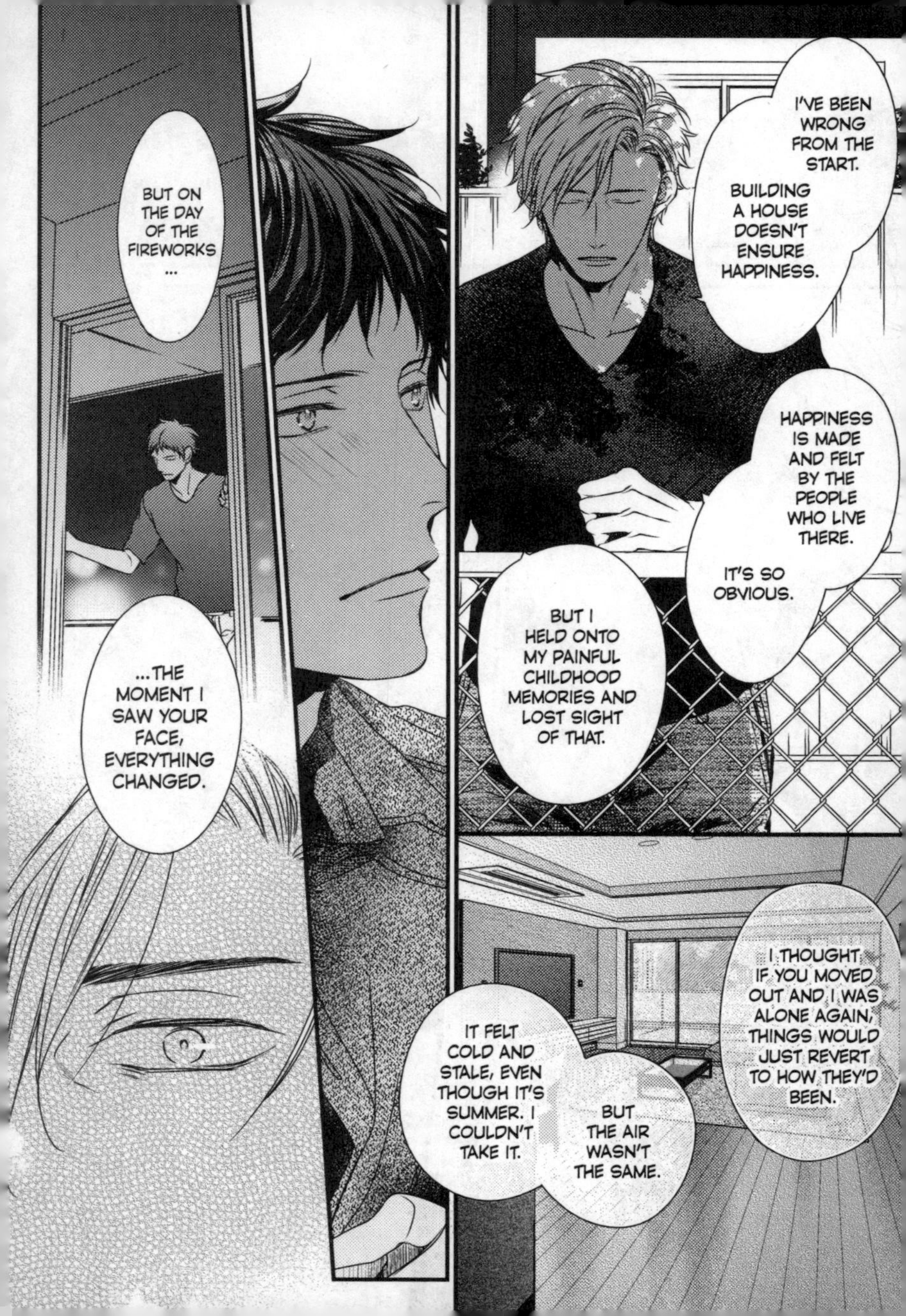
I'VE BEEN WRONG FROM THE START.
BUILDING A HOUSE DOESN'T ENSURE HAPPINESS.
HAPPINESS IS MADE AND FELT BY THE PEOPLE WHO LIVE THERE.
IT'S SO OBVIOUS.
BUT I HELD ONTO MY PAINFUL CHILDHOOD MEMORIES AND LOST SIGHT OF THAT.
I THOUGHT IF YOU MOVED OUT AND I WAS ALONE AGAIN, THINGS WOULD JUST REVERT TO HOW THEY'D BEEN.
BUT THE AIR WASN'T THE SAME.
IT FELT COLD AND STALE, EVEN THOUGH IT'S SUMMER. I COULDN'T TAKE IT.
BUT ON THE DAY OF THE FIREWORKS...
...THE MOMENT I SAW YOUR FACE, EVERYTHING CHANGED.

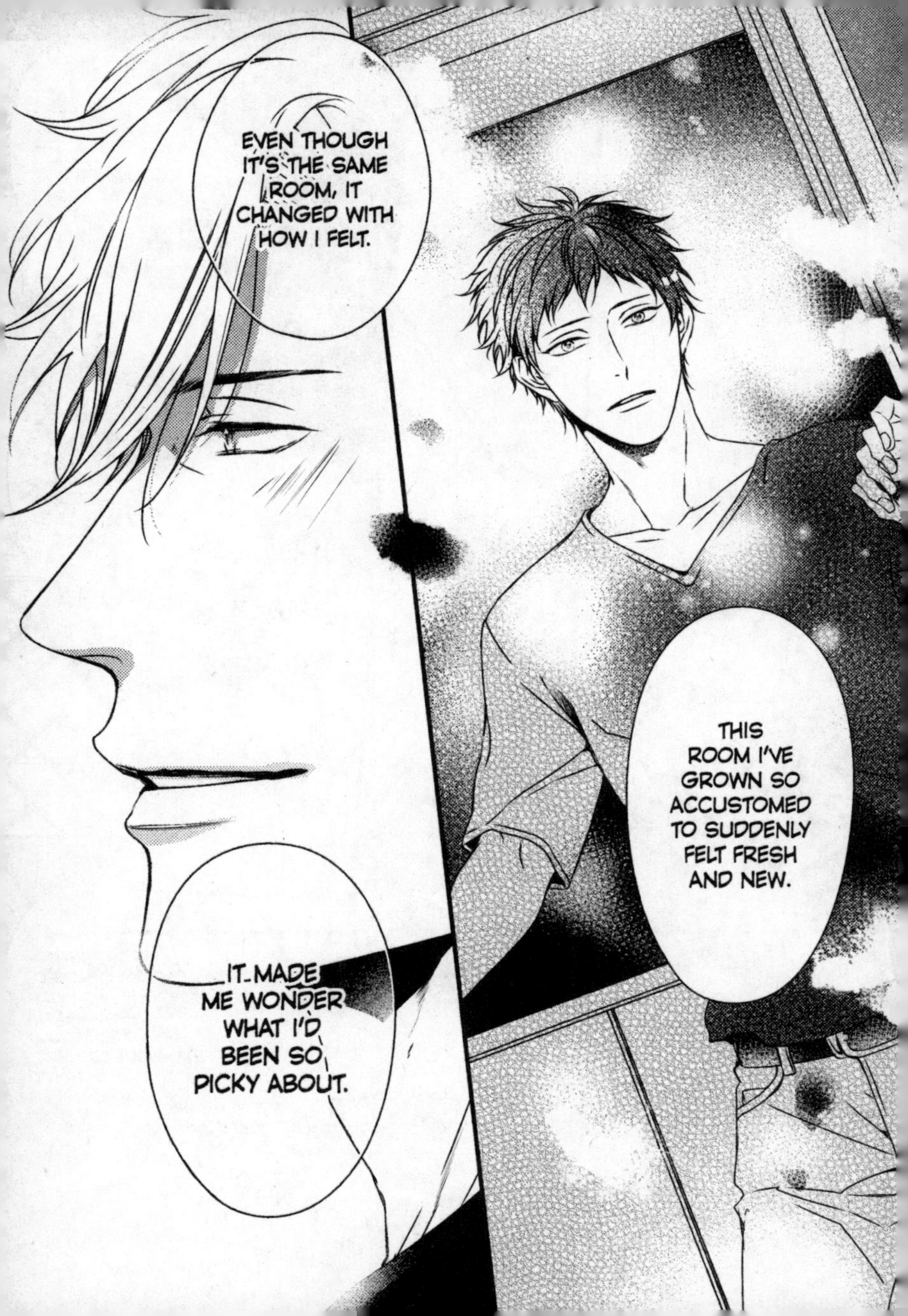
THIS ROOM I'VE GROWN SO ACCUSTOMED TO SUDDENLY FELT FRESH AND NEW.
EVEN THOUGH IT'S THE SAME ROOM, IT CHANGED WITH HOW I FELT.
IT MADE ME WONDER WHAT I'D BEEN SO PICKY ABOUT.

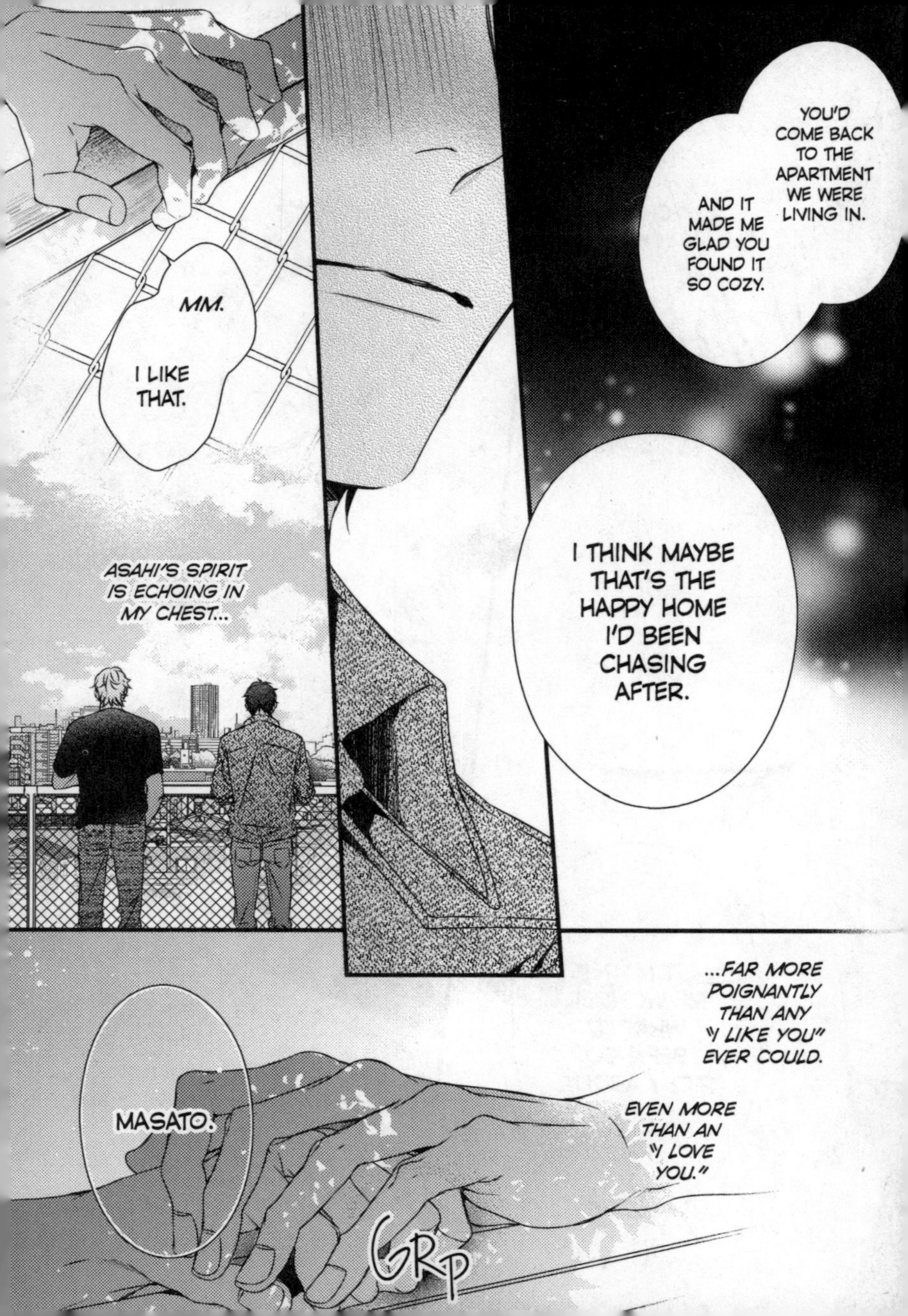
YOU'D COME BACK TO THE APARTMENT WE WERE LIVING IN.
AND IT MADE ME GLAD YOU FOUND IT SO COZY.
I THINK MAYBE THAT'S THE HAPPY HOME I'D BEEN CHASING AFTER.
MM.
I LIKE THAT.
ASAHI'S SPIRIT IS ECHOING IN MY CHEST...
...FAR MORE POIGNANTLY THAN ANY "I LIKE YOU" EVER COULD.
EVEN MORE THAN AN "I LOVE YOU."
MASATO.
GRP

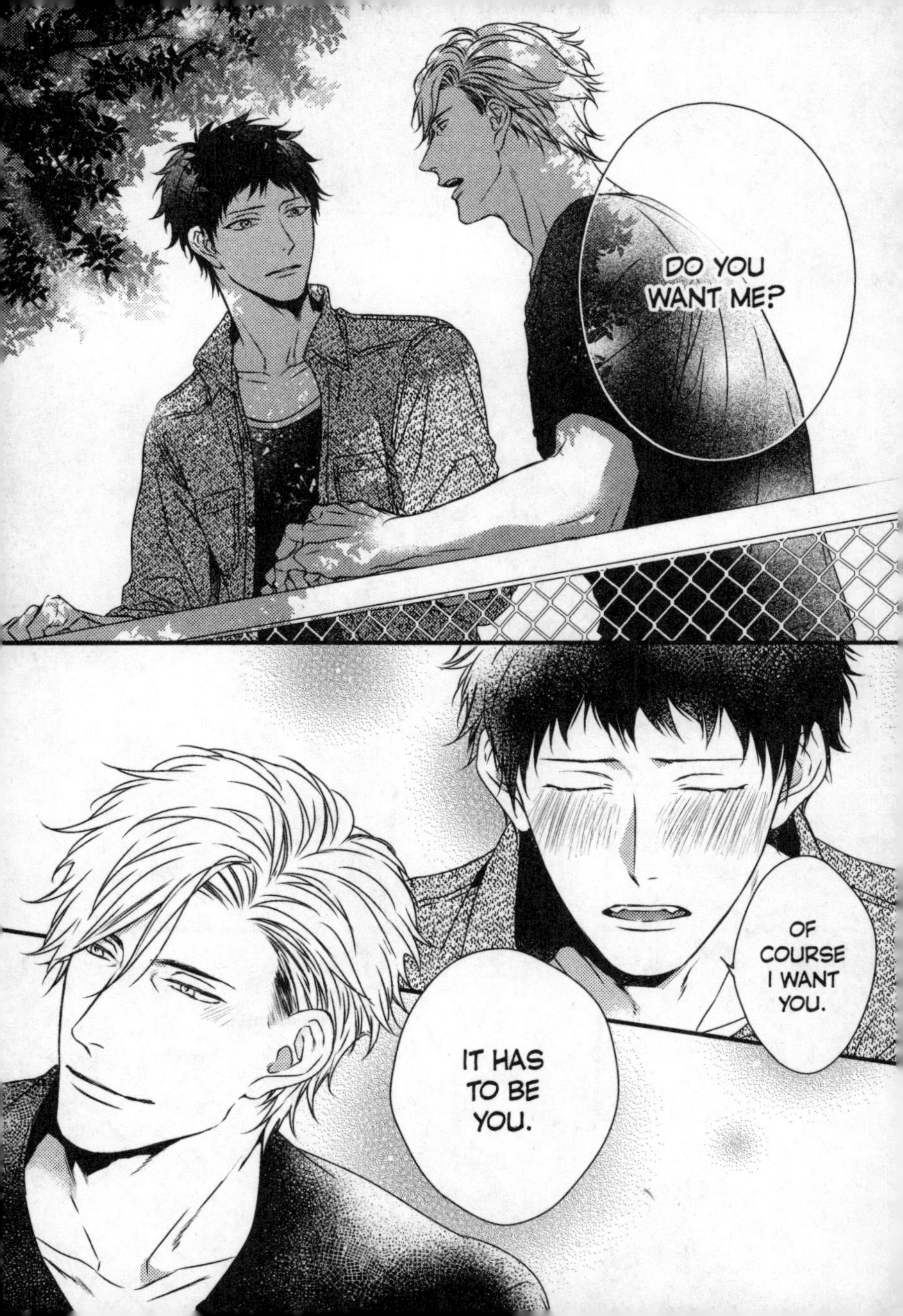
DO YOU WANT ME?
OF COURSE I WANT YOU.
IT HAS TO BE YOU.

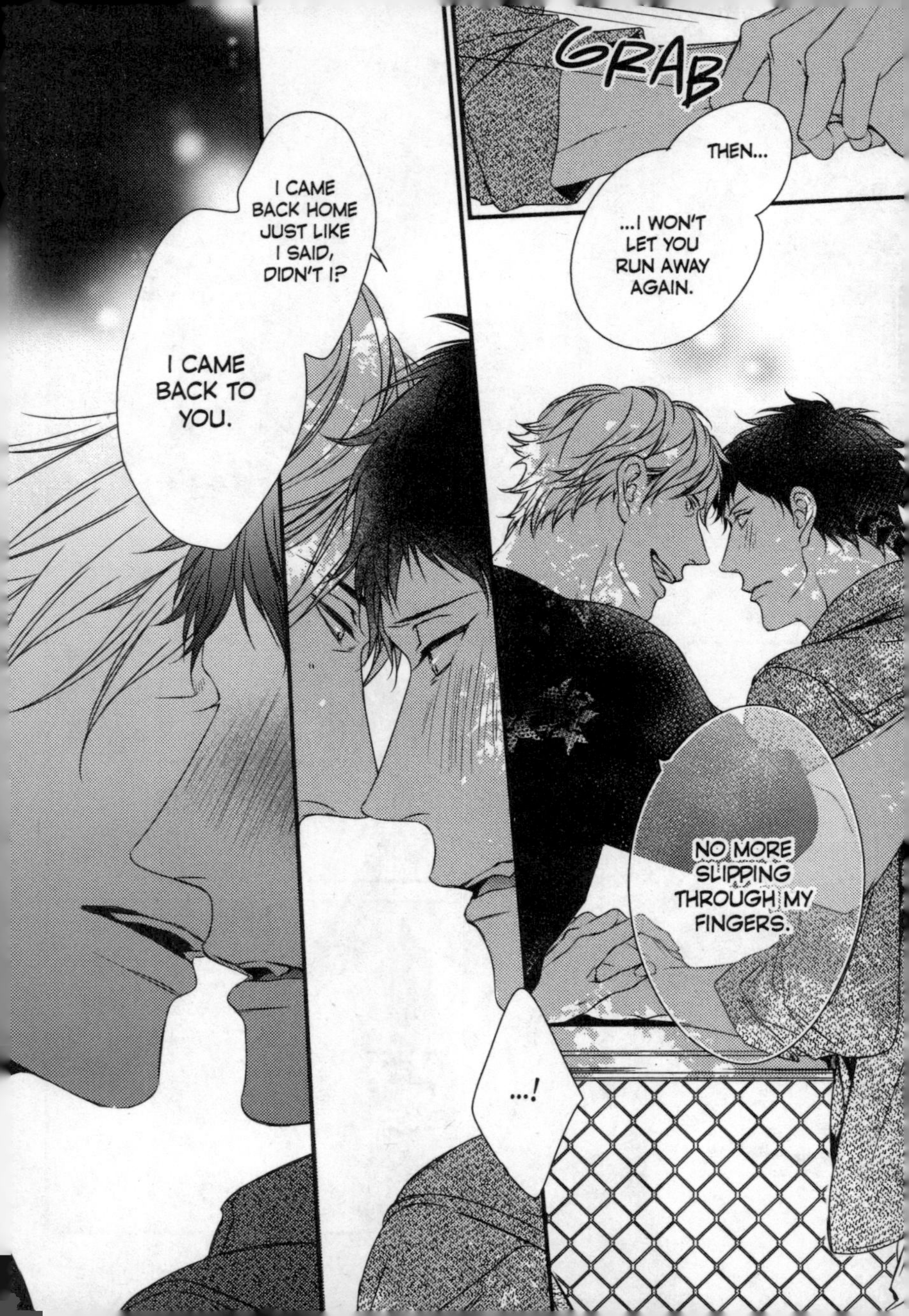
GRAB
THEN...
...I WON'T LET YOU RUN AWAY AGAIN.
NO MORE SLIPPING THROUGH MY FINGERS.
...!
I CAME BACK HOME JUST LIKE I SAID, DIDN'T I?
I CAME BACK TO YOU.

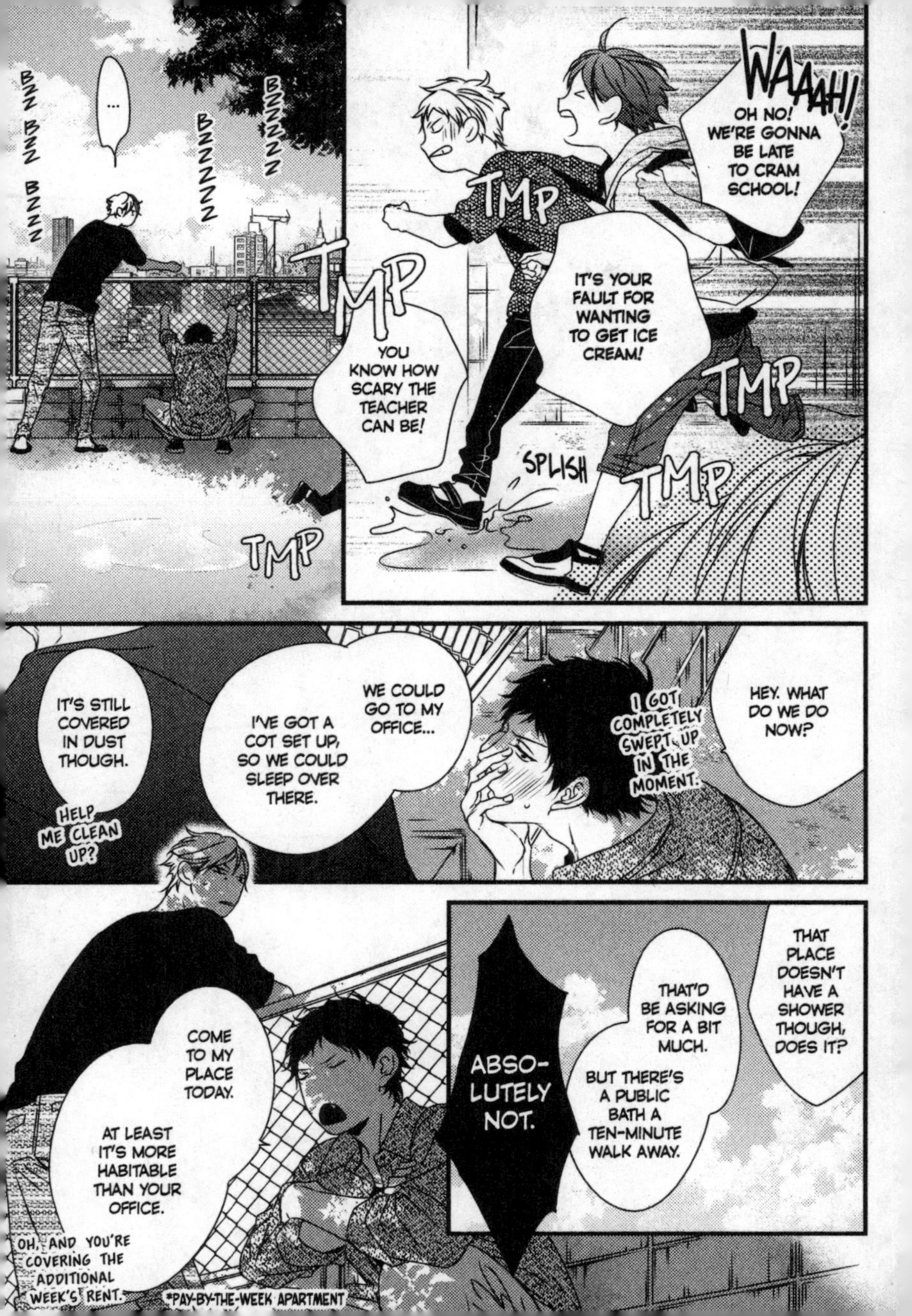
WAAAH!
OH NO! WE'RE GONNA BE LATE TO CRAM SCHOOL!
TMP
IT'S YOUR FAULT FOR WANTING TO GET ICE CREAM!
TMP
YOU KNOW HOW SCARY THE TEACHER CAN BE!
TMP
SPLISH
TMP
TMP
BZZZZZ
BZZZZZZ
...
BZZ BZZ BZZZ BZZZ
HEY. WHAT DO WE DO NOW?
I GOT COMPLETELY SWEPT UP IN THE MOMENT.
WE COULD GO TO MY OFFICE...
I'VE GOT A COT SET UP, SO WE COULD SLEEP OVER THERE.
IT'S STILL COVERED IN DUST THOUGH.
HELP ME CLEAN UP?
THAT PLACE DOESN'T HAVE A SHOWER THOUGH, DOES IT?
THAT'D BE ASKING FOR A BIT MUCH.
BUT THERE'S A PUBLIC BATH A TEN-MINUTE WALK AWAY.
ABSO-LUTELY NOT.
COME TO MY PLACE TODAY.
AT LEAST IT'S MORE HABITABLE THAN YOUR OFFICE.
OH, AND YOU'RE COVERING THE ADDITIONAL WEEK'S RENT.
*PAY-BY-THE-WEEK APARTMENT

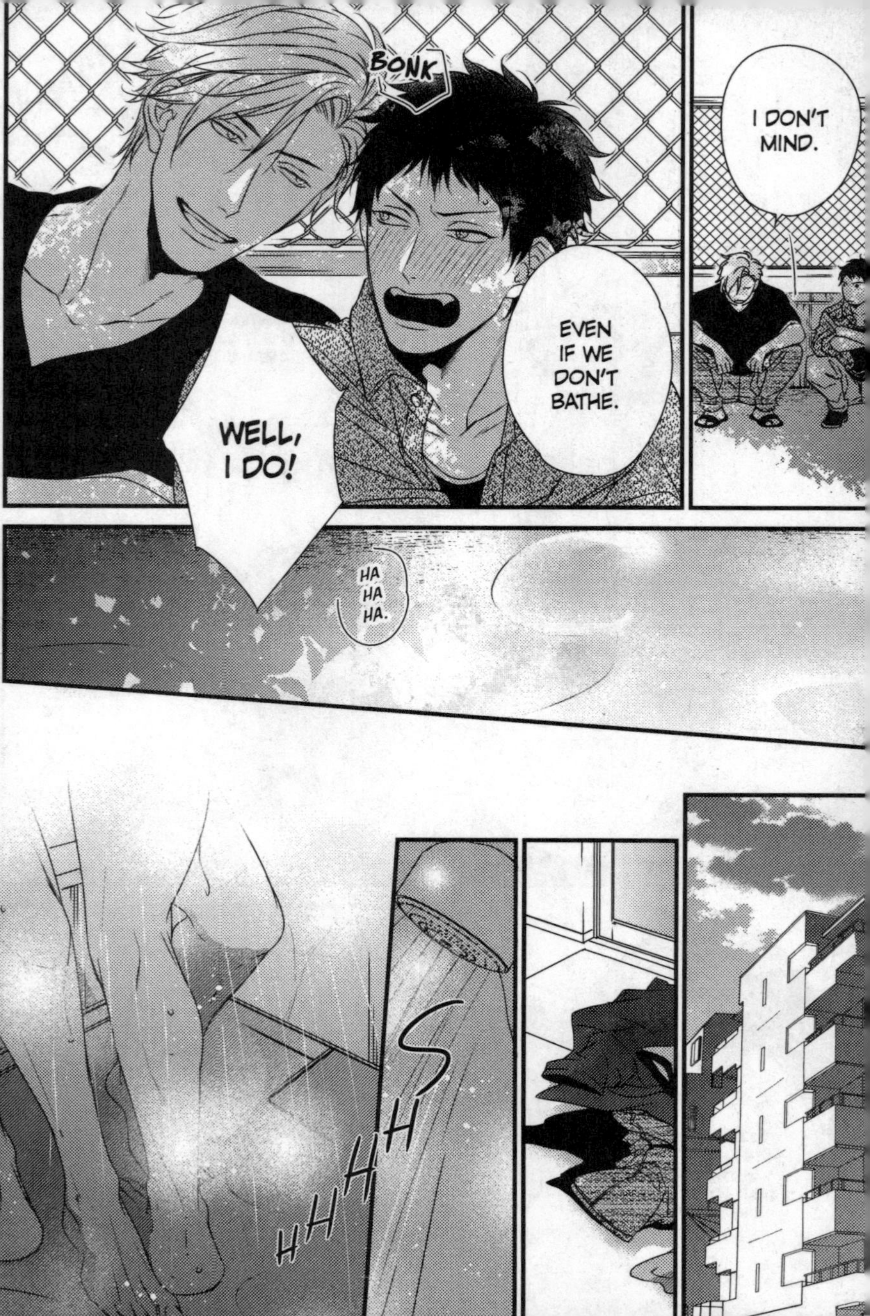
I DON'T MIND.
BONK
EVEN IF WE DON'T BATHE.
WELL, I DO!
HA HA HA.
SHHHHHH

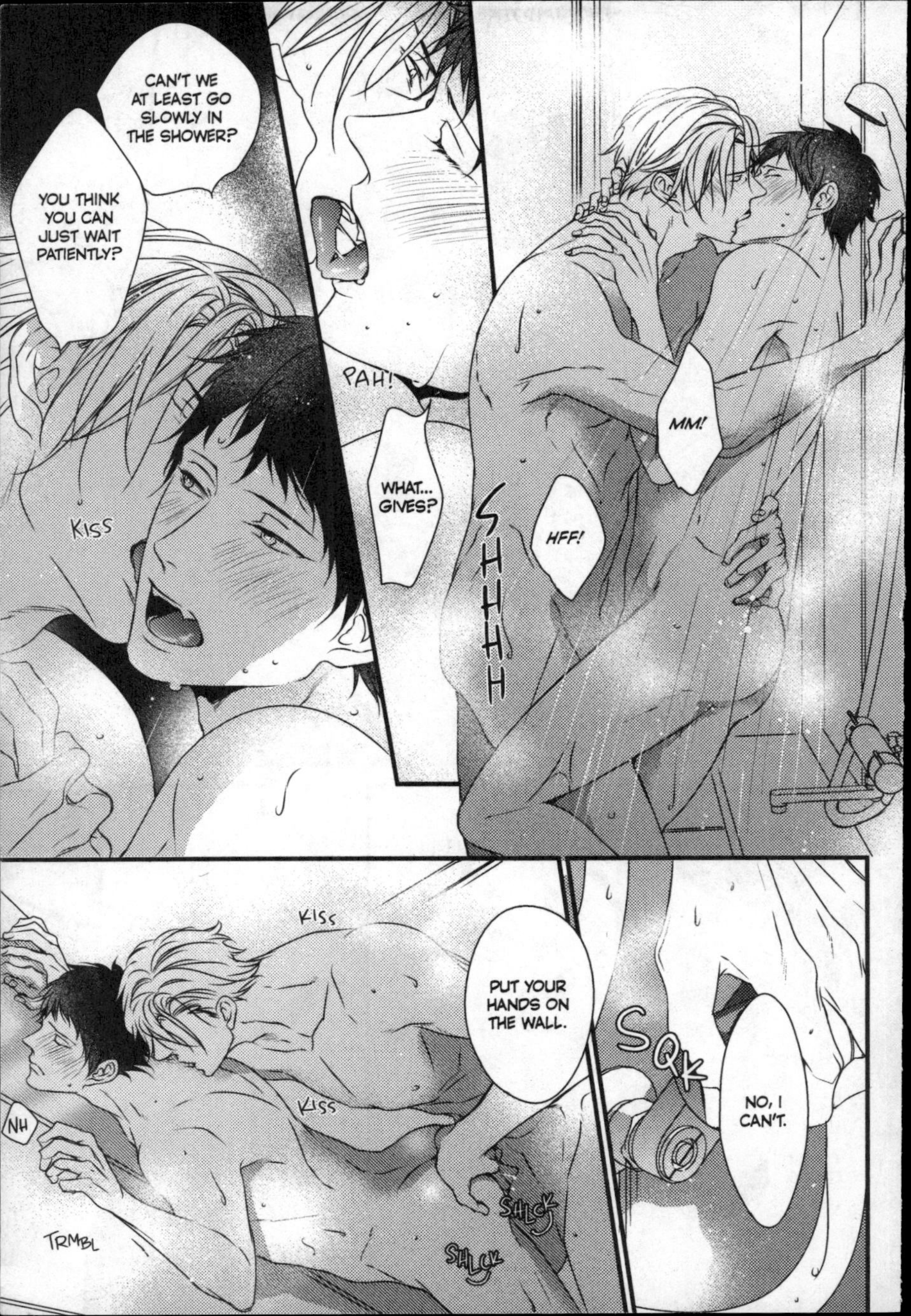
MM!
HFF!
SHHHHH
PAH!
WHAT... GIVES?
CAN'T WE AT LEAST GO SLOWLY IN THE SHOWER?
YOU THINK YOU CAN JUST WAIT PATIENTLY?
KISS
SQK
NO, I CAN'T.
PUT YOUR HANDS ON THE WALL.
KISS
KISS
NH
SHLCK
SHLCK
TRMBL

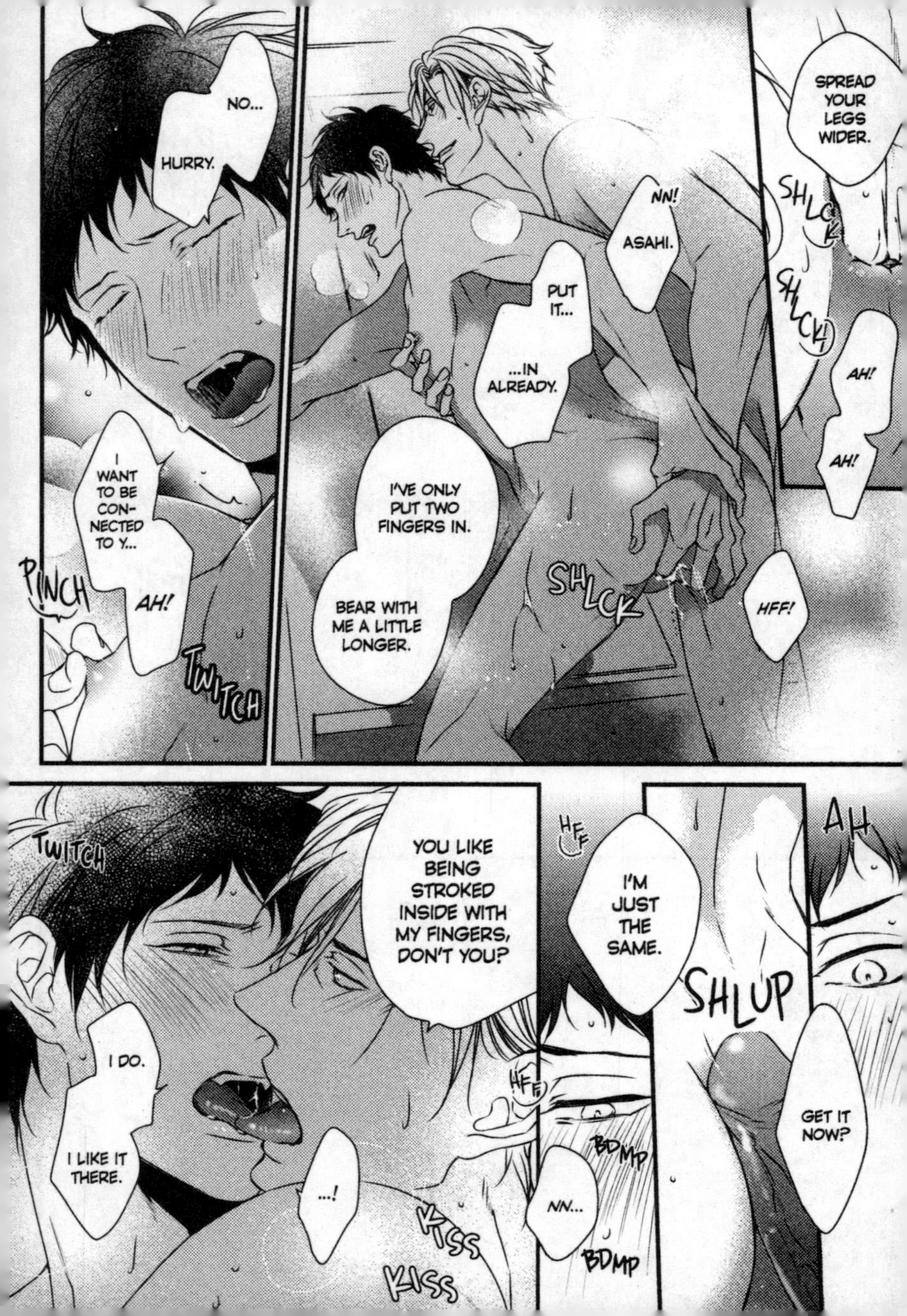
SPREAD YOUR LEGS WIDER.
SHLCK
SHLCK
AH!
AH!
NN!
ASAHI.
PUT IT...
...IN ALREADY.
I'VE ONLY PUT TWO FINGERS IN.
BEAR WITH ME A LITTLE LONGER.
SHLCK
HFF!
NO...
HURRY.
I WANT TO BE CON-NECTED TO Y...
PINCH
AH!
TWITCH
AH
SHLUP
GET IT NOW?
HFF
I'M JUST THE SAME.
HFF
BDMP
NN...
BDMP
TWITCH
YOU LIKE BEING STROKED INSIDE WITH MY FINGERS, DON'T YOU?
I DO.
I LIKE IT THERE.
...!
KISS
KISS

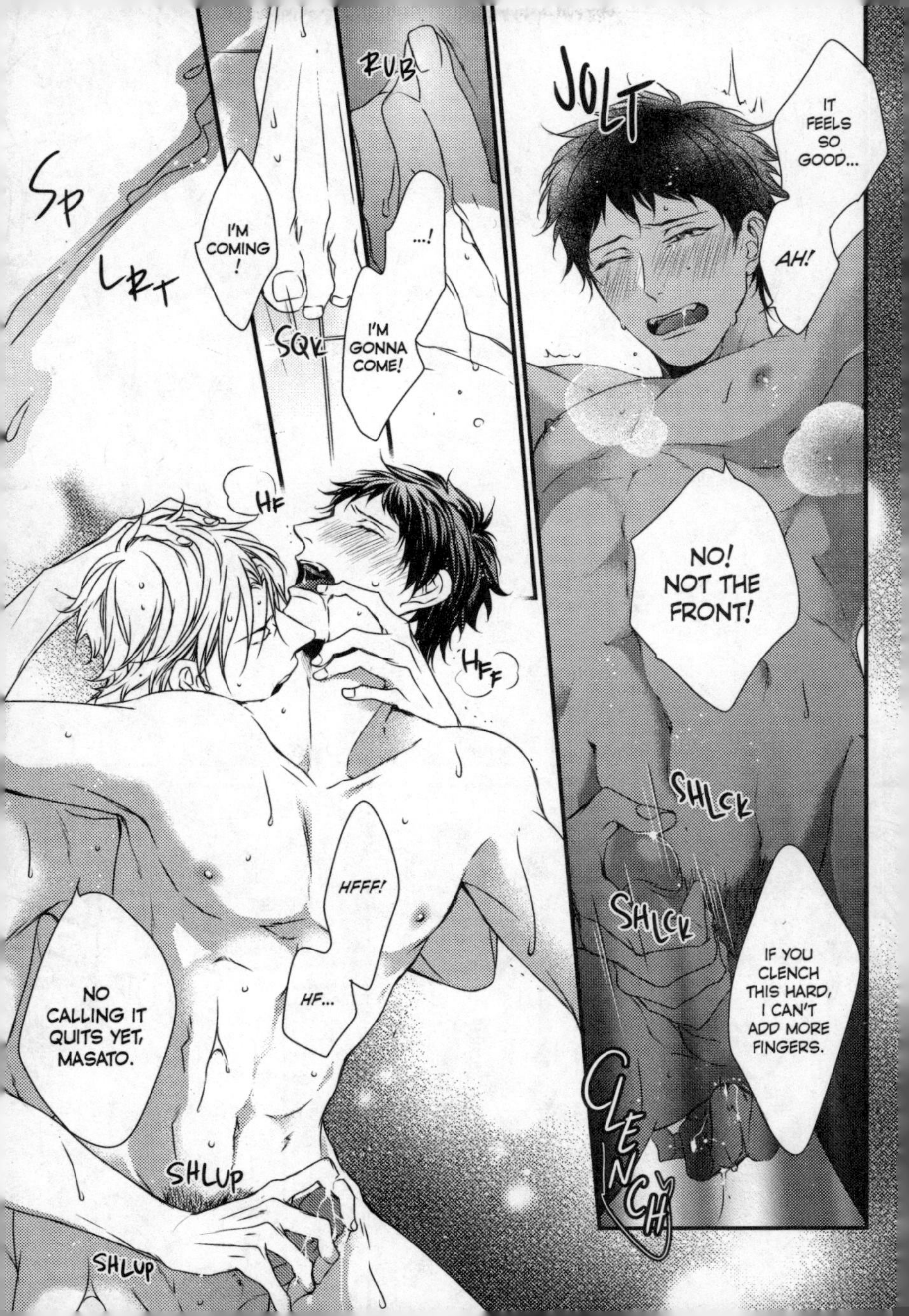
JOLT
IT FEELS SO GOOD...
AH!
NO! NOT THE FRONT!
SHLCK
SHLCK
IF YOU CLENCH THIS HARD, I CAN'T ADD MORE FINGERS.
CLENCH
RUB
...!
I'M GONNA COME!
SQK
I'M COMING!
SP
LRT
HF
HFF
HFFF!
HF...
NO CALLING IT QUITS YET, MASATO.
SHLUP
SHLUP

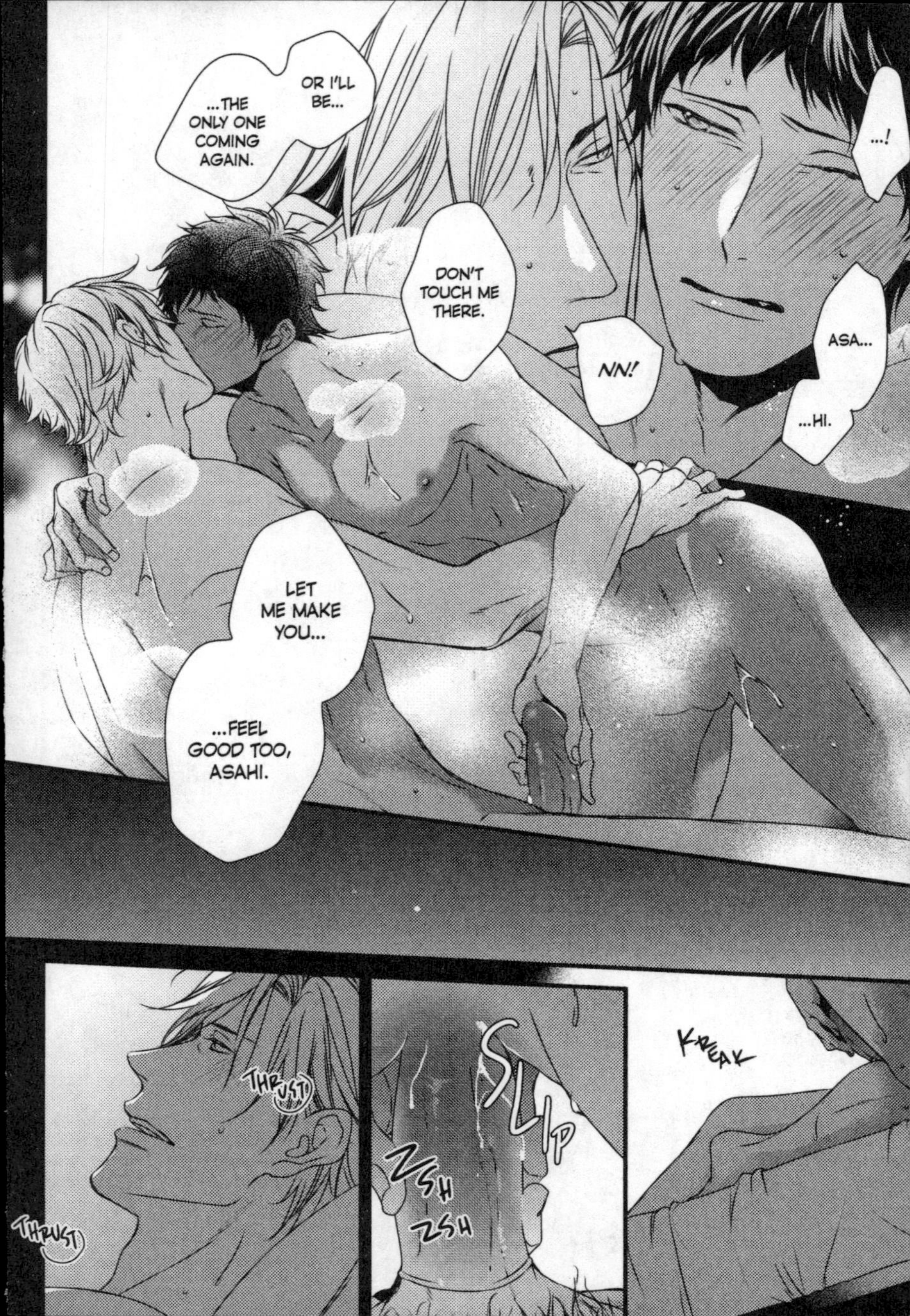
...!
ASA...
...HI.
NN!
DON'T TOUCH ME THERE.
OR I'LL BE...
...THE ONLY ONE COMING AGAIN.
LET ME MAKE YOU...
...FEEL GOOD TOO, ASAHI.
KREAK
SLIP
ZSH
ZSH
THRUST
THRUST

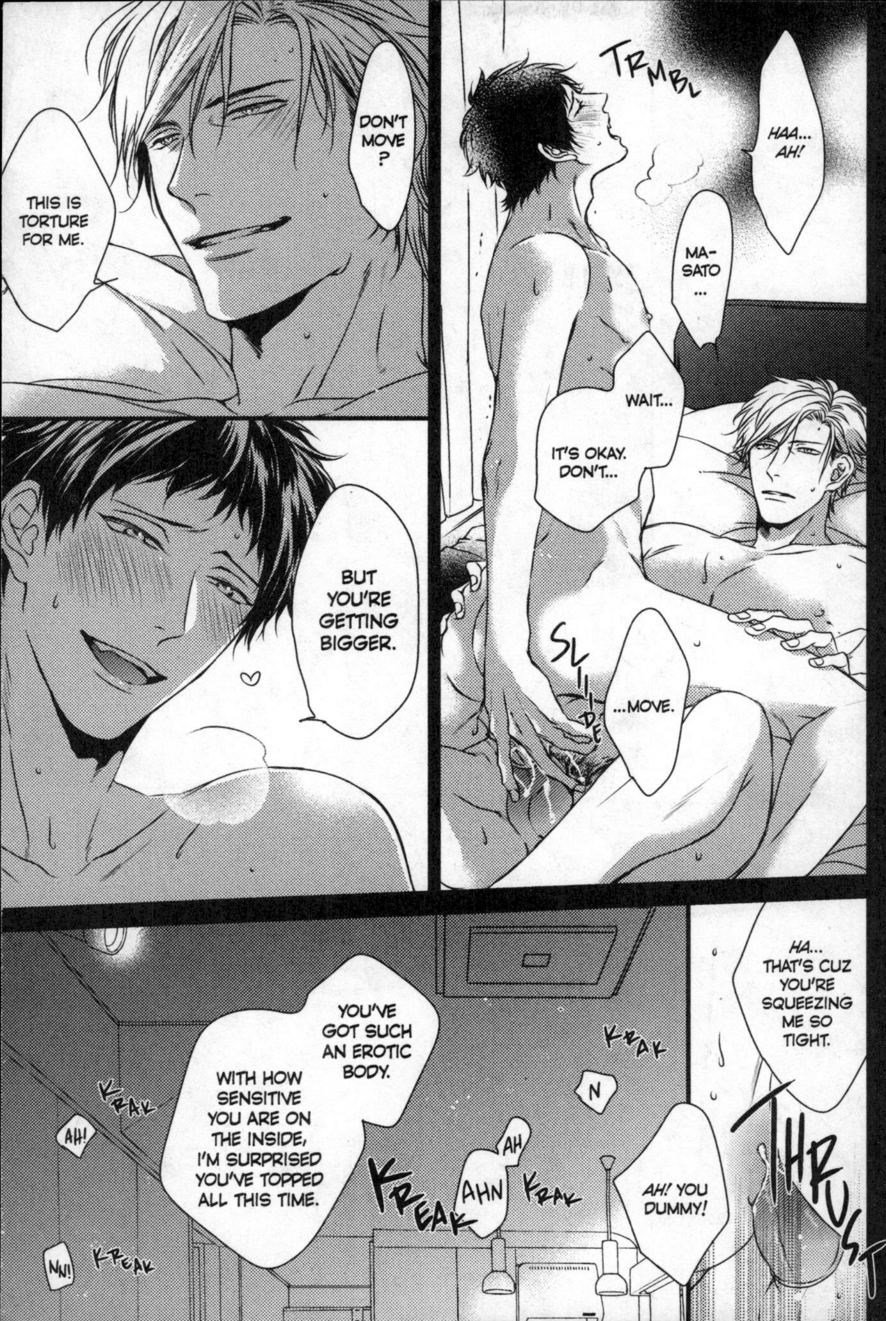
TRMBL
HAA... AH!
MA-SATO...
WAIT...
IT'S OKAY. DON'T...
SLIIIDE
...MOVE.
DON'T MOVE?
THIS IS TORTURE FOR ME.
BUT YOU'RE GETTING BIGGER.
HA... THAT'S CUZ YOU'RE SQUEEZING ME SO TIGHT.
THRUST
AH! YOU DUMMY!
KRAK
N
YOU'VE GOT SUCH AN EROTIC BODY.
WITH HOW SENSITIVE YOU ARE ON THE INSIDE, I'M SURPRISED YOU'VE TOPPED ALL THIS TIME.
AH
AHN
KRAK
KREAK
KRAK
AH!
NN!
KREAK

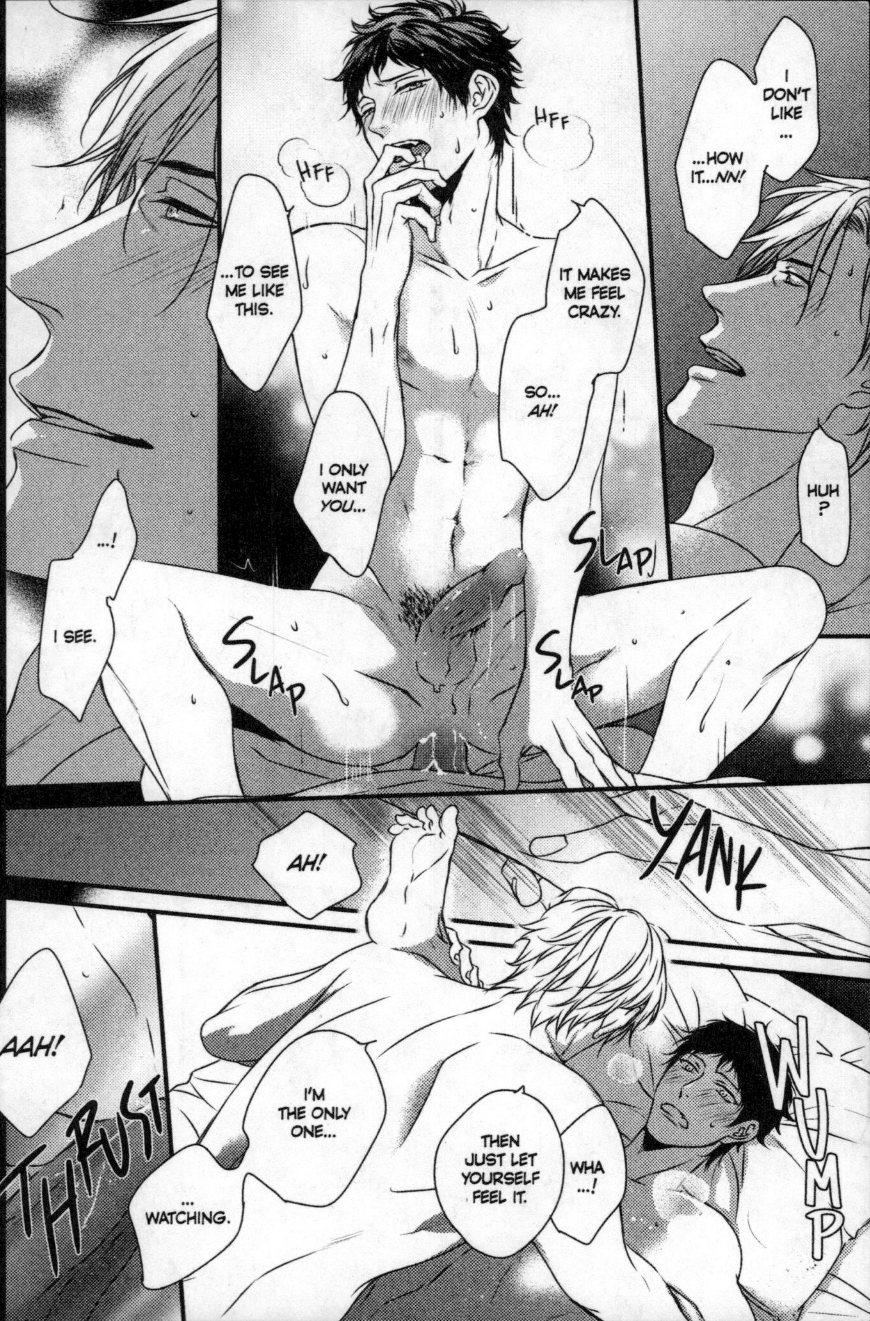
I DON'T LIKE ...
...HOW IT...*NN!*
HUH?
HFF
HFF
IT MAKES ME FEEL CRAZY.
SO... *AH!*
I ONLY WANT *YOU*...
...TO SEE ME LIKE THIS.
SLAP
SLAP
SLAP
...!
I SEE.
YANK
AH!
WUMP
WHA ...!
THEN JUST LET YOURSELF FEEL IT.
I'M THE ONLY ONE...
... WATCHING.
AAH!
THRUST

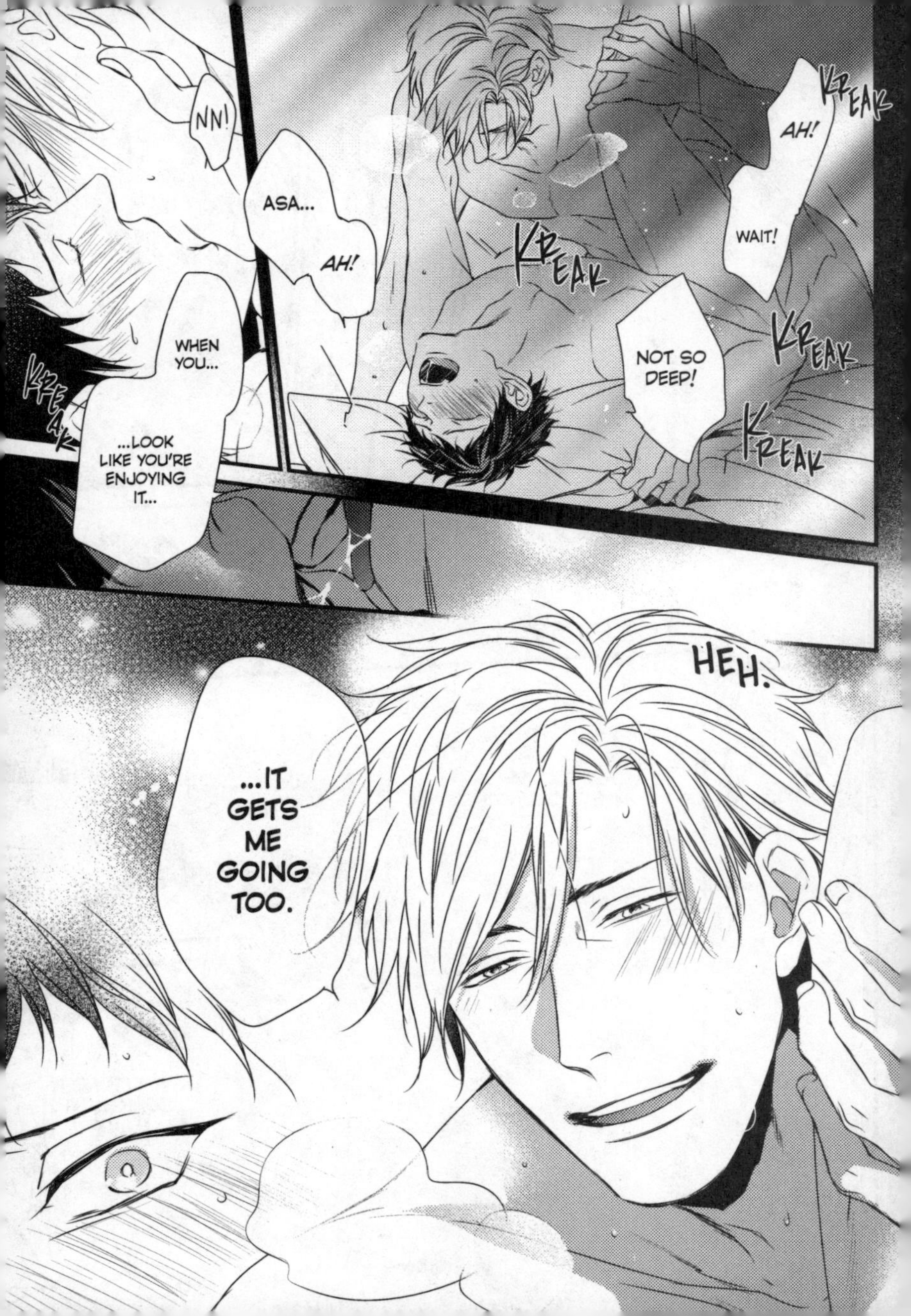
KREAK
AH!
WAIT!
ASA...
AH!
KREAK
KREAK
NOT SO DEEP!
KREAK
NN!
WHEN YOU...
...LOOK LIKE YOU'RE ENJOYING IT...
KREAK
HEH.
...IT GETS ME GOING TOO.

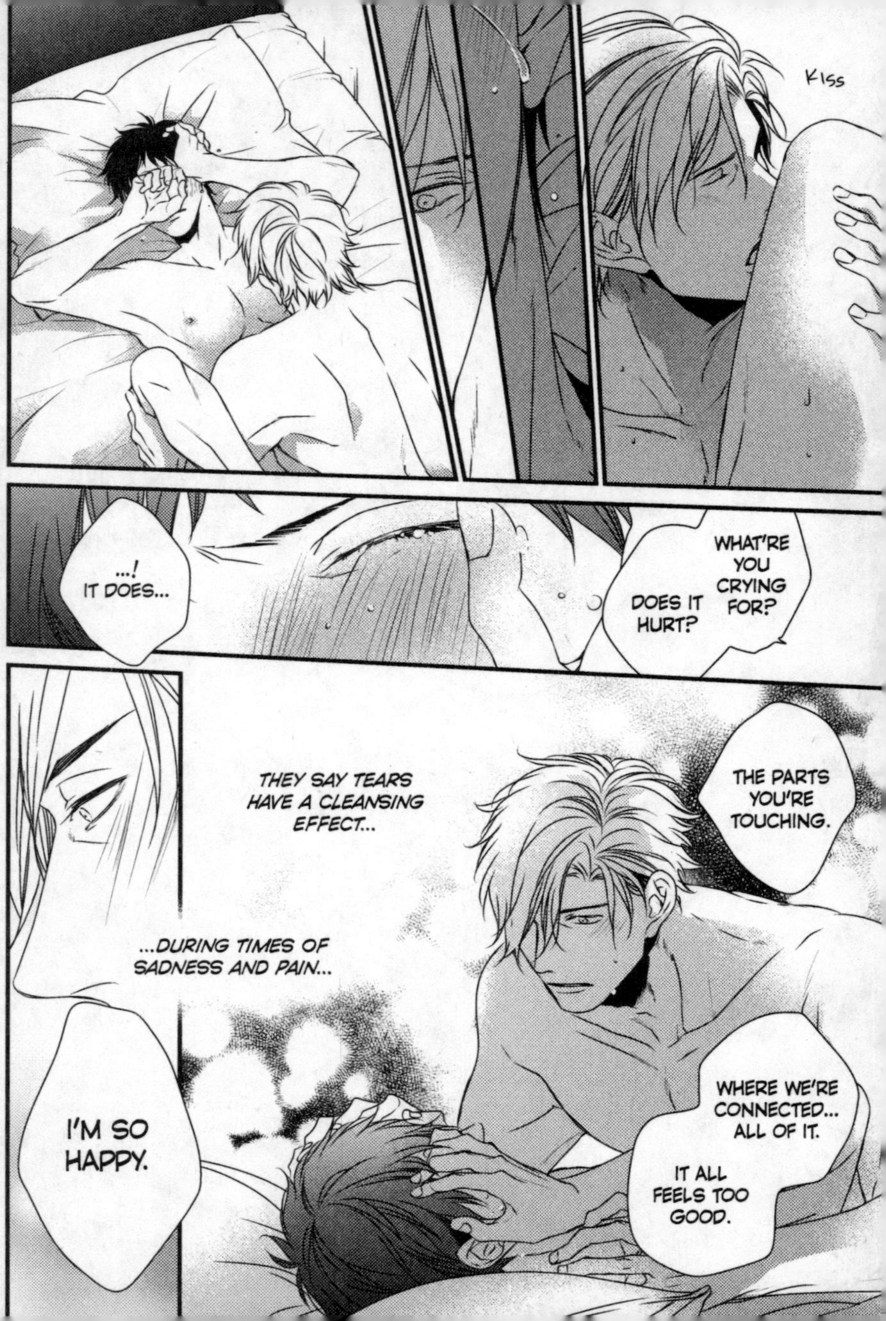
KISS
WHAT'RE YOU CRYING FOR?
DOES IT HURT?
...! IT DOES...
THE PARTS YOU'RE TOUCHING.
THEY SAY TEARS HAVE A CLEANSING EFFECT...
WHERE WE'RE CONNECTED... ALL OF IT.
IT ALL FEELS TOO GOOD.
...DURING TIMES OF SADNESS AND PAIN...
I'M SO HAPPY.

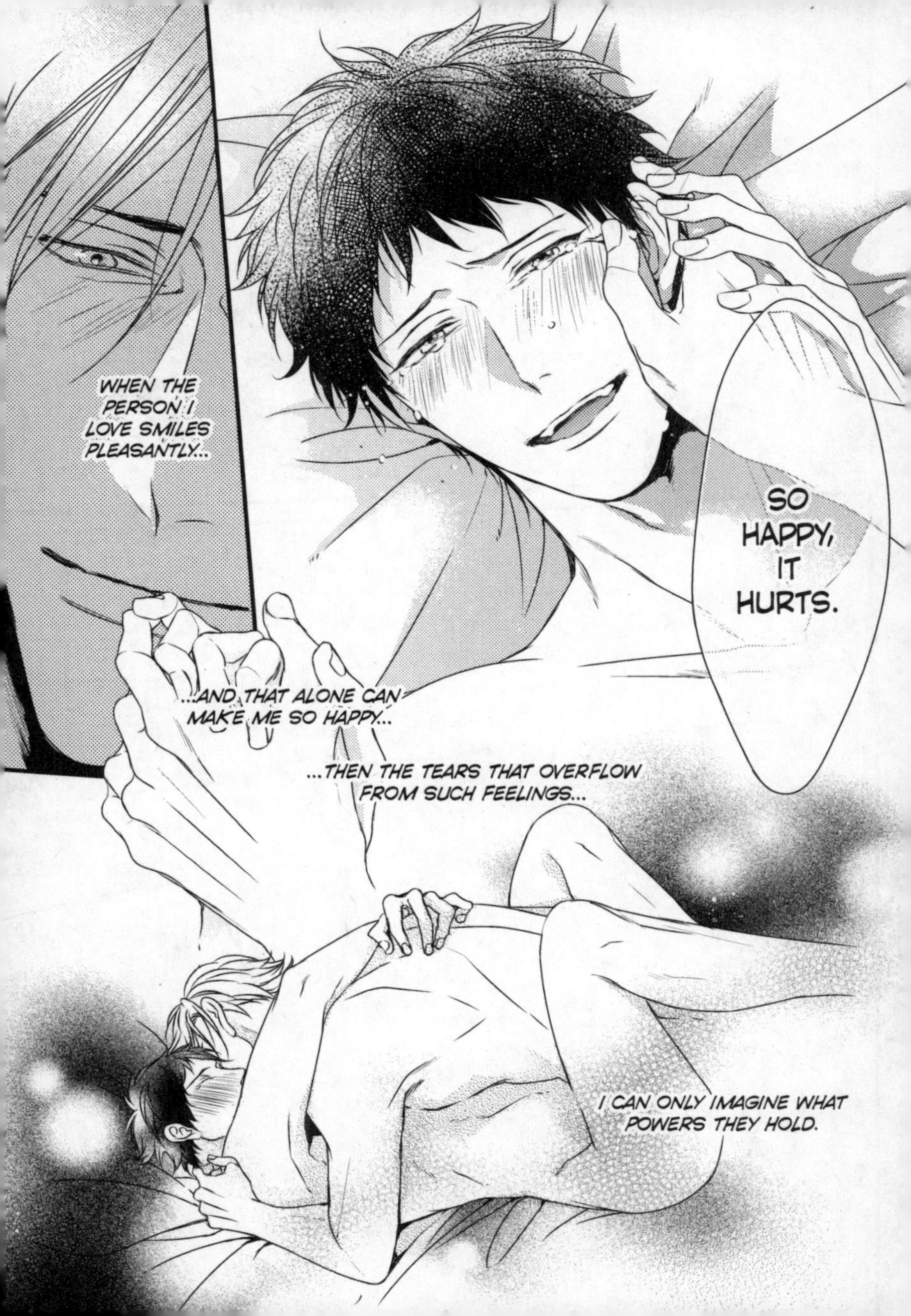
SO HAPPY, IT HURTS.
WHEN THE PERSON I LOVE SMILES PLEASANTLY...
...AND THAT ALONE CAN MAKE ME SO HAPPY...
...THEN THE TEARS THAT OVERFLOW FROM SUCH FEELINGS...
I CAN ONLY IMAGINE WHAT POWERS THEY HOLD.

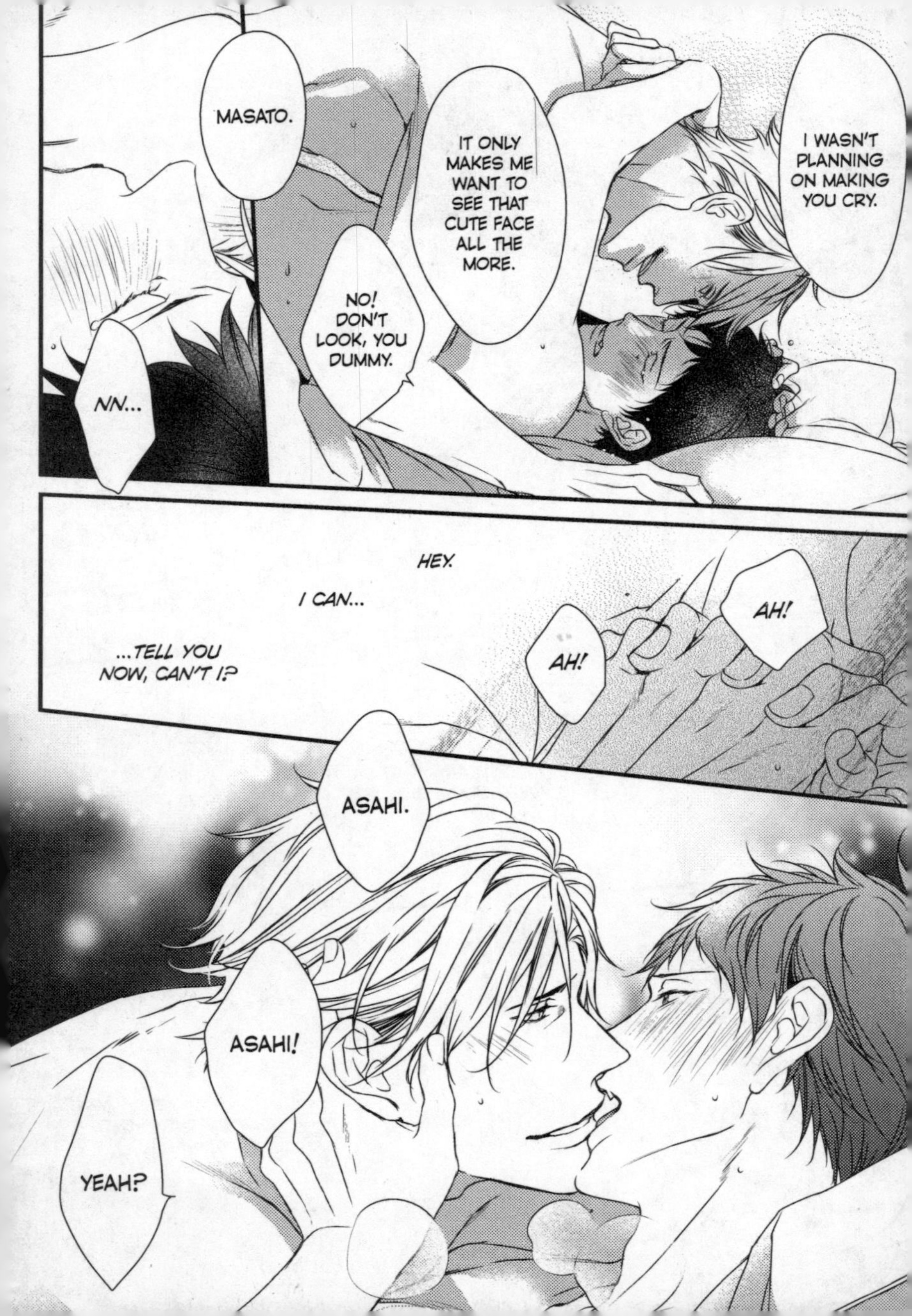
I WASN'T PLANNING ON MAKING YOU CRY.
IT ONLY MAKES ME WANT TO SEE THAT CUTE FACE ALL THE MORE.
NO! DON'T LOOK, YOU DUMMY.
MASATO.
NN...
AH!
AH!
HEY.
I CAN...
...TELL YOU NOW, CAN'T I?
ASAHI.
ASAHI!
YEAH?

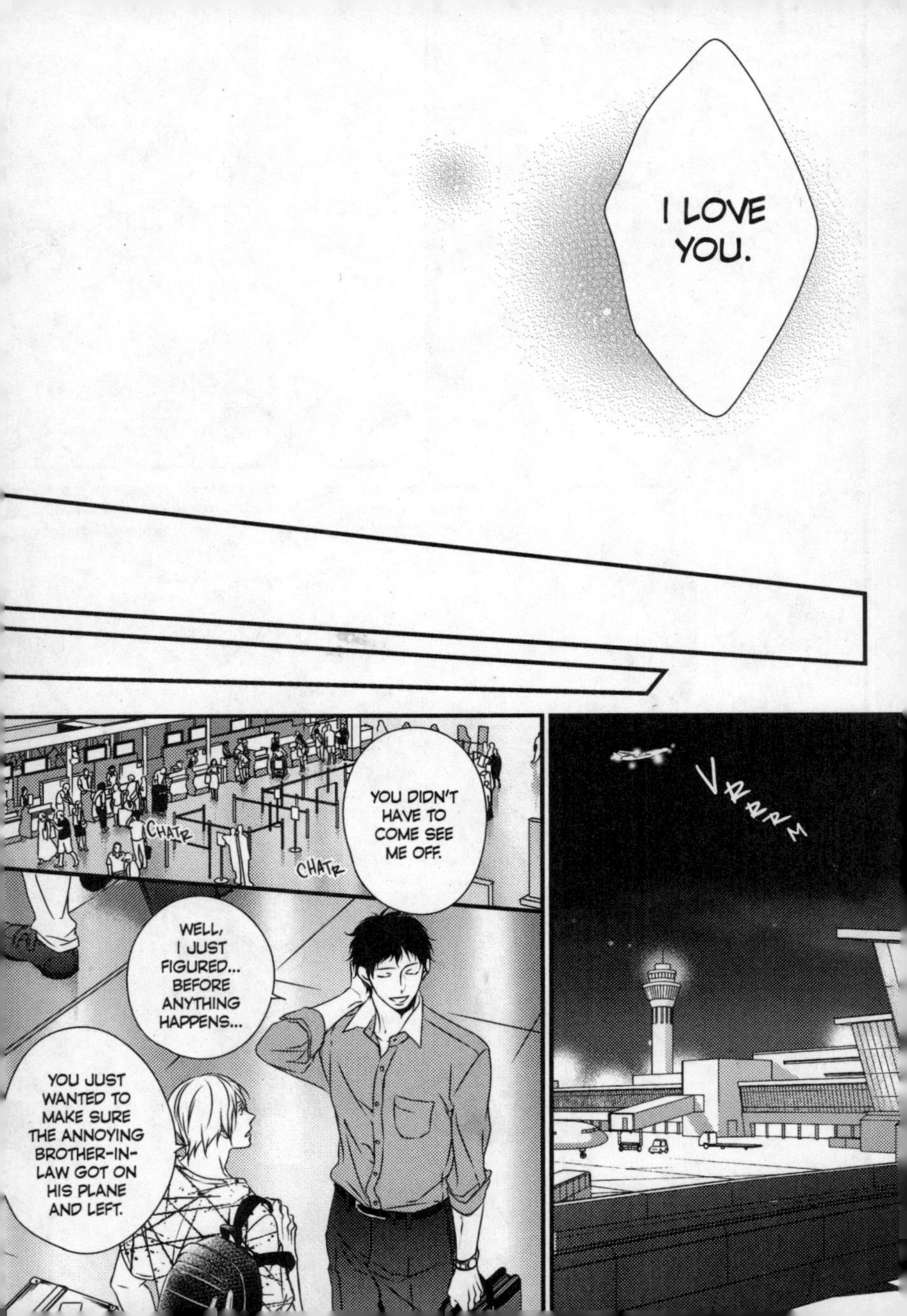
I LOVE YOU.
VRRRM
CHATR
CHATR
YOU DIDN'T HAVE TO COME SEE ME OFF.
WELL, I JUST FIGURED... BEFORE ANYTHING HAPPENS...
YOU JUST WANTED TO MAKE SURE THE ANNOYING BROTHER-IN-LAW GOT ON HIS PLANE AND LEFT.

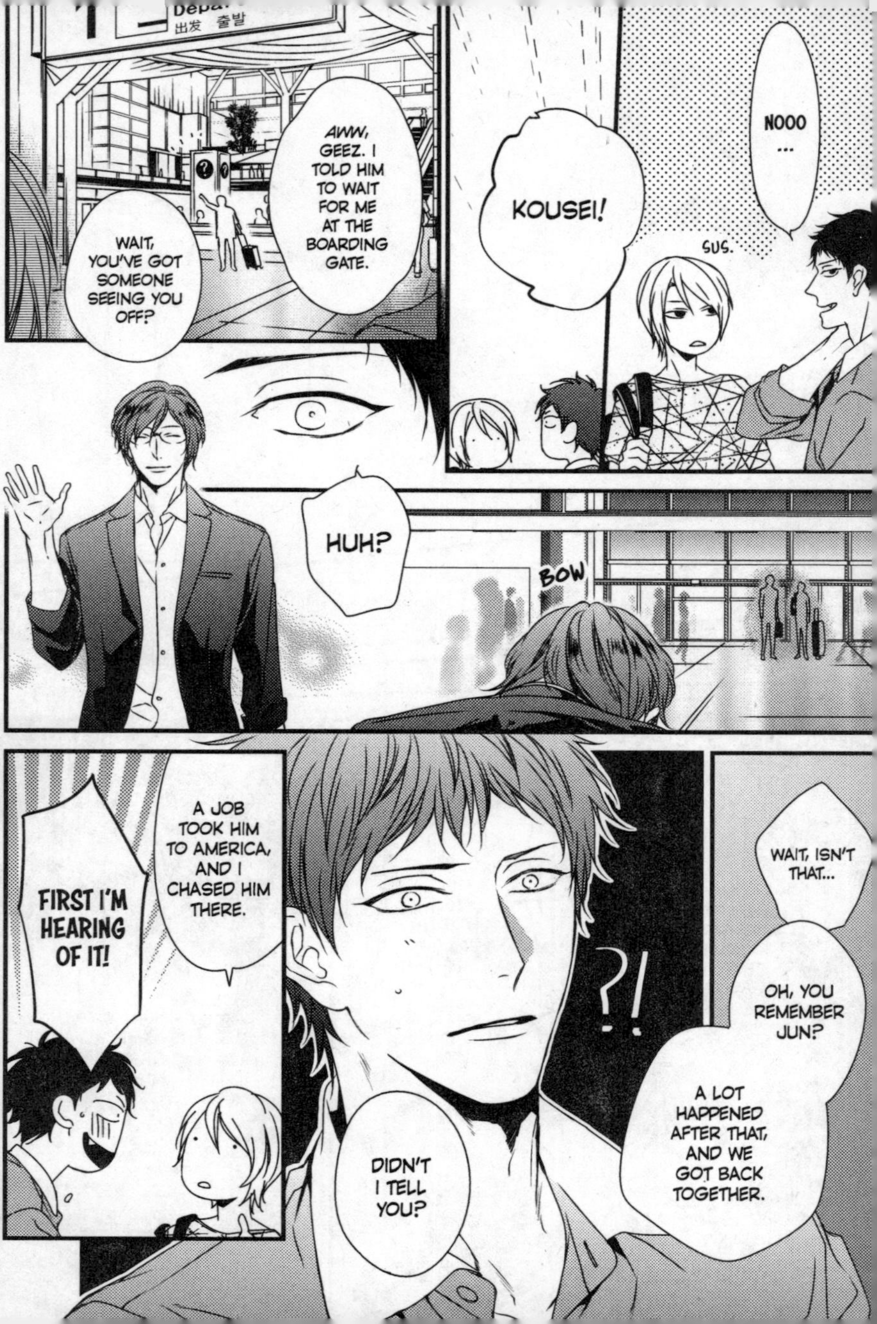
NOOO...
SUS.
KOUSEI!
出发 출발
AWW, GEEZ. I TOLD HIM TO WAIT FOR ME AT THE BOARDING GATE.
WAIT, YOU'VE GOT SOMEONE SEEING YOU OFF?
HUH?
BOW
WAIT, ISN'T THAT...
OH, YOU REMEMBER JUN?
A LOT HAPPENED AFTER THAT, AND WE GOT BACK TOGETHER.
?!
DIDN'T I TELL YOU?
A JOB TOOK HIM TO AMERICA, AND I CHASED HIM THERE.
FIRST I'M HEARING OF IT!

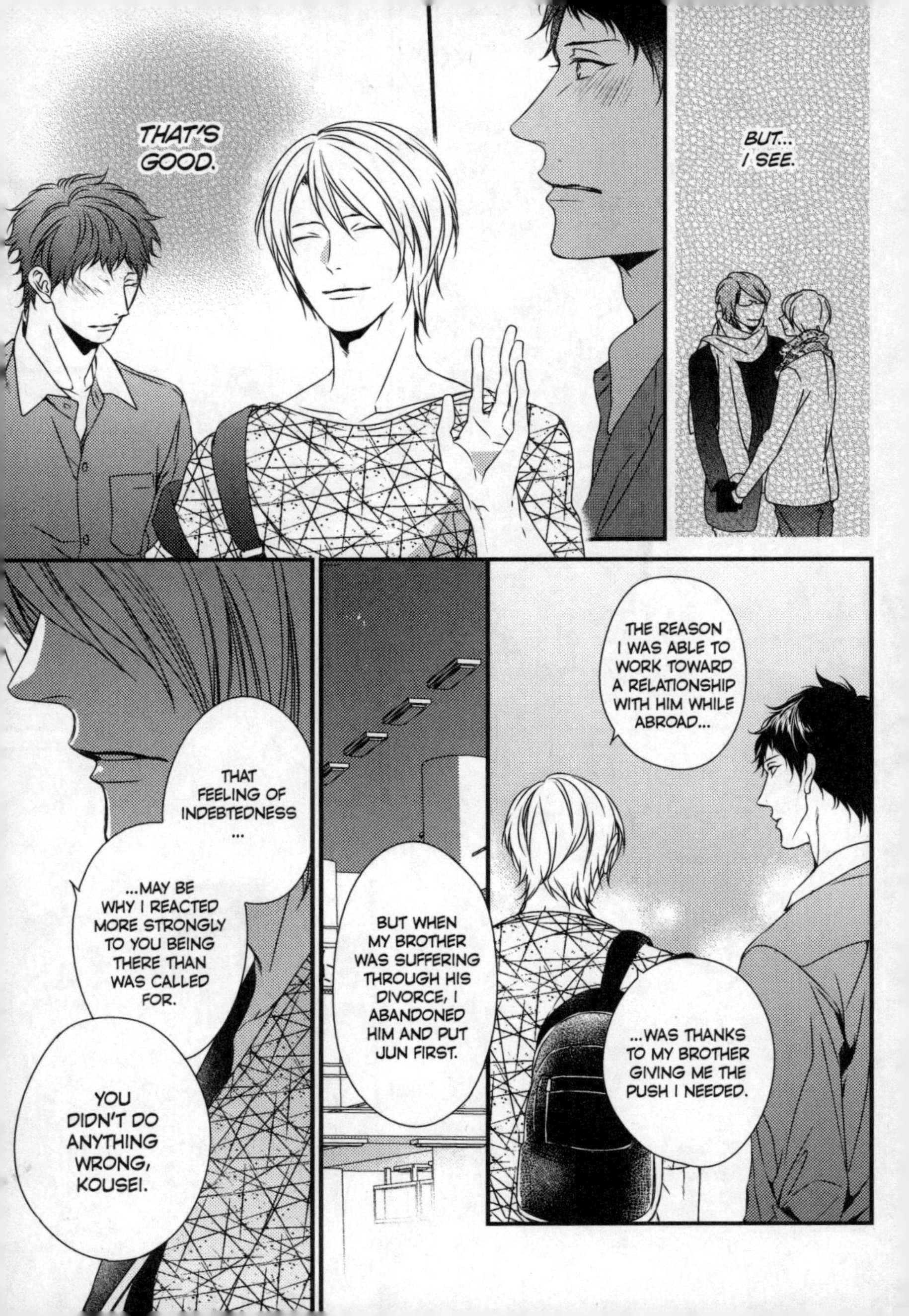
BUT... I SEE.
THAT'S GOOD.
THE REASON I WAS ABLE TO WORK TOWARD A RELATIONSHIP WITH HIM WHILE ABROAD...
...WAS THANKS TO MY BROTHER GIVING ME THE PUSH I NEEDED.
BUT WHEN MY BROTHER WAS SUFFERING THROUGH HIS DIVORCE, I ABANDONED HIM AND PUT JUN FIRST.
THAT FEELING OF INDEBTEDNESS ...
...MAY BE WHY I REACTED MORE STRONGLY TO YOU BEING THERE THAN WAS CALLED FOR.
YOU DIDN'T DO ANYTHING WRONG, KOUSEI.

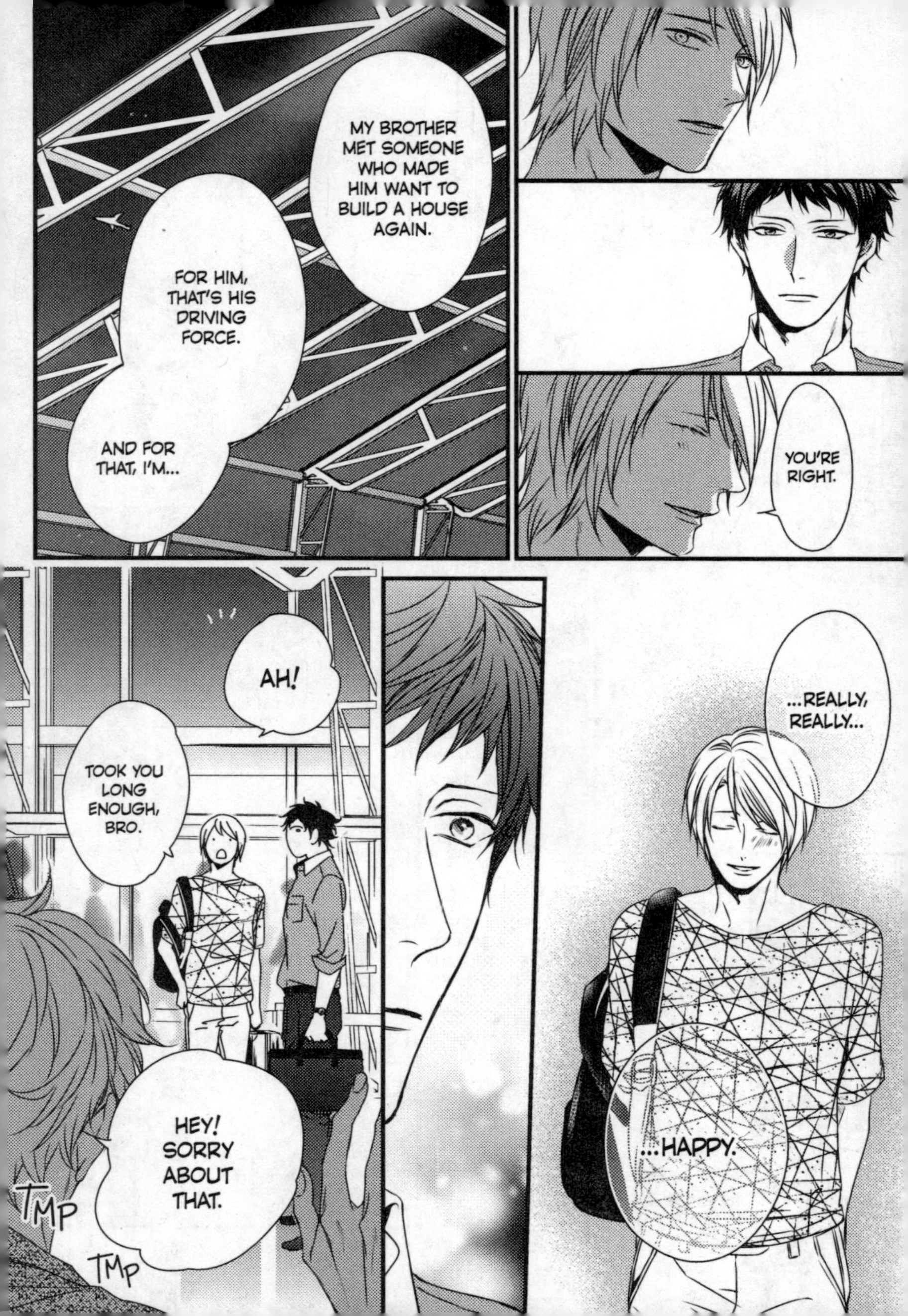
YOU'RE RIGHT.
MY BROTHER MET SOMEONE WHO MADE HIM WANT TO BUILD A HOUSE AGAIN.
FOR HIM, THAT'S HIS DRIVING FORCE.
AND FOR THAT, I'M...
...REALLY, REALLY...
...HAPPY.
AH!
TOOK YOU LONG ENOUGH, BRO.
HEY! SORRY ABOUT THAT.
TMP
TMP

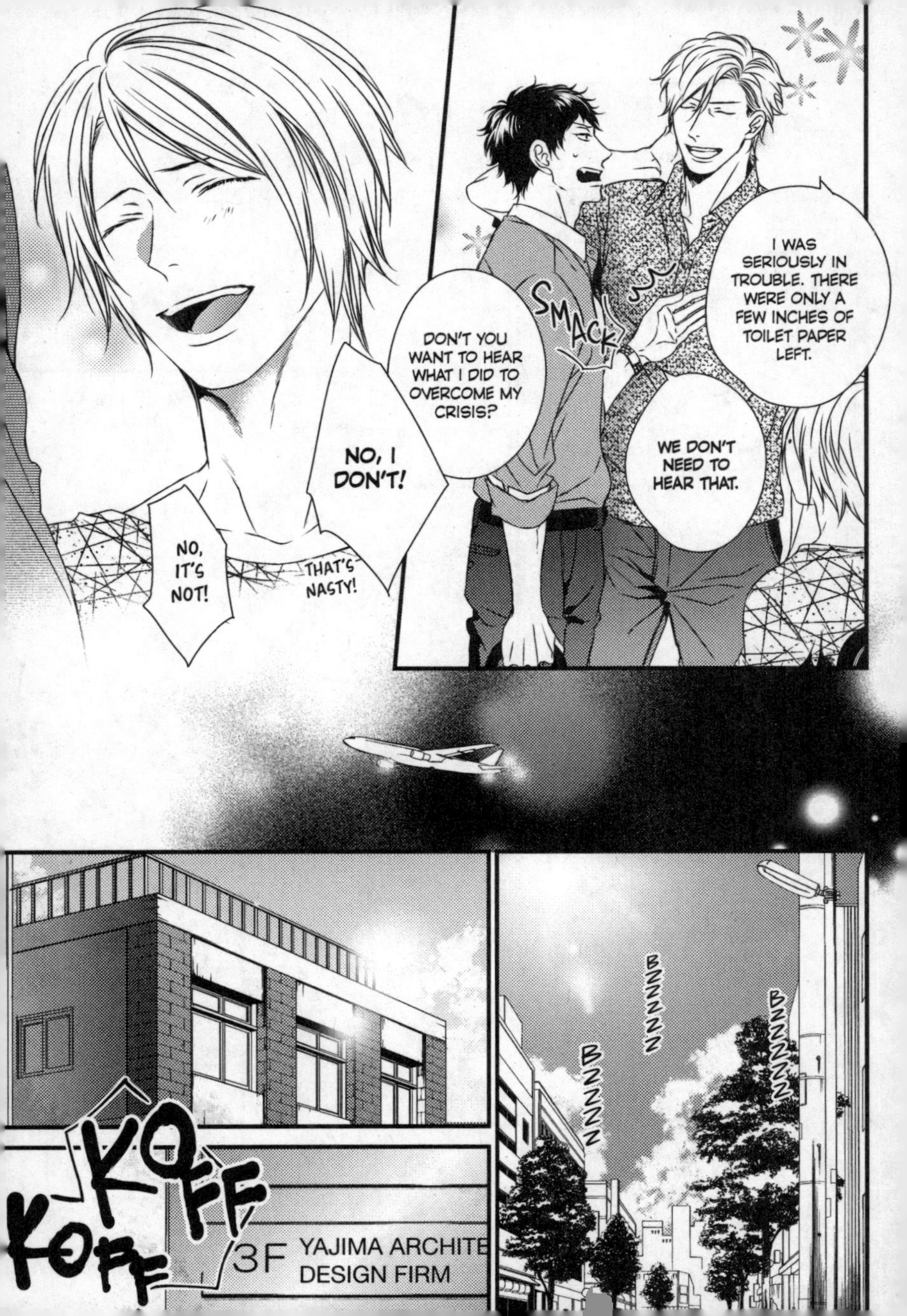
I WAS SERIOUSLY IN TROUBLE. THERE WERE ONLY A FEW INCHES OF TOILET PAPER LEFT.
SMACK
WE DON'T NEED TO HEAR THAT.
DON'T YOU WANT TO HEAR WHAT I DID TO OVERCOME MY CRISIS?
NO, I DON'T!
THAT'S NASTY!
NO, IT'S NOT!
BZZZZZ
BZZZZZ
BZZZZ
KOFF
KOFF
3F YAJIMA ARCHITE
DESIGN FIRM

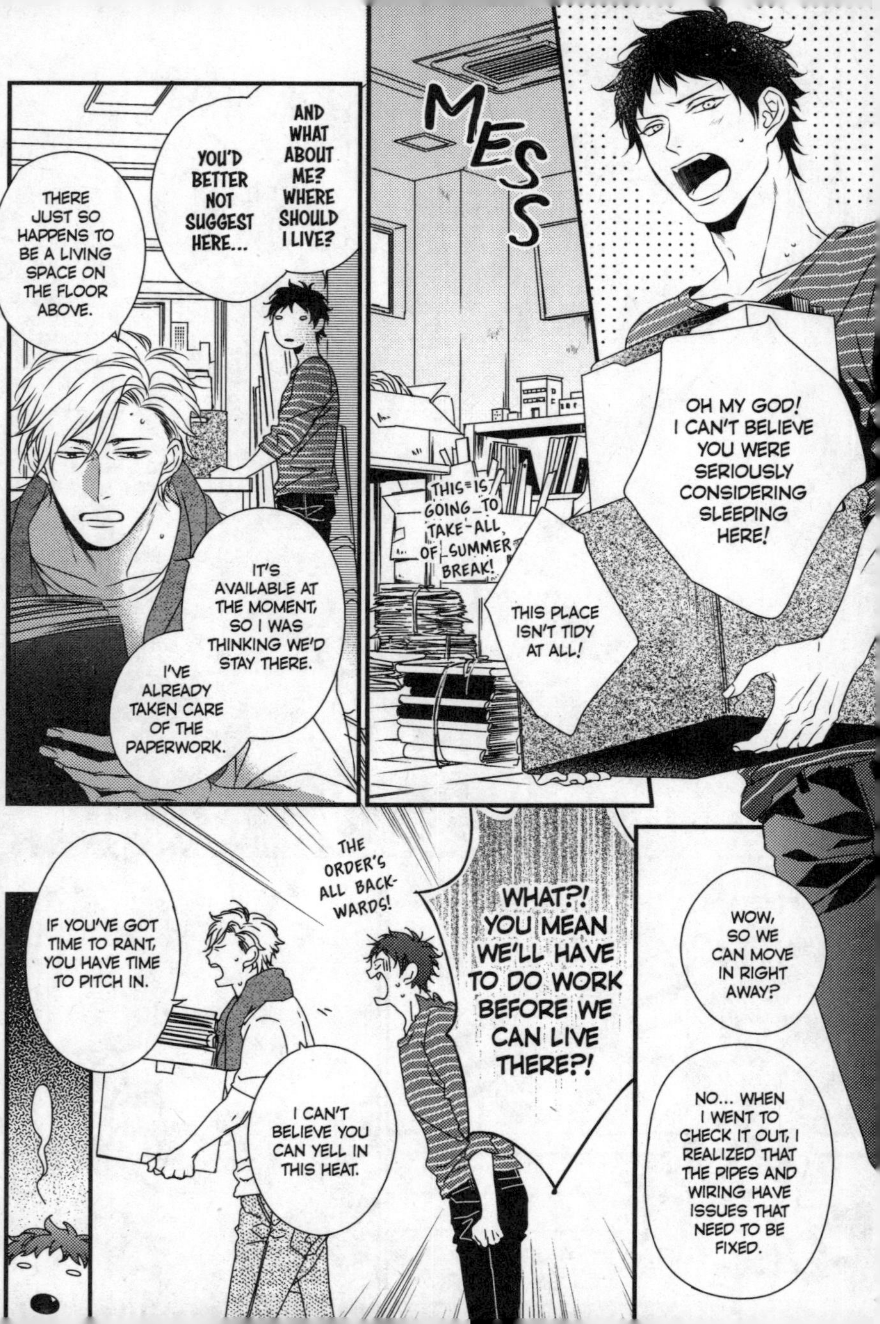
MESS
OH MY GOD! I CAN'T BELIEVE YOU WERE SERIOUSLY CONSIDERING SLEEPING HERE!
THIS PLACE ISN'T TIDY AT ALL!
THIS IS GOING TO TAKE ALL OF SUMMER BREAK!
AND WHAT ABOUT ME? WHERE SHOULD I LIVE?
YOU'D BETTER NOT SUGGEST HERE...
THERE JUST SO HAPPENS TO BE A LIVING SPACE ON THE FLOOR ABOVE.
IT'S AVAILABLE AT THE MOMENT, SO I WAS THINKING WE'D STAY THERE.
I'VE ALREADY TAKEN CARE OF THE PAPERWORK.
WOW, SO WE CAN MOVE IN RIGHT AWAY?
NO... WHEN I WENT TO CHECK IT OUT, I REALIZED THAT THE PIPES AND WIRING HAVE ISSUES THAT NEED TO BE FIXED.
WHAT?! YOU MEAN WE'LL HAVE TO DO WORK BEFORE WE CAN LIVE THERE?!
THE ORDER'S ALL BACK-WARDS!
IF YOU'VE GOT TIME TO RANT, YOU HAVE TIME TO PITCH IN.
I CAN'T BELIEVE YOU CAN YELL IN THIS HEAT.

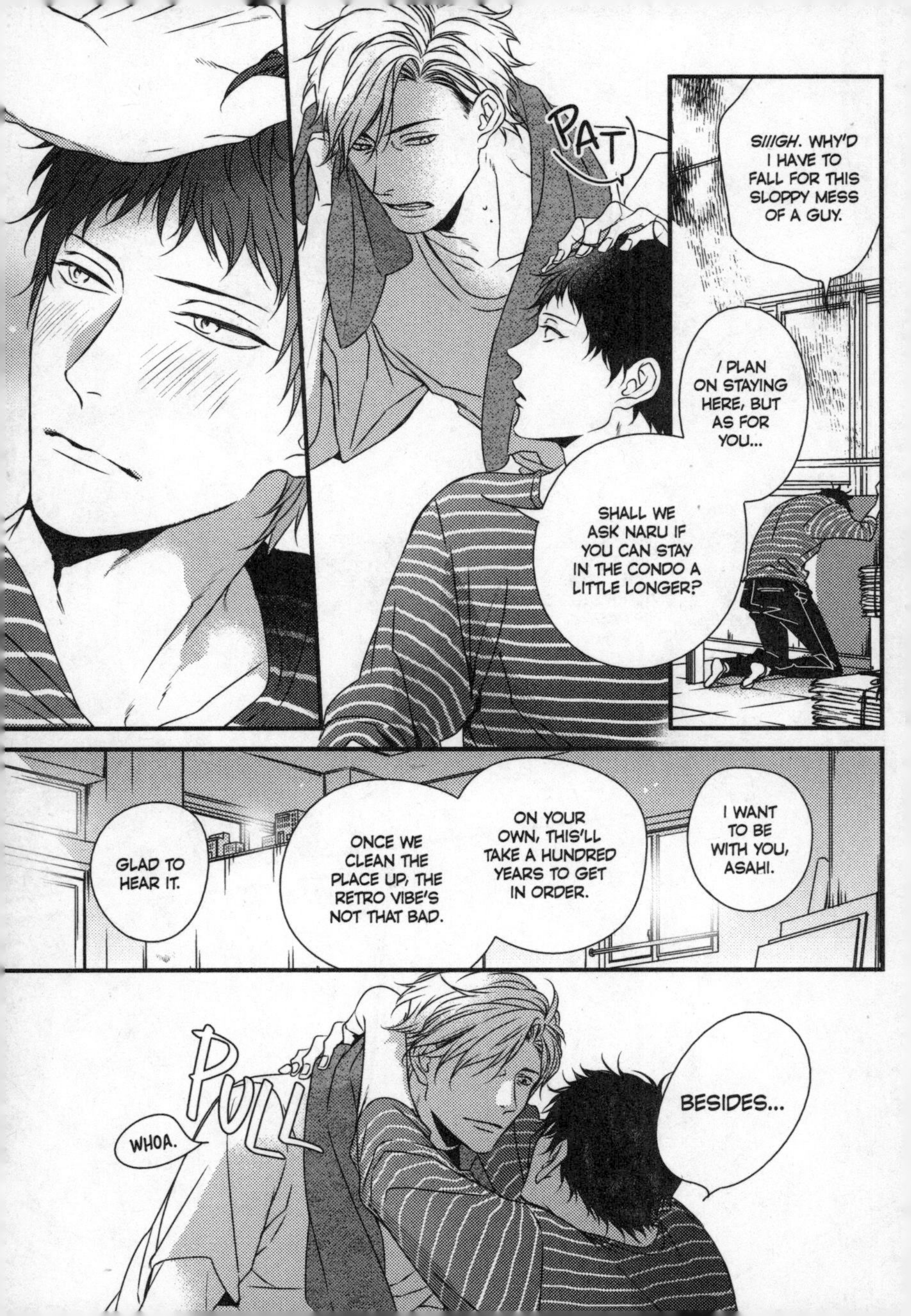
SIIIGH. WHY'D I HAVE TO FALL FOR THIS SLOPPY MESS OF A GUY.
PAT
I PLAN ON STAYING HERE, BUT AS FOR YOU...
SHALL WE ASK NARU IF YOU CAN STAY IN THE CONDO A LITTLE LONGER?
I WANT TO BE WITH YOU, ASAHI.
ON YOUR OWN, THIS'LL TAKE A HUNDRED YEARS TO GET IN ORDER.
ONCE WE CLEAN THE PLACE UP, THE RETRO VIBE'S NOT THAT BAD.
GLAD TO HEAR IT.
BESIDES...
PULL
WHOA.

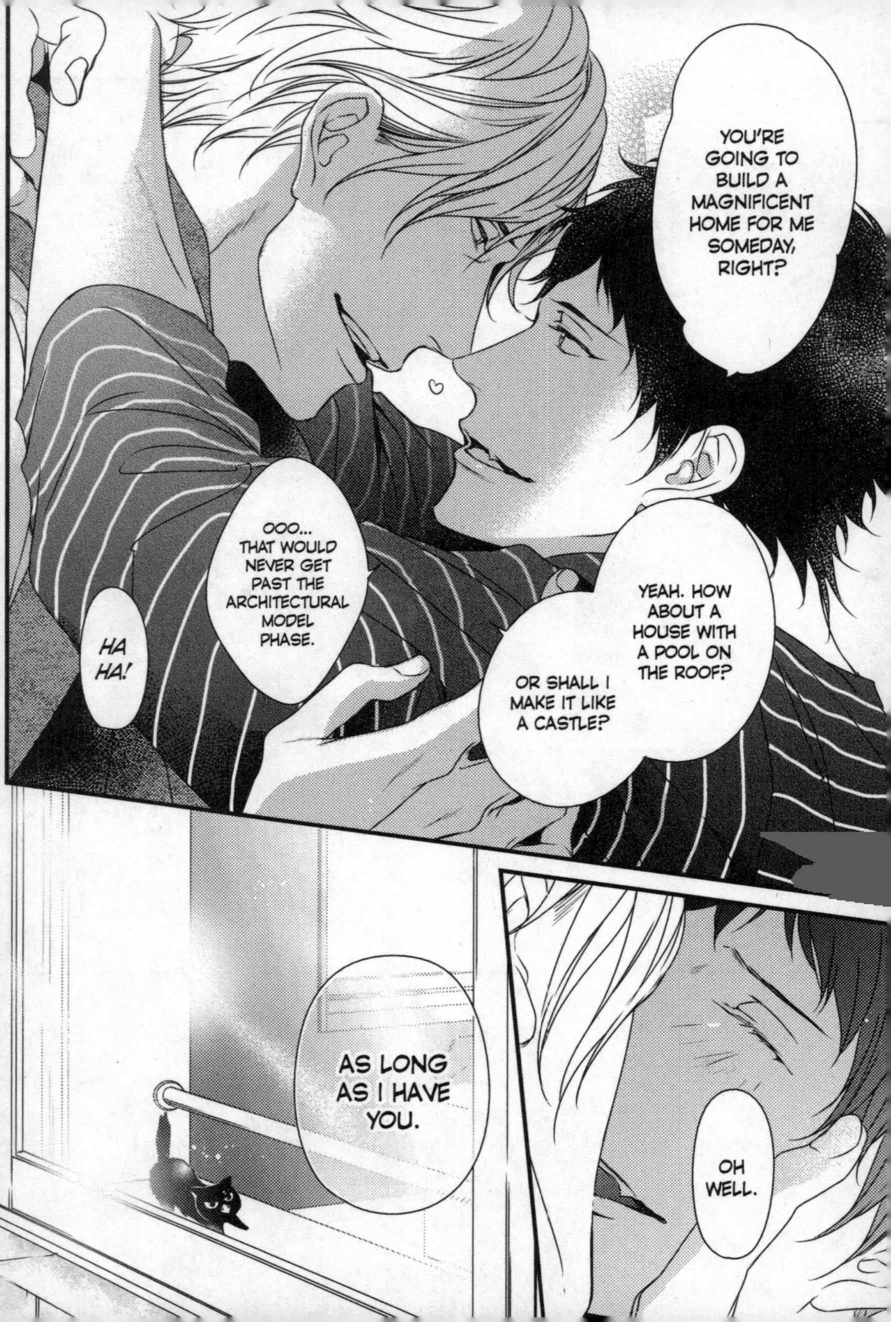
YOU'RE GOING TO BUILD A MAGNIFICENT HOME FOR ME SOMEDAY, RIGHT?
YEAH. HOW ABOUT A HOUSE WITH A POOL ON THE ROOF?
OR SHALL I MAKE IT LIKE A CASTLE?
OOO... THAT WOULD NEVER GET PAST THE ARCHITECTURAL MODEL PHASE.
HA HA!
OH WELL.
AS LONG AS I HAVE YOU.

Love Nest Sequel

LOVE NEST

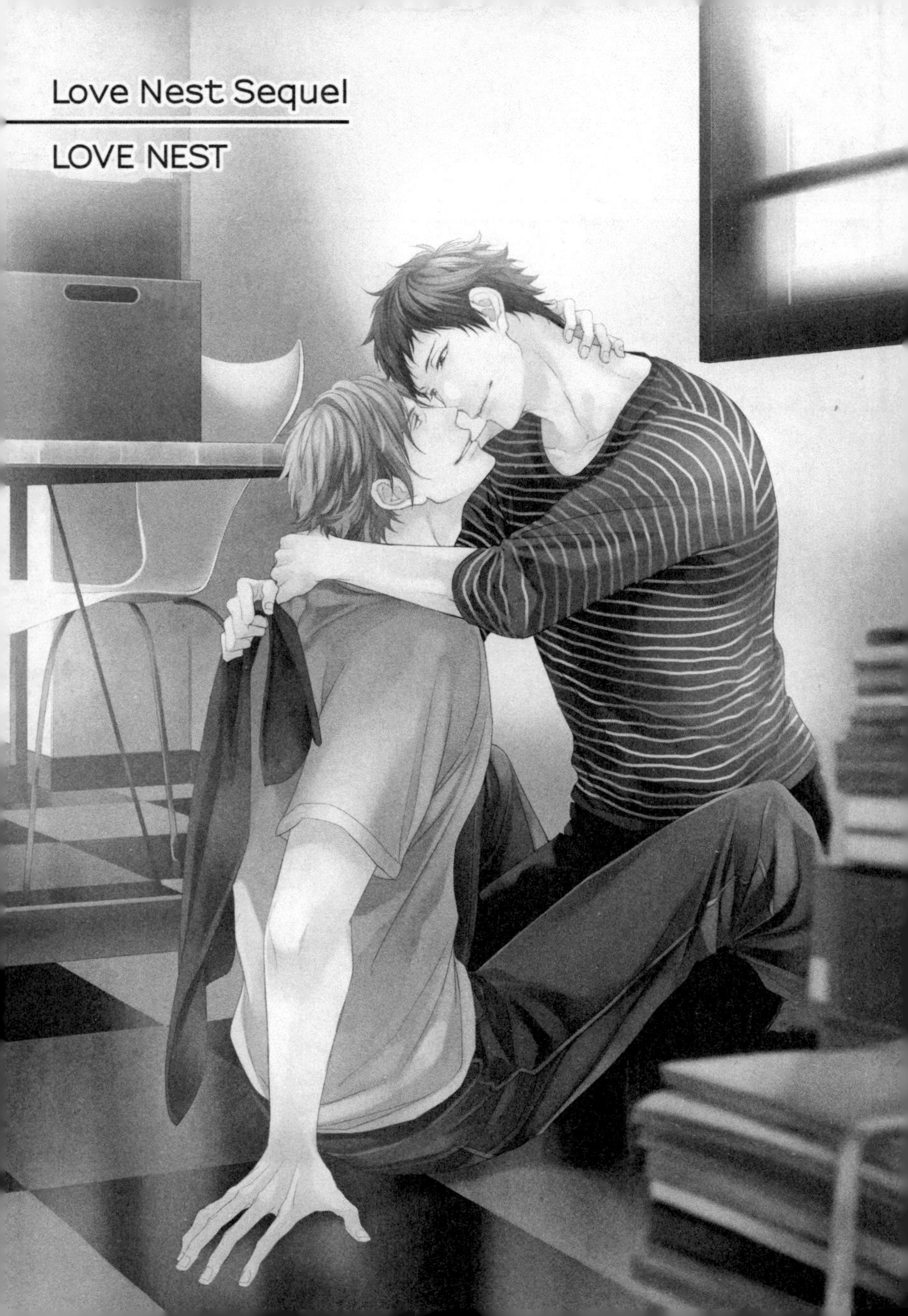

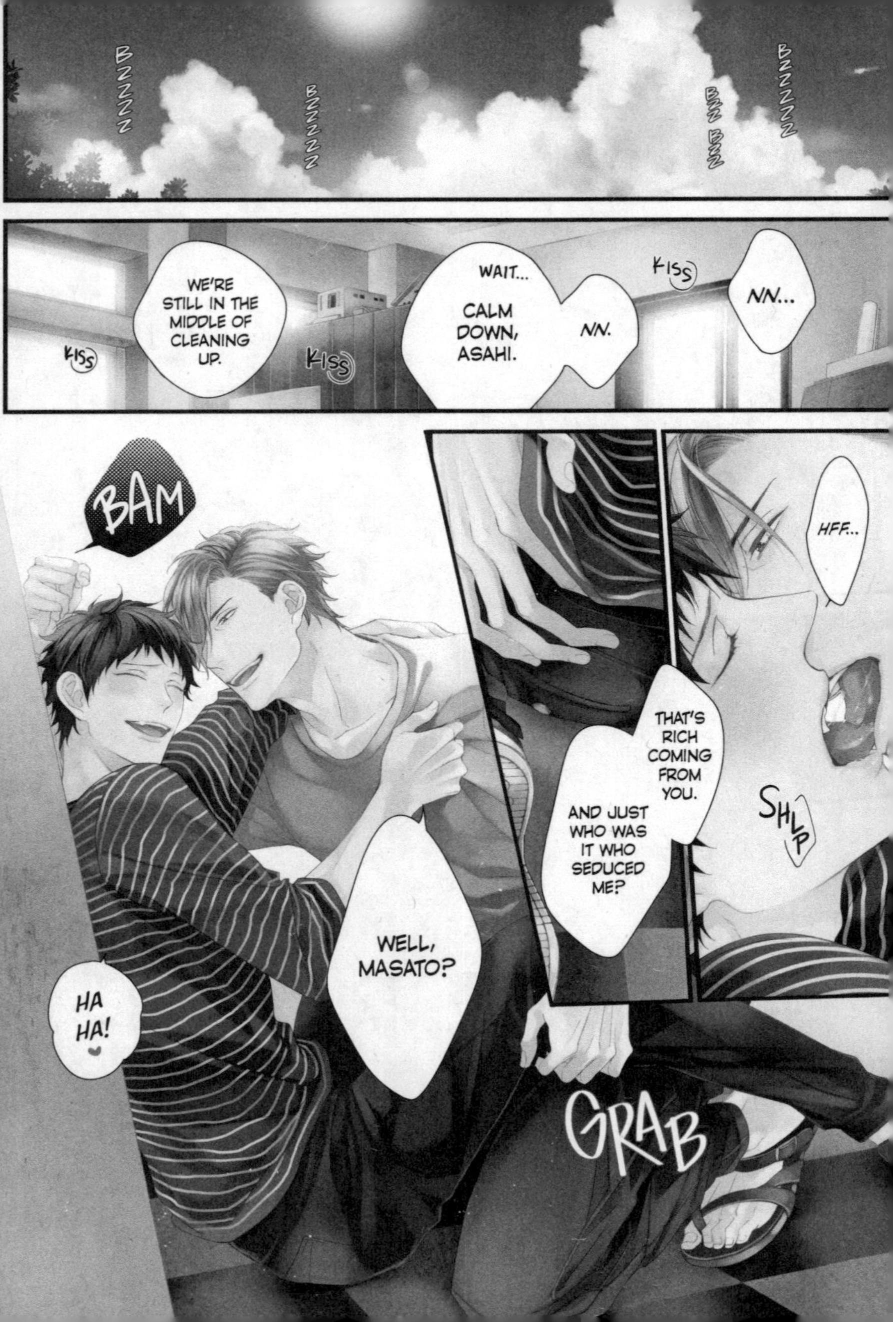
BZZZZZZ
BZZ BZZ
BZZZZZ
BZZZZ
NN...
KISS
NN.
WAIT...
CALM DOWN, ASAHI.
KISS
WE'RE STILL IN THE MIDDLE OF CLEANING UP.
KISS
HFF...
SHLP
THAT'S RICH COMING FROM YOU.
AND JUST WHO WAS IT WHO SEDUCED ME?
BAM
WELL, MASATO?
HA HA!
GRAB

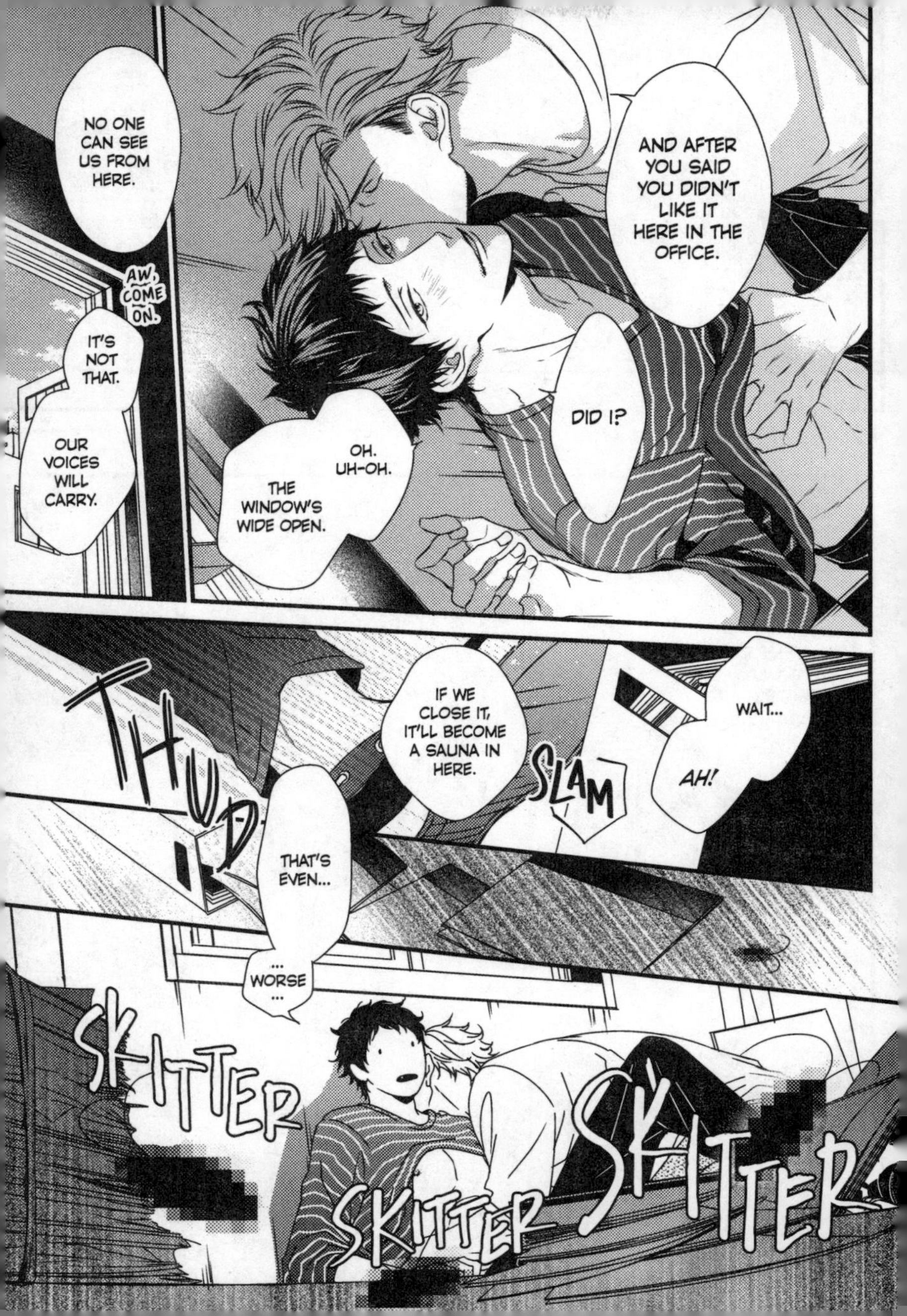
AND AFTER YOU SAID YOU DIDN'T LIKE IT HERE IN THE OFFICE.
DID I?
OH. UH-OH.
THE WINDOW'S WIDE OPEN.
NO ONE CAN SEE US FROM HERE.
AW, COME ON.
IT'S NOT THAT.
OUR VOICES WILL CARRY.
WAIT...
AH!
SLAM
IF WE CLOSE IT, IT'LL BECOME A SAUNA IN HERE.
THUD
THAT'S EVEN...
...WORSE...
SKITTER
SKITTER
SKITTER

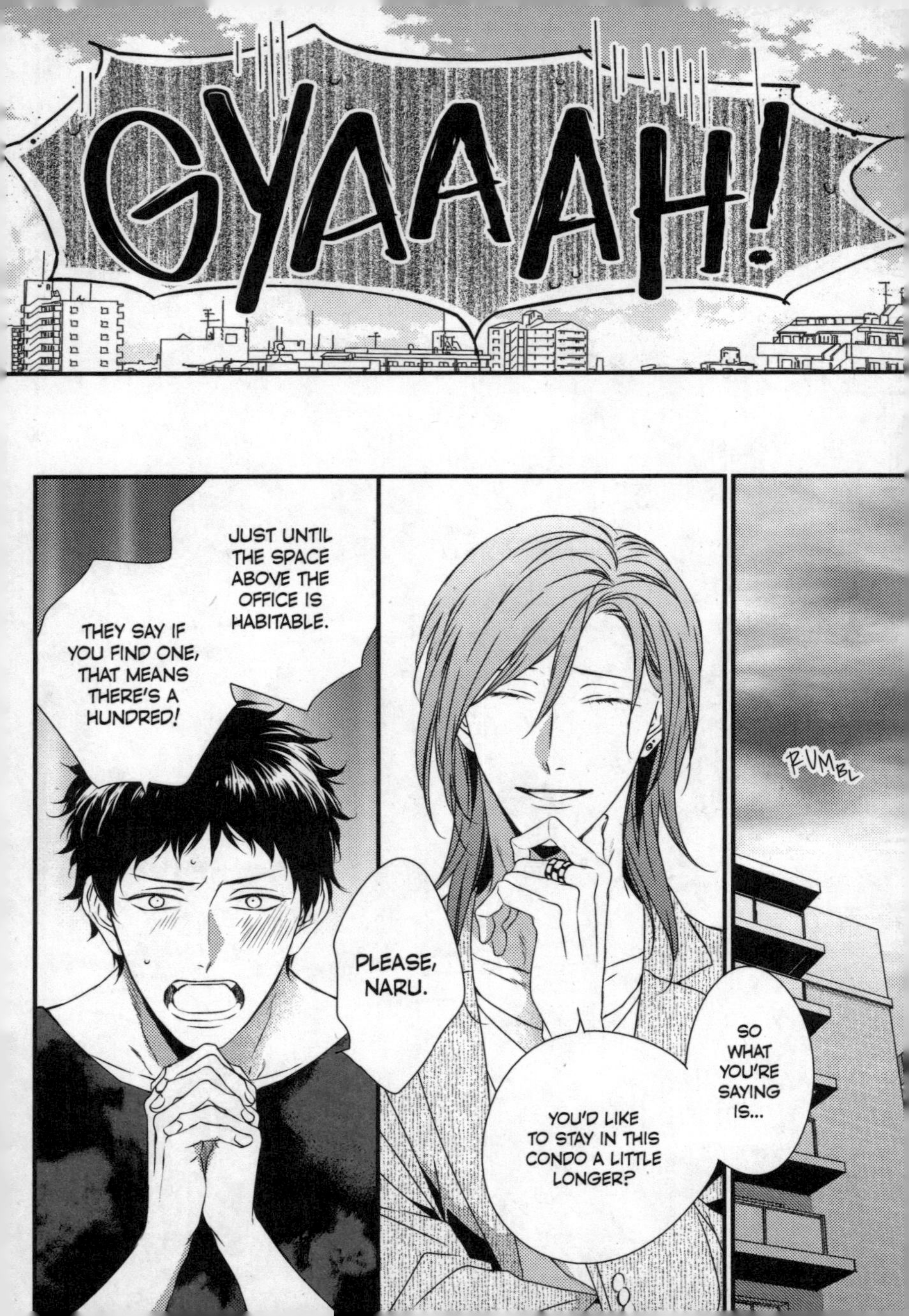
GYAAAH!
RUMBL
SO WHAT YOU'RE SAYING IS...
YOU'D LIKE TO STAY IN THIS CONDO A LITTLE LONGER?
PLEASE, NARU.
JUST UNTIL THE SPACE ABOVE THE OFFICE IS HABITABLE.
THEY SAY IF YOU FIND ONE, THAT MEANS THERE'S A HUNDRED!

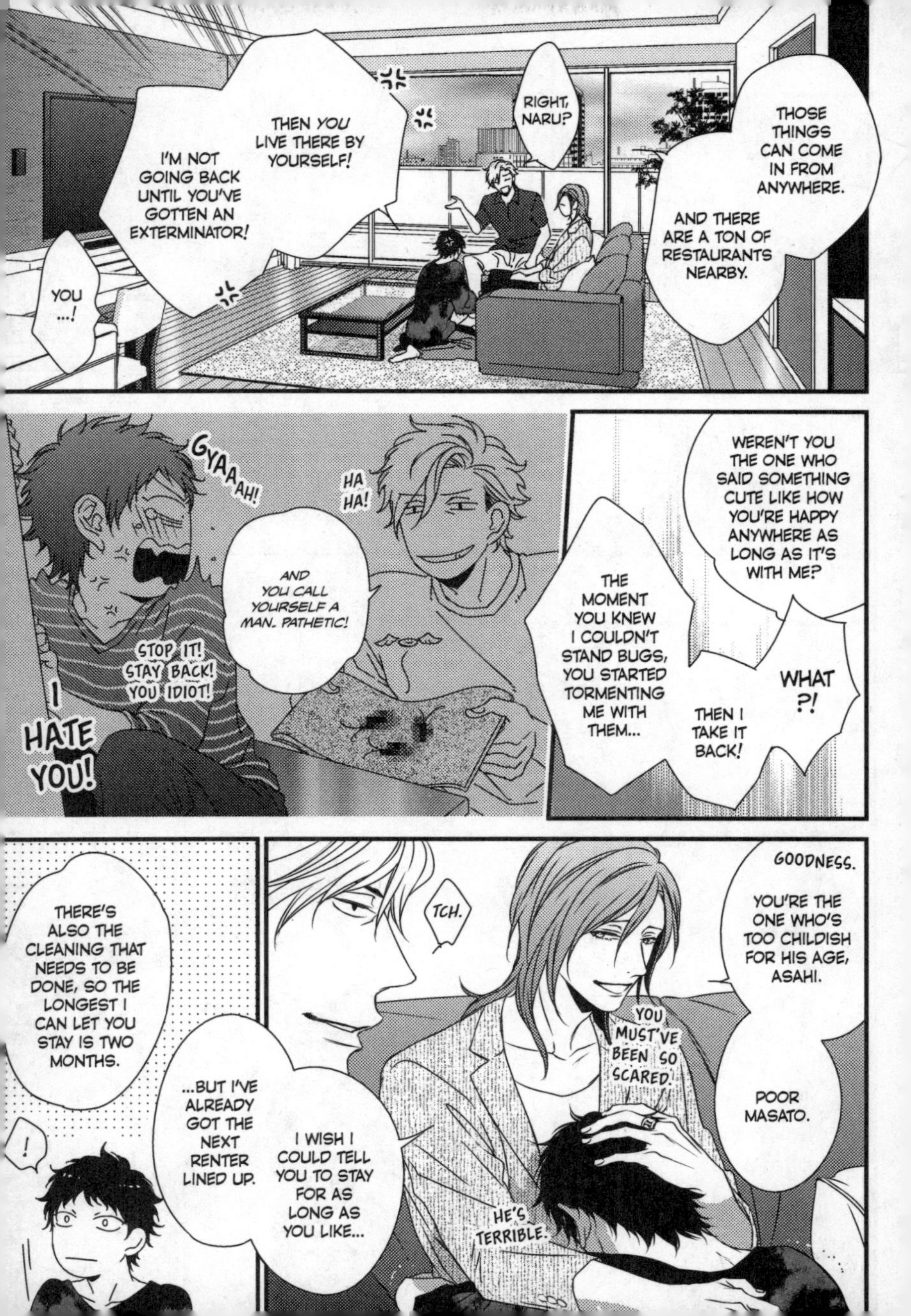
THOSE THINGS CAN COME IN FROM ANYWHERE.
AND THERE ARE A TON OF RESTAURANTS NEARBY.
RIGHT, NARU?
THEN *YOU* LIVE THERE BY YOURSELF!
I'M NOT GOING BACK UNTIL YOU'VE GOTTEN AN EXTERMINATOR!
YOU ...!
WEREN'T YOU THE ONE WHO SAID SOMETHING CUTE LIKE HOW YOU'RE HAPPY ANYWHERE AS LONG AS IT'S WITH ME?
WHAT ?!
THEN I TAKE IT BACK!
THE MOMENT YOU KNEW I COULDN'T STAND BUGS, YOU STARTED TORMENTING ME WITH THEM...
HA HA!
AND YOU CALL YOURSELF A MAN. PATHETIC!
GYAAAAH!
STOP IT! STAY BACK! YOU IDIOT!
I HATE YOU!
GOODNESS.
YOU'RE THE ONE WHO'S TOO CHILDISH FOR HIS AGE, ASAHI.
TCH.
POOR MASATO.
YOU MUST'VE BEEN SO SCARED.
HE'S TERRIBLE.
I WISH I COULD TELL YOU TO STAY FOR AS LONG AS YOU LIKE...
...BUT I'VE ALREADY GOT THE NEXT RENTER LINED UP.
THERE'S ALSO THE CLEANING THAT NEEDS TO BE DONE, SO THE LONGEST I CAN LET YOU STAY IS TWO MONTHS.
!

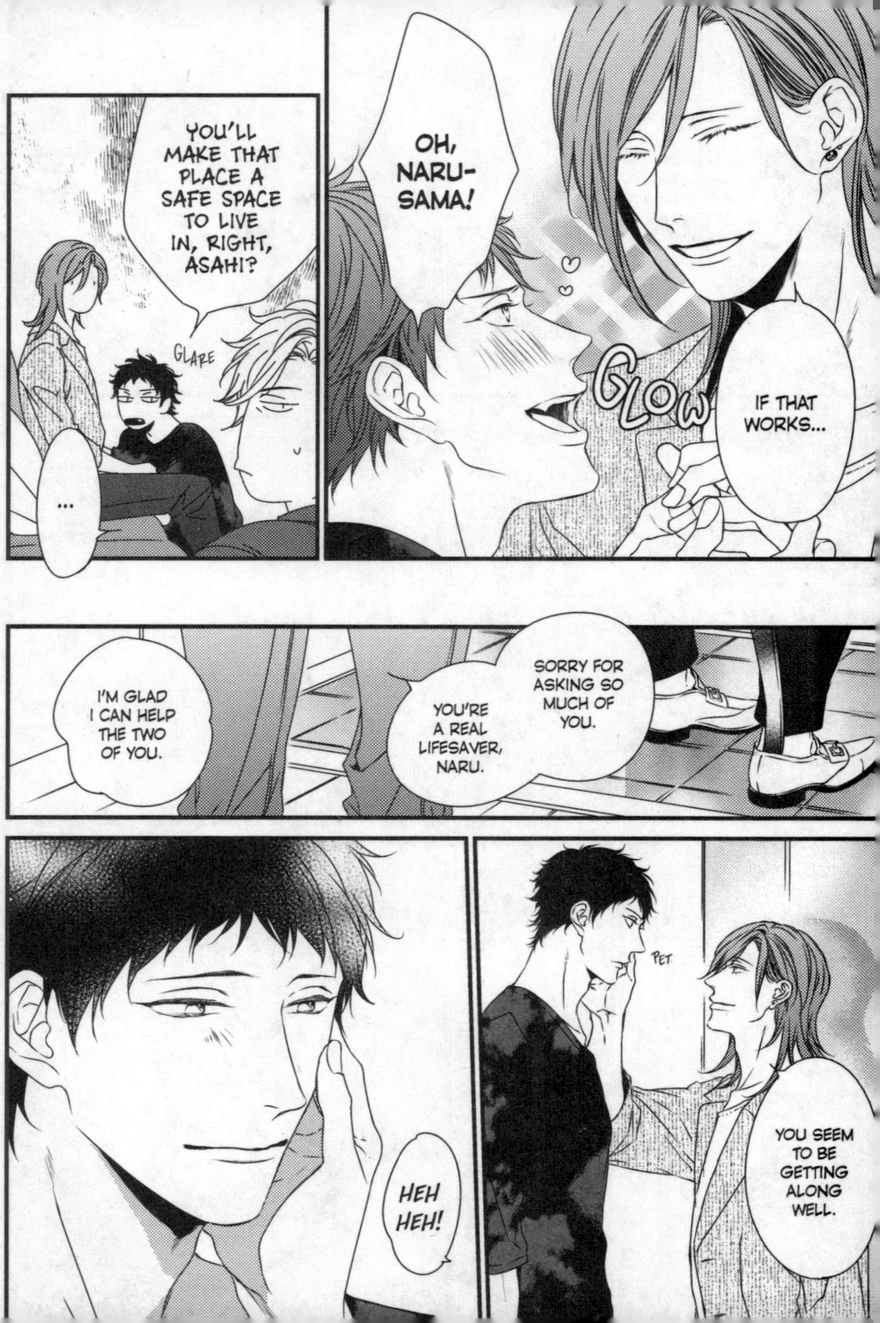
OH, NARU-SAMA!
GLOW
IF THAT WORKS...
YOU'LL MAKE THAT PLACE A SAFE SPACE TO LIVE IN, RIGHT, ASAHI?
GLARE
...
SORRY FOR ASKING SO MUCH OF YOU.
YOU'RE A REAL LIFESAVER, NARU.
I'M GLAD I CAN HELP THE TWO OF YOU.
PET
YOU SEEM TO BE GETTING ALONG WELL.
HEH HEH!

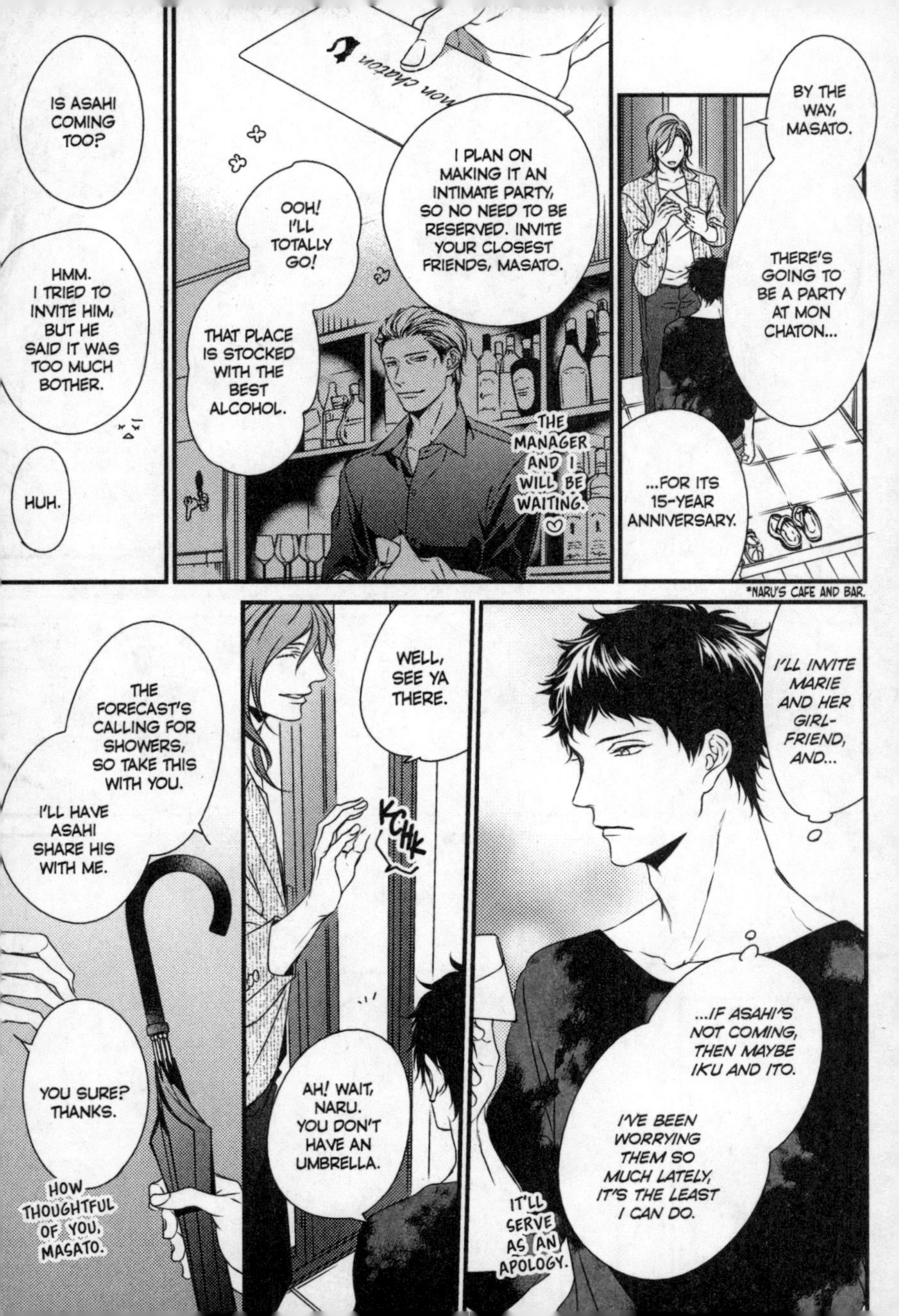
BY THE WAY, MASATO.
THERE'S GOING TO BE A PARTY AT MON CHATON...
...FOR ITS 15-YEAR ANNIVERSARY.
mon chaton
I PLAN ON MAKING IT AN INTIMATE PARTY, SO NO NEED TO BE RESERVED. INVITE YOUR CLOSEST FRIENDS, MASATO.
THE MANAGER AND I WILL BE WAITING.
OOH! I'LL TOTALLY GO!
THAT PLACE IS STOCKED WITH THE BEST ALCOHOL.
IS ASAHI COMING TOO?
HMM. I TRIED TO INVITE HIM, BUT HE SAID IT WAS TOO MUCH BOTHER.
HUH.
I'LL INVITE MARIE AND HER GIRL-FRIEND, AND...
...IF ASAHI'S NOT COMING, THEN MAYBE IKU AND ITO.
I'VE BEEN WORRYING THEM SO MUCH LATELY, IT'S THE LEAST I CAN DO.
IT'LL SERVE AS AN APOLOGY.
WELL, SEE YA THERE.
KCHK
AH! WAIT, NARU. YOU DON'T HAVE AN UMBRELLA.
THE FORECAST'S CALLING FOR SHOWERS, SO TAKE THIS WITH YOU.
I'LL HAVE ASAHI SHARE HIS WITH ME.
YOU SURE? THANKS.
HOW THOUGHTFUL OF YOU, MASATO.

*NARU'S CAFE AND BAR.

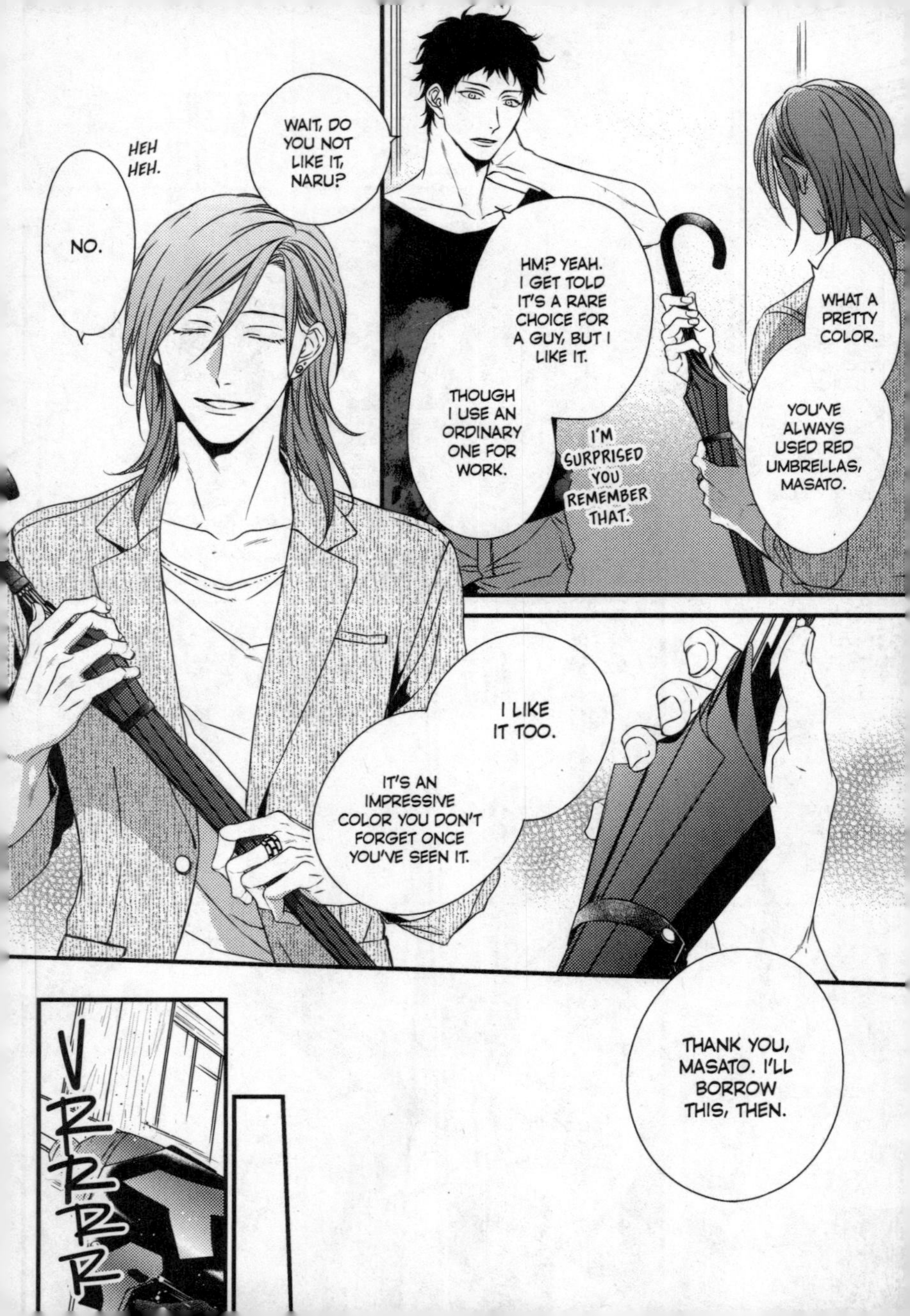
WHAT A PRETTY COLOR.
YOU'VE ALWAYS USED RED UMBRELLAS, MASATO.
HM? YEAH. I GET TOLD IT'S A RARE CHOICE FOR A GUY, BUT I LIKE IT.
THOUGH I USE AN ORDINARY ONE FOR WORK.
I'M SURPRISED YOU REMEMBER THAT.
I LIKE IT TOO.
IT'S AN IMPRESSIVE COLOR YOU DON'T FORGET ONCE YOU'VE SEEN IT.
WAIT, DO YOU NOT LIKE IT, NARU?
HEH HEH.
NO.
THANK YOU, MASATO. I'LL BORROW THIS, THEN.
VRRRRR

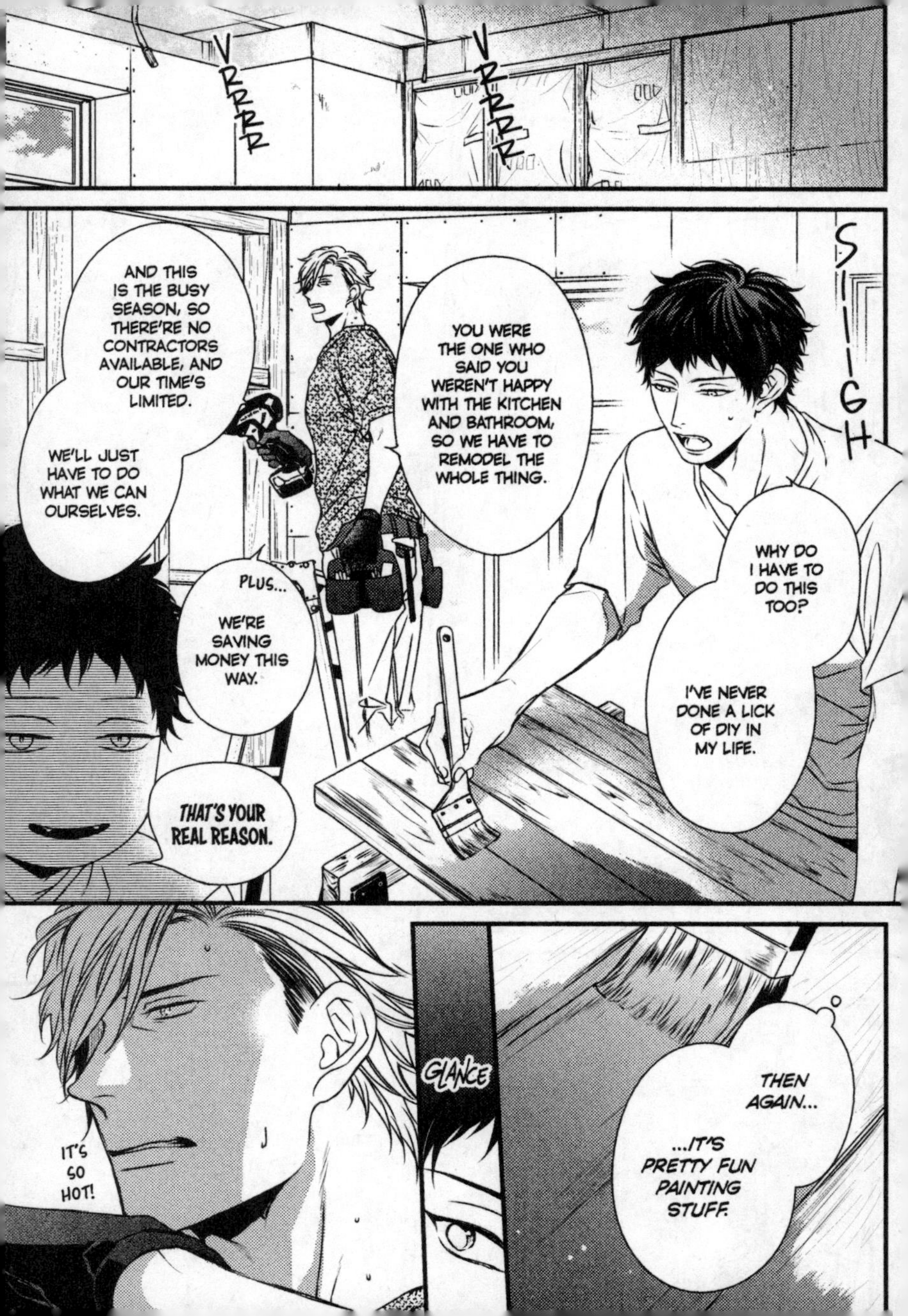
VRRRR
VRRRR
SIIIGH
WHY DO I HAVE TO DO THIS TOO?
I'VE NEVER DONE A LICK OF DIY IN MY LIFE.
YOU WERE THE ONE WHO SAID YOU WEREN'T HAPPY WITH THE KITCHEN AND BATHROOM, SO WE HAVE TO REMODEL THE WHOLE THING.
AND THIS IS THE BUSY SEASON, SO THERE'RE NO CONTRACTORS AVAILABLE, AND OUR TIME'S LIMITED.
WE'LL JUST HAVE TO DO WHAT WE CAN OURSELVES.
PLUS...
WE'RE SAVING MONEY THIS WAY.
THAT'S YOUR REAL REASON.
GLANCE
THEN AGAIN...
...IT'S PRETTY FUN PAINTING STUFF.
IT'S SO HOT!

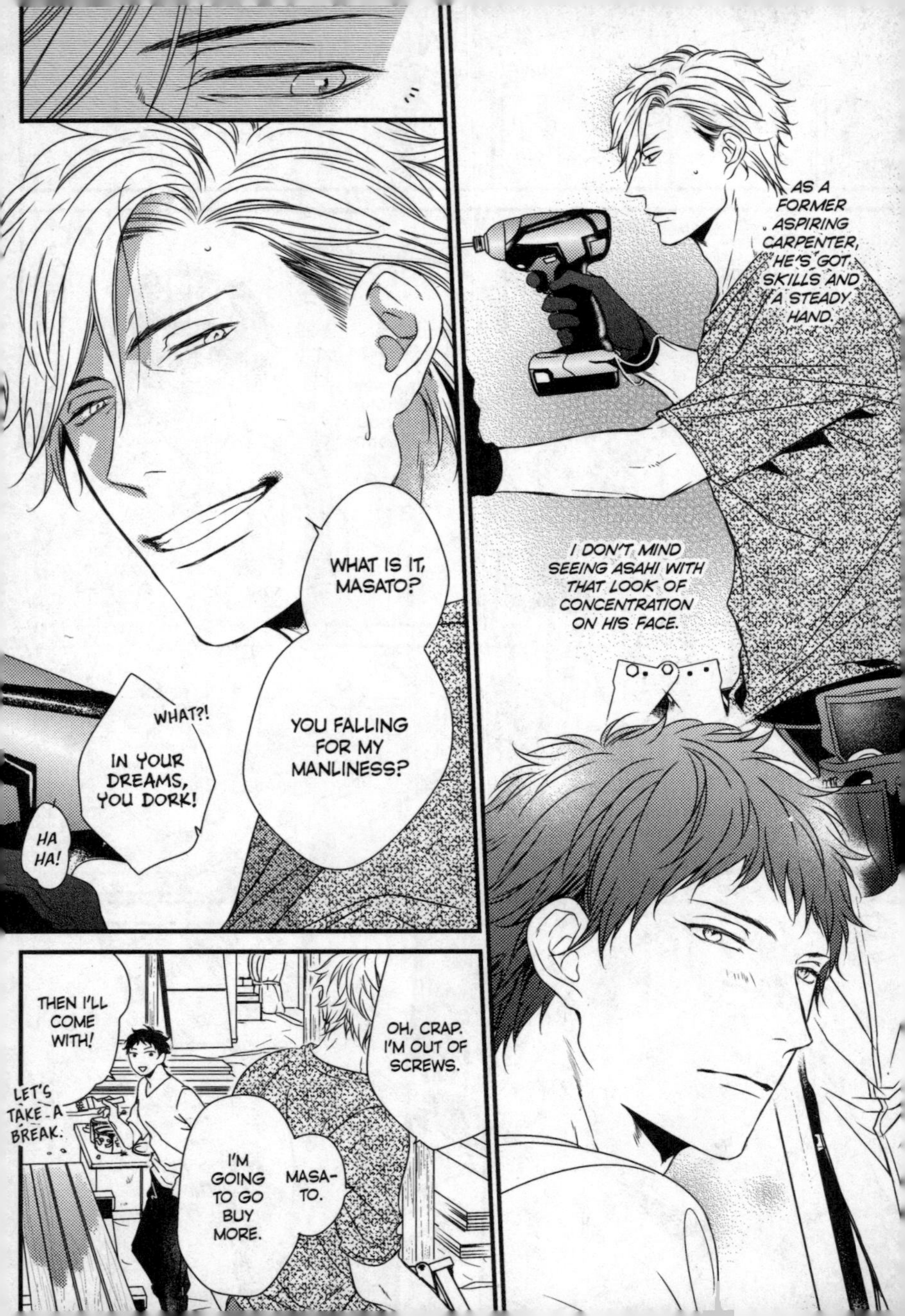
AS A FORMER ASPIRING CARPENTER, HE'S GOT SKILLS AND A STEADY HAND.
I DON'T MIND SEEING ASAHI WITH THAT LOOK OF CONCENTRATION ON HIS FACE.
...
WHAT IS IT, MASATO?
YOU FALLING FOR MY MANLINESS?
WHAT?!
IN YOUR DREAMS, YOU DORK!
HA HA!
OH, CRAP. I'M OUT OF SCREWS.
MASATO.
I'M GOING TO GO BUY MORE.
THEN I'LL COME WITH!
LET'S TAKE A BREAK.

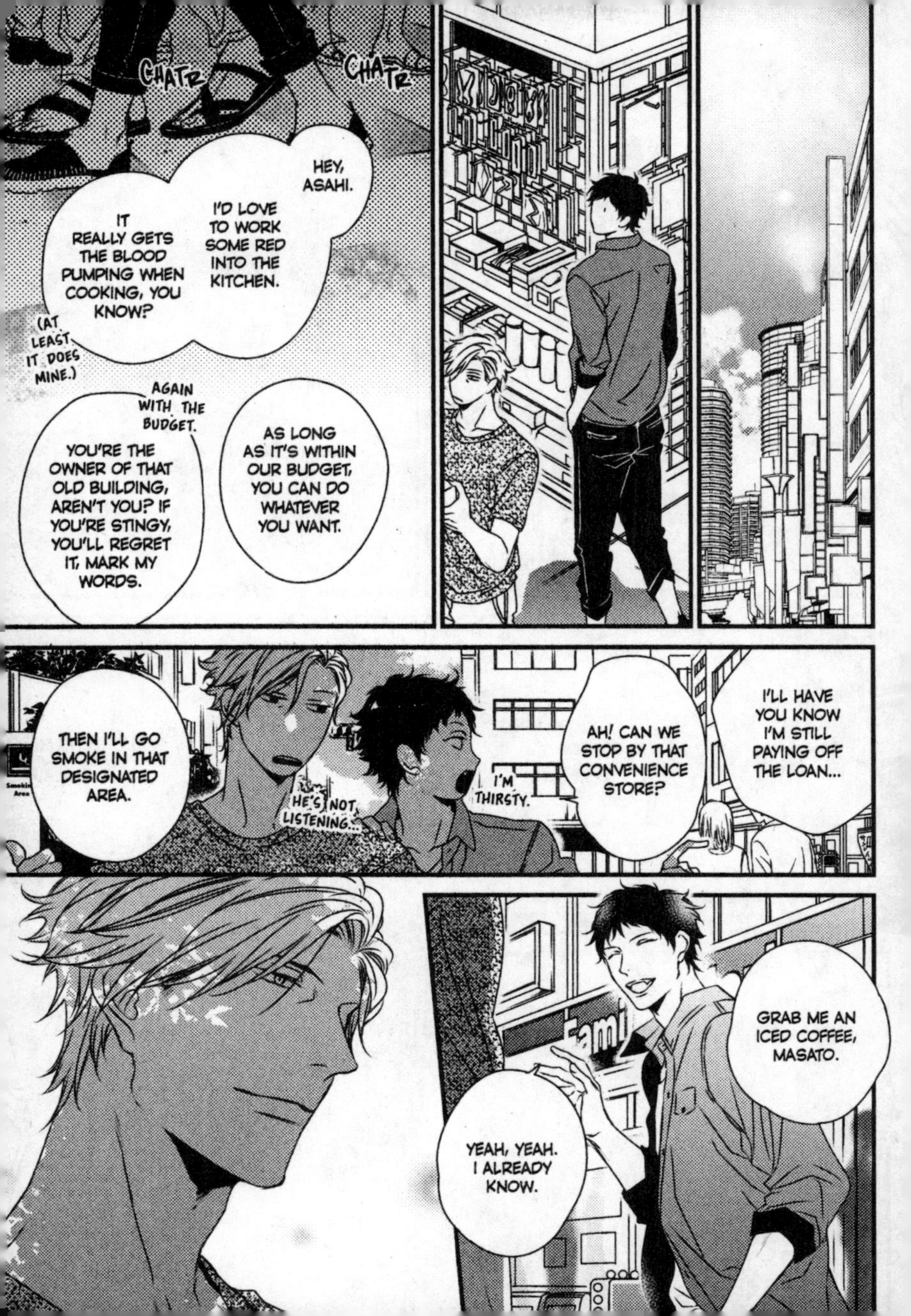
CHATR
CHATR
HEY, ASAHI.
I'D LOVE TO WORK SOME RED INTO THE KITCHEN.
IT REALLY GETS THE BLOOD PUMPING WHEN COOKING, YOU KNOW?
(AT LEAST IT DOES MINE.)
AS LONG AS IT'S WITHIN OUR BUDGET, YOU CAN DO WHATEVER YOU WANT.
AGAIN WITH THE BUDGET.
YOU'RE THE OWNER OF THAT OLD BUILDING, AREN'T YOU? IF YOU'RE STINGY, YOU'LL REGRET IT, MARK MY WORDS.
I'LL HAVE YOU KNOW I'M STILL PAYING OFF THE LOAN...
AH! CAN WE STOP BY THAT CONVENIENCE STORE?
I'M THIRSTY.
HE'S NOT LISTENING...
THEN I'LL GO SMOKE IN THAT DESIGNATED AREA.
GRAB ME AN ICED COFFEE, MASATO.
YEAH, YEAH. I ALREADY KNOW.

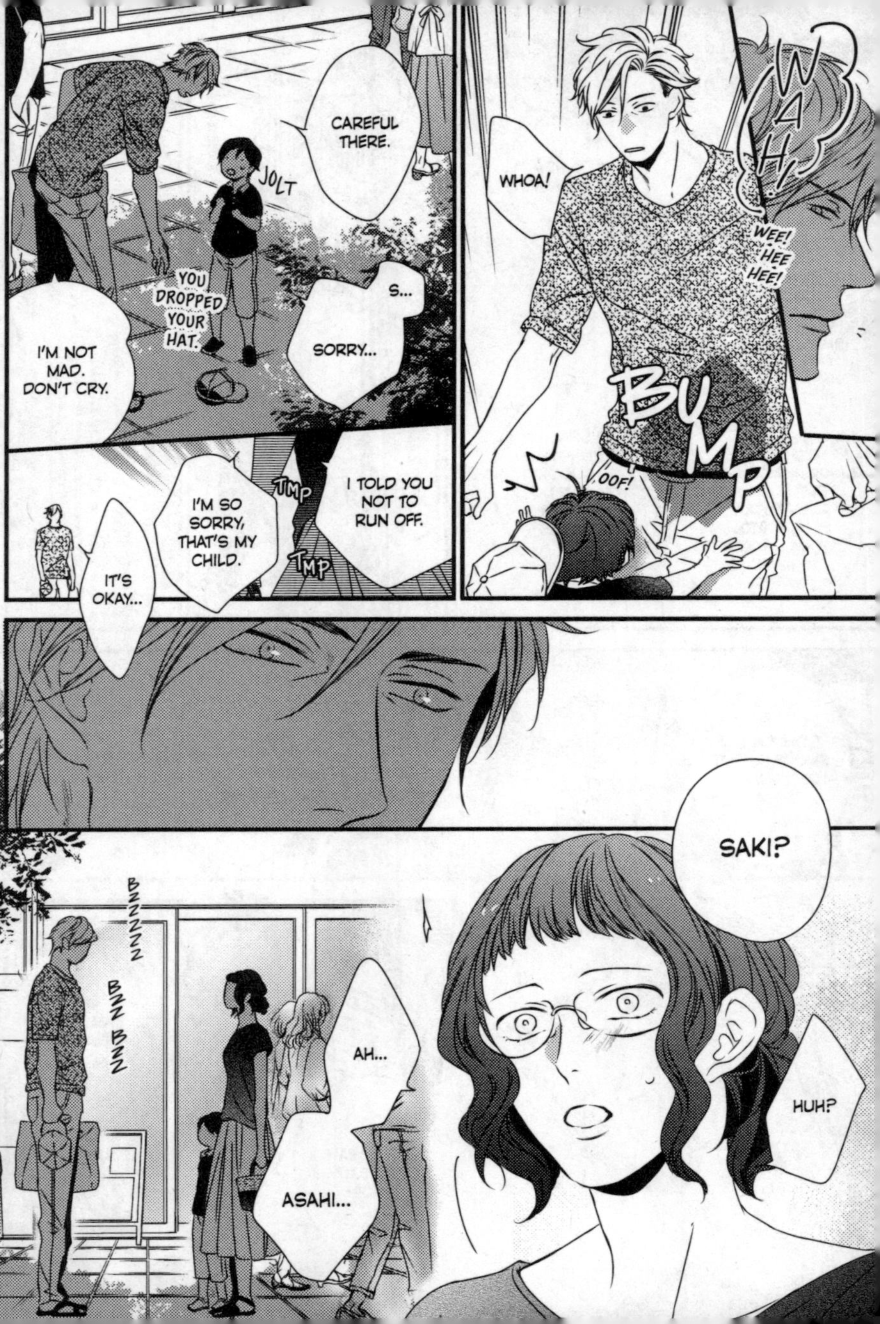
WAH!
WEE! HEE HEE!
WHOA!
BUMP
OOF!
CAREFUL THERE.
JOLT
S...
SORRY...
YOU DROPPED YOUR HAT.
I'M NOT MAD. DON'T CRY.
I TOLD YOU NOT TO RUN OFF.
TMP
TMP
I'M SO SORRY, THAT'S MY CHILD.
IT'S OKAY...
SAKI?
HUH?
AH...
ASAHI...
BZZZZZ
BZZ BZZ

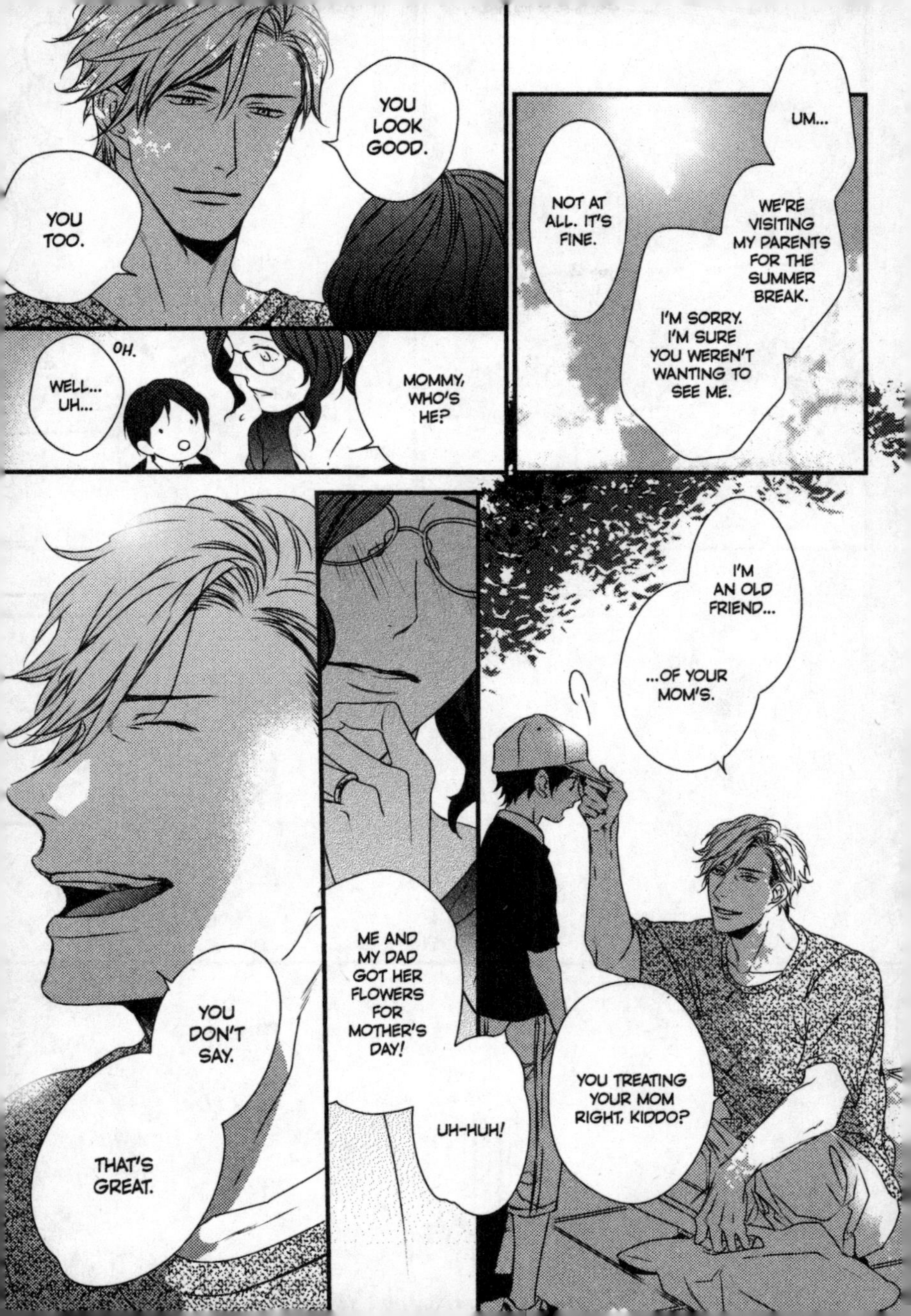
UM...
WE'RE VISITING MY PARENTS FOR THE SUMMER BREAK.
I'M SORRY. I'M SURE YOU WEREN'T WANTING TO SEE ME.
NOT AT ALL. IT'S FINE.
YOU LOOK GOOD.
YOU TOO.
MOMMY, WHO'S HE?
OH.
WELL... UH...
I'M AN OLD FRIEND...
...OF YOUR MOM'S.
YOU TREATING YOUR MOM RIGHT, KIDDO?
UH-HUH!
ME AND MY DAD GOT HER FLOWERS FOR MOTHER'S DAY!
YOU DON'T SAY.
THAT'S GREAT.

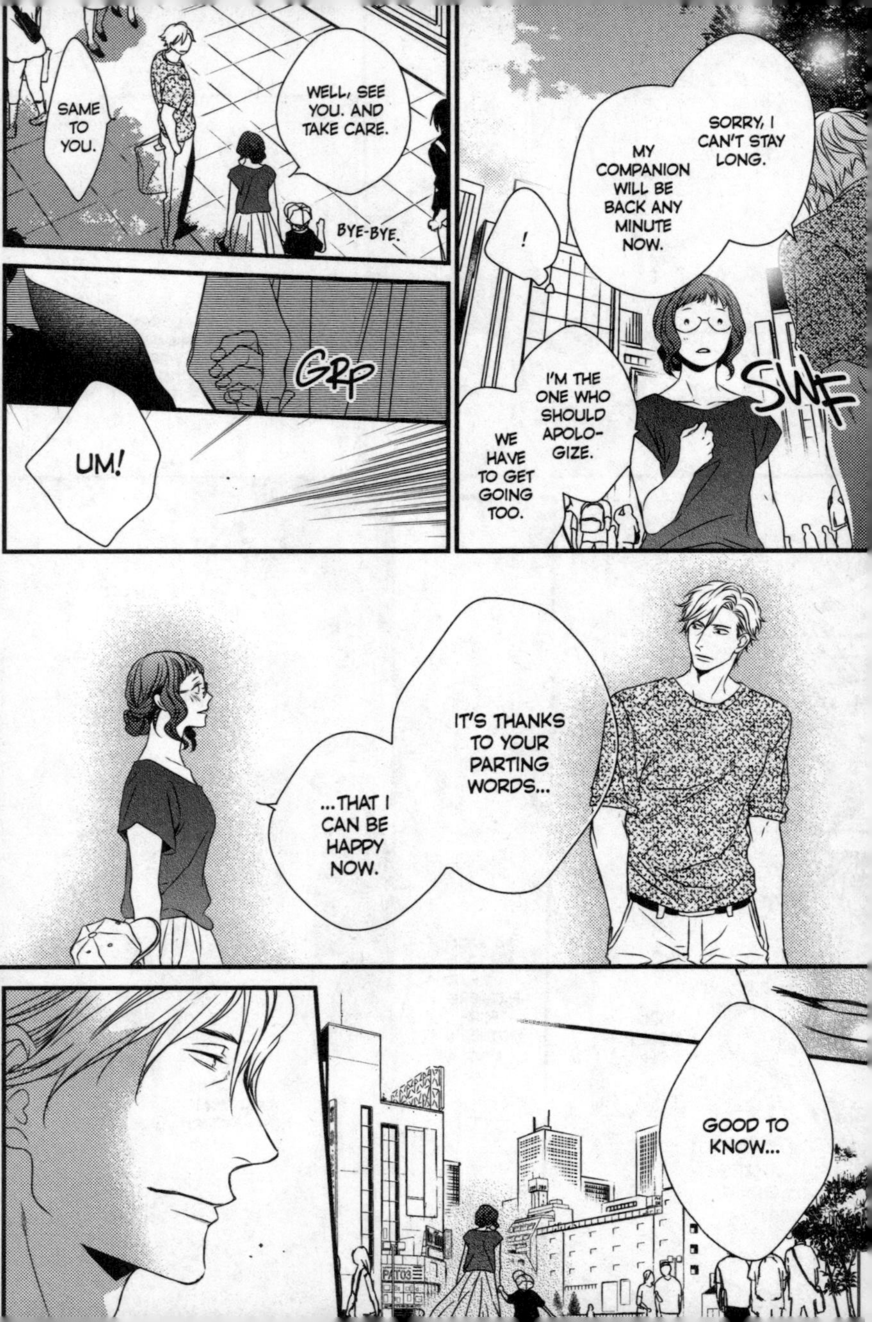
SORRY, I CAN'T STAY LONG.
MY COMPANION WILL BE BACK ANY MINUTE NOW.
!
SWF
I'M THE ONE WHO SHOULD APOLOGIZE.
WE HAVE TO GET GOING TOO.
WELL, SEE YOU. AND TAKE CARE.
SAME TO YOU.
BYE-BYE.
GRP
UM!
IT'S THANKS TO YOUR PARTING WORDS...
...THAT I CAN BE HAPPY NOW.
GOOD TO KNOW...

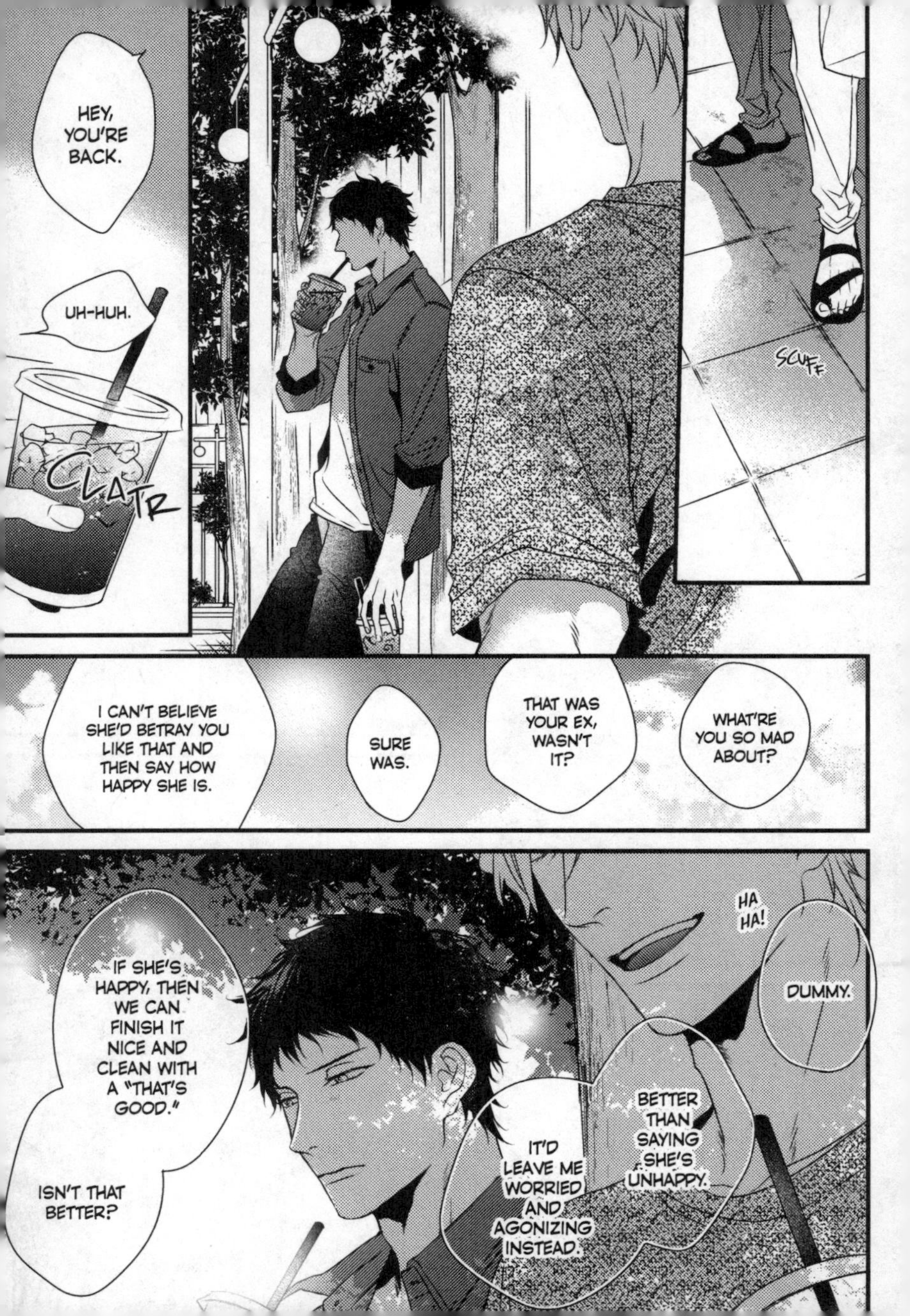
SCUFF
HEY, YOU'RE BACK.
UH-HUH.
CLATR
WHAT'RE YOU SO MAD ABOUT?
THAT WAS YOUR EX, WASN'T IT?
SURE WAS.
I CAN'T BELIEVE SHE'D BETRAY YOU LIKE THAT AND THEN SAY HOW HAPPY SHE IS.
HA HA!
DUMMY.
BETTER THAN SAYING SHE'S UNHAPPY.
IT'D LEAVE ME WORRIED AND AGONIZING INSTEAD.
IF SHE'S HAPPY, THEN WE CAN FINISH IT NICE AND CLEAN WITH A "THAT'S GOOD."
ISN'T THAT BETTER?

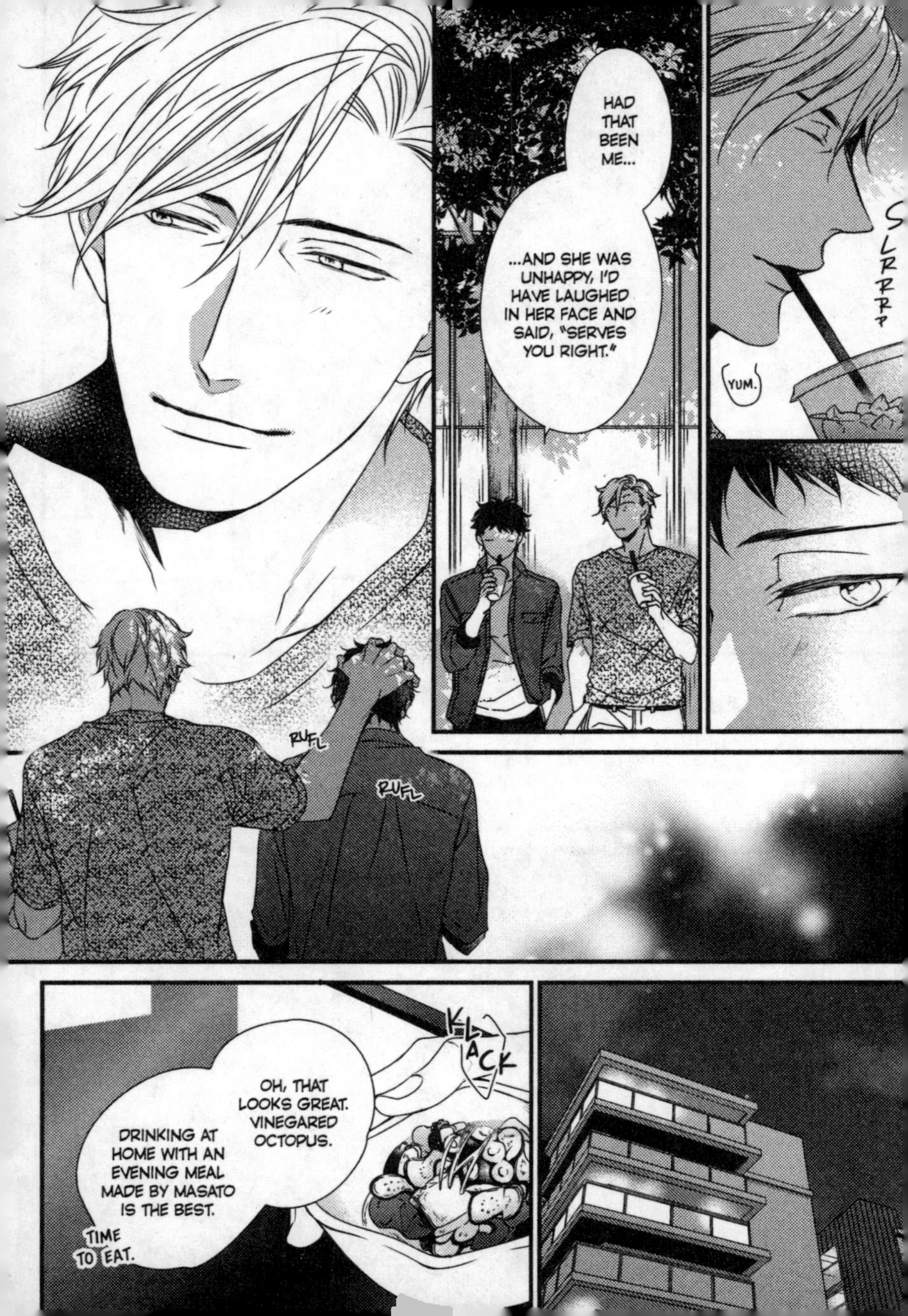
SLRRRP
YUM.
HAD THAT BEEN ME...
...AND SHE WAS UNHAPPY, I'D HAVE LAUGHED IN HER FACE AND SAID, "SERVES YOU RIGHT."
RUFL
RUFL
KLACK
OH, THAT LOOKS GREAT. VINEGARED OCTOPUS.
DRINKING AT HOME WITH AN EVENING MEAL MADE BY MASATO IS THE BEST.
TIME TO EAT.

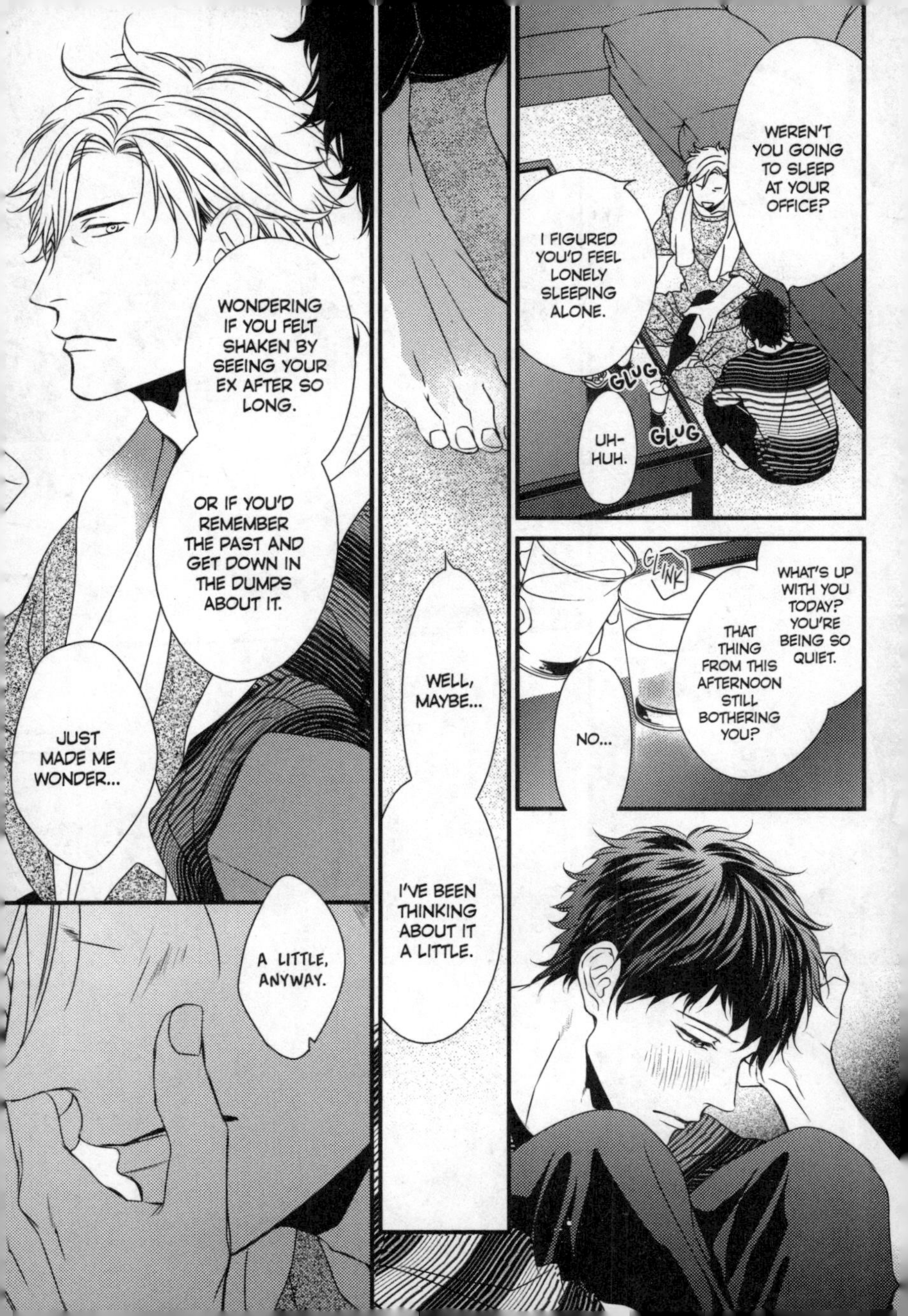
WEREN'T YOU GOING TO SLEEP AT YOUR OFFICE?
I FIGURED YOU'D FEEL LONELY SLEEPING ALONE.
GLUG
GLUG
UH-HUH.
CLINK
WHAT'S UP WITH YOU TODAY? YOU'RE BEING SO QUIET.
THAT THING FROM THIS AFTERNOON STILL BOTHERING YOU?
NO...
WELL, MAYBE...
I'VE BEEN THINKING ABOUT IT A LITTLE.
WONDERING IF YOU FELT SHAKEN BY SEEING YOUR EX AFTER SO LONG.
OR IF YOU'D REMEMBER THE PAST AND GET DOWN IN THE DUMPS ABOUT IT.
JUST MADE ME WONDER...
A LITTLE, ANYWAY.

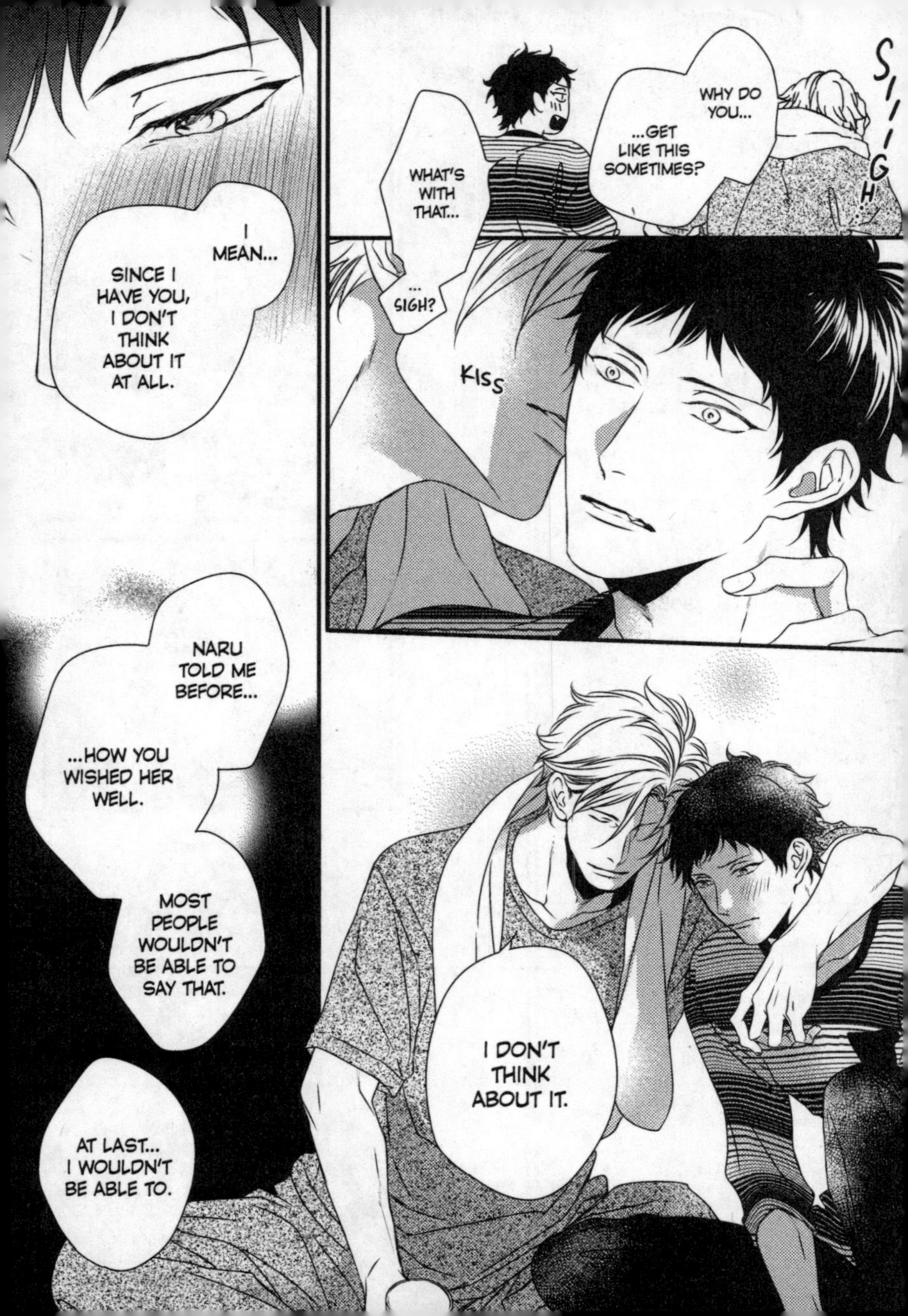

SIIIGH...
WHY DO YOU...
...GET LIKE THIS SOMETIMES?
WHAT'S WITH THAT...
...SIGH?
KISS
I MEAN...
SINCE I HAVE YOU, I DON'T THINK ABOUT IT AT ALL.
I DON'T THINK ABOUT IT.
NARU TOLD ME BEFORE...
...HOW YOU WISHED HER WELL.
MOST PEOPLE WOULDN'T BE ABLE TO SAY THAT.
AT LAST... I WOULDN'T BE ABLE TO.

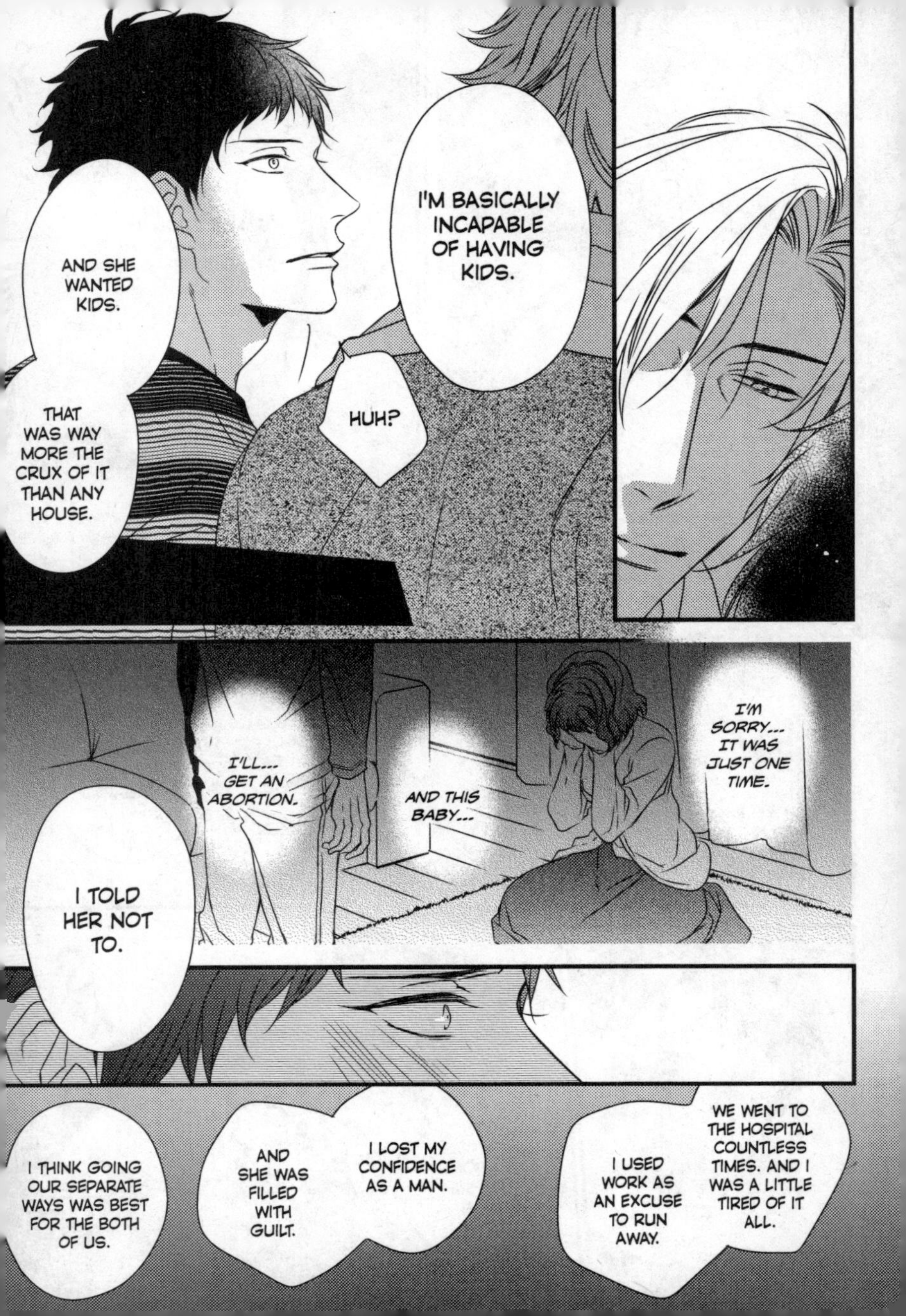
I'M BASICALLY INCAPABLE OF HAVING KIDS.
HUH?
AND SHE WANTED KIDS.
THAT WAS WAY MORE THE CRUX OF IT THAN ANY HOUSE.
I'M SORRY... IT WAS JUST ONE TIME.
AND THIS BABY...
I'LL... GET AN ABORTION.
I TOLD HER NOT TO.
WE WENT TO THE HOSPITAL COUNTLESS TIMES. AND I WAS A LITTLE TIRED OF IT ALL.
I USED WORK AS AN EXCUSE TO RUN AWAY.
I LOST MY CONFIDENCE AS A MAN.
AND SHE WAS FILLED WITH GUILT.
I THINK GOING OUR SEPARATE WAYS WAS BEST FOR THE BOTH OF US.

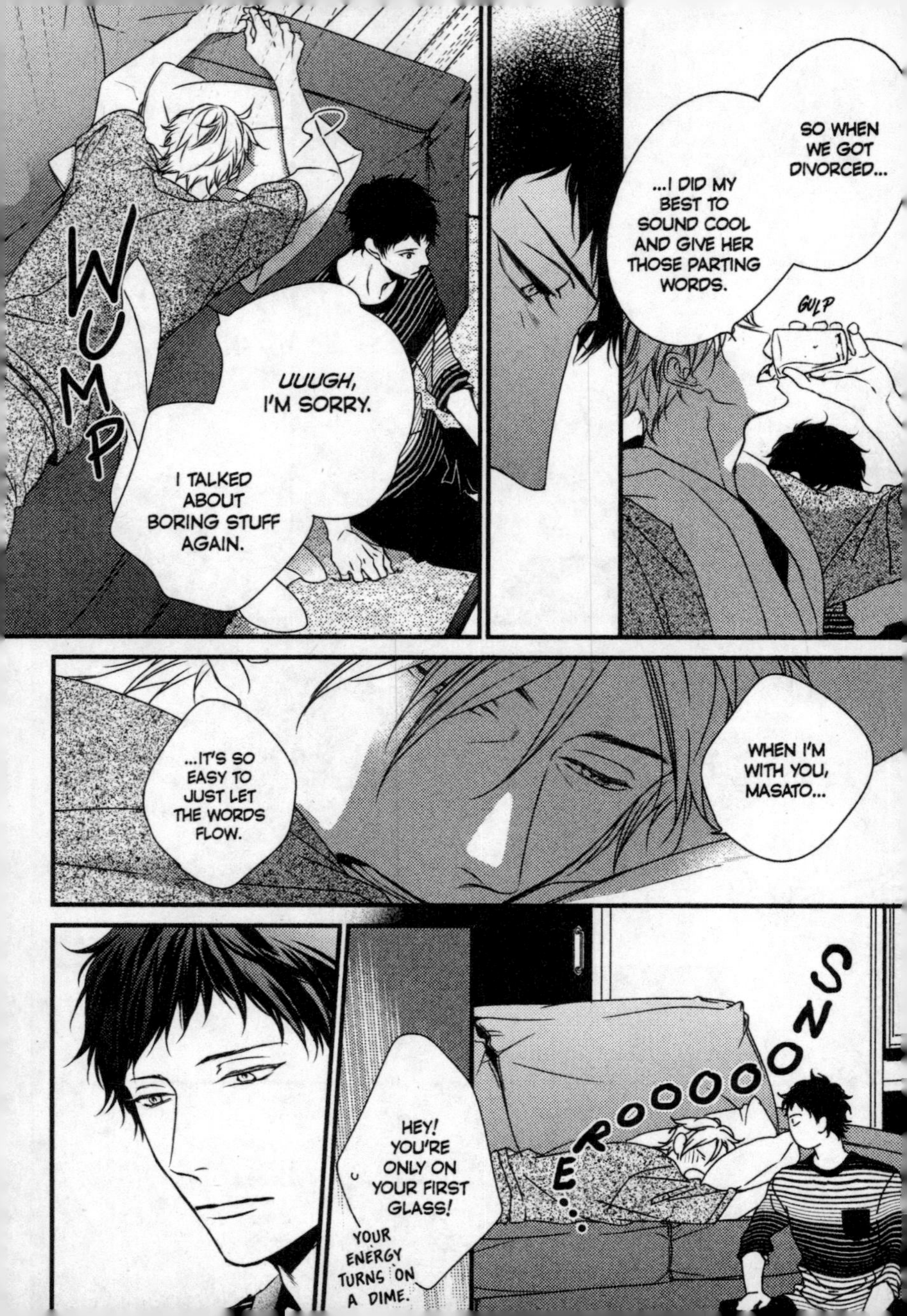
SO WHEN WE GOT DIVORCED...
...I DID MY BEST TO SOUND COOL AND GIVE HER THOSE PARTING WORDS.
GULP
WUMP
UUUGH, I'M SORRY.
I TALKED ABOUT BORING STUFF AGAIN.
WHEN I'M WITH YOU, MASATO...
...IT'S SO EASY TO JUST LET THE WORDS FLOW.
SNOOOOORE...
HEY! YOU'RE ONLY ON YOUR FIRST GLASS!
YOUR ENERGY TURNS ON A DIME.

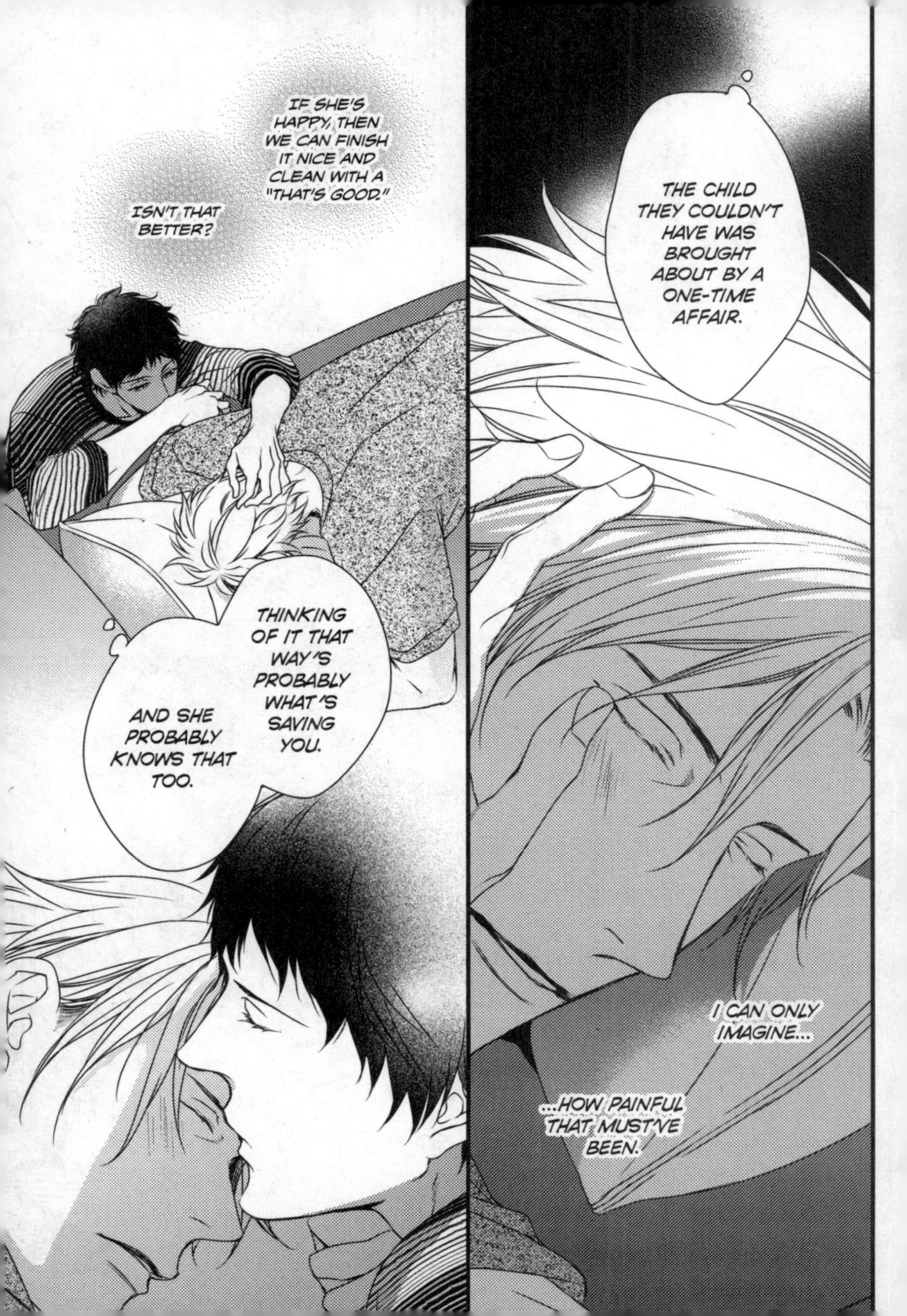
THE CHILD THEY COULDN'T HAVE WAS BROUGHT ABOUT BY A ONE-TIME AFFAIR.
I CAN ONLY IMAGINE...
...HOW PAINFUL THAT MUST'VE BEEN.
IF SHE'S HAPPY, THEN WE CAN FINISH IT NICE AND CLEAN WITH A "THAT'S GOOD."
ISN'T THAT BETTER?
THINKING OF IT THAT WAY'S PROBABLY WHAT'S SAVING YOU.
AND SHE PROBABLY KNOWS THAT TOO.

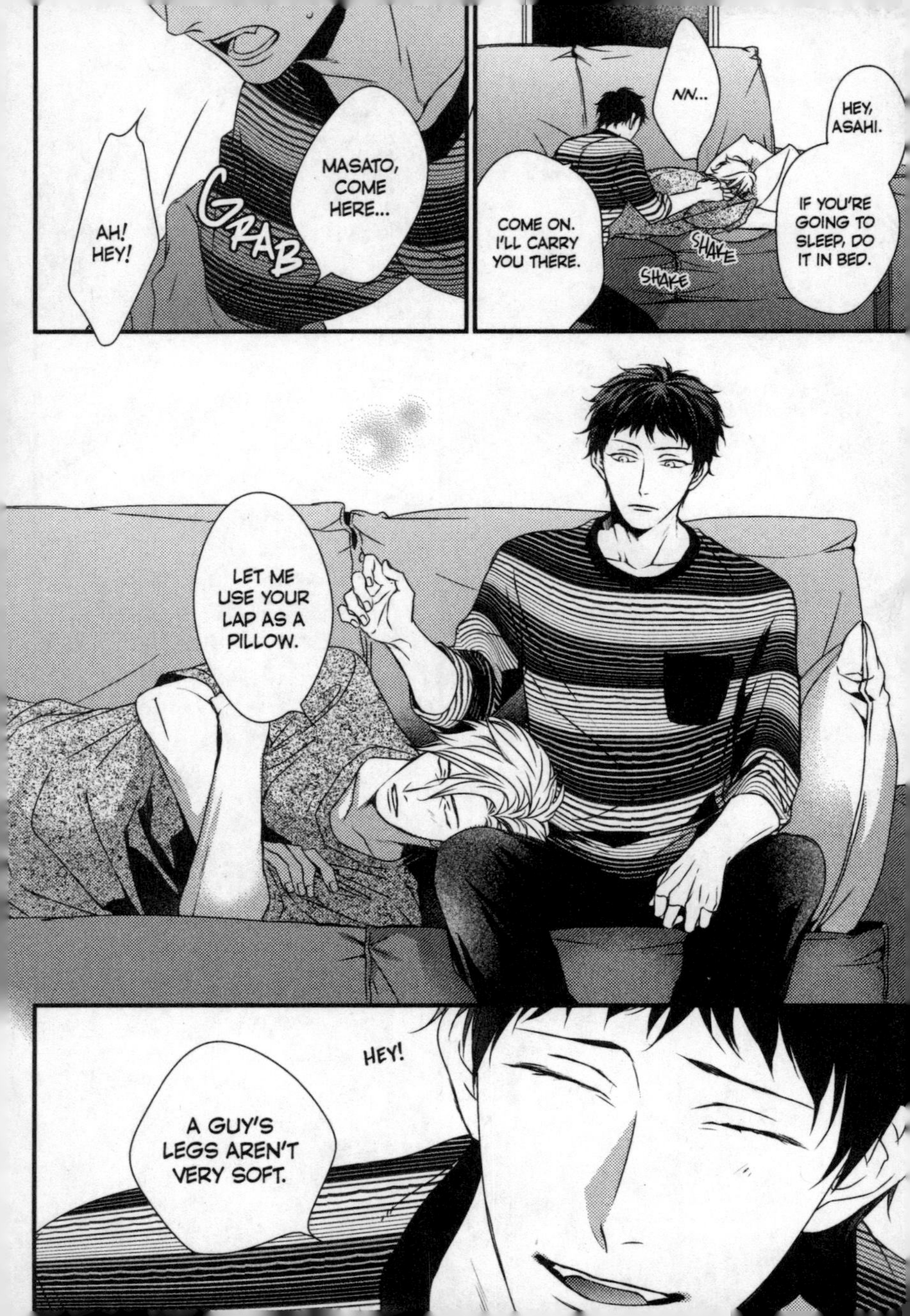
HEY, ASAHI.
IF YOU'RE GOING TO SLEEP, DO IT IN BED.
NN...
SHAKE
SHAKE
COME ON. I'LL CARRY YOU THERE.
MASATO, COME HERE...
GRAB
AH! HEY!
LET ME USE YOUR LAP AS A PILLOW.
HEY!
A GUY'S LEGS AREN'T VERY SOFT.

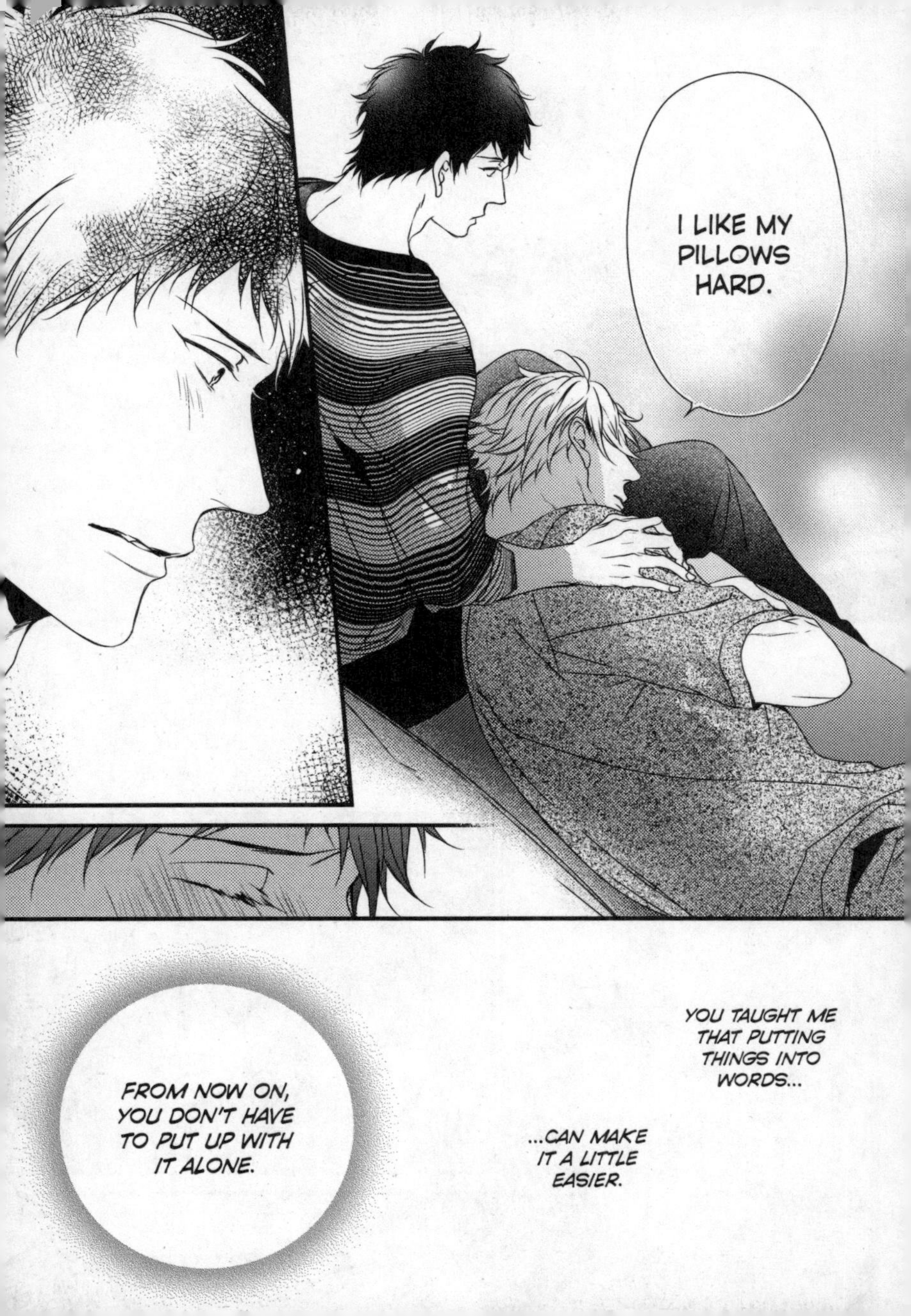
I LIKE MY PILLOWS HARD.
YOU TAUGHT ME THAT PUTTING THINGS INTO WORDS...
...CAN MAKE IT A LITTLE EASIER.
FROM NOW ON, YOU DON'T HAVE TO PUT UP WITH IT ALONE.

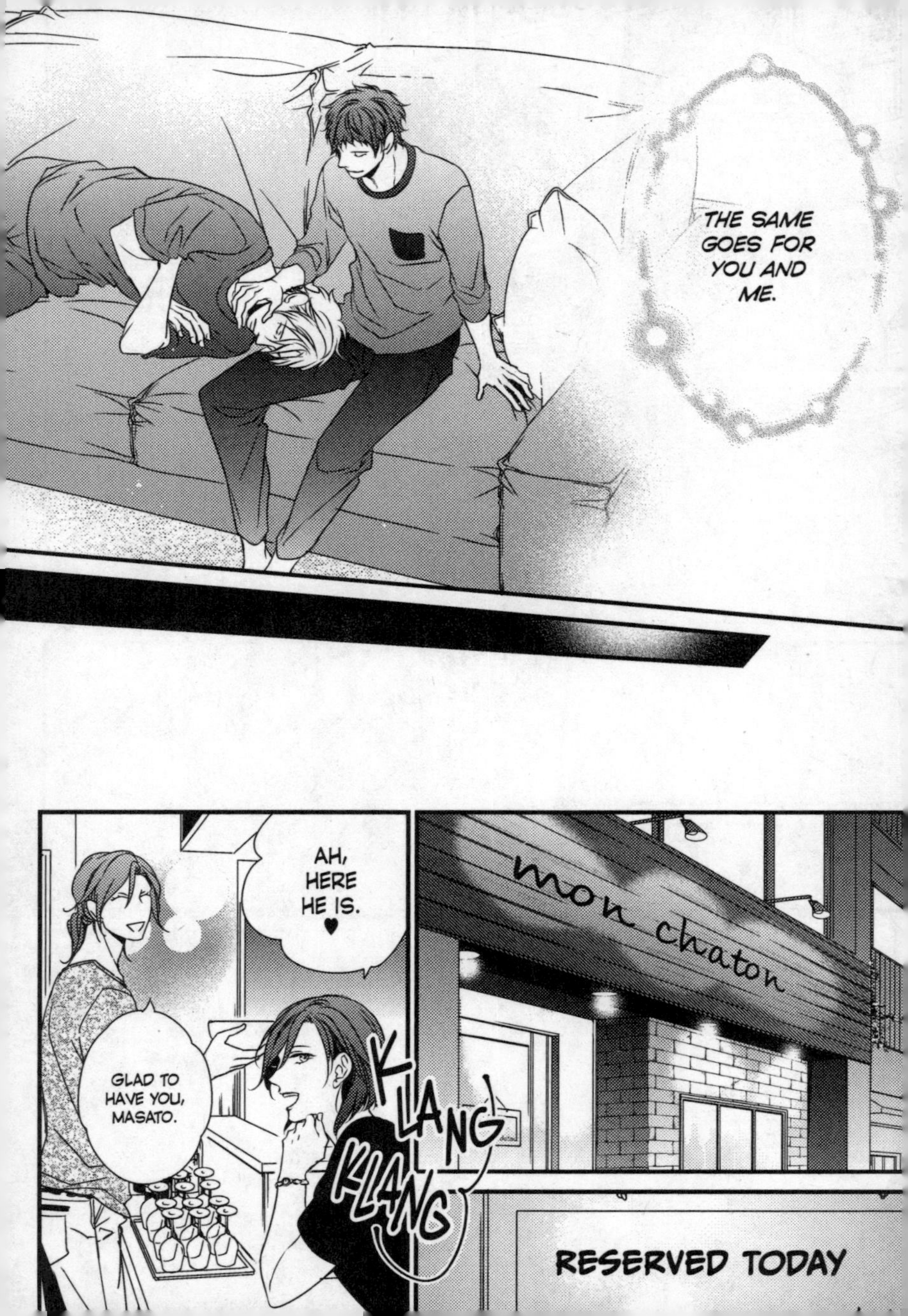
THE SAME GOES FOR YOU AND ME.
mon chaton
RESERVED TODAY
KLANG KLANG
AH, HERE HE IS. ♥
GLAD TO HAVE YOU, MASATO.

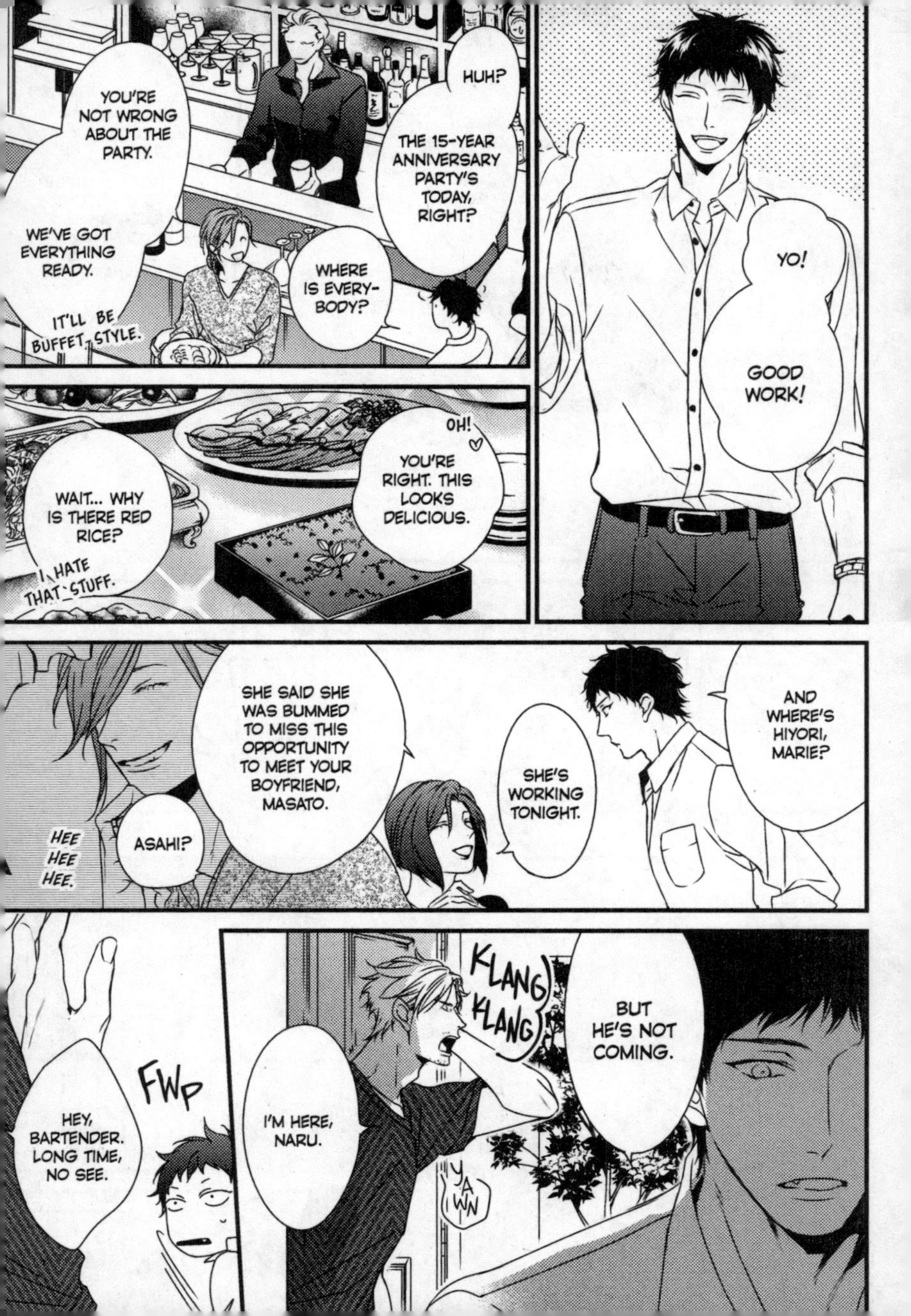
YO!
GOOD WORK!
HUH?
THE 15-YEAR ANNIVERSARY PARTY'S TODAY, RIGHT?
WHERE IS EVERY-BODY?
YOU'RE NOT WRONG ABOUT THE PARTY.
WE'VE GOT EVERYTHING READY.
IT'LL BE BUFFET STYLE.
OH! ♡
YOU'RE RIGHT. THIS LOOKS DELICIOUS.
WAIT... WHY IS THERE RED RICE?
I HATE THAT STUFF.
AND WHERE'S HIYORI, MARIE?
SHE'S WORKING TONIGHT.
SHE SAID SHE WAS BUMMED TO MISS THIS OPPORTUNITY TO MEET YOUR BOYFRIEND, MASATO.
ASAHI?
HEE HEE HEE.
BUT HE'S NOT COMING.
KLANG KLANG
I'M HERE, NARU.
YAWN
FWP
HEY, BARTENDER. LONG TIME, NO SEE.

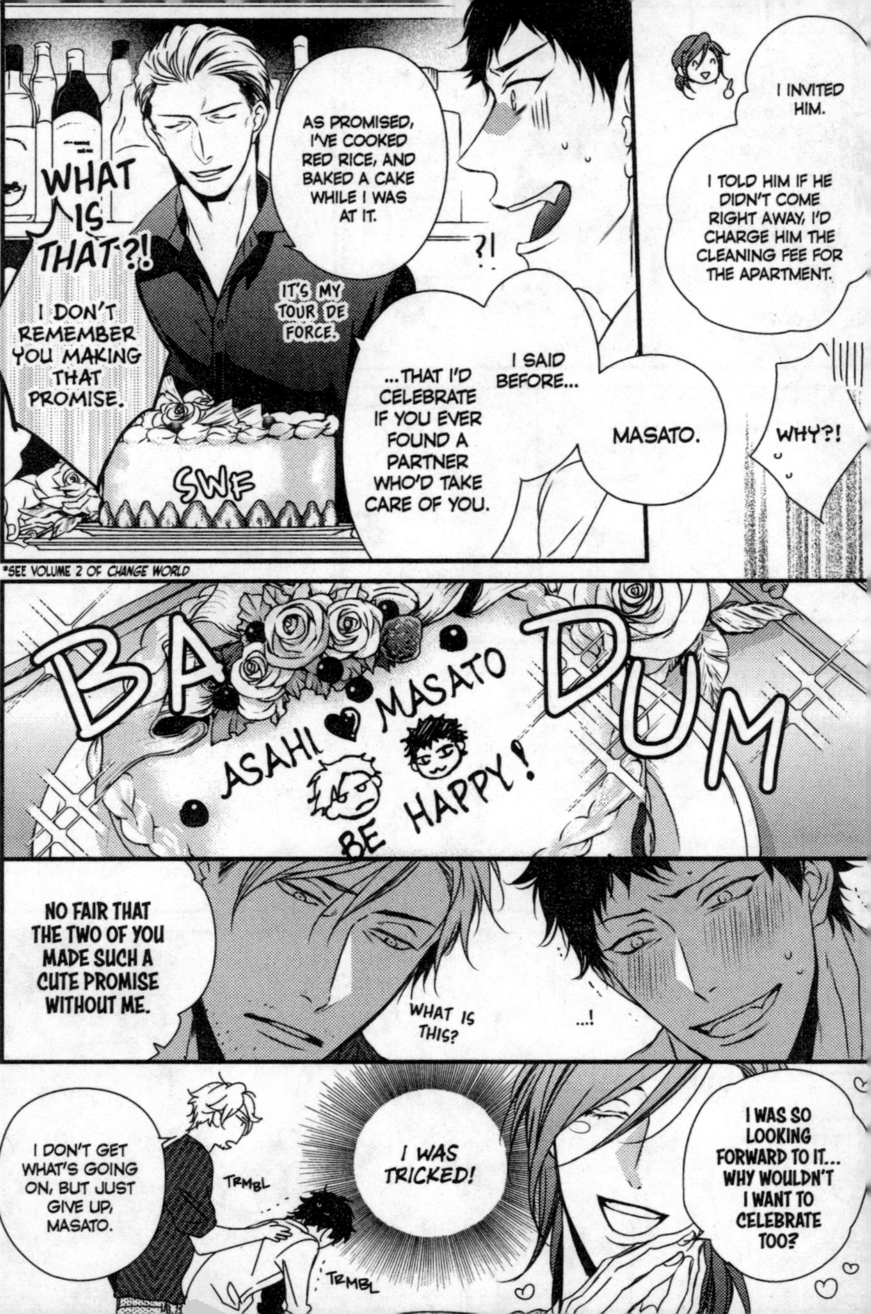
I INVITED HIM.
I TOLD HIM IF HE DIDN'T COME RIGHT AWAY, I'D CHARGE HIM THE CLEANING FEE FOR THE APARTMENT.
WHY?!
MASATO.
I SAID BEFORE...
...THAT I'D CELEBRATE IF YOU EVER FOUND A PARTNER WHO'D TAKE CARE OF YOU.
?!
AS PROMISED, I'VE COOKED RED RICE, AND BAKED A CAKE WHILE I WAS AT IT.
WHAT IS THAT?!
IT'S MY TOUR DE FORCE.
I DON'T REMEMBER YOU MAKING THAT PROMISE.
SWF
BA DUM
ASAHI ♥ MASATO
BE HAPPY!
...!
WHAT IS THIS?
NO FAIR THAT THE TWO OF YOU MADE SUCH A CUTE PROMISE WITHOUT ME.
I WAS SO LOOKING FORWARD TO IT... WHY WOULDN'T I WANT TO CELEBRATE TOO?
I WAS TRICKED!
TRMBL
TRMBL
I DON'T GET WHAT'S GOING ON, BUT JUST GIVE UP, MASATO.

*SEE VOLUME 2 OF *CHANGE WORLD*

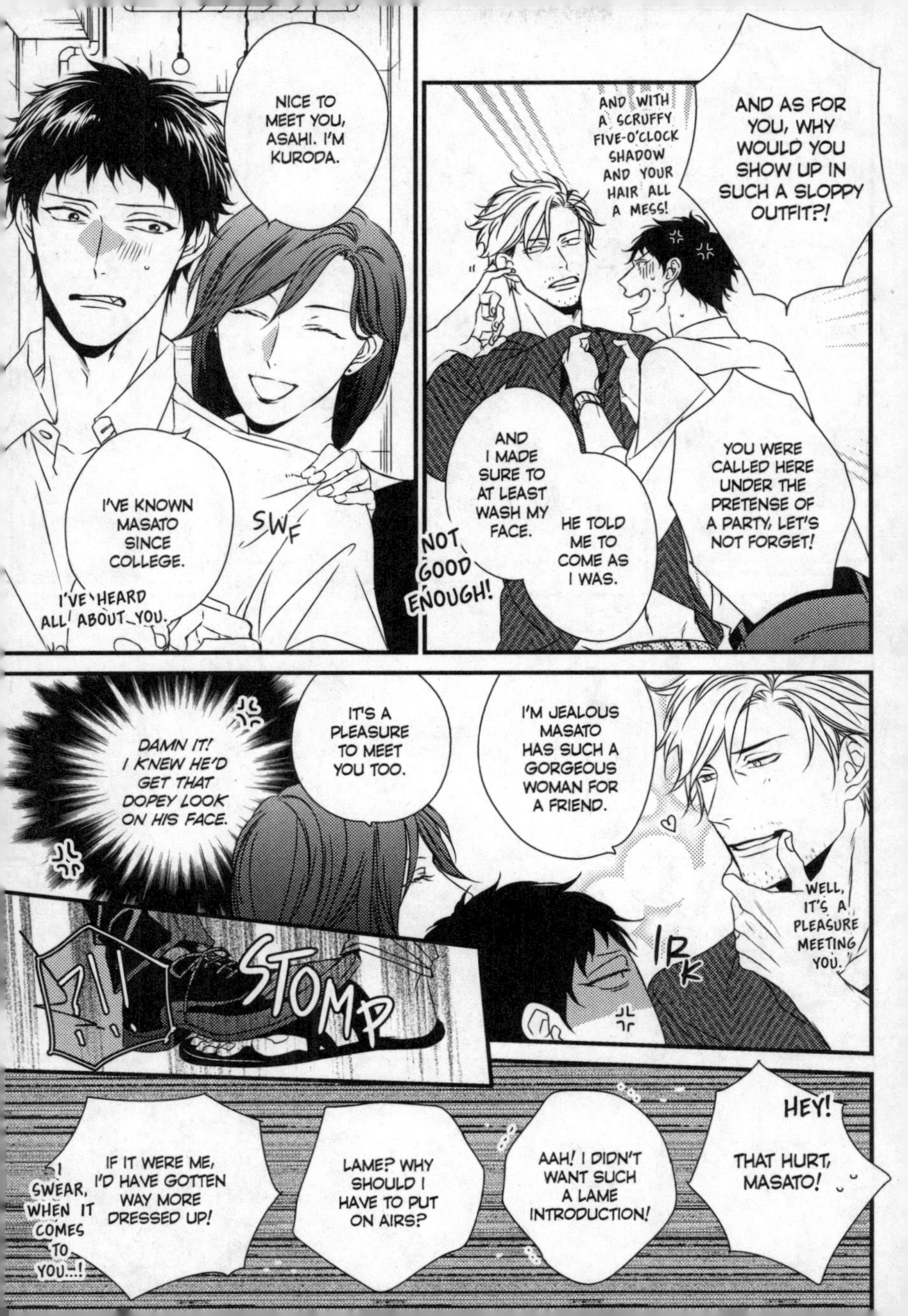
AND AS FOR YOU, WHY WOULD YOU SHOW UP IN SUCH A SLOPPY OUTFIT?!
AND WITH A SCRUFFY FIVE-O'CLOCK SHADOW AND YOUR HAIR ALL A MESS!
YOU WERE CALLED HERE UNDER THE PRETENSE OF A PARTY, LET'S NOT FORGET!
AND I MADE SURE TO AT LEAST WASH MY FACE.
HE TOLD ME TO COME AS I WAS.
NOT GOOD ENOUGH!
NICE TO MEET YOU, ASAHI. I'M KURODA.
SWF
I'VE KNOWN MASATO SINCE COLLEGE.
I'VE HEARD ALL ABOUT YOU.
I'M JEALOUS MASATO HAS SUCH A GORGEOUS WOMAN FOR A FRIEND.
WELL, IT'S A PLEASURE MEETING YOU.
IT'S A PLEASURE TO MEET YOU TOO.
DAMN IT! I KNEW HE'D GET THAT DOPEY LOOK ON HIS FACE.
IRK
STOMP
?!!
HEY!
THAT HURT, MASATO!
AAH! I DIDN'T WANT SUCH A LAME INTRODUCTION!
LAME? WHY SHOULD I HAVE TO PUT ON AIRS?
IF IT WERE ME, I'D HAVE GOTTEN WAY MORE DRESSED UP!
I SWEAR, WHEN IT COMES TO YOU...!

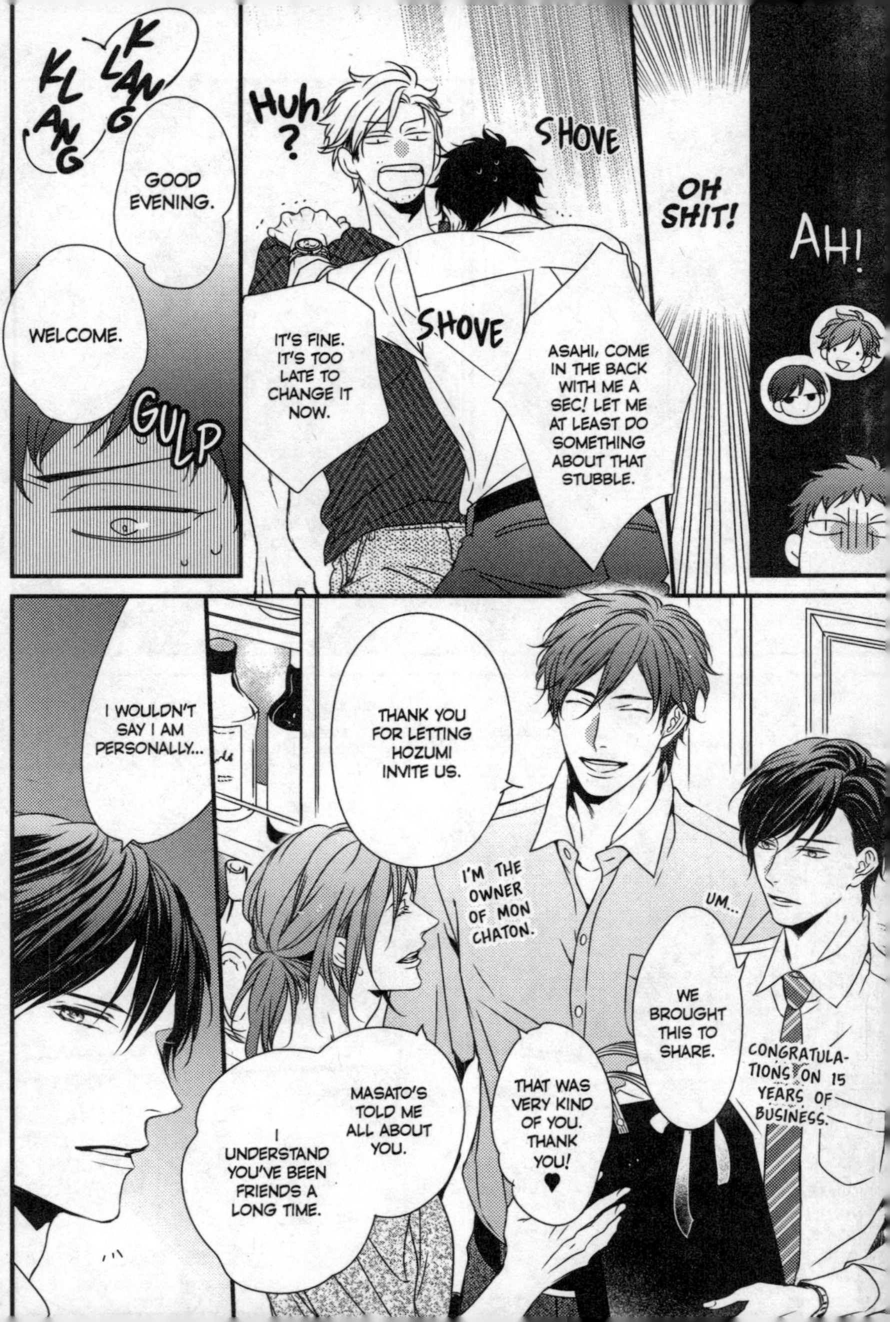
AH!
OH SHIT!
SHOVE
Huh?
ASAHI, COME IN THE BACK WITH ME A SEC! LET ME AT LEAST DO SOMETHING ABOUT THAT STUBBLE.
SHOVE
IT'S FINE. IT'S TOO LATE TO CHANGE IT NOW.
KLANG
KLANG
GOOD EVENING.
WELCOME.
GULP
UM...
CONGRATULATIONS ON 15 YEARS OF BUSINESS.
WE BROUGHT THIS TO SHARE.
I'M THE OWNER OF MON CHATON.
THANK YOU FOR LETTING HOZUMI INVITE US.
I WOULDN'T SAY I AM PERSONALLY...
THAT WAS VERY KIND OF YOU. THANK YOU!
MASATO'S TOLD ME ALL ABOUT YOU.
I UNDERSTAND YOU'VE BEEN FRIENDS A LONG TIME.

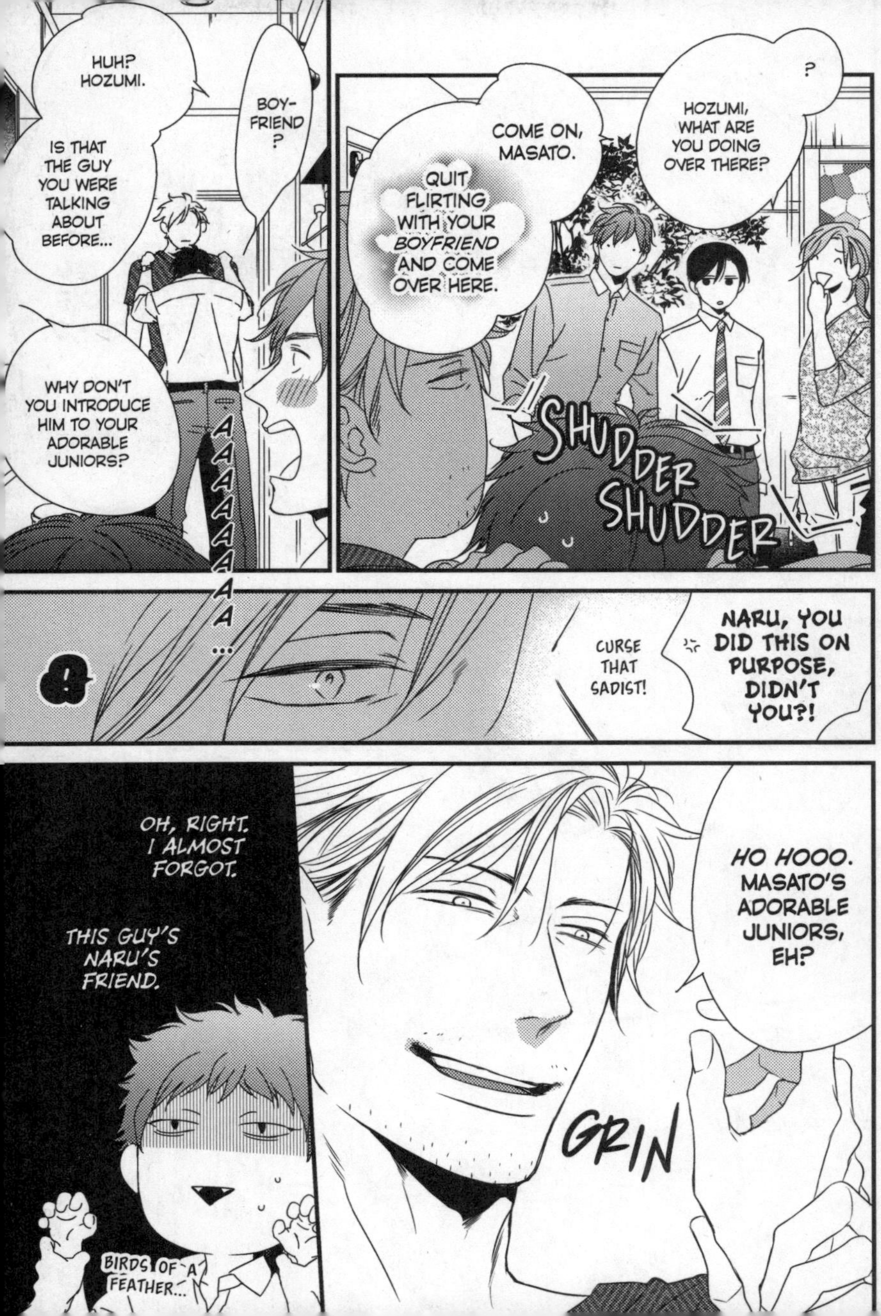
?
HOZUMI, WHAT ARE YOU DOING OVER THERE?
COME ON, MASATO.
QUIT FLIRTING WITH YOUR *BOYFRIEND* AND COME OVER HERE.
SHUDDER SHUDDER
BOY-FRIEND?
HUH? HOZUMI.
IS THAT THE GUY YOU WERE TALKING ABOUT BEFORE...
WHY DON'T YOU INTRODUCE HIM TO YOUR ADORABLE JUNIORS?
AAAAAAAAAA...
NARU, YOU DID THIS ON PURPOSE, DIDN'T YOU?!
CURSE THAT SADIST!
!
HO HOOO. MASATO'S ADORABLE JUNIORS, EH?
GRIN
OH, RIGHT. I ALMOST FORGOT.
THIS GUY'S NARU'S FRIEND.
BIRDS OF A FEATHER...

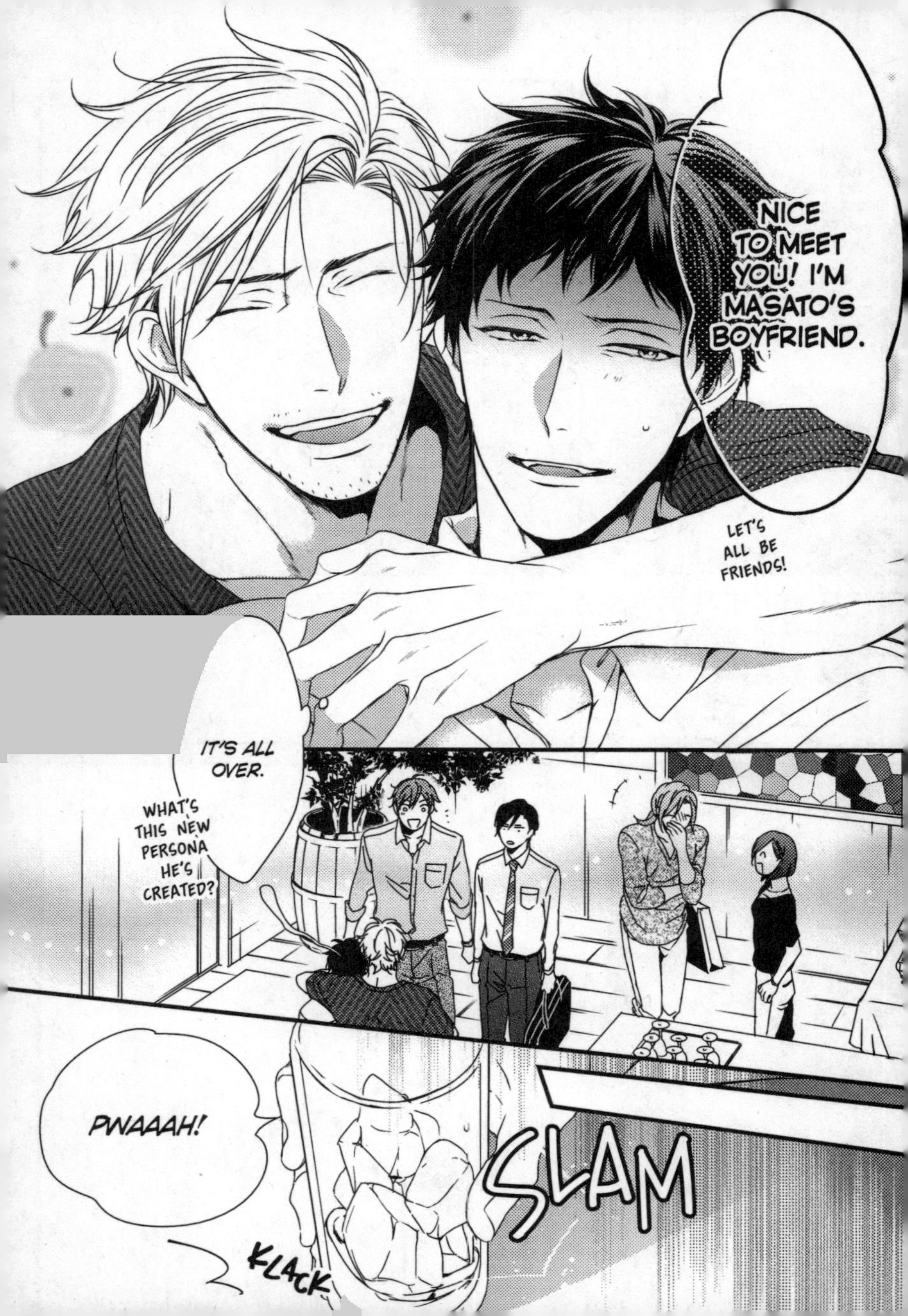
NICE TO MEET YOU! I'M MASATO'S BOYFRIEND.
LET'S ALL BE FRIENDS!
IT'S ALL OVER.
WHAT'S THIS NEW PERSONA HE'S CREATED?
SLAM
PWAAAH!
KLACK

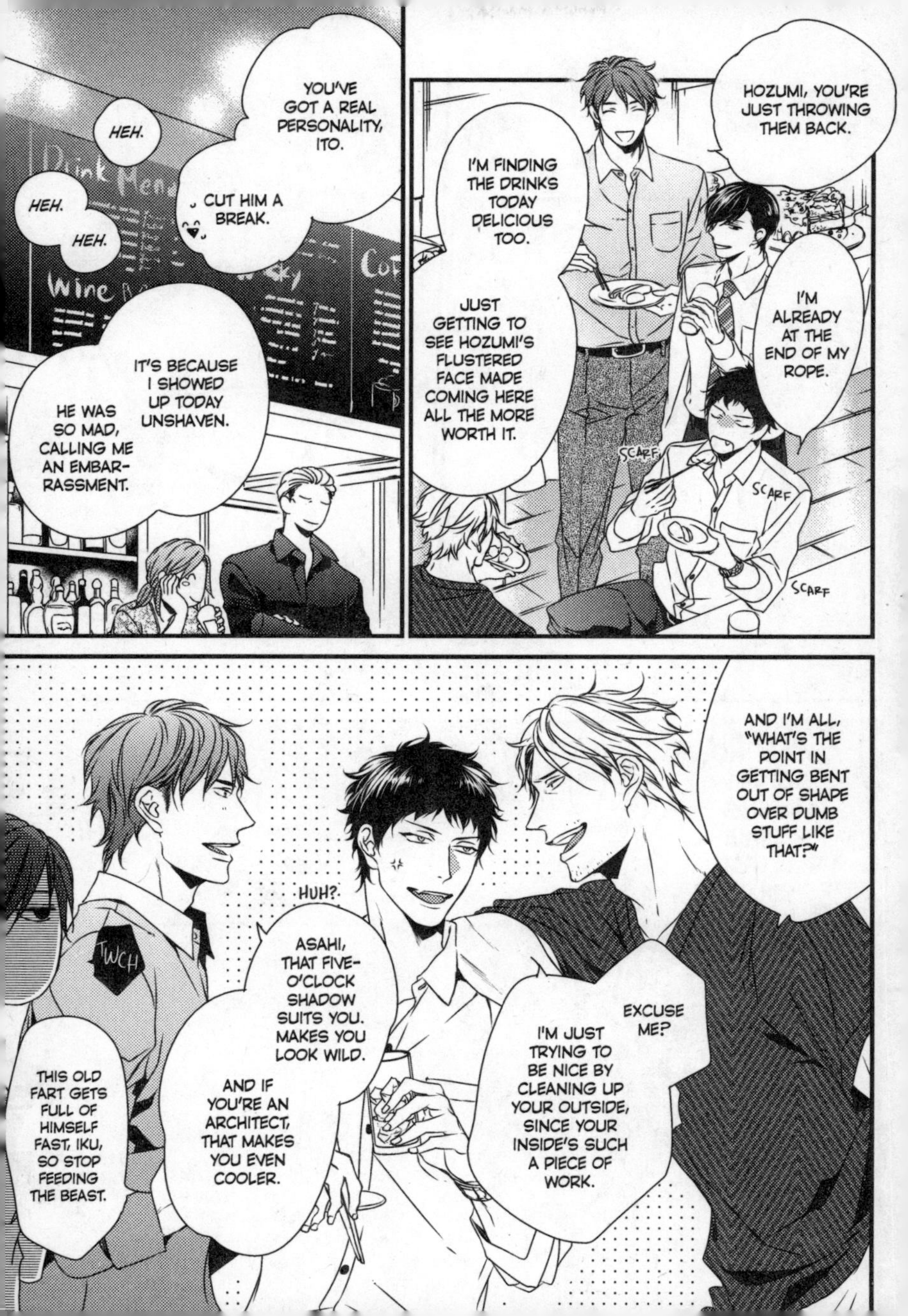
HOZUMI, YOU'RE JUST THROWING THEM BACK.
I'M FINDING THE DRINKS TODAY DELICIOUS TOO.
I'M ALREADY AT THE END OF MY ROPE.
JUST GETTING TO SEE HOZUMI'S FLUSTERED FACE MADE COMING HERE ALL THE MORE WORTH IT.
SCARF
SCARF
SCARF
YOU'VE GOT A REAL PERSONALITY, ITO.
HEH.
CUT HIM A BREAK.
HEH.
HEH.
IT'S BECAUSE I SHOWED UP TODAY UNSHAVEN.
HE WAS SO MAD, CALLING ME AN EMBAR-RASSMENT.
AND I'M ALL, "WHAT'S THE POINT IN GETTING BENT OUT OF SHAPE OVER DUMB STUFF LIKE THAT?"
EXCUSE ME?
I'M JUST TRYING TO BE NICE BY CLEANING UP YOUR OUTSIDE, SINCE YOUR INSIDE'S SUCH A PIECE OF WORK.
HUH?
ASAHI, THAT FIVE-O'CLOCK SHADOW SUITS YOU. MAKES YOU LOOK WILD.
AND IF YOU'RE AN ARCHITECT, THAT MAKES YOU EVEN COOLER.
TWCH
THIS OLD FART GETS FULL OF HIMSELF FAST, IKU, SO STOP FEEDING THE BEAST.

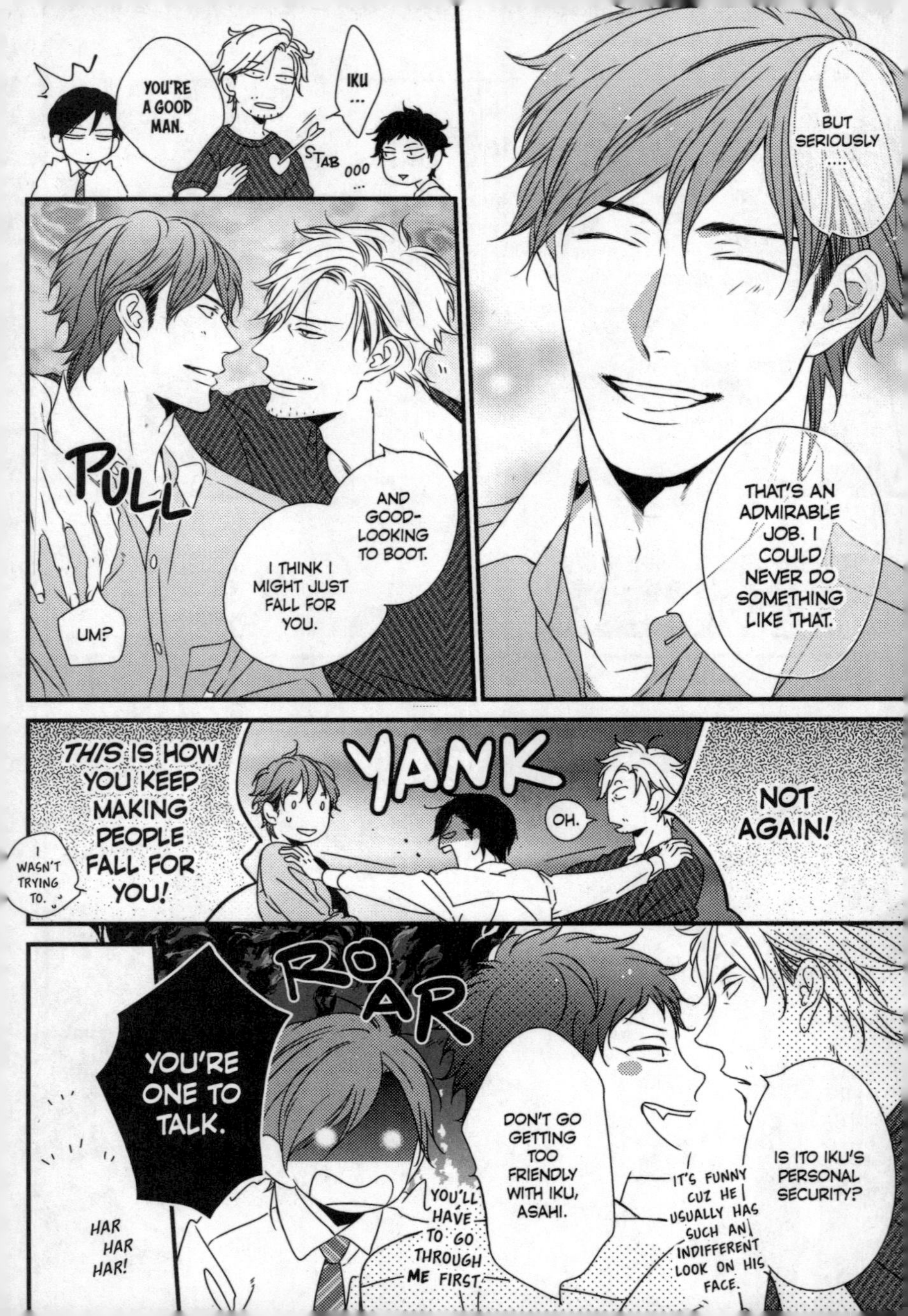
BUT SERIOUSLY....
THAT'S AN ADMIRABLE JOB. I COULD NEVER DO SOMETHING LIKE THAT.
YOU'RE A GOOD MAN.
IKU...
STAB
ooo...
AND GOOD-LOOKING TO BOOT.
I THINK I MIGHT JUST FALL FOR YOU.
PULL
UM?
NOT AGAIN!
OH.
YANK
THIS IS HOW YOU KEEP MAKING PEOPLE FALL FOR YOU!
I WASN'T TRYING TO.
IS ITO IKU'S PERSONAL SECURITY?
IT'S FUNNY CUZ HE USUALLY HAS SUCH AN INDIFFERENT LOOK ON HIS FACE.
DON'T GO GETTING TOO FRIENDLY WITH IKU, ASAHI.
YOU'LL HAVE TO GO THROUGH ME FIRST.
ROAR
YOU'RE ONE TO TALK.
HAR HAR HAR!

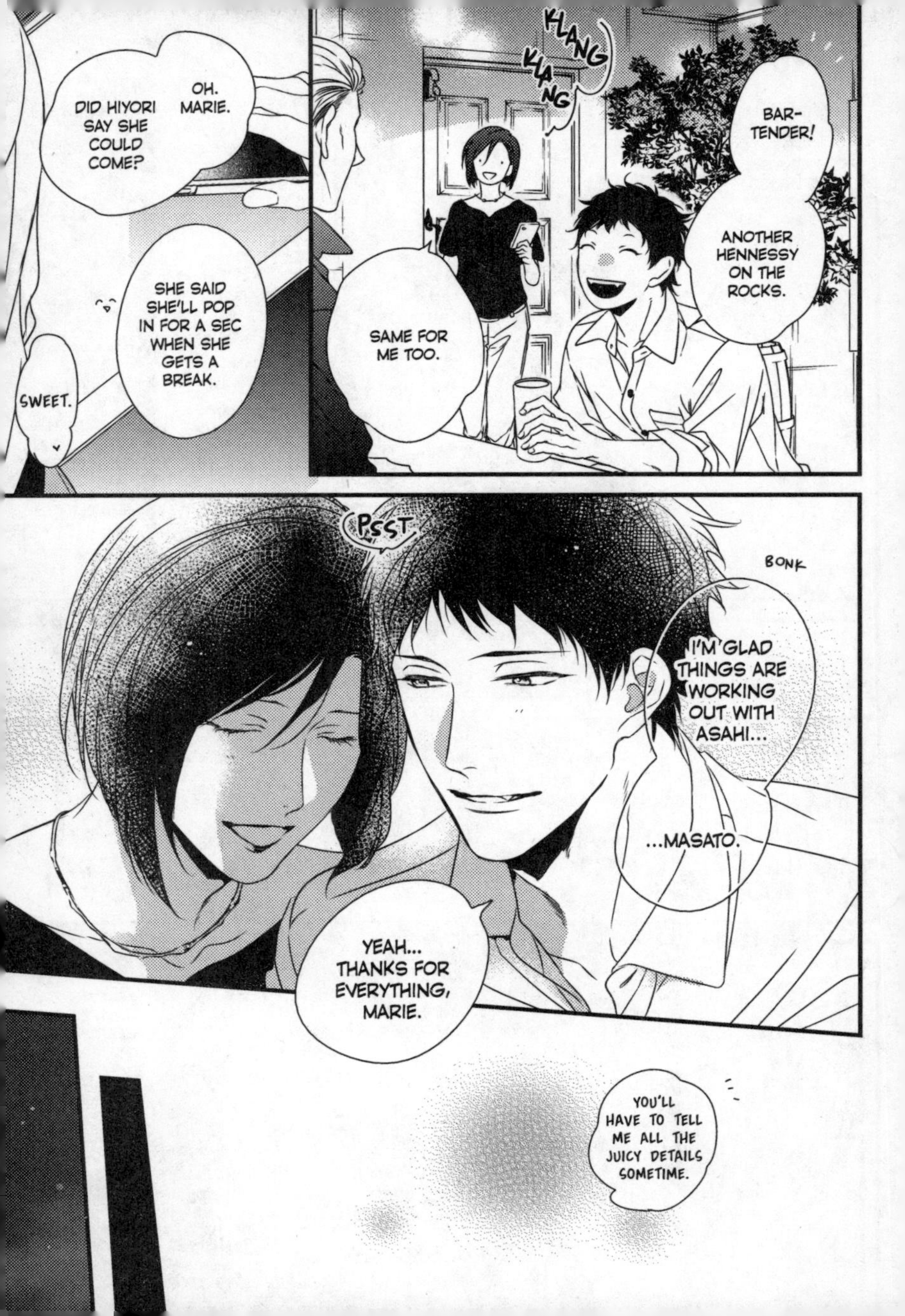
KLANG
KLANG
BAR-TENDER!
ANOTHER HENNESSY ON THE ROCKS.
SAME FOR ME TOO.
OH. MARIE.
DID HIYORI SAY SHE COULD COME?
SHE SAID SHE'LL POP IN FOR A SEC WHEN SHE GETS A BREAK.
SWEET.
PSST
BONK
I'M GLAD THINGS ARE WORKING OUT WITH ASAHI...
...MASATO.
YEAH... THANKS FOR EVERYTHING, MARIE.
YOU'LL HAVE TO TELL ME ALL THE JUICY DETAILS SOMETIME.

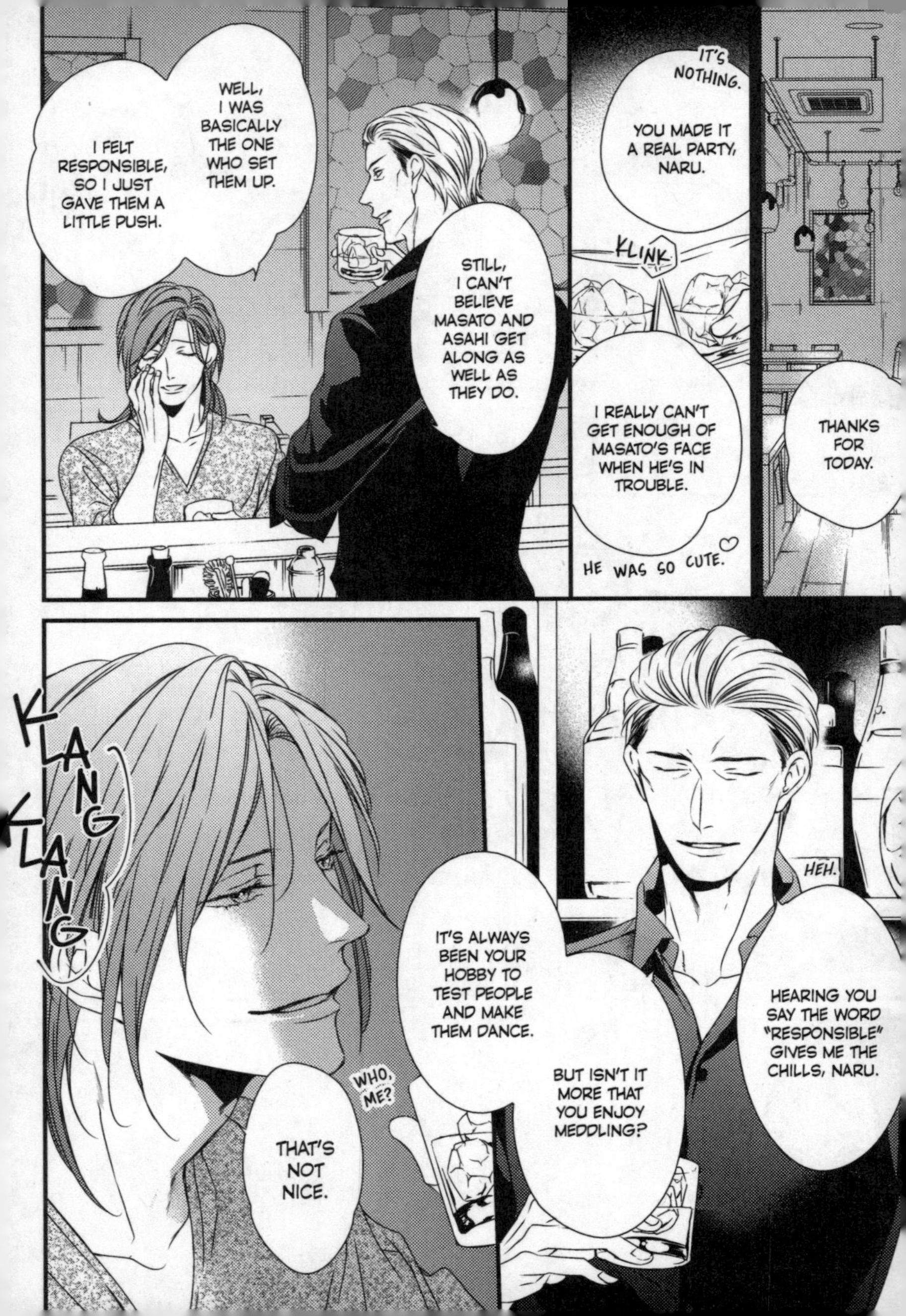
THANKS FOR TODAY.
IT'S NOTHING.
YOU MADE IT A REAL PARTY, NARU.
KLINK
I REALLY CAN'T GET ENOUGH OF MASATO'S FACE WHEN HE'S IN TROUBLE.
HE WAS SO CUTE.
STILL, I CAN'T BELIEVE MASATO AND ASAHI GET ALONG AS WELL AS THEY DO.
WELL, I WAS BASICALLY THE ONE WHO SET THEM UP.
I FELT RESPONSIBLE, SO I JUST GAVE THEM A LITTLE PUSH.
HEH.
HEARING YOU SAY THE WORD "RESPONSIBLE" GIVES ME THE CHILLS, NARU.
IT'S ALWAYS BEEN YOUR HOBBY TO TEST PEOPLE AND MAKE THEM DANCE.
BUT ISN'T IT MORE THAT YOU ENJOY MEDDLING?
KLANG KLANG
WHO, ME?
THAT'S NOT NICE.

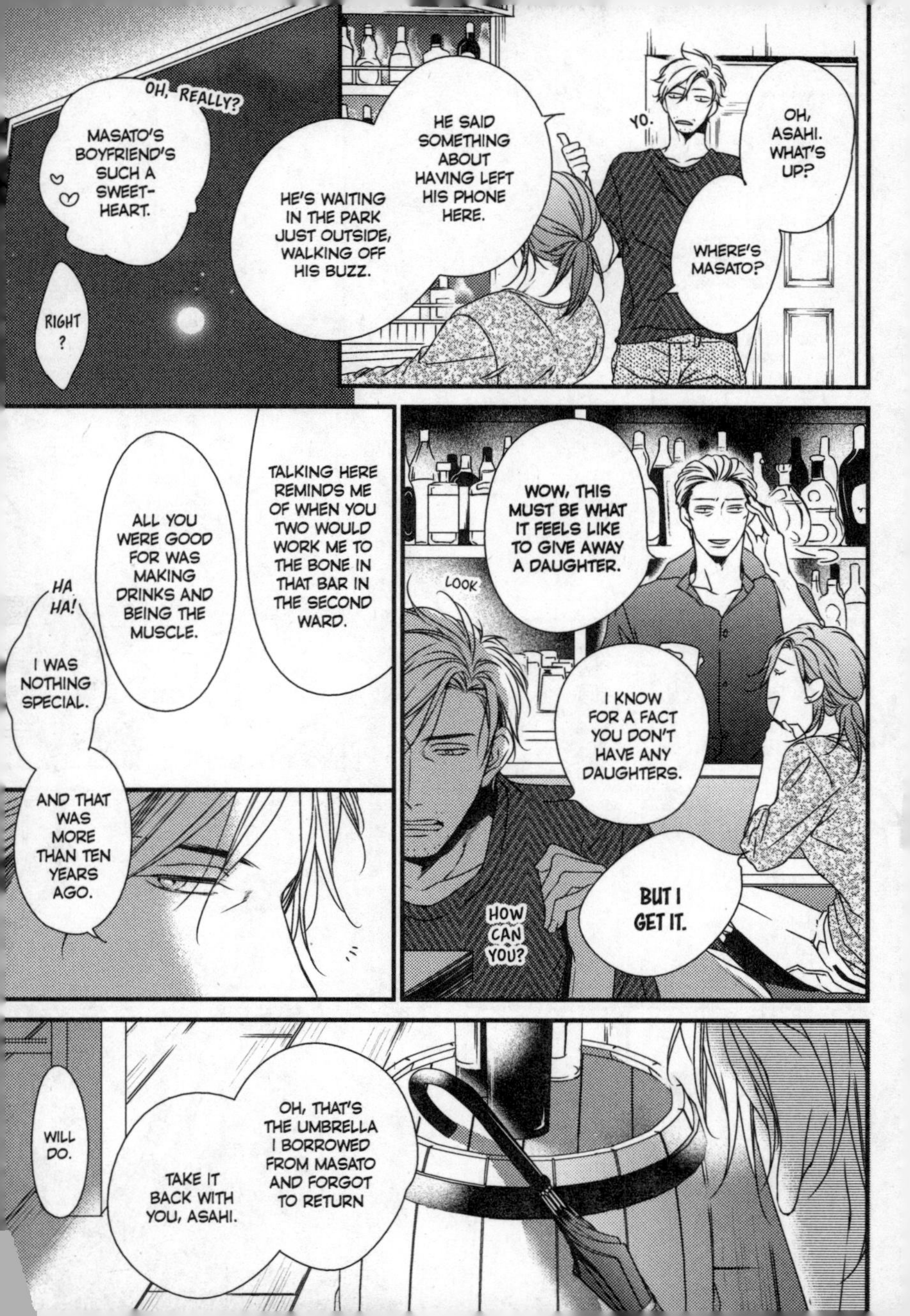
OH, ASAHI. WHAT'S UP?
YO.
WHERE'S MASATO?
HE SAID SOMETHING ABOUT HAVING LEFT HIS PHONE HERE.
HE'S WAITING IN THE PARK JUST OUTSIDE, WALKING OFF HIS BUZZ.
OH, REALLY?
MASATO'S BOYFRIEND'S SUCH A SWEET-HEART.
RIGHT?
WOW, THIS MUST BE WHAT IT FEELS LIKE TO GIVE AWAY A DAUGHTER.
LOOK
I KNOW FOR A FACT YOU DON'T HAVE ANY DAUGHTERS.
BUT I GET IT.
HOW CAN YOU?
TALKING HERE REMINDS ME OF WHEN YOU TWO WOULD WORK ME TO THE BONE IN THAT BAR IN THE SECOND WARD.
ALL YOU WERE GOOD FOR WAS MAKING DRINKS AND BEING THE MUSCLE.
HA HA!
I WAS NOTHING SPECIAL.
AND THAT WAS MORE THAN TEN YEARS AGO.
OH, THAT'S THE UMBRELLA I BORROWED FROM MASATO AND FORGOT TO RETURN
TAKE IT BACK WITH YOU, ASAHI.
WILL DO.

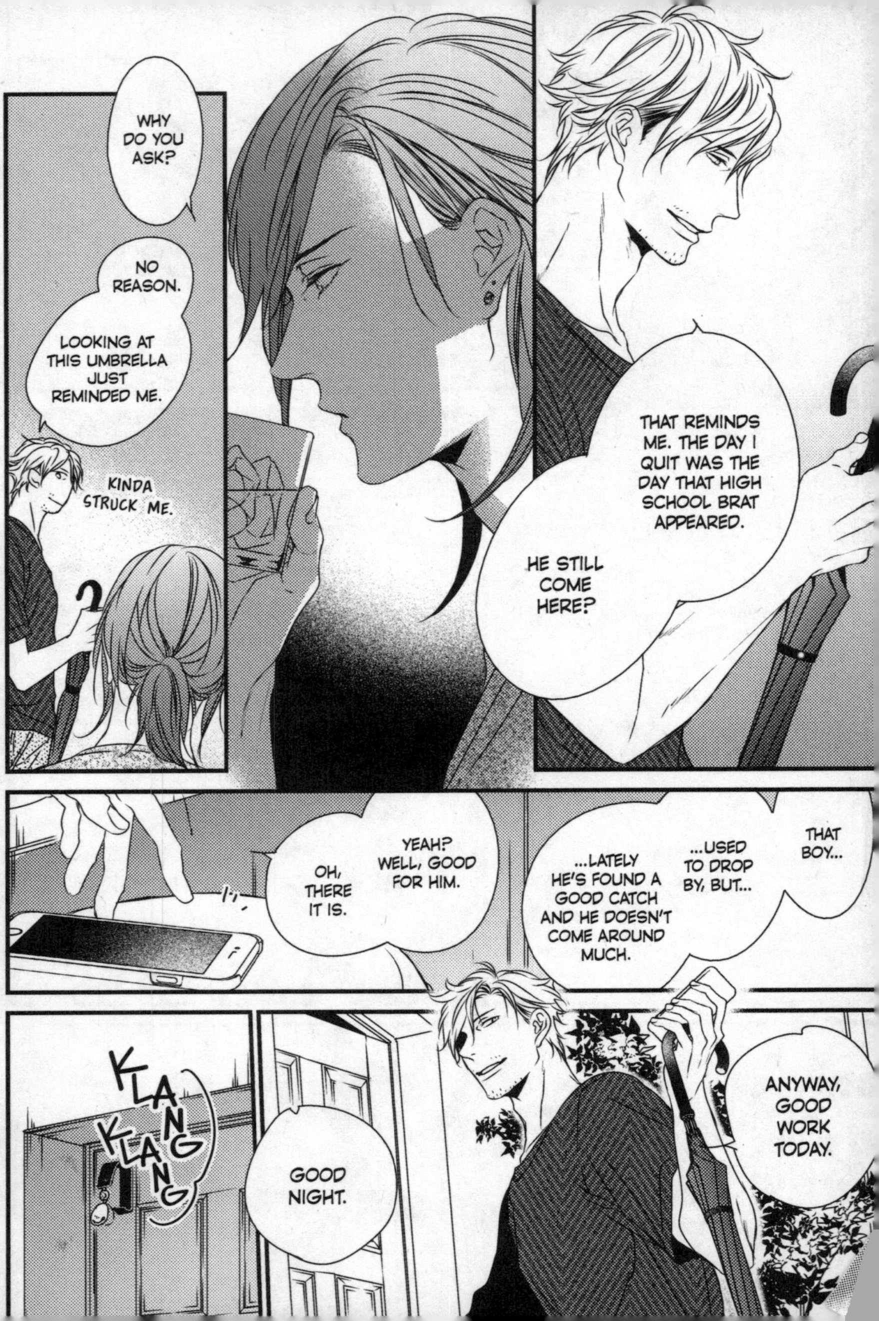
THAT REMINDS ME. THE DAY I QUIT WAS THE DAY THAT HIGH SCHOOL BRAT APPEARED.
HE STILL COME HERE?
WHY DO YOU ASK?
NO REASON.
LOOKING AT THIS UMBRELLA JUST REMINDED ME.
KINDA STRUCK ME.
THAT BOY...
...USED TO DROP BY, BUT...
...LATELY HE'S FOUND A GOOD CATCH AND HE DOESN'T COME AROUND MUCH.
YEAH? WELL, GOOD FOR HIM.
OH, THERE IT IS.
ANYWAY, GOOD WORK TODAY.
GOOD NIGHT.
KLANG KLANG

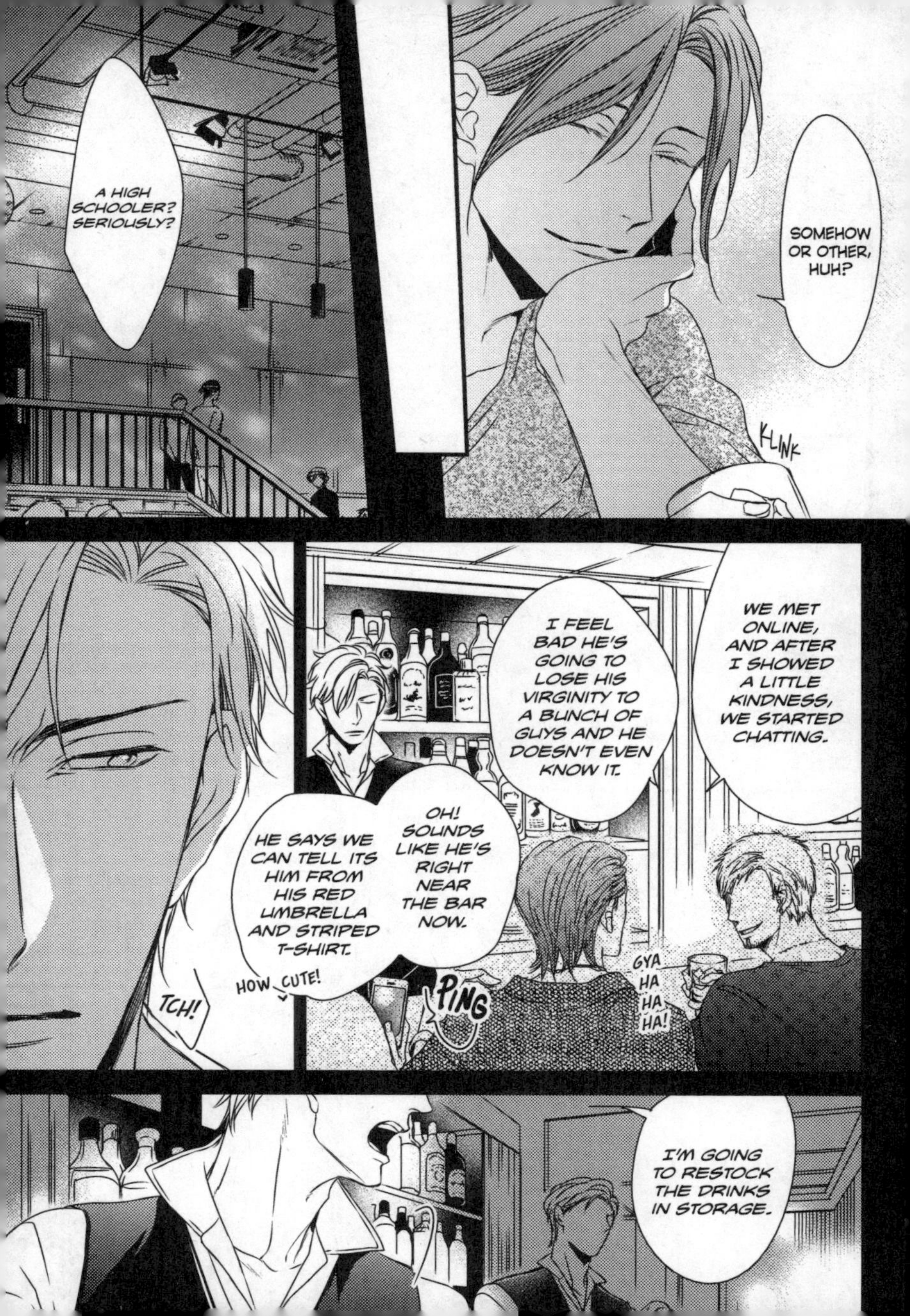
SOMEHOW OR OTHER, HUH?
K-LINK
A HIGH SCHOOLER? SERIOUSLY?
WE MET ONLINE, AND AFTER I SHOWED A LITTLE KINDNESS, WE STARTED CHATTING.
I FEEL BAD HE'S GOING TO LOSE HIS VIRGINITY TO A BUNCH OF GUYS AND HE DOESN'T EVEN KNOW IT.
GYA HA HA HA!
OH! SOUNDS LIKE HE'S RIGHT NEAR THE BAR NOW.
PING
HE SAYS WE CAN TELL ITS HIM FROM HIS RED UMBRELLA AND STRIPED T-SHIRT.
HOW CUTE!
TCH!
I'M GOING TO RESTOCK THE DRINKS IN STORAGE.

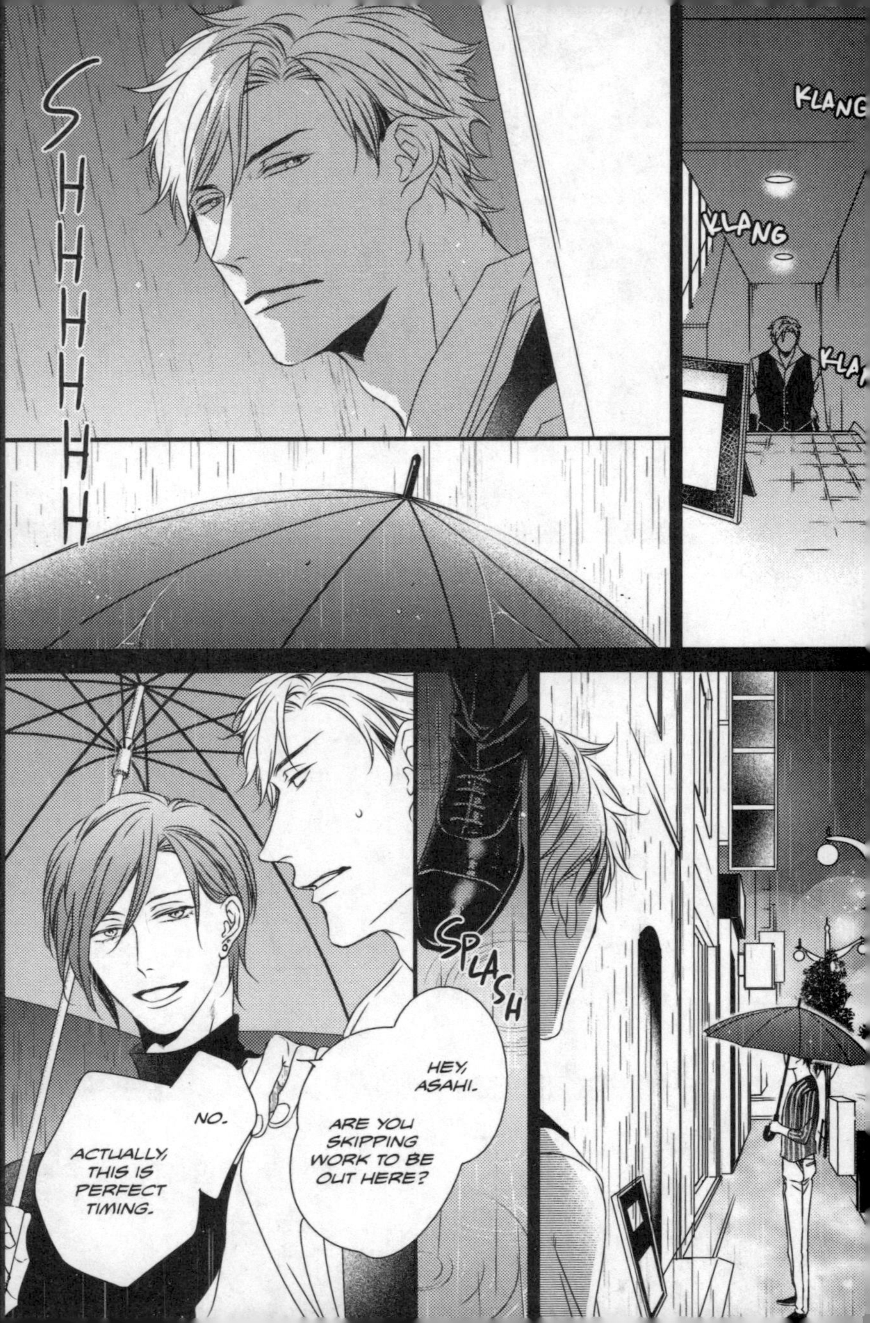
KLANG
KLANG
SHHHHHHHH
SPLASH
HEY, ASAHI.
ARE YOU SKIPPING WORK TO BE OUT HERE?
NO.
ACTUALLY, THIS IS PERFECT TIMING.

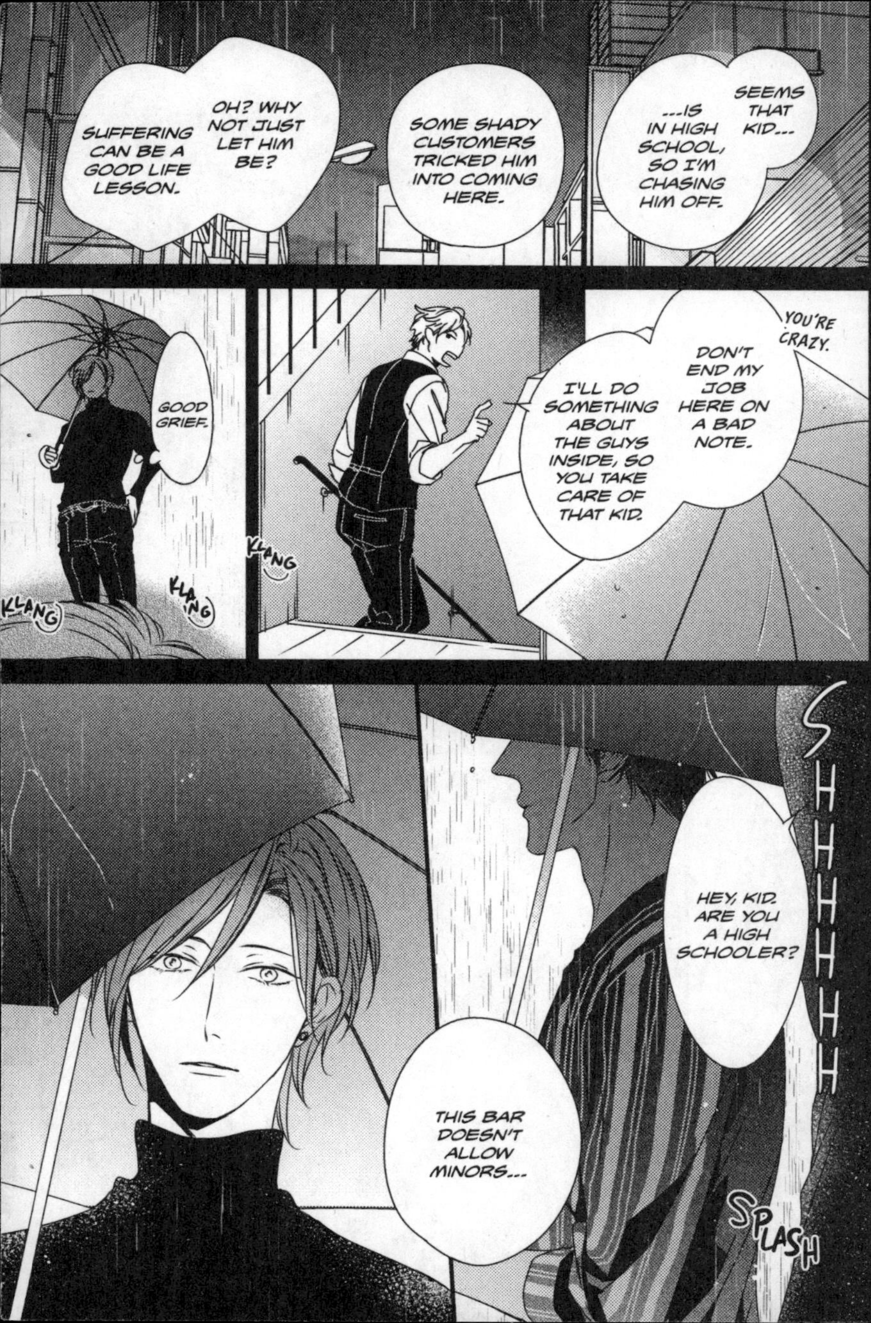
SEEMS THAT KID...
...IS IN HIGH SCHOOL, SO I'M CHASING HIM OFF.
SOME SHADY CUSTOMERS TRICKED HIM INTO COMING HERE.
OH? WHY NOT JUST LET HIM BE?
SUFFERING CAN BE A GOOD LIFE LESSON.
YOU'RE CRAZY.
DON'T END MY JOB HERE ON A BAD NOTE.
I'LL DO SOMETHING ABOUT THE GUYS INSIDE, SO YOU TAKE CARE OF THAT KID.
KLANG
KLANG
GOOD GRIEF.
KLANG
SHHHHHHH
HEY, KID. ARE YOU A HIGH SCHOOLER?
THIS BAR DOESN'T ALLOW MINORS...
SPLASH

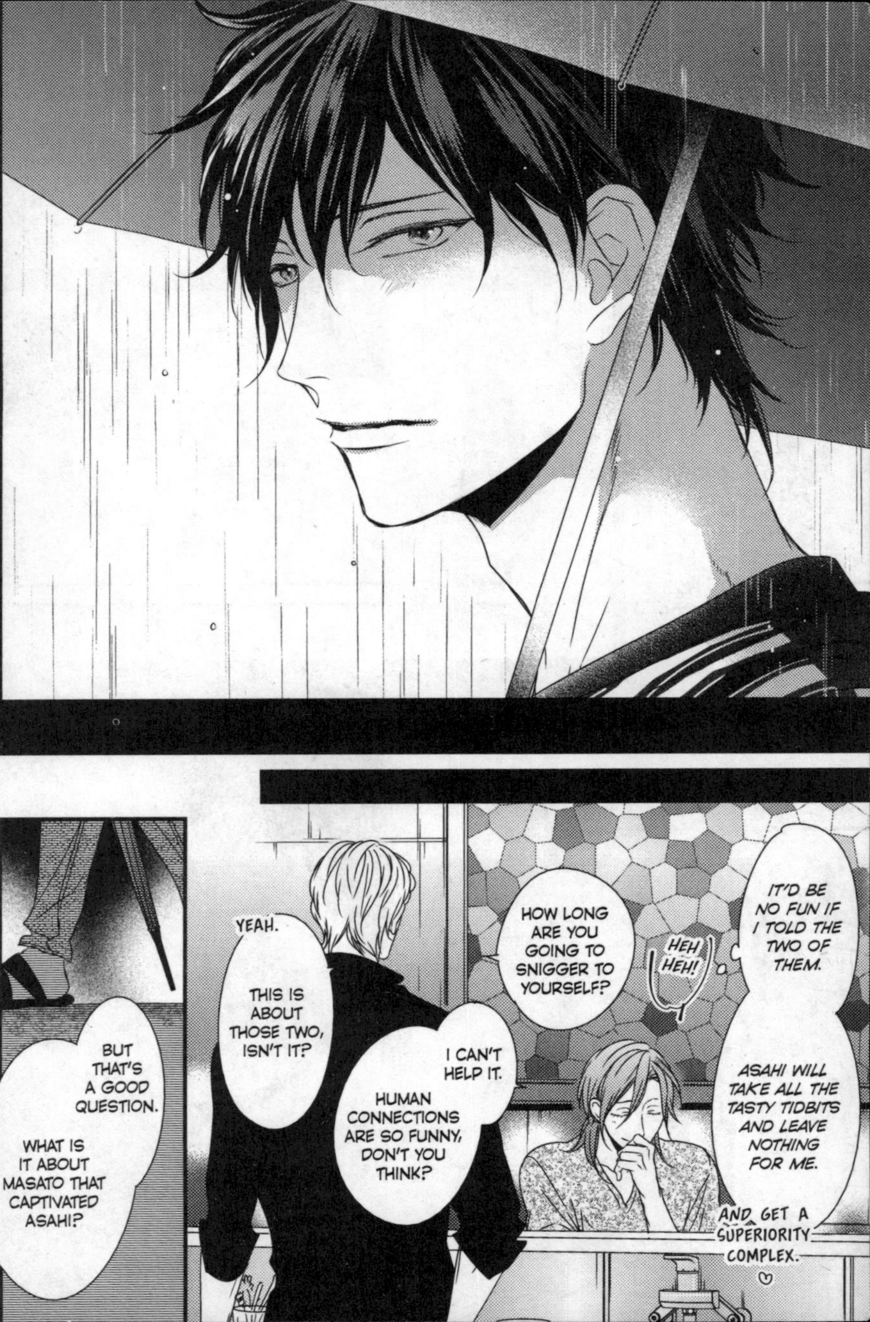
IT'D BE NO FUN IF I TOLD THE TWO OF THEM.
HEH HEH!
HOW LONG ARE YOU GOING TO SNIGGER TO YOURSELF?
ASAHI WILL TAKE ALL THE TASTY TIDBITS AND LEAVE NOTHING FOR ME.
AND GET A SUPERIORITY COMPLEX.
YEAH.
THIS IS ABOUT THOSE TWO, ISN'T IT?
I CAN'T HELP IT.
HUMAN CONNECTIONS ARE SO FUNNY, DON'T YOU THINK?
BUT THAT'S A GOOD QUESTION.
WHAT IS IT ABOUT MASATO THAT CAPTIVATED ASAHI?

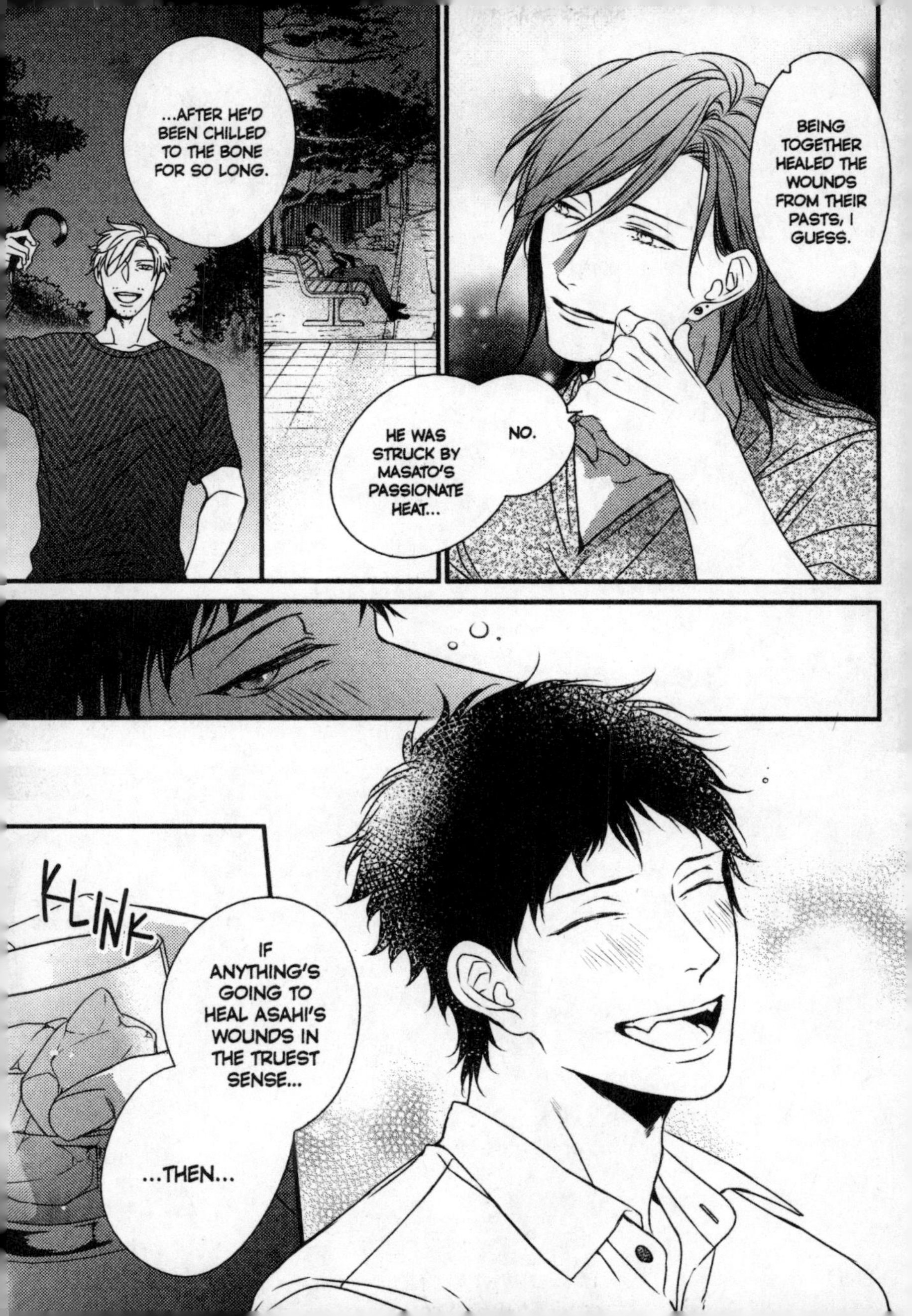
BEING TOGETHER HEALED THE WOUNDS FROM THEIR PASTS, I GUESS.
NO.
HE WAS STRUCK BY MASATO'S PASSIONATE HEAT...
...AFTER HE'D BEEN CHILLED TO THE BONE FOR SO LONG.
KLINK
IF ANYTHING'S GOING TO HEAL ASAHI'S WOUNDS IN THE TRUEST SENSE...
...THEN...

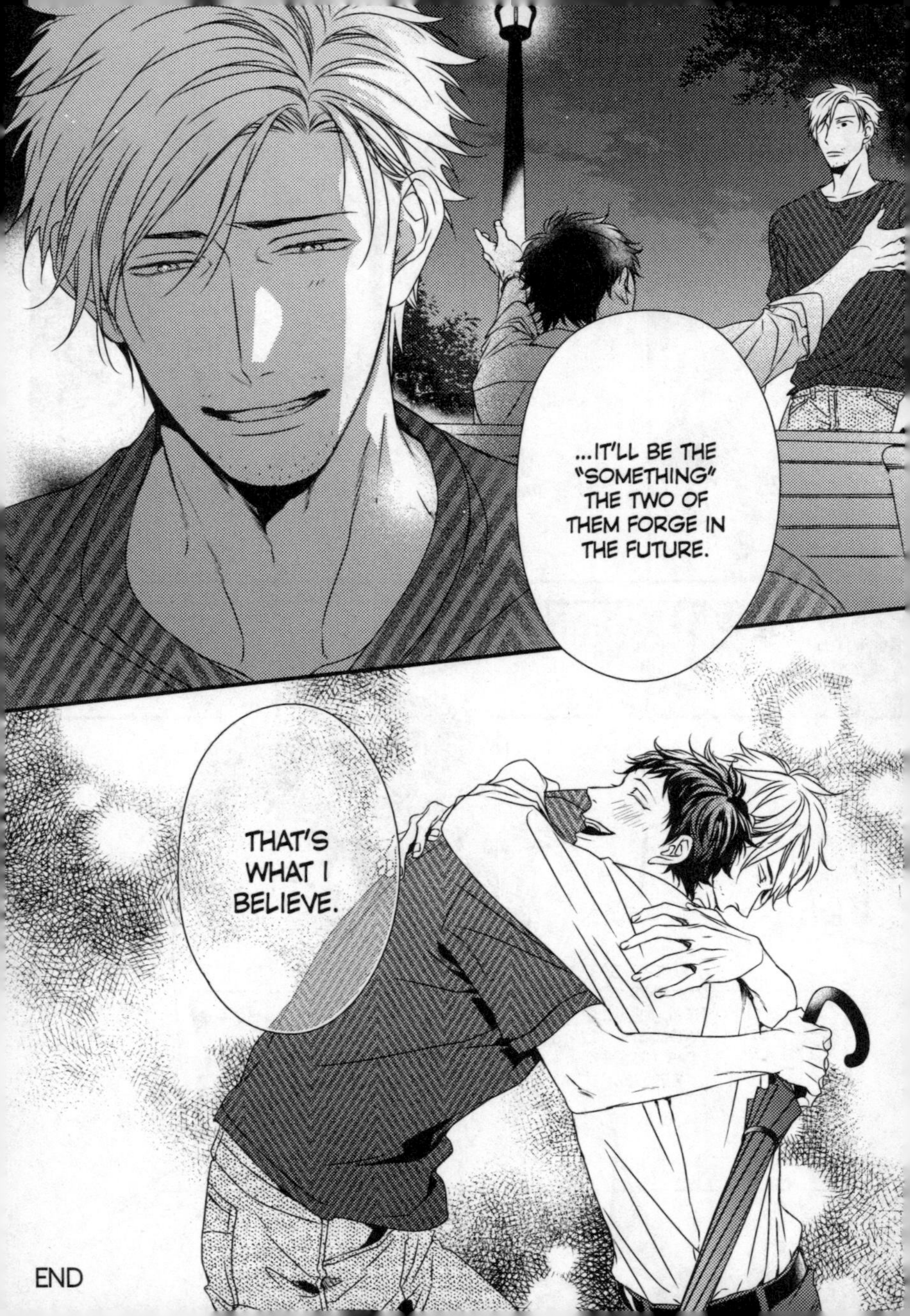
...IT'LL BE THE "SOMETHING" THE TWO OF THEM FORGE IN THE FUTURE.
THAT'S WHAT I BELIEVE.
END

LOVE NEST

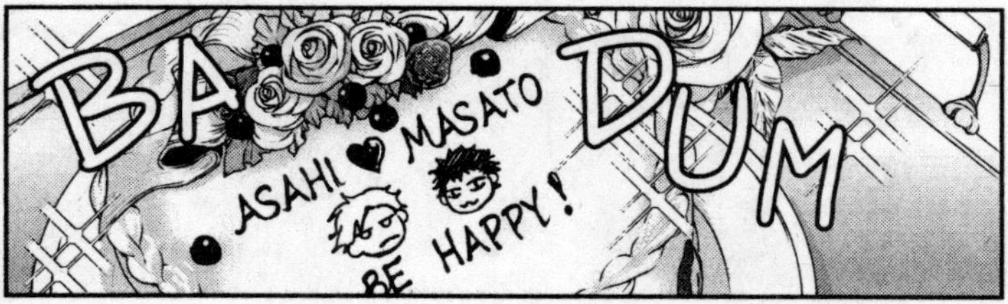
BA DUM
ASAHI ♥ MASATO
BE HAPPY!

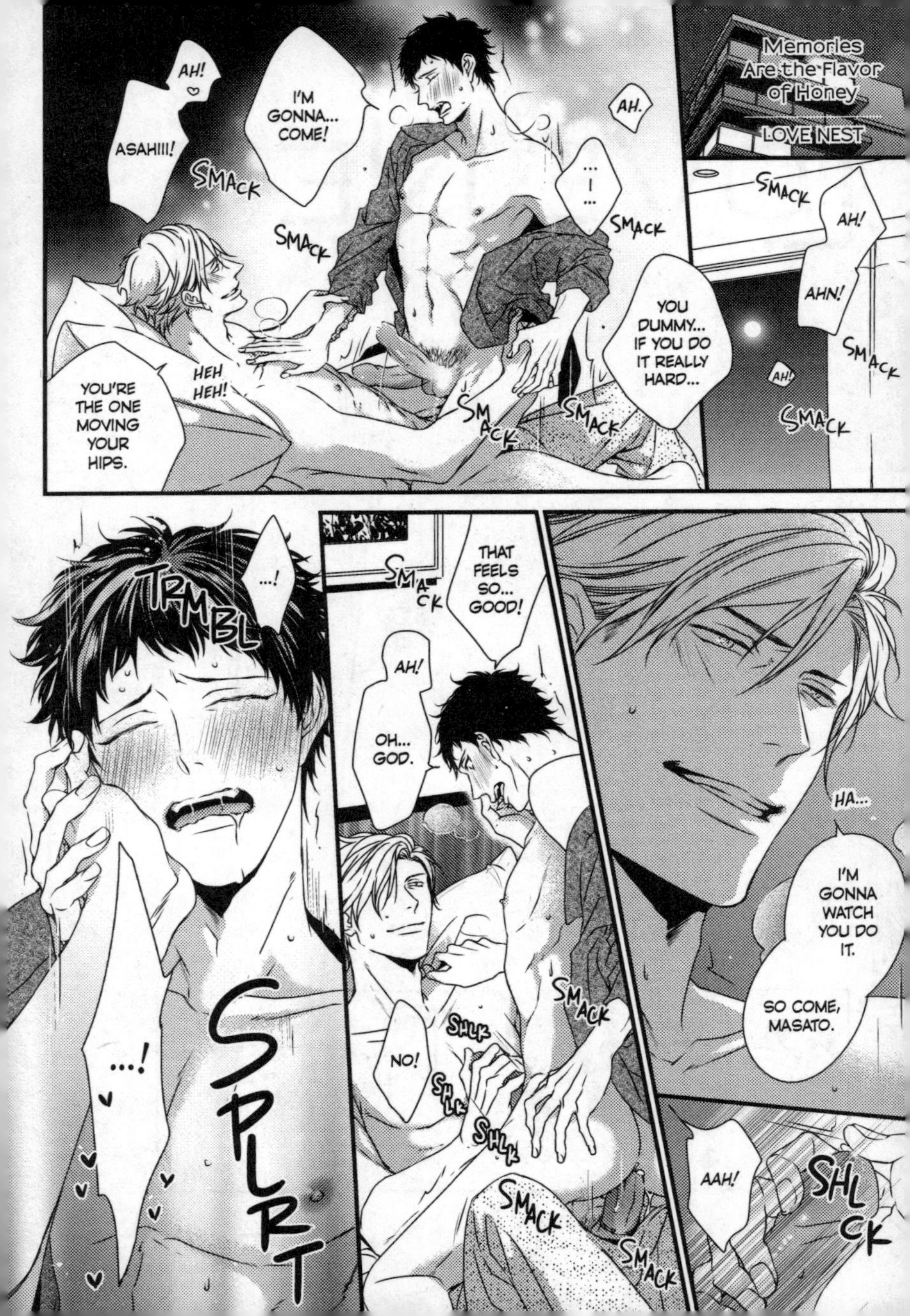
Memories Are the Flavor of Honey
LOVE NEST
SMACK
AH!
AHN!
SMACK
AH!
SMACK
AH.
...!...
SMACK
I'M GONNA... COME!
AH! ♥
ASAHIII!
SMACK
SMACK
YOU DUMMY... IF YOU DO IT REALLY HARD...
SMACK
SMACK
HEH HEH!
YOU'RE THE ONE MOVING YOUR HIPS.
HA...
I'M GONNA WATCH YOU DO IT.
SO COME, MASATO.
AAH!
SHLCK
THAT FEELS SO... GOOD!
SMACK
AH!
OH... GOD.
SMACK
SHLK
NO!
SHLK
SHLK
SMACK
SMACK
...!
TRMBL
SPLRT
...!

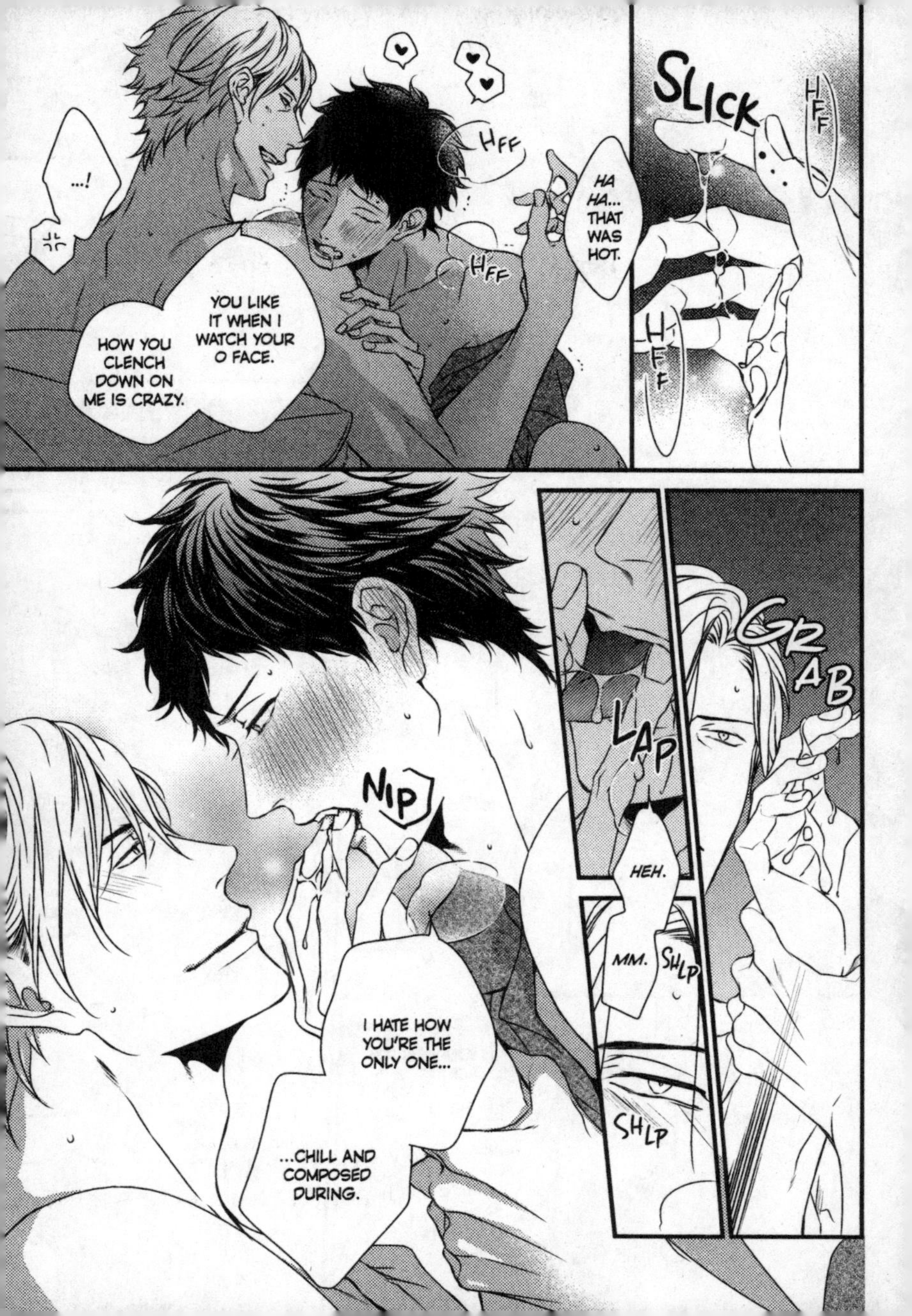
SLICK
HFF
HFF
HA HA... THAT WAS HOT.
HFF
HFF
...!
YOU LIKE IT WHEN I WATCH YOUR O FACE.
HOW YOU CLENCH DOWN ON ME IS CRAZY.
GRAB
LAP
HEH.
MM.
SHLP
SHLP
NIP
I HATE HOW YOU'RE THE ONLY ONE...
...CHILL AND COMPOSED DURING.

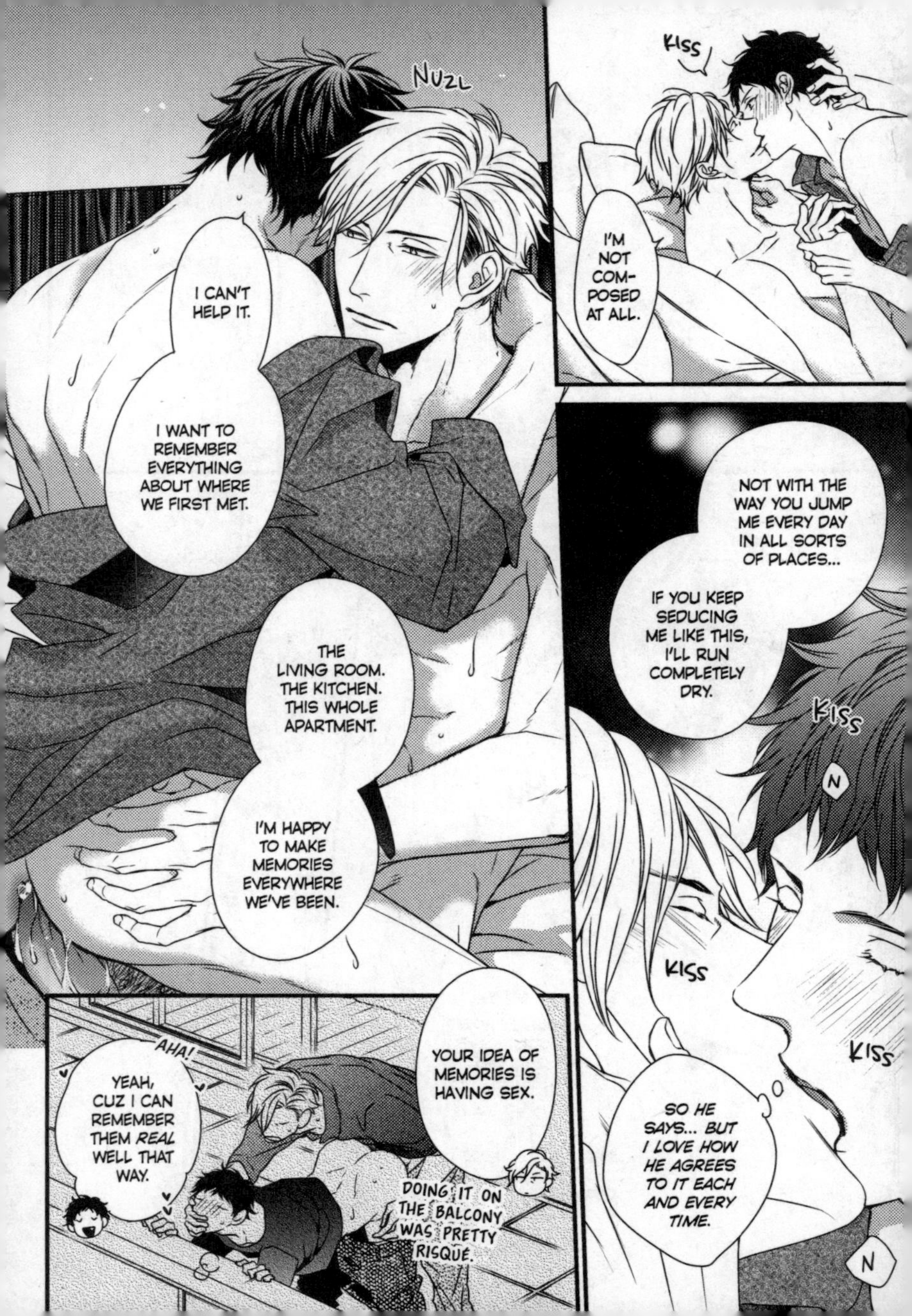
KISS
I'M NOT COMPOSED AT ALL.
NUZL
I CAN'T HELP IT.
I WANT TO REMEMBER EVERYTHING ABOUT WHERE WE FIRST MET.
THE LIVING ROOM. THE KITCHEN. THIS WHOLE APARTMENT.
I'M HAPPY TO MAKE MEMORIES EVERYWHERE WE'VE BEEN.
YOUR IDEA OF MEMORIES IS HAVING SEX.
AHA!
YEAH, CUZ I CAN REMEMBER THEM *REAL* WELL THAT WAY.
DOING IT ON THE BALCONY WAS PRETTY RISQUÉ.
NOT WITH THE WAY YOU JUMP ME EVERY DAY IN ALL SORTS OF PLACES...
IF YOU KEEP SEDUCING ME LIKE THIS, I'LL RUN COMPLETELY DRY.
KISS
N
KISS
KISS
SO HE SAYS... BUT I LOVE HOW HE AGREES TO IT EACH AND EVERY TIME.
N

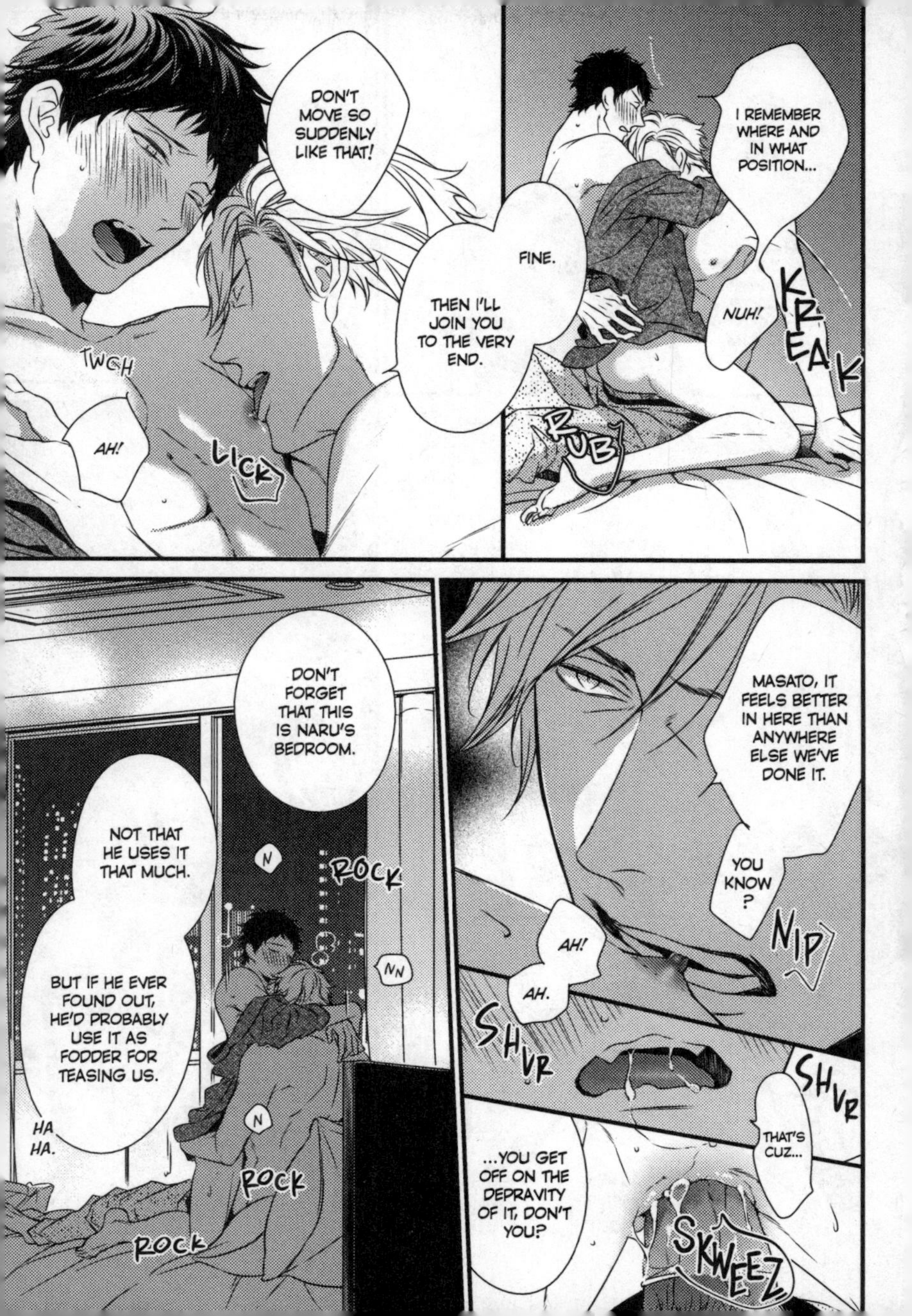
I REMEMBER WHERE AND IN WHAT POSITION...
NUH!
KREAK
RUB
DON'T MOVE SO SUDDENLY LIKE THAT!
FINE.
THEN I'LL JOIN YOU TO THE VERY END.
TWCH
AH!
LICK
MASATO, IT FEELS BETTER IN HERE THAN ANYWHERE ELSE WE'VE DONE IT.
YOU KNOW?
NIP
AH!
AH.
SHVR
SHVR
THAT'S CUZ...
...YOU GET OFF ON THE DEPRAVITY OF IT, DON'T YOU?
SKWEEZ
DON'T FORGET THAT THIS IS NARU'S BEDROOM.
NOT THAT HE USES IT THAT MUCH.
N
ROCK
NN
BUT IF HE EVER FOUND OUT, HE'D PROBABLY USE IT AS FODDER FOR TEASING US.
N
HA HA.
ROCK
ROCK

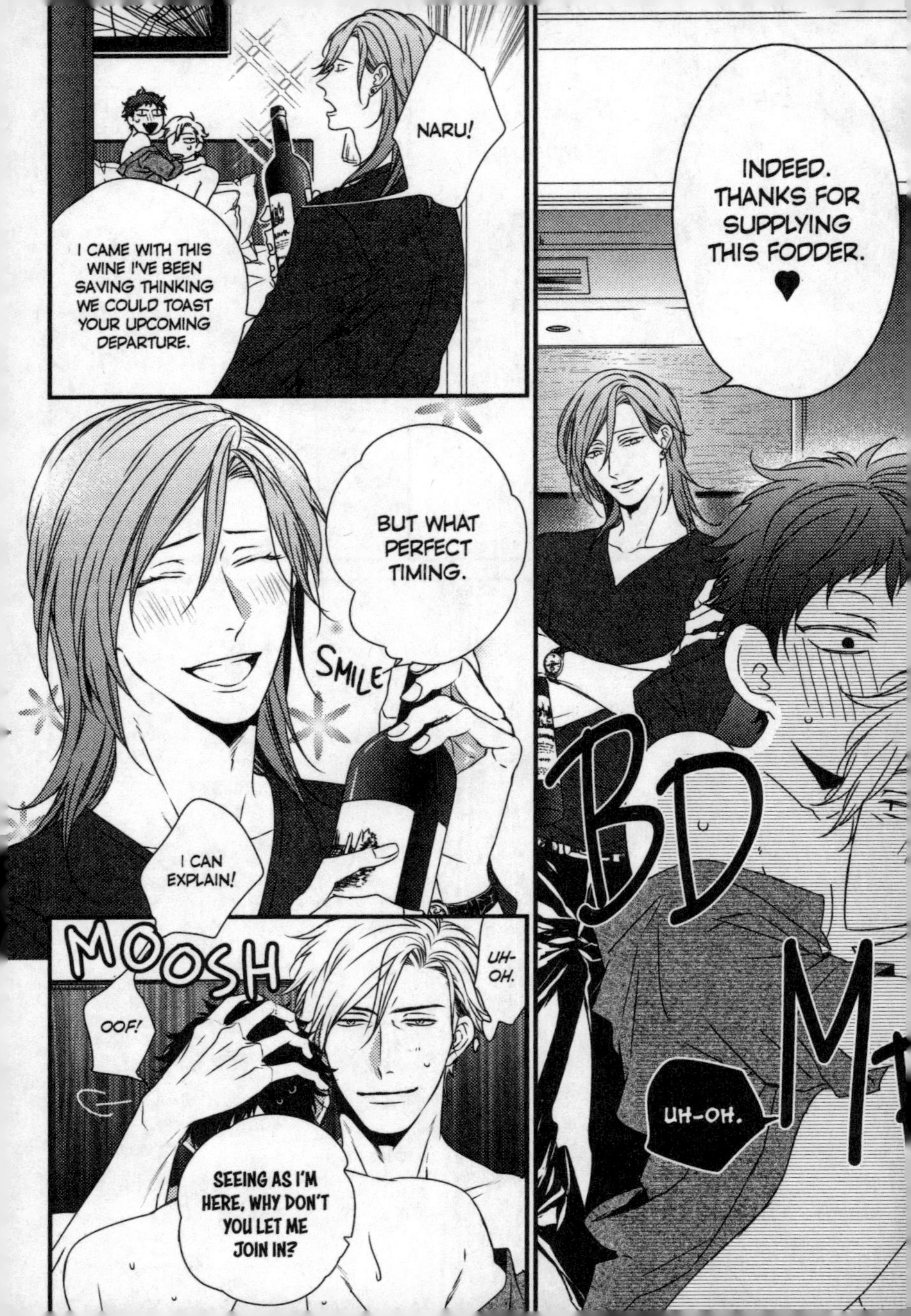
INDEED. THANKS FOR SUPPLYING THIS FODDER. ♥
BDM
UH-OH.
NARU!
I CAME WITH THIS WINE I'VE BEEN SAVING THINKING WE COULD TOAST YOUR UPCOMING DEPARTURE.
BUT WHAT PERFECT TIMING.
SMILE
I CAN EXPLAIN!
MOOSH
UH-OH.
OOF!
SEEING AS I'M HERE, WHY DON'T YOU LET ME JOIN IN?

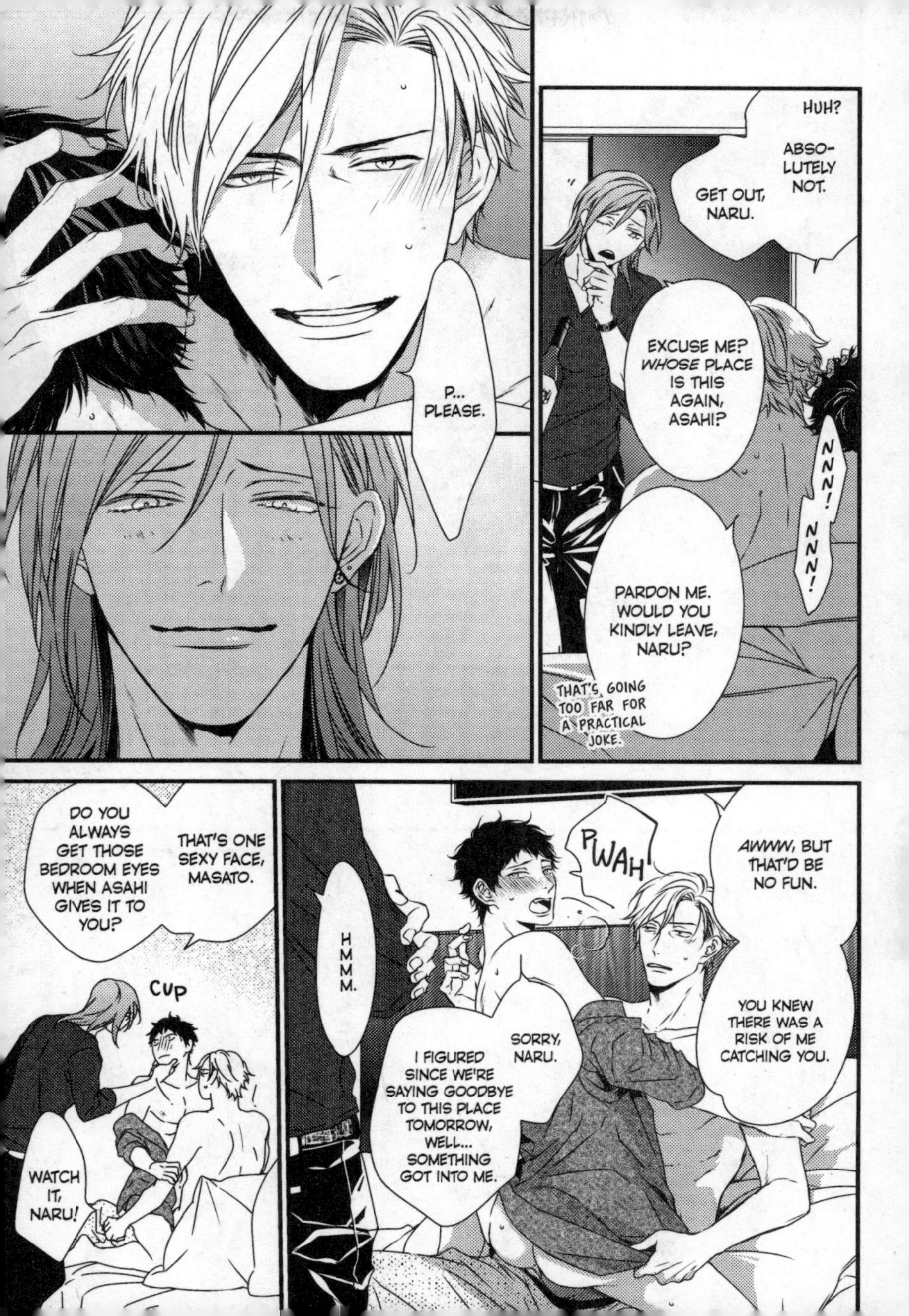
HUH?
ABSO-LUTELY NOT.
GET OUT, NARU.
EXCUSE ME? *WHOSE* PLACE IS THIS AGAIN, ASAHI?
NNN! NNN!
PARDON ME. WOULD YOU KINDLY LEAVE, NARU?
THAT'S GOING TOO FAR FOR A PRACTICAL JOKE.
P... PLEASE.
AWWW, BUT THAT'D BE NO FUN.
PWAH
YOU KNEW THERE WAS A RISK OF ME CATCHING YOU.
SORRY, NARU.
I FIGURED SINCE WE'RE SAYING GOODBYE TO THIS PLACE TOMORROW, WELL... SOMETHING GOT INTO ME.
HMMM.
THAT'S ONE SEXY FACE, MASATO.
DO YOU ALWAYS GET THOSE BEDROOM EYES WHEN ASAHI GIVES IT TO YOU?
CUP
WATCH IT, NARU!

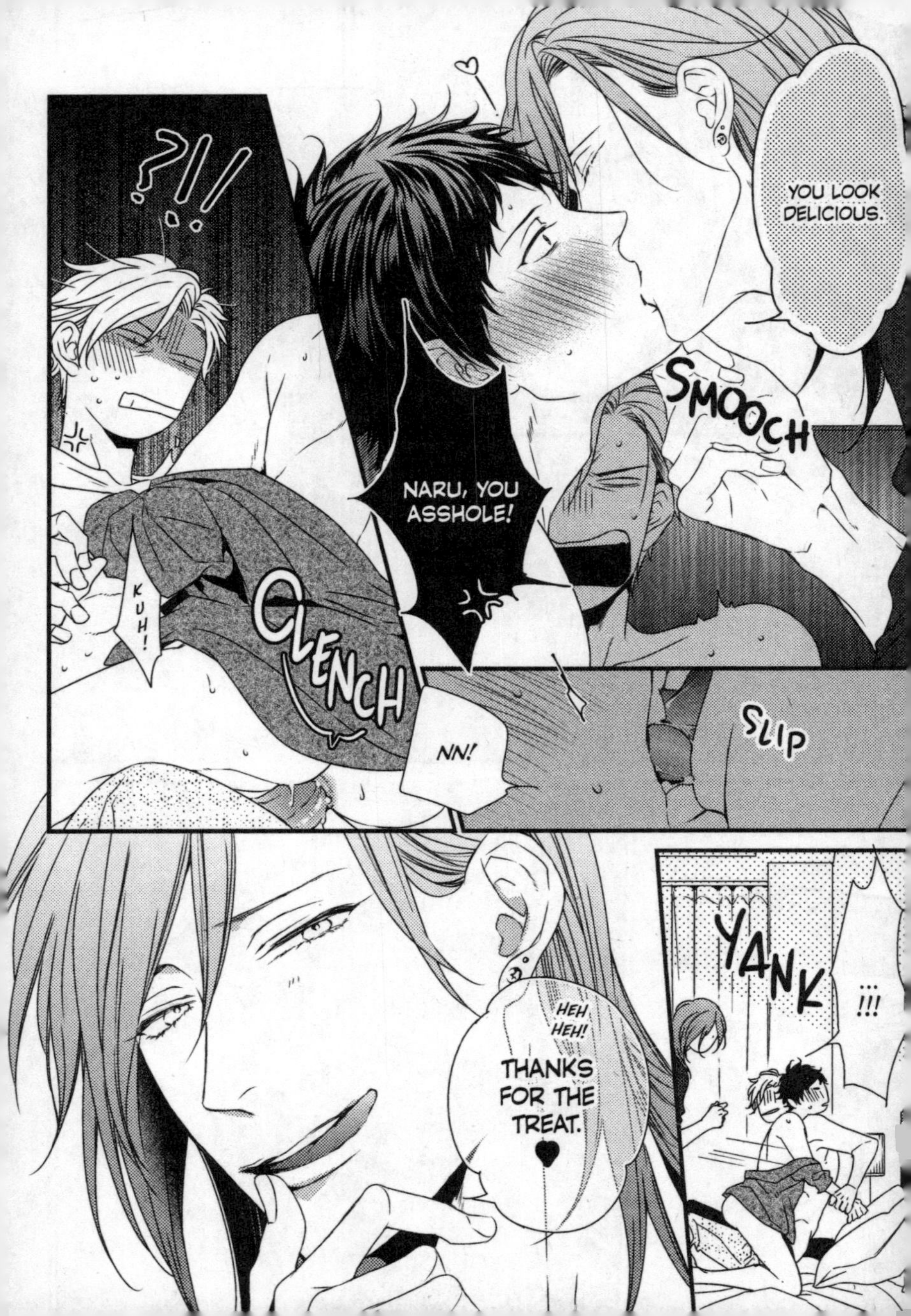
YOU LOOK DELICIOUS.
SMOOCH
?!!
NARU, YOU ASSHOLE!
KUH!
CLENCH
SLIP
NN!
YANK
...!!!
HEH HEH!
THANKS FOR THE TREAT.

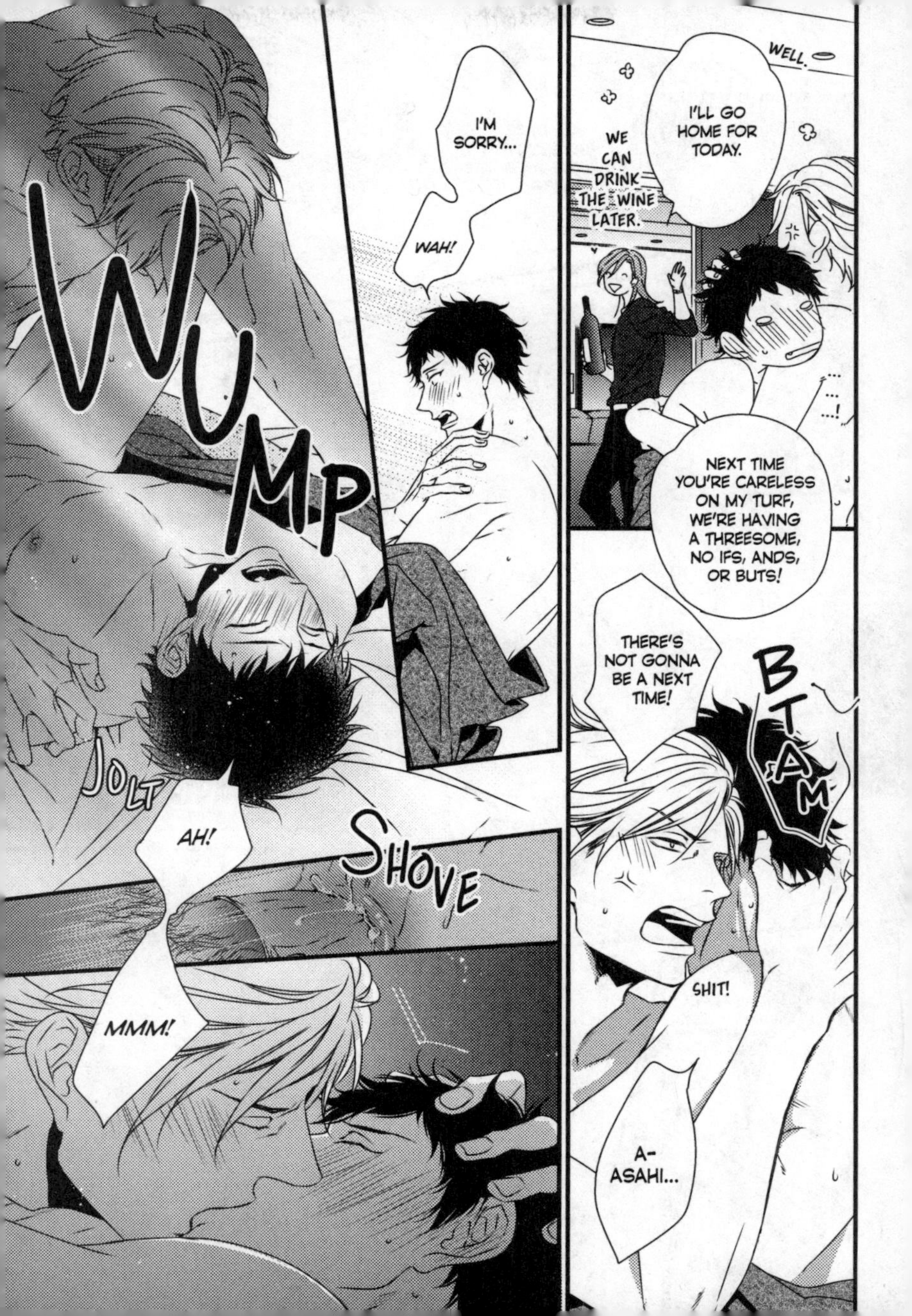
WELL.
I'LL GO HOME FOR TODAY.
WE CAN DRINK THE WINE LATER.
...
...
...!
NEXT TIME YOU'RE CARELESS ON MY TURF, WE'RE HAVING A THREESOME, NO IFS, ANDS, OR BUTS!
THERE'S NOT GONNA BE A NEXT TIME!
BTAM
SHIT!
A- ASAHI...
I'M SORRY...
WAH!
WUMP
JOLT
AH!
SHOVE
MMM!

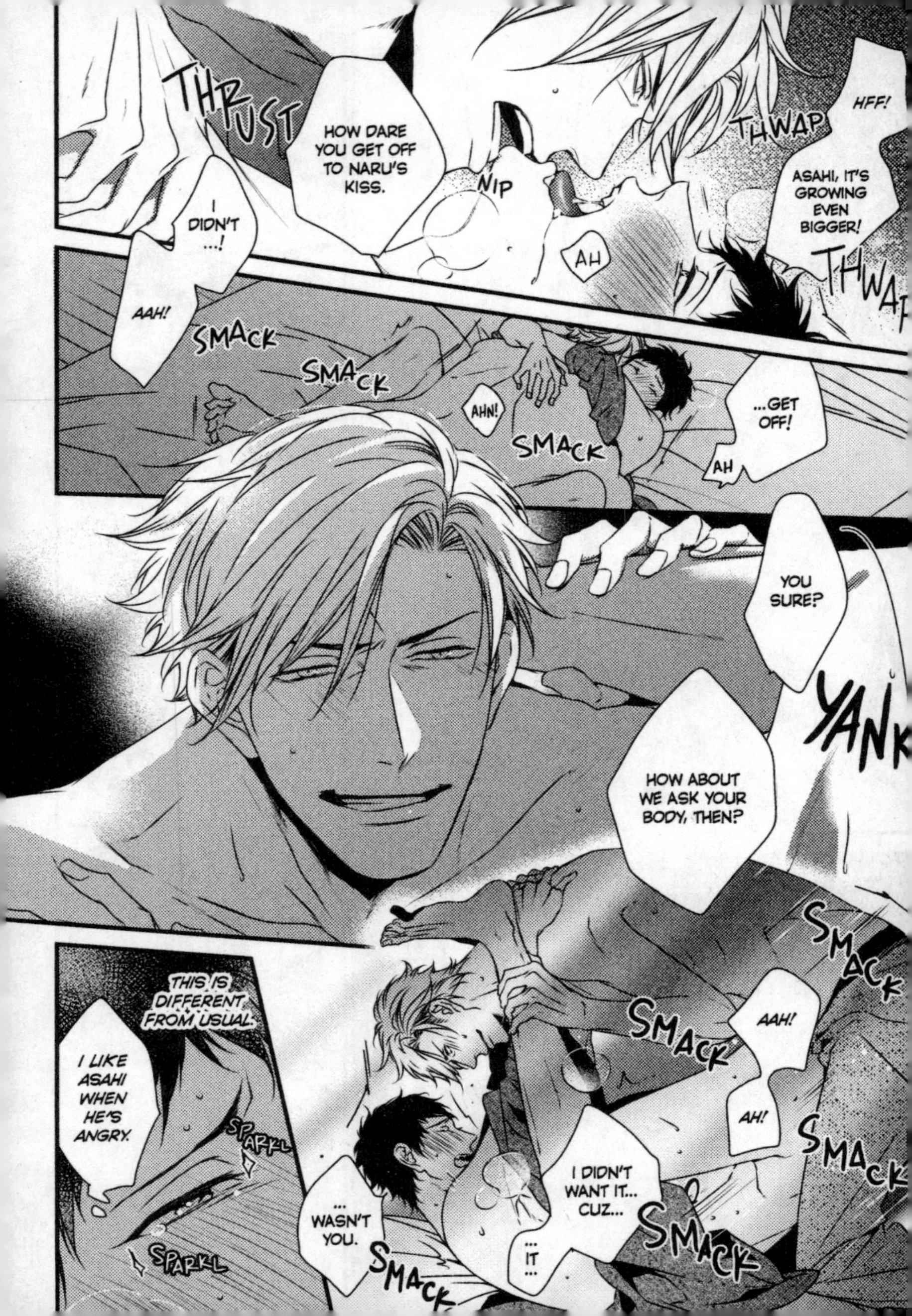
HFF!
THWAP
ASAHI, IT'S GROWING EVEN BIGGER!
THWAP
NIP
AH
HOW DARE YOU GET OFF TO NARU'S KISS.
THRUST
I DIDN'T ...!
...GET OFF!
AH
SMACK
AHN!
SMACK
SMACK
AAH!
YANK
YOU SURE?
HOW ABOUT WE ASK YOUR BODY, THEN?
SMACK
AAH!
SMACK
AH!
SMACK
I DIDN'T WANT IT... CUZ...
SMACK
...IT...
...WASN'T YOU.
SMACK
THIS IS DIFFERENT FROM USUAL.
I LIKE ASAHI WHEN HE'S ANGRY.
SPARKL
SPARKL

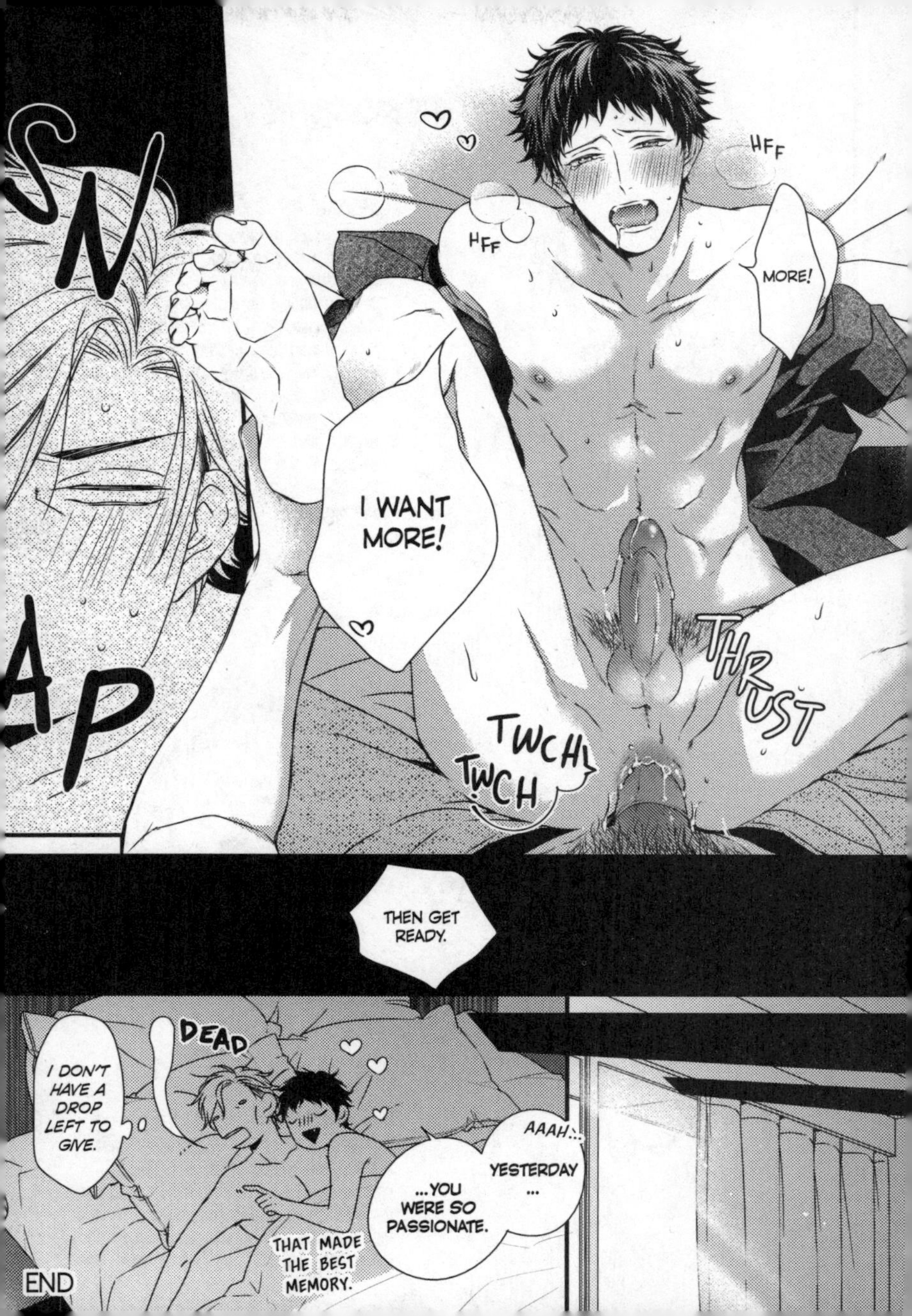
HFF
MORE!
HFF
I WANT MORE!
THRUST
TWCH TWCH
SNAP
THEN GET READY.
AAAH...
YESTERDAY ...
...YOU WERE SO PASSIONATE.
THAT MADE THE BEST MEMORY.
DEAD
I DON'T HAVE A DROP LEFT TO GIVE.
END

THE LOVE NEST CAST'S BACKSTORIES

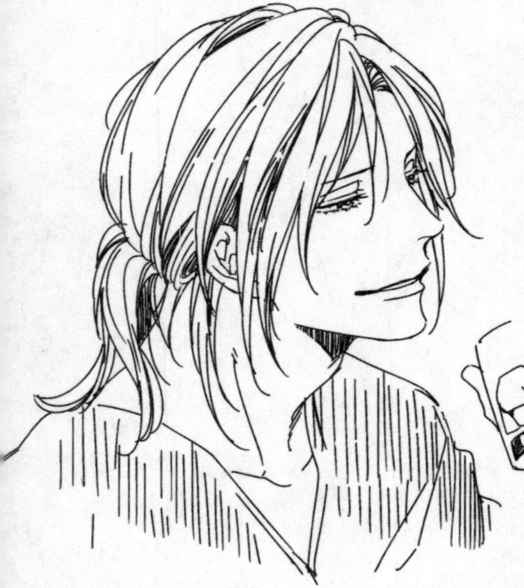

NARU (AGE 38)

HE WAS RAISED IN A HOME ENVIRONMENT FULL OF BETRAYAL AND DECEIT, AND TO PROTECT HIMSELF, HE LEARNED HOW TO READ PEOPLE. HE'S USED THAT TO HIS ADVANTAGE AND HAS BECOME A SUCCESSFUL YOUNG ENTREPRENEUR. HE WON'T HESITATE TO FULLY SUPPORT THOSE HE'S LET INTO HIS HEART, BUT EVERYONE ELSE HE WILL RUTHLESSLY CUT OFF. HE'S A MASTER TACTICIAN (THE KIDNAPPING IN HIS PAST WAS ACTUALLY HIM INTENTIONALLY GETTING HIMSELF CAPTURED TO LURE THE MEN AWAY FROM HIS BROTHER). HE'S CURRENTLY IN A POLYAMOROUS RELATIONSHIP AND HAS THREE LOVERS (A WOMAN AND TWO MEN).

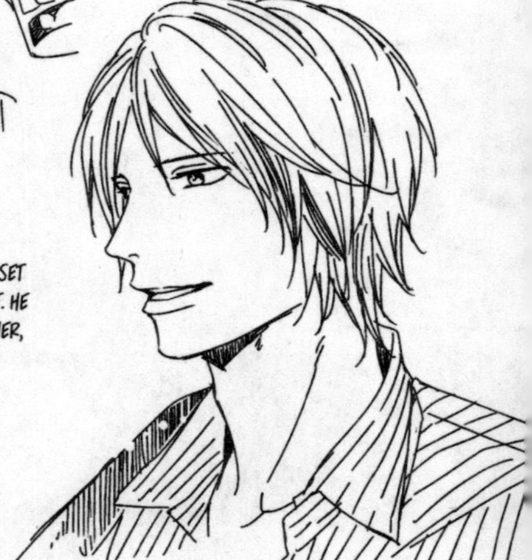

KOUSEI YAJIMA (AGE 29)

UNLIKE HIS OLDER BROTHER, HE'S MORE PUT TOGETHER. ONCE HE'S SET HIS MIND TO SOMETHING, HE'S THE TYPE TO RUSH HEADLONG INTO IT. HE SPECIALIZES IN CLEANING AND LAUNDRY, BUT LIKE HIS OLDER BROTHER, HE'S A POOR COOK. RIGHT NOW, HE'S LIVING IN LOS ANGELES WITH HIS LOVER JUN, A HALF-JAPANESE, HALF-AMERICAN MAN. ONCE HE'S GRANTED PERMANENT RESIDENCY, THEY PLAN TO GET MARRIED.

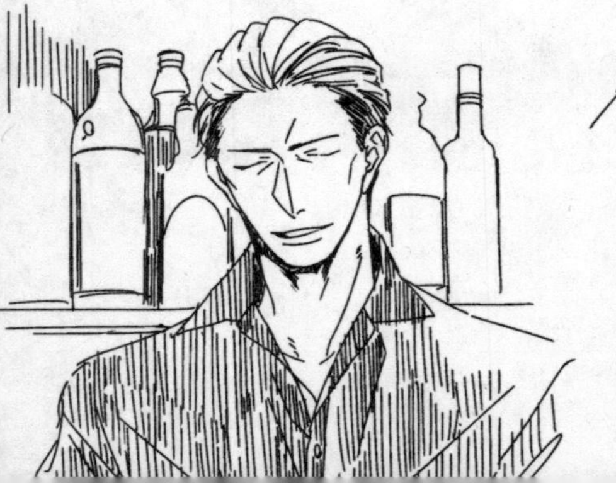

BARTENDER (AGE 47)

HE'S THE MANAGER AT THE CAFE/BAR MON CHATON. HE'S IN CHARGE OF OVERSEEING NARU'S OTHER ESTABLISHMENTS DUE TO NARU'S HECTIC SCHEDULE. HE'S LIKE NARU'S RIGHT-HAND MAN. EVER SINCE ENTRUSTING MASATO TO NARU, HE'S WATCHED OVER HIM AND (DECIDED HIMSELF THAT HE) FEELS LIKE A PARENT TOWARD HIM.

THANK YOU FOR PICKING UP *LOVE NEST*!

IN MY PREVIOUS WORK *CHANGE WORLD*, MASATO HOZUMI PLAYED THE TROUBLEMAKER IN YOSUKE AND IKU'S RELATIONSHIP. BUT AS WE DELVED INTO HIS WORDS, ACTIONS, AND HIS PAST, HIS STORY FLESHED ITSELF OUT, AND I AM VERY SATISFIED TO BE ABLE TO RELEASE IT INTO THE WORLD AS THIS SPIN-OFF SERIES.

IT WAS FUN TO DRAW ASAHI AND MAKE HIM MOVE, AND I ESPECIALLY ENJOYED THE BANTER BETWEEN HIM AND MASATO. THE MORE SERIOUS THINGS GOT IN THE SECOND HALF OF THE STORY, THE MORE PROGRESS MY EVERYDAY FANTASIES MADE...

ACTUALLY, IN THE INITIAL PLOTTING STAGE, ASAHI WAS GOING TO BE YOUNGER, AND I WAS THINKING OF HAVING HIS APPEARANCE AND STORY BE SOMETHING COMPLETELY DIFFERENT. BUT I HAD A BIT OF TROUBLE ALONG THE WAY, SO I TRIED CHANGING UP THE DIRECTION THE CHARACTERS WERE GOING, AND JUST LIKE THAT, ASAHI SLOTTED HIMSELF RIGHT BY MASATO'S SIDE. I REMEMBER IT FELT LIKE THE PIECES OF THE PUZZLE FITTING TOGETHER AT LAST. COMPATIBILITY REALLY IS IMPORTANT...

NARU IS WHAT WE WOULD CALL A KEY PLAYER IN THIS STORY, AND HE REALLY HELPED FLESH IT OUT MORE. HE WAS A DIFFICULT CHARACTER WHO REQUIRED EXQUISITE MODERATION TO PULL OFF, BUT HE'S NEITHER A GOOD GUY NOR A BAD ONE, AND I RATHER LIKED THAT HE WAS SOMEWHAT SHADY.

IT'S THANKS TO MANY PEOPLE THAT I WAS ABLE TO DRAW THIS SERIES FOR A LITTLE LONGER. I HOPE YOU'LL WARMLY WATCH OVER THE TWO OF THEM NOW THAT THEY'VE MOVED OUT OF NARU'S PLACE AND ARE STARTING A NEW LIFE IN A NEW PLACE.

ALSO, I AM VERY HONORED TO ANNOUNCE THAT A DRAMA CD OF THIS STORY HAS BEEN GIVEN THE GREEN LIGHT! I CAN'T WAIT TO SEE HOW THE CAST PERFORM THEIR PARTS... ONCE THE DATE OF RELEASE AND OTHER STATS ARE DECIDED, WE'LL NOTIFY YOU ALL ON SHINSHOKAN'S OFFICIAL WEBSITE AND TWITTER, SO PLEASE AWAIT FURTHER NEWS.

LASTLY, TO MY EDITOR K, MY DESIGNER, MY PARTNER MAMECHOSU, AND ALL MY READERS WHO ALWAYS CHEER ME ON, MY SINCEREST THANKS FROM THE DEPTHS OF MY HEART.

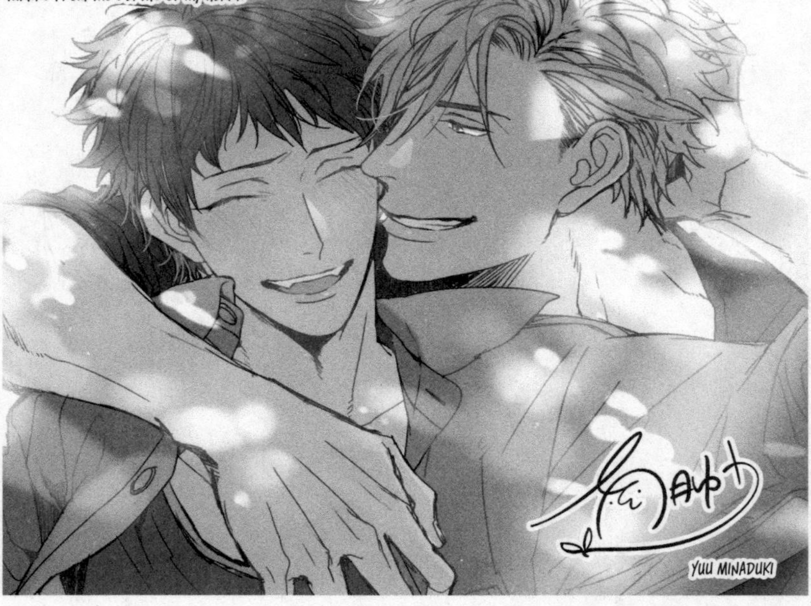
YUU MINADUKI

About the Author

Yuu Minaduki is the creator of over a dozen boys' love manga, some of which have French, Spanish, and German editions. She is a Leo born on August 7 in Saitama with an O blood type. You can find out more about Yuu Minaduki on her Twitter page, **@toriniku_y.**

Love Nest

Volume 2

SuBLime Manga Edition

Story and Art by **Yuu Minaduki**

Translation—**Christine Dashiell**
Touch-Up Art and Lettering—**Deborah Fisher, Sara Linsley**
Cover and Graphic Design—**Alice Lewis**
Editor—**Jennifer LeBlanc**

新書館
SHINSHOKAN

Printed in the U.S.A.

Published by SuBLime Manga
P.O. Box 77010
San Francisco, CA 94107

10 9 8 7 6 5 4 3 2 1
First printing, November 2022

M
MATURE

PARENTAL ADVISORY
LOVE NEST is rated M for Mature and is recommended for mature readers. This volume contains graphic imagery and mature themes.

SUBLIME
SuBLimeManga.com

For more information

on all our products, along with the most up-to-date news on releases, series announcements, and contests, please visit us at:

 SuBLimeManga.com

 twitter.com/**SuBLimeManga**

 facebook.com/**SuBLimeManga**

 instagram.com/**SuBLimeManga**

 SuBLimeManga.tumblr.com

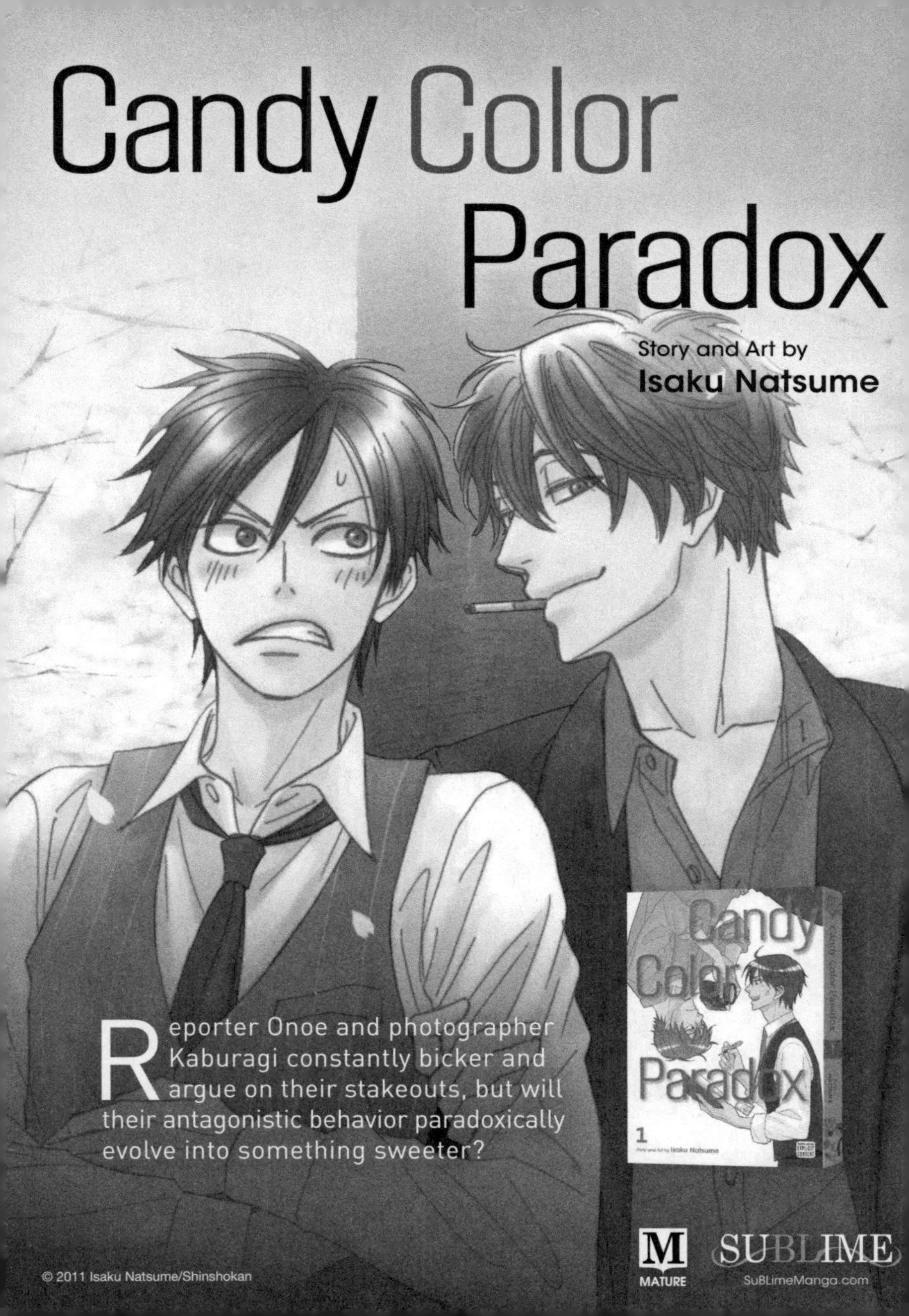
Candy Color Paradox
Story and Art by
Isaku Natsume
Reporter Onoe and photographer Kaburagi constantly bicker and argue on their stakeouts, but will their antagonistic behavior paradoxically evolve into something sweeter?
M
MATURE
SUBLIME
SuBLimeManga.com
© 2011 Isaku Natsume/Shinshokan

Liquor & Cigarettes

Story and Art by
RANMARU ZARIYA

Theo runs the town liquor store—too bad he's a total lightweight! His lifelong best friend, Camilo, runs the cigarette store across the street, and recently, he's been making his attraction to Theo quite clear. Unsure of how he feels about dating a man, Theo accepts Camilo's offer of a trial run at dating, and with a little liquid courage and a lot of heavy petting, Theo sees a whole new side to his childhood friend. Will these new experiences clarify his feelings or only serve to further muddy the waters of love?

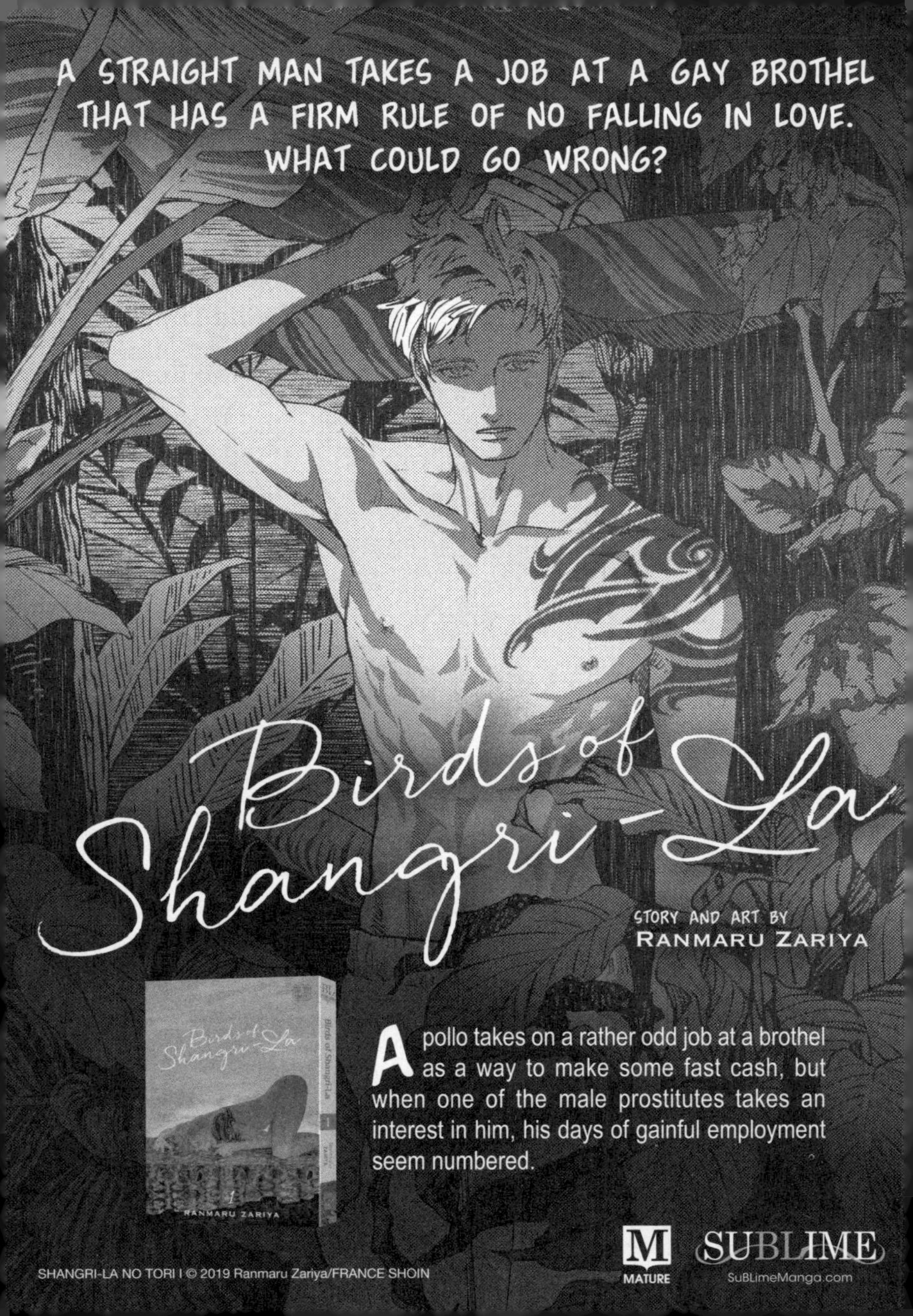
A STRAIGHT MAN TAKES A JOB AT A GAY BROTHEL THAT HAS A FIRM RULE OF NO FALLING IN LOVE. WHAT COULD GO WRONG?
Birds of Shangri-La
STORY AND ART BY
RANMARU ZARIYA
Birds of Shangri-La
1
RANMARU ZARIYA
Apollo takes on a rather odd job at a brothel as a way to make some fast cash, but when one of the male prostitutes takes an interest in him, his days of gainful employment seem numbered.
M
MATURE
SUBLIME
SuBLimeManga.com
SHANGRI-LA NO TORI I © 2019 Ranmaru Zariya/FRANCE SHOIN

TORITAN

Birds of a Feather

Birdsong starts sounding like a love song when bird whisperer Inusaki meets a crow that sounds oddly like a handsome young man he knows!

Story and Art by
KOTETSUKO YAMAMOTO

Inusaki can communicate with birds—and some of them are real jerks! Tired of the incessant chatter, he spends most of his day tuning them out. That is until the day he meets an intriguing and strangely handsome crow he just can't get off his mind!

OLDER TEEN www.SuBLimeManga.com

TORITAN Vol.1 © 2018 YAMAMOTO KOTETSUKO / GENTOSHA COMICS INC.